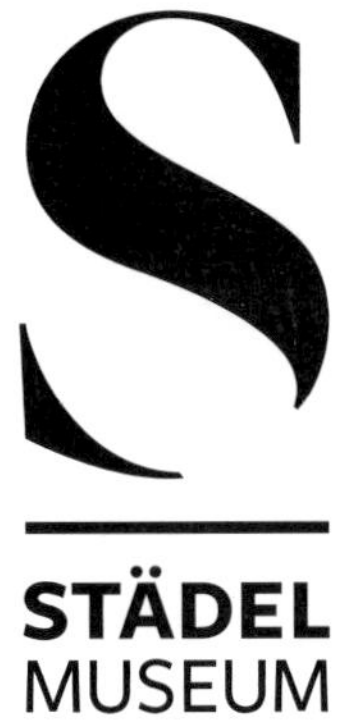

STÄDEL
MUSEUM

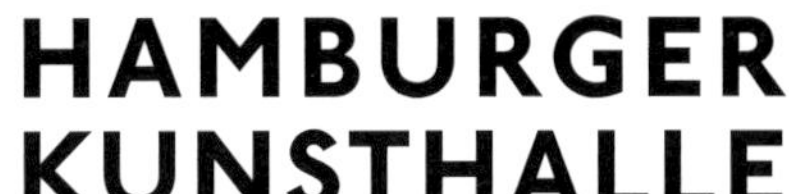

OUTSTANDING!

THE RELIEF FROM RODIN TO PICASSO

Edited by
Alexander Eiling, Eva Mongi-Vollmer and Karin Schick

in collaboration with
Friederike Schütt and Juliane Au

PRESTEL
Munich · London · New York

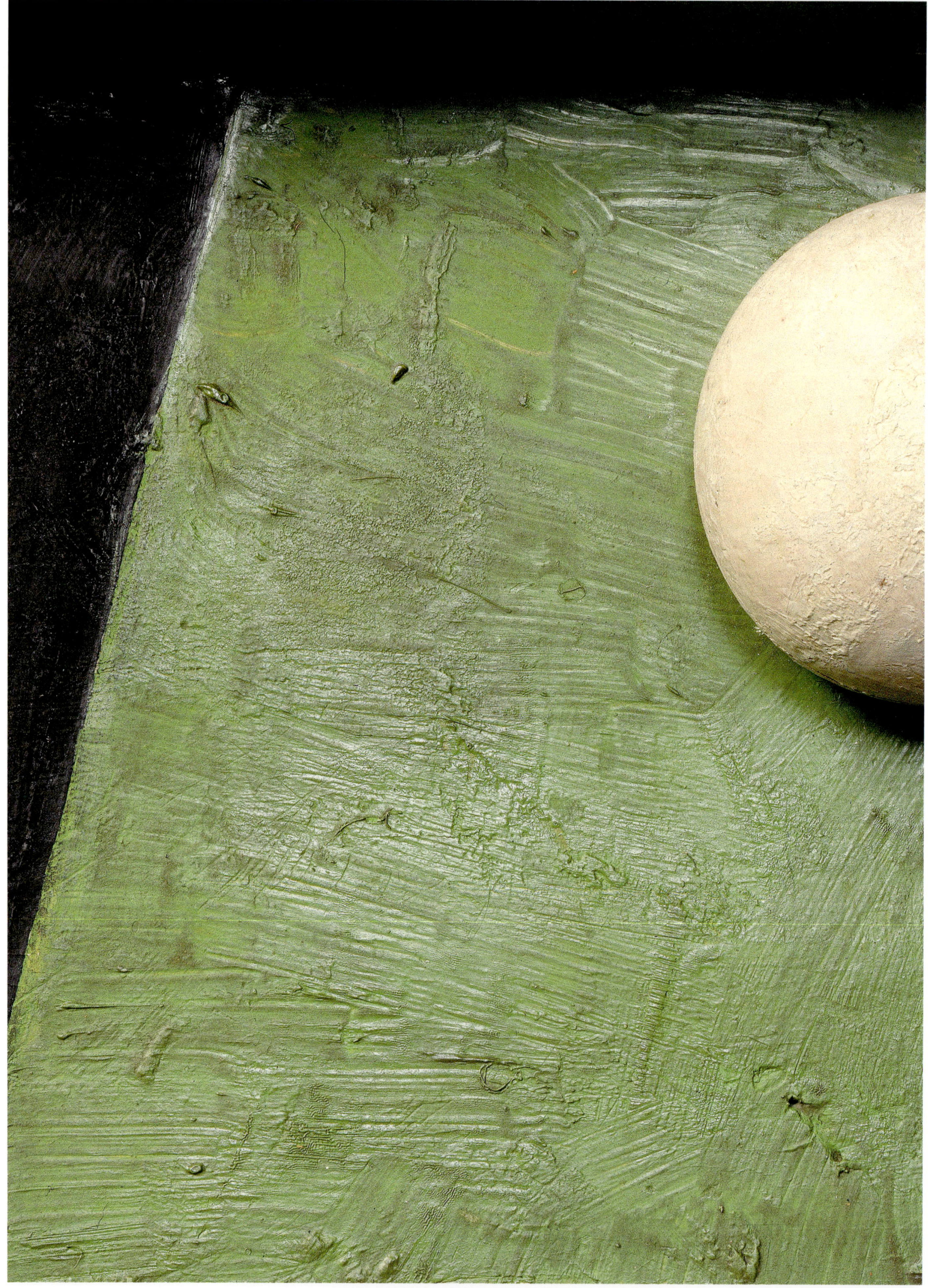

CONTENTS

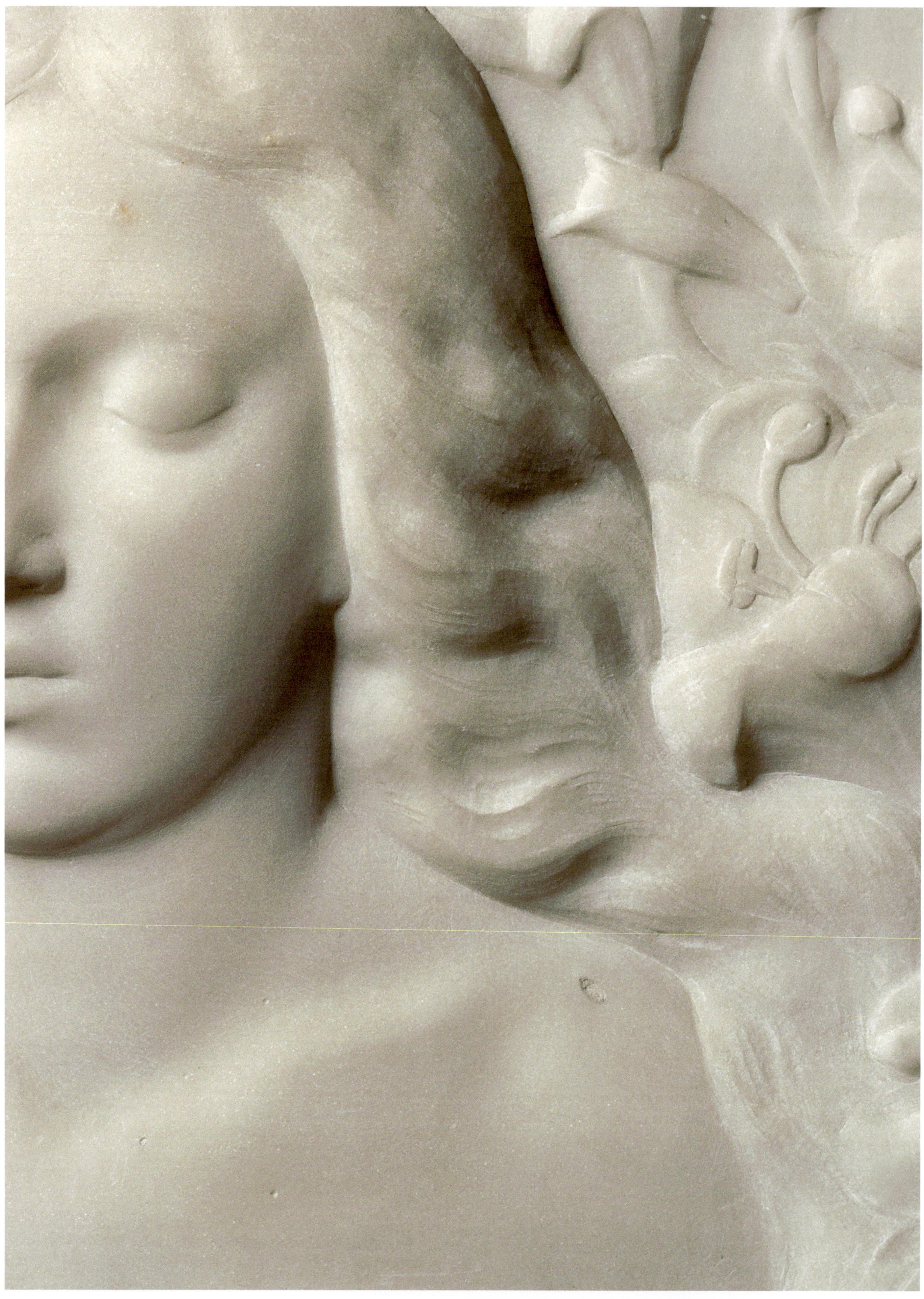

LENDERS

ACKNOWLEDGEMENTS

INSTITUTIONS

Aargauer Kunsthaus Aarau und Gottfried Keller-Stiftung, Bundesamt für Kultur, Bern

Kunstmuseum Basel

Berlinische Galerie – Landesmuseum für Moderne Kunst, Fotografie und Architektur

Galerie Poll, Berlin

Georg Kolbe Museum, Berlin

Staatliche Museen zu Berlin, Nationalgalerie

Pallant House Gallery, Chichester

Kunstsammlungen der Veste Coburg

Ny Carlsberg Glyptotek, Copenhagen

Institut Mathildenhöhe, Städtische Kunstsammlung Darmstadt

Kirchner Museum Davos

Kunstmuseum Den Haag

Albertinum – Skulpturensammlung, Staatliche Kunstsammlungen Dresden

Kunstsammlung Nordrhein-Westfalen, Düsseldorf

Museum Folkwang, Essen

Antikensammlung und Skulpturen-saal der Goethe-Universität Frankfurt am Main

Historisches Museum Frankfurt

Liebieghaus Skulpturensammlung, Frankfurt am Main

Simon Studer Art, Geneva

Museum für Kunst und Gewerbe Hamburg

Kurt und Ernst Schwitters Stiftung, Hannover

Sprengel Museum Hannover

Staatliche Kunsthalle Karlsruhe

Wilhelm-Hack-Museum, Ludwigshafen

Musée des Beaux-Arts de Lyon

Museo Nacional Thyssen-Bornemisza, Madrid

Kunsthalle Mannheim

Museum für Kunst und Kulturgeschichte der Philipps-Universität Marburg

Centre Pompidou, Paris, Musée national d'art moderne – Centre de création industrielle

Musée d'Art Moderne de Paris

Musée d'Orsay, Paris

Musée national Picasso-Paris

Musée Rodin, Paris

Petit Palais, Musée des Beaux-Arts de la Ville de Paris

Museum Boijmans Van Beuningen, Rotterdam

Musée départemental Maurice Denis, Saint-Germain-en-Laye

Sammlung Heinz und Anette Teufel im Kunstmuseum Stuttgart

Staatsgalerie Stuttgart

Stuart Lochhead Sculpture

The Hepworth Wakefield

PRIVATE COLLECTIONS

ahlers collection

Felicitas Baumeister and Jochen Gutbrod

Sammlung Freese

Nachlass Familie Blumenthal

Nachlass Karl Hartung

Emanuel Hoffmann-Stiftung

The William Turnbull Will Trust

and other private collectors who do not wish to be named

Stella Ahlers
Leonie Beiersdorf
Frank Berger
Sandra Bornemann-Quecke
Wolfgang Cilleßen
Simona Ciuccio
Eleanor Clayton
Dennis Conrad
Yvette Deseyve
Hadwig Goez
Imogen Grönninger
Doede Hardeman
Anna Isabella Hartung
Hanne Hartung
Hans-Jürgen Hellwig
Katharina Henkel
Edward Horswell
Michael Ilk
Carolin Jahn
Julia Kloss-Weber
Daniel Koep
Walburga Krupp
Birgit Kümmel
Stuart Lochhead
Gabor Mues
Jenny Mues
Astrid Nielsen
Magdalena Nieslony
Maja Oeri
Christoph Otterbeck
Eva Poll
Nana Poll
Eva Reifert
Fabienne Ruppen
Moya Schönberg
Dorothea Schöne
Dirk Schönfeld
Sandra Simshäuser
MaryAnne Stevens
Alain Tarica
Stefanie and Christian Torner
Robert Travers
Alex Turnbull
Johnny Turnbull
Michael and Yvonne Uva
Julia Wallner
Iris Wenderholm
Sabine Wilhelm

SPONSORS

The exhibition in Frankfurt is supported by

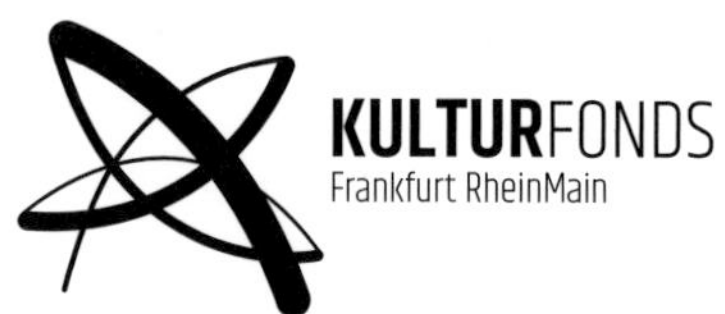

STÄDELSCHER **MUSEUMS-VEREIN** STÄDELFREUNDE 1815

With additional support from

GEORG UND FRANZISKA SPEYER'SCHE HOCHSCHULSTIFTUNG

Media Partner

Cultural Partner

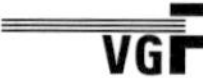

The exhibition in Hamburg is supported by

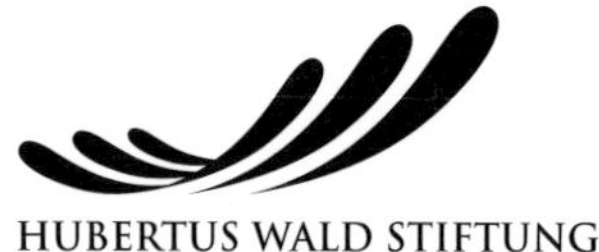

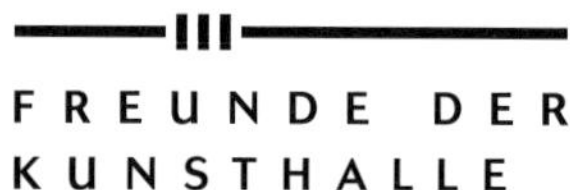

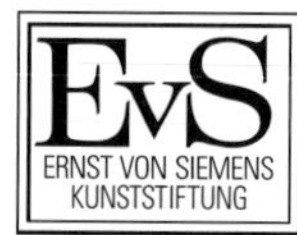

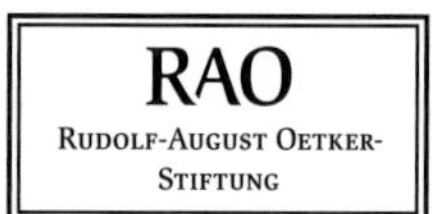

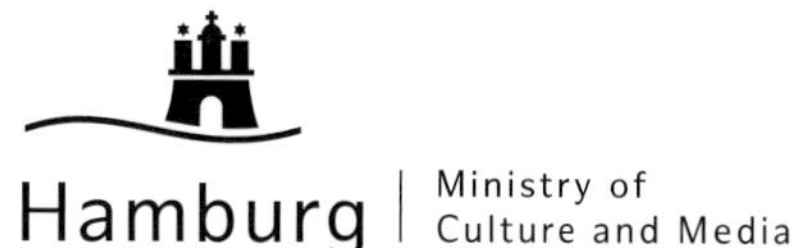

Media Partner

Cultural Partner

GREETINGS

Reliefs are ubiquitous: one need only take a look at buildings in public space to see that they are a part of it. However, they do not always attract our attention. We are primarily familiar with painting and sculpture – as early as in Goethe's day, there was debate over which artistic category the relief belonged to. The exhibition postulates that the relief is a distinct genre with its own aesthetic and its own innovative techniques. With a gaze trained in such way, we can contemplate our immediate surroundings more openly.

We are delighted to see high-quality exhibits from European museums united with outstanding works from the Rhine-Main area. Monumental works such as Bernhard Hoetger's *Equestrian Relief*, originally produced for the Mathildenhöhe in Darmstadt, are placed alongside international artworks, as are the small sculptural portrait reliefs of well-known personalities from Frankfurt from the city's Historisches Museum or designs by the sculptor Hans Mettel, who once taught at the Städelschule and who produced numerous wall reliefs for the Main metropolis. Imbedded in a precise curatorial concept, these works once again develop transregional radiance. Along with exhibits on loan, selected works from the collections of the Städel Museum and Liebieghaus present an opportunity to once again inquire into the various styles and forms of the relief as well as to carry out a scholarly examination of the different techniques. The regional institutions are part of a research network and maintain a close dialogue. Visitors can look forward not only to immersing themselves in a superb exhibition but also to experiencing a tried-and-trusted, broad art outreach programme for people of all ages and backgrounds. We, the Kulturfonds Frankfurt RheinMain, are therefore pleased to be accompanying this exhibition project and wish each and every visitor "outstanding" moments in the presentation and while reading the companion catalogue.

Karin Wolff
Managing Director
Kulturfonds Frankfurt RheinMain

The relief has always been an important element of cultural history. This art genre, which can be traced back to the Stone Age, was valued in Ancient Egypt just as much as in Greek and Roman antiquity. In Europe, it remained palpable from the Romanesque period through the Renaissance up to modernity, and it continues to display its vitality in the art of our own times. Situated between sculpture and painting, the relief has always remained somewhat mysterious – a subject for art experts – and whereas throughout history any number of exhibitions and publications have been dedicated to the two other genres, the last museum presentation on the relief already dates back 40 years.

Therefore, this exhibition at the Hamburger Kunsthalle, in which the public can experience approximately 130 works spanning 150 years, is all the more significant. This strikingly diverse panorama full of surprises not only demonstrates how, as an intermedial art genre, precisely the relief could become an ideal locus for experiments and developments. Because it protrudes from the plane, often far into space, it seems to come towards us as a corporeal vis-à-vis, to touch us and to be tangible itself. Valuable sculptures, reliefs and paintings have now travelled to Hamburg from throughout Europe for the purpose of representing the entire scope of the subject matter. However, more than 40 stem from the Kunsthalle's own collection, which once more proves to be a treasure chamber. The fact that this presentation is taking place at the Hubertus Wald Forum, which served as an exhibition space for the first time in 2004, seems especially apt, as two striking reliefs adorn its vestibule: former fireplace figures, more than two metres tall, sculpted in limestone by Gustav Heinrich Wolff in 1925. The two works, inspired by Greek antiquity, frame the show's title wall and simultaneously invite visitors to enter the main hall.

The Hubertus Wald Stiftung, which has been associated with the Hamburger Kunsthalle for many years, is extremely delighted to be supporting this extraordinary project. I wish the exhibition the great resonance it deserves, and I hope that each and every visitor has an intense encounter with the originals and gains many new insights perusing the accompanying catalogue.

Dr Volkmar Herms
Hubertus Wald Stiftung

FOREWORD STÄDEL MUSEUM

With the exhibition *Outstanding! The Relief from Rodin to Picasso*, the Städel Museum is devoting itself to an area of art that is situated between painting and sculpture: the relief, a "hybrid" consisting of a three- and two-dimensional style of composition that breaks away from the plane but nonetheless adheres to it.

In the period around 1800, it evidently required exceptional courage to make an artistic attempt at the relief; nothing seemed to please the critics. In 1806, Carl Ludwig Fernow, for example, compiled a regular catalogue of errors for reliefs in his *Römische Studien* (Roman Studies): the arrangement of the figures was not to be too painterly or perspectival, and "flattening" was likewise to be avoided, as the figures would otherwise "appear to have flowed apart". In contrast, as early as 1798 Johann Wolfgang von Goethe fulminated in the introduction to the *Propyläen* that one "made the planarly raised works higher and higher" and in doing so "depicted half painting, half puppetry". The fact that works of relief art were created nevertheless delighted the public back then as much it does today. The discussions surrounding how a relief was to be presented in no way abated; rather, they were once more fanned by further questions. How was a relief to be defined? Was it a sculptural work that partially drew on painterly means? Was it painting that extended into the third dimension? Or, owing to its wall-plane relatedness, more like an element of architecture?

In 1899, August Schmarsow discounted these divisive questions and instead expressly cautioned against "erecting Chinese walls" between the so-called sisters of painting, sculpture and architecture. On the contrary, he saw "an advance of modern aesthetic [...] precisely in the fact that it does not solely have to be with a clean separation of the boundaries". In fact, the relief was an area of creative freedom worthy of being rediscovered time and time again. A look at this multifaceted subject seems long overdue, and thus there was no hesitation in enabling the realisation of the exhibition concept put forward by the curatorial team of Alexander Eiling and Eva Mongi-Vollmer. The idea for this project traces back to the results of research conducted by both curators for the highly regarded Städel exhibition *En passant. Impressionism in Sculpture* (2020), on which they wanted to enlarge with this project.

In the process, it was possible to draw in large measure on the collections of both the Städel Museum and the Liebieghaus Skulpturensammlung in Frankfurt. In turn, the cooperation with the Hamburger Kunsthalle further-more provided for fabulous synergies. Just under half of the objects on display stems from the rich collections of both venues. I would therefore like to thank the committed team of the Hamburger Kunsthalle – first and foremost my colleague Alexander Klar, the curator Karin Schick and her research assistant Juliane Au – for all of the collaborative efforts towards realising this wonderful project. I am also greatly indebted to the numerous lenders from throughout Europe, whose generosity made the exhibition possible in the first place. In this context, I would also like to express my appreciation to the Städel curators Regina Freyberger and Svenja Grosser as well as to the meanwhile retired Liebieghaus curator Maraike Bückling, who loaned us important works from her department for the duration of the presentation.

This exhibition would not have come to fruition without the support of committed partners and patrons of the Städel Museum. My gratitude goes to the Kulturfonds Frankfurt RheinMain gGmbH, represented by the advisory board presided over by Professor Dr h.c. Klaus-Dieter Lehmann and the cultural committee chaired by Dr Ina Hartwig. I would particularly like to thank Karin Wolff, the managing director of the Kulturfonds Frankfurt RheinMain, as well as her deputy Dr Julia Cloot for the unfailingly professional dialogue and the ongoing support of our work.

I would furthermore like to extend my thanks to the Städelscher Museums-Verein e.V., and not lastly to the circle of "Städelfreunde 1815", who stood by us during this exhibition project with their support as well as their deep personal interest. I wish to express special thanks to the executive board with its chairwoman Sylvia von Metzler for the tireless support of our work. Further words of gratitude go to the Georg und Franziska Speyer'sche Hochschulstiftung, who are assisting us with the implementation of the educational activities accompanying this presentation. Acting on behalf of the foundation, I would like to express my appreciation to their chairman Professor Dr Salomon Korn and their executive director Günter Hampel. We extend our heartfelt thanks to our supporters for their commitment and their close cooperation!

Another round of thanks goes to our media partner, the Verkehrsgesellschaft Frankfurt am Main, as well as to our cultural partner hr2-kultur for their cooperation and support within the scope of the exhibition.

The presentation developed in close collaboration with all of the museum's departments. For their passionate and professional effort, I thank the staff of our exhibition organisation, conservation, technical department and installation crew, education and communication, marketing, graphics and corporate design, press and public relations, sponsorship, fundraising, administration, IT department, events, museum shop, library, assistants to the director, catalogue management, and external partners and international relations. Deserving of special mention are Sven Lubinus and Hannah Vietoris for their coordination of the exhibition, along with conservators Jutta Keddies, Stephan Knobloch, Miguel González de Quevedo and Harald Theiss, as well as Gabi Schulte-Lünzum for the coordination of the new images by photographer Horst Ziegenfusz. Our appreciation likewise goes out to Steffen Gehrmann for the detailed and delicate installation of the artworks in the exhibition.

We are indebted to Nicole Miller for the striking exhibition architecture. In combination with the keen graphics by the visual design studio tonique, in particular Alexander Horn, Lukas Schmidt and Tim Schötensack, visiting the exhibition becomes a genuine experience. The tonique team is also responsible for the outstandingly beautiful design of the catalogue developed in conjunction with the Hamburger Kunsthalle. We took great pleasure in realising it in collaboration with the Prestel Verlag and its meticulous team around Katharina Haderer, Markus Eisen and Cilly Klotz, as well as translators Judith Rosenthal and Rebecca van Dyck and copyeditors Holger Steinemann and Sarah Quigley.

Linon, in particular Christian Hillengaß, was once again entrusted with developing the audio guide accompanying the presentation. We are furthermore grateful to Christoph Weigand for the wonderful film produced for the exhibition.

I am deeply indebted to the curators of the exhibition, Alexander Eiling and Eva Mongi-Vollmer, and in equal measure to project manager Friederike Schütt, who unfailingly handled all scholarly and organisational concerns with care and precision. This team has succeeded in staging the heterogeneous material in a thought-provoking and visually convincing way and in developing a highly stimulating tour of the exhibition.

I now want to wish each and every visitor an enjoyable time and an inspiring perusal of the catalogue.

Philipp Demandt
Director

FOREWORD HAMBURGER KUNSTHALLE

For some years now, the science of sociology has been detecting mounting isolation and loneliness in our society. At the same time, the need for physical contact remains existential and most recently continued to increase in a period in which quarantine and social distancing restricted our everyday life. The genre of the relief, situated between painting and sculpture, predestines people to exercise their sense of touch: reliefs reach from the plane into space, and their visible and palpable materiality invites an encounter with them. They constitute a physical vis-à-vis with the human body and induce tactile vision – something that is becoming increasingly rare in a digital world with long periods spent in front of a screen. In a reality that is still frequently defined by polarity and binarity, the exhibition *Outstanding!* is also a case for the power of synergies and for the potential that lies in the indefinite in-between. The authenticity of the relief and its ability to embody depth and vitality can be arrestingly experienced in this presentation of icons of the art of the relief from a period of approximately 150 years. *Outstanding!* is intended to open one's eyes to an art form that nowadays is hardly taken into consideration in art academies and artists' studios alike – which is an unmistakable indicator that this will soon change. This exhibition will contribute to such a renaissance of the relief.

The extensive show brings together substantial loans from Europe as well as the valuable collections at the Städel Museum and the Liebieghaus in Frankfurt and at the Hamburger Kunsthalle. In Hamburg, the exhibition, curated by Karin Schick, primarily feeds on the Modern Art Department for which she is responsible: owing to the commitment of the two post-1945 directors Carl Georg Heise and Alfred Hentzen as well as their successors, our modern art collection alone embodies a unique blend of painting, sculpture and relief. Thanks to the curators of nineteenth-century art, contemporary art, and prints and drawings – Markus Bertsch, Brigitte Kölle and Andreas Stolzenburg – important works from other departments at our museum could be included.

Outstanding! is programmatic for the scholarly work performed by the Hamburger Kunsthalle, in particular against the backdrop of the research project "From the Second to the Third Dimension" that has been ongoing since 2020. This comprises the first scholarly processing and contextualisation of our collection of coins, medals and badges, which was concealed for decades. The first director of the Kunsthalle, Alfred Lichtwark, had begun collecting these small-scale reliefs – which include high-quality artists' medals, primarily from the nineteenth and twentieth centuries – as a "basis for the sculpture collection" (*Die Wieder-erweckung der Medaille* [The Reawakening of the Medal], Dresden 1897). Beginning in 2025, curator Annabelle Görgen-Lammers will make the examined collections and their connections to graphic art, painting and sculpture, accessible to the public in a new presentation. With its focus on the twentieth century, *Outstanding!* considers the subject from the perspective of modern art and marks the start for the publication of the Hamburger Kunsthalle's long-term involvement with the artistic alternation between the dimensions.

I would like to begin by thanking the generous lenders from Germany and abroad as well as our unstinting patrons for the current exhibition and the accompanying catalogue: this ambitious project would not have been possible without their openness and enthusiasm. In Hamburg, the exhibition is being supported by the Hubertus Wald Stiftung with a veritably outstanding sum, and so our deep gratitude goes to Dr Volkmar Herms and the foundation's advisory board. Heartfelt thanks go to the Freunde der Kunsthalle: Dr Ekkehard Nümann and the executive board provided the first start-up funds for our project. Many thanks similarly go to the Ernst von Siemens Kunststiftung for the generous support of the present publication. We are likewise very grateful to the Rudolf-August Oetker-Stiftung for having made urgently needed restorations possible. We also thank our media partner Hamburger Abendblatt and our cultural partner NDR Kultur, whose participation ensures that the exhibition acquires media presence. A further expression of gratitude goes to the Department of Art History at the University of Hamburg, with whom we, among other things, are able to implement a seminar on the relief in front of the originals. We would once again like to extend our appreciation to the Freunde der Kunsthalle for an extensive supporting programme within the newly founded Gustav-Pauli-Kolleg with events concerning the genre of the relief and its special brisance in modernity.

An exhibition of this dimension is always a collaborative effort: hence I would like to express my thanks to the team in Frankfurt – specifically my colleague Philipp Demandt, the curators Alexander Eiling and Eva Mongi-Vollmer, and the project manager Friederike Schütt – for the realisation of this extraordinary project. We have Alexander Horn, Lukas Schmidt and Tim Schötensack from tonique to thank for the congenial design of our collective catalogue, as well as the Prestel Verlag and its team around Katharina Haderer, Markus Eisen and Cilly Klotz. We also thank the translators Judith Rosenthal and Rebecca van Dyck as well as copy-editors Holger Steinemann and Sarah Quigley.

As always, we are indebted to all of the departments at the Hamburger Kunsthalle for their achievements with respect to the multitude of concerns surrounding exhibition coordination, conservation, the library, communication, press and public relations, art education, event management, clerical services, administration, building and technology, and visitor services. In this case my special thanks go to Meike Wenck for the comprehensive organisation, Nicoline Zornikau for the demanding conservational supervision, the collection management team for the elaborate installations, and Monika Wildner for her support in the area of scholarly research. Photographs of reliefs pose a challenging task, which our artistic photographer Christoph Irrgang mastered brilliantly. We once again thank m I W a A Scénographie and Susanne Bax in Berlin for the keen design of the exhibition.

In closing, I would like to extend my great appreciation to the curator of the exhibition in Hamburg, Karin Schick, and her research assistant Juliane Au. In close collaboration with the team in Frankfurt they have brought together important works of art with a high level of expertise, passion and a wealth of ideas, bringing an extraordinary presentation and a stimulating catalogue to fruition. Numerous people can now take pleasure in viewing and reading the impressive result. I wish everyone an enjoyable experience!

Alexander Klar
Director

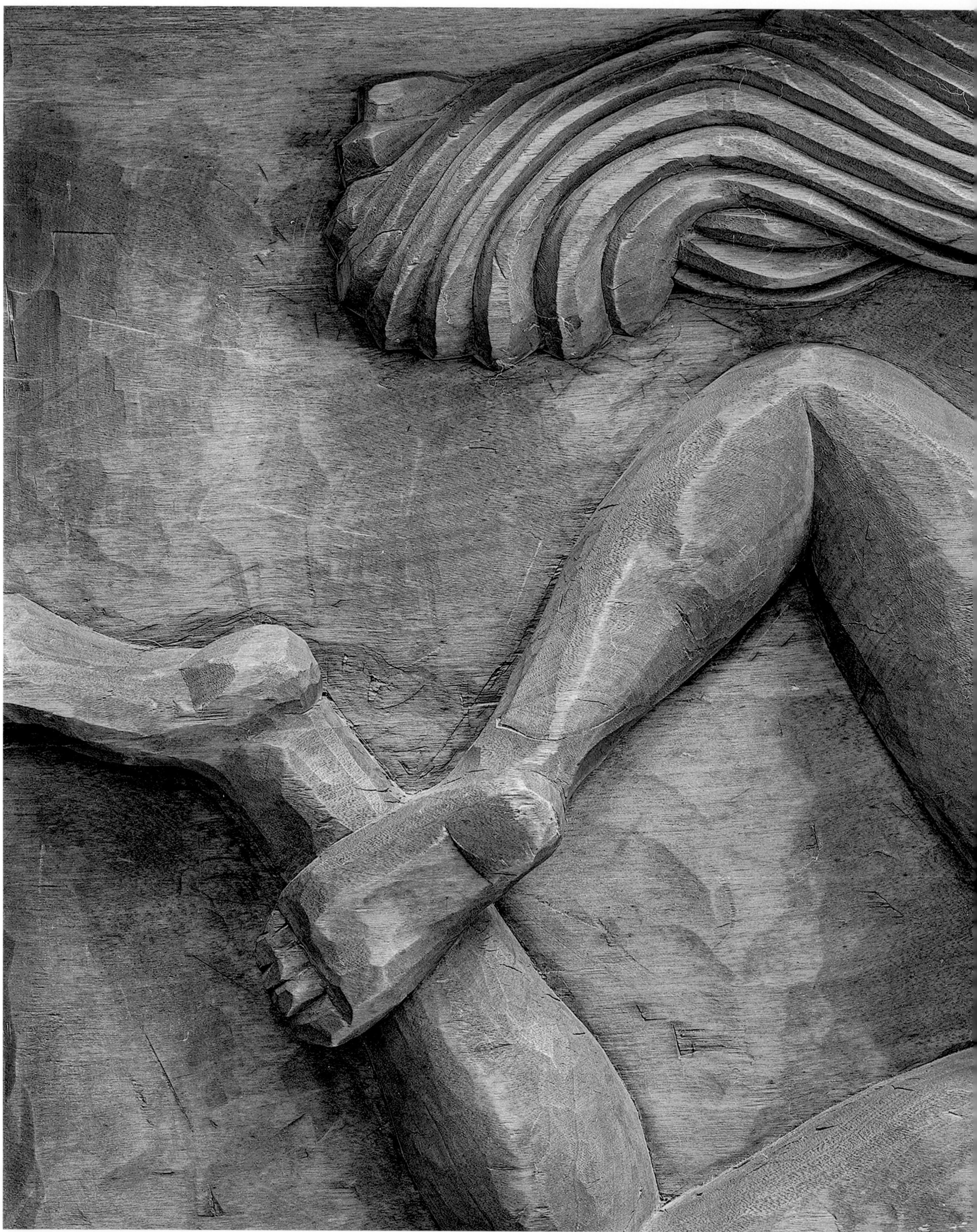

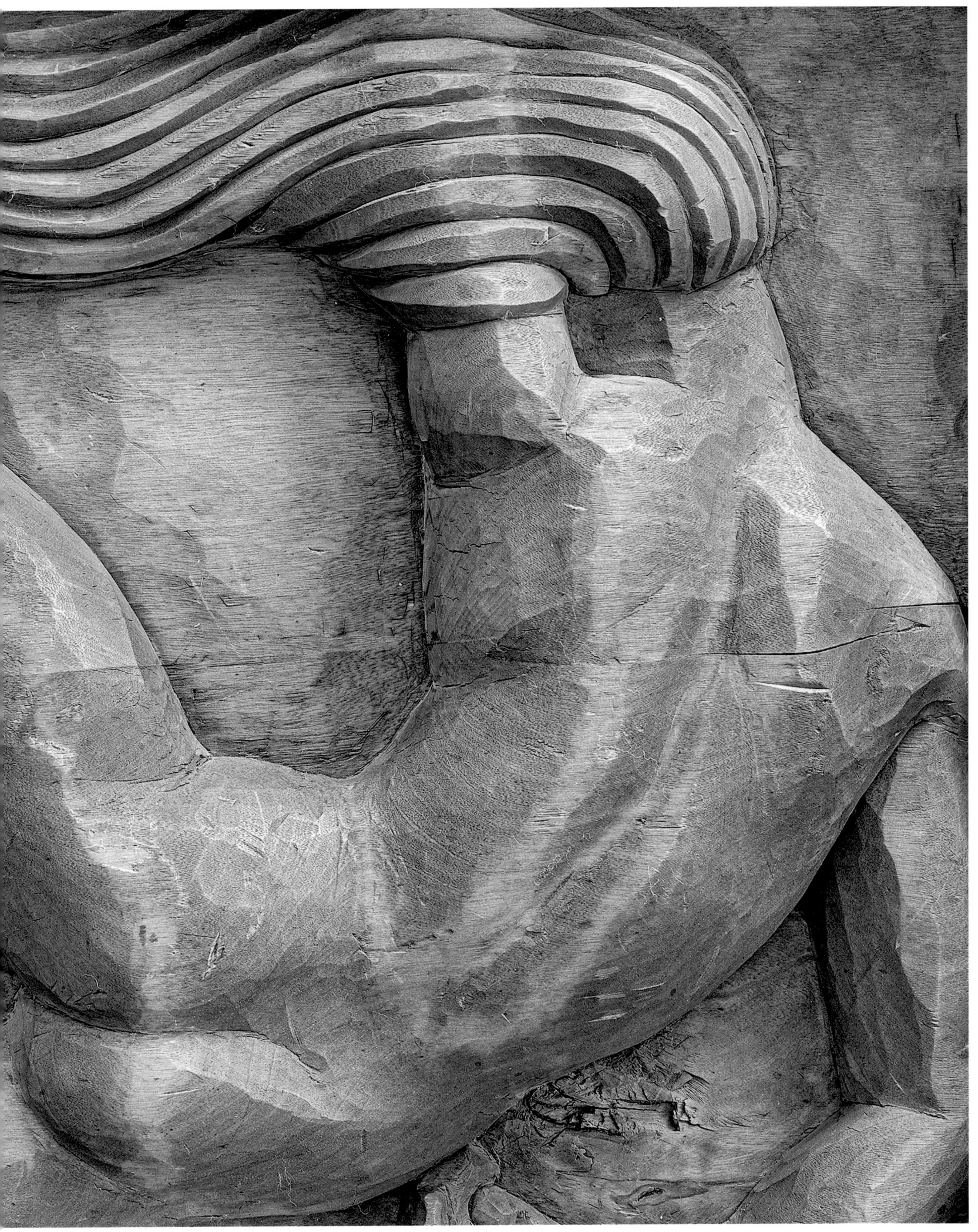

THE RELIEF

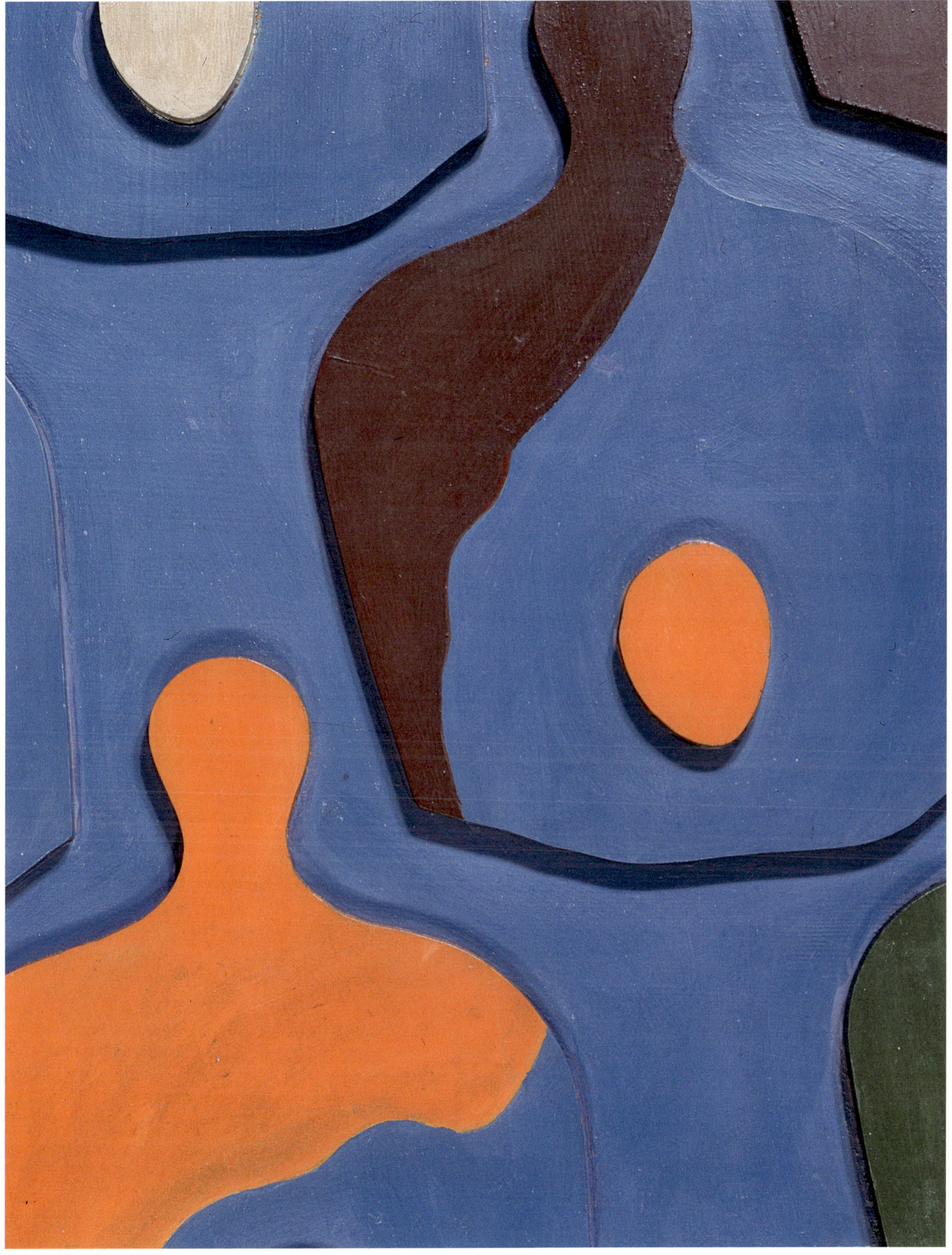

Alexander Eiling
Eva Mongi-Vollmer
Karin Schick

THE RELIEF

An Introduction to the Subject and the Exhibition

In an age of smooth, flat touchscreens (fig. 1) that serve as gateways to enter virtual worlds, the artistic relief projecting into real space appears to be archaic, but at the same time more topical than ever. Reliefs (from the Latin *relevare*, to raise) protrude from the surface or are embedded in it in recessed form. For raised reliefs, the terminological differentiation between low, half and high relief – already in use in art historiography for centuries – is still serviceable as an initial approximation, even if over the course of the twentieth century other aspects above and beyond those categories came to our attention.[1] Depending on the era and artistic context, various forms have been favoured in the history of the relief. Whereas Greek antiquity and the European Renaissance, for example, had a predilection for the subtle low relief (*bas-relief*; fig. 2), the far more three-dimensional high relief (*haut-relief*; fig. 3) was widespread in the Baroque. In the latter, figures and forms can even become partially freestanding through undercutting and other methods of detachment. In sunk or hollow relief (*relief en creux*; fig. 4), a rarer type known above all from ancient Egyptian art, the figures or lines are worked into the surface of the block as hollow forms and therefore are lower than that reference plane.

As the last-named example from ancient Egypt shows, reliefs are among mankind's oldest pictorial media. Yet despite their omnipresence in the world, often as decorative ornaments, they are frequently overlooked. Perhaps that is at least partly because, by definition, the relief is ambiguous. After all, it is a hybrid that holds a place between artistic mediums and thus goes against the grain of well-practised expectations on the part of the viewer. In view of its dependence on a supporting surface it is closely related to painting. Yet it also has spatiality at its disposal, quite in accordance with sculpture; it protrudes from the architectural wall into the third dimension and thus into the viewer's sphere. And this plasticity is doubly coded because the relief possesses factual corporeality

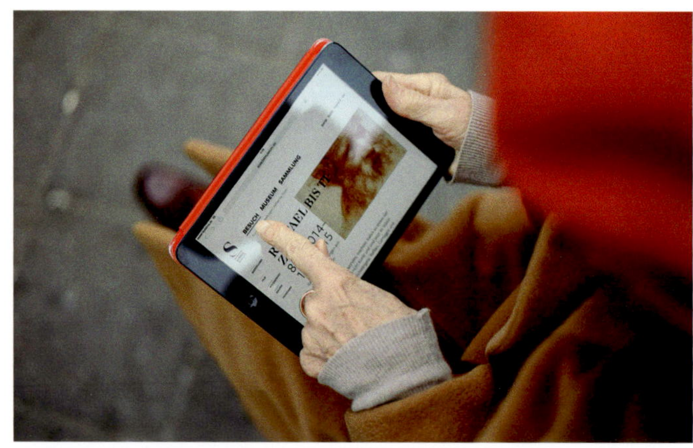

Fig. 1 Points of contact with virtual worlds

while at the same time, in analogy to painting, it is also capable of simulating a spatial construction, for instance by means of central perspective. The fact that the relief not only occupies a place between two artistic media, but also, where its perception is concerned, between the senses of sight and touch, does not make it easier to comprehend: Peter Bexte's recent observation that reliefs are "outsiders" rings true.[2] At the same time, the relief develops a tremendous independence that grasps the medium's openness as an opportunity.

Carl Ludwig Fernow's concept of the "groping eye"[3] dating from 1806 is symbolic of a complex epistemological issue that continues to resonate into our own time and is once again under discussion now in the natural sciences, humanities and arts. Is sight itself tactile? Does visual perception represent a form of touching?[4] To what extent are human sensory experience, trained by reality, and the perception of art – particularly contemporary art, which is often medial in character – related? How do we "grasp" with pure sight in analogy to touching in the physical sense? In view of such questions, it is worth our while to look back at the history

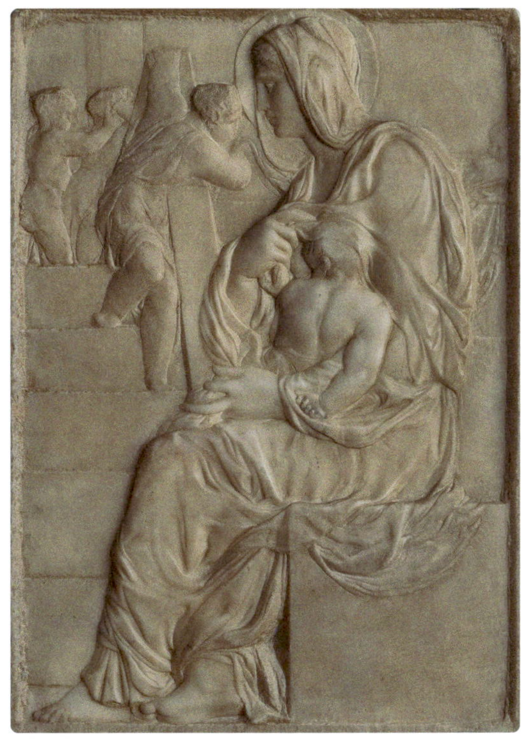

Fig. 2

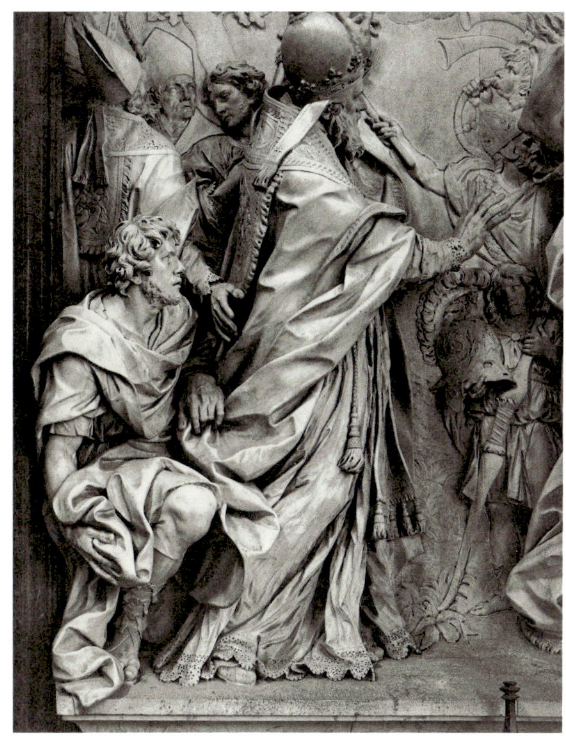

Fig. 3

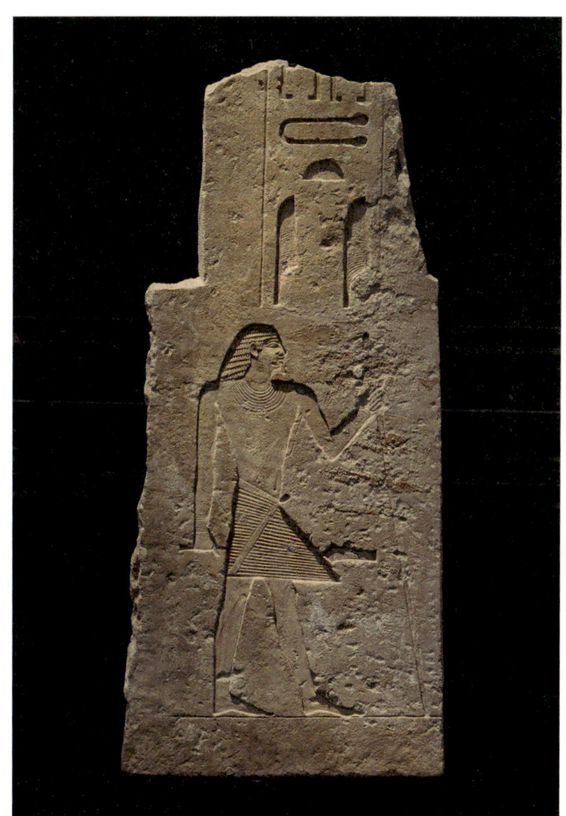

Fig. 4

Fig. 2   Michelangelo Buonarroti: *Madonna of the Stairs* (*Madonna della Scala*), ca. 1490, marble, Casa Buonarroti, Florence

Fig. 3   Alessandro Algardi: *Meeting of Leo I and Attila* (detail), 1646–53, marble, St. Peter's Basilica, Rome

Fig. 4   Egyptian relief, Memphis, Old Kingdom, 6th Dynasty, ca. 2300 BCE, limestone, Staatliche Museen zu Berlin, Ägyptisches Museum und Papyrussammlung

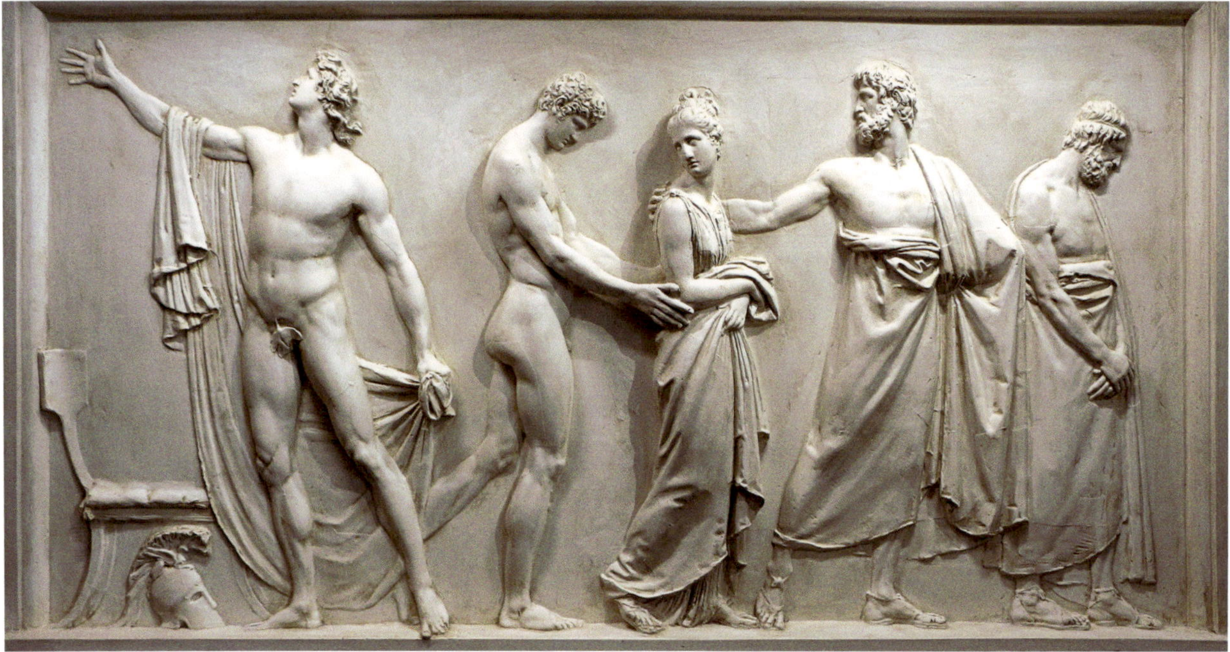

Fig. 5   Antonio Canova: *Achilles Delivers Briseis to Agamemnon's Heralds*, 1787–92, plaster, Fondazione Musei Civici di Venezia, Museo Correr, Venice

of art: For the very reason that the relief unites plane and space, surface and depth, and addresses both the sense of sight and the sense of touch, a closer look at it is as stimulating as it is challenging.

Taking these special possibilities and opportunities into account, we have devoted our exhibition project to the relief in art from 1800 to the 1960s as exemplified in works by more than a hundred European and American artists. We chose this timeframe for several reasons. On the one hand, the saddle period around 1800, with its reorientation towards classical antiquity, represents a distinct break as regards the meaning and the aesthetic of the relief. After the exuberance of the Baroque and Rococo, reliefs were now distinguished by rigorous, almost uniformly raised frieze compositions depicting figures in isocephalic rows – that is, with their heads at the same level – in front of grounds left entirely smooth (fig. 5). At the other end of the period examined, in the 1960s, the "departure from painting" and the associated transfer of sculptural into spatial concepts mark yet another pivotal point (figs. 6, 7). Thus our exhibition does not provide a comprehensive history of the relief; after all, in view of the medium's vast dimensions, such an undertaking would scarcely be achievable. In the following,

we will begin with a brief look at the state of research on the relief with the aid of selected art-theoretical sources. Then we will turn our attention to the important aspects of material and technique as carriers of meaning, before finally devoting ourselves to the exhibition itself.[5]

The Discussion of the Relief in Theory and Research

Our knowledge about the relief draws on several studies of various epochs pre-dating and within the period we have chosen to examine,[6] as well as on investigations of individual artists such as Bertel Thorvaldsen and Jean Arp, a number of whose works are featured in the show. Similarly important for our exploration of the relief were in-depth looks at certain manifestations of the medium such as Alfred Lichtwark's seminal work on the medal published in 1897,[7] at selected time segments such as Symbolism,[8] at phenomena such as the painterly-sculptural much discussed around 1900,[9] and at the tactile aspect of the relief,[10] as well as key passages in surveys and applicable investigations of sculpture.[11] The work by Claire Barbillon, published in 2014, provided valuable insights into the relief in nineteenth-century France.[12] And for the twentieth-century relief, the exhibition catalogues *The Planar Dimension* (1979), *Reliefs: Formprobleme zwischen Malerei und Skulptur im 20. Jahrhundert* (1980) and *Transform: BildObjektSkulptur im 20. Jahrhundert* (1992) are still as fundamental as ever.[13] What all these publications (and many of our other sources) have in common is the decision to narrow the subject matter down to a more or less manageable magnitude.

A look back at the history of art theory reveals that the word *rilievo* already turns up as early as the Italian quattrocento. Back then it was used as a term for the three-dimensional effect of painting, but also to generally refer to the three-dimensional depiction of a figure, that is, to sculpture. It does not, however, specifically designate an object worked in relief. It was not until the sixteenth century and the writings of Giorgio Vasari that the relief medium gained independence, if as a subcategory of sculpture. It is also Vasari to whom we owe the terminological differentiation between high relief, low relief and *rilievo stiacciato* (Tuscan for *schiacciato*, flattened or "squashed" relief[14]).[15] Vasari lavished particular praise on Donatello for the astonishing sense of spatiality he created in these so-called squashed reliefs with elevations of no more than a few millimetres (p. 51, fig. 4). Even before Vasari, Leonardo da Vinci recorded his thoughts on painting in the early sixteenth century in a text that went down in history as the posthumously published *Trattato della pittura*. In it, he expounded on the advantages of painting as compared to sculpture, thus contributing fundamentally to the competition that emerged in the Renaissance between the different visual arts and later became known as *paragone* (Italian for "comparison").[16] One topic that came up in that context was the relief, which Leonardo acknowledged as a contribution of sculpture because it approximated painting by way of spatial perspective. Its shortcomings, he pointed out, were the impossibility of colour perspective and its dependence on the lighting.[17]

The idea of *paragone* was also one that preoccupied Benvenuto Cellini in his writings.[18] Unlike Leonardo, the Florentine sculptor and goldsmith attached more importance to the interconnections between relief, sculpture and painting, which he regarded as being in a quasi "familial" relationship of dependence with one another: "[T]he greatest praise one can bestow upon a beautiful painting is to say of it: it looks like a relief. The relief is thus the true father of sculpture, and painting is one of its [that is, sculpture's] children."[19] This assessment would later be encountered again in modified form, in statements by Auguste Rodin.[20]

In the following centuries, the relief was repeatedly an object of comparison between artistic mediums and of discussion about their respective predominance in a constructed hierarchy of the arts. In theory, therefore, the mediums were in competition with one another. In practice, however, the relief was often the outcome of a division of labour between

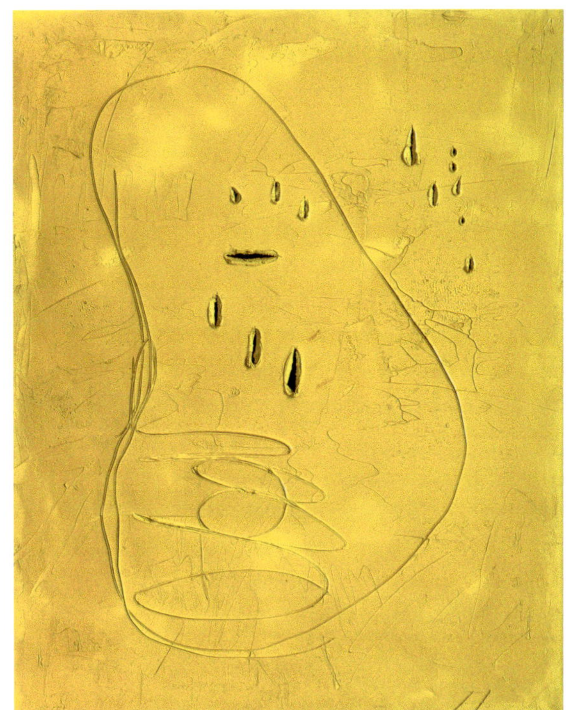

Fig. 6

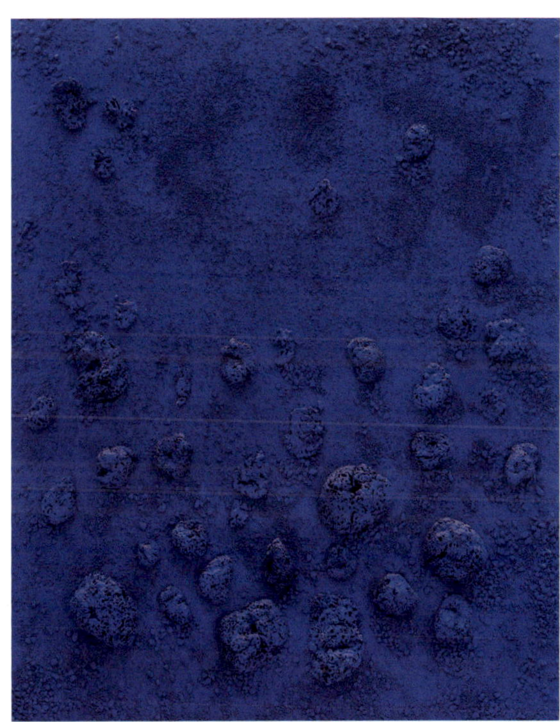

Fig. 7

Fig. 6   Lucio Fontana: *Spatial Concept* (*Concetto spaziale*), 1960, oil on canvas, Hamburger Kunsthalle (cat. 135)

Fig. 7   Yves Klein: *Blue Sponge Relief* (*Little Night Music*), 1960, sponge, stone and colour pigments on wood and canvas, Städel Museum, Frankfurt am Main (cat. 94)

the painter or draughtsman, who supplied the design, and the sculptor, who executed the work on that basis. In fact, for the various stages of the complex processes sculptural and three-dimensional work involves, artists are frequently dependent on cooperation with other trades to this day. The answer to the question of who has authority and control over the overall process differs from one case to the next. These days, for example, we not uncommonly encounter bronze reliefs whose makers never planned their execution in this material, or whose realisation they did not live to see (cats. 42, 59).[21]

In the modernist age, the necessary collaboration in the artistic process from design to execution would collide with the "problem" of invention that had only then become especially virulent.[22] The early nineteenth century had seen the assertion of a new conception of art – and accordingly a new self-conception of the artist – which ranked the significance of the idea over its practical realisation. At the same time the contest between the mediums, as well as the classification and assessment of the relief in and of itself, came to be discussed in a different vein, with far more autonomy now being attributed to the individual mediums and more attention paid to the incomparability of the different arts. As we will see in the following, over the course of the nineteenth century the relief no longer figured as an object of dispute but as a synthesis of the mediums of painting and sculpture.

In 1801, in an era when theoretical reflections on the autonomous mediums and their boundaries intensified, August Wilhelm von Schlegel defined the relief as the "intermediary member" between sculpture and painting. This halfway position led, on the one hand, to its shady reputation as an "eternal lie", to quote Schlegel.[23] Yet Schlegel also recognised the relief's great potential and declared it a "complete field of art" for select connoisseurs: "From the point of view of the self-consciousness of art [...], the bas-relief stands very high: it is destined from the outset only for learned eyes; artist and observer concur, outside the generally valid truth, about a third thing, in which they find a common truth. It is peculiar and destroys, in one stroke, the inane principles of deception and natural reality, such that, in the most material of all the arts, where the correctness of the imitation of nature can otherwise almost be grasped with one's hands, a kind of arbitrary sign has formed and expanded into a complete field of art."[24] For the execution of reliefs Schlegel recommended, quite in the classicist spirit, availing oneself of clear profile depictions of subjects. Carl Ludwig Fernow

followed suit in his *Roman Studies* published between 1806 and 1808, while at the same time expressly rejecting the idea of composing in the manner of painting for what he called the "intermediate medium".[25] Only a "small degree of optical deception" in the sense of perspective should be allowed, as, after all, the relief itself disposed of a "closer" and a "further away" by virtue of its slight elevation.[26]

Already these recommendations bespoke a tension that would persist throughout the nineteenth century and ultimately came to be discussed on several levels around 1900. In that context, the "sculptural" relief, which had gained recognition as an intermediate medium, was contrasted with the "painterly" – that is, a form of relief distinguished by its painting-like qualities.[27] The sculptural relief, whether high or low, worked with representations of space arising from the materiality or its thickness, and avoided illusionistic and imitative devices. The painterly relief, on the other hand, depended solely on the means of painting; that is, it employed perspective, atmospheric effects and other modes of depiction equated with the painterly. Not the least prominent of the historical examples of the painterly relief was Lorenzo Ghiberti's *Gates of Paradise* (fig. 8) – which Schlegel had already considered an expression of "vile taste" as far back as 1801.[28] *Meyers Großes Konversations-Lexikon* of 1908, for its part, cited antiquity in a similarly judgmental manner, to arrive at its assessment: "Relief: [...] a sculpture medium [...] intermediate medium between true sculpture, from which it derives its manner of depiction, and painting, from which it takes its arrangement – in such a way that the three-dimensional principle prevails more in the simple, calm reliefs of the older Greek art (fig. 9), while the painterly predominates in the overcrowded, often vehemently dynamic ones of the later Roman art (fig. 10)."[29]

In Germany, this discussion took on nationalistic undertones around 1900 when the painterly relief was vilified as French, in which context the modern medal (→ Faces in Relief) – a medium gaining ever more significance at the time – was sometimes referred to as a *Schaumünze* (medallion; literally "display coin") in an expression of anti-French sentiment.[30] Alfred Lichtwark, the greatest proponent of the medal in those days, was not nationalistic; rather, he had dedicated himself to a more broadly conceived artistic modernism. In his 1897 paper *Wiedererweckung der Medaille* on the rediscovery of the medal, in which he steadfastly favoured the French designs, Lichtwark began by pointing out the close

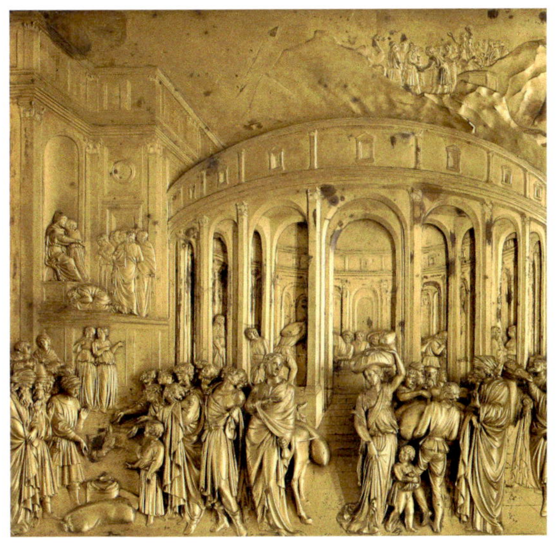

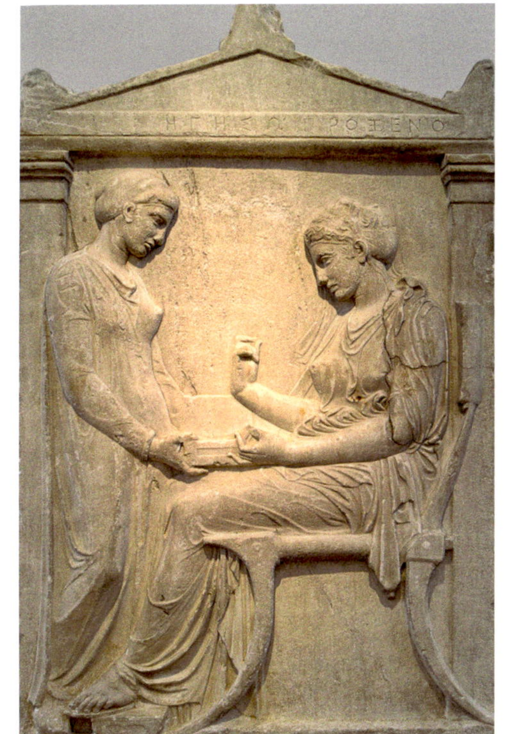

Fig. 8

Fig. 9

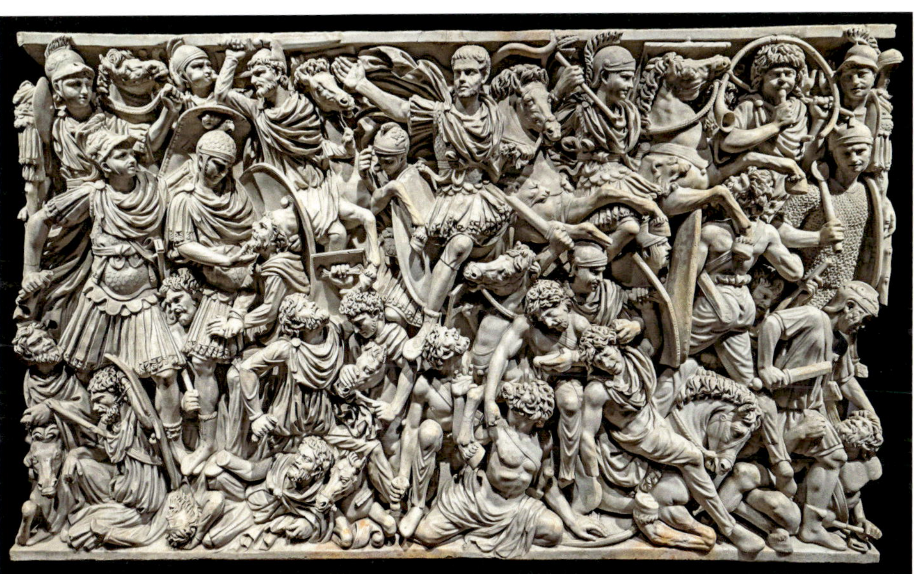

Fig. 10

Fig. 8   Lorenzo Ghiberti: *Gates of Paradise* (detail), 1425–52, bronze,
         gilded, Baptistery of San Giovanni, Florence

Fig. 9   *Grave Stele of Hegeso*, Kerameikos, Athens, 5th century BCE,
         marble, National Archaeological Museum, Athens

Fig. 10   So-called *Ludovisisi Battle Sarcophagus*, Rome, 251 CE, marble,
         Museo Nazionale Romano, Rome

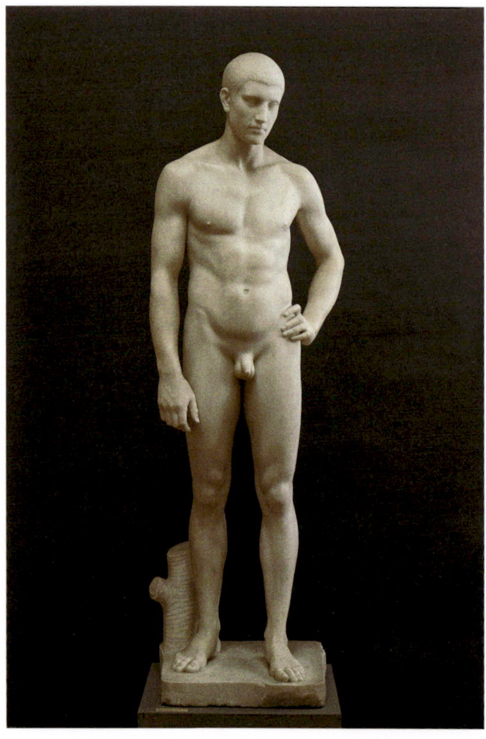

Fig. 11 Adolf von Hildebrand: *Standing Young Man*, 1883/84, marble, Staatliche Museen zu Berlin, Alte Nationalgalerie

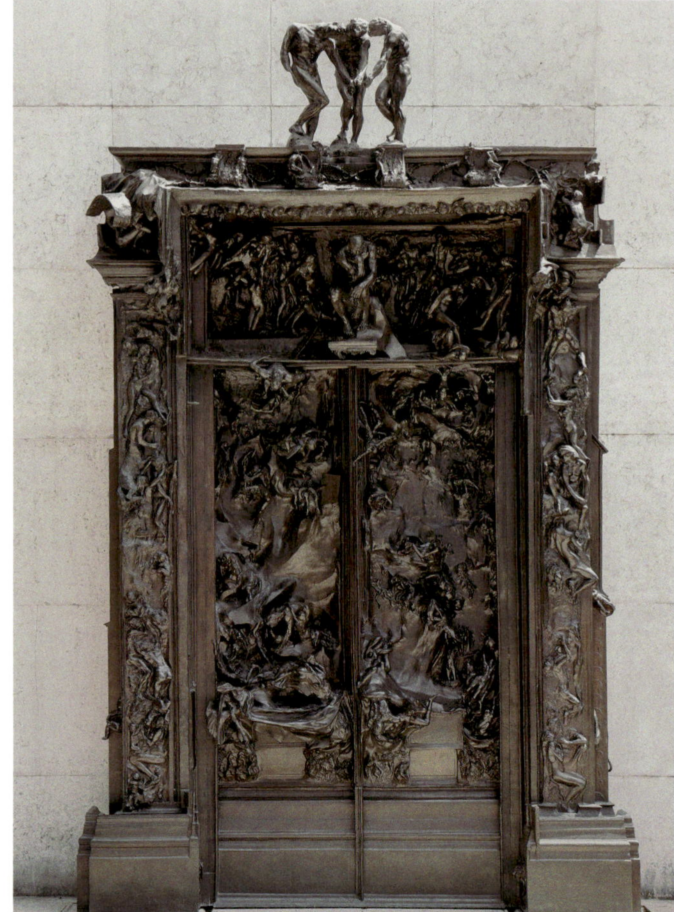

Fig. 12 Auguste Rodin: *The Gates of Hell* (*La Porte de l'Enfer*), 1880–1917, bronze, Musée Rodin, Paris

relationship between sculpture and painting as an aspect of key importance to the medal: "A painterly nature trained as a sculptor: that brings forth the great medallist."[31] He supplemented his remarks with an important observation: "Through the medal, the field of sculpture has undergone an expansion akin to that of painting through the engraving, because the fine technique takes its relief close to drawing, and is thus capable of expressing thoughts that, for the sculpture medium in the narrower sense, are unsuitable and inadequate."[32]

In his *Grammaire des arts du dessin* (1867), the French art critic Charles Blanc had already likewise broadened the field of reference by citing not drawing but poetry. He described the low relief he so appreciated as something made by a poet, a dreamer, whose vision was to make images emerge from hard stone.[33] Deliberations on the relief were thus open to other art forms.

Adolf von Hildebrand and Auguste Rodin were two sculptors who would impact the development of their medium, each in his own way, for decades to come. The differing conceptions of the relief they subscribed to constituted yet another thread of discussion around the turn to the twentieth

century, and a complex one at that. In his treatise *The Problem of Form in Painting and Sculpture*, first published in German in 1893, Hildebrand drew on hypotheses about the perception and effect of the relief formulated back in the Renaissance. Using somewhat cumbersome language,[34] he described the "conception of the relief"[35] as a sensory experience. In the so-called distant view, an object or scene initially appears two-dimensionally as a uniformly self-contained and direct pictorial impression. Bodies, he explained, articulate themselves from a flat surface into layers, or in a relief-like manner. On the other hand, its actual three-dimensionality – and here Hildebrand spoke of the figure in the round (fig. 11) – only becomes apparent successively and partially from close up, making a synthesis of the two modes of perception necessary. As with a painting, this type of observation requires only minimal effort in the sense of adaptation or movement.[36] These notions, classicist and methodical in nature, contrasted starkly with the sculptural practice of Hildebrand's contemporary, Auguste Rodin (fig. 12), who, in keeping with his claim to *"l'effet"*, rejected precisely that systematic separation of levels in favour of an obscuration of spatial and surface

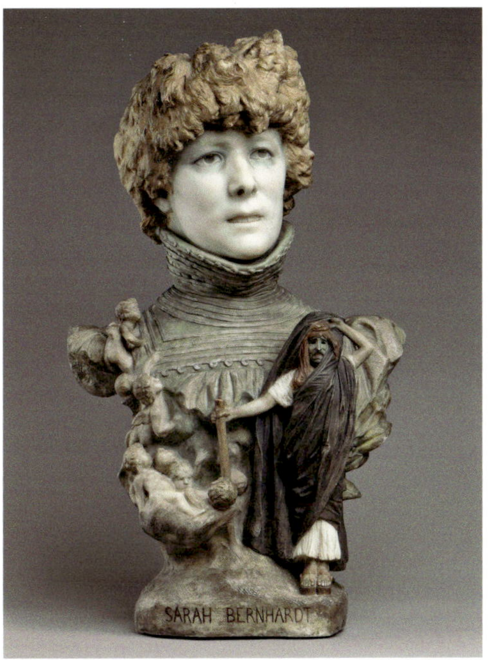

Fig. 13   Jean-Léon Gérôme: *Sarah Bernhardt,* ca. 1895, marble, painted, Musée d'Orsay, Paris

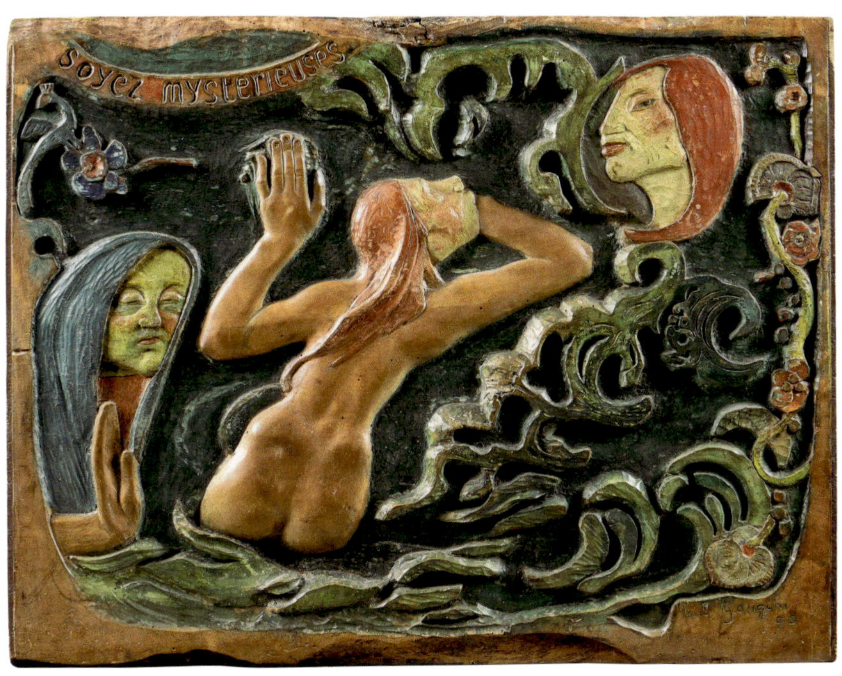

Fig. 14   Paul Gauguin: *Be Mysterious* (*Soyez mystérieuses*), 1890, lime wood, polychrome, traces of dark pencil, Musée d'Orsay, Paris (cat. 16)

references calculated in dramatic chiaroscuro.[37] Formed of surfaces both concave and convex, in their unbounded relief space Rodin's figures flow freely from high relief to low and back again. The ground holding the figures resembles a fluid mass from which they appear to emerge almost completely in the round – or into whose depths they seemingly disappear entirely. In view of this special character, Julius Meier-Graefe referred to Rodin's work as a "new personal relief" in contrast to the "old academic" conception.[38]

Rodin's dramatically expressive approach was also the focus of those early twentieth-century publications in which art critics and artists such as Edmond Claris, Albert Bartholomé and said Meier-Graefe rose up against Charles Baudelaire's legendary Salon review of 1846, and therein his condemnation of modern sculpture lock, stock and barrel. According to Baudelaire, particularly sculptures' lack of single, defined vantage points for viewers – in other words, their viewability from all sides – constituted a fundamental drawback of the medium compared to painting. He observed: "Sculpture has several disadvantages which are a necessary consequence of its means and materials. Though as brutal and positive as nature herself, it has at the same time a certain vagueness and ambiguity, because it exhibits too many surfaces at once. [...] Painting has but one point of view; it is exclusive and absolute, and therefore the painter's expression is much more forceful."[39] Even if Baudelaire tempered this blow against the medium in a review of the Salon of 1859, it was still a subject of fierce discussion around the turn of the century. And sculpture's salvation was deemed to lie in its close relationship to painting, and thus also in the relief.[40] Like painting, the relief initially dictates the beholder's vantage point; at the same time, however, it works with the means of three-dimensional modelling and thus offers more than one point of view. Since time immemorial, the colour of the relief had also played a prominent role, and this was particularly true around the end of the nineteenth century. Like sculpture in the round, the relief medium was now at the heart of an embittered discussion about the pros and cons of sculptural polychromy. Drawing on the newest findings with regard to the original flamboyantly coloured decoration of ancient marble sculptures, artists likewise began conceiving coloured works (→ Polychrome Reliefs). The natural multiplicity of hues brought about by material combinations, the use of deliberately coloured materials and not least classical colouring made for numerous interfaces between three-dimensional sculptures and reliefs. However strange they might appear today, the results of polychrome sculpture in the round were considered expressions of specific modernity, and were intended to open up new possibilities for the medium (fig. 13).[41] Because of the proximity to painting, colour appears to integrate more organically with the relief (fig. 14). What is more, the employment of paint offers a means of emphasising the three-dimensional qualities of the relief independently of the actual lighting conditions. It is hardly surprising, therefore, that numerous painters tried their hand at this art form.

There were painters who sculpted and sculptors who painted. From the late nineteenth century onwards, that also had consequences for painting. The critic Jules Claretie, for instance, wrote about the painter Jules Dupré that his palette resembled geographic maps worked in relief (→ Approximating Nature). And in view of the haptic surfaces of his paintings, the artist Adolphe Monticelli dubbed himself "Croûsticelli", thus playing on the pejorative term "croûte" (crust) for pastose paintings.[42] In the twentieth century, it was above all the Surrealists, especially Max Ernst, who used an entire range of relief-like textures in their works as a means of triggering fanciful associations. Thus, not only did the relief tend towards the painterly, but also the surface of painting towards relief-like qualities.[43] By figuring ever more prominently in the relief and painting alike, the fundamental haptic aspect became an object of perception and a subject of debate in its own right. The relief was now no longer just an object, but also an attribute ("to have relief").

The relief was thus also the prototypical expression of a development that called firmly established artistic categories increasingly into question. In the nineteenth century, this initially applied to the traditional hierarchy of the painting genres (history painting, portrait, genre painting, landscape, still life), whose boundaries painters successively blurred and broke, as Zacharie Astruc observed in his review of the 1870 Paris Salon: "The genres are mixing more and more; the figures have invaded the landscape, which virtually becomes more a genre painting; the genre ascends to history painting; the history is demoted to genre. It is a veritable confusion of modes, of ideas – the strangest amalgam. There's no spirit today that isn't fleeing the old classification, that isn't denying its rank in the established order of the compositions."[44]

It is therefore no coincidence that the number of artists who produced reliefs rose steadily in the late nineteenth century, an age in which not only traditional iconography but also the line between painting and sculpture became ever more fluid, and the relief appeared to be a way of combining the best of both worlds. It was a development that Theodor W. Adorno would later refer to as the *Verfransungsprozess* – that is, the "fraying" of traditional boundaries and functions of art genres.[45] In 1974, in the light of several artworks executed in 1913, for example Pablo Picasso's *Guitars* and *Violins*, Alexander Archipenko's *sculpto-paintings* and Jean Arp's biomorphic

constructions, Albert E. Elsen described the successful convergence of painting and sculpture as an instance of rivalry overcome, thus neatly summing up the results of the theoretical discussion in progress at the time.[46] And regardless of whether one considered it "frayed" or pacified, the terrain of art now offered the relief entirely new possibilities. Thanks to the fact that Futurist, Cubist and DADA impulses had tremendously broadened the conception of art, the variety of materials virtually exploded over the course of the twentieth century, and with it the means of creating reliefs, as this exhibition shows. At the same time, the terrain itself expanded to include subject matter that previously had hardly been considered worthy of the "spatial" artwork. Drawing on his experience with Cubist painting, Picasso began assembling reliefs from found everyday objects (fig. 15). From 1912 onwards, he produced these constructs from layered, flat and curved planes, thus enhancing the reliefs he had modelled or developed directly from the material. The wall took on the function of the relief ground and became the underlying support for a great number of three-dimensional inventions that played with the associative power of everyday objects and their manifold construction and stratification.[47] The relief therefore entered a state of dynamic transformation in which it underwent an undreamt-of boost of vitality that in turn inspired artists of vastly differing backgrounds, for example the Cubo-futurist Ivan Puni[48] (cat. 107), the Constructivist Antoine Pevsner (cat. 148) or the Dadaists Jean Arp and Sophie Taeuber-Arp (cats. 137–143, 155), to explore the medium in depth. At the same time, this creative process of renewal also made itself felt in three-dimensional works by artists like Archipenko (cats. 78, 82, 83) and Naum Gabo (cats. 85, 146), who increasingly approached the relief in a similar way (→ The Polyperspectival Gaze). In the process, real space with its play of light and shade, as well as the viewer's sense of perception, became integral parts of the works and so in a sense part of the expanded range of materials artists now had to work with (→ Boundary and Space of Possibility). After all, it ultimately took the movement of the recipients – their changing vantage point and additive sight – to form the complete work.[49] The relief constructions that came about around 1900 under the influence of rapid technical progress and new scientific findings now demanded an "active" viewer who relinquished old visual habits and entered into a dialogical relationship with the artwork. With the interpenetration

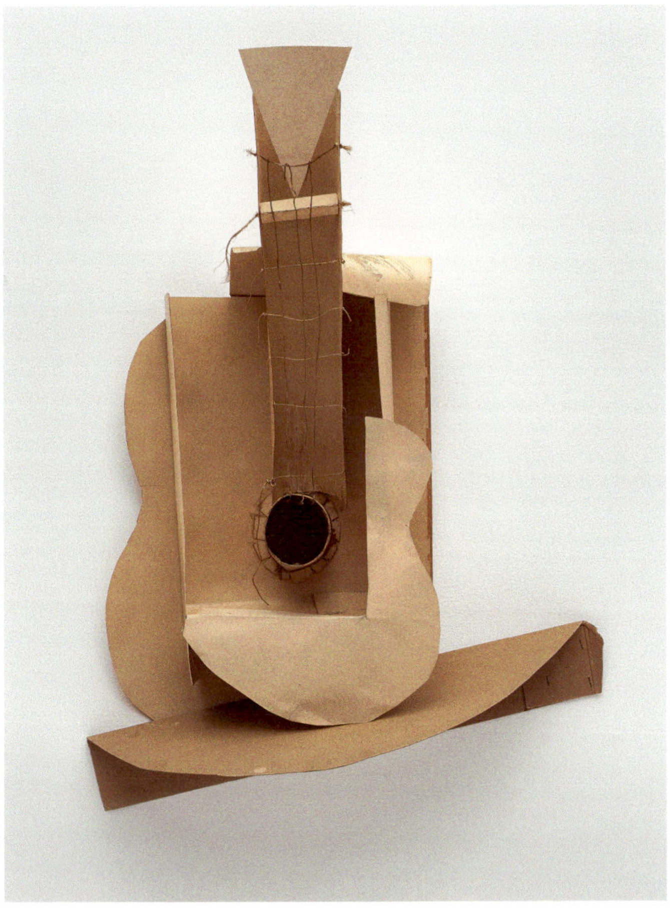

Fig. 15

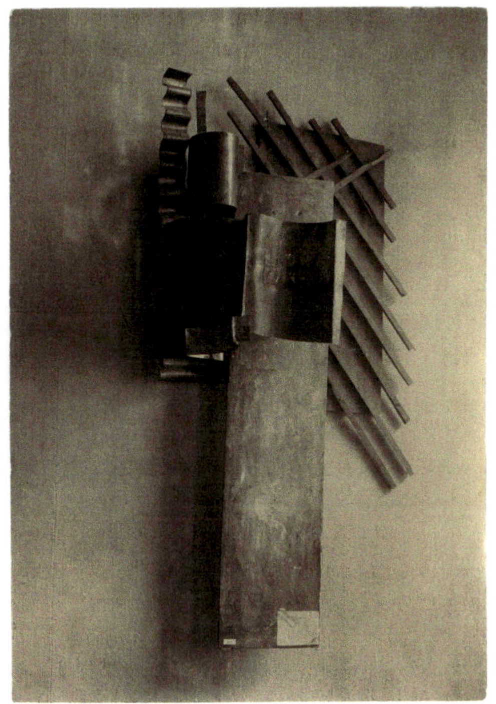

Fig. 16

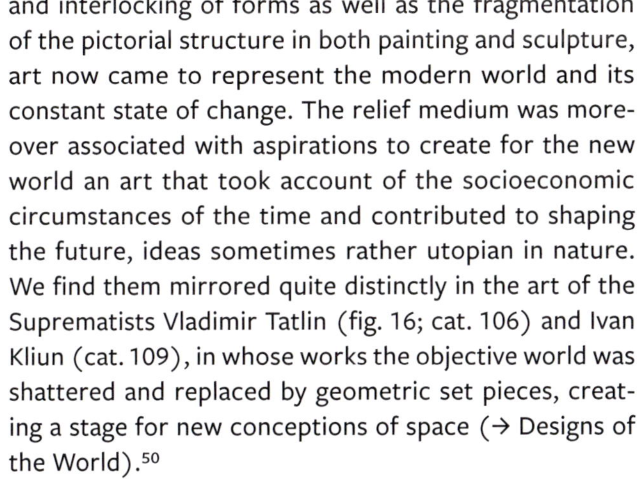

Fig. 15 Pablo Picasso: *Guitar* (*Guitare*), 1912, cardboard, paper, wire, string, The Museum of Modern Art, New York

Fig. 16 Vladimir Tatlin: *Counter-Relief*, 1916, wood and sheet metal, whereabouts unknown, photograph, Russian State Archive for Literature and Art, Moscow (see cat. 106)

and interlocking of forms as well as the fragmentation of the pictorial structure in both painting and sculpture, art now came to represent the modern world and its constant state of change. The relief medium was moreover associated with aspirations to create for the new world an art that took account of the socioeconomic circumstances of the time and contributed to shaping the future, ideas sometimes rather utopian in nature. We find them mirrored quite distinctly in the art of the Suprematists Vladimir Tatlin (fig. 16; cat. 106) and Ivan Kliun (cat. 109), in whose works the objective world was shattered and replaced by geometric set pieces, creating a stage for new conceptions of space (→ Designs of the World).[50]

Detached from its former strict connection to architecture, the relief now finally claimed the status of an autonomous artwork and, with the newfound artistic liberties it offered, animated artists to engage in all kinds of experimentation.

The discussion about how to categorise the relief among the artistic media remained as topical as ever, not least for Kurt Schwitters who, in 1920, remarked: "I nailed pictures in such a way as to create a sculptural effect alongside the painterly pictorial one. This came about as a way of blurring the boundaries of the art forms."[51]

On Material and Technique as Carriers of Meaning

In addition to motif, composition and mode of depiction, the material and its processing are integral aspects of the language that constitutes the substance of a relief.[52]

For their sculpted reliefs, the artists initially had the entire spectrum of traditional sculptural materials at their disposal. Several of them have long been used in the cultural history of mankind. This is particularly true of all types of stone.[53] In addition to being robust, stone is also characterised by an impressive variety with regard to hardness, structure, granularity, and colour. These qualities led to the emergence of different processing techniques for different materials, as P. M. Sprengel described in 1772, for example, for the alabaster relief.[54] The combination of different types of stone in turn guaranteed appealing and expressive results. A case in point is the bust of a man made of light-hued alabaster and mounted on marble in the work *Allegory of Winter* formerly attributed to Antonio Canova (fig. 17). Its materiality alone conveys the frosty chill of the dark season even before the eye has grasped the behatted and beshawled figure in all detail.

Apart from stone, materials such as wood, wax, clay, terracotta, plaster, stucco and cast stone, not uncommonly gilded, painted or glazed, remained in use for reliefs until well into the modernist age. Wood, for its part, was extremely popular among the Post-Impressionists and Expressionists, for instance Paul Gauguin (fig. 14; cat. 16), Ernst Ludwig Kirchner and Jenny Wiegmann-Mucchi (cats. 17, 69), because it was considered an honest, direct material and was associated with the supposedly unfeigned expression of medieval artworks.[55] In the nineteenth century, when waxworks sprang up all over Europe, wax also gained significance as a material.[56] In his relief *The Three Fairies* (cat. 9), Henry Cros made direct reference to the motifs and modes of depiction of courtly portraits of the Late Middle Ages (→ Polychrome Reliefs), and Xaver Heuberger's *Portrait of the Father of the Frankfurt Actress Karoline Lindner* (cat. 52) to Renaissance-era portrait medallions. For both artists, therefore, the work with wax did not represent merely a preliminary stage in the creation process but the final act. This is noteworthy in that, like clay and plaster, wax had traditionally been used above all for creating models for transmission into other materials (and sizes). Edgar Degas was one of the artists whose revolutionary, impressionistically understood sculptures would not have been possible without wax and newly invented modelling compounds such as plastiline (cats. 6, 40).[57] Aristide Maillol's work *Desire* (cat. 68), on the other hand, is an example of a multiple transfer of materials: designed in clay and plaster, it was then realised in stone and later cast in terracotta and lead (→ Relief and Frame).

Regardless of the technique, the direct processing by the artist leaves traces on the relief that contribute to its ultimate appearance. Chisels, rasps and files make their marks on stone, which can moreover be broken, coarsely hewn, sanded or polished to obtain a rough crystalline

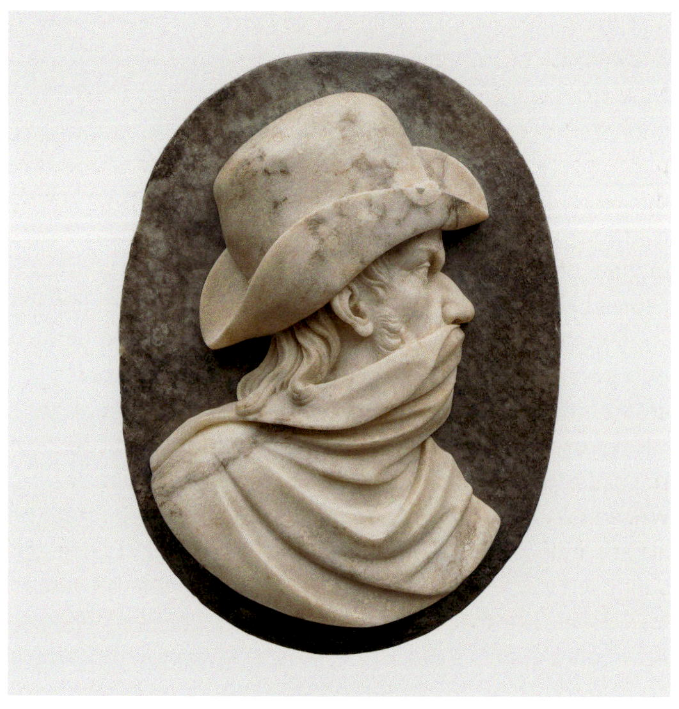

Fig. 17   Antonio Canova (once attributed to): *Allegory of Winter*,
1779, alabaster and marble, Liebieghaus Skulpturensammlung,
Frankfurt am Main

surface, a refined shimmer or a transparent character. Wood can reveal the employment of the saw, carving knife or hook knife, as seen in reliefs by Erich Buchholz (cat. 71), but can also be smoothed and sanded. The creative process inscribes itself in wax, plastiline and clay with fingers, modelling tools, scrapers and rasps, whose traces translate through the casting process into plaster or metal, as encountered in works by Constantin Brancusi and Henri Matisse (cats. 60, 36). In the reception of sculptural works, the surface was always understood as an important carrier of meaning: the artist's individual style was said to manifest itself there in particular. Whereas in the eighteenth century that "signature" showed itself primarily in the artist's manner of representing different textures, especially human skin,[58] in modernism the free, often non-representative interplay between peaks and crevices, rough and smooth, sketchy and refined, gained ever more significance over the motivic depiction. The opening of the artwork through its surface into the surrounding space and towards the viewer transported a language of its own and invited reaction and communication.[59]

At the dawn and over the course of the twentieth century, traditional materials were developed further, bringing forth such innovative works as Karel Appel's ceramic with its deeply rutted, coloured surfaces (cat. 64). The technical possibilities were considerably expanded, not least to include modern substances such as cement, acrylic glass and steel, which Auguste Herbin, Naum Gabo, Lee Bontecou and others staged in their works (cats. 163, 146, 147, 149). Now, moreover, artists took to combining things taken from nature or everyday life – sand, bark, tin, wire, cardboard, paper, paste, textiles and plastic – to make reliefs in unorthodox ways. The works of Kurt Schwitters in particular testify to these new realms of material (cats. 105, 112, 113). And in view of such material diversity, the relief's production process also transformed: it no longer came about solely by traditional sculptural methods but could be assembled by gluing to arrive at flatter reliefs, or by nailing or screwing to create more space-filling structures, so-called "assemblages". Works of this kind no longer bore the personal touch of the sculptor in the classical sense of a sculpted surface; it was equally the concept and realisation that manifested the artist's individuality. Artists now incorporated chance and supposedly inferior materials as creative elements and allowed even the most ordinary objects to bear significance. As a consequence, the whole world potentially became a co-originator of an art that corresponded profoundly to modern reality – and that at the same time was out to create an entirely new reality (→ Designs of the World).

The Exhibition

Exhibitions on the relief are rare; the last surveys took place some 40 years ago. That is astonishing considering how many reliefs there are in museum collections around the globe.[60] Already this exhibition is a case in point: nearly half of the works on view come from the two museums, in Frankfurt and Hamburg, that collaborated on the project. And even if the composition of the exhibition differs somewhat at the respective venues, each can draw on a rich fund that mirrors the medium's diversity at the highest level of quality. Variants were chosen where the two collections contained equivalent works, for instance from the oeuvres of Käthe Kollwitz (cats. 58, 59), Alberto Giacometti (cats. 44, 45) and Paul Klee (cats. 97, 98). Both locations, moreover, introduce a local touch; Hans Mettel (cats. 129–133), for example, a sculptor influential in Frankfurt after 1945, is featured with several designs for wall reliefs only at the Städel, while Karl Hartung's (cats. 125–128) importance for Hamburg is emphasised more strongly in the Kunsthalle. The Hamburg exhibition omits the section on casts of ancient cameos, medals and plaquettes (cats. 46–51, 53–57) because the Kunsthalle will soon be dedicating a presentation to this aspect of its collection. And of course conservatorial caution

also accounts for a number of differences – not every work proved as fit to travel as initially hoped. Furthermore, the fact that the exhibition was conceived for two venues early on in the process led to an extensive renouncement of light-sensitive and fragile works on paper and aspects such as the sculptor's drawing.

Our use of the jointly examined material was not intended as a basis for developing a stringent history of the relief. In part, this was because we were aware that the histories of our respective collections already brought certain emphases with them, for example a concentration on the art of Europe or a surplus of male sculptors. We made a deliberate effort to compensate for the latter with external works by, for instance, Sophie Taeuber-Arp (cats. 73, 138, 139), Lee Bontecou (cats. 147, 149), Jenny Wiegmann-Mucchi (cat. 69), Louise Nevelson (cats. 134, 154) and Niki de Saint Phalle (cat. 72).[61] Despite several constraints, the exhibition does succeed in shedding light on the theme's historical dimensions. The thirteen sections – of which some span the entire period of investigation while others focus on shorter time periods – inquire into the special possibilities and limitations of relief art above and beyond developmental lines or stylistic labels. To an extent the themes are based on motif, for example "Echo of the Parthenon", "Faces in Relief" and "Approximating Nature". Others concentrate on formal criteria, such as "Polychrome Reliefs", "Painterly-Sculptural Reliefs", "Relief and Frame", "The Polyperspectival Gaze", "Boundary and Space of Possibility" and "A Spotlight on Structure". And whereas "Designs of the World" and "Monumental Tasks" have their place in the spectrum between the history of ideas and questions of mediums, the chapters "Sculptural Narration" and "Optical Illusion in the Relief" are devoted more to conceptual deliberations. The assignment of the individual objects to the respective theme was based on curatorial decisions, which in many cases could have been made differently. We could have grouped the reliefs, for instance, according to the functions they were intended to fulfil, and thus united numerous works from the area of monument and memorial sculpture. And in fact, to this day, the relief often enjoys more public presence on buildings (fig. 18), monuments or at cemeteries than, for example, painting.[62] Particularly collections like ours encompass preparatory models for precisely such monumental realisations of what are usually competition works or commissions. A telling example is Ernst Barlach's model (fig. 19) for the Hamburg memorial commemorating the victims of the First World War, which was erected in 1931, reproduced in 1949 and restored in 2005.[63] Motifs from the context of commemorative sites, however, are also discussed in other chapters of this publication: Käthe Kollwitz's *Lament* (cats. 58, 59) in the section entitled "Faces in Relief", Christian Daniel Rauch's *Frederick II after the*

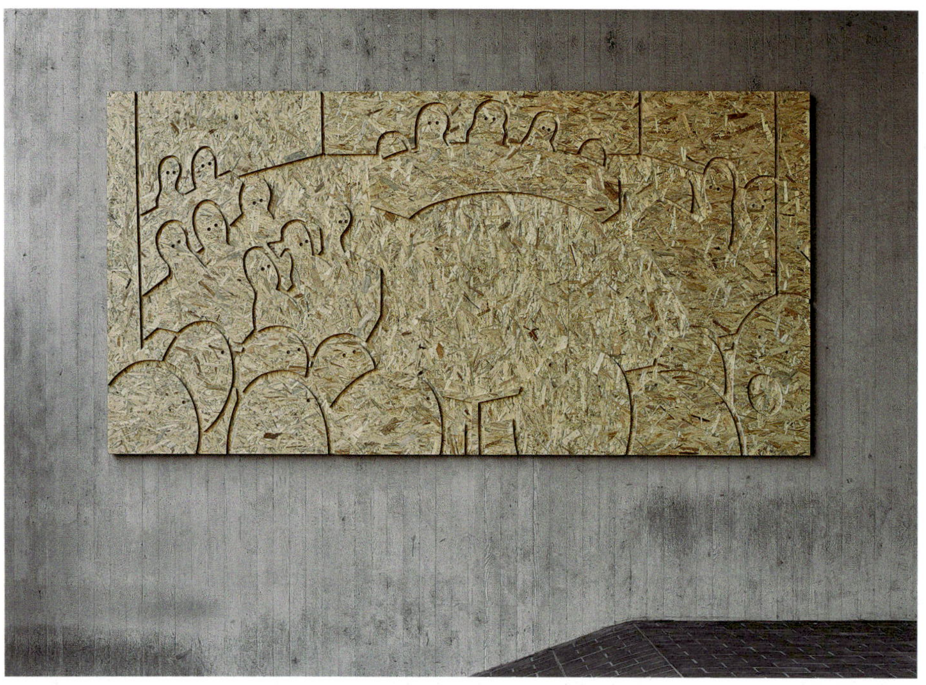

Fig. 18   Sebastian Jung: *Relief of the NSU Trial,* 2020, wood, Strafjustizzentrum München, Munich

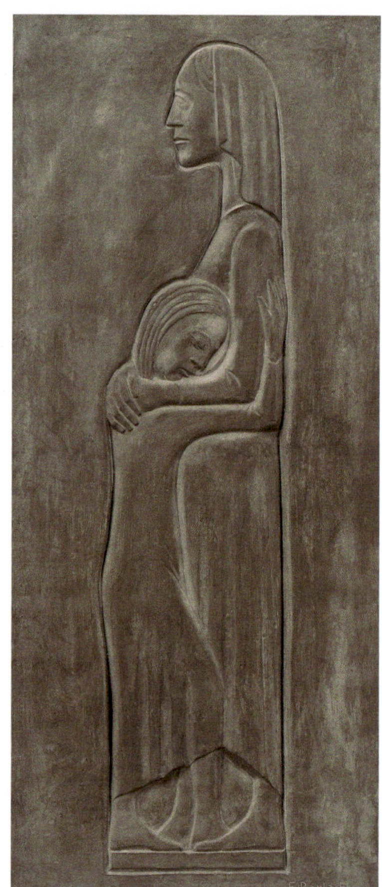

Fig. 19   Ernst Barlach: *Hamburg Memorial*, 1931, stucco (cast after the working model), Hamburger Kunsthalle

Battle of Kolin (cat. 18) in "Sculptural Narration". None of the categorisations we made are absolute. On the contrary, a flexible and sometimes surprising web of interrelations evolves from the many cross-references. It is precisely the differing perspectives that contribute piece by piece to an understanding of the relief as an "intermediary member" holding great appeal for artists.

It proved especially challenging to illustrate the featured works: the corporality inherent to the relief defies reproduction in photographs and, accordingly, in print. In the illustrations the relief shrinks from spatial to planar image, particularly when it has been photographed from the front. In many cases, therefore, we had the pictures taken from different angles in an effort to convey the spatial dimension.[64] We hope that visitors and readers alike will be able to experience the fascinating – and still too little known – hybrid medium of the relief in all its sensorial diversity via the exhibition and its accompanying catalogue.

We thank Juliane Au and Friederike Schütt for their invaluable input in the preparation of this introduction.

1   On the definition, forms and history of the relief, see *The Dictionary of Art*, ed. Jane Turner, vol. 26, London 1996, pp. 132–137; *Brockhaus Enzyklopädie*, vol. 18, Mannheim 1992, pp. 264–266; *Meyers Großes Konversations-Lexikon*, vol. 16, Leipzig 1908, p. 782.

2   Peter Bexte: "Tastaufnahmen: Reliefs im 20. Jahrhundert", in: Kristin Marek and Carolin Meister (eds.): *Berührung: Taktiles in Kunst und Theorie*, Paderborn 2022, pp. 133–149, here p. 147.

3   Carl Ludwig Fernow: "Über den Begriff des Kolorits", in: idem: *Römische Studien*, 3 vols., Zürich 1806–1808, vol. 2, pp. 175–252; see Monika Wagner: "'Das Auge ward Hand, der Lichtstrahl Finger.' Bildoberfläche und Betrachterraum", in: Markus Rath, Jörg Trempler and Iris Wenderholm (eds.): *Das haptische Bild: Körperhafte Bilderfahrung in der Neuzeit*, Berlin 2013, pp. 253–266, here p. 260.

4   See for example Marek/Meister 2022 (see note 2); Tina Zürn, Steffen Haug and Thomas Helbig (eds.): *Bild, Blick und Berührung: Optische und taktile Wahrnehmung in den Künsten*, Paderborn 2019; Rath/Trempler/ Wenderholm 2013 (see note 3).

5   Only the attempt by Leonard Robert Rogers is to be mentioned here: *Relief Sculpture*, London et al. 1974.

6   Selected examples of studies of the relief before 1800: Rath/ Trempler/Wenderholm 2013 (see note 3); Andrea Niehaus: *Florentiner Reliefkunst von Brunelleschi bis Michelangelo*, Munich/ Berlin 1998; Wilhelm Messerer: *Das Relief im Mittelalter*, Berlin 1959; Erica Tietze-Conrat: "Die Erfindung im Relief: Ein Beitrag zur Geschichte der Kleinkunst", in: *Jahrbuch der Kunsthistorischen Sammlungen in Wien*, vol. 35, no. 1, 1920/21, pp. 99–176.

7   Alfred Lichtwark: *Die Wiedererweckung der Medaille*, Dresden 1897; for further secondary literature, see the contribution "Faces in Relief" in this catalogue, pp. 99–103.

8   Claire Barbillon: "The Influence of Symbolism on the Formal Evolution of Sculptural Relief between 1900 and 1940", in: Rosina Neginsky (ed.): *Symbolism, Its Origins and Its Consequences*, Cambridge 2011, pp. 203–208.

9   August Schmarsow: *Beiträge zur Aesthetik der bildenden Künste*, vol. 3: *Plastik, Malerei und Reliefkunst in ihrem gegenseitigen Verhältnis*, Leipzig 1899.

10   See notes 2 and 4.

11   Let us here cite a small selection of publications: Bernhard Maaz: *Skulptur in Deutschland zwischen Französischer Revolution und Erstem Weltkrieg*, Berlin 2010; Rosalind E. Krauss: *Passages in Modern Sculpture*, Cambridge/ London 1977; Albert E. Elsen: *Origins of Modern Sculpture: Pioneers and Premises*, New York 1974.

12   Claire Barbillon: *Le Relief au croisement des arts du XIXe siècle*, Paris 2014.

13   *Transform: BildObjektSkulptur im 20. Jahrhundert*, ed. Theodora Vischer, exh. cat. Kunstmuseum Basel and Kunsthalle Basel, Basel 1992; *Reliefs: Formprobleme zwischen Malerei und Skulptur im 20. Jahrhundert*, ed. Ernst-Gerhard Güse, exh. cat. Westfälisches Landesmuseum für Kunst und Kulturgeschichte Münster, Bern 1980; *The Planar Dimension: Europe 1912–1932*, ed. Margit Rowell, exh. cat. The Solomon R. Guggenheim Museum, New York, 1979.

14   See Frank Fehrenbach: "Rilievo schiacciato: Donatello und die Kräfte der Skulptur", in: *Donatello: Erfinder der Renaissance*, ed. Neville Rowley, exh. cat. Staatliche Museen zu Berlin, Preußischer Kulturbesitz, Berlin 2022, pp. 58–67.

15   See Niehaus 1998 (see note 6), p. 45.

16   On the paragone and its waning importance in the nineteenth-century discussion, see Ulrich Pfisterer: "Der Paragone", in: Wolfgang Brassat (ed.): *Handbuch der Rhetorik der Bildenden Künste* (*Handbücher Rhetorik*, vol. 2), Berlin/Boston 2017, pp. 283–312, esp. pp. 305–307; Barbillon 2014 (see note 12), pp. 144–157.

17   Leonardo da Vinci: "How Effects Should Be Achieved", in: *The Painter's Practice*, Part V of *Leonardo on Painting*: *An anthology by Leonardo da Vinci with a selection of documents relating to his career as an artist*, ed. Martin Kemp, New Haven and London 1989, pp. 208–214, here p. 209. On Leonardo's further differentiation between relief types, see Wencke Deiters: *Der Paragone in der italienischen Malerei des Cinquecento: Mittel im Wettstreit der Künste bei Mazzola Bedoli, Tizian, Pontormo, Bronzino, Daniele da Volterra und Vasari*, Heidelberg 2002, p. 68.

18   See Alessandro Nova and Anna Schreurs (eds.): *Benvenuto Cellini: Kunst und Kunsttheorie im 16. Jahrhundert*, Cologne et al. 2003, esp. chap. IV: "Die Paragone-Debatte", pp. 183–237.

19   "[…] e le maggior lode che si dà a una bella pittura e' se gli dice: la par propiamente di rilievo. Adunque il rilievo è il vero padre della scultura, e la pittura è un de' sua figliuoli." Benvenuto Cellini: "Sopra l'arte del disegno" (1568), in: idem: *I trattati dell'oreficeria e della scultura di Benvenuto Cellini*, ed. Carlo Milanesi, Florence 1857, pp. 215–219, here p. 217.

20   "Dire d'une telle peinture qu'elle se détache de telle façon qu'elle semble en relief, n'est-ce pas le plus grand éloge qu'en puisse faire? d'où: il faut conclure que le relief est le véritable père de la peinture, et que la peinture est la charmante et gracieuse fille du relief." Auguste Rodin, in: Henri Dujardin-Beaumetz: *Entretien avec Rodin* (1913), Paris 1992, p. 24; quoted in Barbillon 2014 (see note 12), p. 145.

21   On the complex issue of posthumous casts of works by Jean Arp, Ernst Barlach, Alberto Giacometti, Käthe Kollwitz, Aristide Maillol, Henry Moore and others, see Ursel Berger, Klaus Gallwitz and Gottlieb Leinz (eds.): *Posthume Güsse: Bilanz und Perspektiven*, Munich 2009.

22   A noteworthy early study is: Tietze-Conrat 1920/21 (see note 6).

23   August Wilhelm von Schlegel: "Die Kunstlehre. Vorlesungen über schöne Litteratur und Kunst (gehalten 1801/02)", in: idem: *Kritische Schriften und Briefe*, ed. Edgar Lohner, vol. 2: *Die Kunstlehre*, Stuttgart 1963, pp. 100–139, here p. 132.

24 Ibid. p. 135.

25 See Carl Ludwig Fernow: "Über den Bildhauer Canova und dessen Werk", in: Fernow 1806–1808 (see note 3), vol. 1, pp. 1–248, here p. 115.

26 Ibid.

27 See Niehaus 1998 (see note 6), p. 12, who rightly points out that the German specialist literature has never come up with a consistent definition for "the painterly".

28 Schlegel 1963 (see note 23), p. 137.

29 *Meyers Großes Konversations-Lexikon* (see note 1), vol. 16, Leipzig 1908, p. 782.

30 For a more detailed discussion of this topic, see: Martin Heidemann: *Medaillenkunst in Deutschland von 1895 bis 1914*, Berlin 1998, p. 22.

31 Lichtwark 1897 (see note 7), p. 30.

32 Ibid., p. 13.

33 "L'inventeur du bas-relief fut un poète, un rêveur, qui voulut réaliser une vision, en taillant dans la pierre dure les images qui lui étaient apparues saillantes et remuées." Charles Blanc: *Grammaire des arts du dessin: Architecture, Sculpture, Peinture*, Paris 1867, p. 421. His compatriot Emile Zola also addressed himself to this matter: in his review of the sculpture on display in the Salon of 1868, he wrote about its evolution which, in his conception, had successively liberated itself from architecture until it ultimately became completely three-dimensional. The relief represented a stage in this development: "At the very start, sculpture is one with architecture. The statues are united with the temple; they enhance them, they are intergrown with them through their marble feet. Initially, coarse images were hewn in stone, then low reliefs lifted the images away from the walls of the built structure; finally the statues detached from the walls entirely and were stood on their bases." Émile Zola: "Der Salon von 1868", in: idem: *Schriften zur Kunst: Die Salons von 1866 bis 1896*, Frankfurt am Main 1988, pp. 93–125, here p. 121.

34 Developed from perceptual psychology, Hildebrand's conception of the relief was widely embraced especially in artistic circles, but reading it was a challenge. Heinrich Wölfflin, for example, wrote: "Difficult to read for the uninitiated, but perfectly transparent for them that are capable of imbuing words with visual conceptions." Heinrich Wölfflin: "Adolf von Hildebrand: Zu seinem siebzigsten Geburtstag am 6. Oktober", in: *Kunst und Künstler*, vol. 16, 1918, pp. 6–21, here p. 10; see idem: "Ein Künstler über Kunst, Rezension von Adolf Hildebrand, Das Problem der Form in der bildenden Kunst", in: *Beilage zur Münchner Allgemeinen Zeitung*, vol. 157, 11 July 1893.

35 Adolf von Hildebrand: "The Conception of Relief", in: idem: *The Problem of Form in Painting and Sculpture*, trans. Max Meyer and Robert Morris Ogden, New York et al., 1907, chap. V, pp. 80–99; see Sigrid Braunfels-Esche: "Reliefs und Reliefauffassung von Adolf von Hildebrand", in: exh. cat. Münster 1980 (see note 13), pp. 24–34; Christof Belmann: *Adolf von Hildebrand und die Skulptur der Moderne zwischen 1900 und 1925*, Master thesis, Bochum 2015, p. 3. We are grateful to Julia Wallner, formerly Georg Kolbe Museum, Berlin, now Arp Museum Bahnhof Rolandseck, Remagen, for her valuable pointer to this research contribution.

36 In his deliberations on the conception of a sculpture, surprisingly Hildebrand did not regard the flat background surface – that is, in the case of the relief, the background – as the most important reference surface but rather the foremost plane of depiction. And he was decidedly against anything coming in front of this front plane: "[N]othing can be permitted to thrust itself toward us out of the picture. On the contrary, the dominant idea is that we should move into the picture." Hildebrand 1907 (see note 35), p. 68. Hildebrand thus aspired towards an effect diametrically opposed to that achieved today with the aid of 3D goggles, which cause objects to appear to bulge optically towards the viewer.

37 Dominik Brabant: "Auguste Rodin and Impressionism", in: *En passant: Impressionism in Sculpture*, ed. Alexander Eiling and Eva Mongi-Vollmer, exh. cat. Städel Museum Frankfurt am Main, Munich 2020, pp. 174–183; Barbillon 2014 (see note 12), p. 48.

38 Julius Meier-Graefe: *Entwicklungsgeschichte der modernen Kunst*, 3 vols., 2nd ed., Munich 1915, vol. 3, p. 471.

39 Charles Baudelaire: "The Salon of 1846" (1846), in: idem: *The Mirror of Art: Critical Studies by Baudelaire*, ed. and trans. Jonathan Mayne, New York 1956, pp. 38–130, here p. 120.

40 Julius Meier-Graefe: *Entwickelungsgeschichte der modernen Kunst: Vergleichende Betrachtung der Bildenden Künste als Beitrag zu einer neuen Aesthetik*, 3 vols., Stuttgart 1904, vol. 1, p. 310; M. Bartholomé, in: Edmond Claris: *Der Impressionismus in der Skulptur: Auguste Rodin und Medardo Rosso*, trans. (from French) Etha Fles, Utrecht 1902, pp. 31–33. For a detailed discussion of this matter, see exh. cat. Frankfurt am Main 2020 (see note 37); L. Cassandra Hamrick: "Baudelaire et la sculpture ennuyeuse de son temps", in: *Nineteenth-Century French Studies*, vol. 35, no. 1: *Sculpture et poétique: Sculpture and Literature in France, 1789–1859*, autumn 2006, pp. 110–131.

41 For a general discussion, see: *En couleurs: La sculpture polychrome*

en France 1850–1910, ed. Édouard Papet, exh. cat. Musée d'Orsay, Paris, Vanves and Paris 2018.

42 In the process of finishing a painting, the artist reportedly sometimes cried out, "Euh! voici un crousticelli …"; quoted in Matthias Krüger: *Das Relief in der Farbe: Pastose Malerei in der französischen Kunstkritik 1850–1890*, Munich and Berlin 2007, p. 40.

43 Ibid.

44 "De plus en plus, les genres sont confondus […]. Les figures ont envahi le paysage, devenu à peu près tableau de genre; […] le genre se hausse à l'histoire; l'histoire se rapetisse au genre […]. C'est une véritable confusion de modes, d'idées, – le plus singulier mélange. Il n'est pas d'esprit, aujourd'hui, qui n'échappe à l'ancien classement et ne se refuse au numéro d'ordre établi pour les séries de composition." Zacharie Astruc, "Salon de 1870", in: *L'Écho des Beaux-Arts,* vol. 7, 12 June 1870, pp. 1–3, here p. 1, reprinted in Dianne Pitman: *Bazille: Purity, Pose and Painting in the 1860s*, University Park, PA 1998, p. 214.

45 Theodor W. Adorno: "Die Kunst und die Künste", in: idem: *Ohne Leitbild: Parva Aesthetica*, Frankfurt am Main 1967, pp. 168–192, esp. p. 189.

46 Elsen 1974 (see note 11), p. 144. Elsen speaks of a "battleground".

47 For a detailed discussion, see "Picasso, vom Relief zum Reliefhaften" in: Roland Bothner: *Grund und Figur: Die Geschichte des Reliefs und Auguste Rodins Höllentor*, Munich 1993, pp. 117–129.

48 See Magdalena Nieslony: "Iwan Puni zwischen Paris und Petersburg", in: Ada Raev and Isabel Wünsche (eds.): *Kursschwankungen: Russische Kunst im Wertesystem der europäischen Moderne*, Berlin 2007, pp. 76–82.

49 See Doede Hardeman: "De bevrijding van sculptuur: Hoe de moderne beeldhouwkunst de ruimte veroverde", in: *Van Rodin tot Bourgeois: Sculptuur in de 20ste eeuw*, ed. idem and Patrick Elliott, exh. cat.

Gemeentemuseum Den Haag 2016, pp. 9–13; Andreas Franzke: "Picasso, Boccioni, Duchamp: Wegbereiter der modernen Plastik", in: *Von Rodin bis Giacometti: Plastik der Moderne*, ed. Siegmar Holsten, exh. cat. Staatliche Kunsthalle Karlsruhe, Heidelberg 2009, pp. 25–28.

50 See *Auf der Suche nach 0.10: Die letzte futuristische Ausstellung der Malerei*, ed. Matthew Drutt, exh. cat. Fondation Beyeler, Riehen/Basel, Ostfildern 2015.

51 Kurt Schwitters: "MERZ (Für den 'Ararat' geschrieben 19. Dezember 1920)", in: *Der Ararat*, vol. 2, no. 1, January 1921, pp. 3–9, here p. 7.

52 On the research field of material iconography, see the foundational works by Monika Wagner and Dietmar Rübel, not least importantly the source collection: Dietmar Rübel, Monika Wagner and Vera Wolff (eds.): *Materialästhetik: Quellentexte zu Kunst, Design und Architektur*, Berlin 2005.

53 Iris Wenderholm (ed.): *Stein: Eine Materialgeschichte in Quellen der Vormoderne*, Berlin and Boston 2021.

54 P. M. Sprengel: *Handwerke und Künste in Tabellen*, Berlin 1772, p. 149: "A Low Relief in Alabaster".

55 On this subject, see Theresa Nisters: "Zurück zum Ursprung, zu den Quellen, zur Natur und zum Material': Holz – Material mit Geschichte", in: *Geheimnis der Materie: Kirchner, Heckel, Schmidt-Rottluff*, ed. Regina Freyberger, exh. cat. Städel Museum, Frankfurt am Main, Dresden 2019, pp. 30–47.

56 On the history of wax portraits, see Maraike Bückling: "Wachs und Marmor – Augenblick und Ewigkeit: Kunsttheoretische Überlegungen der Neuzeit", in: *Die große Illusion: Veristische Skulpturen und ihre Techniken*, ed. Stefan Roller, exh. cat. Liebieghaus Skulpturensammlung, Frankfurt am Main, Munich 2014, pp. 120–137.

57 See for example Daphne S. Barbour and Shelley G. Sturman: "Degas the Sculptor and His Technique", in: *Edgar Degas*

Sculpture, ed. Suzanne Glover Lindsay et al., exh. cat. National Gallery of Art, Washington, D.C., Princeton 2010, pp. 35–45; and the respective contributions in: exh. cat. Frankfurt am Main 2020 (see note 37).

58 See for example Ursula Ströbele: *Die Bildhaueraufnahmestücke der Académie Royale de Peinture et de Sculpture in Paris 1700–1730*, Petersberg 2012, chap. 8: "Metamorphosen in Stein: Die Bedeutung der Oberfläche", pp. 159–176; Daniela Bohde and Mechthild Fend (eds.): *Weder Haut noch Fleisch: Das Inkarnat in der Kunstgeschichte*, Berlin 2007.

59 See for example the contributions in: Gundolf Winter, Jens Schröter and Christian Spies (eds.): *Skulptur: Zwischen Realität und Virtualität*, Munich 2006.

60 Exh. cat. Münster 1980; exh. cat. New York 1979 (see note 13).

61 On this subject, see *Bildhauerinnen in Deutschland*, ed. Marc Gundel, Arie Hartog and Frank Schmidt, exh. cat. Städtische Museen Heilbronn/Gerhard-Marcks-Haus and Museen Böttcherstraße, Bremen, Cologne 2018.

62 One of the countless more recent examples: Sebastian Jung: "Relief zum NSU-Prozess am Oberlandesgericht in München", 27 August 2020, https://www.jungjungjung.com/2020/08/27/relief-zum-nsu-prozess-am-oberlandesgericht-in-muenchen/ (accessed 13 February 2023).

63 For detailed insights into the eventful history of that project, see Antje Rhauderwiek: "Ernst Barlach: Das Hamburger Ehrenmal", in: *Ernst Barlach: Das Hamburger Ehrenmal*, ed. Uwe M. Schneede, exh. cat. Hamburger Kunsthalle 2004, pp. 7–43.

64 See Bexte 2022 (see note 2), pp. 138f.; Heinrich Wölfflin: "Wie man Skulpturen aufnehmen soll [I]", in: *Zeitschrift für bildende Kunst*, Neue Folge 8, 1897, pp. 294–297.

THE WORKS

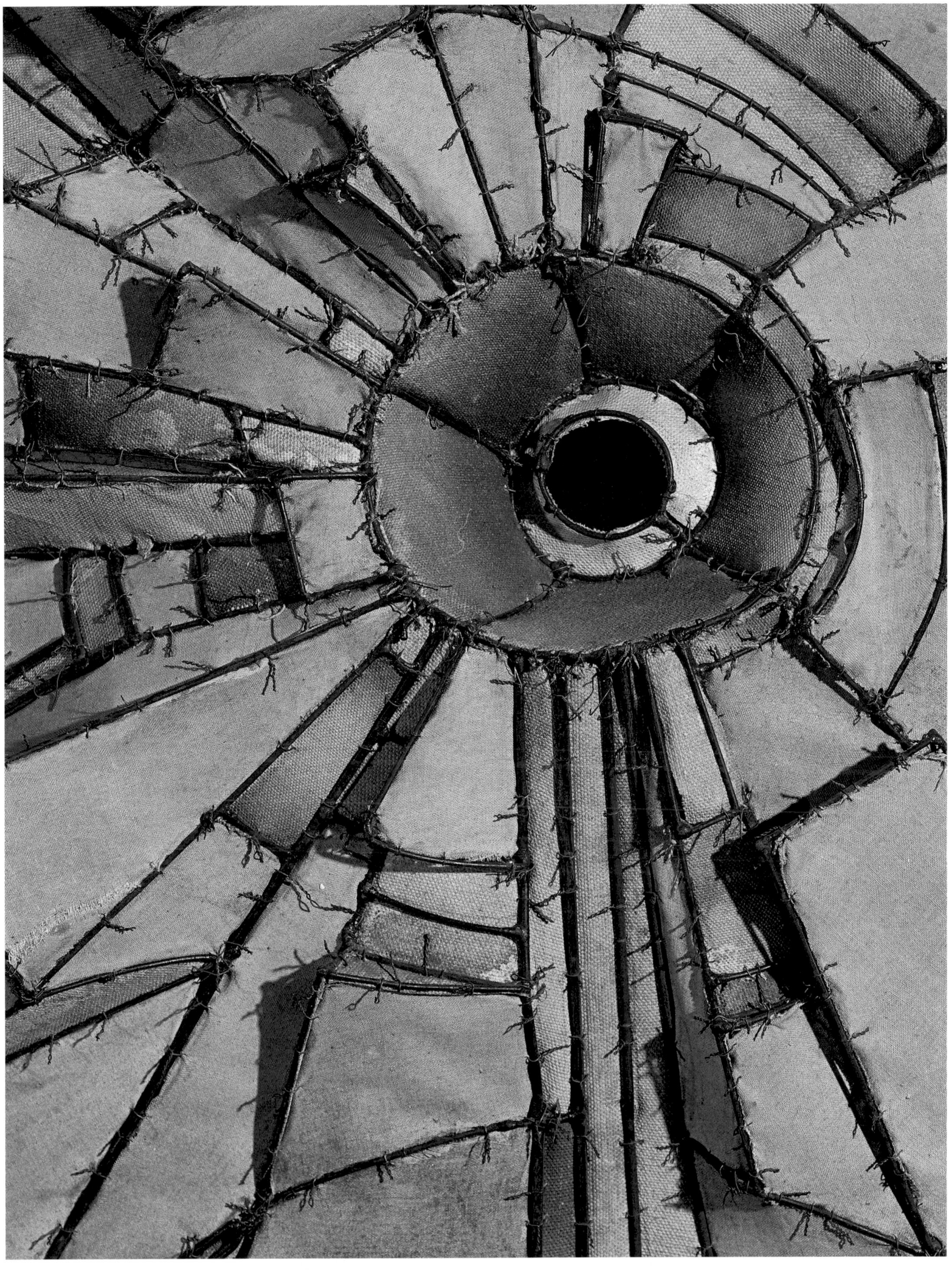

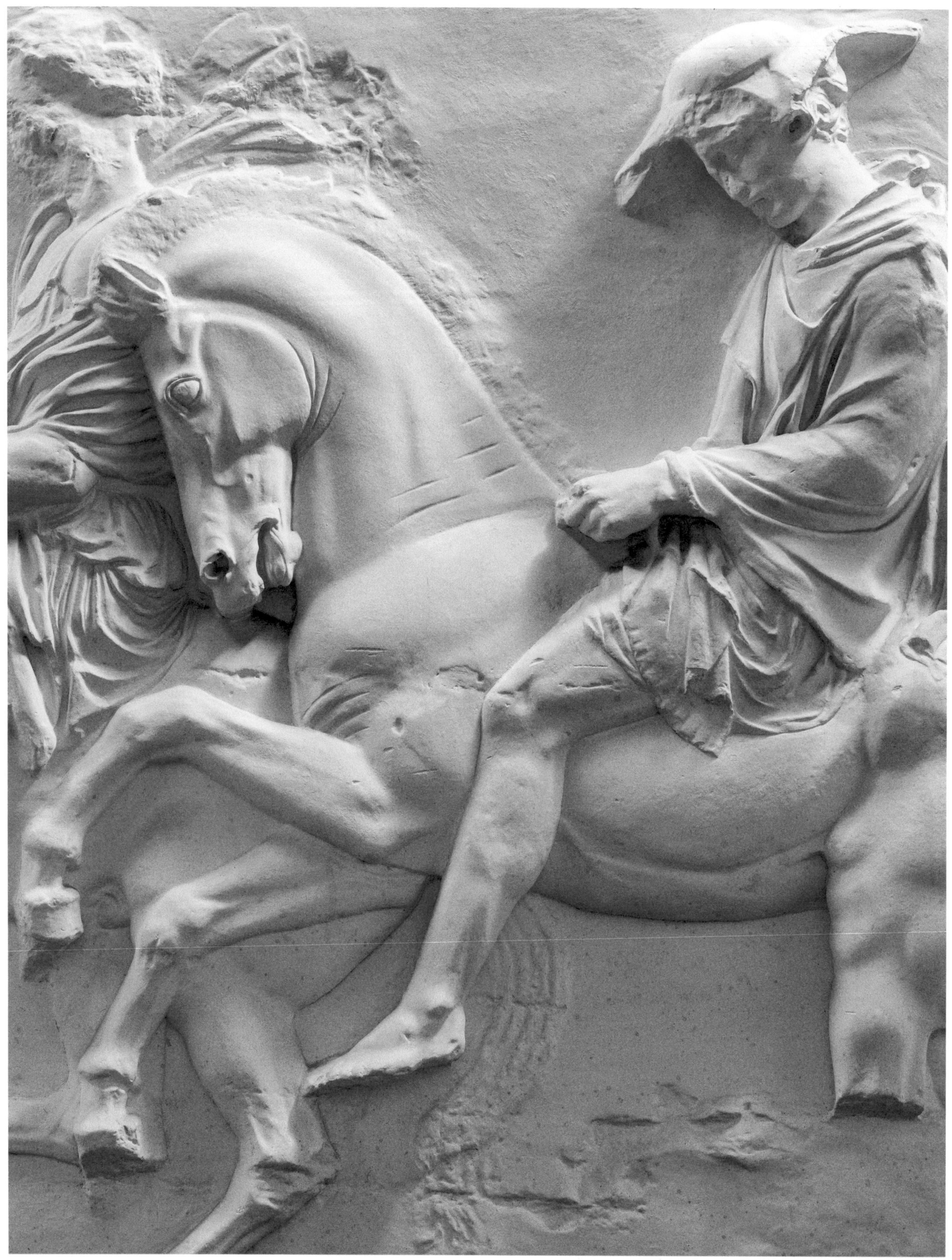

Cats. 1—8

Eva Mongi-Vollmer

"IF YOU HAVEN'T SEEN THE ELGIN MARBLES, YOU HAVEN'T SEEN ANYTHING"

The Parthenon Reliefs and Their Echo

The Parthenon temple has crowned the Athenian Acropolis for nearly 2,500 years. Yet it was only a little over 200 years ago that its extant marble sculptural decorations began to electrify archaeologists, artists and the European public at large. In an undertaking whose legality is still questioned to this day, the transfer of key pieces to London got underway in 1801 under the direction of Lord Elgin, the British ambassador to the Ottoman Empire at the time. The action drew considerable attention even then, but the acquisition of the artefacts by the British Museum in 1816 is what put them in the global limelight once and for all.

Long known as the "Elgin Marbles" after the main protagonist of that controversial acquisition, the works consist of figures from the temple pediments, 92 metope panels featuring battle scenes between humans and mythical beasts in high relief and the frieze running 160 metres along the outer wall of the core structure, worked in low relief and depicting festivities in honour of the goddess Athena. About one metre in height, this frieze is particularly striking by virtue of the sophisticated rhythmicity characterising its dense figural arrangements. One behind the other or staggered side by side in relief no more than six to seven centimetres deep, the 378 humans and 245 animals make their way towards a group of seated gods.[1] The frieze consists of 114 rectangular blocks altogether. As seen in block IX of the west frieze (plaster cast, cat. 1), the bodies are astonishingly lifelike – many of them are represented in motion, with the moving body parts foreshortened accordingly – and their relationship to the surface plane is entirely clear despite the absence of spatial perspective. Artists of the nineteenth and twentieth centuries were especially fascinated by the more than 100 equestrian figures, men of downright casual elegance on powerful steeds.

To this day, many of the questions raised by the frieze have yet to be answered in full. What exactly does the procession depict? Does it represent a specific moment, or combine various temporal and narrative levels (→ Sculptural Narration)? What was the original colour scheme (fig. 1; → Polychrome Reliefs)? Who apart from Phidias – whose authorship we know of from Pausanias – was involved in the creation of the frieze, a work as extensive as it is complex? Were the reliefs carried to completion before or after their installation? The debates over conservation and reconstruction, but also restitution, are equally impassioned.[2]

To whatever degree the sculptural decoration of the Parthenon was and is an object of fascination, the impact it has borne is no less widespread and multifaceted. In the early nineteenth century, for example, the Danish artist Bertel Thorvaldsen was declared the "northern Phidias",[3] the first world's fair in London in 1851 presented a tapestry with a depiction of the frieze,[4] in France a play was devoted to it,[5] and Auguste Rodin adopted the word "Parthenon" as a generic term for something sublime.[6] By the threshold to the twentieth century, both the Parthenon as a whole and its individual elements had become a permanent feature of the collective consciousness and the quintessential iconic symbol of ancient Greek civilisation and culture.[7]

In the words of the Italian sculptor and connoisseur of antiquity Antonio Canova: "If you haven't seen the Elgin Marbles, you haven't seen anything."[8] Of course not everyone had the privilege of studying the originals in London as Canova did as far back as 1815. But the visual means of acquainting oneself with the figures and reliefs were manifold and constantly increasing.[9] What is more, the approaches to the works' artistic reception ranged from faithful copying to various degrees of transformation and even free association, as the examples cited in the following will show.

Even before the treasures left Athens, images of them were available in the form of engraved illustrations in publications such as James Stuart and Nicholas Revett's

Antiquities of Athens (1762–1816). Reference works of this kind circulated among experts, whose ranks, in the period around 1800, included visual artists such as the successful sculptor Johann Gottfried Schadow of Berlin. In productive exchange with his friend Canova, Schadow had studied antiquity in Rome in depth. Nevertheless, for his modelled design for the façade of the Ritter- und Reit-akademie (Academy of Knights) in Berlin, he evidently looked to rider and chariot scenes of the Greek Parthenon frieze for orientation (cats. 2, 3). In keeping with the Athenian work, he consistently refrained from the perspectival opening of the space to create the illusion of depth, anchoring the narrative on the horizontal base line instead. At the same time, Schadow's equestrians and horse teams are surprising in that, rather than pressing forward in a loose procession, the protagonists are depicted reining in their steeds, coming to a halt, or even collapsing.[10]

Schadow would have had another important source at his disposal soon afterwards – plaster casts, not only of the large collection in the British Museum but also of the few original Parthenon reliefs in the Louvre as well as those remaining in Athens. Such casts entered the holdings of Frankfurt's Städel (fig. 2),[11] for example, as early as 1817, and the public Städtische Gemälde-Gallerie in Hamburg from 1852 onwards,[12] while also making their way into countless artists' studios (fig. 3).

In 1855 the young art student Edgar Degas carried out about 20 drawings of Parthenon casts in the study collections of the Écoles des Beaux-Arts in Paris and Lyon, thus laying the foundation for his lifelong preoccupation with the depiction of horses and riders.[13] Showing the relief on block VII of the west frieze (cat. 5), the drawing from Hamburg testifies to the artist's interest in certain isolated details, for instance the three-dimensional representation of one of the horses' heads. Yet the rigorous parallelism to the pictorial plane, an aspect distinguishing the frieze as a whole, would have a lasting impact on Degas. It inspired not only his painterly oeuvre but also his sculptural works, most of which he kept for and to himself. His *Horse Trotting* (cat. 6), for example, like the frieze relief, is viewable only in profile and only from one side, its regular movement and strong forward orientation unfolding exclusively along the plane but never into spatial depth.[14]

Whether or not Degas had photographs of the frieze in his possession has remained a mystery. His contemporary Auguste Rodin, on the other hand, is known to have purchased photographs of the originals in Paris and London, as well as of plaster casts, for the purpose of studying the works.[15] By the turn of the nineteenth to the twentieth century, if not before, the Parthenon frieze was presumably accessible in a wide range of mediums, both two- and three-dimensional, and many sizes. Artists moreover increasingly had the means to travel to Greece. Yet we must not suppose that the Parthenon was always considered an example worthy of emulation. In addition to outright negative reactions – for instance on the part of the Italian Futurists – there were also contradictory views. A case in point is Paul Gauguin, who opined that a child's drawing was better than the Parthenon horses – but took a photographic reproduction to the South Seas with him anyway.[16]

We encounter this kind of ambivalence in the work of Bernhard Hoetger as well. It was under the influence of the west frieze that, in 1914, he created 20 wrought copper sheet relief panels, including the one here on view (cat. 4), for the Lions' Gate designed by Albin Müller for the Mathildenhöhe in Darmstadt:[17] five closely spaced riders gallop into the scene from the left, bridling five steeds rearing up in unison. The dense and extremely shallow staggering of the figures serves to heighten the dynamic movement dramatically. As in the Greek frieze, the all-but-unclothed men differ from one another in hairstyle and facial features representing different types and ages. An artist who took his orientation primarily from non-European examples and in principle rejected antiquity on the grounds that it was decadent, Hoetger here nevertheless drew on the meanwhile canonical ancient Greek masterwork. In the syncretic manner typical of his art, he incorporated Asian stylistic features into his two-dimensional conceptions of both the body and the ornamental vegetation.[18] The pride he took in the relief he had conceived for an outdoor installation is evident in his reuse of it over the fireplace of the Large Club Room in Bremen's Haus Atlantis in 1931.[19]

Other artists had more unreservedly positive associations with Greek art and thus with its High Classical period, which the Parthenon manifests. A movement known as "Modern Classicism"[20] that had taken hold in art in 1920s Germany would branch out in various forms under the National Socialist art and culture policies in effect from 1933 onwards. Hermann Blumenthal, for his part, remained true to the lyrical arcadian style he had developed before the National Socialists' accession to power,[21] as reflected in his 1934 designs for the fountain room of the Museum Folkwang in Essen (cats. 24–28) and continued in his low reliefs of equestrian

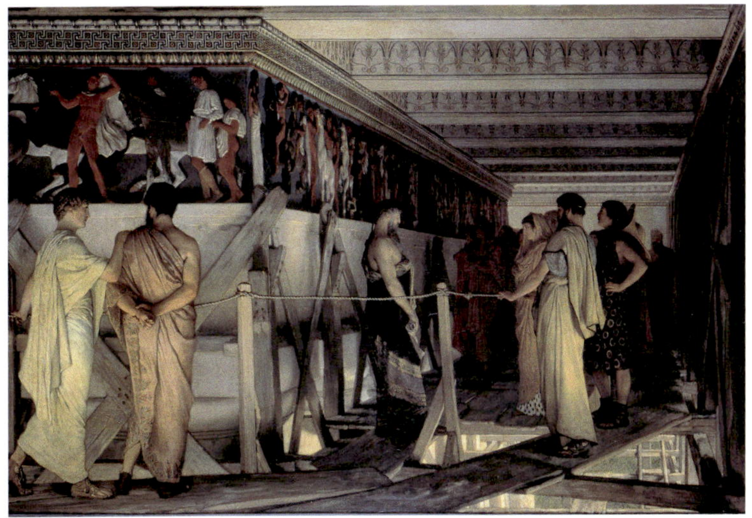

Fig. 1

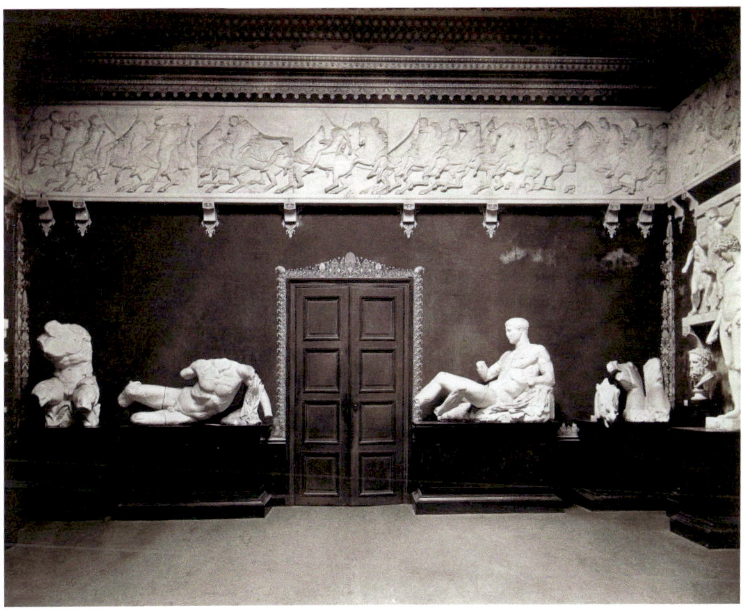

Fig. 2

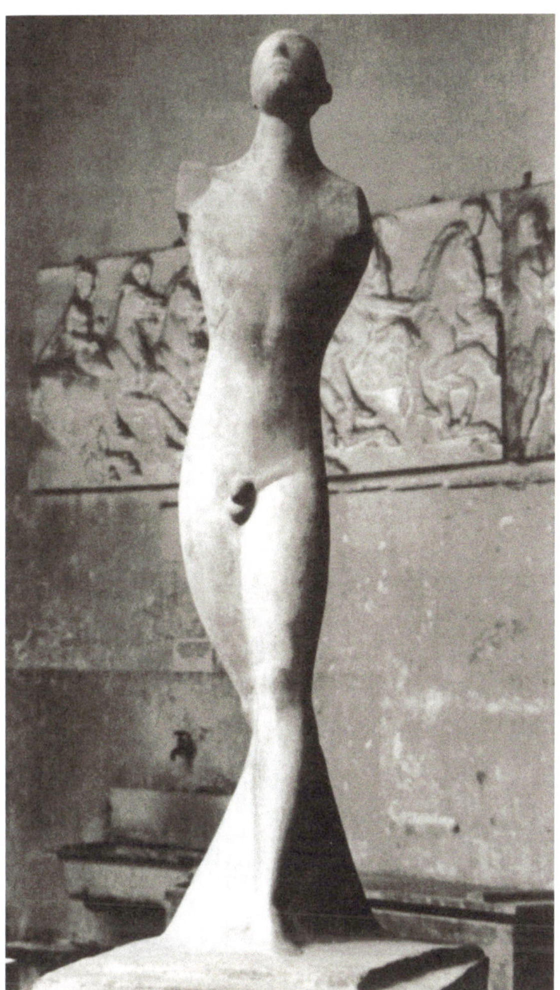

Fig. 3

Fig. 1   Lawrence Alma-Tadema: *Phidias Showing the Parthenon Frieze to His Friends*, 1868, oil on canvas, Birmingham Museums Trust

Fig. 2   View into plaster cast collection of the Städelsches Kunstinstitut in Neue Mainzer Straße, 1833–73, photograph by Joseph Bamberger, Städel-Archiv, Frankfurt am Main

Fig. 3   Edwin Scharff: *Large Striding Man*, parts of the Parthenon frieze in the background (casts), photograph, before 1920

figures. In the example of the latter seen here (cat. 7), the calm, erect pose of the rider – again only scantily dressed – as well as the pronounced verticals and horizontals of all three bodies and the omission of any spatial context lend the depiction a dignified serenity.[22] Although some of the artist's works were defamed as "degenerate" in 1937 and confiscated, he also received public recognition and support on many occasions, for instance with the award of the Cornelius-Preis of the city of Düsseldorf for his plaster model of this relief in 1939 – one of many examples of the contradictions within the National Socialist art system. This warm-hued cast was produced in Berlin in early 1940 for the collector Carl Hagemann.[23]

Blumenthal died a soldier in Russia in August 1942. Several well-known personages had spoken out in favour of his withdrawal from the front, including the state-sanctioned sculptor Arno Breker.[24] In 1939, Werner Hager wrote of the latter artist: "But the decisive factor for Breker's work is his preoccupation with antiquity in all its stages from Archaic to Classical to Hellenistic. […] It was there that he found what he sought – the corporeal being and its elevation to the heroic and mythical."[25] In fact, Breker took the "elevation" of the state-prescribed classicism to dizzying heights. He worked, for instance, on a relief frieze 240 metres in length intended to flank the new north-south axis in Albert Speer's redesign of the Reich capital Berlin. The ten-metre-high reliefs depicted exaggeratedly athletic male figures, many of them nude, as heroic allegories such as *Sacrifice*, *Guardian*, *Comradeship* and *The Avenger*. A five-metre-high version of the last-named was on display in the *Great German Art Exhibition* in Munich in 1941, and a special-issue publication on the show (cat. 8) featured an illustration of it. For his conceptions of ideal art and the ideal body, Breker drew in part on classical battle scenes like those of the Parthenon metopes (fig. 4), taking them to new extremes with regard to both form and content. His penchant for immaculate surfaces led to the cold, dehumanised aesthetic often inherent to National Socialist art. Willi Baumeister, for his part, remained insubordinate to the regime and was ostracised for it accordingly. And it was he who returned the human dimension to Breker's work – or at least to the photographic reproduction of it – by means of ridicule. The Brekerian figure, its genital region overdrawn with a bulbous-nosed face, implodes with a single blow. The "avenger" Baumeister has wielded

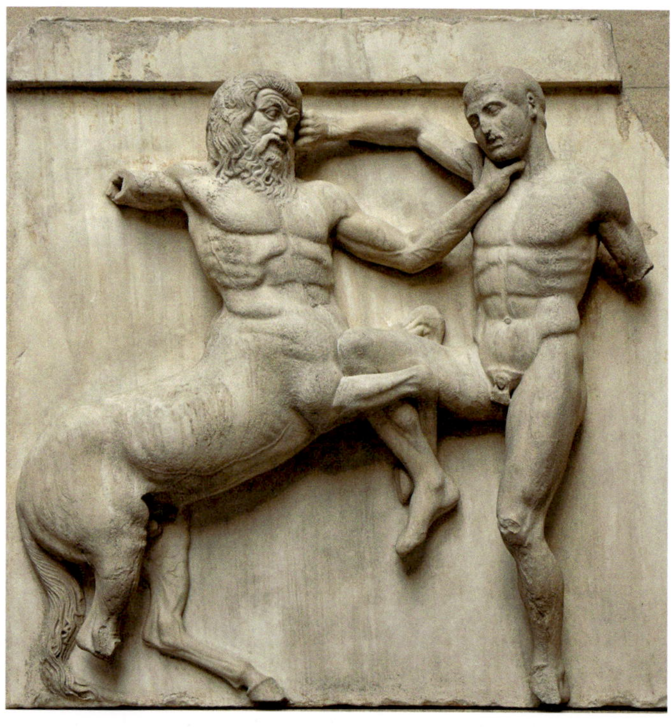

Fig. 4   South Metope XXXI of the Parthenon, 5th century BCE, marble, British Museum, London

not a sword but the pen and brush of the draughtsman and painter as his weapons.[26]

This overdrawing of the photographic reproduction of a relief design not only marks the endpoint of a complex transfer of mediums, but also exemplifies the great arc spanned by artistic responses to the architecture-bound Parthenon relief. Not one of the artists introduced here shared the artistic ambitions and goals of the classical sculptors around Phidias. Nevertheless, the Parthenon reverberates through the ages when it comes to addressing core aspects of the relief – the tension between volume and surface or between the reality of the material dimension and the illusion of space, the colouration, the narrative mode, et cetera – in ever new ways. And above and beyond these many issues of content, form and style, the Parthenon has been and still is an aesthetic ideal for artists, even if in some cases they did not immediately recognise it as such. As Henry Moore summed it up at age 62: "There was a time when […] I believed that Greek and Renaissance art were the enemy. […] It was only perhaps ten or fifteen years ago that I realised how wonderful the Elgin Marbles are."[27]

1   On the history of the Parthenon Frieze, see Jenifer Neils: *The Parthenon Frieze*, Cambridge 2001; also see the numerous publications by Ian Jenkins, for example "Der ionische Fries des Parthenon", in: *Zurück zur Klassik: Ein neuer Blick auf das alte Griechenland*, ed. Vinzenz Brinkmann, exh. cat. Liebieghaus Skulpturensammlung, Frankfurt am Main, Munich 2013, pp. 195–201; also see: Barbillon 2014, pp. 97–108.

2   Ulrike Kvech-Hoppe: *Der Fries im 19. Jahrhundert: Ästhetische und gattungsspezifische Aspekte einer Kunstform*, Weimar 2001, p. 21. The restitution debate permeates all fields of specialist literature as well as international politics. The UNESCO recently made a renewed effort to facilitate the works' return.

3   Quoted in ibid., p. 40 (also see the sources there).

4   Ibid., p. 61.

5   Ibid., p. 29.

6   Bénédicte Garnier: "'My dream as a sculptor' – The Thousand Parthenons of Auguste Rodin", in: *Rodin and the Art of Ancient Greece*, ed. Celeste Farge et al., exh. cat. The British Museum, London, London 2018, pp. 34–53, here p. 49.

7   Artists were naturally also inspired by many other ancient works of architecture and art such as the Temple of Apollo at Bassae and the Temple of Zeus in Olympia.

8   Quoted in Kvech-Hoppe 2001 (see note 2), p. 12.

9   Stelios Lydakis: "The Impact of the Parthenon Sculptures on 19th and 20th Century Sculpture and Painting", in: Panayotis Tournikiotis (ed.): *The Parthenon and Its Impact in Modern Times*, Athens 1994, pp. 230–257.

10   *Johann Gottfried Schadow und die Kunst seiner Zeit*, ed. Bernhard Maaz, exh. cat. Städtische Kunsthalle Düsseldorf et al., Cologne 1994, p. 262; on the bronze casts of works by Schadow commissioned by director Lichtwark for the Hamburg Kunsthalle, see

Anna Seidel: *Skulptur für Hamburg: Alfred Lichtwarks Gründung einer Skulpturensammlung in der Hamburger Kunsthalle*, Hamburg 2021, pp. 42–46; *Johann Gottfried Schadow: Berührende Formen*, ed. Yvette Deseyve, exh. cat. Staatliche Museen zu Berlin, Alte Nationalgalerie, Munich 2022.

11   Ursula Mandel: "Die Abguß-sammlung des Städelschen Kunstinstitut und ihre Erweiterung als Sammlung des Archäologischen Instituts der Universität", in: Marlene Herfort-Koch et al. (eds.): *Begegnungen: Frankfurt und die Antike*, Frankfurt am Main 1994, pp. 231–252, here p. 232.

12   Seidel 2021 (see note 10), pp. 13–17. My thanks to Ute Haug and Felix Krebs of the Hamburger Kunsthalle for breaking down the history of the acquisitions.

13   See *Degas: Klassik und Experiment*, ed. Alexander Eiling, exh. cat. Staatliche Kunsthalle Karlsruhe, Munich 2014, pp. 202f. (Sonja Maria Krämer).

14   See *En passant: Impressionism in Sculpture,* ed. Alexander Eiling and Eva Mongi-Vollmer, exh. cat. Städel Museum, Frankfurt am Main, Munich 2020, pp. 110–121 (Alexander Eiling).

15   Exh. cat. London 2018 (see note 6), pp. 86–89.

16   On Gauguin's statement, see Lydakis 1994 (see note 9), p. 244. On the photograph in question, see Neils 2001 (see note 1), p. 230; Martin Schwander: "Paul Gauguin, der untröstliche Magier: Eine Einführung", in: *Paul Gauguin*, ed. Raphaël Bouvier and idem, exh. cat. Fondation Beyeler, Riehen/Basel, Ostfildern 2015, pp. 11–27, here p. 21.

17   Initially installed on the Lions' Gate in conjunction with the Mathildenhöhe exhibition of 1914, the reliefs were then placed in storage until the reinstallation of the gate on the Rosenhöhe. At that time, a selection of only eight or ten of the 20 reliefs were mounted, and those in turn replaced by casts in the 1970s. My thanks to Moya Schönberg of the Institut

Mathildenhöhe Darmstadt for clarifying the history of the panels' installation.

18   Ingo Kerls: "'Wie Ahasver treibt es ihn durch die Kunstgeschichte der Menschheit.' Inhaltliche Kontinuität im Werk Bernhard Hoetgers", in: *Faszination Nofretete: Bernhard Hoetger und Ägypten*, ed. Katja Lembke, exh. cat. Niedersächsisches Landesmuseum Hannover, Petersberg 2013, pp. 13–27.

19   Ill. in: *Bernhard Hoetger: Bildhauer, Maler, Baukünstler, Designer*, ed. Dieter Golücke, exh. cat. Museum am Ostwall, Dortmund, Lilienthal 1984, p. 162.

20   *Ateliergemeinschaft Klosterstraße 1933–1945: Künstler in der Zeit des Nationalsozialismus*, ed. Angela Lammert, exh. cat. Akademie der Künste Berlin, Berlin 1994.

21   *Sterngucker: Hermann Blumenthal und seine Zeit*, ed. Josephine Gabler, exh. cat. Georg Kolbe Museum, Berlin, 2006.

22   Josephine Gabler: "'Bleiben wir heiter und schreiben wir weiter.' Hermann Blumenthals Bemühungen um öffentliche Förderung nach 1933", in: ibid., pp. 55–72, esp. pp. 62f.

23   Letter from Hermann Blumenthal to Carl Hagemann, 29 January 1940, in: Hans Delfs et al. (eds.): *Kirchner, Schmidt-Rottluff, Nolde, Nay … Briefe an den Sammler und Mäzen Carl Hagemann*, Ostfildern 2004, no. 1136; see Christian Adolf Isermeyer: *Hermann Blumenthal: Das plastische Werk*, Stuttgart 1993, catalogue raisonné no. R 27.

24   Magdalena Bushart: "Arno Breker (geb. 1900) – Kunstproduzent im Dienst der Macht", in: *Skulptur und Macht: Figurative Plastik im Deutschland der 30er und 40er Jahre*, ed. ders., exh. cat. Städtische Kunsthalle Düsseldorf, Berlin 1983, pp. 155–158.

25   Werner Hager: "Der Bildhauer Arno Breker", in: *Kunst für Alle*, vol. 54, no. 5, February 1939, pp. 18–25, here p. 20.

26   See Peter Chametzky: "Marginal Comments, Oppositional Work:

Willi Baumeister's Confrontation with Nazi Art", in: *Willi Baumeister: Zeichnungen, Gouachen, Collagen*, exh. cat. Staatsgalerie Stuttgart et al., Stuttgart 1989, pp. 251–272, here pp. 257f.; idem: "Willi Baumeister, 1889–1955", in: *Kunst für Keinen: 1933–1945*, ed. Ilka Voermann, exh. cat. Schirn Kunsthalle Frankfurt, Munich 2022, pp. 60–65.

27   Henry Moore, quoted in Christa Lichtenstern: *Henry Moore: Werk – Theorie – Wirkung*, Munich and Berlin 2008, p. 146.

Cat. 1   Block IX of the west frieze on the Parthenon, plaster cast,
103 × 144 × 12 cm, Antikensammlung und Skulpturensaal
der Goethe-Universität Frankfurt am Main (Frankfurt only)

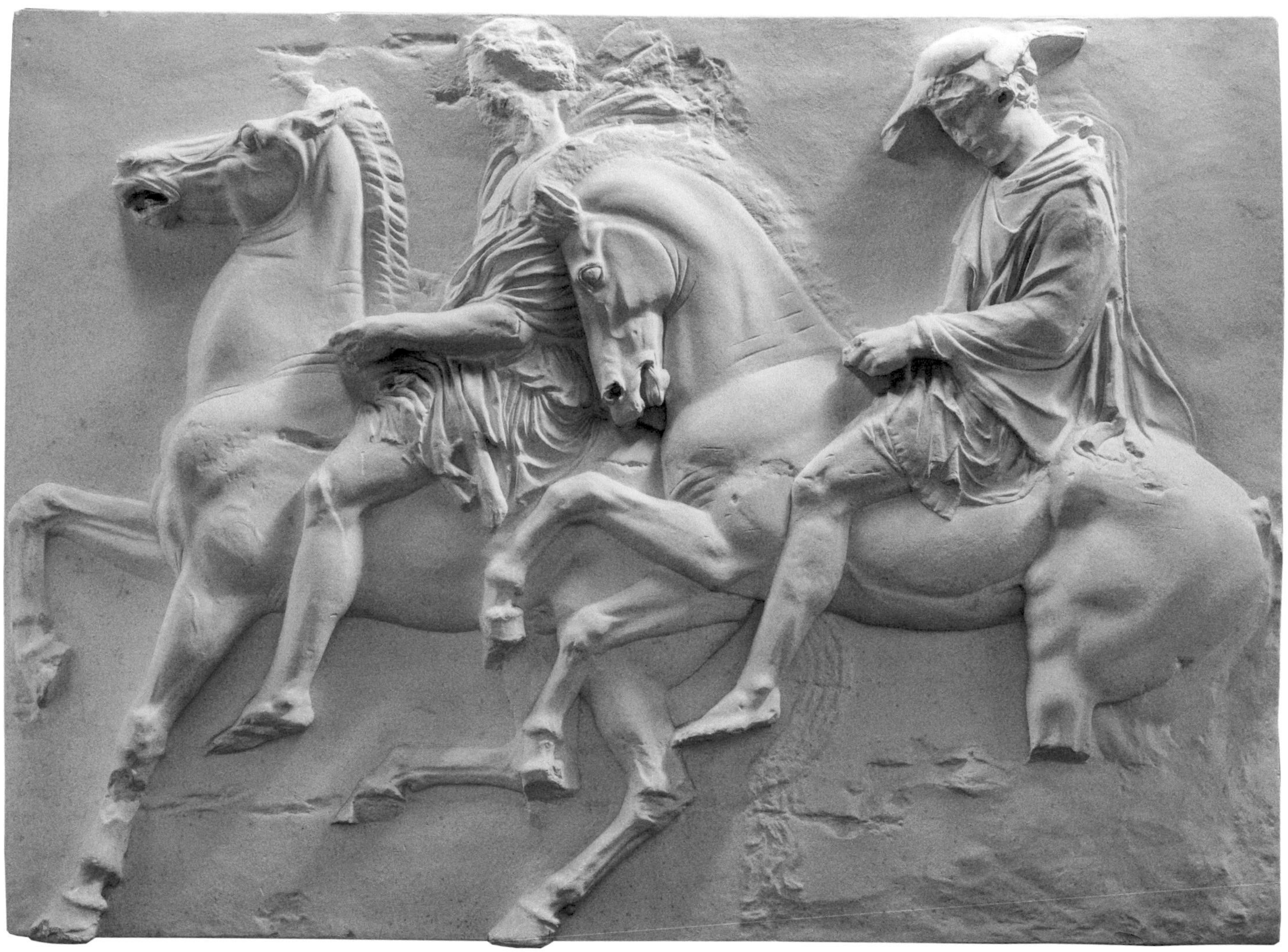

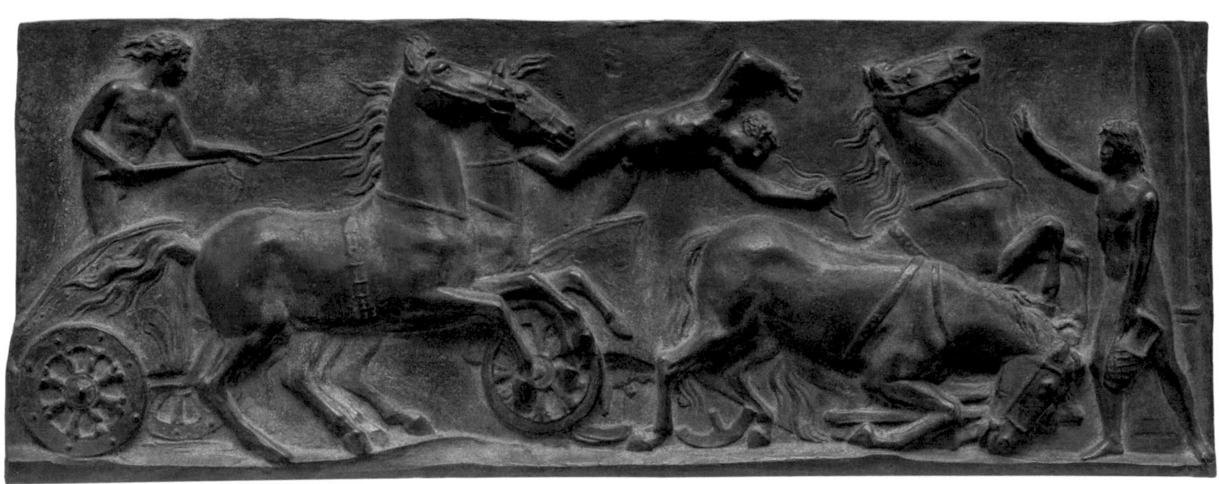

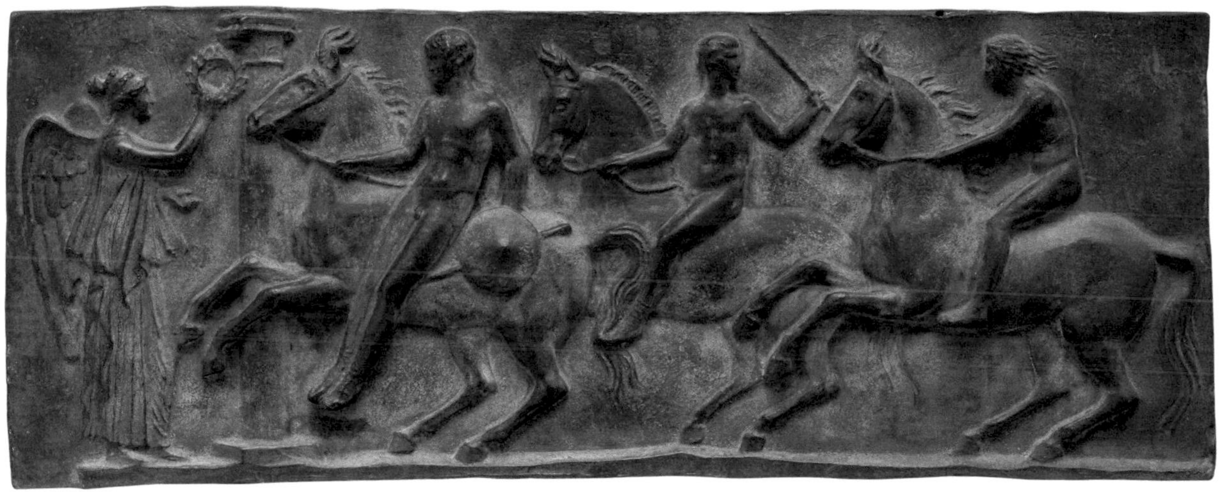

Cat. 4   Bernhard Hoetger: *Equestrian Relief, Former Right Gate-Wing in the Lions' Gate by Albin Müller*, 1914, copper sheet, wrought, 132 × 139 cm, Institut Mathildenhöhe, Städtische Kunstsammlung Darmstadt, inv. no. 128/03 PL

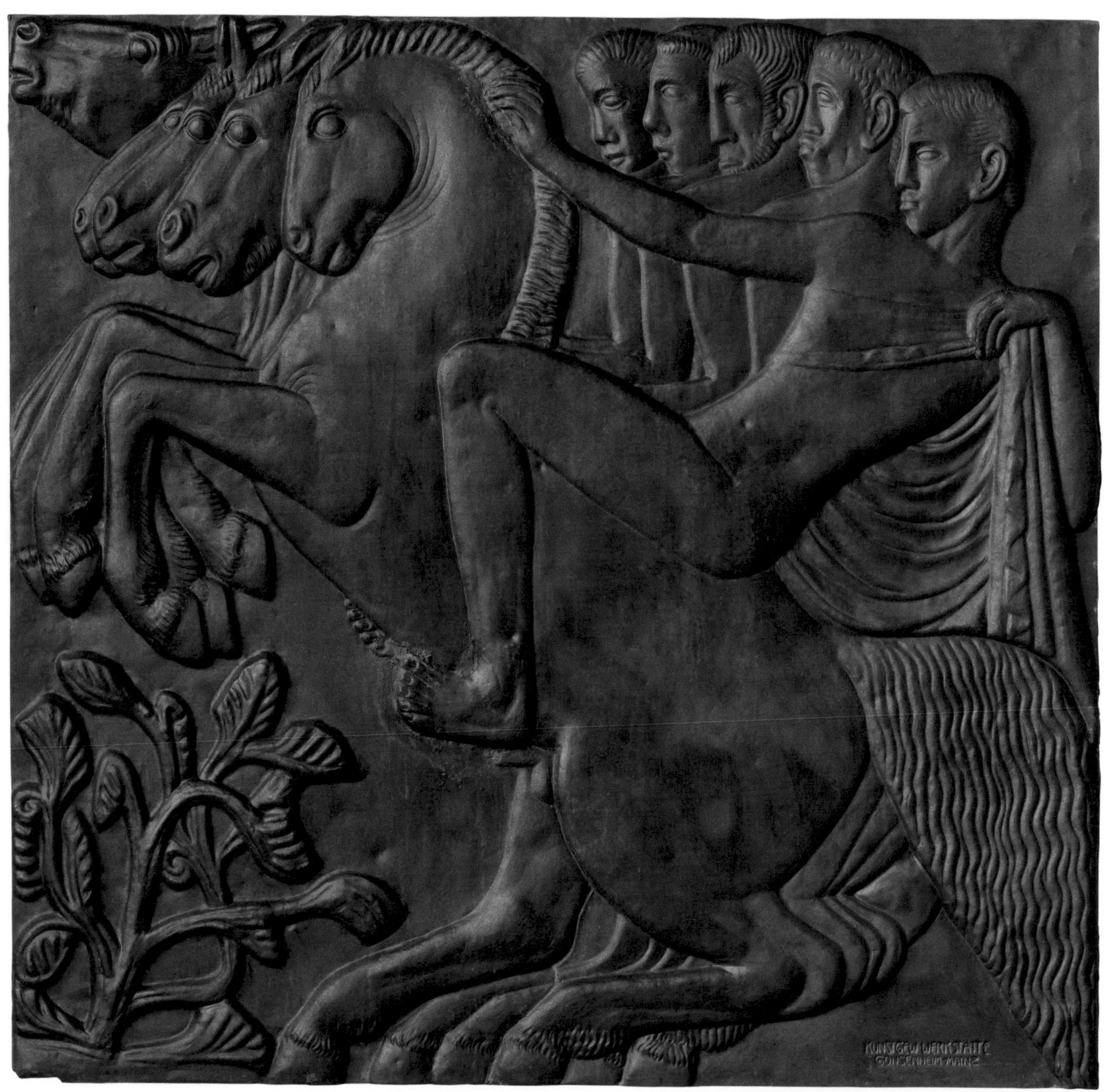

Cat. 5   Edgar Degas: *Study after the Parthenon Frieze*, 1857,
           pencil on brown paper, 26.8 × 38 cm, Hamburger Kunsthalle,
           Kupferstichkabinett, inv. no. 1976-223 (Frankfurt only)

Cat. 6   Edgar Degas: *Horse Trotting, the Feet Not Touching the
           Ground* (*Cheval au trot, les pieds ne touchant pas le sol*),
           1870–80, cast 1919–26, bronze, 22.5 × 27 × 12.7 cm,
           Städel Museum, Frankfurt am Main, inv. no. SGP 62

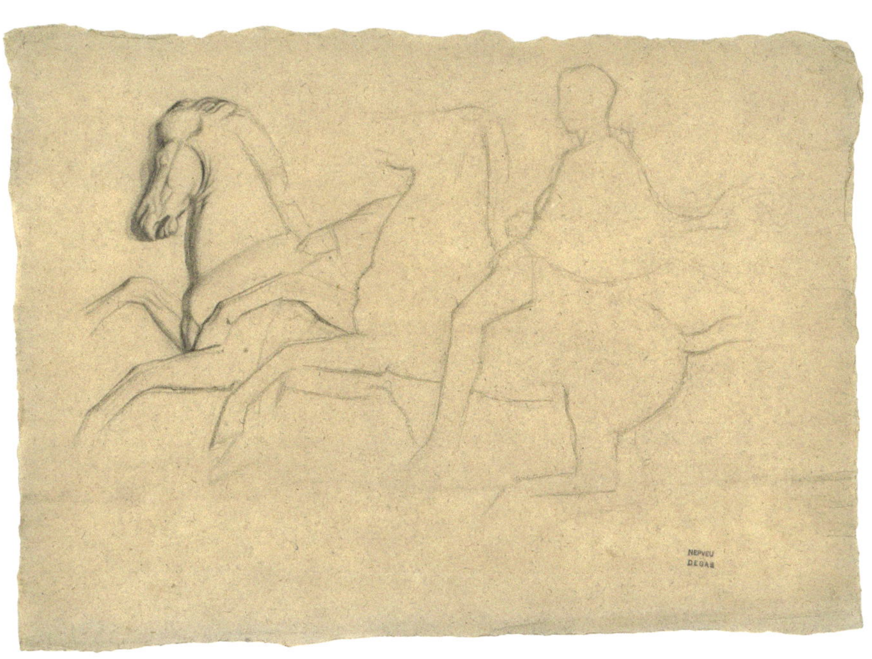

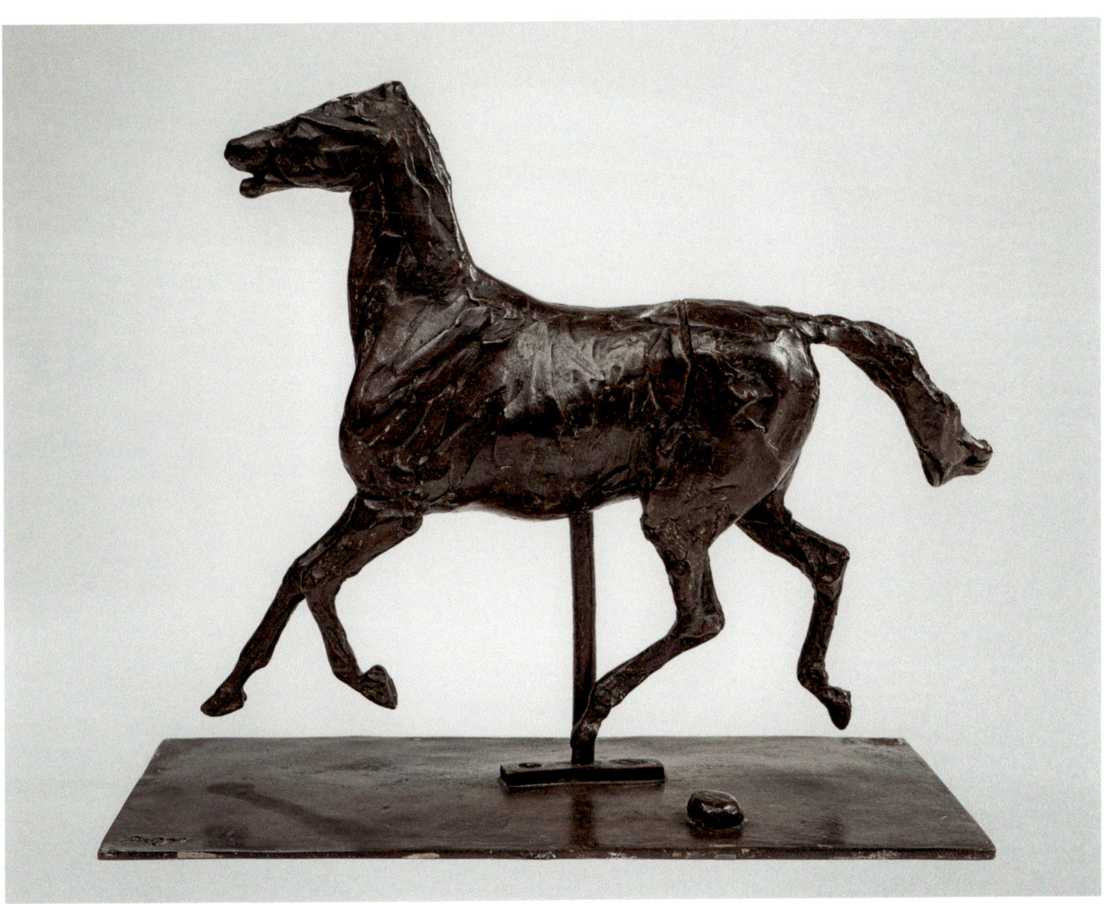

Cat. 7 Hermann Blumenthal: *Equestrian at the Watering Place* (*Schwemmereiter*), 1940, bronze, 69.4 × 64.9 × 5.6 cm, Städel Museum, Frankfurt am Main, permanent loan from private collection, inv. no. LG 152

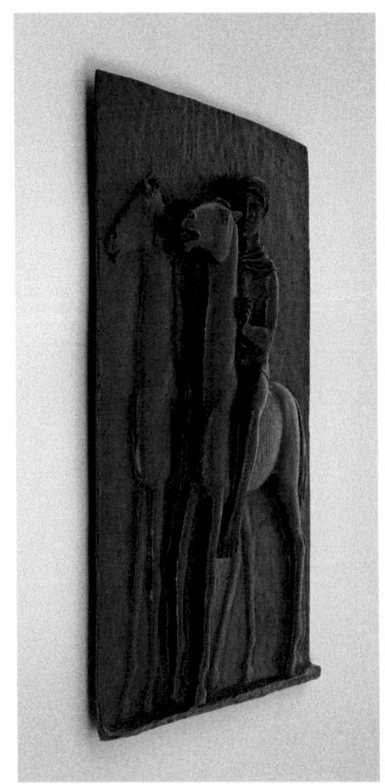

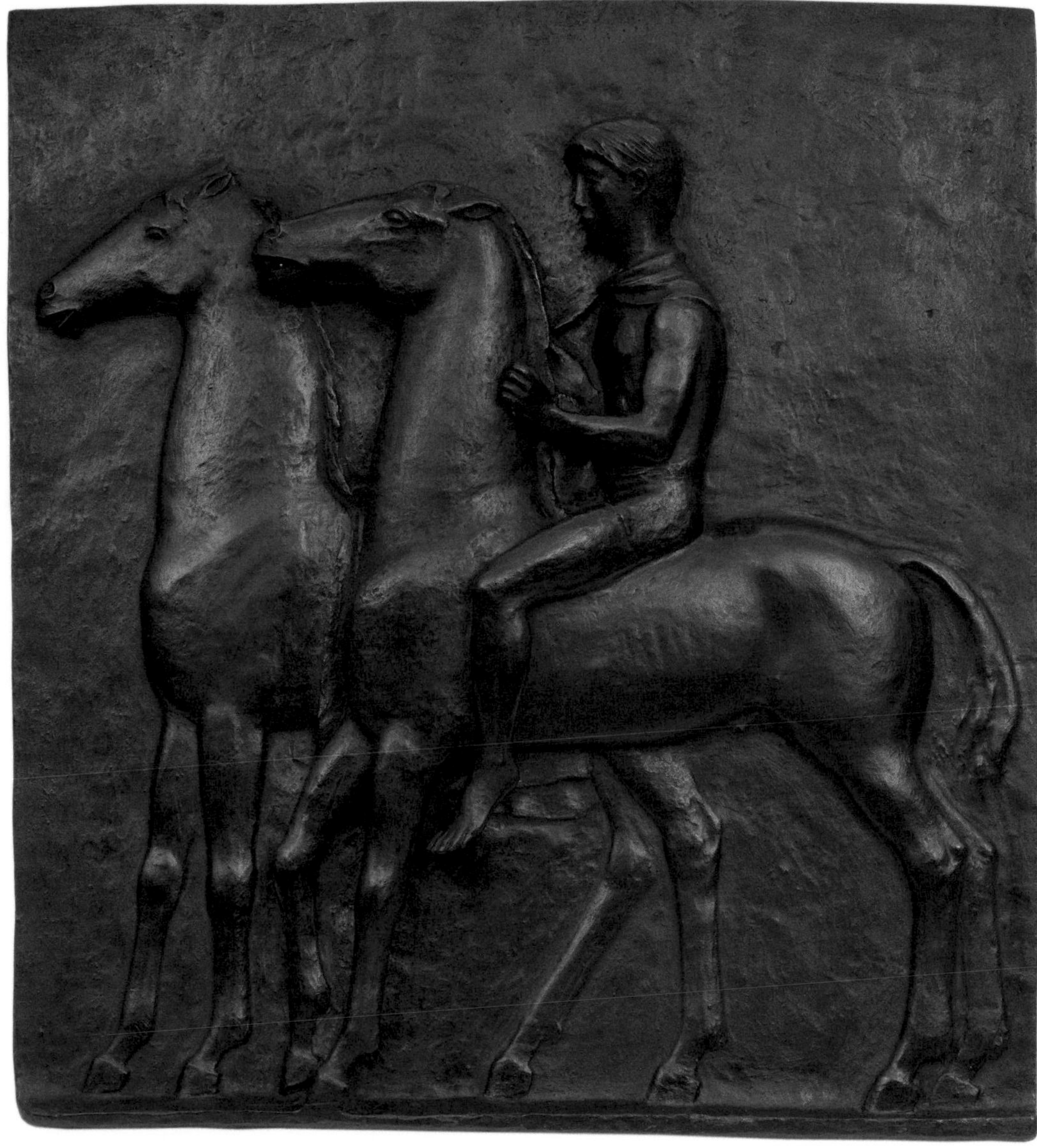

Willi Baumeister: *The Avenger (Overpainting with Ink)*, ca. 1941, in: Special issue *Grosse Deutsche Kunstausstellung*, 1941, part II, page 12: "Arno Breker, Berlin: Der Rächer / The Avenger (Relief)", 30.8 × 23.5 cm, private collection

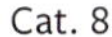

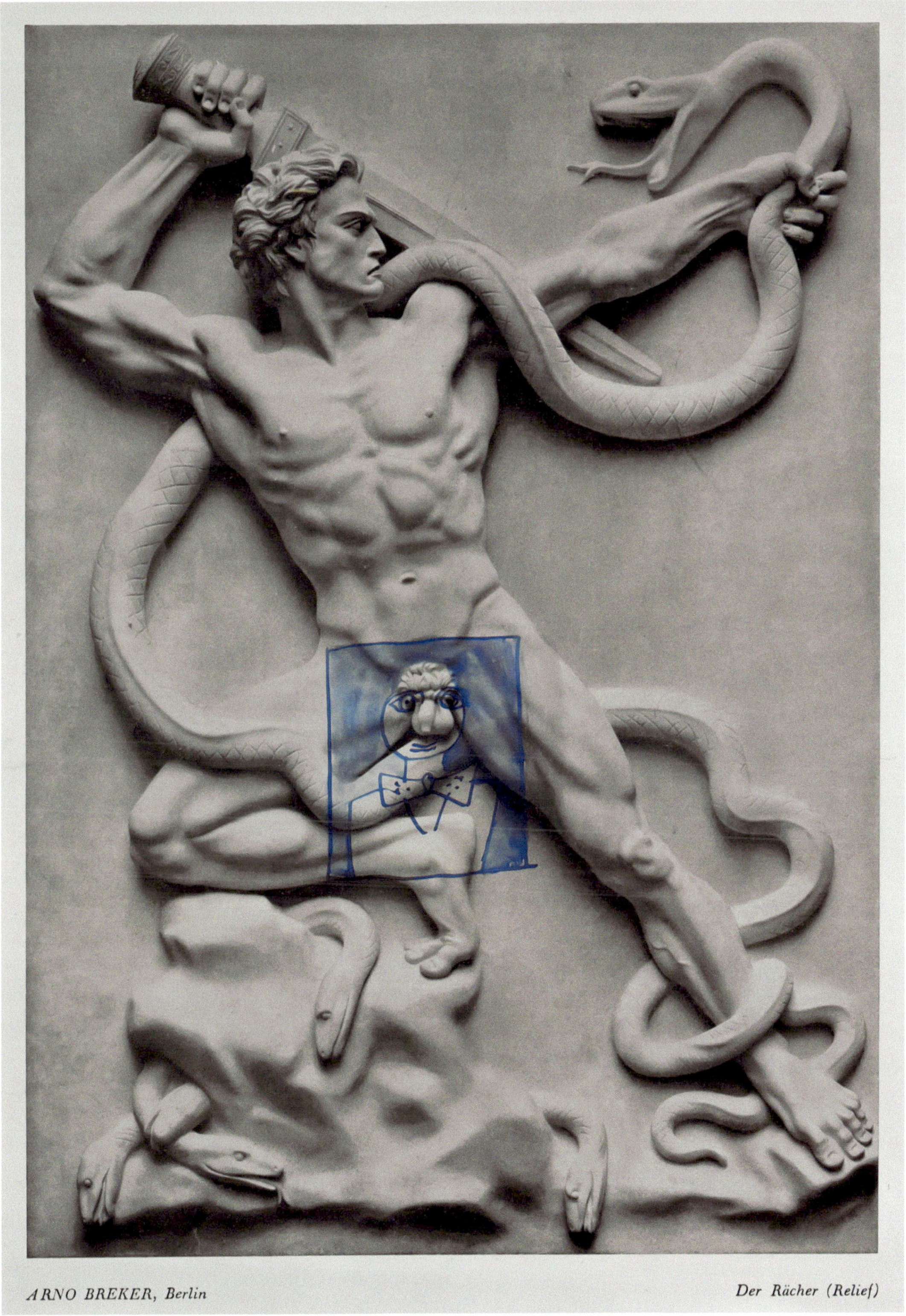

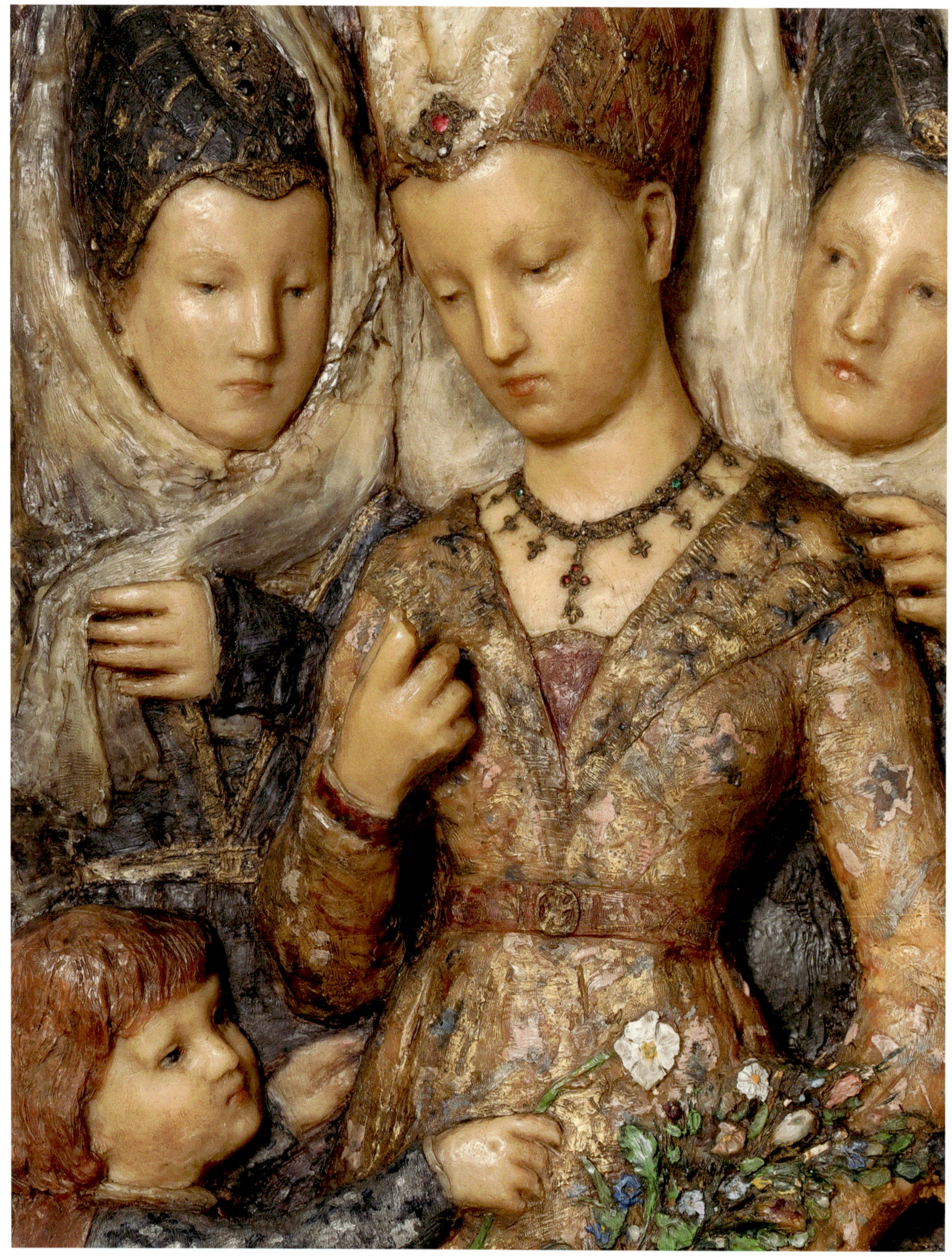

Cats. 9 — 17

POLYCHROME RELIEFS

"The producing generation of the present is convinced of the necessity that, already now, the colour of sculpture must be regained, and it will have its will."[1] It was with these words that, in 1885, the German art historian and later director of the Hamburg Kunsthalle Alfred Lichtwark commented on a large-scale polychrome sculpture exhibition project carried out by the Nationalgalerie in Berlin.[2] In doing so, he was joining a discussion revolving around the pros and cons of colour as an attribute of sculpture – a quite contentious topic in artists' circles of the fin de siècle.[3] Controversial since as far back as the Renaissance, the issue now came to a head in fierce conflicts over the question of the original polychromy of ancient marble sculptures. The defenders of monochrome purism were rapidly losing ground in view of research by Antoine-Chrysostôme Quatremère de Quincy, Gottfried Semper, Georg Treu and others offering ever more tangible evidence of the original polychrome conception of ancient sculpture.[4] And it was Treu, the director of the Königliche Sächsische Antiken- und Abgusssammlung (Royal Saxon Antiquities and Cast Collection) in Dresden, who provided the impulse for an exhibition project in Berlin intended to present an overview of the history of coloured sculpture through more than 330 objects. The show left no doubt that polychrome sculptures had been common across geographical and temporal boundaries from ancient Egypt and classical antiquity to the Middle Ages and the Renaissance, as well as in Eastern Asia. Moreover, it featured works by artists such as Arnold Böcklin, Henry Cros, Adolf von Hildebrand and Artur Volkmann testifying to the widespread contemporary artistic interest in sculptural polychromy. By virtue of their number alone, polychrome reliefs already held a prominent place in this show.

The two female portraits Cros contributed to the Berlin exhibition (today no longer clearly identifiable) were on display in the section devoted to "reliefs modelled in coloured wax".[5] In 1885, the artist was known not only as an innovator of the glass paste (*pâte de verre*) technique but also, and especially, for his historicist works in wax. In fact, he had written an extensive treatise on the artistic application of this material the previous year.[6] Even if wax had been in use for sculpture since antiquity, it had a decidedly mixed if not downright bad reputation among nineteenth-century experts on art. Because its surface resembled the appearance of human skin more closely than any other known material, it was used for wax figures as well as for models of body parts and organs in anatomical collections, but art critics usually condemned its use in artistic sculpture.[7] They were quite favourably disposed towards Cros' wax sculptures, however, owing above all to his adoption of medieval and Renaissance motifs that had become very popular again in the age of historicism.[8] Moreover, they underscored the elaborate working process in which the artist initially poured the wax into a plaster mould, then modelled it in more detail after it had cooled and finally gave it a lifelike appearance by applying oil paints enhanced with coloured-glass inlays.[9] Cros' wax relief known as *The Three Fairies* (cat. 9) – a title presumably bestowed on it by posterity – is a representative example of these works, which the artist produced until the mid-1880s. Executed in a narrow vertical format and probably exhibited as early as 1882 under the title *L'Horoscope*,[10] the relief depicts three women clad in Burgundian court attire. Despite their medieval dress, however, the names scratched into the foundation identify them as figures of classical mythology. Flora, the goddess of spring, is flanked at the left by Circe, an enchantress of *Odyssey* fame, and at the right by Medea, the wife of Jason in the myth of the Argonauts and likewise endowed with magical powers. The constellation is puzzling. According to one explanation, the artist's intention was – quite in the vein of the symbolist fascination with the "femme fatale" – to assemble three female figures who, according to ancient tales, had used their charms to ensnare men and lead them morally astray. Yet this reading may fall short of the mark; at any rate, the artist seems to have deliberately toned down the erotic connotations of the names by dressing the figures in chaste clothing and introducing a small child and a dog to the scene.

In the late nineteenth century, few characters embodied the dangers of female seduction better than the Gorgon Medusa, at the sight of whom every mortal turned to stone. Having advanced from dread of antiquity to seductress par excellence, she was a favoured subject among symbolist artists. One of the most impressive examples is *Shield with the Head of Medusa* by Arnold Böcklin and his son-in-law, the sculptor Peter Bruckmann.[11] The severed head juts out from a dark, round, convex surface in high relief. The eyes are frozen in a piercing, horror-filled stare; the mouth is open in a silent scream. In terms of motif, the two artists took orientation from a pictorial type known since antiquity: the use of the head of Medusa to decorate the shields of deities as a deterrent to would-be attackers. Caravaggio's painted Medusa shield (fig. 1) also seems to have been a major source of inspiration. Böcklin and Bruckmann showed their joint work at the 1885 exhibition in Berlin, where it was on display side by side with polychrome antique sculptures.[12] After it suffered damage during the return transport, the two artists created a second version in papier-mâché from which several plaster casts were subsequently taken (cat. 10).[13] The relief is a three-dimensional formulation of a pictorial idea Böcklin had already realised in painting, his primary artistic medium, in 1878 (fig. 2). Now the realism of his painted Medusa competed with the hyperrealism of the coloured relief in an intra-oeuvre paragone. Like many painters who also worked with sculpture, Böcklin had no reservations about colouring his objects. He regarded the practice as a continuation of a tradition of polychrome sculpture that had existed since antiquity – and thus took an explicit stand against the proponents of monochromy.[14]

Like Böcklin, the Belgian painter Fernand Khnopff produced only a few three-dimensional works, many of which he repeated in different materials and colour schemes.[15] He was equally fascinated with the figure of Medusa. Yet in contrast to Böcklin's shield, Khnopff created his *Mask* of around 1897 (cat. 14) as a relief object without a support, so that the viewer is left in the dark about the nature of the figure depicted. He had presumably taken his formal inspiration from the Medusa on the shield of Athena on the Parthenon (fig. 3; → Echo of the Parthenon). It is not snakes, however, but vegetal forms and blossoms that frame the face of his ideally beautiful, androgynous being. The wings sprouting from the head are moreover reminiscent of Hypnos, the god of sleep, whom the artist had depicted around the same time in the form of a bust modelled on a Roman bronze head in the British Museum.[16] Khnopff painted his *Mask* in delicate pastel shades and gold, thereby transporting it to an otherworldly realm. This effect must have been more pronounced in the first version, made of ivory, enamel and gilded bronze, than in the second version now in Hamburg, made of the plaster-like material gesso duro.[17] In the few sculptures he produced, Khnopff explored the pictorial language of his paintings and drawings in the round. In the process, he created a world of symbols that – in an expression of his personal mythology – became a defining element of his private sphere. In this context the line between painting and sculpture was fluid, and the polychromy of the reliefs closely echoed the colours and forms of his art as a whole.

For the marble relief *Sleep* (cat. 13), on the other hand, artist Albert Marque relied entirely on the discreet colouration of the chosen material. After all, even supposedly monochrome reliefs can exhibit chromaticity, for example in the ever-unique grain of marble. A young woman with closed eyes appears as a half-length figure next to a lily. Not only its rendition as a low relief but also the framing architecture place Marque's depiction in the tradition of Italian reliefs of the quattrocento. It was with good reason that, in view of a sculpture on display at the 1905 Salon d'Automne amid paintings by Henri Matisse, André Derain and Maurice de Vlaminck, the art critic Louis Vauxcelles referred to Marque as "Donatello chez les Fauves".[18] The Renaissance had elevated to an ideal the aesthetic of ancient marble sculpture in which the marble surface was visible. This inspired artists such as Donatello to create works of their own that derive their appeal from the individual veining of the stone (fig. 4). In his relief, Marque adopted this tradition, availing himself more of a shallow, precise cut of the lines than of three-dimensional modelling. A decisive aspect here are the light effects that play out between the subtly worked parts of the depiction and vitalise the marble surface. The work is a symbolist devotional image alluding not only to the Virgin Mary but also to the penchant for internalisation and the evocation of unbodied transparency so widespread in the years around 1900.

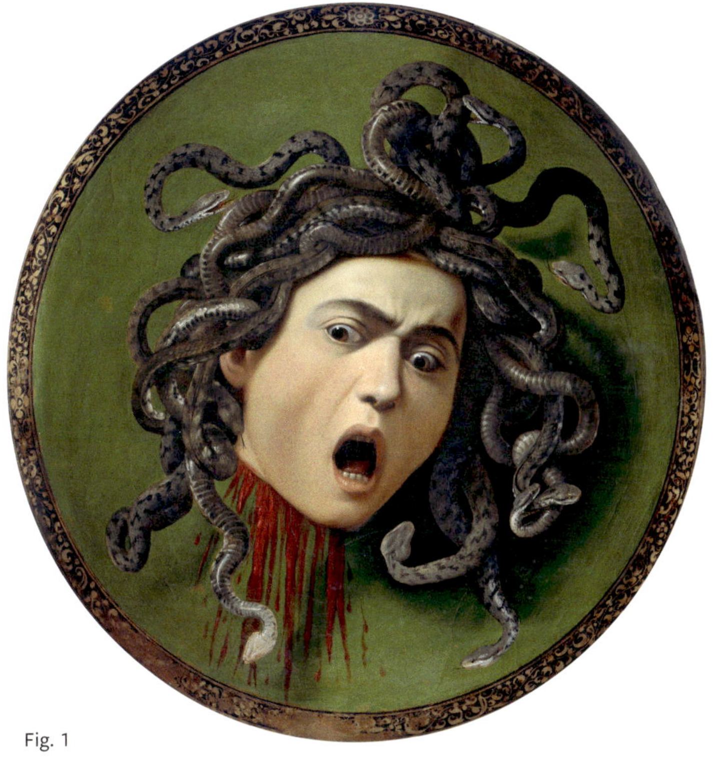

Fig. 1

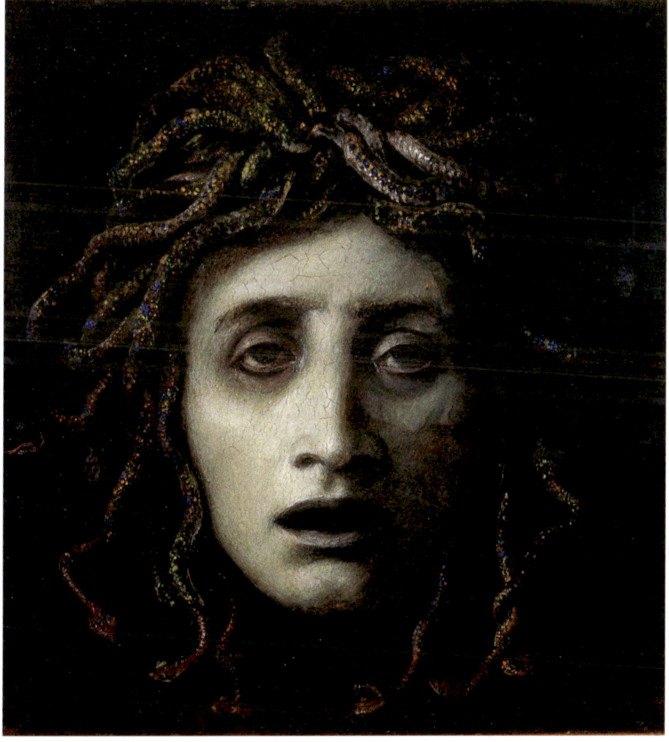

Fig. 2

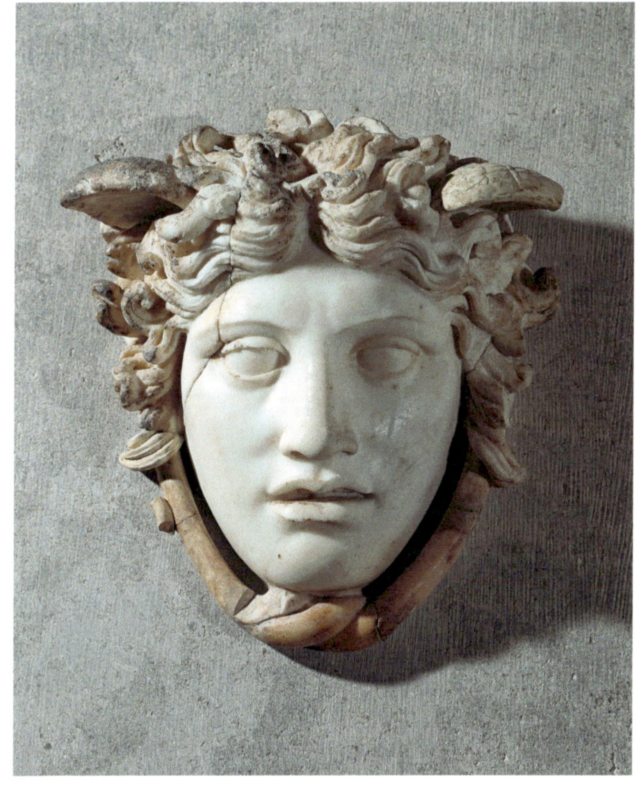

Fig. 3

Fig. 1   Michelangelo Merisi da Caravaggio: *Head of the Medusa*, 1597, oil on canvas on wood, Gallerie degli Uffizi, Florence

Fig. 2   Arnold Böcklin: *Medusa*, ca. 1878, oil on wood, Germanisches Nationalmuseum, Nuremberg

Fig. 3   *Medusa Rondanini*, Roman copy of the head of Medusa on the shield of the Athena statue on the Parthenon, 2nd century BCE, marble, Staatliche Antikensammlung und Glyptothek, Munich

Like Marque's work, Adolf von Hildebrand's *Elisabeth von Herzogenberg as Saint Cecilia* (cat. 12) also follows the tradition of classical relief art, which the artist strongly advocated in his theoretical writings.[19] Executed in terracotta as a low relief, the scene is a downscaled version of a funerary monument created by the sculptor in 1893 in memory of Elisabeth von Herzogenberg, née Stockhausen (1847–1892) (fig. 5).[20] The work in white majolica depicts the pianist and patron of music as Saint Cecilia playing the organ in a loggia before a balustrade and two arches. To approximate the appearance of the monochrome white gravestone, the artist painted the surface of the terracotta relief in shades of white and pink. For the saint's hair and the background behind the arcade, moreover, he used gold in a reminiscence of Renaissance images of saints. The work is a telling example of his Neoclassicist conception of the relief, according to which no part of the depiction was to pierce the foremost plane.[21] On the contrary, the volumes of the figure and the space were to be staggered on receding planes. The artist referred to this relief ideal as "a surface impression with a strong impulse for the conception of depth".[22]

Hildebrand had developed his relief concept from theories of perceptual psychology as well as intensive exchanges with the painter Hans von Marées. The latter's figural compositions – characterised as they are by the complete absence of any non-essential elements or details, and above all by their relief-like modelling on two-dimensional supports – also inspired many other sculptors, including Artur Volkmann.[23] Between 1876 and 1887, the two artists collaborated closely in Rome, and Volkmann designed Marées' grave relief. He repeatedly alternated between painting and sculpture so as to apply the insights gained in one medium to his work in the respective other. Volkmann's ideal was not the Italian Renaissance, however, but the relief art of antiquity, from which he took orientation in terms of form and content alike. Motifs with putti are especially numerous in his oeuvre. He created the *Putto with Snakes* (cat. 11) in Frankfurt, where he held a professorship at the Städelschule, during the First World War. The tightly bounded framed scene depicts a naked kneeling boy wrestling with two snakes. The composition is distinguished by its balanced distribution of the masses; its ascending and descending diagonals and the ornamentally twisting and turning snakes keep the viewer's gaze circling (→ Sculptural Narration).[24] The motif combines the aesthetic of ancient sarcophagus reliefs with a reference to the famous *Laocoön Group*. In keeping with Volkmann's notion of the ideal relief, the background serves not to suggest depth but rather acts as a foil against which the figures stand out all the more. The colouration of the white marble is extremely restrained and has the effect of emphasising the material more than concealing it. Evidently the artist was striving to evoke the impression of a faded artefact.

Whereas Volkmann devoted himself to marble as the quintessential material of classical relief art, Paul Gauguin made his reliefs primarily in wood (cat. 16). Late-nineteenth-century French critics such as Joris-Karl Huysmans held the view that sculptors should abandon the materials in use since antiquity – marble, stone and bronze – and instead work with wood on the grounds that it was especially appropriate for a vibrant art of the present.[25] Huysmans's advocacy of wood is to be understood against the background of a newfound enthusiasm not just for medieval church art but also for folk art. During his summer stays in Brittany (between 1886 and 1891), Gauguin began to take an interest in local woodcarving and decorative ceramics. The simplified forms and expressive colours of these objects immediately made their way into his work. He executed his relief *Be Mysterious* in Pont-Aven, Brittany – thus even before his first trip to the South Seas. Nevertheless, in terms of style and motif it already mirrors his explorations of Javanese and Polynesian carving, examples of which he had encountered at the Paris World Fair of 1889.[26] The relief shows three female figures whose relationship to one another is indeed "mysterious", executed as a bust, a half-length and a full-length figure; in other words, in very different ways. All three are incorporated into a surface enlivened with tossing waves and aquatic plants and coloured with vivid hues.[27] Rather than waiting until the carving work was finished before applying the pigments, Gauguin constantly alternated between the two processes. The result is a relief whose content and form run contrary to the classical conception of beauty and evoke the ideal of a remote, strange and enigmatic world. The deliberate simplification of forms and bold colouration in turn impacted the artist's painting.

The mutual enrichment of relief art and painting in the artists' circle at Pont-Aven is especially evident in the oeuvre of Maurice Denis. In the case of *Audi filia*, the artist realised the same motif in both mediums (fig. 6; cat. 15).[28] The subject of the composition is the religious awakening of Jeanne, a young woman who, in the eyes of the deeply devout Denis, was filled with the grace of God. The artist relegated this

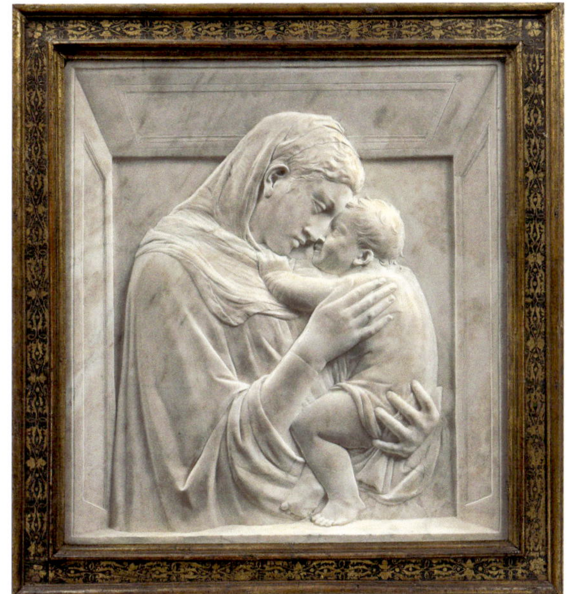

Fig. 4

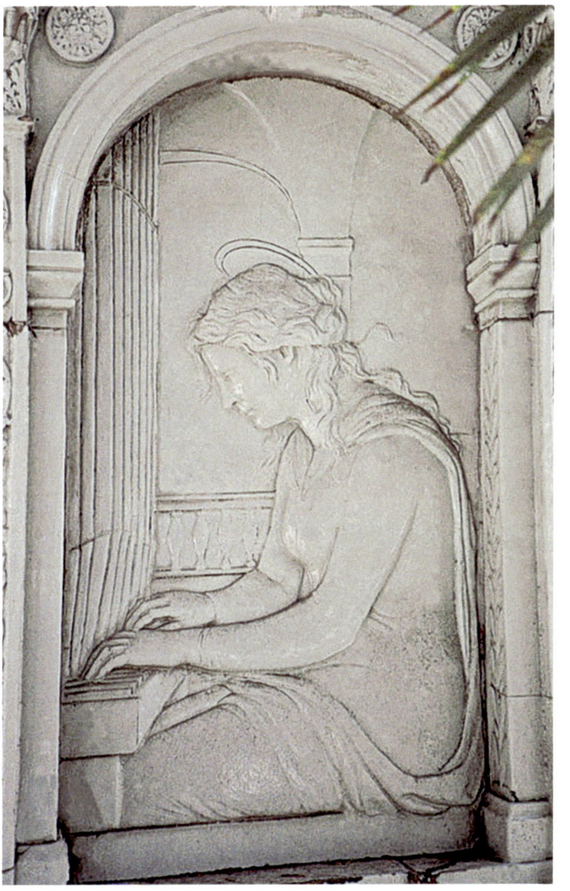

Fig. 5

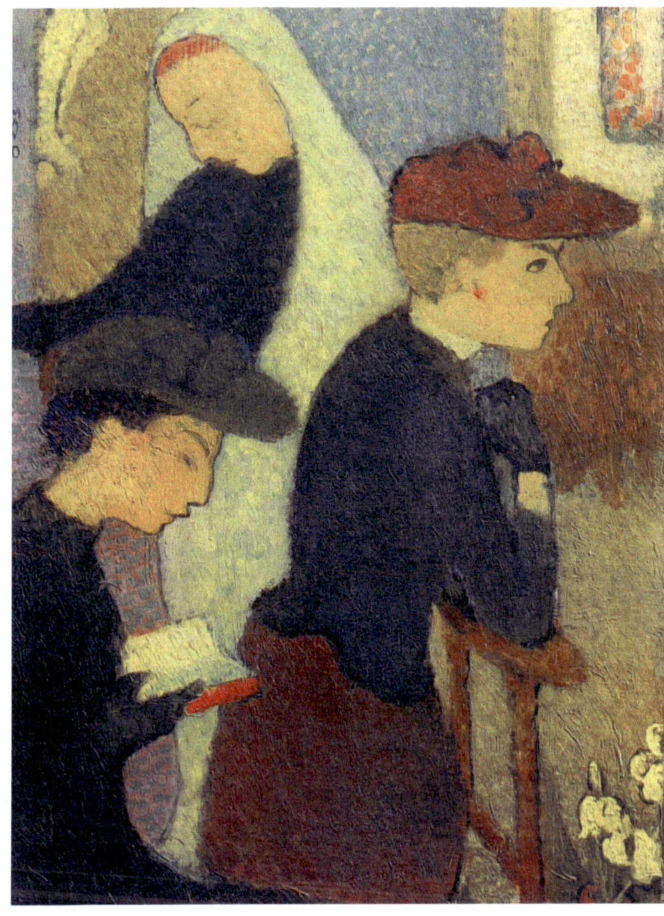

Fig. 6

Fig. 4   Donatello: *Pazzi Madonna*, ca. 1420, marble, Staatliche Museen zu Berlin, Skulpturensammlung und Museum für Byzantinische Kunst

Fig. 5   Adolf von Hildebrand: *Tomb of Elisabeth von Herzogenberg*, 1893, majolica relief, Cimitero Monumentale della Foce, Sanremo

Fig. 6   Maurice Denis: *Listen, Daughter* (*Audi filia*), ca. 1890, oil on canvas, private collection

theme to the background, however, where he depicted the young woman kneeling before a crucifix with her eyes closed. In the relief, he carved the exhortation "Audi filia" ("Hearken, O daughter") from Psalm 45 – an element not found in the painting – into the wood surface next to her head. On the whole, however, he adhered relatively accurately to his two-dimensional model when translating the pictorial idea into the relief medium. From the painted version he adopted the tightly framed box-like space, the staggering of the figures and even the colouration, although the relief substantially reduces the range of hues and the variation in the brushwork. To an extent, the grain of the wood creates the lifelike quality achieved in the painting with dabs and striae of paint. The constraints of woodcarving make the figures in the relief appear more simplified than in his emphatically two-dimensional way of painting.

The interplay between painting and woodcarving is even more pronounced in the work of Ernst Ludwig Kirchner, who described the production of his wooden sculptures as a process of consolidation that helped him clarify his ideas about form.[29] In the manner typical of his approach, the long process of developing the wood relief for the entrance portal of the schoolhouse in Davos-Frauenkirch (cat. 17) began with drawing. In this medium the artist tried out various figural constellations before finally arriving at the form of the high relief.[30] The work depicts the teacher Florian Bätschi as a half-length figure at the centre with two pupils on either side, represented as full-length figures seated at their desks. Kirchner carved all five individually from rectangular blocks of Swiss pine wood which he then assembled to form a whole. In their spatially confined arrangement and *en face* depiction, the figures are reminiscent of sculptural decorations on Romanesque and Gothic cathedrals. From the very start of his career, Kirchner had had a predilection for medieval art, to which he attributed great expressiveness and formal rigour. Compared to the other – more abstract – works of his late phase, he rendered these figures highly realistically and coloured them in just a few unobtrusive shades. After the harsh criticism he had so often reaped for his works in his adopted hometown of Davos, he appears to have exercised restraint in the execution of this public commission so as not to lose the goodwill of the community.

The schoolhouse relief was his last three-dimensional work. And here it also marks the end of the era of the polychrome relief, which had flourished from the late nineteenth century until well into the 1930s. Many of the makers of coloured reliefs had been painters who used this medium to try out their individual artistic conceptions of colour and form, two- and three-dimensionality, and illusionism and abstraction, experimenting with new or revived materials in the process, and often entering into artistic competition with their own painterly oeuvres.

1 Alfred Lichtwark: "Eine Ausstellung farbiger Skulptur", in: *Die Gegenwart, Wochenschrift für Literatur, Kunst und öffentliches Leben*, vol. 28, no. 41, 1885, pp. 234–236, here p. 234.

2 *Ausstellung farbiger und getönter Bildwerke in der Königlichen National-Galerie zu Berlin*, ed. Georg Treu, exh. cat. Königliche National-Galerie, Berlin, 14 November–31 December 1885, Berlin 1885.

3 For a general discussion on the colour of sculpture in the nineteenth and early twentieth century, see *The Colour of Sculpture 1840–1910*, ed. Andreas Blühm, exh. cat. Van Gogh Museum, Amsterdam/ Henry Moore Institute, Leeds, Zwolle 1996.

4 On the history of research into polychrome sculpture in antiquity, see Vinzenz Brinkmann: "Die Farben der antiken Bildhauerkunst: Anmerkungen zur Forschungsgeschichte und zur Rezeption", in: *Bunte Götter: Die Farben der Antike – Golden Edition*, ed. idem and Ulrike Koch-Brinkmann, exh. cat. Liebieghaus Skulpturensammlung, Frankfurt am Main, Munich 2020, pp. 29–44, esp. pp. 34f.

5 Exh. cat. Berlin 1885 (see note 2), nos. 151, 152.

6 Henry Cros and Charles Henry: *L'Encaustique et les autres procédés de peinture chez les anciens : Histoire et technique*, Paris 1884. Some twenty works in wax by Cros are extant today; see Dominique Morel: "Henry Cros, *La Belle Viole* and *Circe, Flora, and Medea*", in: *Nineteenth-Century Art Worldwide*, vol. 16, no. 1, Spring 2017, https://doi.org/10.29411/ ncaw.2017.16.1.5 (accessed 13 February 2023). For a general discussion of Cros, see *Henry Cros. 1840–1907*, ed. Léonce Bénédite, exh. cat. Salon d'Automne, Paris, 1922, pp. 369–376.

7 See, among others, Charles Blanc: "Grammaire des arts du dessin: Architecture, sculpture, peinture", in: *Gazette des Beaux-Arts*, vol. 18, no. 1, 1 January 1865, chap. XIV, pp. 42–45, here pp. 43f.

8 *En couleurs: La sculpture polychrome en France 1850–1910*,
ed. Édouard Papet, exh. cat. Musée d'Orsay, Paris, Vanves and Paris 2018, p. 68.

9 Morel 2017 (see note 6), notes 8–10.

10 Société des Artistes Français pour l'Exposition des Beaux-Arts de 1882: *Salon de 1882*, Paris 1882, p. 375, no. 4252.

11 Exh. cat. Amsterdam/Leeds 1996 (see note 3), no. 17.

12 "Bruckmann in Hottingen bei Zürich: Gorgoschild, Gyps mit lackierter Ölfarbe bemalt von Arnold Böcklin in Hottingen, Eigentum des Malers", in: exh. cat. Berlin 1885 (see note 2), no. 63.

13 See Alain Moirandat: "Der Plastiker Böcklin", in: *Arnold Böcklin, 1827–1901: Gemälde, Zeichnungen, Plastiken*, ed. Susanne Burger and Dorothea Christ, exh. cat. Kunstmuseum Basel, Stuttgart 1977, pp. 81–84, here p. 84.

14 Exh. cat. Amsterdam/Leeds 1996 (see note 3), no. 17.

15 Maria Golovteeva: "Forming the Symbolist Identity: The Materiality of Fernand Khnopff's Sculptures", in: *North Street Review*, 15 April 2016, https:// northstreetreview.wordpress. com/2016/04/15/forming- the-symbolist-identity-the- materiality-of-fernand-khnopffs- sculptures/ (accessed 13 February 2023).

16 Bronze head of Hypnos, Roman copy of a Hellenistic original, first/second century, The British Museum, London. Michael Sagroske does not count the *Mask* among Khnopff's depictions of Medusa but associates it with the artist's bust of Hypnos; see Michael Sagroske: "Zur Medusendarstellung im Werk von Fernand Khnopff", in: *Fernand Khnopff*, ed. Frederik Leen, exh. cat. Königlich-Belgische Kunstmuseen, Brussels et al., Ostfildern 2004, pp. 53–63, here pp. 62f.

17 Until recently, plaster was given as the material. On recent research, see Golovteeva 2016 (see note 15); Rachel Sloan: "The Archaeology of Dreams: Fernand Khnopff, Henri Cros and
the Mask", in: Claire O'Mahony (ed.): *Symbolist Objects: Materiality and Subjectivity at the Fin de Siècle*, High Wycombe 2009, pp. 165–189, here p. 175.

18 Louis Vauxcelles: "Le Salon d'Automne", in: *Supplément à Gil Blas*, 17 October 1905, p. 2.

19 Adolf von Hildebrand: *Das Problem der Form in der bildenden Kunst*, Strasbourg 1893, esp. chap. V: "Reliefauffassung", pp. 63–82. On Adolf von Hildebrand's conception of relief, also see: Liliana Albertazzi: *Visual Thought: The Depictive Space of Perception*, Amsterdam and Philadelphia 2006, pp. 140–142.

20 Sigrid Esche-Braunfels: *Adolf von Hildebrand (1847–1921)*, Berlin 1993, pp. 181–183, 370–372.

21 Sigrid Esche-Braunfels: "Reliefs und Reliefauffassung von Adolf von Hildebrand", in: exh. cat. Münster 1980, pp. 23–34.

22 Hildebrand 1893 (see note 19), p. 65.

23 See Christa Lichtenstern: "Der Bildhauer Hans von Marées und seine verborgene Aktualität in der Plastik des 20. Jahrhunderts", in: *Hans von Marées*, ed. Christian Lenz, exh. cat. Neue Pinakothek and Schack-Galerie, Munich, Munich 1987, pp. 163–178.

24 See Anette Niethammer: *Wie auf den Tag das Abendsonnenlicht … Hans von Marées' Meisterschüler Artur Volkmann (1851–1941)*, Nordhausen 2006, p. 271.

25 Joris-Karl Huysmans: "L'Exposition des indépendants en 1881", in: idem.: *L'Art moderne*, Paris 1883, pp. 225–257, here pp. 229f.; see David Scott: "Matter for Reflexion: Nineteenth-Century French Art Critics' Quest for Modernity in Sculpture", in: Richard Hobbs (ed.): *Impressions of French Modernity: Art and Literature in France 1850–1900*, Manchester and New York 1998, pp. 99–117, here p. 114.

26 *The Art of Paul Gauguin*, ed. Richard R. Brettell et al., exh. cat. National Gallery of Art, Washington, D.C. et al., Washington, D.C. 1988, pp. 190f., no. 110 (Françoise Cachin).
27 On polychromy, see Juliette Levy-Hinstin and Patrick Mandron: "Le Regard du restaurateur: Soyez mystérieuses", in: *Gauguin : L'alchimiste*, ed. Claire Bernadi and Ophélie Ferlier-Bouat, exh. cat. The Art Institute of Chicago and Musée d'Orsay, Paris, Paris 2019, p. 294.

28 See *Maurice Denis 1870–1943*, ed. Philippe Duret et al., exh. cat. Musée des Beaux-Arts, Lyon et al., Spaden 1994, pp. 131f., nos. 12, 13; exh. cat. Amsterdam/ Leeds 1996 (see note 3), p. 234, no. 93.

29 Louis de Marsalle [= Ernst Ludwig Kirchner]: "Über Kirchners Graphik", in: *Genius*, vol. 3, 1921, pp. 251–263, here p. 252.

30 For a detailed account of the work's development, see: Wolfgang Henze: *Die Plastik Ernst Ludwig Kirchners: Monographie und Werkverzeichnis*, Wichtrach/ Bern 2002, catalogue raisonné no. 1936/03.

Cat. 9   Henry Cros: *The Three Fairies* (*Les trois fées*), 1881,
coloured wax with glass inlays and oil-painting additions,
mounted on wood, 48 × 33 × 6 cm, Kunstsammlungen
der Veste Coburg, inv. no. Pl.194

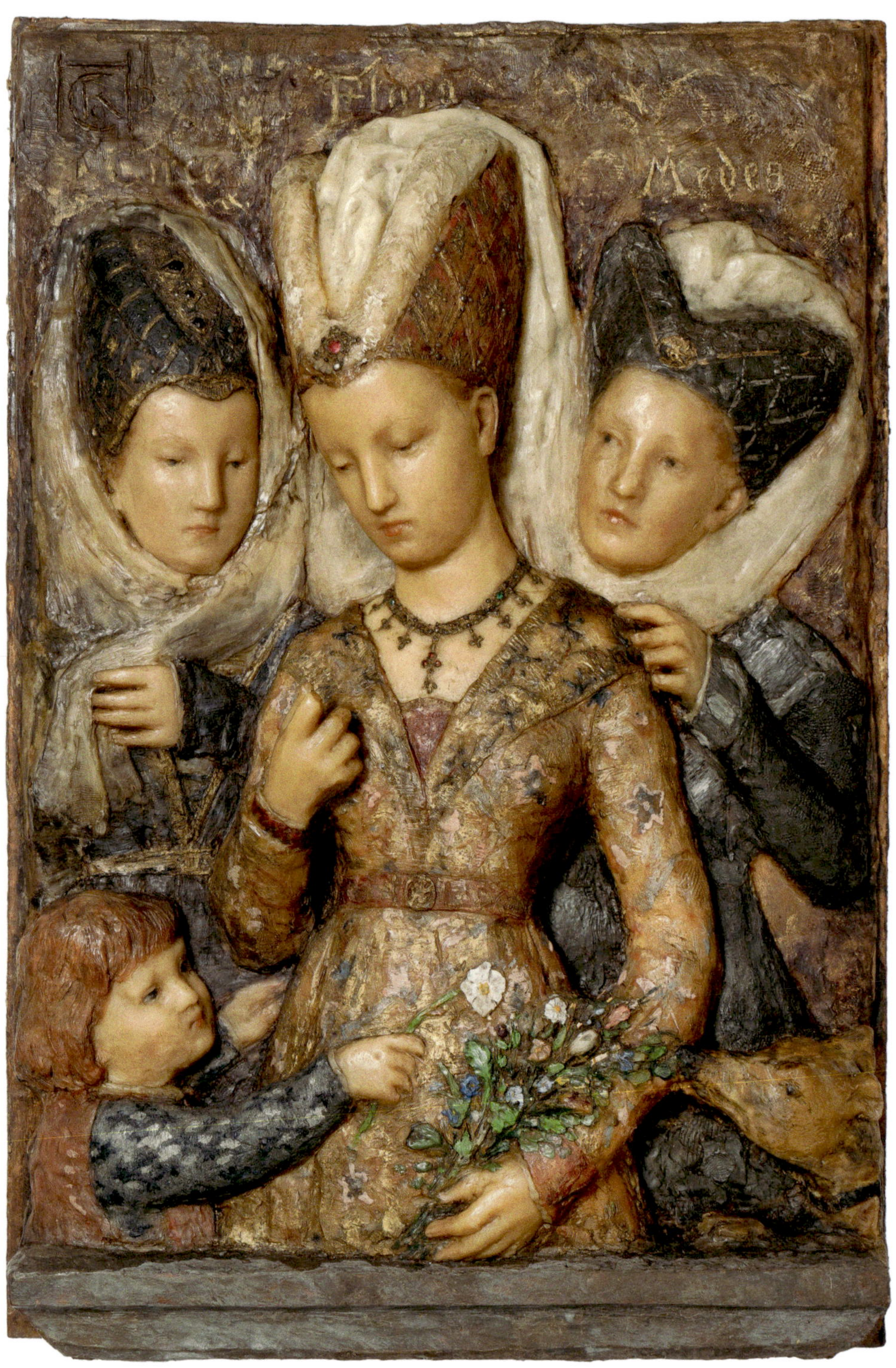

Cat. 10   Arnold Böcklin and Peter Bruckmann: *Shield with the Head of Medusa*, 1887, plaster, painted, diameter: 60.5 cm, Kunstmuseum Basel, inv. no. P 5 (Frankfurt only)

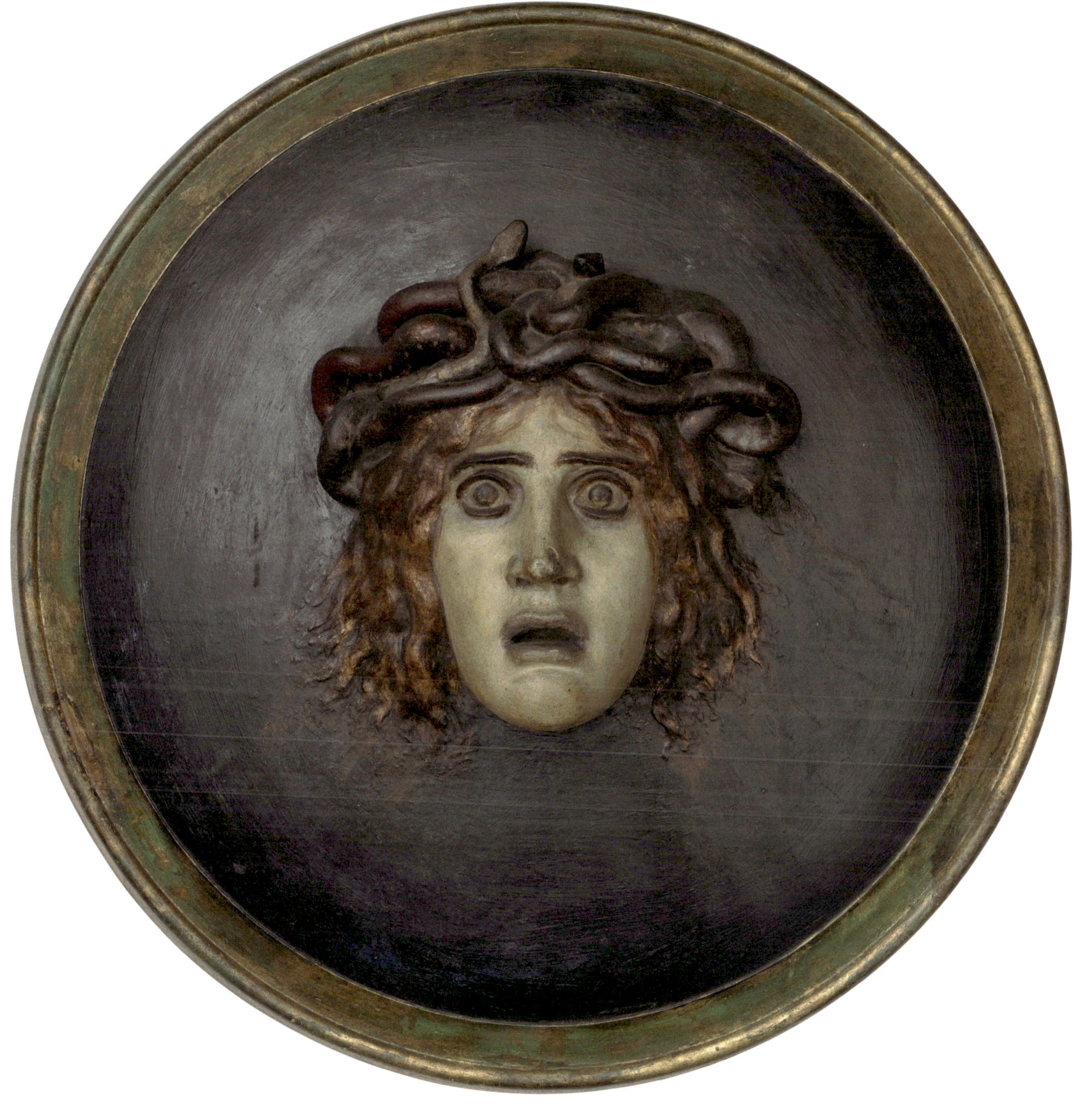

Cat. 11   Artur Volkmann: *Putto with Snakes*, 1915–18, marble, painted, 52 × 45 cm, Städel Museum, Frankfurt am Main, inv. no. SGP 224 (Frankfurt only)

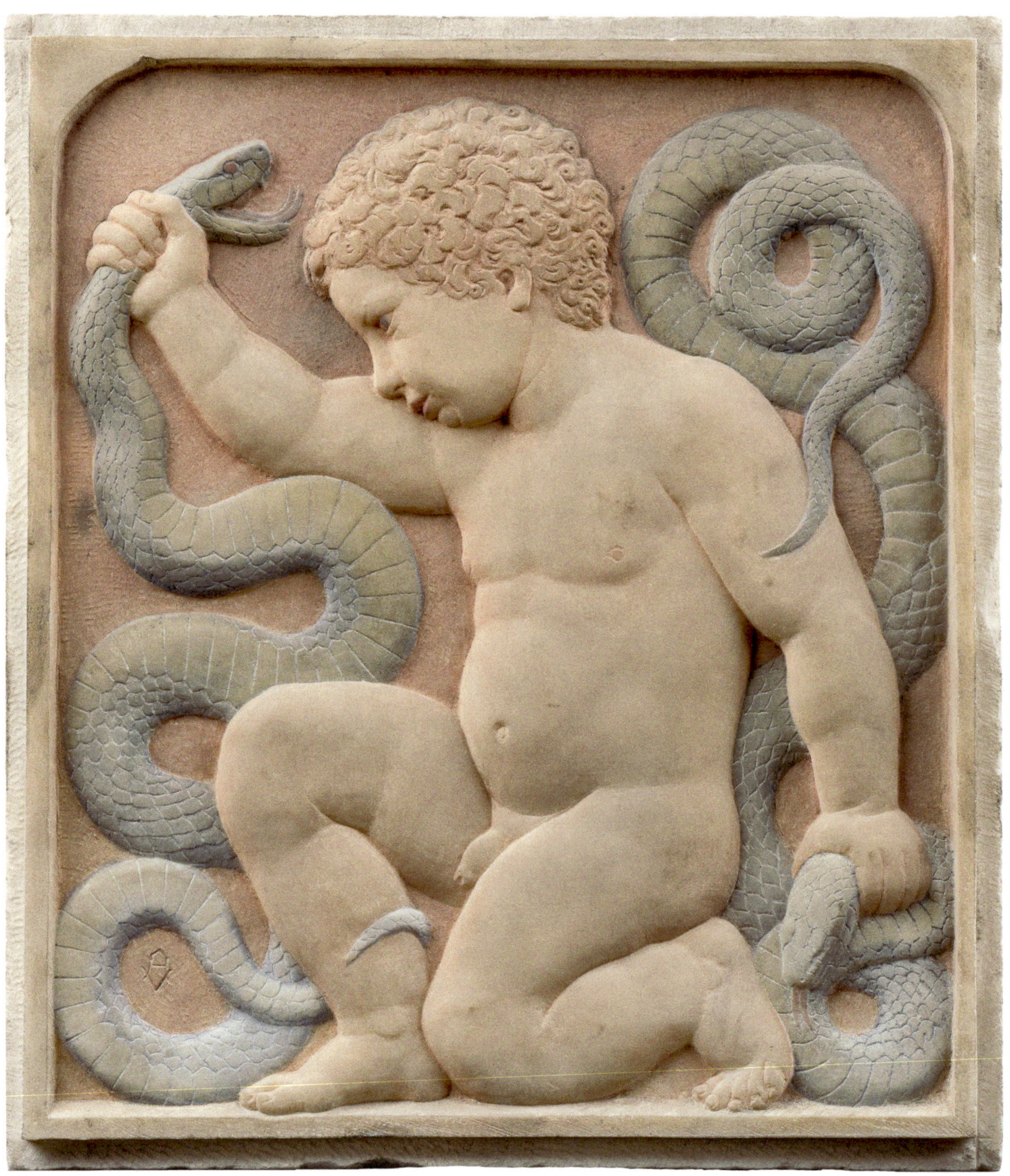

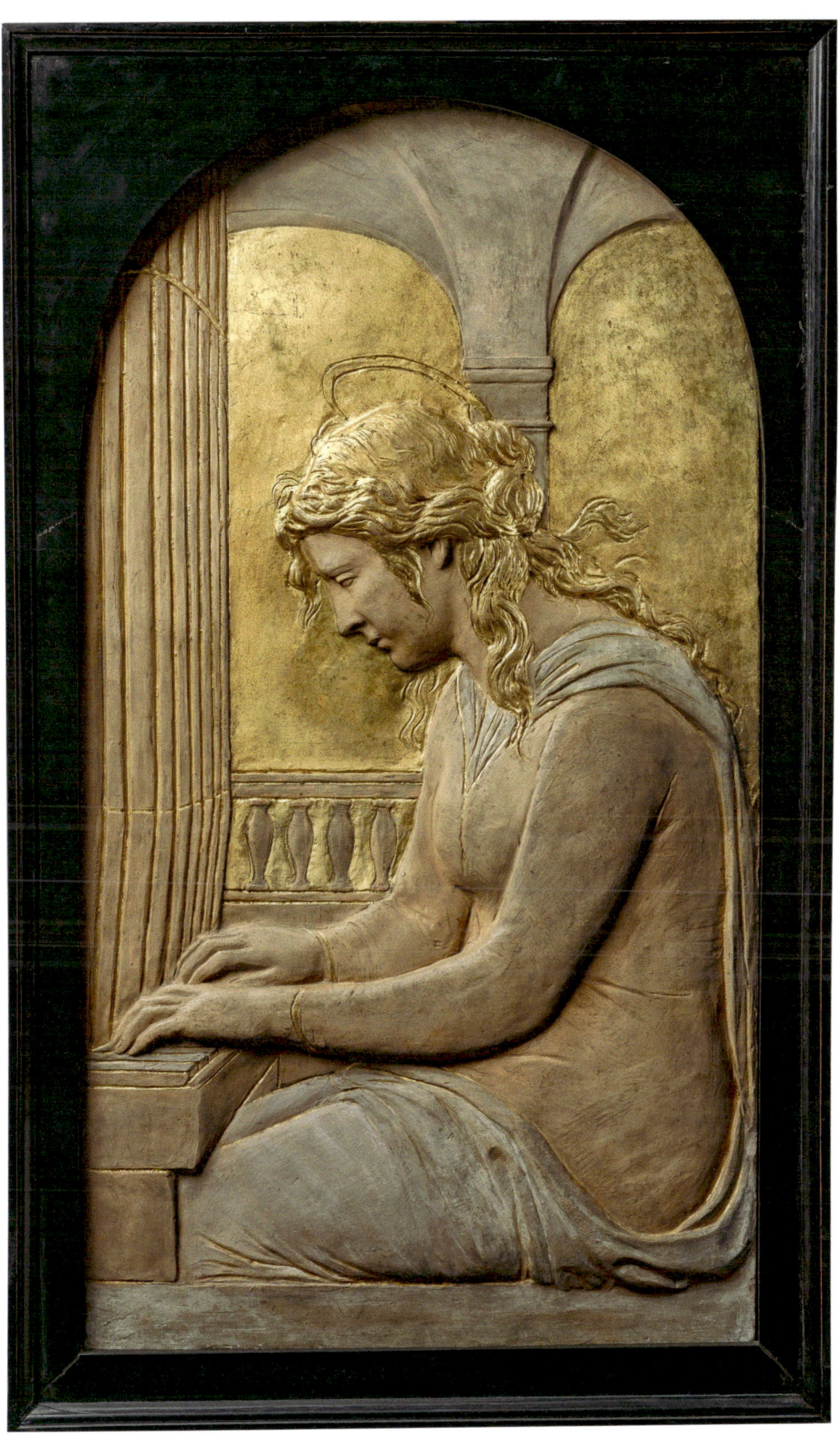

Cat. 12   Adolf von Hildebrand: *Elisabeth von Herzogenberg as Saint Cecilia*, 1893–97, terracotta, painted, 79 × 44 cm, Museum für Kunst und Kulturgeschichte der Philipps-Universität Marburg, inv. no. 16666

Cat. 13   Albert Marque: *Sleep (Sommeil)*, ca. 1899, marble,
59.5 × 44.5 cm, courtesy of Stuart Lochhead Sculpture

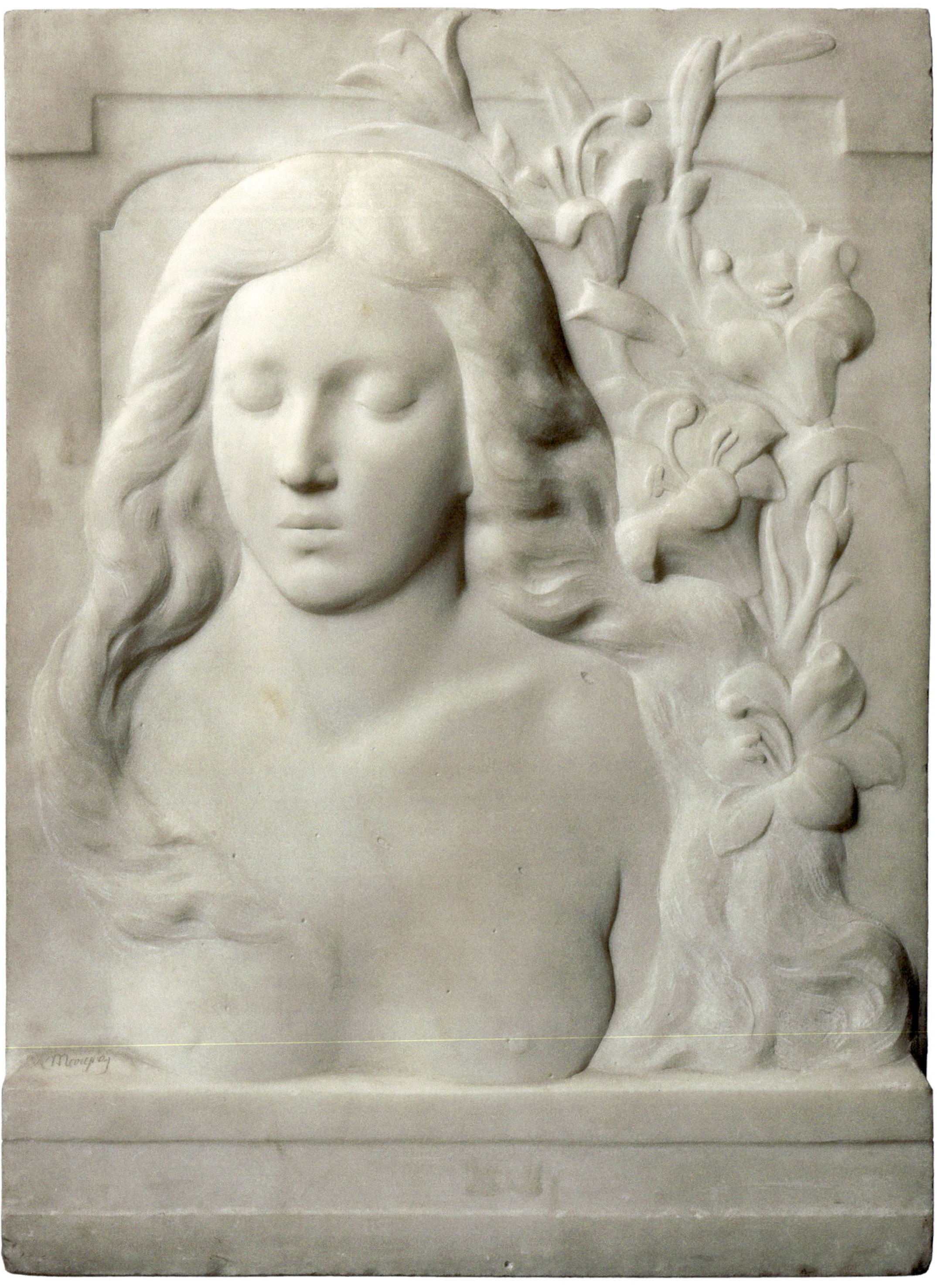

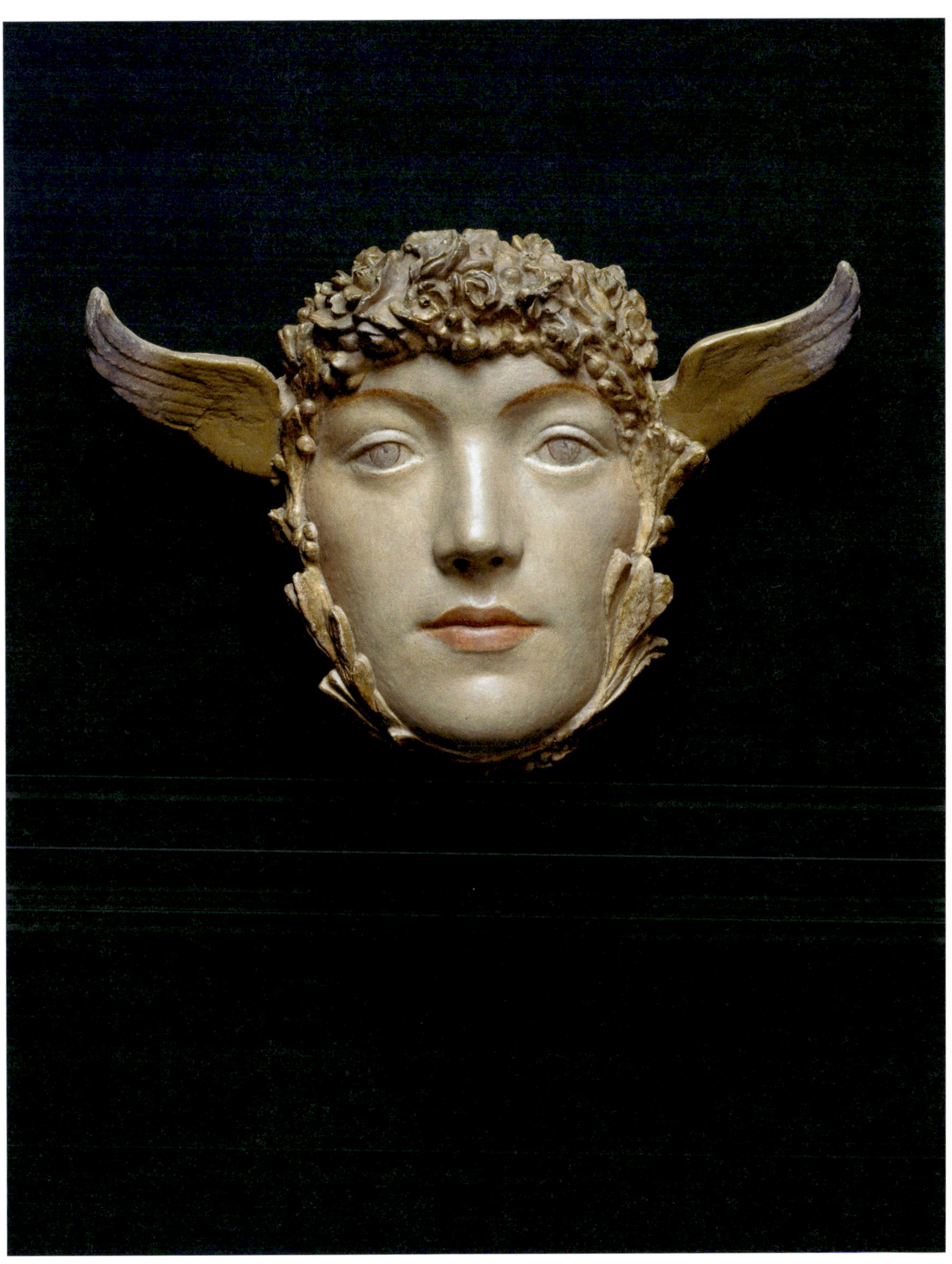

Cat. 14 Fernand Khnopff: *A Mask* (*Un masque*), ca. 1897, gesso duro, painted, 18.5 × 28 × 6.5 cm, Hamburger Kunsthalle, inv. no. S-1986-4

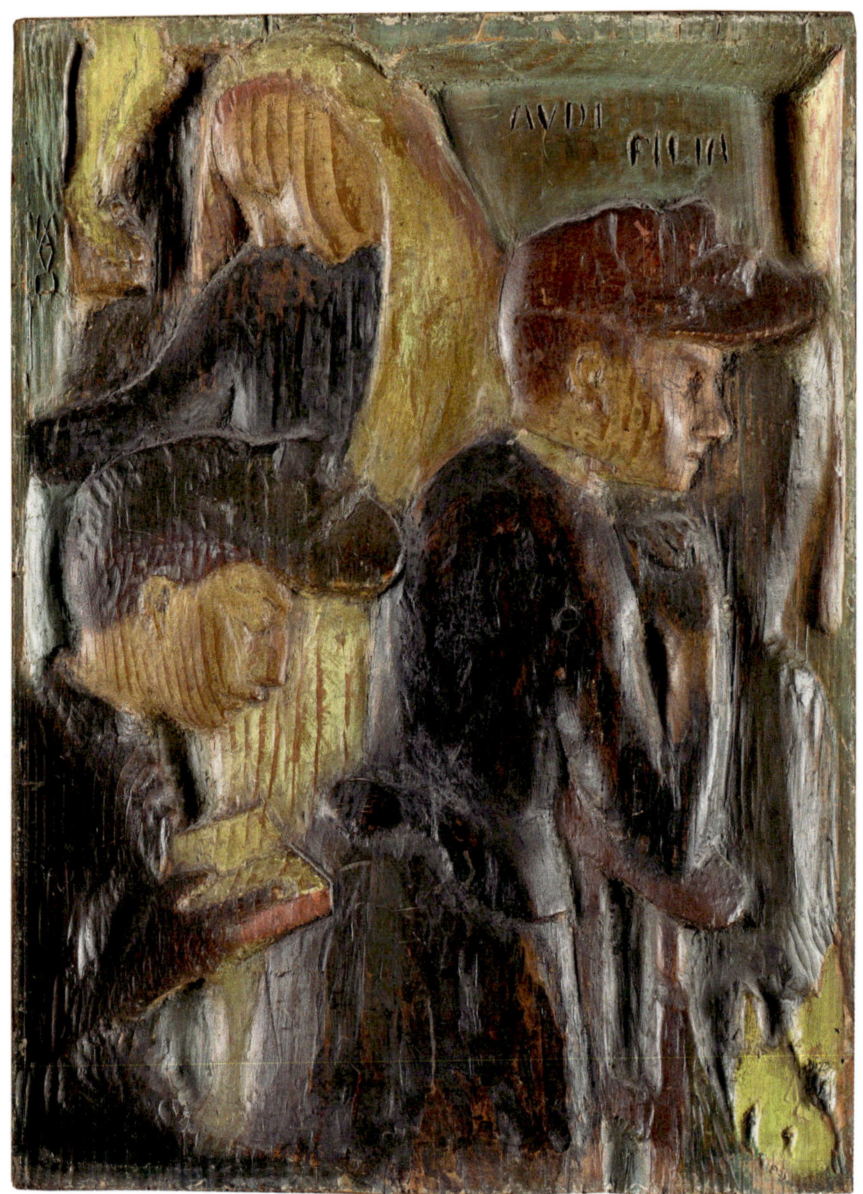

Cat. 15   Maurice Denis: *Listen, Daughter (Audi filia)*, 1899, wood, painted, 41 × 30 cm, Musée départemental Maurice Denis, Saint-Germain-en-Laye, inv. no. PMD 980.13.1

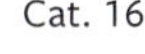

Cat. 16   Paul Gauguin: *Be Mysterious* (*Soyez mystérieuses*), 1890,
lime wood, polychrome, traces of dark pencil, 73 × 95 × 5 cm,
Musée d'Orsay, Paris, inv. no. RF340

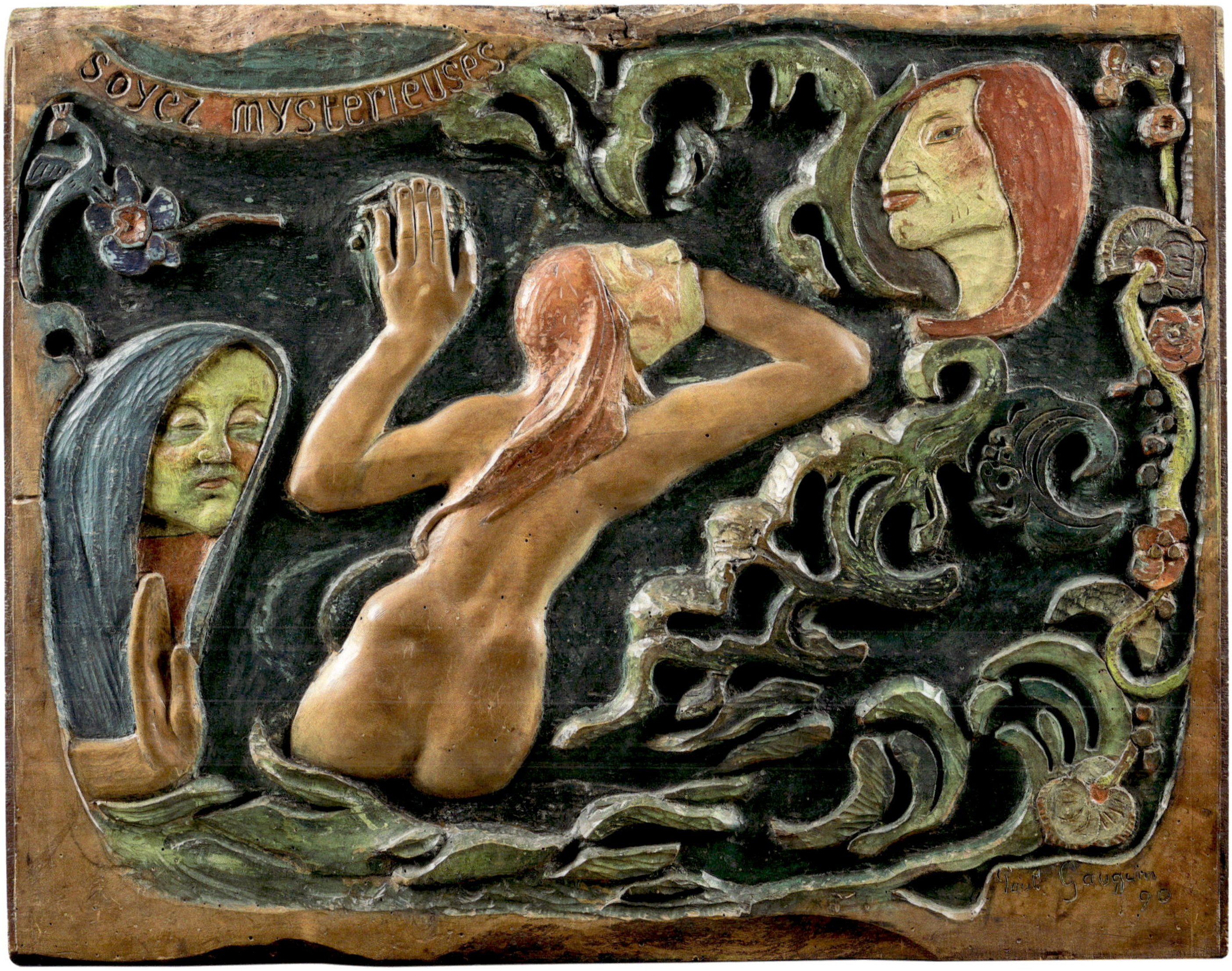

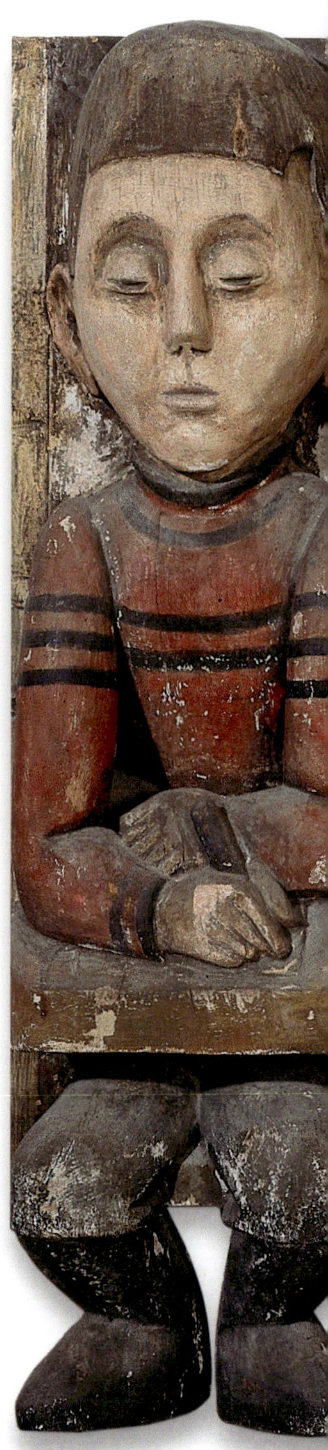

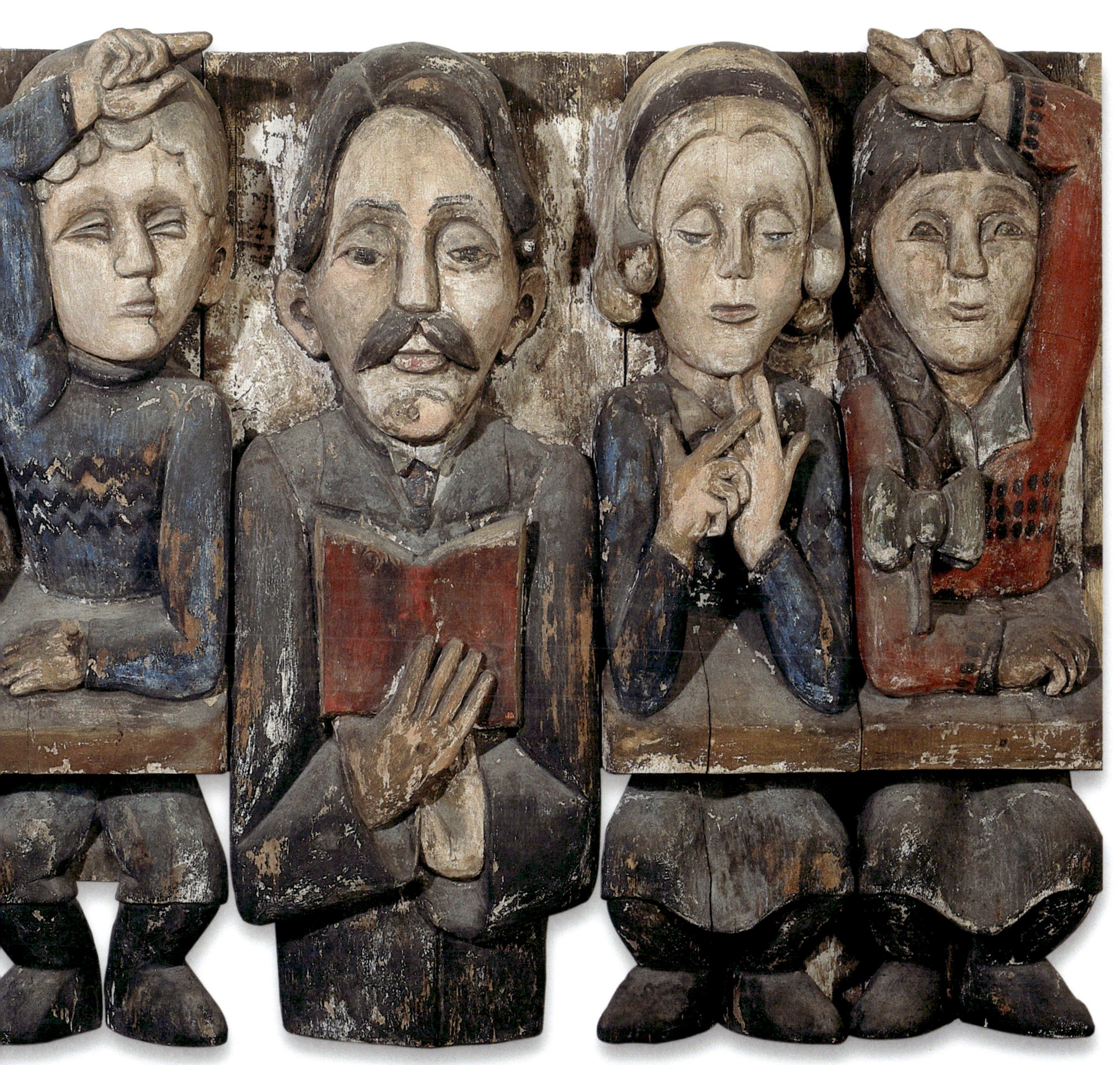

Cat. 17   Ernst Ludwig Kirchner: *Teacher Florian Bätschi with Schoolchildren*, 1936, Swiss pine, painted, 83 × 120.5 × 14.5 cm, Kirchner Museum Davos, inv. no. 1982/Davos-3/00013/P

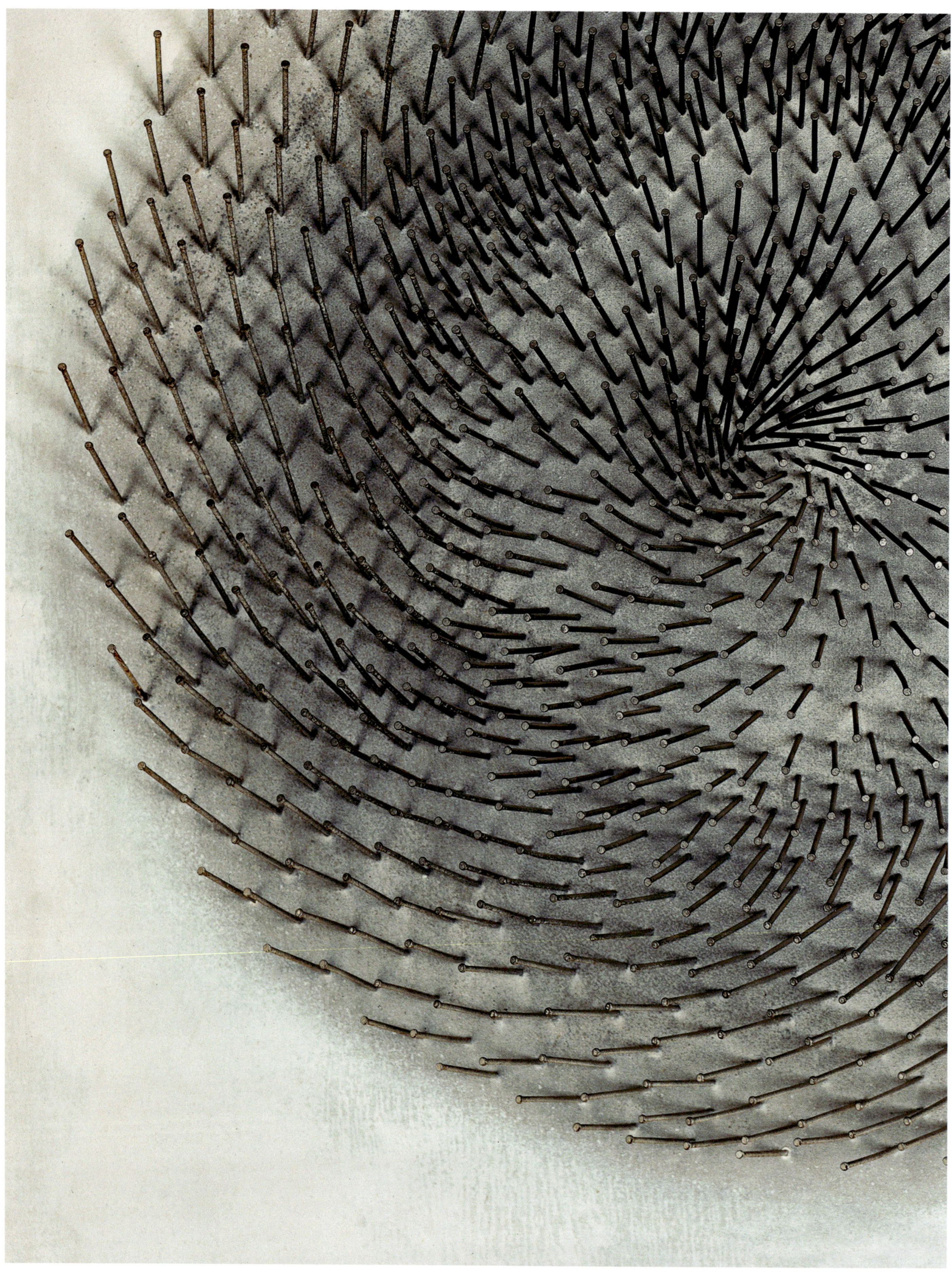

Cats. 18 — 31

SCULPTURAL NARRATION

The shield of Achilles, the shield of Heracles – these famous weapons are only known to us from the epic narratives in antique literature of the eighth and seventh centuries BCE. When artists began addressing them beginning in the nineteenth century, lending form to the shields, they therefore did not make reference to specific sculptures but rather to descriptions of the shields. In Ludwig Schwanthaler's *Shield of Heracles*, his visualisation, produced between 1832 and 1842, of an anonymous text once mistakenly attributed to Hesiod, a serpent is surrounded by four concentric rings, the narrative logic of which becomes apparent from the centre towards the edge (cat. 19). The entire antique universe is included within it: the first ring shows battles and pursuits, followed in the second ring by scenes from the world of gods and heroes; the third ring presents occurrences from the life of ordinary mortals, and the outer, recessing edge the Oceanus surrounding the earth.[1] Although the evenly cambered artwork, presumably commissioned by the Duke of Devonshire, was conceived as a display object, due to its meaning as a battle shield it implicitly carries the potential of turbulent action within itself.

In contrast, Günther Uecker, using the nail as his preferred tool of composition since 1957, operated very explicitly: in the supports with rounded corners, by hammering on nails spirally in 1962 he introduced not only the third dimension but also his own body movement (cat. 20). Consequently, the one-time result is vividly evident to this day; furthermore, there is a narrative element in the re-enactment of the artistic action.[2]

Both Schwanthaler's as well as Uecker's work belong in the complex field of narratives – narratives that consist of specific story lines just as they do synthesised depictions of occurrences or situations. On the one side there is the artist, and on the other, viewers with their behaviour towards what they see and how they see it (fig. 1). Whereas the two autonomous reliefs are arranged and readable from the centre outwards, the examples discussed below demand very different behaviour on the part of the viewer. The research area of narratology, which is situated at the interface between several disciplines, such as the history of literature, film and art, systematically pursues these questions around elements of action, narrative structures and directing the path of the viewer's eye.[3] In this respect, the relief harbours peculiarities for both the artists as well as the addressees – because this is where not only the plane is available as a field of action but also the material-related plasticity and, as the case may be, the spatial-situative context. Depictive elements can thus lie on different levels of meaning and illumination or engender them in the first place.

The first example takes us to Italy. "Because the three bas-reliefs alone make reference to one another, comprise a coherent visual narrative, I would have all three of them, like in the sketch, mounted on the front of the sarcophagus."[4] This precisely worded request by the Frankfurter Susanne Bethmann-Hollweg reached the famous sculptor Bertel Thorvaldsen in Rome in 1813. In the more than 16 years it took to create the funerary monument for her son, who died at the age of just 21, the client's extremely decisive attitude collided with the sculptor's exalted understanding of himself – as he had recently caused a furore with his *Alexander Frieze* for Christiansborg Castle in Copenhagen, of which the Bethmann family immediately ordered a cast. Nevertheless, the artist complied with the mother's request with all due consistency, namely by completely dispensing with the multi-sided sarcophagus in favour of a flat, three-part wall epitaph (cat. 21).[5] In fact, in the case of the three relief fields it is a matter of an arrangement to be comprehended at one glance and to be read from left to right: from the earthly depiction of the grieving mother in the company of her two daughters; the central field, which, with the younger brother's handing of the wreath to the deceased, leaning against the genius of death, illustrates the transition into the afterworld; to the right field with the abstract allegories of the river god Arno and the annalist Nemesis. In terms of composition as well, the fields are linked by the subtle up-and-down of the sequence of figures – dispensing with any illusionism, the artist focuses in a typically classicistic manner on the clear legibility of the planarly designed, sharply contoured figures on a flat ground, hence presented in an even flux of light and shadow.

A narrative and aesthetic coherency of this kind was not conceivable for Christian Daniel Rauch's plaster model for a bronze relief depicting *Frederick II after the Battle of Kolin* (cat. 18), as it was part of an intrinsically complex equestrian monument for the Prussian king Frederick the Great (fig. 2). It was produced during the politically turbulent period between 1822 and 1850, and it is not for nothing that, after its completion, the artist wrote: "I am exhausted mentally, my body and soul weary."[6] The monument, including the circumferential relief frieze, links biographical aspects with political acts, and history with the present. The relief with the seated sovereign occupied a prominent position at its narrow front edge. It describes an episode from the Seven Years' War: following the Prussians' lost battle against Austria, the king was found sitting on a well pipe and drawing a further strategy in the sand with a cane.[7] While the depiction that captures the precise instant of his melancholy gesture as he ponders his failure develops out of the surface into space to become nearly three-dimensional, Frederick's vision of the future triumph[8] – flanked by Victoria and Minerva – is a subtle bas-relief in the background. In terms of both form as well as content, Rauch, a pupil of Schadow, presents Frederick on two different relief levels, once in a genre-like and once in an allegorising setting.[9]

In 1916/17, the sculptor Ernst Barlach designed his three-part relief *Death and Life* (cat. 22) to be neither linear or separated into levels. Indeed, in terms of content the work strikes an arc from the love in life to death – yet it does not exact a specific perspectival logic. On the contrary, the gaze oscillates back and forth between the restlessly contoured complementary fields. With the multi-figure entombment scene, death, mentioned first in the title, dominates the two overlying fields with the lovers.[10] Supported by the clear format, the work can be perceived as a whole at each instant it is viewed, hence allowing for – analogous to reading a comic book – peripheral vision.[11] However, this relief is distinguished by a

second feature related to the path the eye takes: Barlach dispensed with perspectival-spatial clarification in the style of the Middle Ages, which was typical of his time, within the intrinsically modelled-animated fields,[12] but he all the more decidedly opened the marked top view of the expressive robed figures towards the viewer's elevated point of sight. Thanks to this artfully chosen path of the eyes, the figures achieve a pronounced plasticity visually.

In order to appreciate the eight (or nine) reliefs by Hermann Blumenthal that he created in 1934 for the competition to redesign the famous polygonal Fountain Room at the Museum Folkwang in Essen (fig. 3), a 360-degree view would have been necessary (cats. 24–28).[13] Five differently coloured plaster panels from this series of reliefs, entitled *Sun and Art,* have survived; however, based on three further photographs it is known that nothing has been passed down from the ninth relief called for in the competition. Each of the groups of figures, recorded in pairs in a recessed outline, float in the spatial void surrounding them. This dispensing with formal concretisation continues in terms of content when virtually unimportant essential things of life are described, such as hunting as well as music and human bonds. Today, the sequence in which Blumenthal had envisaged the reliefs, which were to be adapted to the more than 2.3-metre-high wall niches, can no longer be reconstructed; the only thing that is certain is that the figures would have been larger than life-sized. It is primarily the sum of the fields that produces an aesthetic and spiritual climate of calm beyond a concrete narrative by means of the gentle rhythm of the harmoniously interacting figures.

Five years before Blumenthal created his Arcadian world, Jean Arp, at the time regarded as a notorious troublemaker, designed a work of cosmic nature (cat. 23) using similarly reduced means. Arp formed his protagonists, floating in a diffuse sphere and facing one another in dialogue, from a string sewn to the canvas – an idea rooted in his artistic exchange with Kurt Schwitters.[14] The artist constantly operated playfully between the genres. In this case, he brought the wall-dominating effect of painting into a sensitive synthesis with the flowing lines of the drawing as well as with the spatial presence of the string.[15] At the same time, the content-related and technical buoyancy delightfully contradict the monochrome coolness.

Arp started out with a canvas when he created his relief employing an application. Under completely different circum-

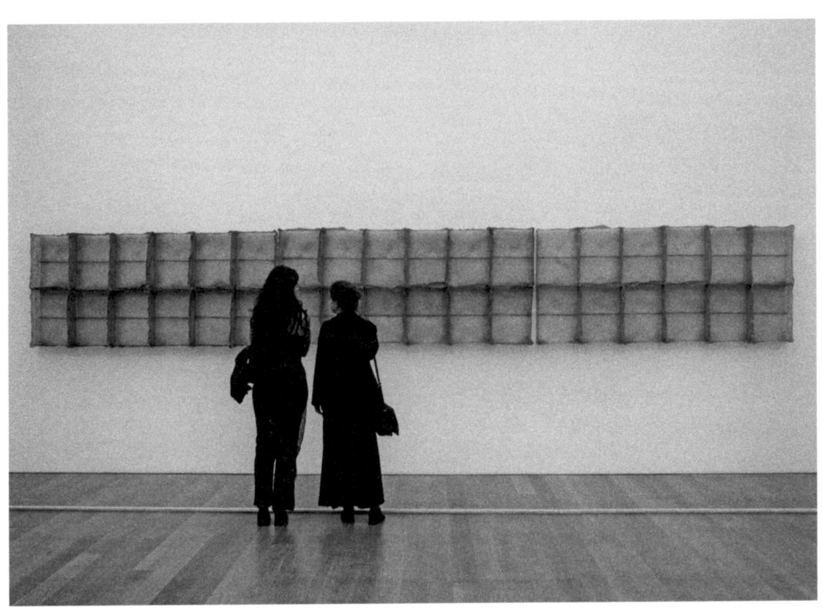

Fig. 1

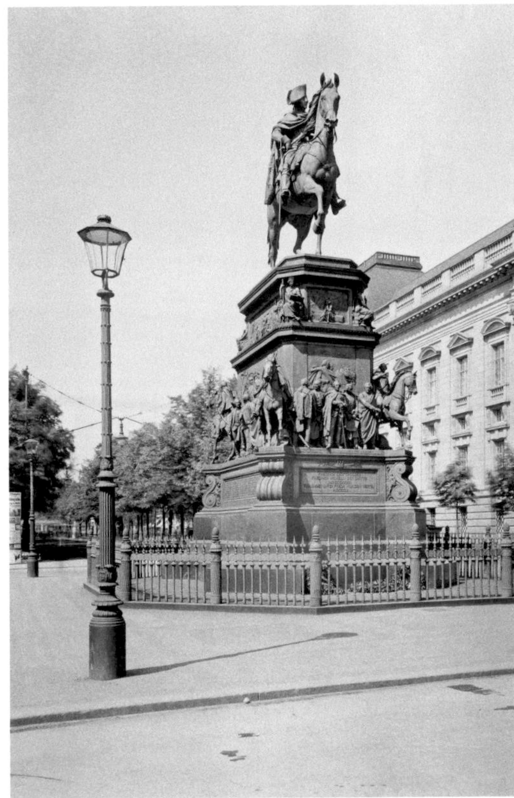

Fig. 2

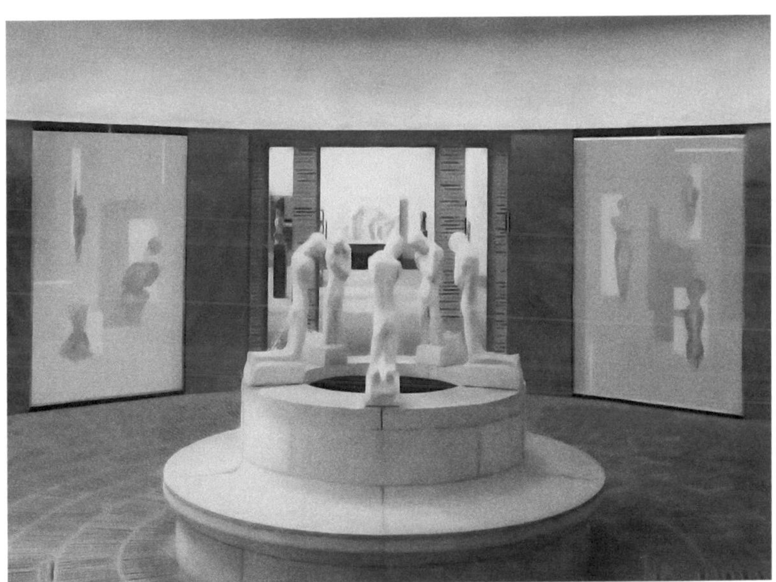

Fig. 3

Fig. 1   Barbara Klemm: *Eva Hesse Exhibition, Wiesbaden, 2002,*
          photograph, Städel Museum, Frankfurt am Main, property of
          Städelscher Museums-Verein e.V.

Fig. 2   Christian Daniel Rauch: *Equestrian Sculpture of Frederick the
          Great,* 1822–50, Berlin, view from the southeast with the
          Preußische Staatsbibliothek in the background, photograph, 1914

Fig. 3   Hall at Museum Folkwang, Essen, with the central fountain
          by George Minne and paintings by Oskar Schlemmer, state:
          1933/34, photograph

stances, when he designed the monument at the tomb of the painter Théodore Géricault, who died in 1824 (cat. 30), in 1841 the French sculptor Antoine Étex dealt with the transfer of a canvas painting into the third dimension of the relief and at the same time with that of the colouration of the painting into the tonality of the bronze. For Étex integrated – besides the painter resting like an Etruscan tomb figure – three of Géricault's most famous paintings, starting at the front with *The Raft of the Medusa* (fig. 4), also reproduced in this model at a reduced scale.[16] There was muted criticism at the time, especially for the realisation of this painting, theatrically incorporated into the depth around several shipwrecked men in distress under scandalous circumstances: a relief could only badly imitate a painting; one should preferably not interfere with the individual character of any work of art.[17] However, Étex did not imitate but instead creatively transferred the maelstrom produced using painterly means into the perspectively tapering pictorial depth, in relief heights flattening from bottom to top.[18] For dramaturgical reasons, he only lent greater plasticity and therefore greater attention to the depth of the narrative space to the rear-view figure seated on the highest point of the pyramid of bodies and waving a cloth.

In 1885, in his bronze relief entitled *The Punishments* (cat. 29), Étex's fellow countryman Jules Dalou did not address the depth of the space, but rather the depth of the fall. The naked, writhing male bodies form a vertical cascade, but at the same time the figures sink, successively transforming, in the powerful light modelling, from a high into a low relief on the reverse surface. As a result, gravity annoyingly seems to act in two directions: vertically as well as, orthogonal to that, into the surface ground. This relief was rooted conceptionally in an unrealised design for a tomb for Victor Hugo and a short time later served Félix Bracquemond as a model for an etching in which he employed a simplified rendering of the exciting arrangement of light and dark (fig. 5).[19] A good ten years later, Dalou pursued a different narrative concept and a different staging of relief and space associated with it. His design for the monument in honour of the racing-car driver Émile Levassor, who died in 1897 as a result of a collision – his was the first motorsport fatality – visualises an almost overwhelming occurrence when the driver, accompanied by the cheering crowd, breaks out of the surface ground directly toward the viewer.[20] Following his death, Dalou's plaster model (cat. 31), produced between 1898 and 1902, was rendered by his student Camille

Lefèvre (fig. 6). Dalou was initially opposed to the commission – he saw himself in dangerous proximity to automobile advertising and at the same time shunned the depiction of what, in his opinion, was an aesthetically unattractive vehicle. With his plastic-dynamic composition in high relief, Lefèvre moved not only in analogy to painting, for instance in the manner of William Turner's painting *Rain, Steam and Speed – The Great Western Railway* (1844, National Gallery, London), but also in analogy to the still young medium of film. With their short film *Arrivée d'un train en gare de La Ciotat* (*Train Pulling into a Station*), shot in 1895, the Lumière brothers had amazed or otherwise thrown their audience into a state of panic as a result of the locomotive racing towards them.[21] In 1900 in Great Britain, Cecil M. Hepworth's film *How It Feels to Be Run Over* succeeded in achieving this no less effectively.[22]

The ascetic to theatrical treatment of surfaces and volumes – for their narrative reliefs, in terms of technique and form artists exhaust the extraordinary possibilities of the medium in order to produce perspectives, movements, actions, interactions and even levels of time directed towards the viewer. In doing so, they benefit from the permeability of neighbouring genres and as a result achieve a high degree of different readings: centred, linear, oscillating, descending, deepening, frontal – hence an unusually wide field of experience opens itself up to the recipient.

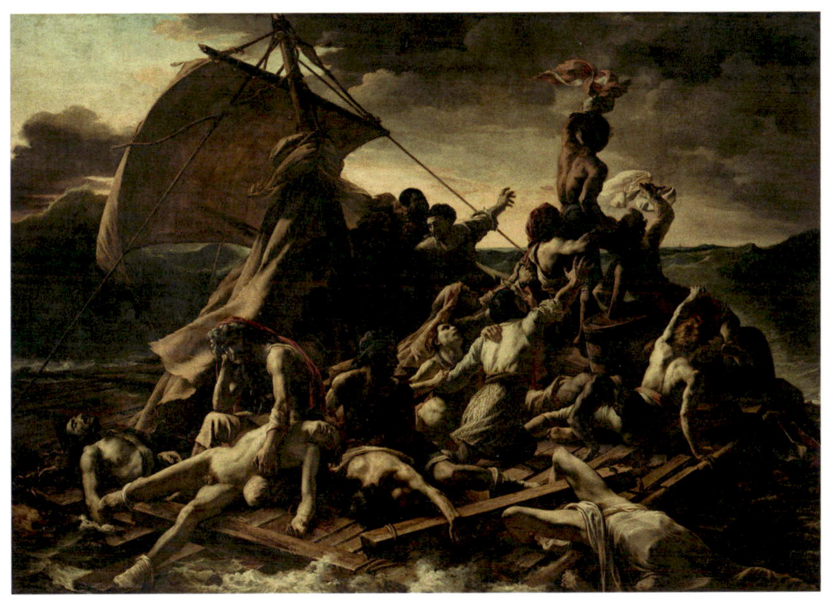

Fig. 4

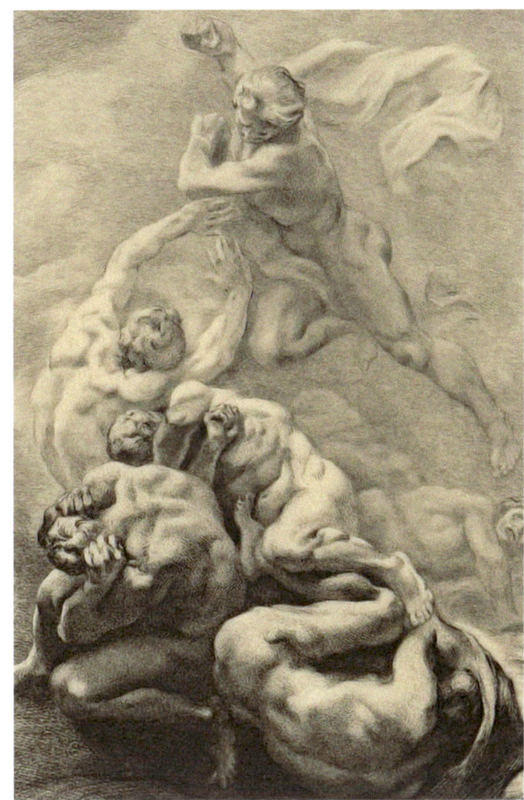

Fig. 5

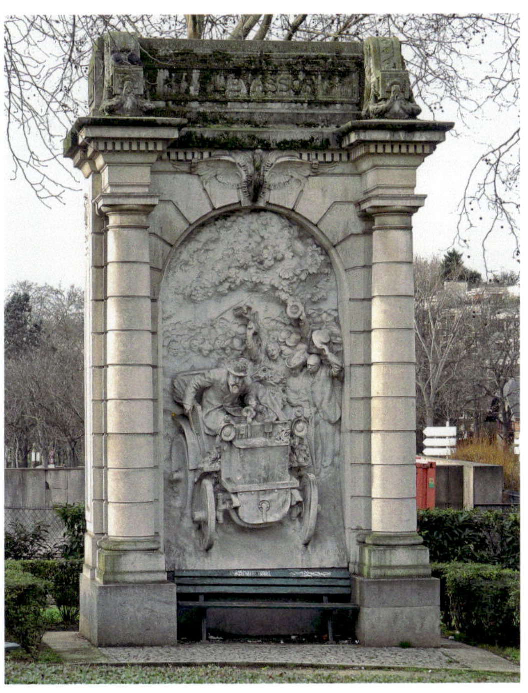

Fig. 6

Fig. 4   Théodore Géricault: *The Raft of the Medusa* (*Scène de naufrage*), 1819, oil on canvas, Musée du Louvre, Paris

Fig. 5   Félix Bracquemond: *Society Has Been Saved* (*La Société est sauvée*), 1885/86, etching, New York Public Library

Fig. 6   Camille Lefèvre after Jules Dalou: *Monument to Émile Levassor*, 1907, marble, Porte Maillot, Paris

1   Claire Barbillon: *Le Relief au croisement des arts du XIXe siècle*, Paris 2014, p. 223; Herbert Beck: *Liebieghaus – Museum alter Plastik: Führer durch die Sammlungen. Bildwerke des Klassizismus*, Melsungen 1985, pp. 108f.; Frank Otten: *Ludwig Michael Schwanthaler 1802–1848: Ein Bildhauer unter König Ludwig I von Bayern. Monographie und Werkverzeichnis*, Munich 1970, p. 149; Ludwig von Schwanthaler: *Der Schild des Herakles*, 1840, K-L372, https://sammlungonline. muenchner-stadtmuseum.de/ objekt/der-schild-des-herakles-10005151.html (accessed 13 February 2023).

2   Alexander Tolnay: "Bildgewordene Handlungen: Zum Werk von Günther Uecker", in: *Günther Uecker*, exh. cat. Ca' Pesaro, Galleria Internazionale d'Arte Moderna, Venice, Milan 2011, pp. 50–57; Stephan Mann: *Das 20. Jahrhundert im Städel*, ed. Sabine Schulze, Ostfildern 1998, p. 161.

3   Johannes Grave provided a concise summary of the research area: Johannes Grave: *Bild und Zeit: Eine Theorie des Bildbetrachtens*, Munich 2022.

4   Letter from Susanne Bethmann-Hollweg to Bertel Thorvaldsen, 16 August 1813, quoted in: Barbara Bott: "Das Epitaph für Johann Philipp Bethmann-Hollweg in Frankfurt am Main", in: Gerhard Bott (ed.): *Bertel Thorvaldsen: Untersuchungen zu seinem Werk und zur Kunst seiner Zeit*, Cologne 1977, pp. 449–460, esp. p. 453.

5   For more detail on this, see *Schönheit und Revolution: Klassizismus 1770–1820*, ed. Maraike Bückling and Eva Mongi-Vollmer, exh. cat. Städel Museum, Frankfurt am Main, Munich 2013, pp. 266–268 (Alexander Kaczmarczyk); Karlheinz Hemmeter: *Studien zu Reliefs von Thorvaldsen: Auftraggeber – Künstler – Werkgenese: Idee und Ausführung*, Munich 1984, pp. 151–198; Bott 1977 (see note 4).

6   On the monument, see Jutta von Simson: *Christian Daniel Rauch: Œuvre-Katalog*, Berlin 1996, cat. nos. 179–188; on the relief in particular, see Lars Eisenlöffel: "Die Melancholie des Königs: Politische Rhetorik und historische Semantik an Rauchs Friedrich-Denkmal", in: Birgit Kümmel and Bernhard Maaz (eds.): *Christian-Daniel-Rauch-Museum Bad Arolsen*, Munich and Berlin 2002, pp. 41–49; quoted in ibid., p. 42.

7   *Nationalgalerie Berlin: Das XIX. Jahrhundert. Bestand der Skulpturen*, ed. Bernhard Maaz, inv. cat. Nationalgalerie Berlin, Leipzig 2006, pp. 566f. (Rolf H. Johannsen); Kümmel/Maaz 2002 (see note 6), p. 160 (Brigitte Schmitz).

8   According to Brigitte Schmitz (Kümmel/Maaz 2002 [see note 6], p. 160), the triumphant equestrian in the background is Frederick himself; however, according to Rolf H. Johannsen (Inv. cat. Berlin 2006 [see note 7], p. 567), it is his ancestor, the Grand Elector Frederick William of Prussia, who is referred to there.

9   Karl Arndt: "Christian Daniel Rauch – der Mensch, der Künstler – im Lichte der Briefe", in: Birgit Kümmel and Bernhard Maaz (eds.): *Kolloquium zur Skulptur des Klassizismus: Bad Arolsen*, Korbach 2004, pp. 13–32. The fact that the relief panels of the memorial proved popular becomes apparent in view of the full-scale casts that found entry as architectural decoration into the Villa Kogge in Berlin-Charlottenburg in 1864; see Inv. cat. Berlin 2006 (see note 7), p. 567 (Rolf H. Johannsen).

10   In this connection, Barlach recombined motifs he had already developed in another context; see Elisabeth Laur: *Ernst Barlach: Das bildnerische Werk. Plastik, Zeichnung, Druckgraphik. Werkverzeichnis II. Das plastische Werk*, ed. Volker Probst, Güstrow 2006, cat. no. 249; *Tod und Klage: Arbeiten von Käthe Kollwitz und Ernst Barlach*, comp. Ursula Grzechca-Mohr, exh. cat. Städtische Galerie im Städelschen Kunstinstitut, Frankfurt am Main, 1995.

11   Very interesting in this respect is an article by the comic illustrator Rutu Modan: "Was wir sehen, wenn wir Comics lesen", *FAZ*, 21 May 2022, p. 18; cf. Grave 2022 (see note 3), pp. 73–77, who speaks of "differential structures".

12   On this phenomenon in general: Magdalena Bushart: *Der Geist der Gotik und die expressionistische Kunst: Kunstgeschichte und Kunsttheorie 1911–1925*, Munich 1990, esp. p. 156.

13   Mario-Andreas von Lüttichau: "Hermann Blumenthal im Folkwang 1934", in: *Sterngucker: Hermann Blumenthal und seine Zeit*, ed. Josephine Gabler, exh. cat. Georg Kolbe Museum, Berlin, 2006, pp. 93–103; Christian Adolf Isermeyer: *Hermann Blumenthal: Das plastische Werk*, Stuttgart 1993, cat. no. R 17, 1–8.

14   Gabriele Mahn: "Die Reliefs von Hans Arp", in: *Hans Arp*, ed. Christine Hopfengart, exh. cat. Kunsthalle Nürnberg, Ostfildern 1994, pp. 44–55, esp. p. 50.

15   Dieter Schwarz: "Vorwort", in: *Hans Arp*, exh. cat. Kunstmuseum Winterthur 2016, pp. 5–19, esp. p. 6.

16   On the design verso the names of the donors; on the monument, see Stefan Eric Püngel: *L'Œuvre sculptée de Jean-Antoine Étex. L'expressivité comme source de l'inspiration artistique*, Ph.D. diss. Frankfurt am Main 2010, pp. 477f.; Bruno Chenique: "Le Tombeau de Géricault", in: Régis Michel (ed.), *Géricault*, 2 vols., Paris 1996, vol. 2, pp. 721–758.

17   "Je ne trouve pas une idée heureuse dans la reproduction fort imparfaite du tableau de *la Méduse* dans un bas-relief en bronze, sur la face du monument; un bas-relief imite mal un tableau, il faut laisser à chaque art son caractère individuel." L'Amateur, "Salon de 1841 (5e et dernier article)", *La Quotidienne*, 6 June 1841, pp. 1–3, esp. p. 3; quoted in: Püngel 2010 (see note 16), p. 484.

18   Barbillon 2014 (see note 1), pp. 202–204, esp. p. 204.

19   The etching was intended to decorate the frontispiece of a new edition of Victor Hugo's volume of poetry of the same time, directed against Napoleon III, that he had published for the first time in 1851 in Belgian exile; see *Jules Dalou, le sculpteur de la Republique: Catalogue des sculptures de Jules Dalou conservées au Petit Palais*, ed. Amélie Simier, exh. cat. Petit Palais and Musée Cognacq-Jay, Paris, 2013, pp. 106–115 (Amélie Simier).

20   Barbillon 2014 (see note 1), p. 132; exh. cat. Paris 2013 (see note 19), pp. 142–145 (Marine Kisiel); Amélie Simier et al. (eds.): *Dalou à Paris*, Paris 2010, p. 61 (Marine Kisiel).

21   Exh. cat. Paris 2013 (see note 19), p. 142 (Marine Kisiel).

22   Dietmar Rübel: *Plastizität: Eine Kunstgeschichte des Veränderlichen*, Munich 2012, pp. 27f.

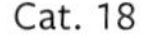

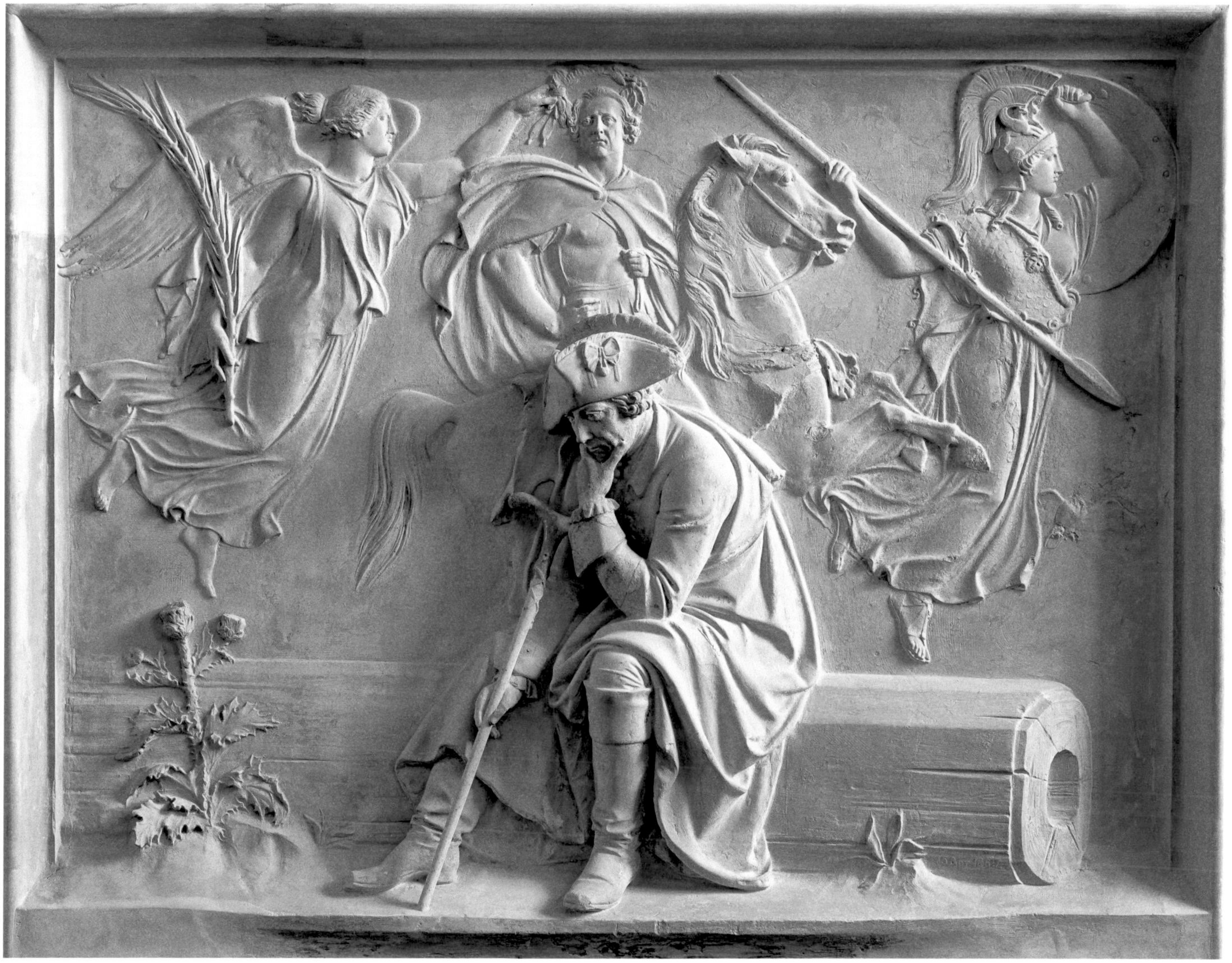

Cat. 19   Ludwig Schwanthaler: *Shield of Heracles*, 1832–42,
bronze, diameter: 89 cm, Liebieghaus Skulpturensammlung,
Frankfurt am Main, inv. no. St.P 4 (Frankfurt only)

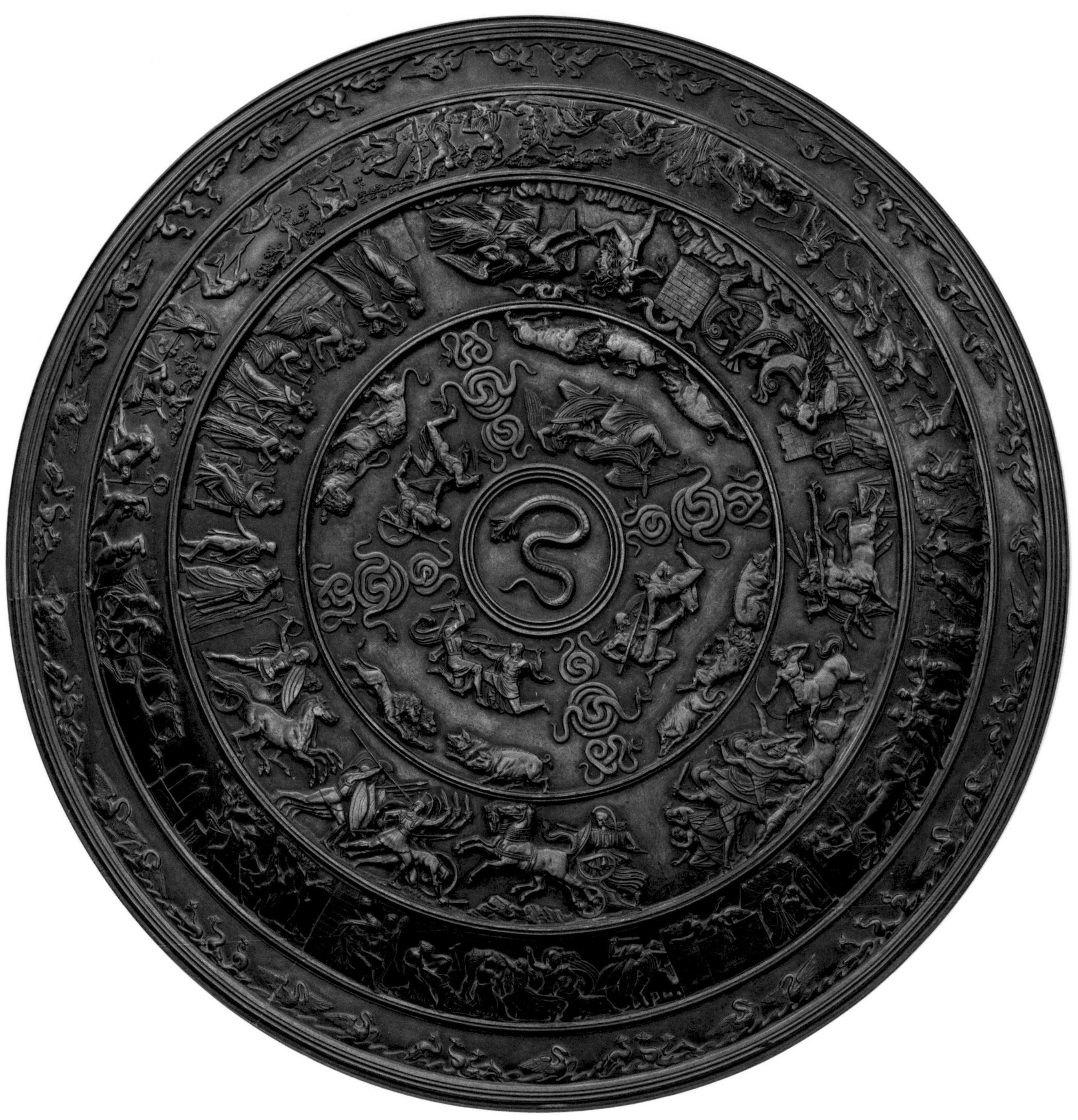

Cat. 20   Günther Uecker: *Organic Structure*, 1962, nails and
oil on canvas on wood, 110 × 110 × 8 cm, Städel Museum,
Frankfurt am Main, inv. no. SG 1241 (Frankfurt only)

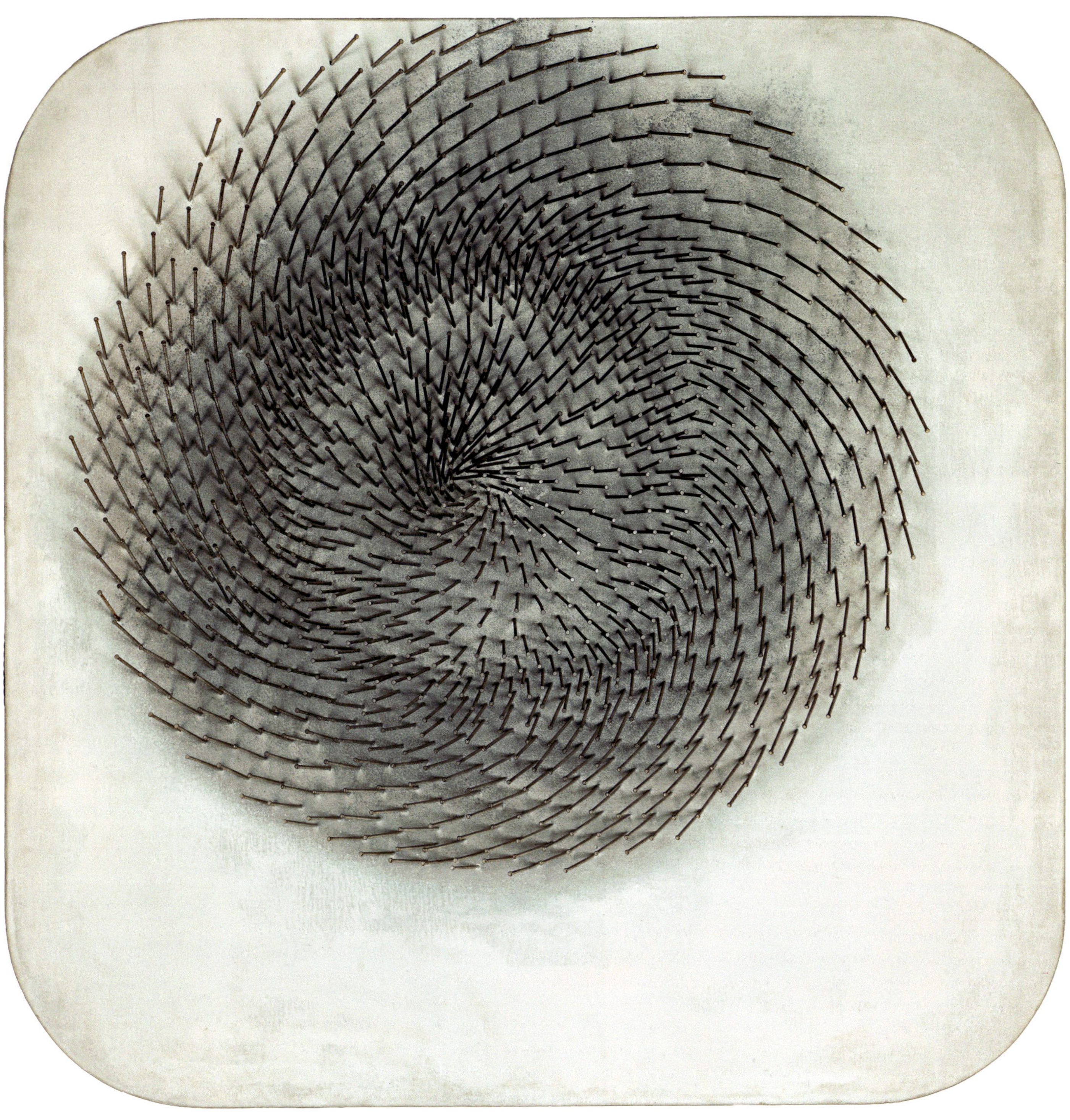

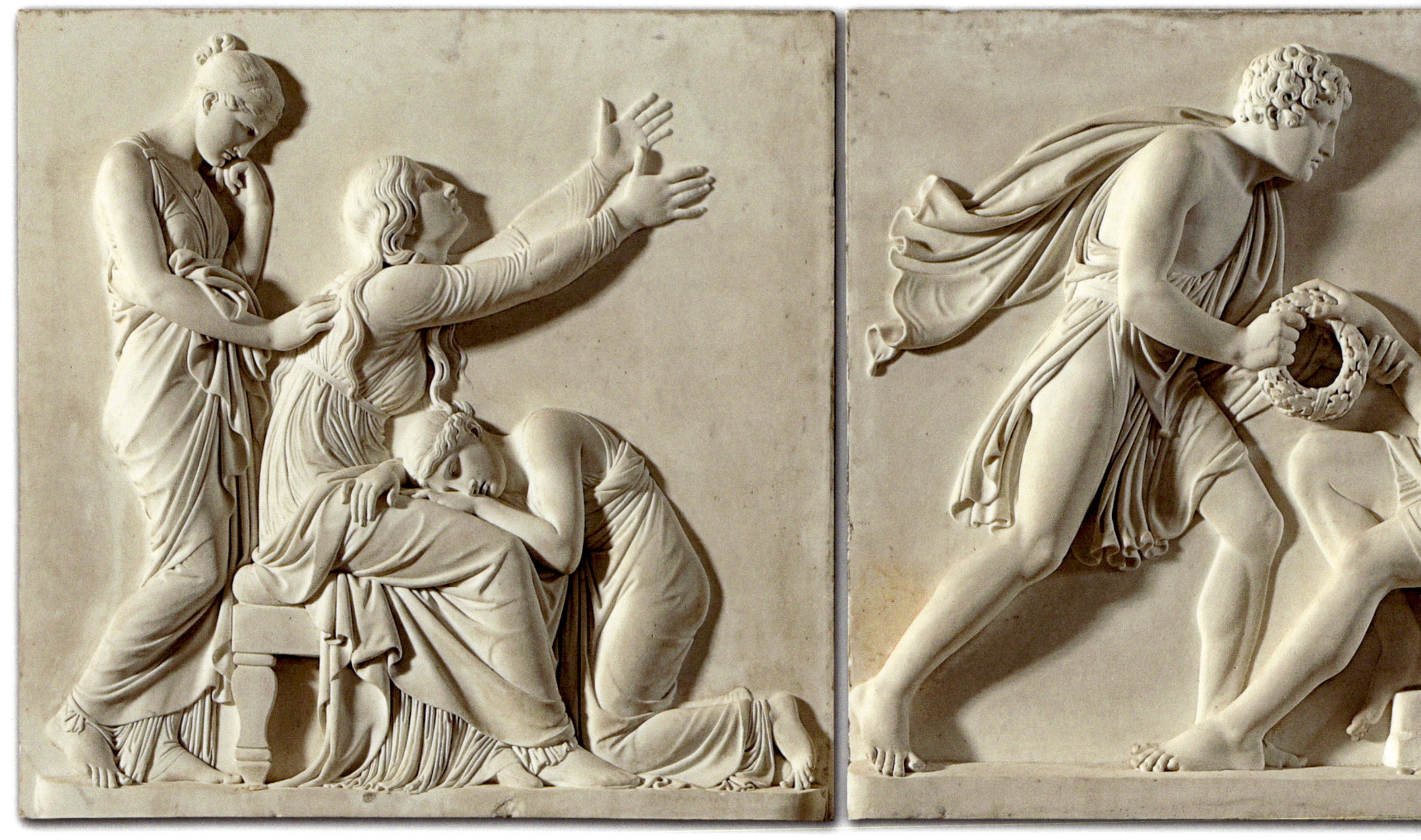

Cat. 21   Bertel Thorvaldsen: *Epitaph for Johann Philipp Bethmann-Hollweg*, 1830, marble, 91 × 198 × 14 cm, Liebieghaus Skulpturensammlung, Frankfurt am Main, inv. no. 2354 a–c

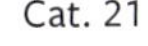

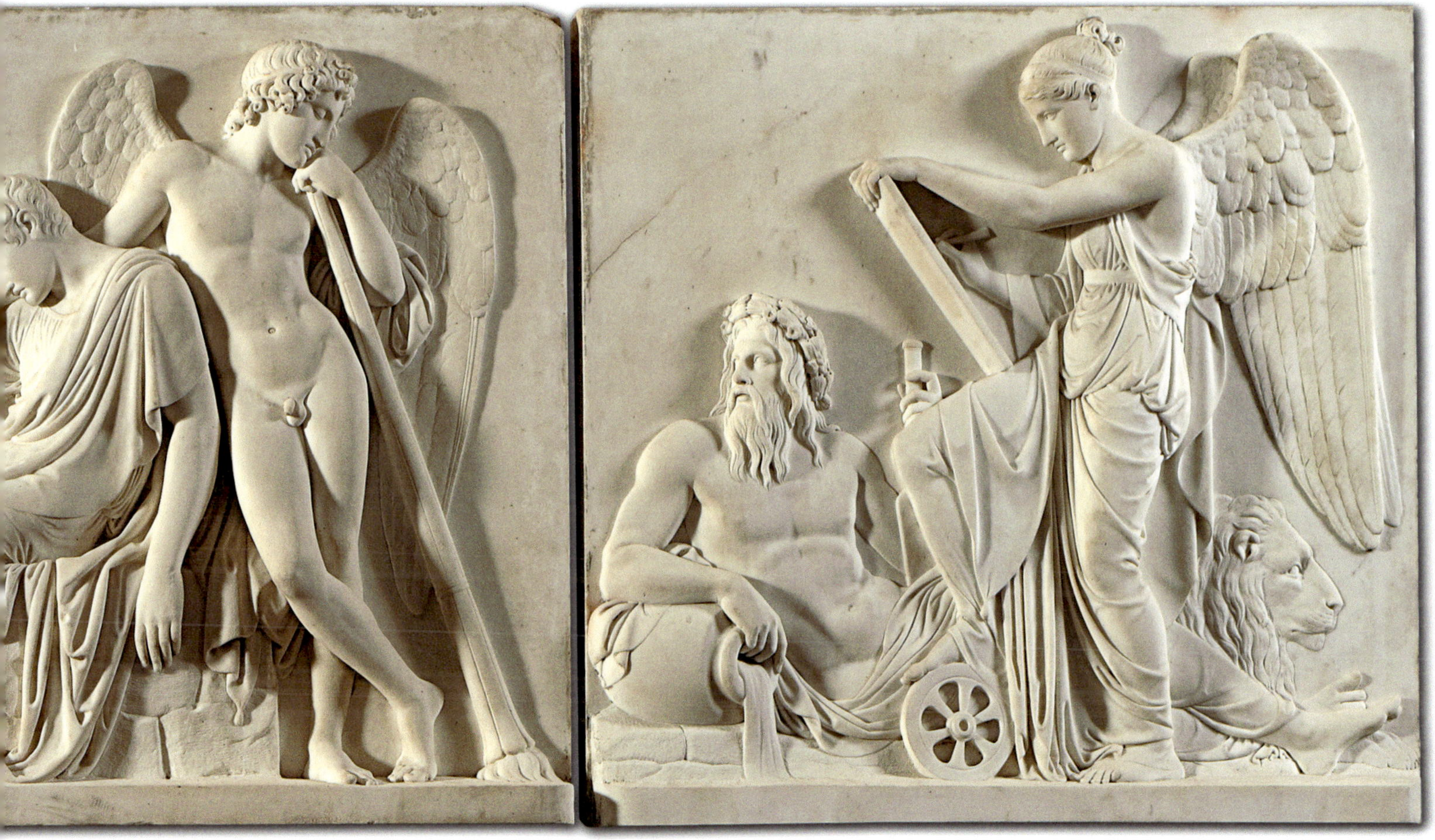

Cat. 22   Ernst Barlach: *Death and Life*, 1916/17, bronze,
50.5 × 41.7 × 1.5 cm, Städel Museum, Frankfurt am Main,
inv. no. St.P 446

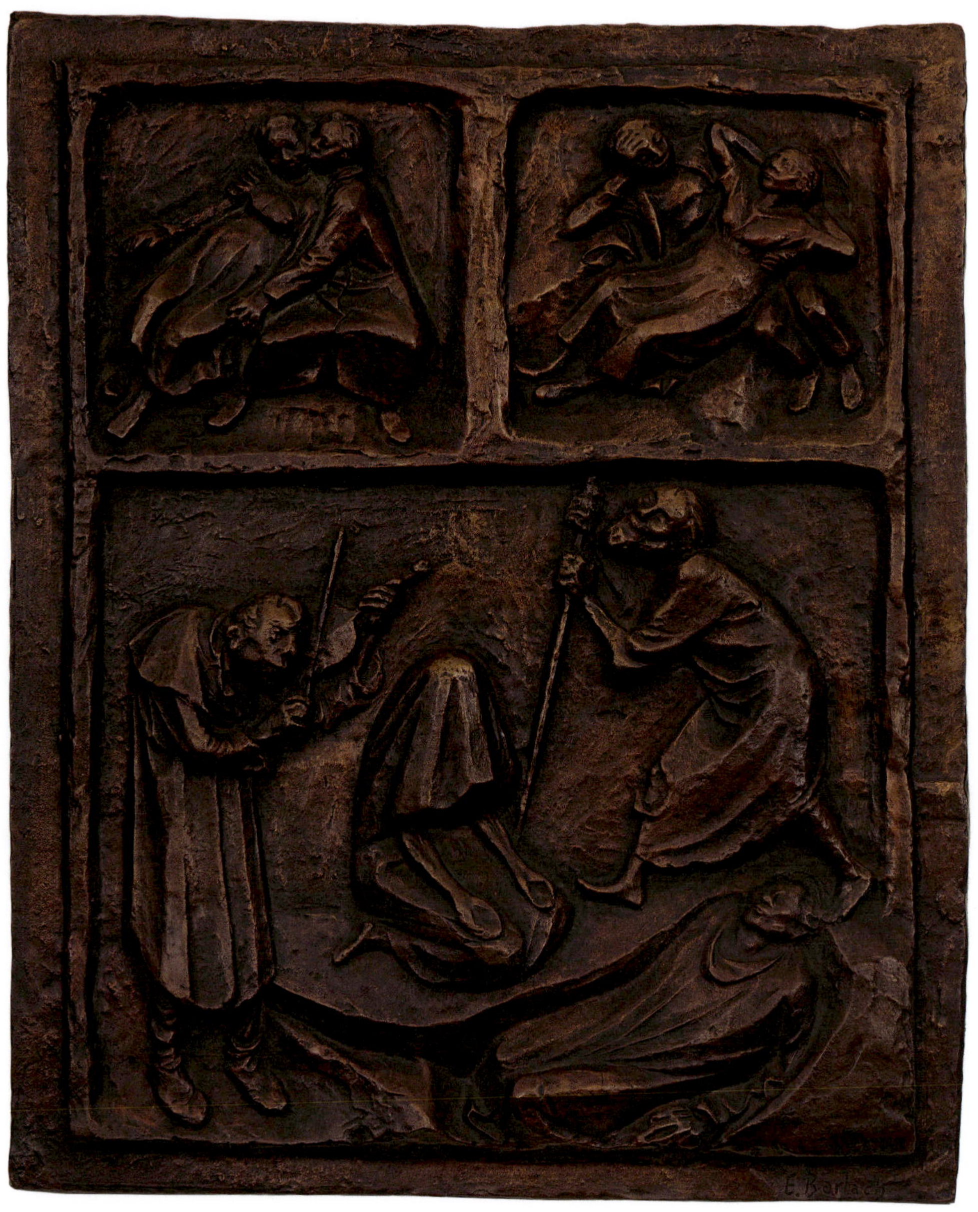

Cat. 23   Jean Arp: *Two Heads* (*Deux Têtes*), 1927, oil and string on
canvas, 64.8 × 80.6 cm, private collection

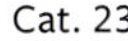

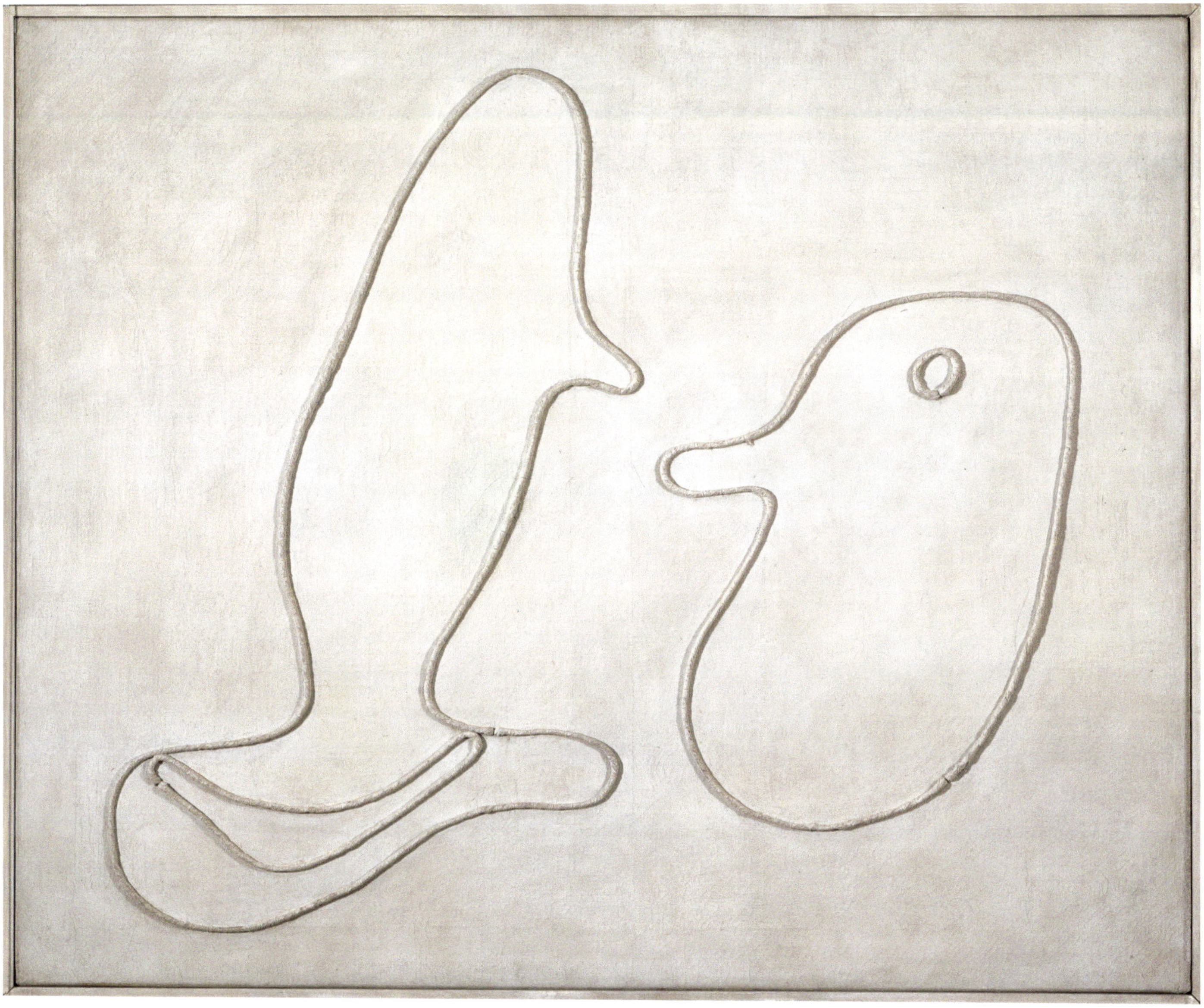

Cats. 24–26 Hermann Blumenthal: *Man with Foal / Two Archers / Man with Woman*, 1934, plaster, 58 × 40 cm each, Georg Kolbe Museum, Berlin, permanent loan (Nachlass Familie Blumenthal), inv. nos. DL119, DL120, DL131

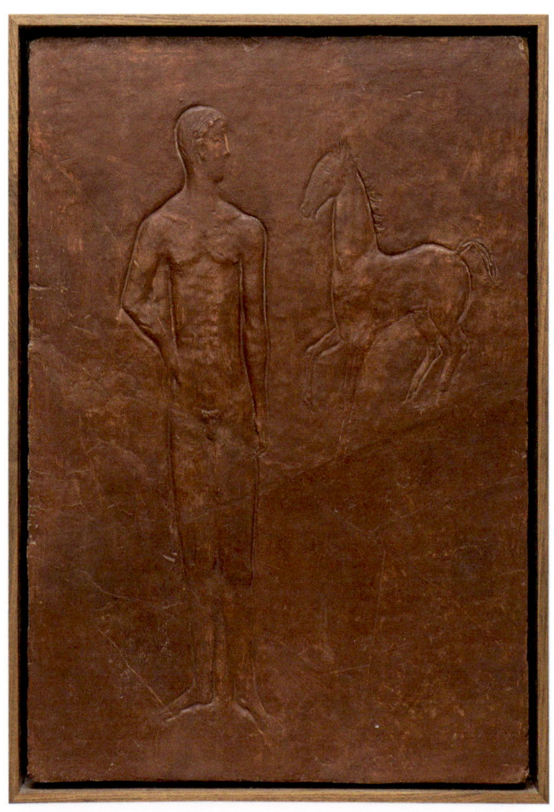

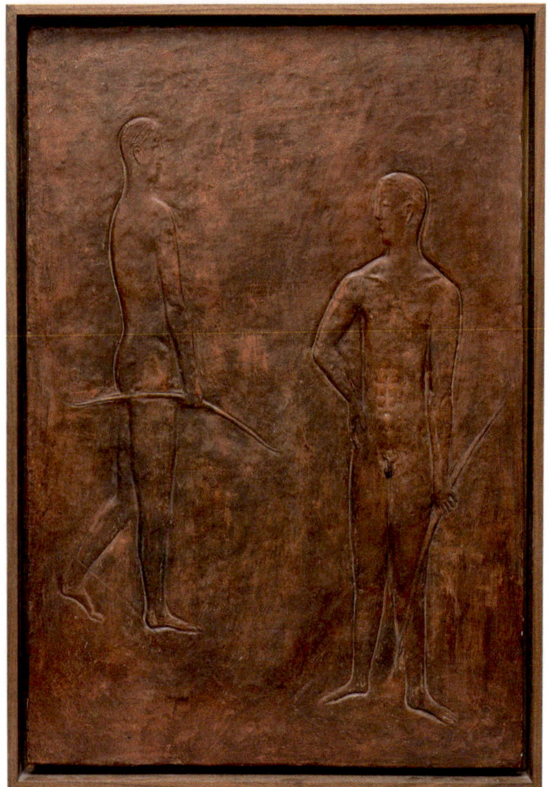

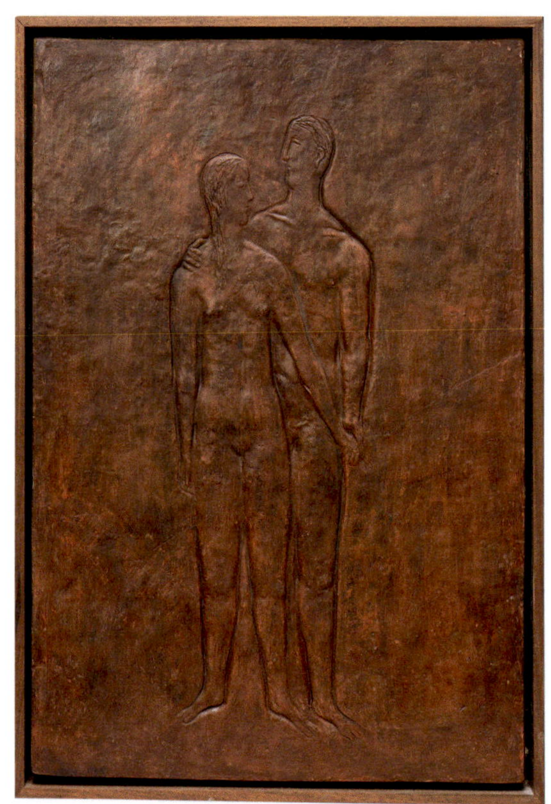

Cats. 27, 28 Hermann Blumenthal: *Resting Shepherds / Two Women*,
1934, plaster, 58 × 40 cm each, Georg Kolbe Museum, Berlin,
permanent loan (Nachlass Familie Blumenthal), inv. no.
DL126, DL127

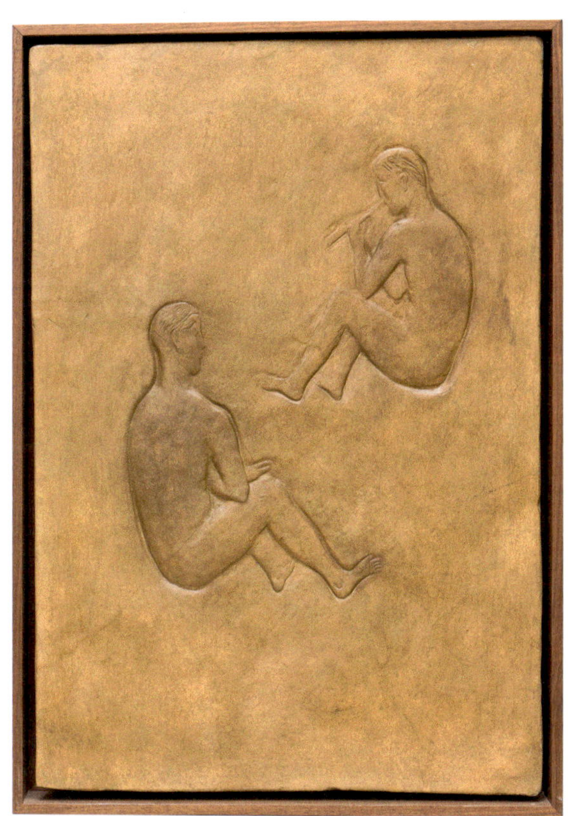

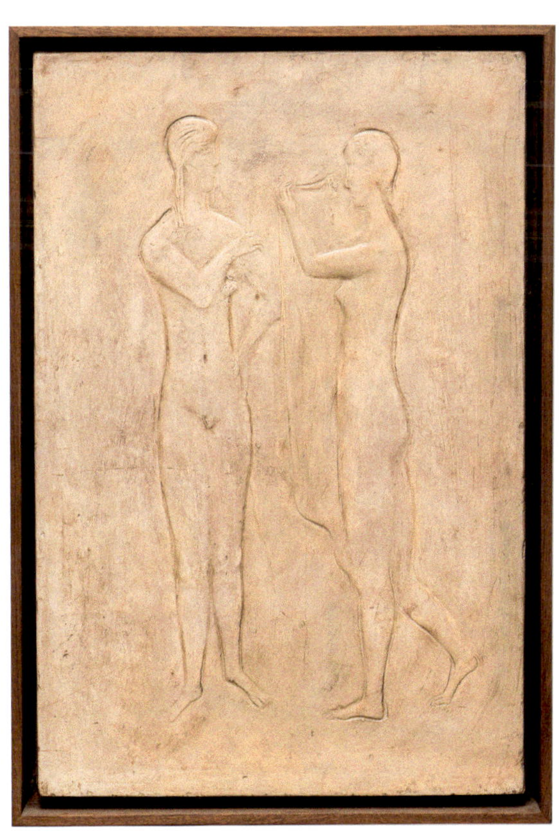

Cat. 29   Jules Dalou: *The Punishments (Les Châtiments)*, 1885, bronze, 35 × 25 × 8 cm, private collection, London

Cat. 30   Antoine Étex: *Model for the Tomb of Théodore Géricault*, 1840, bronze, 43 × 36 × 16 cm, private collection, Paris, courtesy of Stuart Lochhead Sculpture

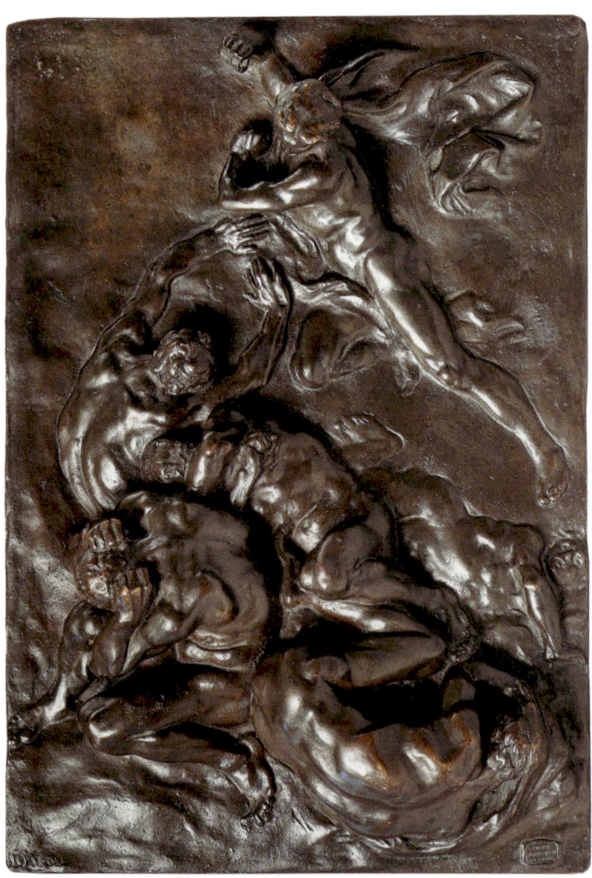

Cat. 29

Cat. 30

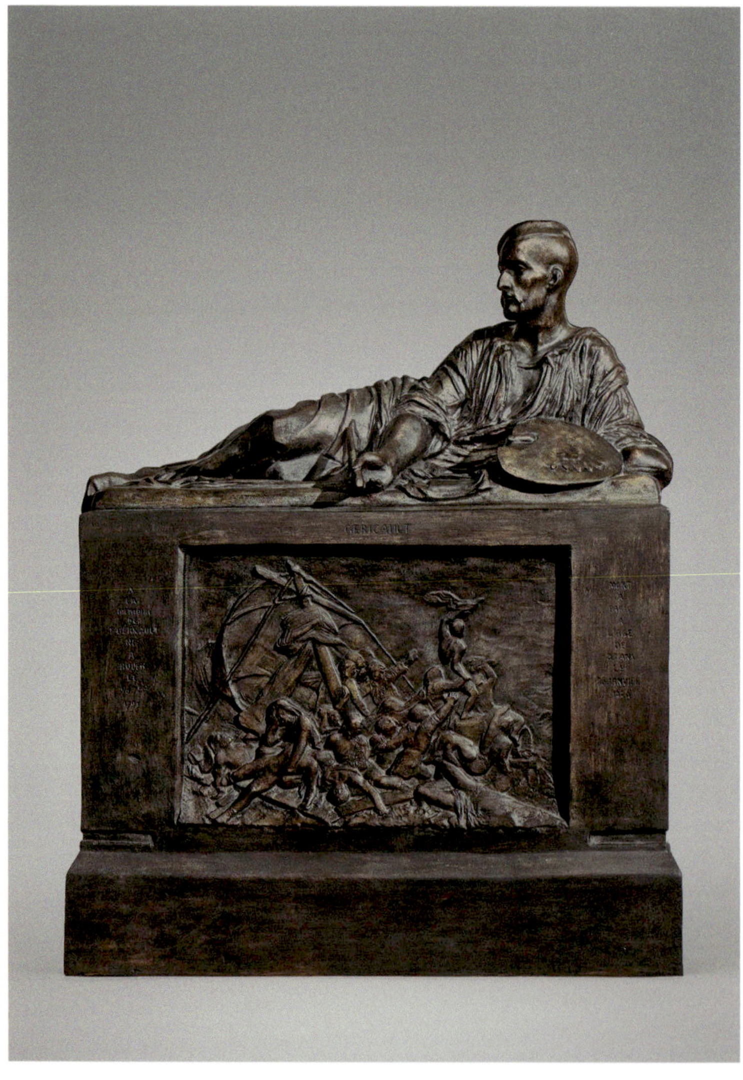

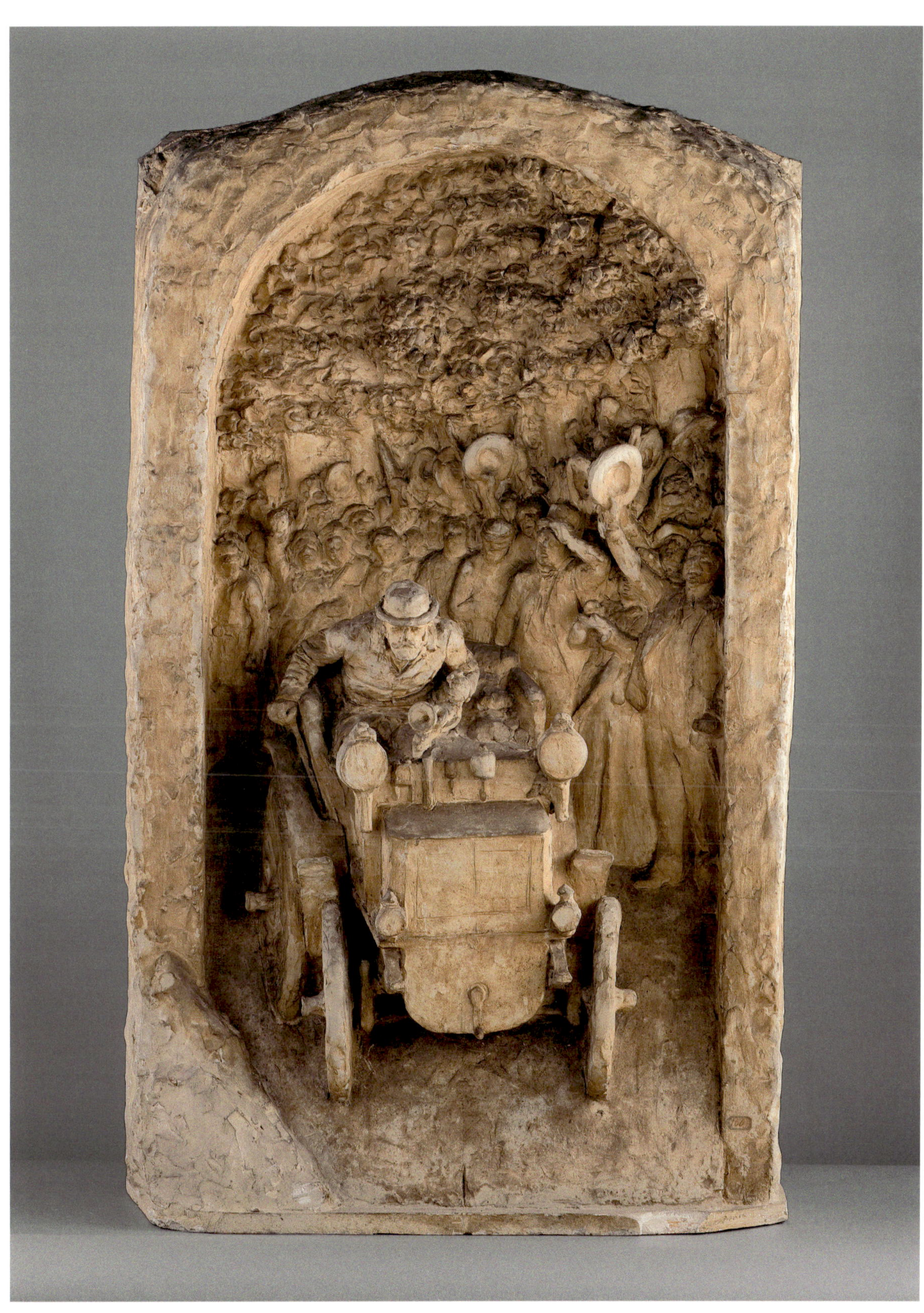

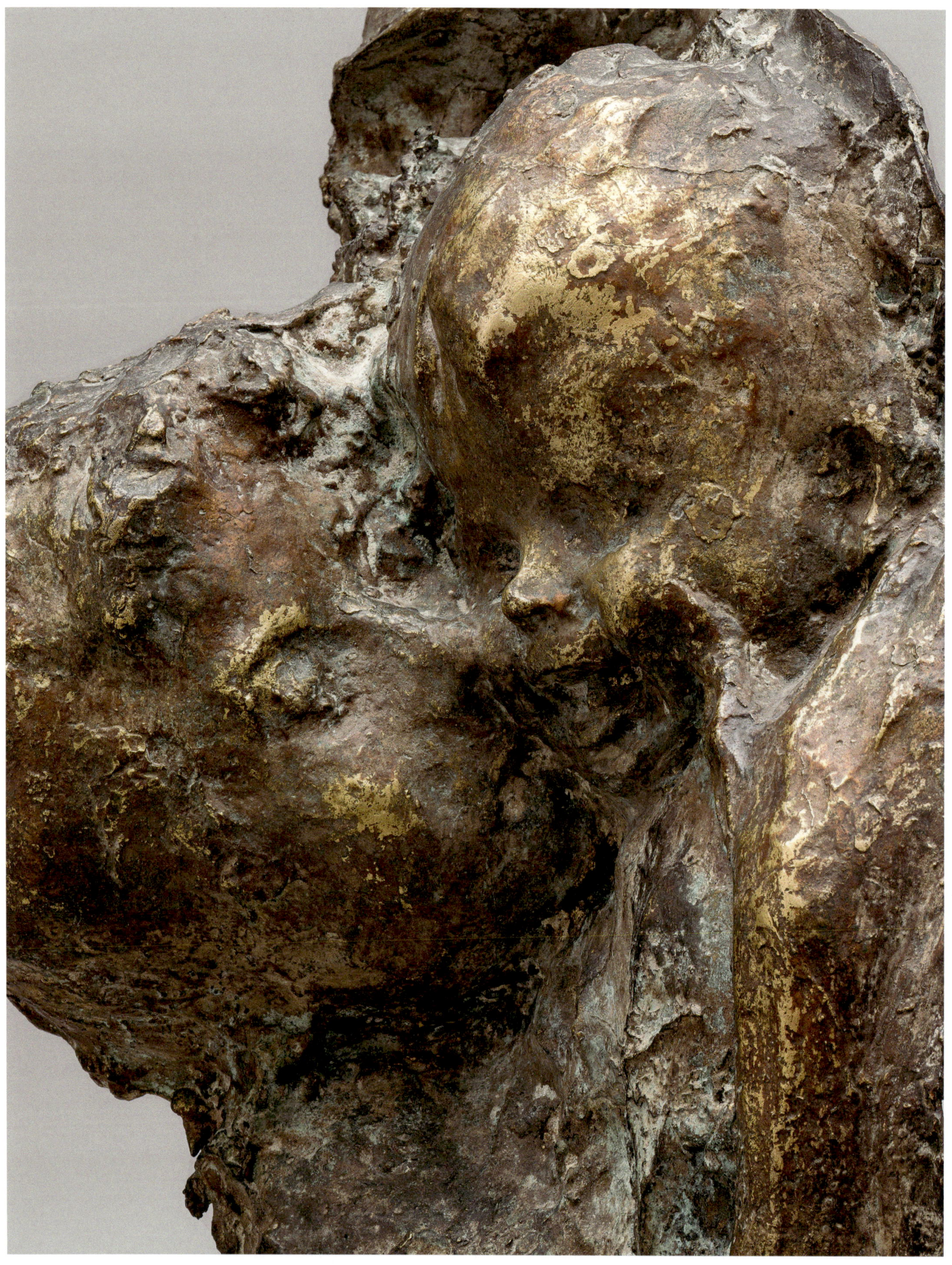

Cats. 32—40

Alexander Eiling

PAINTERLY-SCULPTURAL RELIEFS

In 1899 August Schmarsow published his essay on the inter-relationship between sculpture, painting, and relief art, thus joining in the ongoing discussion about artistic mediums, the specific possibilities they offered and their relationships to one another – a topic that inflamed passions around the turn of the century. He located relief in the realm between painting and sculpture, arguing that, as a "former of bodies", it not only availed itself of sculptural means but also succeed-ed in representing "body and space at once", as did paint-ing.[1] Thanks to this hybrid status, it was capable of uniting elements of both mediums. Unlike sculpture in the round, it permitted the representation of the space surrounding a motif, and with it the creation of atmospheric effects. As aptly phrased by Roland Bothner in his study of the history of the relief, it proved itself "in the sculptural mastery of the painterly".[2] The traditional criterion for evaluating re-liefs – the relationship between "figure and ground" – now gave way to those applied to painting. This is evident not least of all in works executed in an open style of modelling, in which the depiction and the underlying support enter into productive interplay between protrusion and fusion, plasticity and planarity. In this case, sculpture often takes orientation from the loose mode of painting that had devel-oped above all in Impressionism. We accordingly encounter painterly-sculptural relief depictions more frequently in the oeuvres of artists who worked in both techniques, such as Honoré Daumier, Edgar Degas, Constantin Meunier and Henri Matisse. On the other hand, such reliefs were also produced by sculptors who were particularly interested in painting and strove to compete with it, including Medardo Rosso and Auguste Rodin.

The close interweave of painting and sculpture is espe-cially clear in a work by Honoré Daumier known today primarily as *The Fugitives* (*Fugitifs*; cat. 32). Two very similar complete versions of the motif executed by the artist in clay between 1848 and 1878 have come down to us.[3] To this day there are conflicting opinions on ex-actly when Daumier executed the work and how we are to interpret it. The long human procession extending across the entire width of the surface has been associ-ated with various historical events. Speculations range from the mass deportations following the May Revolution of 1848, to the Polish uprisings of 1863, to the events of the Franco-Prussian War of 1870/71. Daumier probably took inspiration from plaster casts of reliefs on Trajan's Column (112/13 CE) which he had hanging in his studio.[4] Yet his loose modelling and sketchy narrative style con-trast starkly with the precisely worked reliefs of classi-cal antiquity. Closer in character to a study or bozzetto, his depiction derives its vitality from the subtle balance between allusion and description that is far easier to achieve in painting. Daumier succeeds in creating this state of uncertainty by means of a compositional device in which the figures are guided past the viewer not in a line parallel to the picture but rather in a curve. What is more, contrary to the usual direction of reading, they approach from out of the depths at the right and fade into indeterminacy again at the left. This explains their gradual emergence into corporality and their subsequent retrogression back to planarity that lend the composi-tion greater dynamic and already anticipate attributes of Rodin's *Gates of Hell* (p. 22, fig. 12; → Introduction). For Daumier, who had never trained as a sculptor, the medi-um served as a kind of testing ground for transcending conventions and experimenting with compositions that he also utilised for his paintings (fig. 1) and drawings.[5] Edgar Degas, too, alternated freely between mediums with-out regard for academic rules. His only extant relief, known today by the narrative title *Picking Apples*[6] (cat. 40), illus-trates how he in fact obscured the narrative action with the rudimentary development of the figures from the ground. For even with plenty of imagination, the group of five sitting

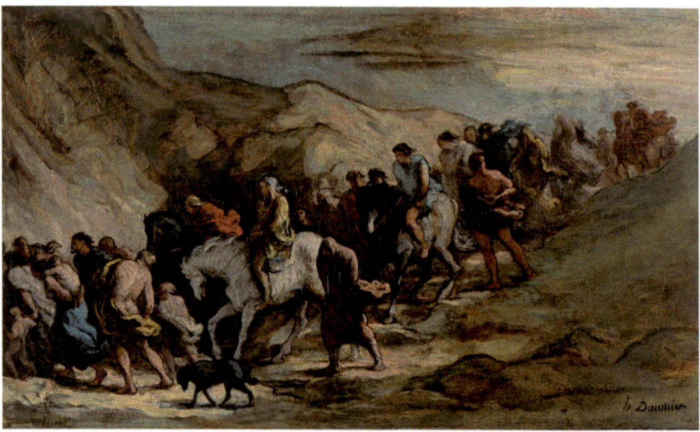

Fig. 1   Honoré Daumier: *The Fugitives* (*Fugitifs*), ca. 1848–52, oil on paper, mounted on canvas, Sammlung Oskar Reinhart "Am Römerholz", Winterthur

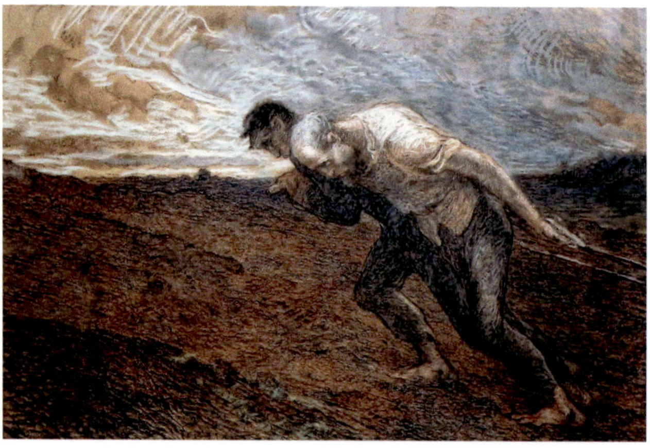

Fig. 2   Constantin Meunier: *The Glebe* (*La Glèbe*), 1872, pastel on paper, mounted on canvas, Musée d'Ixelles, Brussels

and standing figures offers nothing in the way of a discernible storyline related to apple-harvesting. The hands raised to mouths constitute the only possible allusion to the eating of fruit. In the related literature, the relief has been associated with a significantly larger clay model which the artist reportedly abandoned to decay. Some scholars have speculated that the relief in question may have been a study for a gravestone for the artist's niece Marie Fevre.[7] No such epitaph has come down to us. In its arrangement of the composition parallel to the surface plane and the staggering of the figures, however, the work mirrors Degas' intense preoccupation with ancient relief art, especially the Parthenon frieze, with which he had already become fascinated back in his student days (→ Echo of the Parthenon). Statements by the artist also testify to his keen interest in the characteristics offered by the relief.[8] In *Picking Apples*, he made use of the medium's entire range from low to half to high relief. At the same time, with his dynamic modelling of the background he created the illusion of the sketchy execution style frequently encountered in his paintings and pastels.

In painting, the space surrounding the figures can be convincingly represented with the aid of colour. For sculptors, on the other hand, the depiction of space poses a fundamental problem, as it is hardly possible to model air. One solution can be found in Constantin Meunier's work of 1892 entitled *The Glebe* (cat. 33). Using the

means offered by relief, the artist virtually created a stage on which he succeeded in depicting both the soil and the sky with clouds in great detail.[9] A view from the side reveals the concave shape of the underlying support which serves to create the impression that the fieldworkers are embedded in a natural space. Sculpted in high relief, their bodies strain forward dynamically. The relief is the sculptural realisation of a composition that the artist had developed in pastel some twenty years earlier (fig. 2), when he was still primarily active as a painter. Meunier's penchant for materiality is already apparent in the drawing, where the rugged gouges in the earth look almost real enough to touch. To translate the atmospheric elements of the two-dimensional composition into sculpture, he availed himself of the relief, whose support became the canvas on which his pictorial idea took three-dimensional shape. In his "sculptural painting", Meunier defined the viewer's vantage point – and thus seems to have been reacting to Charles Baudelaire's highly consequential criticism that sculpture was inferior to painting on account of its viewability from multiple angles and the resulting indeterminacy of its perception (→ Introduction).[10]

Whereas Meunier strove to translate his two-dimensional work into relief in as much detail as possible, Henri Matisse used the medium for a successive reduction of the formal language arrived at in painting. All his life, Matisse

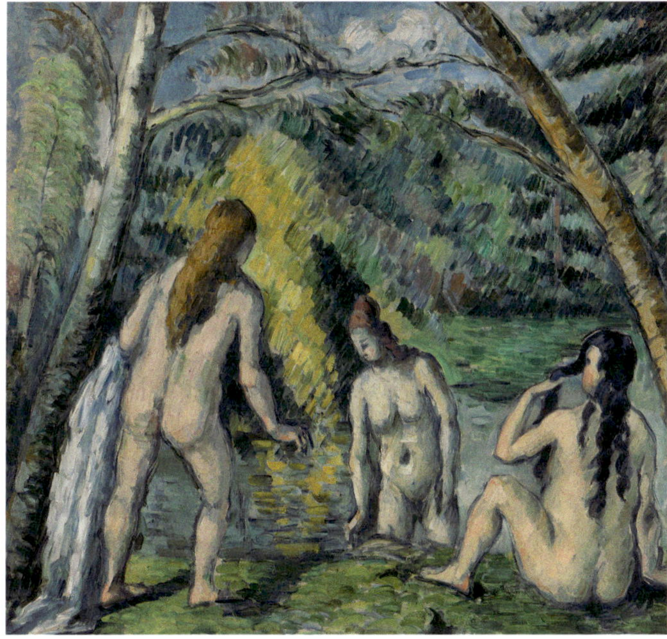

Fig. 3   Paul Cézanne: *Three Bathers* (*Trois baigneuses*), 1879–82,
oil on canvas, Petit Palais, Musée des Beaux-Arts de la Ville de Paris

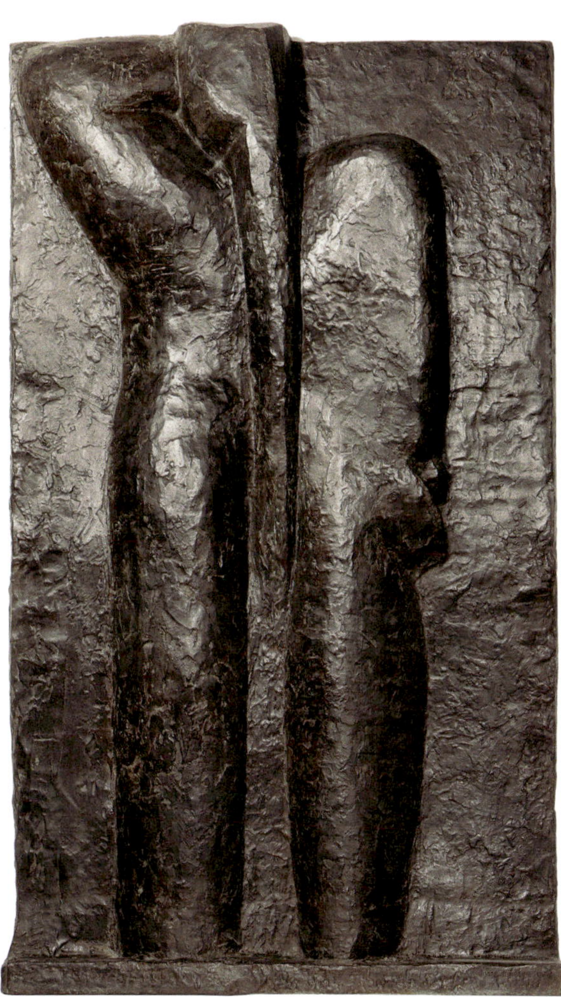

Fig. 4   Henri Matisse: *The Back IV* (*Nu de dos IV*), 1930, bronze,
Staatsgalerie Stuttgart

considered himself more a painter than a sculptor, even if his oeuvre is characterised by the productive interplay between the two techniques and he assigned sculpture a special status within his work.[11] His sculptures are for the most part small-scale works modelled in clay or wax and later cast in bronze. They appear in many of his paintings as quotations and thus lose their viewability from all sides, which in turn – and quite logically – led the artist to the relief medium. Inspired by Paul Cézanne's painting *Three Bathers* (fig. 3), which he had had in his possession since 1899, Matisse embarked on the execution of a life-size bronze relief (cat. 36). It depicts an isolated female nude, seen from the back, in front of a background enlivened with traces of the modelling process. Standing in classical contrapposto, the figure has her left arm raised above her head, thus adopting a pose explored by the artist again and again throughout his career, also in paintings and drawings. Yet her body is defined primarily by the distribution of weighty volumes that draws on the anti-classical idea of Cézanne's bathers and manifests Matisse's ongoing search for a clarity of expression befitting of modernism. He accordingly created neither a stage-like space nor a landscape for his

figure, nor even the studio setting alluded to in his painted depictions of nudes. Particularly the omission of the model's feet underscores this radical abandonment of perspectival spatiality.[12] Defined not as space but rather as a spatial boundary, the relief support served the artist as a medium for exploring the ideal relationship between mass and surface. In the years until 1930, he would go on to create three further relief versions of the same subject and size in which he increasingly abstracted the figure and condensed it formally (fig. 4).[13]

The lessons learned from Matisse's formal experiments are clearly reflected in a relief by the artist Karl Hartung of Hamburg which strikes a subtle balance between figuration and abstraction (cat. 35).[14] The row of closely spaced, standing nudes appears to detach only tentatively from the ground of the relief plate. Hartung has translated Matisse's isolated nude seen from behind into an abstract figural pattern repeat that defies narrative interpretation. The human body has transformed into an animated surface ornament set in motion by the play of light and exhibiting painterly qualities in its slurred transitions.

The reliefs thus far discussed in this chapter share the formal limitation to a rectangular support plate that defines the atmospheric space of the depiction. However modern in appearance, they are therefore all solidly based on the formal ideal of the relief originating in ancient art. Medardo Rosso's *The Golden Age* (cat. 37) introduced a different means of making space visible in sculpture – and one that ventured away from the territory previously staked out for the relief.[15] The artist designed the work to be viewed solely from the front. Its subject matter is hardly discernible at first sight. Like a detail from a larger depiction, a mother presses her child's small body to her mouth and cheek. Rosso's wife Giuditta Pozzi and their son Francesco, born in November 1885, served him as models. He considered the motif the quintessence of earthly bliss, to which he lent universal meaning with a reference to an ideal state of the world in the title. In his works he strove to capture the initial impression of a motif, quite in the manner of the ideas the Impressionist painters had adopted as their creed around the same time. To underscore the brevity and transience of the moment, Rosso deliberately employed a blurred quality that inextricably interweaves figure and space. Here, fragments of the surrounding space appear around the heads as fleeting impressions of things seen in passing – a key component of Rosso's sculptural works (cat. 38). And by virtue of their partially porous surfaces, nuanced patination, and visible traces of the working process, these works also have an effect similar to that of Impressionist paintings. Owing to this approach, the French press paid tribute to Rosso as the "founder of impressionist sculpture".[16]

Rosso's affinity to Impressionism is an important aspect of his work, but the materiality of his sculptures also bears a connection to the mode of pastose painting practised by artists such as Gustave Courbet and Adolphe Monticelli since the middle of the century.[17] Monticelli, in particular, cultivated a highly idiosyncratic method of applying the paint in several thick layers; it was for this reason that he coined the byname "Croûsticelli" (from the French *croûte*, or "crust") for himself.[18] The fissured, relief-like surface of his painting of a house painter (cat. 39) emphasises the intrinsic value of paint as material to such a degree that it almost relegates the depiction to secondary status. At the same time, the motif can be read as a cryptic reference to the fact that contemporary art critics compared Monticelli's unorthodox application of the paint to crafts practices.[19] The juxtaposition of Rosso's sculpture and Monticelli's painting testifies to the fact that the two mediums converged and influenced one another in the haptic, relief-like treatment of the surfaces – an observation also mirrored in a quotation by Rosso: "Painting? Sculpture? There is only one art."[20] The integration of the surrounding space into his sculptures was also a concern of Rosso's greatest rival Auguste Rodin, who would have liked to claim the title of first impressionist sculptor for himself, at least for a time. He also produced a depiction of a mother and child – a motif rare in his oeuvre – likewise presented in detail-like manner but as full-length figures in a grotto (cat. 34).[21] Reminiscent of an earthen womb, the hollow space modelled in plaster encloses the mother and child, who appear to both emerge from and sink into it. The child's legs jut forward from the grotto space, while its head disappears into the depths. In this way, Rodin created a relief entirely in the round that transcends the boundaries of the genre. It differs from the example by Rosso in that here figure and space are distinctly separate. Whereas Rosso modelled the immaterial emptiness directly around his mother and child, Rodin detached – albeit barely – his figures from the surrounding block. Nevertheless, the close relationship between the bodies and the roughly worked plaster, the interplay between light and shaded areas, and the irregular transition from the inner walls of the grotto to the work's edges all contribute so well to fusing the structures optically that the eye of the beholder perceives the image sometimes as three- and sometimes two-dimensional. The tension thus arising between openness and consummation is also encountered in many other works by Rodin, including the marble version of the same motif.[22] By only partially disjoining the figures from the block of stone, Rodin seemingly allows us to share in the artistic process. He increasingly questioned both the function of the relief support and the figure's allegiance to the surface, thereby representing the tendency to circumvent the classical conception of the relief – a development that would come to a head in the reliefs of the twentieth century.

1 "Like painting [...], the relief represents body and space at once. Thus it treats [...] the same subject we have assigned to painting. But it tries to solve this problem entirely with the means of sculpture, that is, as a matter for the former of bodies. Relief art thus belongs in the intermediate zone between painting and sculpture [...]." August Schmarsow: *Beiträge zur Aesthetik der bildenden Künste*, vol. 3: *Plastik, Malerei und Reliefkunst in ihrem gegenseitigen Verhältnis*, Leipzig 1899, pp. 153f.

2 Roland Bothner: *Grund und Figur: Die Geschichte des Reliefs und Auguste Rodins Höllentor*, Munich 1993, p. 68.

3 See the in-depth discussion in Edouard Papet: "Fugitifs", in: *Daumier 1808–1879*, ed. Henri Loyrette et al., exh. cat. Musée des Beaux-Arts du Canada, Ottawa, et al., Paris 1999, pp. 288–295; *"Daumier ist ungeheuer!" (Max Liebermann): Gemälde, Zeichnungen, Graphik, Bronzen von Honoré Daumier*, ed. Claude Keisch, responsible for the publication: Stiftung Brandenburger Tor, exh. cat. Max Liebermann Haus, Berlin, Berlin 2013, pp. 196–198.

4 Arsène Alexandre: *H. Daumier, l'homme et l'œuvre*, Paris 1888, p. 339, note 3.

5 See the general discussion by Martin Sonnabend: "Zeichnung und Skulptur bei Daumier", in: *Honoré Daumier: Zeichnungen*, ed. Colta Ives et al., exh. cat. Städtische Galerie im Städelschen Kunstinstitut, Frankfurt am Main/The Metropolitan Museum of Art, New York, Frankfurt am Main 1992, pp. 29–39.

6 The work received this title not from Degas but in connection with the production of the bronze cast. On the history of the relief, see *Degas*, ed. Jean Sutherland Boggs, exh. cat. Galeries Nationales du Grand Palais, Paris, et al., Paris 1988, p. 358.

7 For a detailed discussion, see *Edgar Degas Sculpture*, ed. Suzanne Glover Lindsay et al., inv. cat. National Gallery of Art, Washington, D.C., Princeton 2010, pp. 331–337.

8 "En dehors du bas-relief lui-même, la sculpture ne serait-elle pas l'art singulier de donner l'idée des formes en trompant tout de même sur le relief? C'est le relief qui gâte tout, qui trompe le plus et c'est à lui qu'on croit [Apart from bas-relief itself, is sculpture not the singular art of conveying the idea of forms by pretending relief? It is the relief that spoils everything, that deceives the most, and it is the relief in which we believe]." Letter from Edgar Degas to Paul-Albert Bartholomé, undated (dated 14 April 1889 by Guérin), in: Edgar Degas: *Lettres de Degas*, ed. Marcel Guérin, revised and enlarged edition, Paris 1945, pp. 138f.; trans. JR.

9 *The Colour of Sculpture 1840–1910*, ed. Andreas Blühm, exh. cat. Van Gogh Museum, Amsterdam/Henry Moore Institute, Leeds, Zwolle 1996, pp. 208f.

10 Charles Baudelaire: "Warum die Bildhauerei ein Ärgernis ist" (1846), in: idem: *Juvenilia – Kunstkritik: 1832–1846 (Sämtliche Werke/Briefe in 8 Bänden*, vol. 1), Munich 1977, pp. 273–276.

11 See Alexandra König: "Henri Matisse: 'Ich habe Skulpturen gemacht wie ein Maler'", in: *Die Maler und ihre Skulpturen: Von Edgar Degas bis Gerhard Richter*, ed. Gerhard Finckh, exh. cat. Museum Folkwang Essen, Cologne 1997, pp. 81–86.

12 See Sabine Kricke-Güse and Ernst-Gerhard Güse: "Einleitung", in: exh. cat. Münster 1980, pp. 14–18, here p. 16.

13 See Claudine Grammont: "'Lebende Pfeiler': Die Rückenakte von Henri Matisse", in: *Matisse – Metamorphosen*, ed. Sandra Gianfreda, exh. cat. Kunsthaus Zürich/Musée Matisse, Nice, Zurich 2019, pp. 162–171.

14 *Karl Hartung 1908–1967. Metamorphosen von Mensch und Natur. Monographie und Werkverzeichnis*, ed. Markus Krause, exh. cat. Germanisches Nationalmuseum Nürnberg u.a., Munich 1998, pp. 160–162.

15 For a detailed discussion, see Eva Mongi-Vollmer: "'He is already quite the painter here ...'", in: *En passant: Impressionism in Sculpture*, ed. Alexander Eiling and idem, exh. cat. Städel Museum, Frankfurt am Main, Munich 2020, pp. 141f.

16 Eva Mongi-Vollmer: "'He is masterfully founding Impressionist sculpture' – Medardo Rosso", in: ibid., pp. 126–133, here pp. 126f.

17 Matthias Krüger: *Das Relief der Farbe: Pastose Malerei in der französischen Kunstkritik 1850–1890*, Munich 2007, pp. 12f.

18 See ibid., p. 40.

19 Ibid., chap. IV: "Das Handwerk der Malerei", pp. 197–228.

20 Medardo Rosso, in: Camille de Sainte-Croix: "Medardo Rosso", in: *Mercure de France*, vol. 17, no. 75, March 1896, pp. 378–391, here p. 379.

21 On the motif, see *The Bronzes of Rodin: Catalogue of Works in the Musée Rodin*, Paris 2007, vol. 2, pp. 469–472.

22 Auguste Rodin: *Young Mother in the Grotto (Jeune mère à la grotte)*, after 1885, marble, Philadelphia Museum of Art.

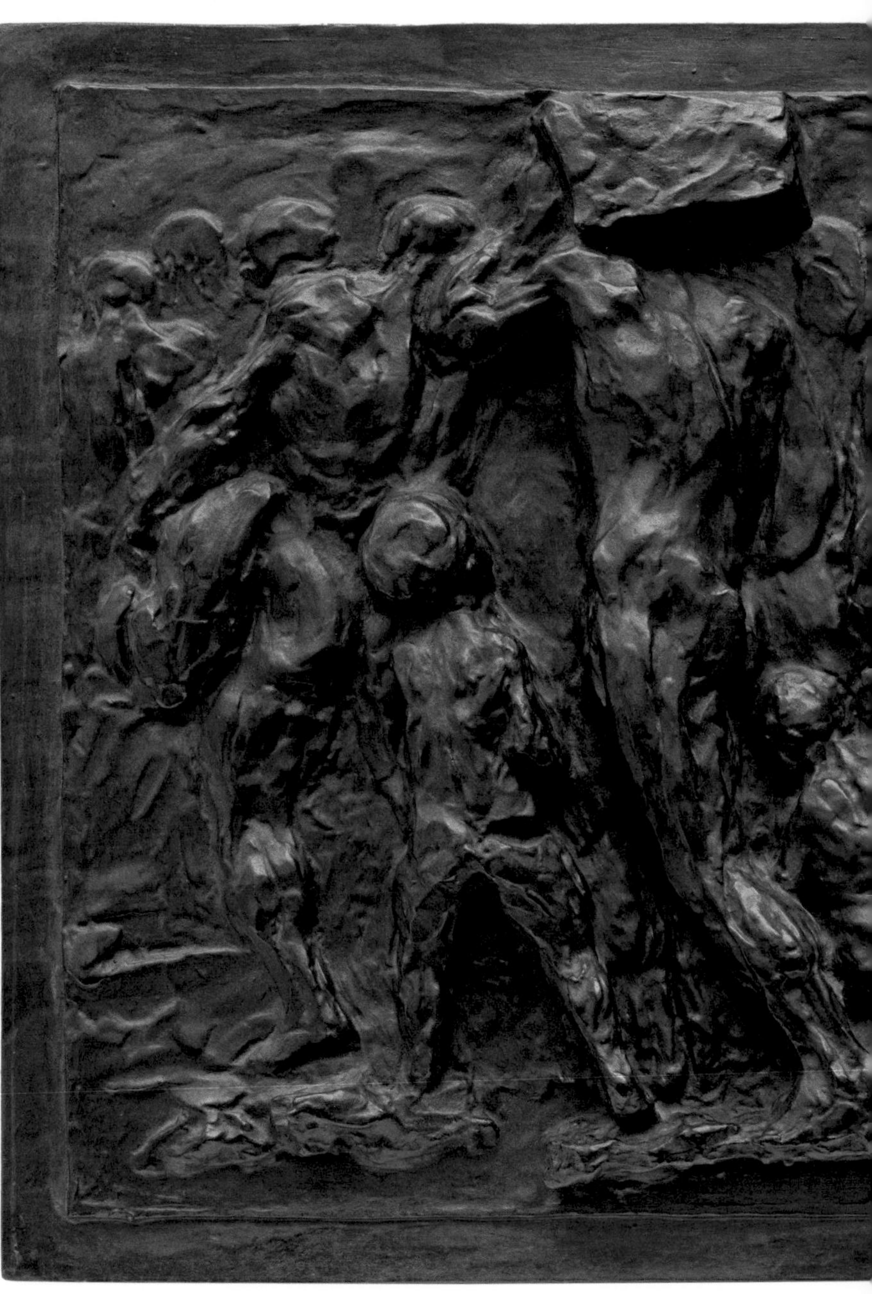

Cat. 32 Honoré Daumier: *The Fugitives* (*Fugitifs*), second version, 1862–78, cast after 1960, bronze, 36.8 × 76.2 × 7 cm, private collection (Frankfurt only)

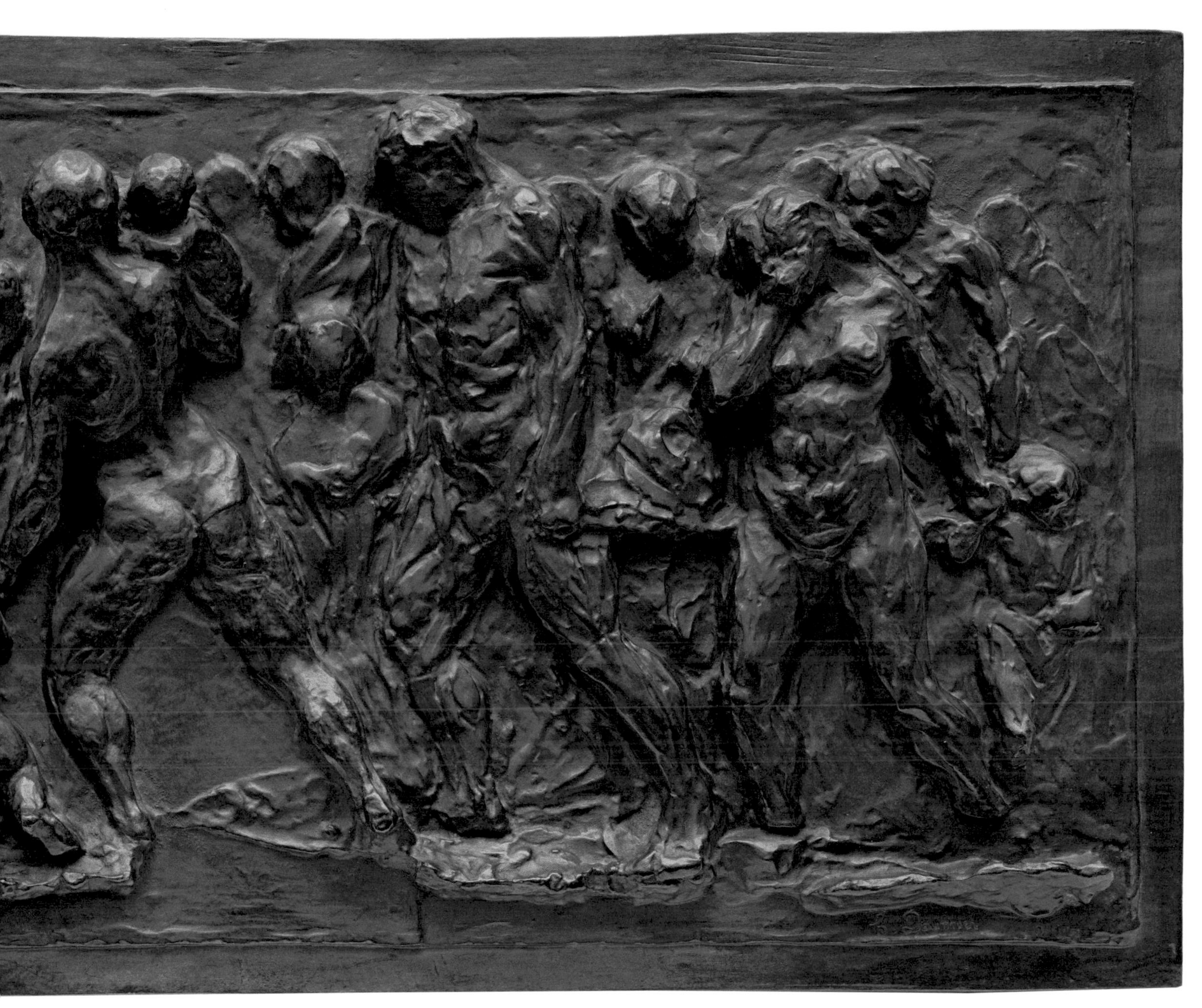

Cat. 33   Constantin Meunier: *The Glebe* (*La Glèbe*), 1892, bronze,
43.6 × 44.5 × 8.5 cm, private collection, London

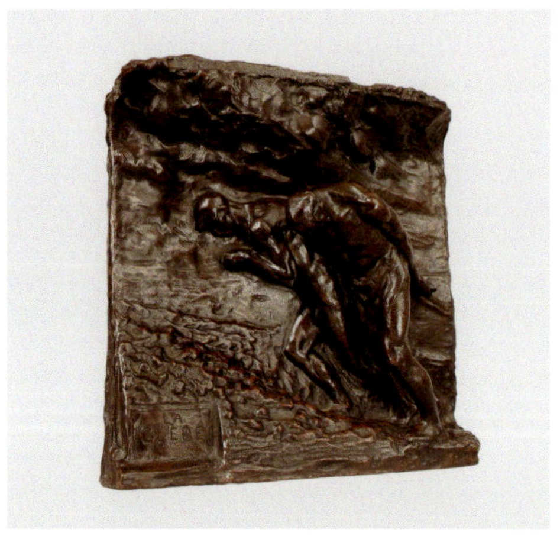

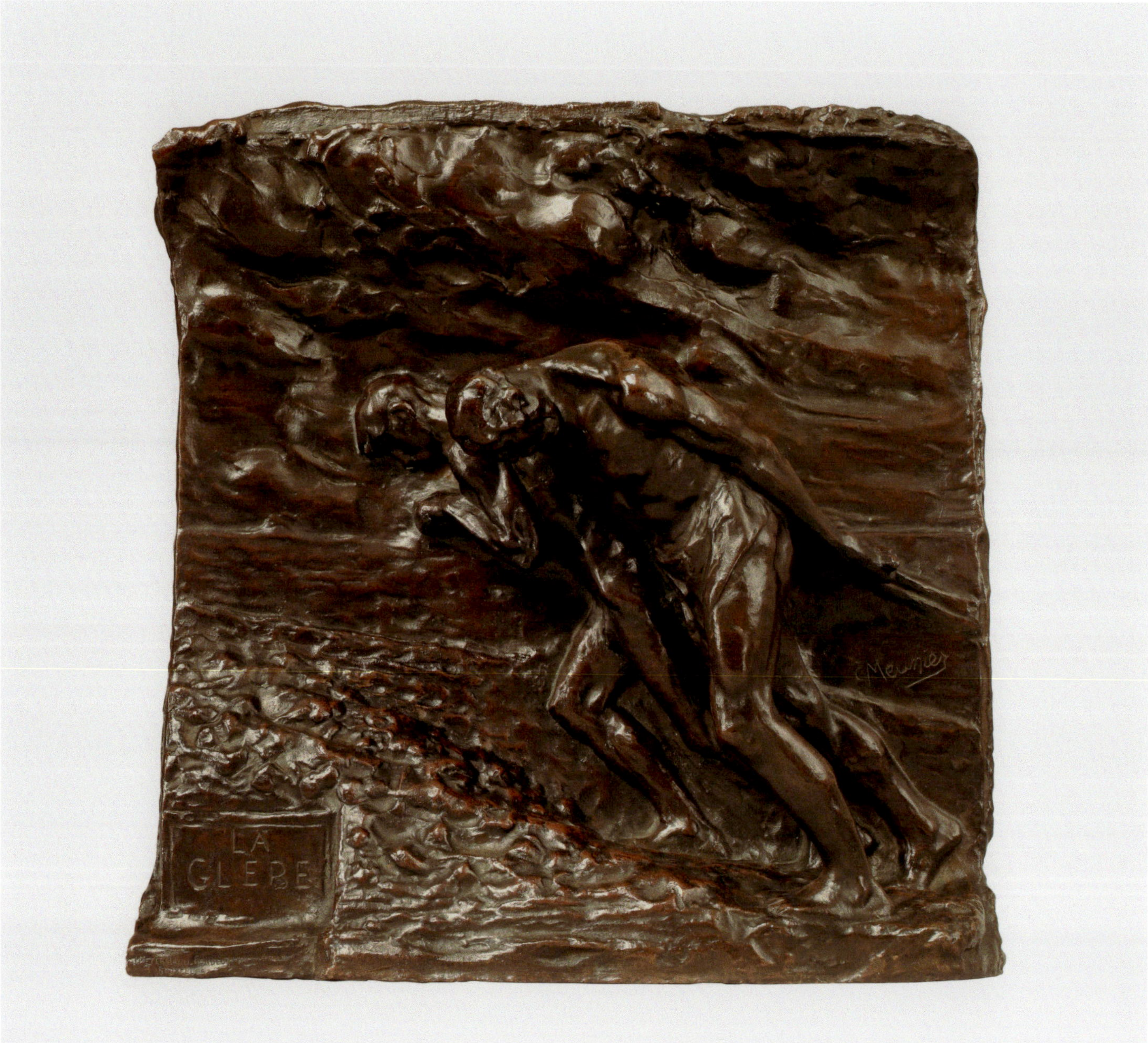

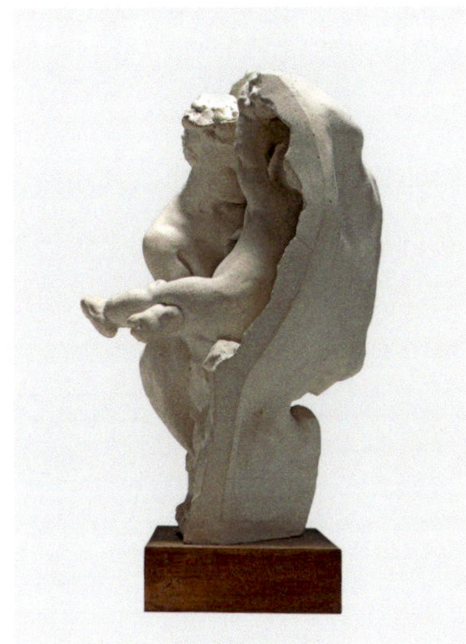

Cat. 34   Auguste Rodin: *Young Mother in the Grotto* (*Jeune mère à la grotte*), 1885, plaster, 36.3 × 26.8 × 24 cm, Musée Rodin, Paris, inv. no. S.01196

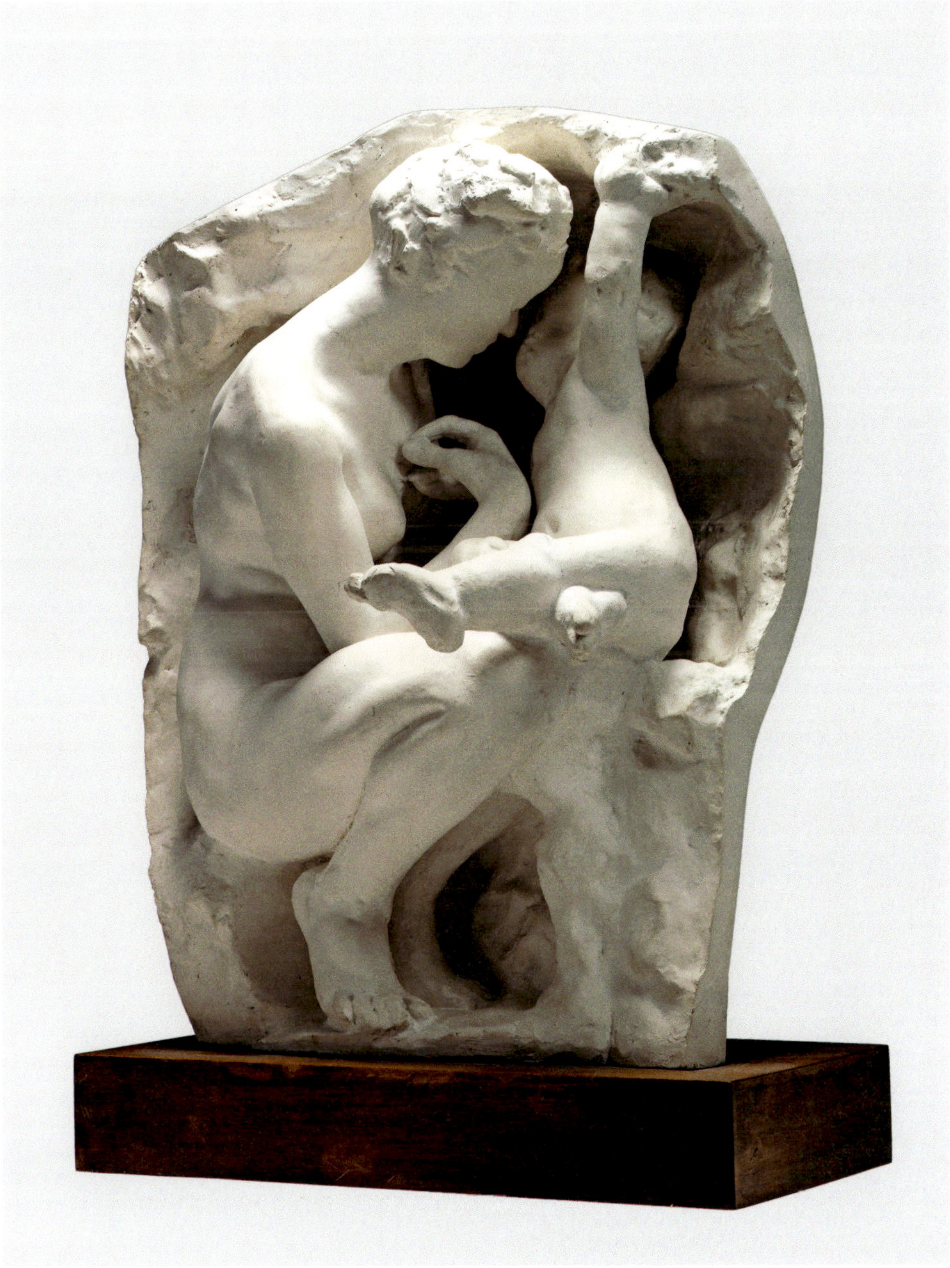

Cat. 35   Karl Hartung: *Figure Relief*, 1967, bronze, 74 × 91 × 7 cm,
Nachlass Karl Hartung

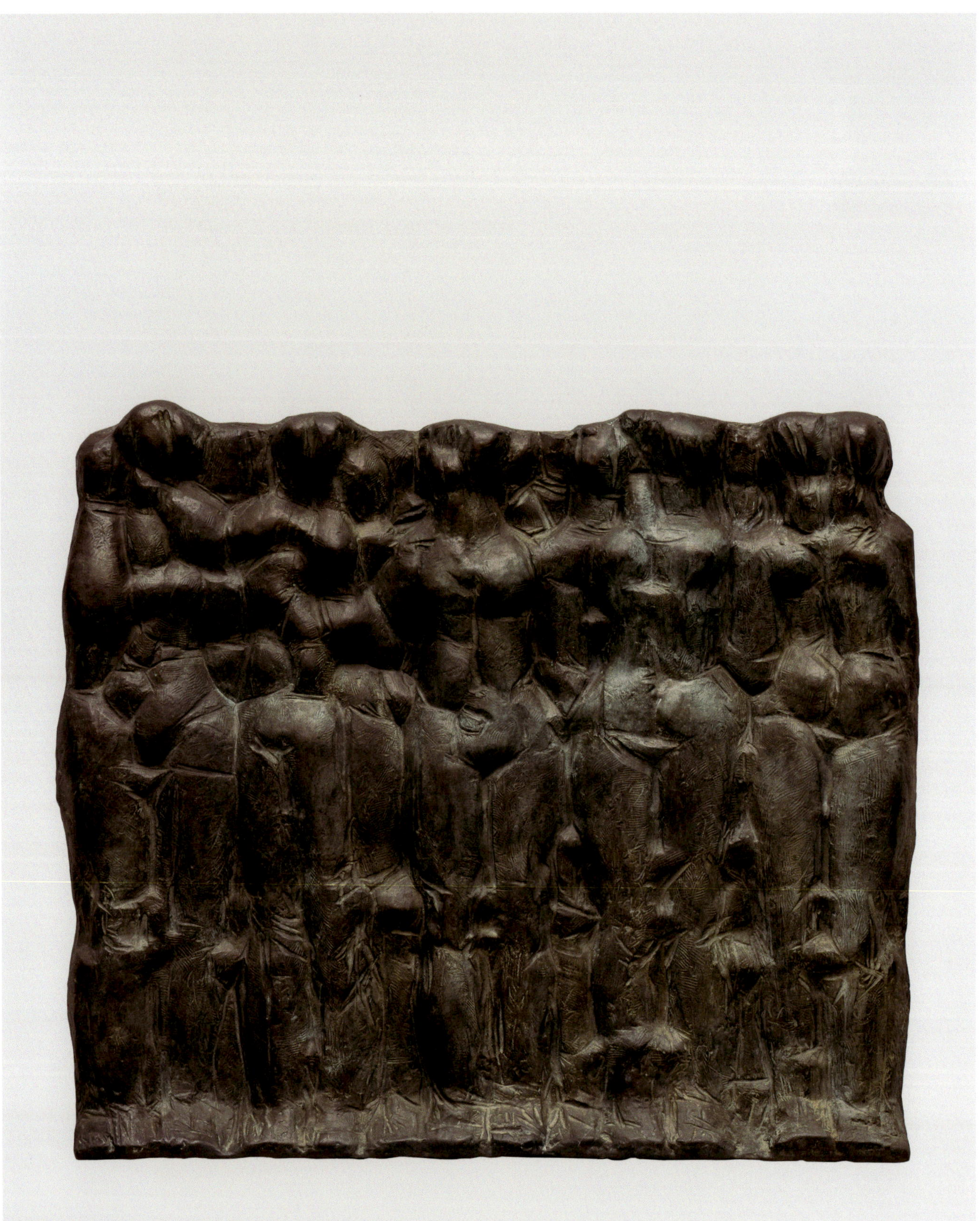

Cat. 36   Henri Matisse: *The Back I* (*Nu de dos I*), 1909, bronze,
188 × 114 × 16.5 cm, Hamburger Kunsthalle, inv. no. S-1963-9

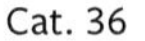

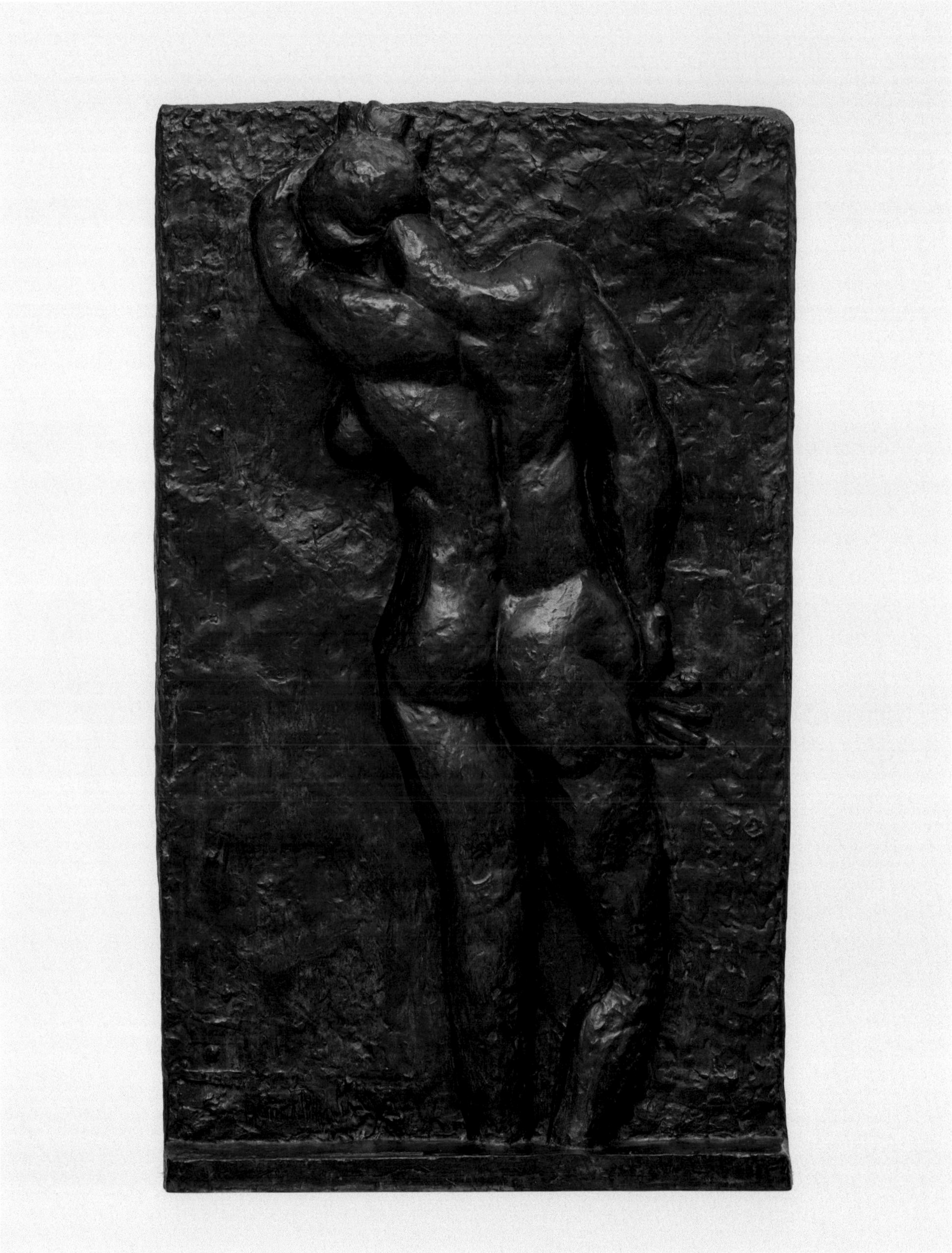

Cat. 37   Medardo Rosso: *The Golden Age* (*Aetas Aurea*), 1886, bronze, 52.5 × 38 × 23 cm, Städel Museum, Frankfurt am Main, inv. no. St.P 670

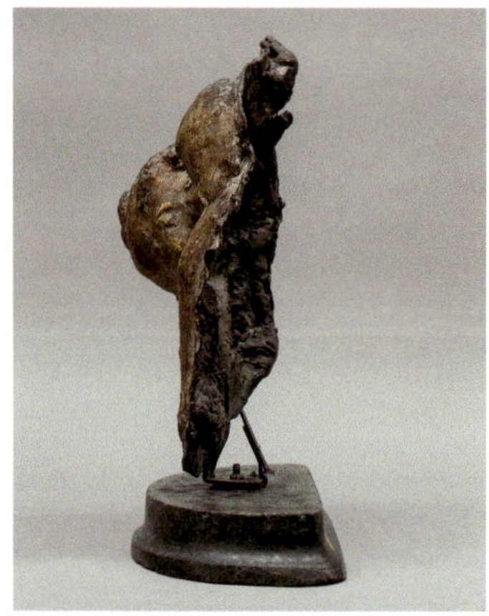

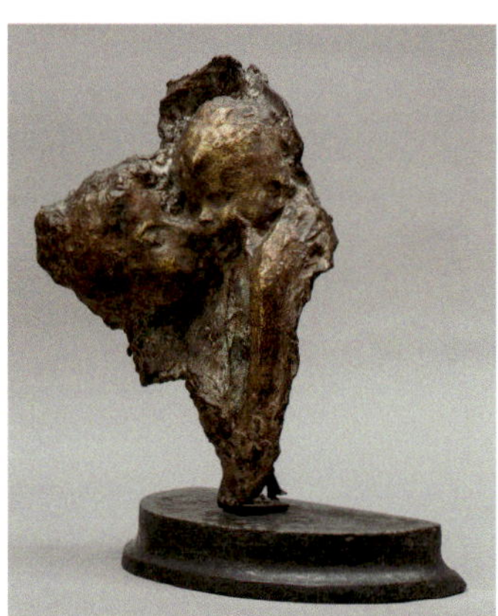

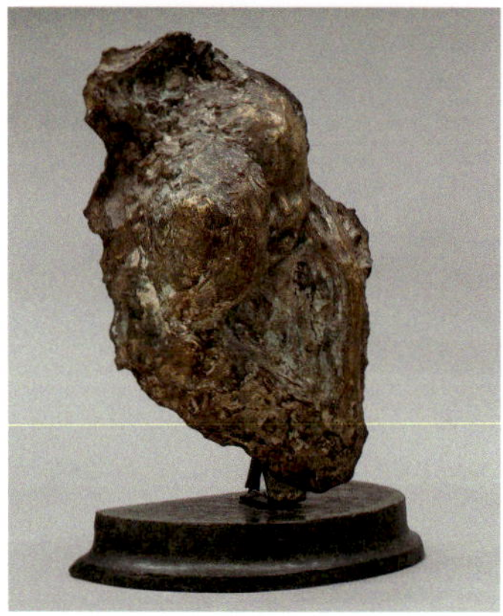

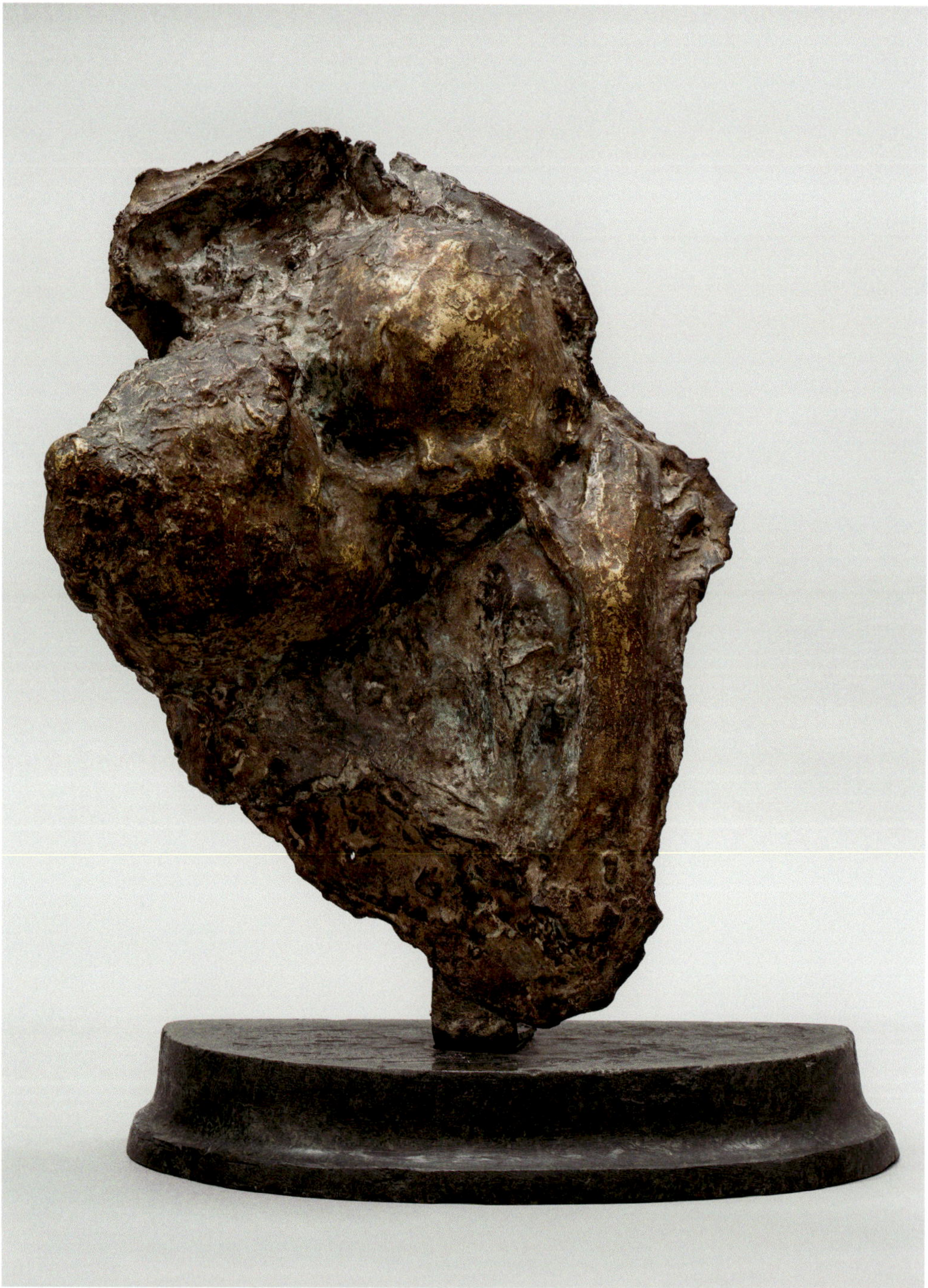

Cat. 38   Medardo Rosso: *Man Reading*, 1894, bronze, patinised, 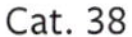
25.5 × 28.5 × 28 cm, Hamburger Kunsthalle, inv. no. S-1977-6
(Hamburg only)

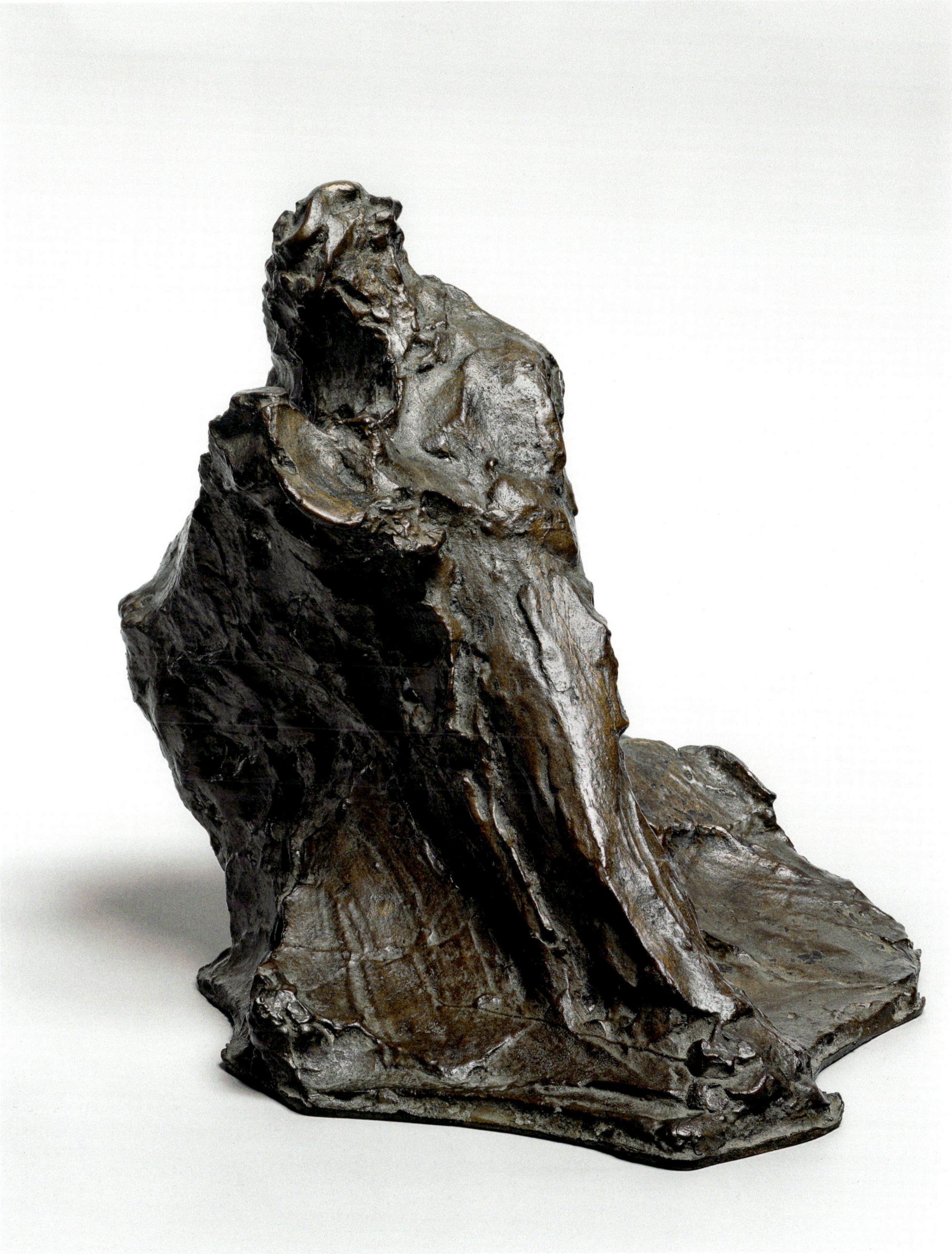

Cat. 39   Adolphe Monticelli: *A Painter at Work on a House Wall*, 1875, oil on wood, 45.7 × 29.3 cm, Städel Museum, Frankfurt am Main, inv. no. 1658

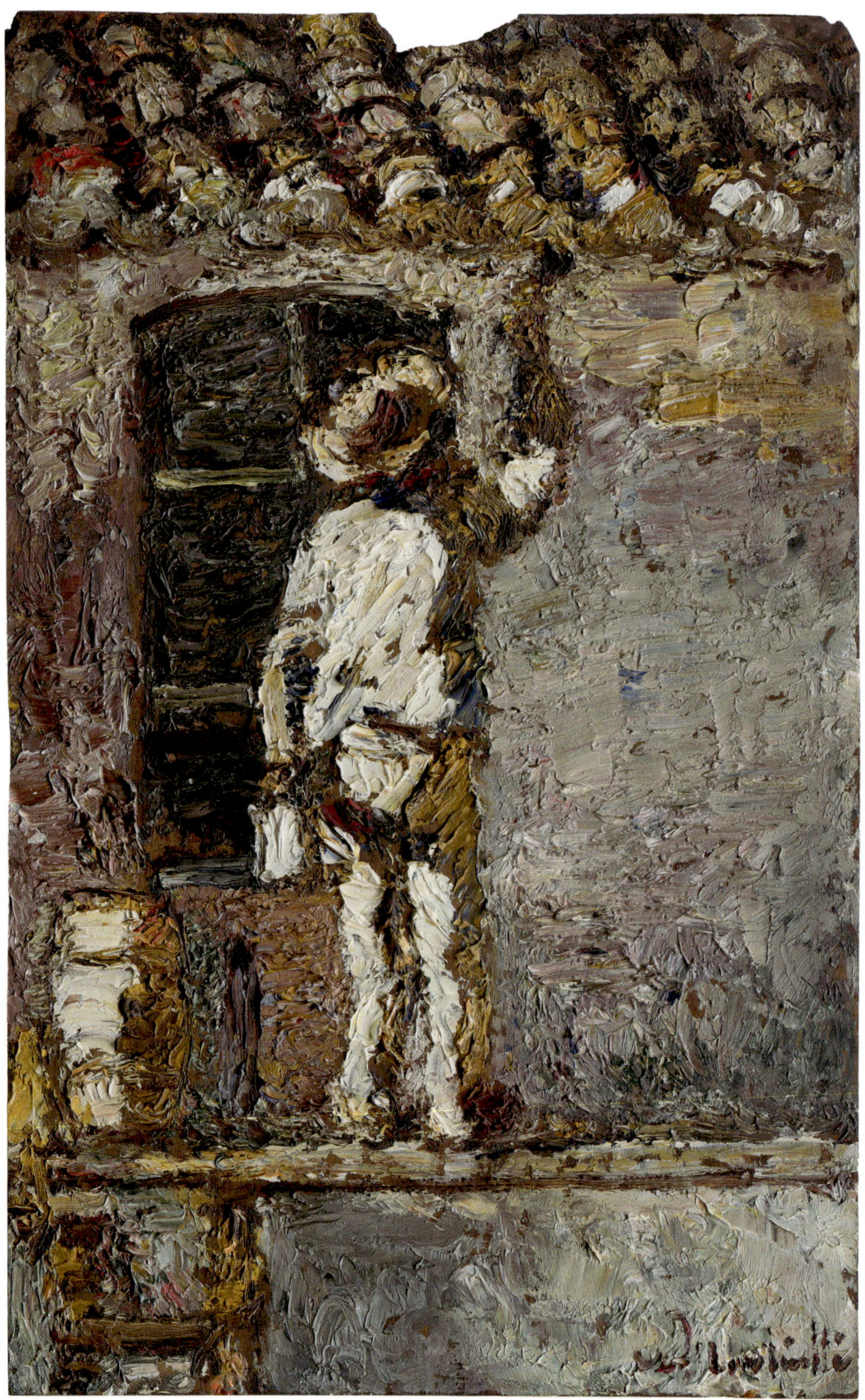

Cat. 40   Edgar Degas: *Picking Apples* (*Cueilleuses de pommes*),
1868–72, cast 1919–21, bronze, 45.6 × 48.5 × 6 cm,
Ny Carlsberg Glyptotek, Copenhagen, inv. no. MIN 2634

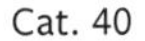

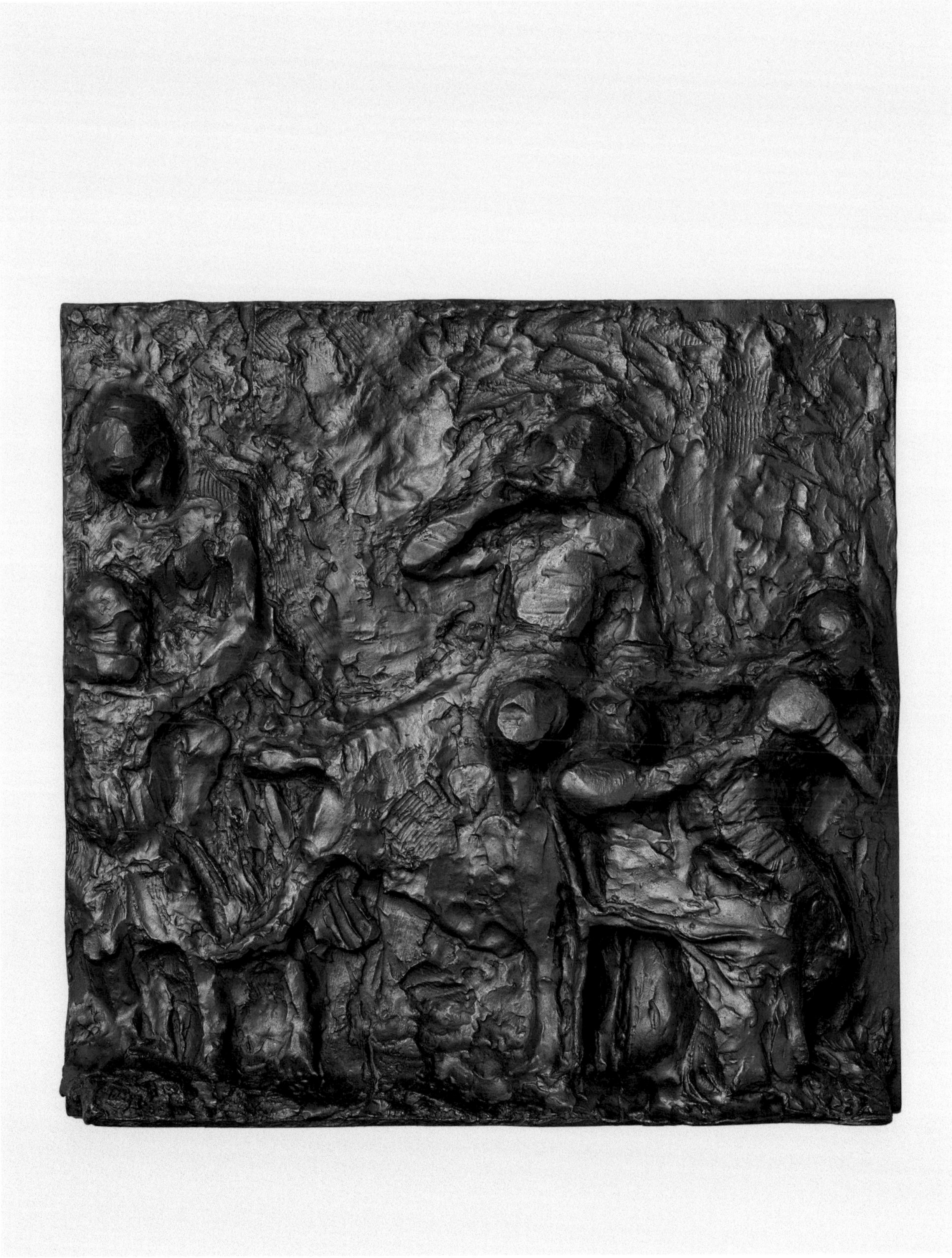

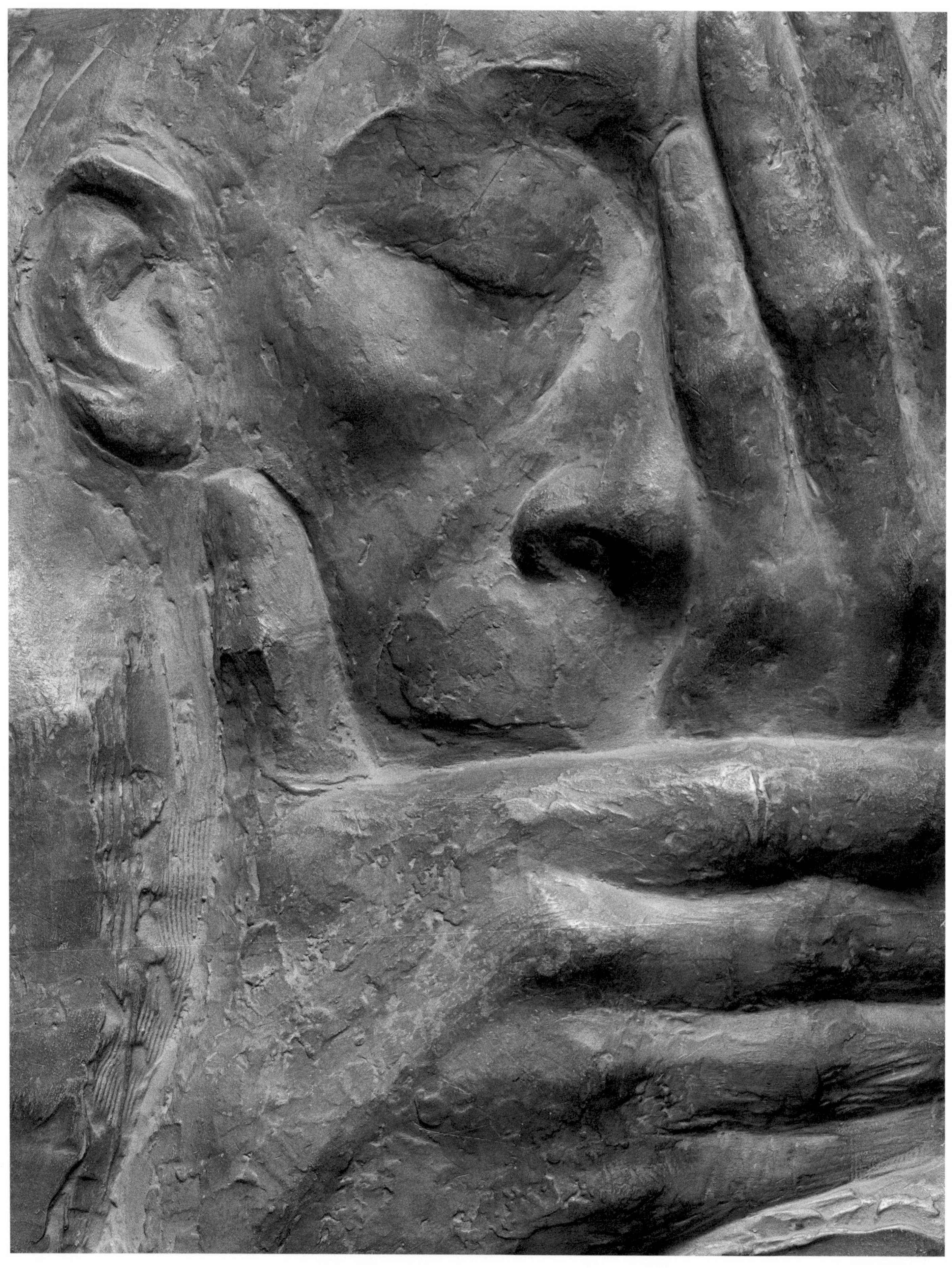

Cats. 41—65

Friederike Schütt

FACES IN RELIEF

Protrusions and depressions from the eyebrows to the chin fold characterise the appearance and facial expression of every individual. People have always desired to have likenesses of their own face captured and preserved. Modelling faces sculpturally and yet bound to the surface is one of the most tradition-steeped artistic tasks there is. In the period between 1800 and the 1960s, the relief proved to be a productive field of experimentation for the examination of the human face.[1] In portraits, the variety of forms possible between sculpture and surface seems to be particularly suited for exploring realism and emotional depth, presence and volatility, in the field of tension between tradition and innovation.

> In order to create an anonymous or portrait-like head depiction as a relief, one suitable starting point can be the reduction of a three-dimensional sculpture to a face. Pablo Picasso and Alberto Giacometti opted for this approach, albeit in different ways, for the production of their works *Head of a Picador with a Broken Nose* (cat. 41) and *Head of a Woman (Flora Mayo)* (cat. 42). While Picasso developed the male physiognomy as a mask on the surface of a hollow form, Giacometti condensed the head of his lover to create a life-sized flat disc, subsequently defining the face on it as the only viewing side and immortalising it as a living snapshot in time.

The internal modelling could not be more contrary: Giacometti captures the eyes, nose and lips of the American artist Flora Mayo, who had studied with him in Paris in the 1920s, as a flat relief. In the bronze cast produced after his death, the areas that he had accentuated in the original plaster by using bold colours (fig. 1), become apparent merely as slight projections.[2] The incisions, as sketchy as they are precise, resemble the densification of the line strokes that Giacometti later employed in the painted portraits of his wife Annette for the purpose of opaquely distinguishing the sitter from the indistinct studio space and of placing figure and space in relation in a way that was as consistent as possible with perception (cats. 44, 45).[3]

> Whereas Giacometti came close to forcing Flora Mayo's face back into the two-dimensional, Picasso focussed on curvatures and bulges. The mask gives the impression of being the cast of a face. However, for Picasso it was a matter not of an individual portrait with a resemblance that was as authentic as possible but one of exploring forms for the creation of expression: the closed mouth and the rigidly opened eyes cause the facial expression to alternate between sadness and lifelessness. The broken nose in particular serves to heighten the expression. With this motif, Picasso, who at the time had been working as a sculptor for only a year, ambitiously placed himself in the tradition of Auguste Rodin and Paul Gauguin in order to intensify the vividness of the face by means of deformation.[4]

Giacometti's and Picasso's head compositions can be seen alongside portrait reliefs that developed from a pictorial two-dimensionality and for which the rigorous profile is often the preferred form. Paul Gauguin staged himself in the style of this traditional view in 1893, following his first trip to Tahiti (cat. 43). He outlined his face using only a few curved lines on the uneven surface area. The lines end at the level of the forehead in the blossom of a Tahitian gardenia, a tiaré, which, like the marked profile, was predestined to become his trademark. The formal arrangement is the expression of his identification with the hoped-for "primitiveness" in the distance. Gauguin understood this as *oviri*, Tahitian for "wild", and he integrated the word as a symbol for his artistic mystification directly next to his signature.[5]

> Gauguin employed the classic side view for the purpose of "exoticising" it. However, the portrait relief in profile is rooted in antiquity and its reception in (Neo-)Classicism in the eighteenth and nineteenth centuries. Artists of this period could find inspiration for ideal portraits

and depictions of heads in impressions of antique gems. These plaster reproductions of cut stones served to relay antiquity. They were brought out in so-called dactyliothecae and collected with encyclopaedic ambition.[6] In 1842, the Städelsches Kunstinstitut acquired the "Collezione Cades" that consisted of 75 volumes and comprised more than 8,000 gems (figs. 2, 3), presenting a different selection of them every fourteen days.[7] Bound in leather, from the outside the boxes with gems systematically arranged according to subjects seem to be folios. Each gem has been provided with a circumferential band and a number, which is itemised in an accompanying handwritten catalogue with concise information about the depiction, material and origin of the original gem.[8] For the best possible interpretation and illustration of the antique objects, the impressions feature a wide variety of relief forms. Volume 1 shows the head and body of Jupiter, the father of the gods, as *intaglio* cut deep into the surface as well as *cameo* with a variously pronounced raised relief and from a diverse number of perspectives, from profile to front view (cat. 46). Compared to graphic reproductions, because of their plasticity the gem impressions were thought to be more authentic and more suitable for the aesthetic cultivation of the educated middle class. Beside the precision of the impressions, what was decisive for this estimation were the haptics of the miniature reliefs, which one could hold in one's hand for study purposes.[9]

They share the advantages of such intimate reception with small-format sculptures such as the medal, which in the late nineteenth century were praised as "portable memorials"[10] and became the arena for the discourse on the superiority of the painterly or sculptural qualities of the relief (→ Painterly-Sculptural Reliefs). The first director of the Hamburger Kunsthalle, Alfred Lichtwark, who fuelled this discussion through the publication of *Die Wiedererweckung der Medaille* (1897), declared the acquisition of contemporary medals and medallions to be the "foundation of the sculpture collection".[11] With a wide reach, he campaigned for the recognition of the modern medal as a high-quality small-format relief.[12] Exemplary for Lichtwark were works by French medallists such as Hubert Ponscarmes and his pupil Ovide Yencesse, who had portrayed one another (cat. 49, 50).[13] Ponscarmes was the first to dispense with a raised edge as the boundary of the medal and developed the relief in a "painterly" fashion out of the matte instead of brightly polished ground (cat. 48).[14]

It was also considered modern to dispense with the standardised block letters in the circumferential lettering that were so typical for coins and embossed medals.[15] This innovation was also adopted by German medallists, in part by handwritten lettering and their unrestricted positioning (cats. 56, 57).

The variations of creating portraits in the medium of the medal ranged from Yencesse's greatest possible "flattening of the relief positive"[16] while maintaining the detailed differentiation of the textures (cats. 47, 51), to something more reminiscent of Adolf von Hildebrand (→ Introduction), to smooth and depth-perspectivally graduated head modelling, as is discernible in Karl Dautert's plaquette of Elise Bamberger-Pundt (cat. 55).[17] Before Dautert, in Frankfurt the sculptor Josef Kowarzik had contributed to a material-oriented modernisation of the embossed and cast medal both in terms of theory and practice.[18] In comparison to the "painterly character with its indistinct relief",[19] Kowarzik advocated an idealising style characterised by clear lines in the spirit of Hildebrand.[20] His medal with the portrait of Johann Friedrich Städel (cat. 53) was recast in iron in 1916 on the occasion of the hundredth anniversary of the museum founder's death. This new edition, which ranges between local patriotism and propaganda, is exemplary of the public memorial function that portrait medals performed.[21]

As handy souvenirs, small-scale sculptural portraits also enjoyed popularity among private persons. Augusto Varnesi's double portrait of the May couple (cat. 54), commissioned by the family in memory of the parents' golden anniversary, is an example of this, as is the miniature relief portrait of the Swiss wax embosser Xaver Heuberger from the 1820s (cat. 52).

Käthe Kollwitz resisted the small-scale sculpture. She wanted to work "monumentally".[22] "[U]nder the impression of Barlach's death and the terrible injustice he had suffered",[23] on the basis of a mask taken of her face, in 1938/39 she created *Lament*, which was posthumously modelled in stucco and cast in bronze (cats. 58, 59).[24] From the narrow side, the relief rises gently upward. In contrast, the front is palpably "block like":[25] the close-up of the face heightens the impression of confinement and involuntary silence. Kollwitz created a timeless emotional expression for lamenting grief with the melancholy gesture of the hands, which cover half of the face.[26]

Constantin Brancusi's *Kiss* (cat. 60) is likewise characterised by a concentration of emotions. The intertwined figures are not based on individual portraits. Rather,

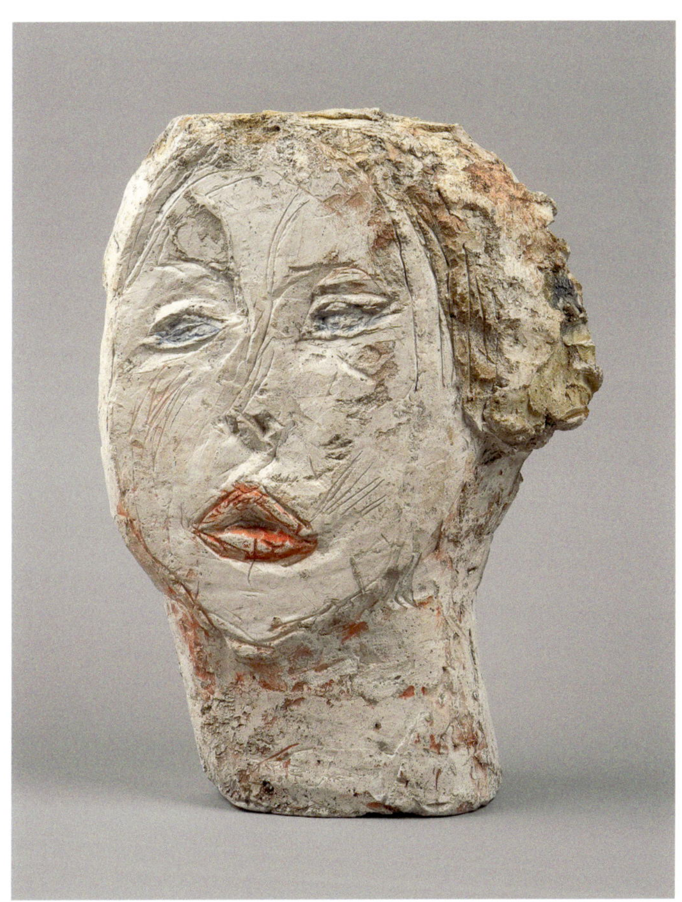

Fig. 1

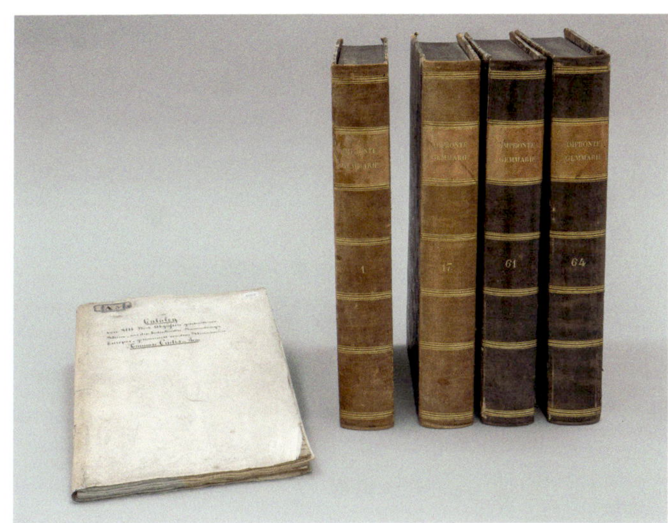

Fig. 2

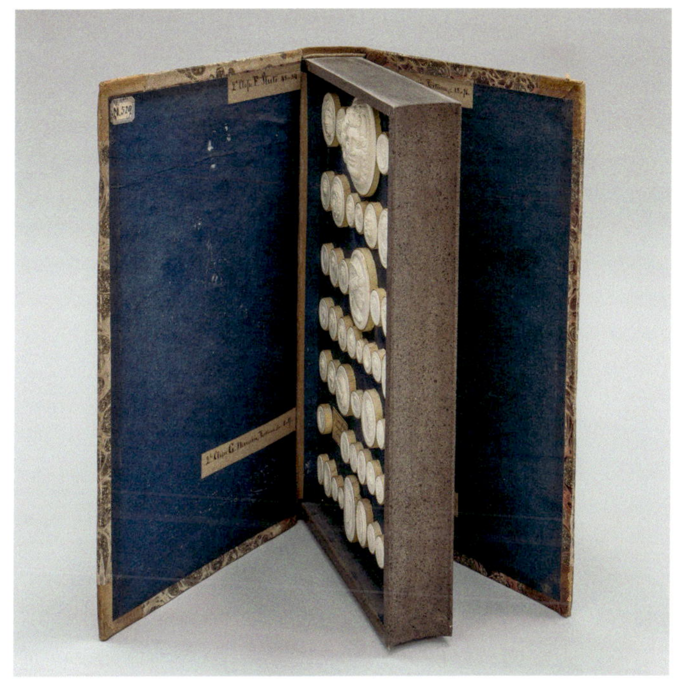

Fig. 3

Fig. 1   Alberto Giacometti: *Head of a Woman* (*Flora Mayo*)
         (*Tête de femme,* [*Flora Mayo*]), ca. 1927, plaster,
         painted, Fondation Giacometti, Paris

Fig. 2   Tommaso Cades: *Impronte Gemmarie* ("Collezione
         Cades"), 1831–49, Städel Museum, Frankfurt
         am Main – Bibliothek

Fig. 3   Tommaso Cades: *Impronte Gemmarie* ("Collezione
         Cades"), 1831–49, vol. 17, Städel Museum,
         Frankfurt am Main – Bibliothek

the bodies and faces are structured by means of just a few curves and incisions. In their conciseness, they become universally understandable ciphers for love. In the free-standing plaster block, designed to be viewed from all sides, Brancusi developed each side as a relief. The execution as a flat relief reinforces the coalescence in the block and accommodates the overriding message of intimate union.[27]

In his portraits after 1945, Jean Dubuffet exaggerated the simplification Brancusi had achieved into a seemingly naïve, childlike manner of representation in order to elevate it to become an anti-aesthetic principle (cats. 61, 62). In his portrait of the art critic and collector Michel Tapié, the rudimentary sketch of the face was inspired by children's drawings and non-European art, as well as works by people with cognitive impairments – models that Dubuffet interpreted as "raw art" (Art Brut).[28] Dubuffet used them by dispensing with perspectival accuracy in the structuring of the head. The crannied application of material aimed at a radical break with portrait conventions of any kind, and he caused a scandal when he exhibited the work in Paris in 1947 for the first time along with other *Haute Pâtes*. The crusted surface is not characterised by seemingly logical raised areas; it is far from the realistic reproduction of physiognomic forms. Thus, Dubuffet reduces the principle of the illusionistic creation of plasticity to absurdity. The haptic surface relief becomes a complex foil on which he questions the relationship between painting and modelling and pushes the representational role of the portrait to its limits.[29]

> Karel Appel, another artist likewise promoted by Michel Tapié, embraced these stimuli for the purpose of heightening the degree of abstraction of the figural depiction.[30] In his ceramic *Face* (cat. 64), he limited the execution of the face to rough finger marks drawn in the wet clay, subsequently glazing them with little accuracy. Thus Dubuffet and Appel challenge the traditional concept of the recognisability of the face by means of formal alienation. Rolf Nesch (cat. 63) subverts the expectations made on a portrait when he declares a metal objet trouvé with eye sockets and tongue to be the head of a bull, presents it in a nested frame, and ties into Kurt Schwitters' Dadaist assemblages with this translation of established conventions of portrayal.[31]

In the years following the Second World War, Eugène Leroy was interested in how the surface of a painting can be sculpturally structured (→ Painterly-Sculptural Reliefs) solely by means of oil-based paint. Inspired to use an opaque application of earthy tones by Rembrandt's painting, in his *Self-Portrait* (cat. 65) he modelled the layers of paint to produce a tactile impasto that, pressed out of the tube directly onto the canvas, appears in some places to be kneaded.[32] The relief consisting of paint lends the painting an independent physicality in whose mass he did not *paint* his portrait but rather *formed* it out of paint. However, the top of the head and chest do not become evident until the gaze has organised the structures on the surface.[33] By emphasising materiality, Leroy, like Dubuffet, draws attention to the haptics of the surface: a quality that – whether in the medal or the material picture – is invariably defining for the perception and effect of portraits and portrayals of heads in the relief.

1   See Ursula Merkel: "Ausdrucks-suche und Formexperiment: *Aspekte der Bildnisplastik von Rodin bis Giacometti"*, in: *Von Rodin bis Giacometti: Plastik der Moderne*, ed. Siegmar Holsten, exh. cat. Staatliche Kunsthalle Karlsruhe, Heidelberg 2009, pp. 15–23; idem, *Das plastische Porträt im 19. und frühen 20. Jahrhundert: Ein Beitrag zur Geschichte der Bildhauerei in Frankreich und Deutschland*, Berlin 1995, here p. 12.

2   See Casimiro Di Crescenzo; "1925–1929: Erste avantgar-distische Jahre", in: *Alberto Giacometti: Material und Vision. Die Meisterwerke in Gips, Stein, Ton und Bronze*, ed. Philippe Büttner, exh. cat. Kunsthaus Zürich, Zurich 2016, pp. 64–67; Véronique Wiesinger: "On Wom-en in Giacometti's Work (and Some Women in Particular)", in: *The Women of Giacometti*, ed. Louise Tolliver Deutschmann, exh. cat. Pace Gallery, New York/ Nasher Sculpture Center, Dallas, New York 2005, pp. 15–29, esp. p. 17f.

3   See Annabelle Görgen: "Alberto Giacometti, Annette im Atelier, 1961", in: Felix Krämer and Kris-tine von Oehsen (eds.): *Bildnisse in der Hamburger Kunsthalle: Für Uwe M. Schneede*, Hamburg 2006, pp. 73–75; Stephan Mann, *Das 20. Jahrhundert im Städel*, ed. Sabine Schulze, Ostfildern 1998, pp. 58f.

4   On the work's genesis in clay and on the early bronze casts from 1905 onwards, see *Picasso: Sculpture*, ed. Ann Temkin and Anne Umland, exh. cat. The Mu-seum of Modern Art, New York, London 2011, pp. 36–38; *Picasso: Das plastische Werk*, comp. Werner Spies and Christine Piot, exh. cat. Nationalgalerie Berlin/ Kunsthalle Düsseldorf, Stuttgart 1983, pp. 14, 18.

5   See *Paul Gauguin: Why Are You Angry?*, ed. Anna Kærsgaard Gregersen and Anna Manly, exh. cat. Ny Carlsberg Glyptotek, Copenhagen/Alte Nationalgalerie, Berlin, Copenhagen 2022; Alastair Wright: "Gauguin's Self-Portraits: Egos and Alter-Egos", in: *Gauguin. Portraits*, ed. Cornelia Homburg and Christo-pher Riopelle, exh. cat. National Gallery of Canada, Ottawa/ The National Gallery, London, New Haven and London 2019, pp. 23–55; Jean-David Jumeau: "Head of a Savage, Mask", in ibid., pp. 57–63; Andreas Franzke: *Skulpturen und Objekte von Malern des 20. Jahrhunderts*, Cologne 2000, pp. 27f.; Kuno Mittelstädt: *Die Selbstbildnisse Paul Gauguins*, Berlin 1966, p. 72.

6   See *Daktyliotheken. Götter & Caesaren aus der Schublade: Antike Gemmen in Abdruck-sammlungen des 18. und 19. Jahrhunderts*, ed. Valentin Kockel and Daniel Graepler, exh. cat. Römisches Museum Augsburg/Staats- und Univer-sitätsbibliothek Göttingen, Munich 2006.

7   On their presentation at the Städel, see the *Verzeichniss der öffentlich ausgestellten Kunst-Gegenstände des Städel'schen Kunst-Instituts* from the years 1844 to 1879.

8   See Helge C. Knüppel: *Dakty-liotheken. Konzepte einer historischen Publikationsform*, Ruhpolding and Mainz 2009, esp. pp. 13, 16–18, 42, 95–98.

9   Matthias Buschmeier: "Schub-ladenklassizismus oder Das Fest-halten der Antike: Die Gemme als Sammel-, Bildungs- und Konsumobjekt der Goethezeit", *Euphorion*, vol. 107, no. 1, 2013, pp. 81–104, esp. pp. 90–92.

10   Alfred Lichtwark: *Die Wieder-erweckung der Medaille*, Dresden 1897, p. 14.

11   Ibid., p. 18.

12   See Anna Seidel: *Skulptur für Hamburg: Alfred Lichtwarks Gründung einer Skulpturen-sammlung in der Hamburger Kunsthalle*, Hamburg 2021, pp. 25–33; Wolfgang Steguweit and Martin Heidemann: "Medaillenkunst vom Beginn des Jahrhunderts bis zum Ende des Ersten Weltkriegs", in: *Die Medaille und Gedenkmünze des 20. Jahrhunderts in Deutschland*, ed. Wolfgang Steguweit, exh. cat. Münzkabinett, Staatliche Museen zu Berlin, Berlin 2000, pp. 12–25, esp. p. 19.

13   See Lichtwark 1897 (see note 10), pp. 20f.

14   See Wolfgang Steguweit, *Euro-päische Medaillenkunst von der Renaissance bis zur Gegenwart*, Berlin 1995, pp. 20, 127.

15   See Nicolas Maier: *Französische Medaillenkunst 1870–1940*, Munich 2010, p. 14.

16   Paul Herrmann: "Ein neuer Meister der französischen Plakette: Ovide Yencesse", in: *Dresdner Jahrbuch*, Dresden 1905, pp. 161–166.

17   On Adolf von Hildebrand's con-cept of the portrait, see Angela Hass: *Adolf von Hildebrand: das plastische Portrait*, Munich 1984, in particular pp. 40–55, esp. p. 50.

18   See Josef Kowarzik: "Zeitgemäße Betrachtung über moderne Medaillen", *Deutsche Kunst und Dekoration*, vol. 23, 1908, pp. 334–342; Felix Dessoff: "Ausstellung moderner Medaillen in Frankfurt am Main", *Frank-furter Münzblätter*, vol. 13–15, 1900, pp. 143–149, esp. p. 148.

19   Josef Kowarzik, quoted in Wolfgang Steguweit: *Das Münz-kabinett der Königlichen Museen zu Berlin und die Förderung der Medaillenkunst. Künstlerbriefe von der Jahrhundertwende bis zum Ersten Weltkrieg*, Berlin 1998, p. 73.

20   See Manfred Großkinsky: "Der Frankfurt-Cronberger Künstler-bund", *Archiv für Frankfurts Geschichte und Kunst*, vol. 69, 2003, pp. 11–38, esp. pp. 23–25.

21   See Werner Kilitschka: "Zur Funktion der historischen Medaillen", in: *Der Traum vom Glück: Die Kunst des Historismus in Europa*, ed. Hermann Filitz and Werner Telesko, exh. cat. Künstlerhaus and Akademie der Bildenden Künste, Vienna, Vienna 1996, pp. 257–265.

22   Käthe Kollwitz, quoted in Annette Seeler: "'Ich möchte im Großen arbeiten' – Käthe Kollwitz als Bildhauerin", in: *Die erste Generation: Bildhauerinnen der Berliner Moderne*, ed. Julia Wallner and Günter Ladwig, exh. cat. Georg Kolbe Museum, Berlin, 2018, pp. 37–41, esp. p. 40.

23   Quoted in Gudrun Fritsch: *Käthe Kollwitz: Schmerz und Schuld. Eine motivgeschichtliche Betra-chtung*, exh. cat. Käthe Kollwitz Museum, Berlin, 1995, p. 193.

24   See Annette Seeler: *Käthe Kollwitz: Die Plastik. Werkver-zeichnis und Online-Katalog*, Munich 2016, pp. 212f., 216, 221, cat. no. 38.I.B.5. (Hamburger Kunsthalle) and 38.I.B.18 (Städel Museum), https://www.kollwitz. de/werkverzeichnis-plastik (accessed 13 February 2023).

25   *Die dritte Dimension: Plastiken, Konstruktionen, Objekte*, comp. Georg Syamken, inv. cat. Hamburger Kunsthalle, Hamburg 1988, p. 249.

26   See Annette Seeler: *Käthe Koll-witz: Die Plastik. Werkverzeich-nis*, Munich 2016, pp. 354–369, esp. pp. 363f.

27   See exh. cat. Karlsruhe 2009 (see note 1), pp. 172–174, esp. p. 173 (Siegmar Holsten).

28   See Mechthild Haas: "Gegenkul-tur – ganz alltäglich", in: *Jean Dubuffet: Figuren und Köpfe. Auf der Suche nach einer Gegen-kultur*, ed. Ernst-Gerhard Güse and Andreas Franzke, exh. cat. Saarland Museum Saarbrücken, Ostfildern 1999, pp. 23–38; idem, in ibid., pp. 67f.

29   See Andreas Franzke: "'Die Men-schen sind doch viel schöner als sie glauben: Es lebe ihr wahres Gesicht.' Dubuffets Portraits 1946–1947", in ibid., pp. 10–22.

30   See Michel Ragon: "Die Besessen-heit des Malens", in: *Karel Appel*, exh. cat. Galerie Beyeler, Basel 1988, n.p.

31   Ulrike Bestgen: "'Romantik der Klempnerei': Materialbilder von Rolf Nesch", in: *Rolf Nesch 1893–1975: Retrospektive zum 100. Geburtstag*, exh. cat. Schleswig-Holsteinisches Landesmuseum Kloster Cismar et al., Schleswig 1993, pp. 97–124, here pp. 108f., 119.

32   *Eugène Leroy, to paint*, exh. cat. Musée d'Art Moderne de Paris, 2022, p. 22.

33   See Martin Engler and Max Hollein (eds.): *Gegenwartskunst 1945–heute im Städel Museum*, Ostfildern 2016, p. 25.

Cat. 41   Pablo Picasso: *Head of a Picador with a Broken Nose* (*Tête de picador au nez cassé*), 1903, cast 1960, bronze, dark patina, 19 × 14.5 × 12 cm, Hamburger Kunsthalle, inv. no. S-1961-21

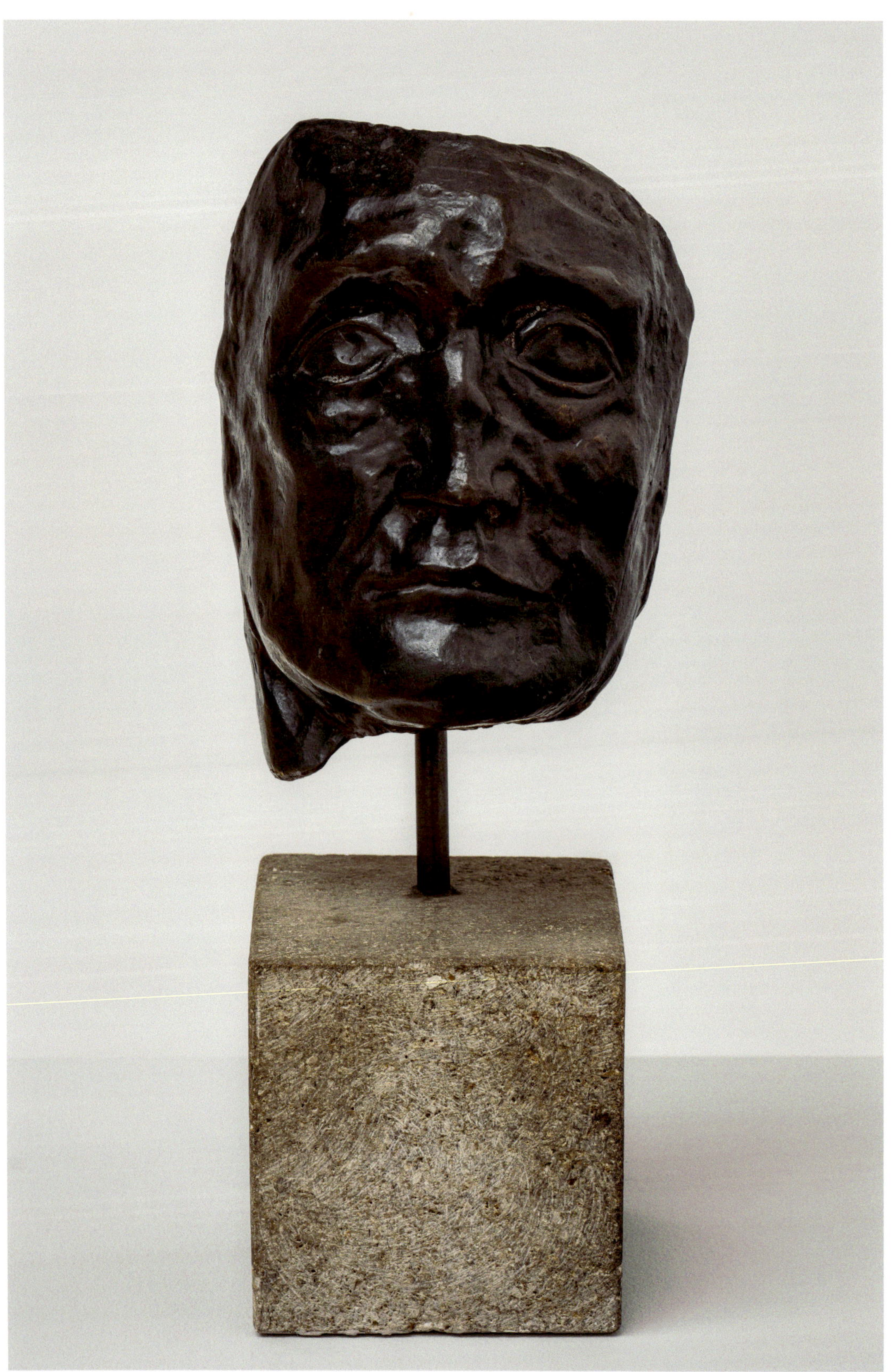

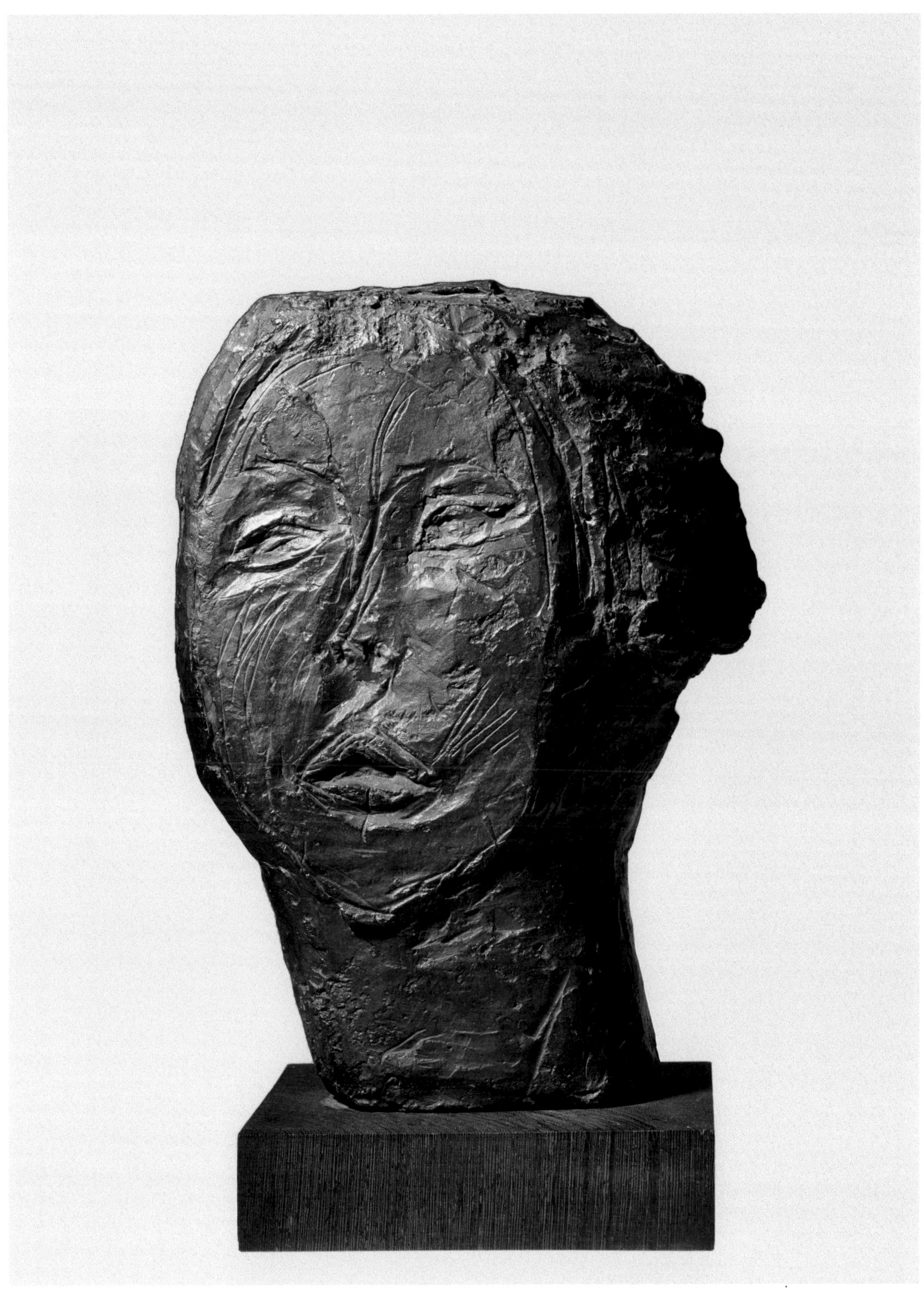

Cat. 42   Alberto Giacometti: *Head of a Woman* (*Flora Mayo*) (*Tête de femme* [*Flora Mayo*]), ca. 1927, cast ca. 1990, bronze, green-brown patina, 30.2 × 22.5 × 8 cm, private collection, London

Cat. 43   Paul Gauguin: *Self-Portrait Oviri (Autoportrait Oviri)*,
1893, bronze, 36.5 × 34.5 × 3 cm, Museum Folkwang, Essen,
inv. no. P 13

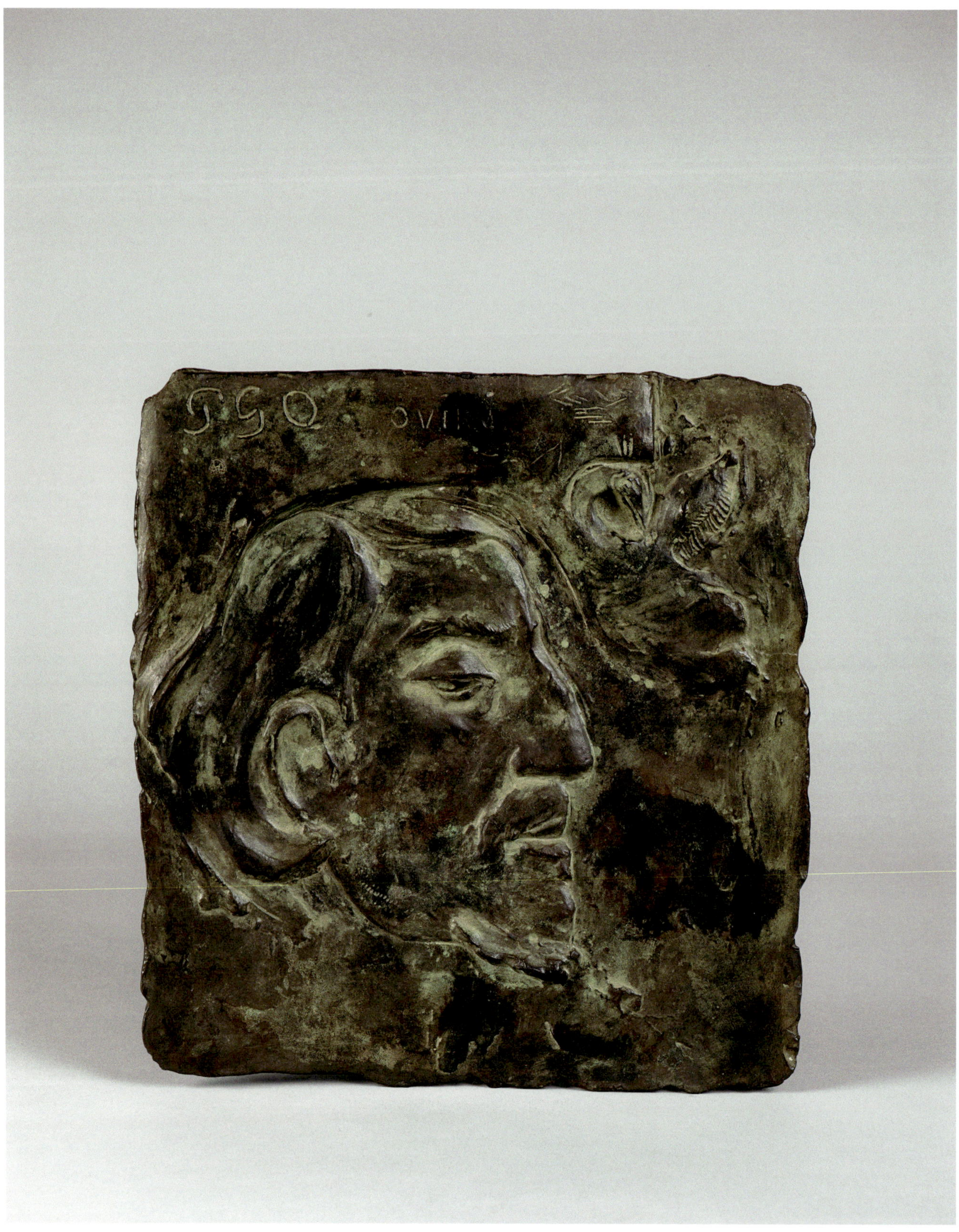

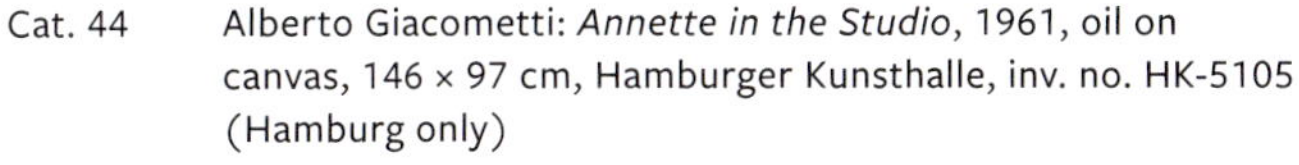

Cat. 44   Alberto Giacometti: *Annette in the Studio*, 1961, oil on canvas, 146 × 97 cm, Hamburger Kunsthalle, inv. no. HK-5105 (Hamburg only)

Cat. 45   Alberto Giacometti: *Great Sitting Nude* (*Grand nu assis*), 1957, oil on canvas, 154 × 59 cm, Städel Museum, Frankfurt am Main, inv. no. SG 1261 (Frankfurt only)

Cat. 45

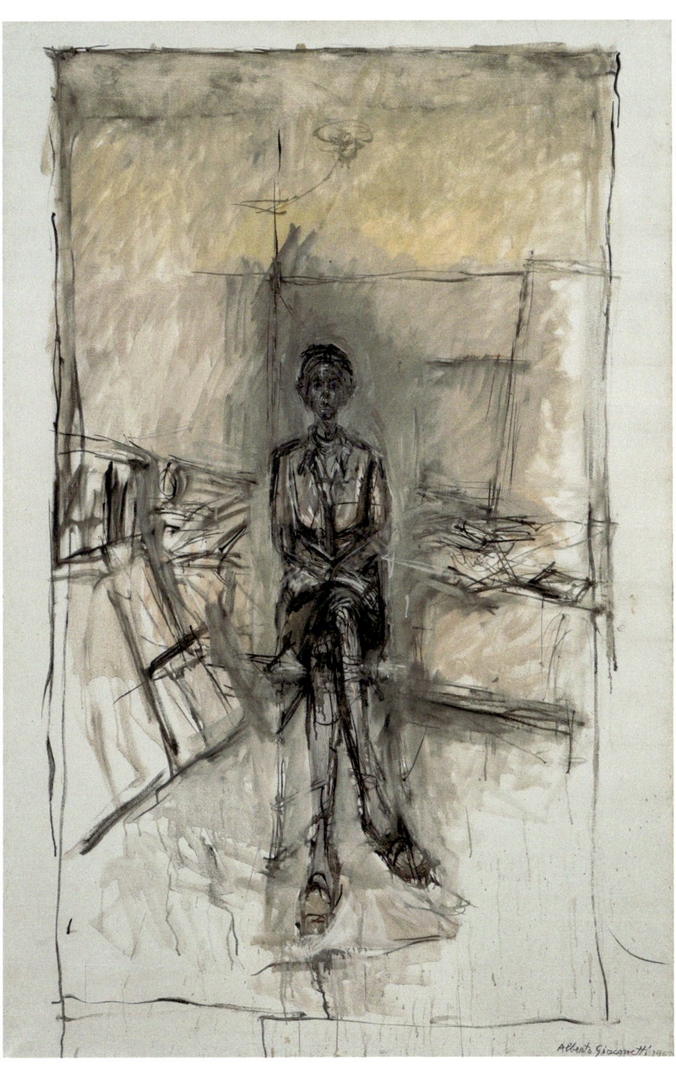

Cat. 44

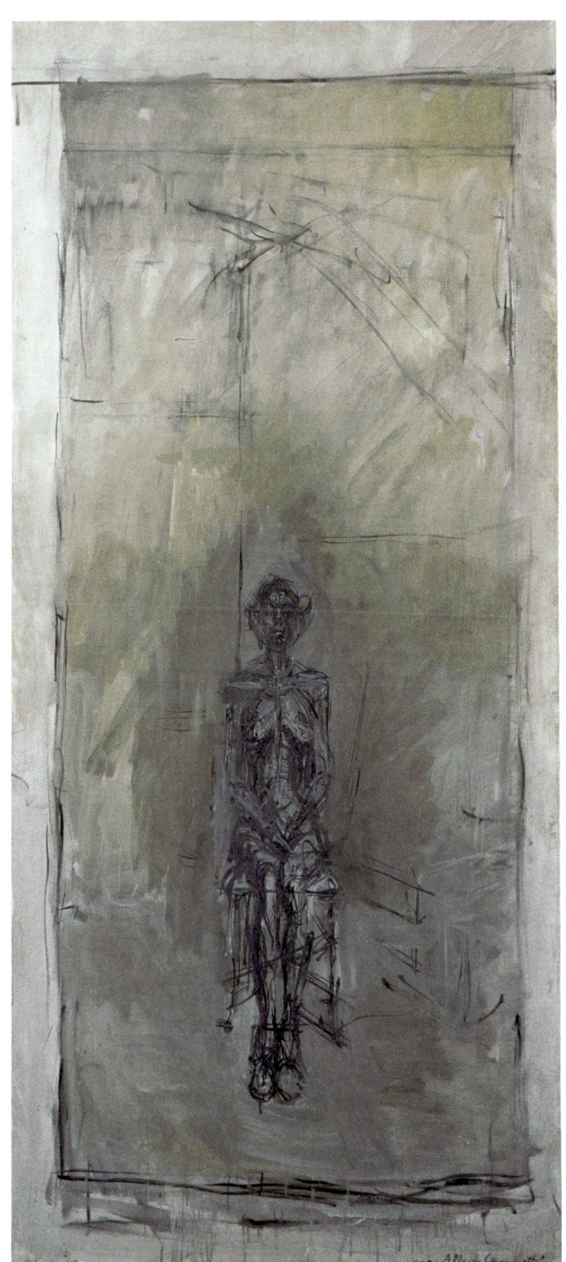

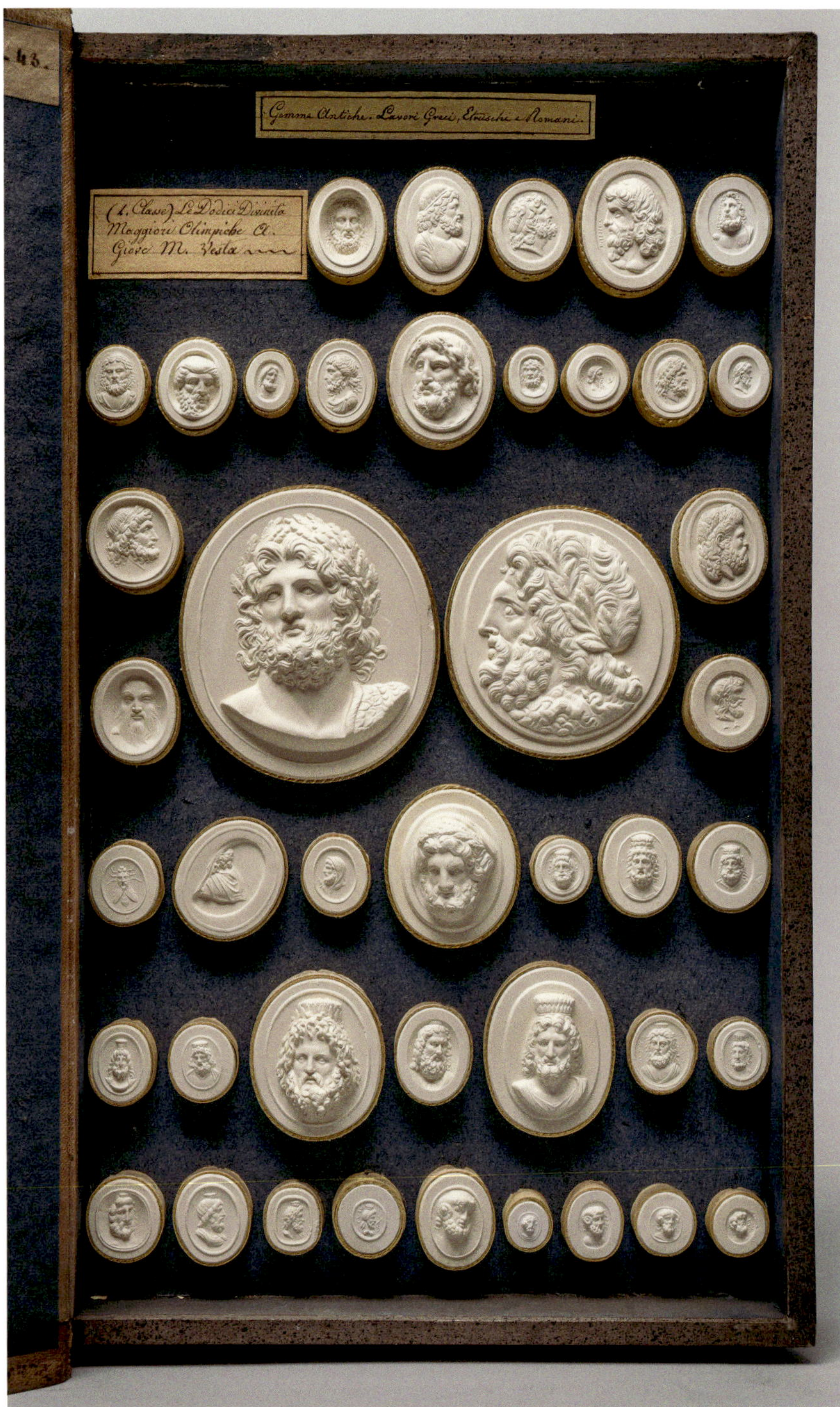

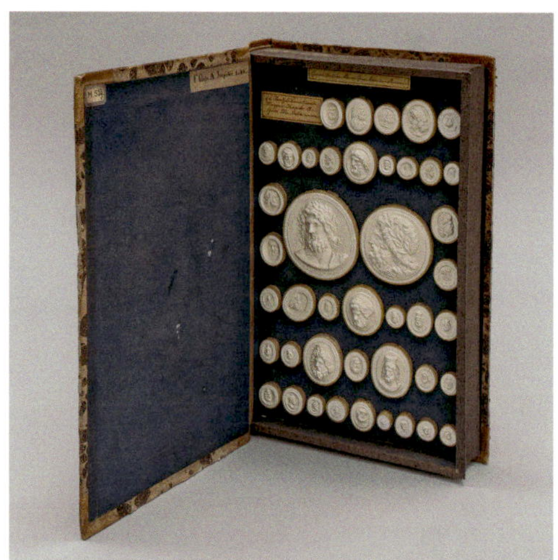

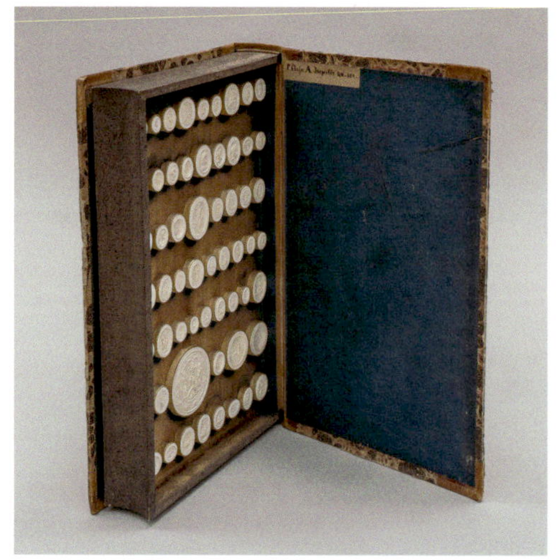

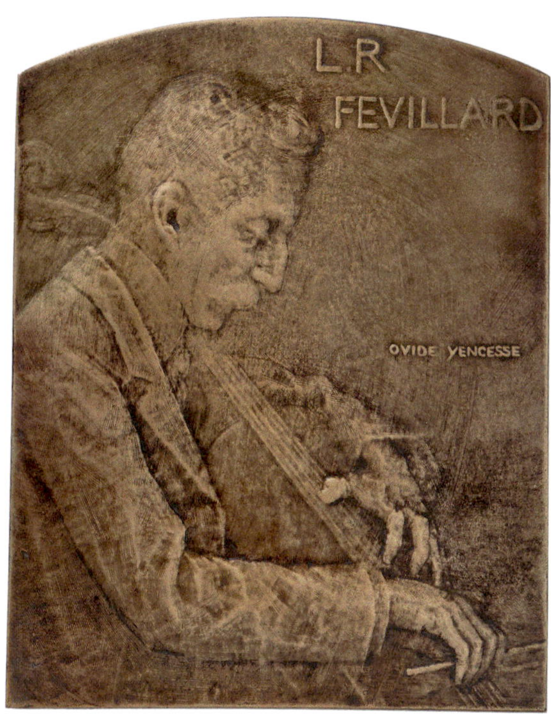

Cat. 47

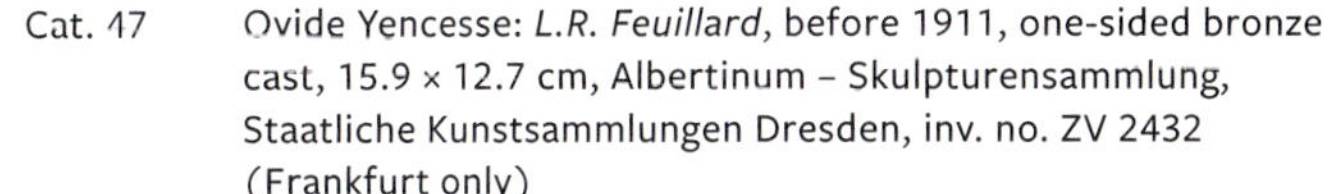

Cat. 47   Ovide Yencesse: *L.R. Feuillard*, before 1911, one-sided bronze cast, 15.9 × 12.7 cm, Albertinum – Skulpturensammlung, Staatliche Kunstsammlungen Dresden, inv. no. ZV 2432 (Frankfurt only)

Cat. 48   Hubert Ponscarme: *Dr. Walther*, before 1900, one-sided bronze cast, diameter: 14.4 cm, Albertinum – Skulpturensammlung, Staatliche Kunstsammlungen Dresden, inv. no. ZV 1861 (Frankfurt only)

Cat. 49   Hubert Ponscarme: *Ovide Yencesse and His Wife*, before 1902, one-sided pewter cast, galvano, diameter: 6.5 cm, Albertinum – Skulpturensammlung, Staatliche Kunstsammlungen Dresden, inv. no. ZV 1948 (Frankfurt only)

Cat. 50   Ovide Yencesse: *Hubert Ponscarme*, before 1902, one-sided galvano cast, silver-plated, 11 × 6.7 cm, Albertinum – Skulpturensammlung, Staatliche Kunstsammlungen Dresden, inv. no. ZV 2189 (Frankfurt only)

Cat. 51   Ovide Yencesse: *Eugène Spuller*, ca. 1896, one-sided bronze cast, 19.5 × 11.6 cm, Albertinum – Skulpturensammlung, Staatliche Kunstsammlungen Dresden, inv. no. ZV 1878 (Frankfurt only)

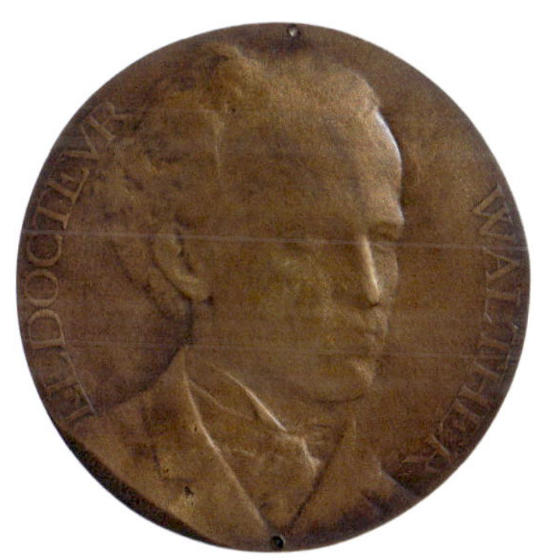

Cat. 48

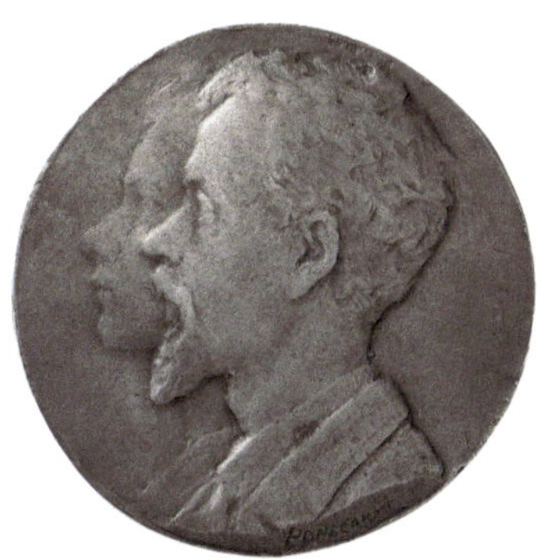

Cat. 49

Cat. 50   Cat. 51

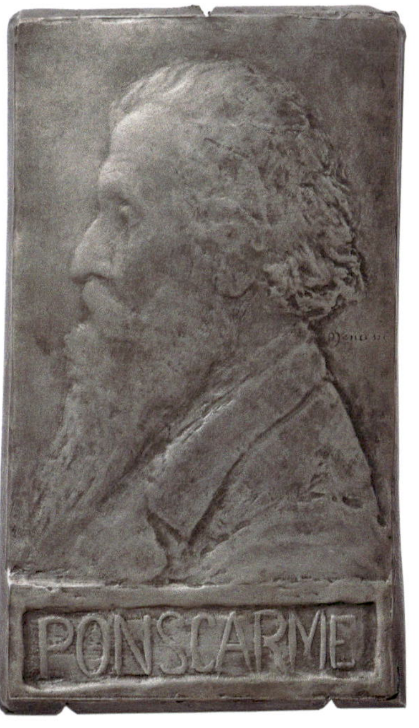

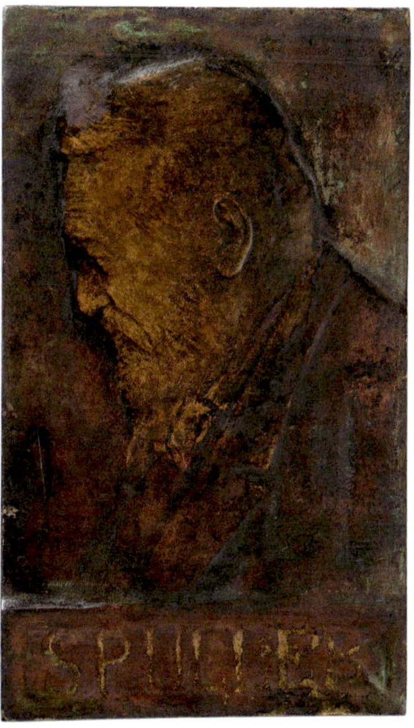

Cat. 52   Xaver Heuberger: *Portrait of the Father of the Frankfurt Actress Karoline Lindner*, 1827, wax, diameter: 10 cm, Liebieghaus Skulpturensammlung, Frankfurt am Main, inv. no. St.P 225

Cat. 53   Josef Kowarzik: *Johann Friedrich Städel*, 1916, two-sided iron cast (Avers), diameter: 8 cm, Historisches Museum Frankfurt, inv. no. MJF 4562 (Frankfurt only)

Cat. 54   Augusto Varnesi: *Mr and Mrs May*, 1897, one-sided bronze cast, 20.7 × 30.1 cm, Historisches Museum Frankfurt, inv. no. MJF 2304 (Frankfurt only)

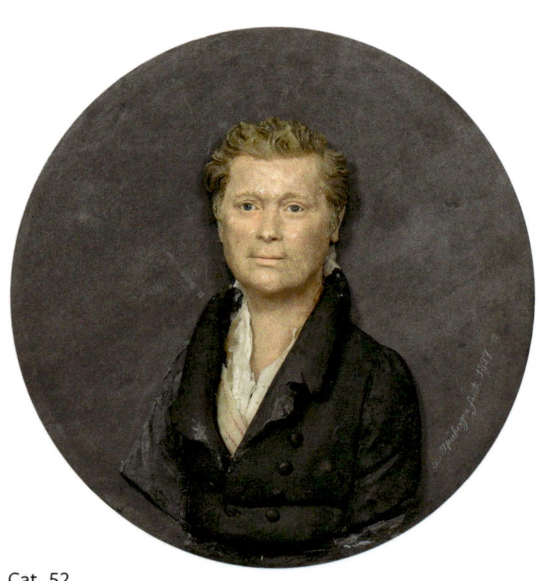

Cat. 52

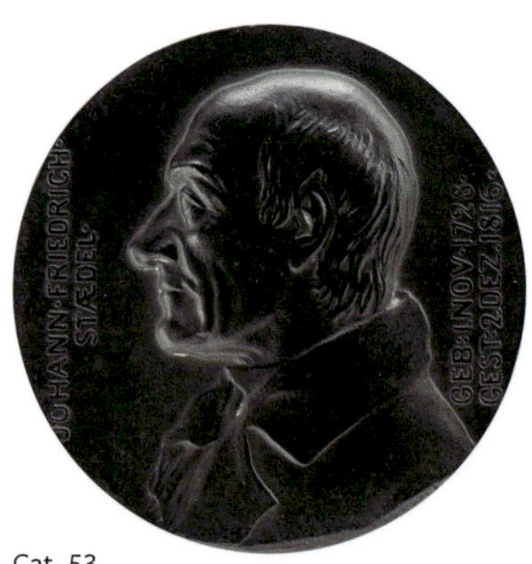

Cat. 53

Cat. 54

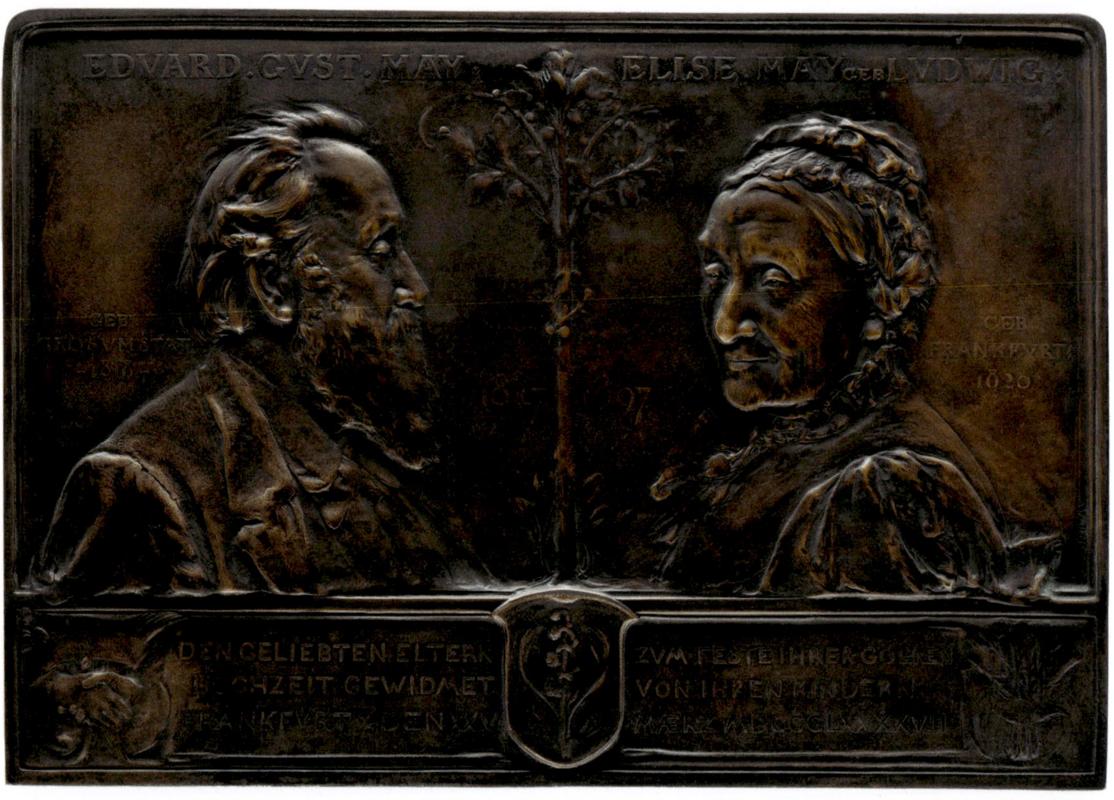

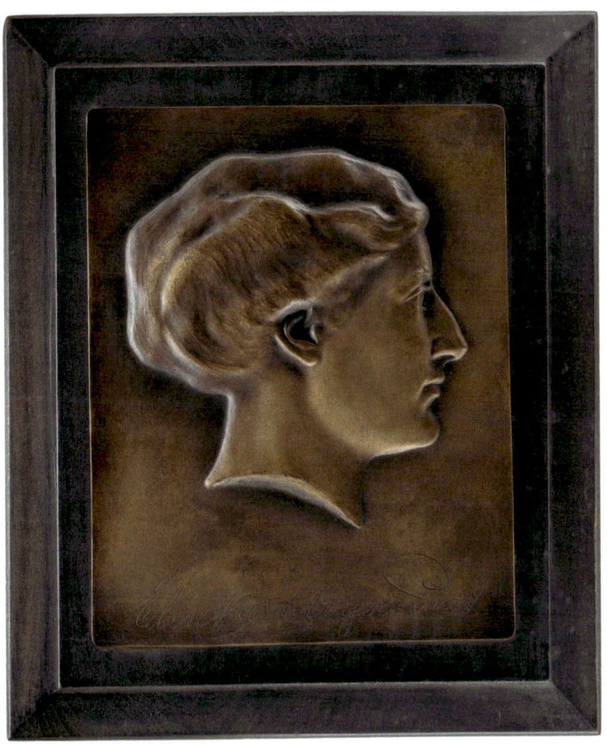

Cat. 55

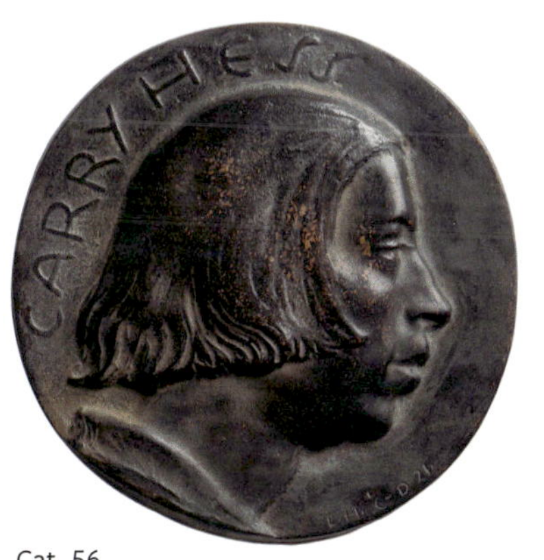

Cat. 56

Cat. 57

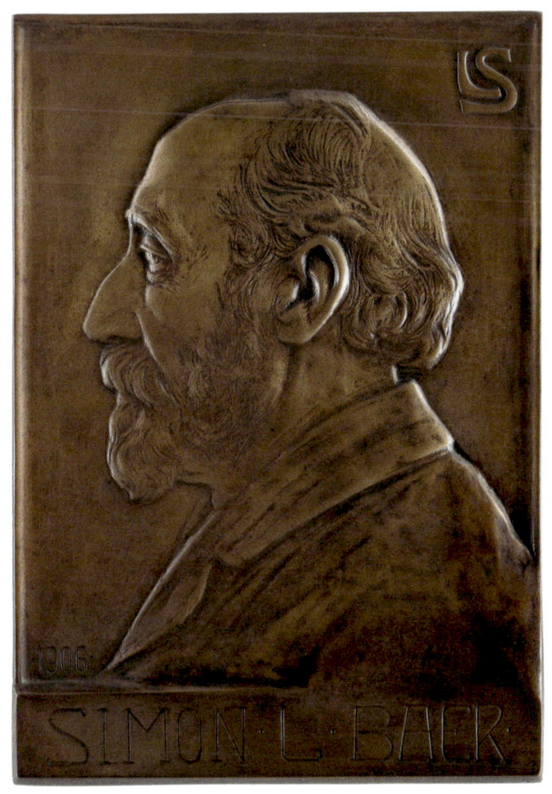

Cat. 55   Karl Dautert: *Elise Bamberger-Pundt*, 1921, one-sided
           bronze cast, 22.4 × 18.1 cm, Historisches Museum Frankfurt,
           inv. no. MJF 3478 (Frankfurt only)

Cat. 56   Lina Cornill-Dechent: *Carry Hess*, 1921, one-sided bronze
           cast, diameter: 8.1 cm, Historisches Museum Frankfurt,
           inv. no. MJF 3486 (Frankfurt only)

Cat. 57   Luise Federn-Staudinger: *Simon L. Baer*, 1906, one-sided
           bronze cast, 23 × 16.5 cm, Historisches Museum Frankfurt,
           inv. no. MJF 3108 (Frankfurt only)

Cat. 58   Käthe Kollwitz: *Lament*, 1938–1941, cast probably 1948,
stucco, 27.8 × 26.4 × 9.9 cm, Hamburger Kunsthalle,
inv. no. S-1949-1 (Hamburg only)

Cat. 59   Käthe Kollwitz: *Lament*, 1938–1941, cast 1960 at the latest,
bronze, 27.3 × 26.2 × 9.8 cm, Städel Museum, Frankfurt
am Main, inv. no. SGP 209 (Frankfurt only)

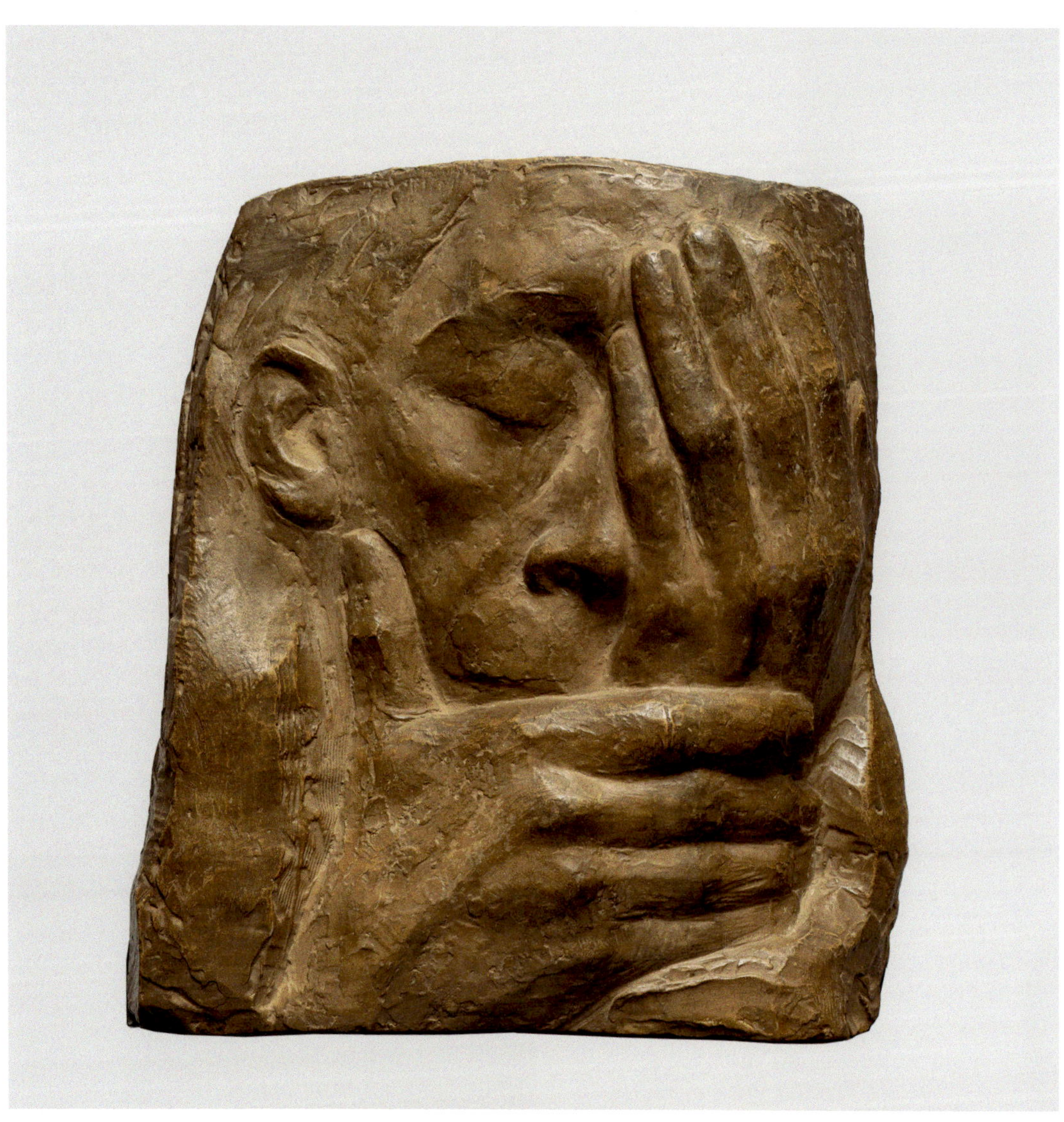

Cat. 58

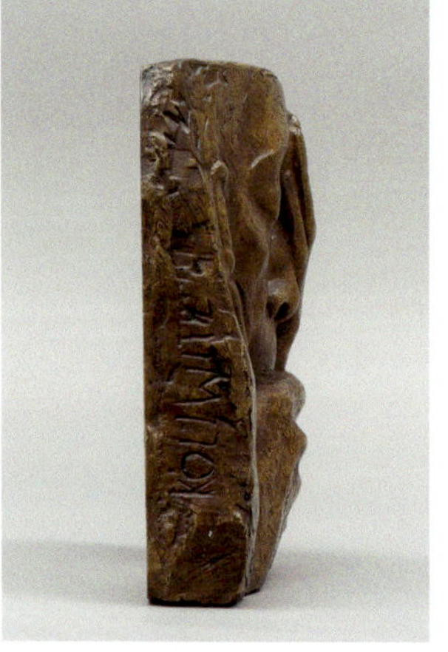
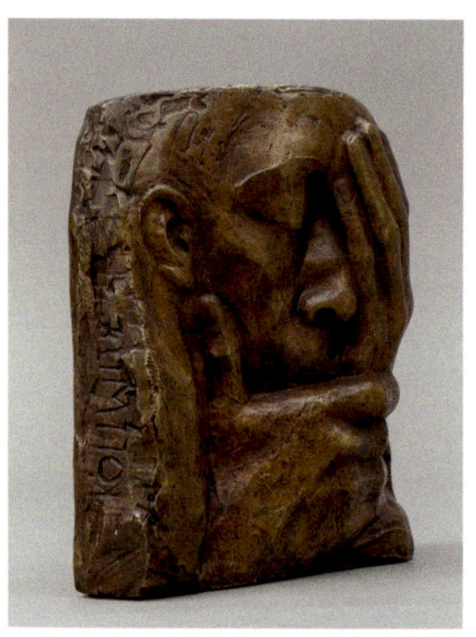
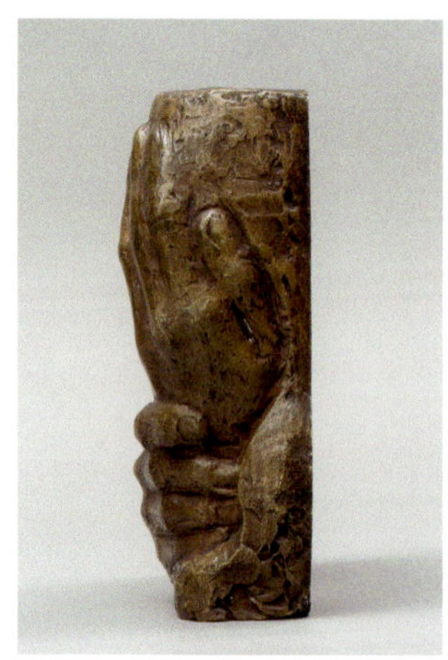

Cat. 59

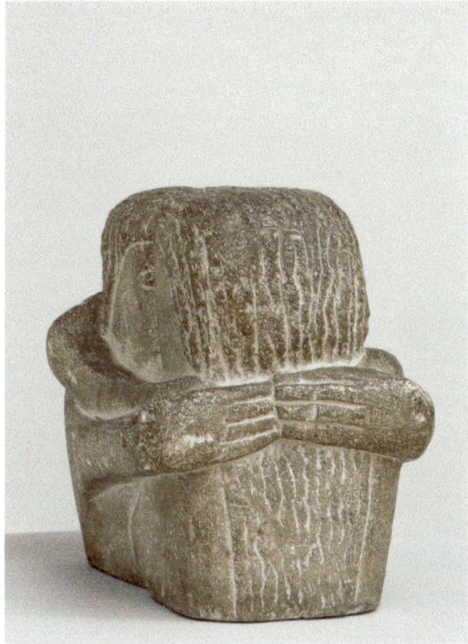

Cat. 60   Constantin Brancusi: *The Kiss* (*Le Baiser*), 1907/08, plaster, overlaid, 28 × 26 × 21.5 cm, Hamburger Kunsthalle, inv. no. S-1955-13

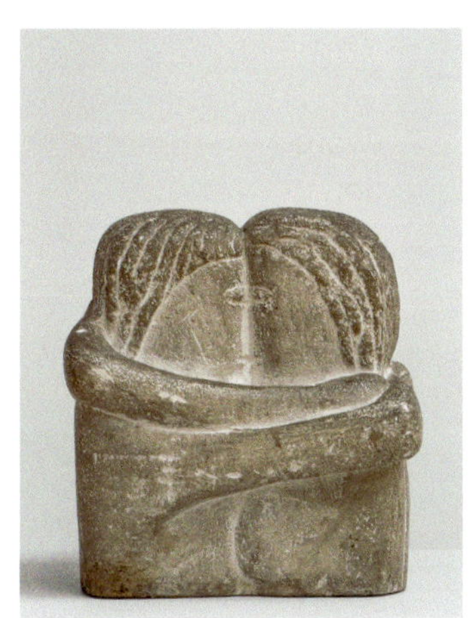

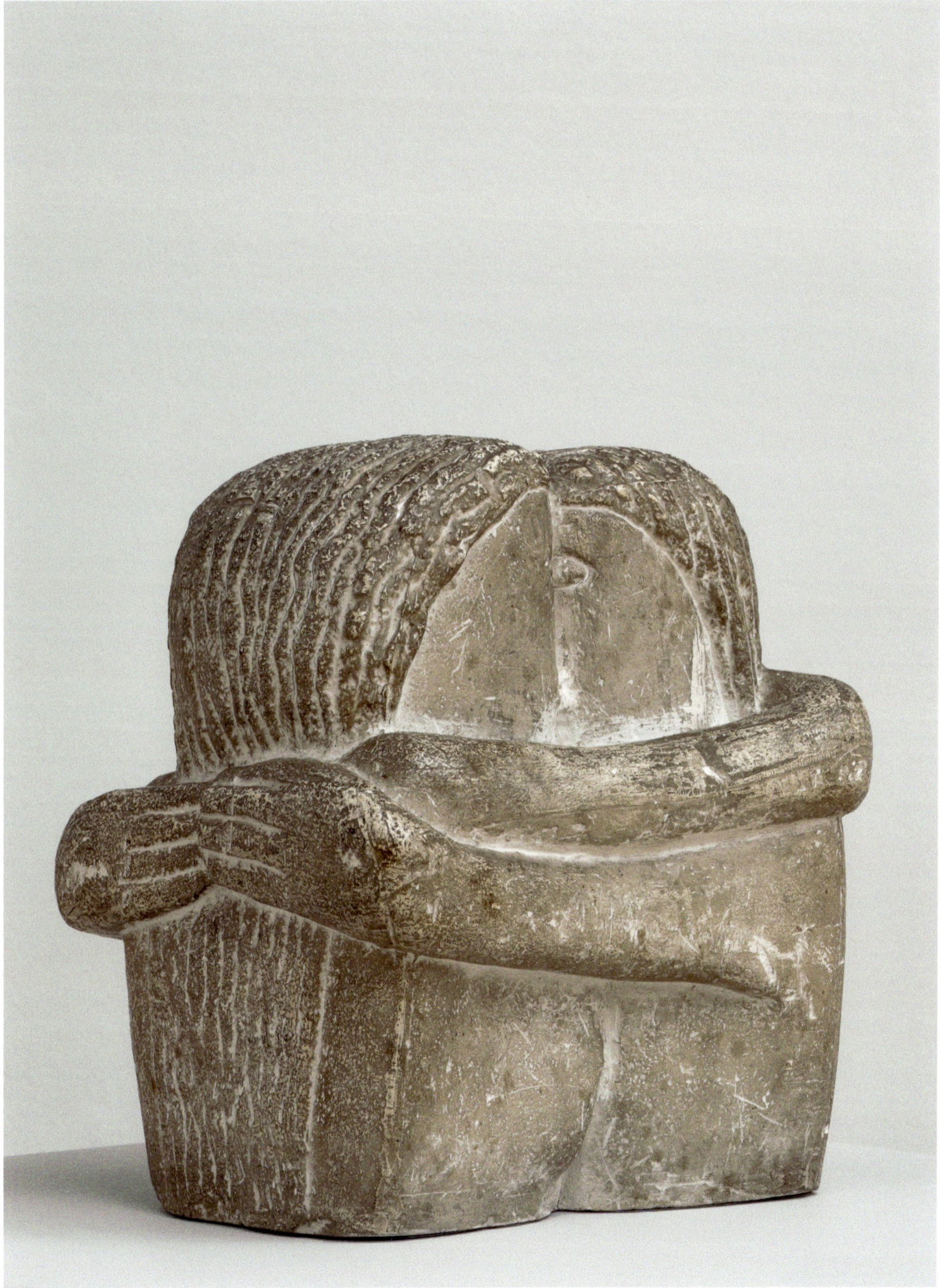

Cat. 61   Jean Dubuffet: *Duke Tapié* (*Tapié grand-duc*), 1946,
oil on plaster on canvas, 83 × 67.5 cm, Städel Museum,
Frankfurt am Main, inv. no. SG 1252 (Frankfurt only)

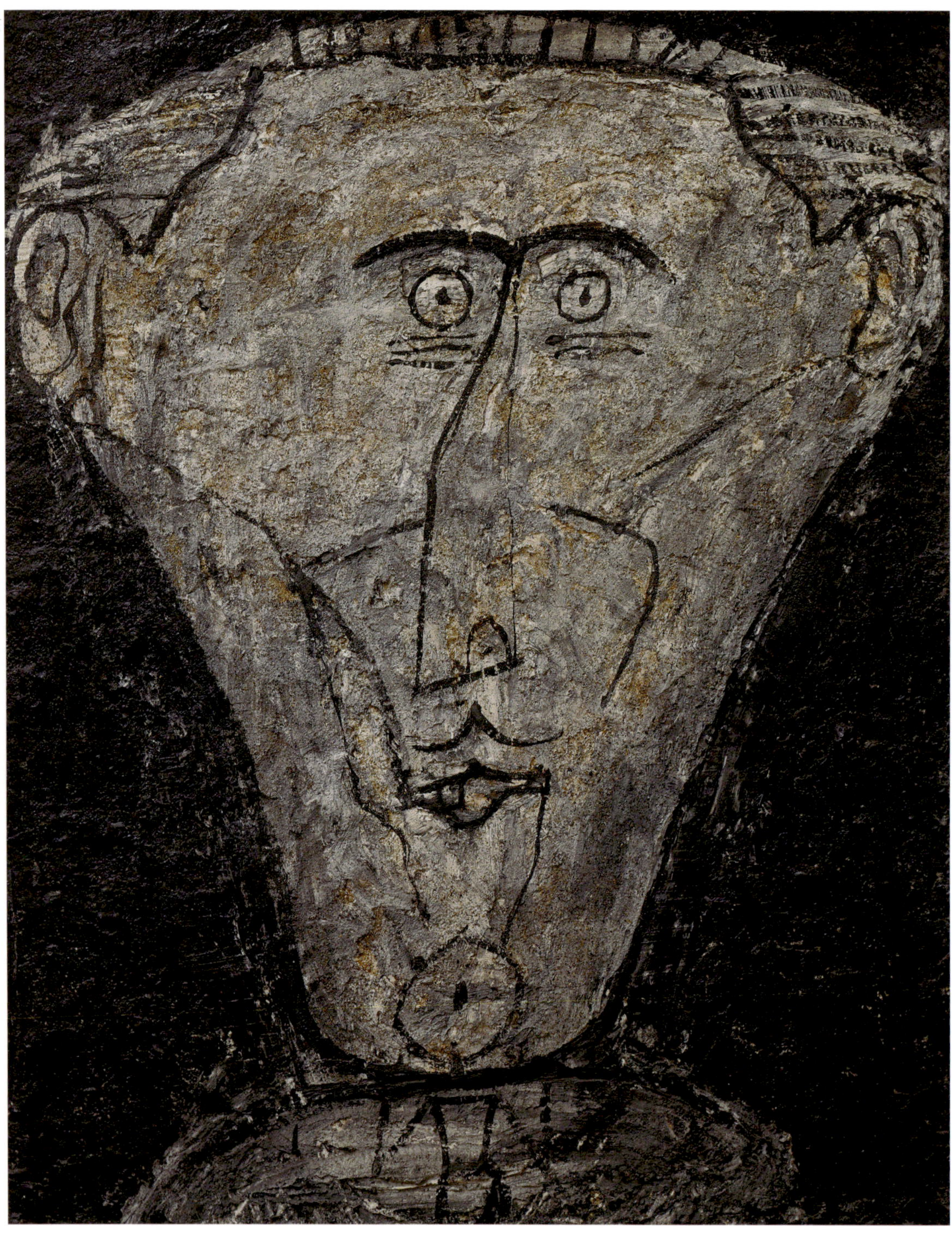

Cat. 62   Jean Dubuffet: *He Has Taken Off His Sandals*
(*Il a ôté les naïls*), 1947, oil on canvas, 99.5 × 81 cm,
Hamburger Kunsthalle, inv. no. HK-5364 (Hamburg only)

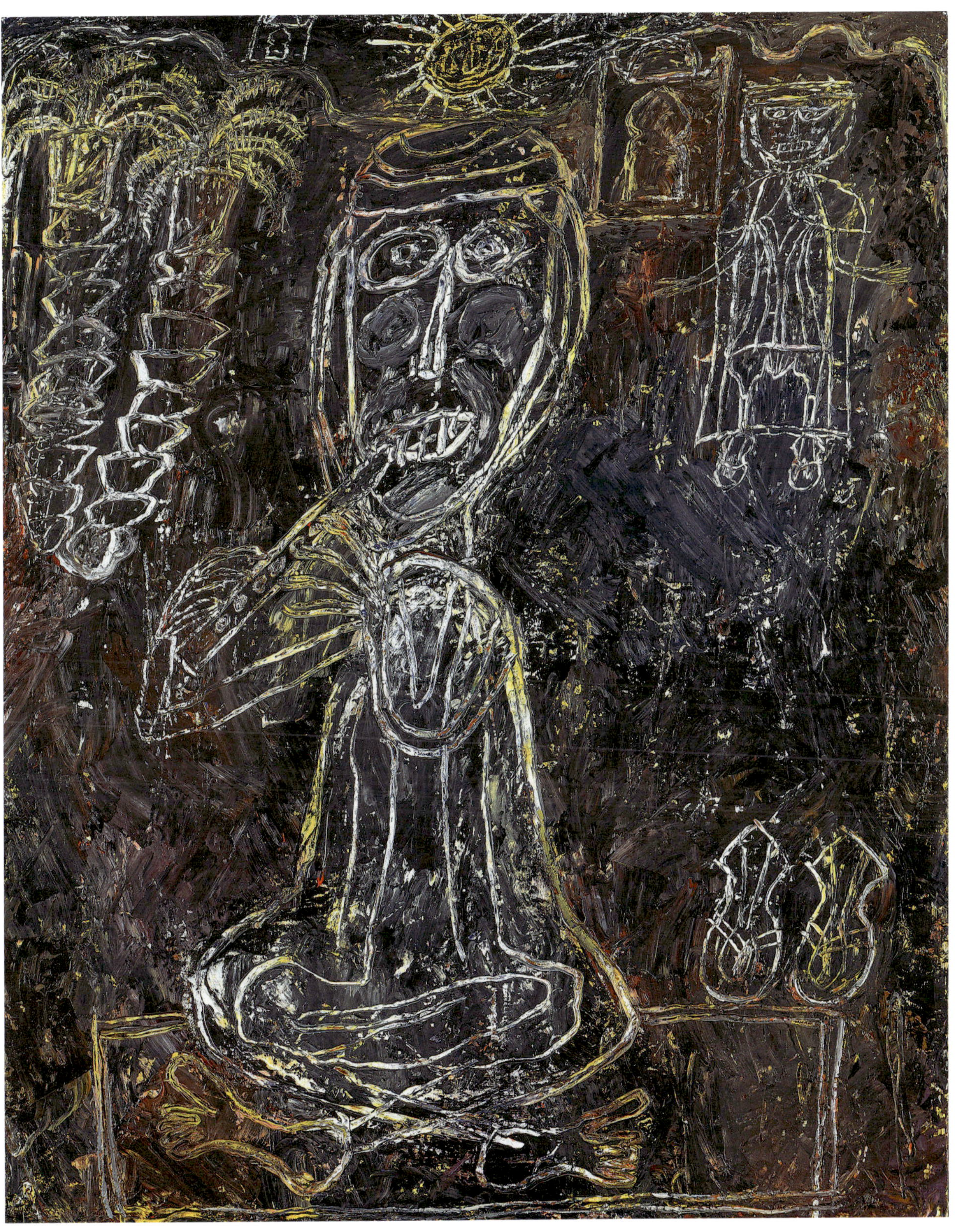

Cat. 63   Rolf Nesch: *Minotaur*, 1952–57, copper plate with perforated pieces of brass, zinc, soldered-on pieces of copper, inlaid mica, wood and coloured glass, 56.3 × 44 cm, Hamburger Kunsthalle, inv. no. HK-5126

Cat. 64   Karel Appel: *Face*, 1954–56, ceramic, painted, 48 × 48 × 6 cm, private collection

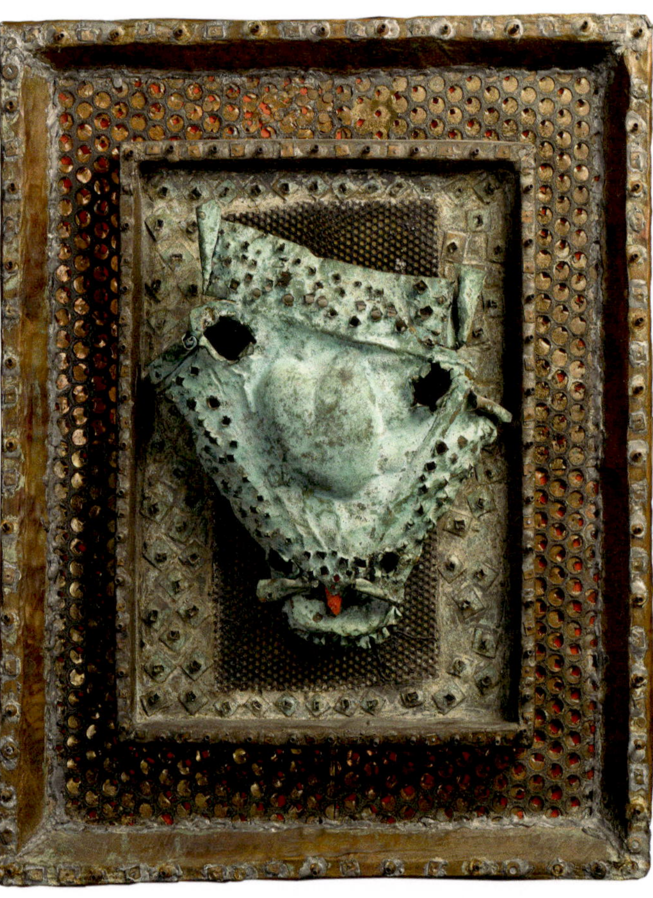

Cat. 63

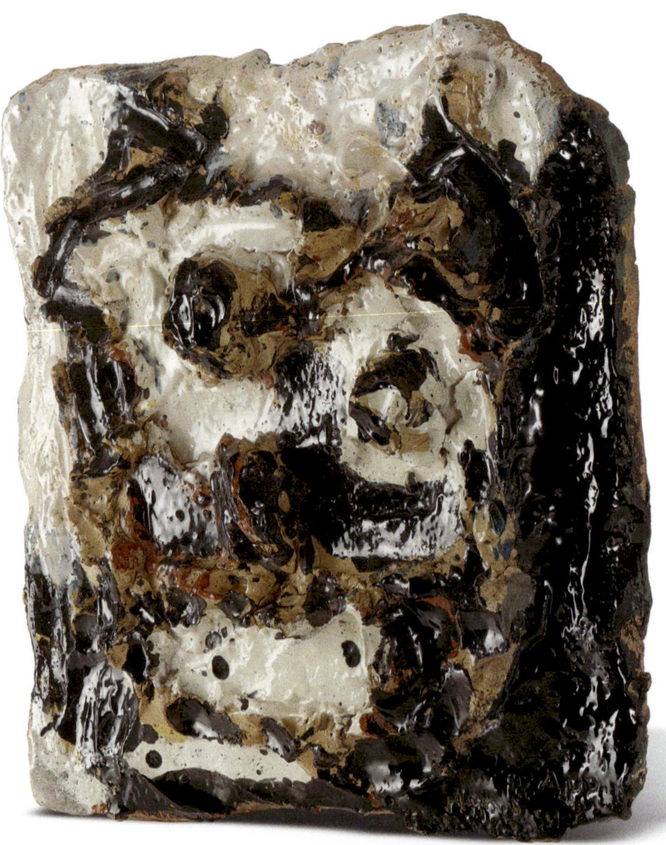

Cat. 64

Cat. 65   Eugène Leroy: *Autoportrait*, 1962, oil on canvas, 82.5 × 60.5 cm,
Städel Museum, Frankfurt am Main, inv. no. 2382

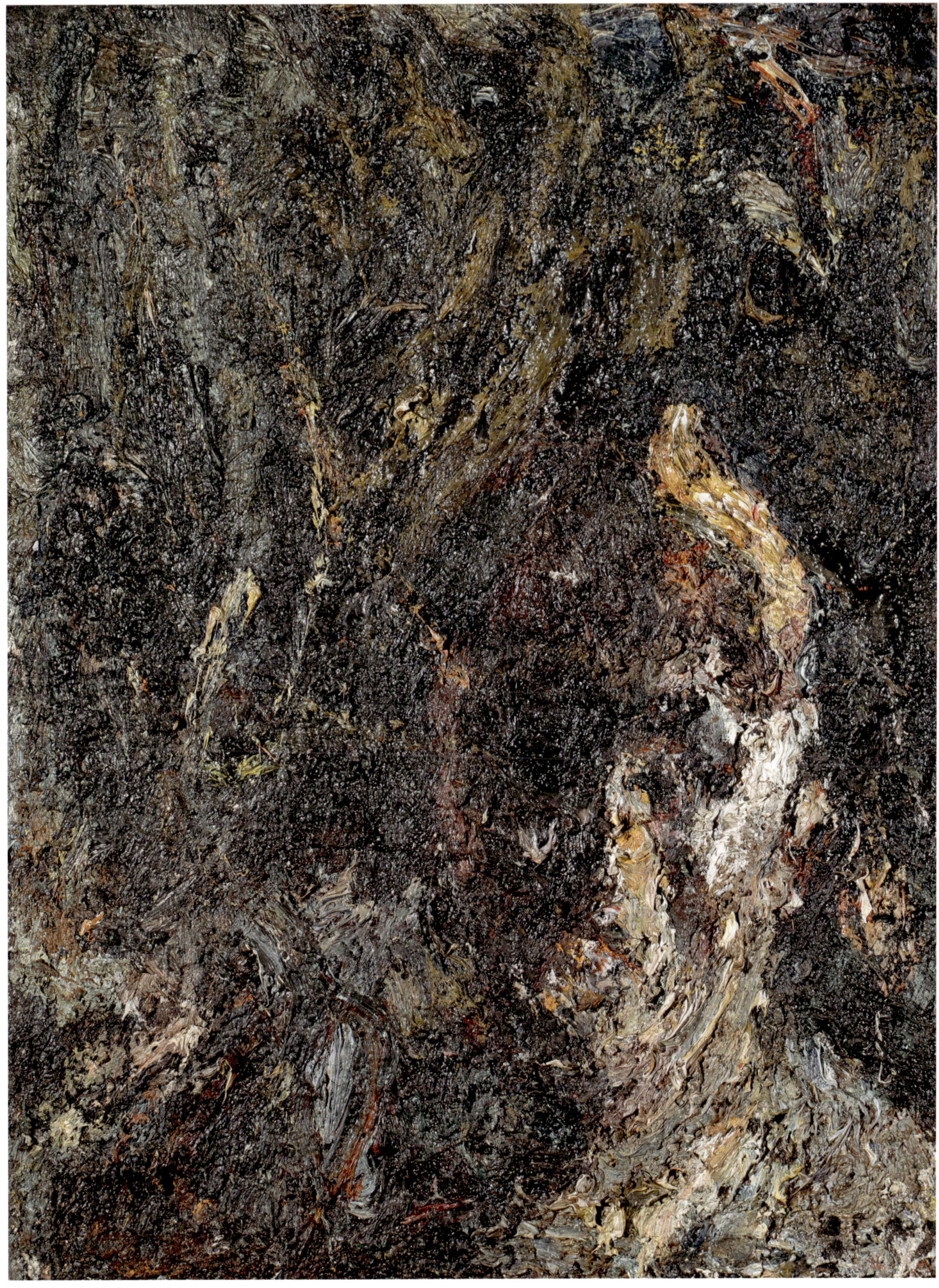

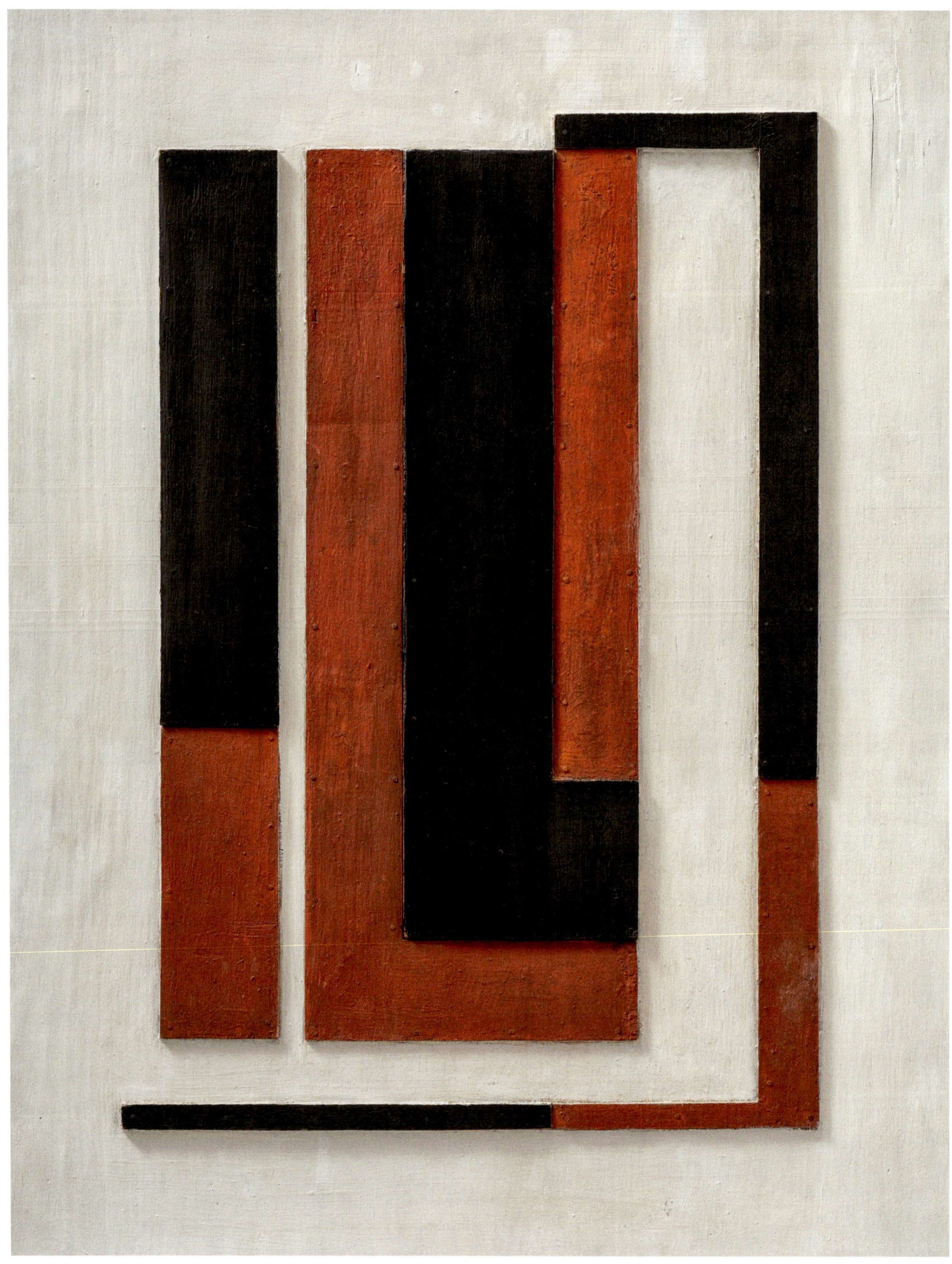

Cats. 66—73

Karin Schick

CONTAINED FORMS, OPEN PLANES

The Relief and Its Frame

Since time immemorial, picture frames have served to artistically surround and protect a work of art.[1] At the same time, they serve a content-related purpose: by delimiting the work inwards and against an outside, it becomes a recognisable, identifiable entity. The frame creates the autonomy of art vis-à-vis reality, provides it with its own space and turns it into an "island in the world".[2] The meaning of the frame itself, whether it belongs to the work or to its surrounding space, whether it is boundary, transition or intermediate zone – these are questions in an ongoing discourse that relates not just to art history.[3]

It was in the mid-nineteenth century in particular that painters began including the frame in their concepts for a painting.[4] Because modernists sought a new reality in which art was to be part of life, and life itself art, they also inquired into the "insular" position of the work.[5] This became visible not least in the handling of the frame: one no longer allowed the strips of frame to descend into the painting and did not distinguish it from the canvas in terms of colour, but often painted it in the same fashion: the illusion of a window frame through which one looked at the world gave way in favour of a pictorial reality that expanded in all directions. Thus, in Robert Delaunay's *Simultaneous Windows* from 1912 (cat. 74), the abstracted view of Paris with the Eiffel Tower in the distance seems to flow in a rhythmic-dynamic movement beyond the frame into the space of reality (→ The Polyperspectival Gaze).

By nature, the relief already makes reference to space. Because it actually opens out from the plane, the question of its presence as a unified entity and its materiality calls for the inclusion of the outer edges from the outset: whether the relief is hewn in stone or wood, cast in plaster, terracotta or metal, its frame has to be taken into account at an early stage. There is a wide variety of compositional solutions; they can emphasise boundaries and open up planes.

Whereas today Aristide Maillol is regarded as an influential sculptor of twentieth-century Europe, his artistic beginnings were in two-dimensional art, in painting, graphic art and tapestry. It was not until the mid-1890s that he produced plastic artworks, initially small reliefs and statuettes, and from 1905 on monumental figures that could be viewed from all sides. At the suggestion of his German patron, Harry Graf Kessler, in the summer of 1907 he created the high relief *Desire* (cat. 68).[6] It features two figures – the male one muscular, the female one softly rounded – entangled in a conflict of turning towards and away from, attacking and resisting. After completing sculptural designs in clay and plaster, Maillol initially carried out the composition in stone, followed by terracotta and then, twice, in lead.[7] The dark metal causes the surface of the depicted bodies to shimmer, at the same time heightening the drama of the scene: mounted in a nearly square frame, the three-dimensional figures not only push their way from the planar ground far into the space. In the confined field, they apparently generate such a strong force that two of their feet bend the lower corners of the relief.

Maillol had explored framing a figure in his earliest works. However, whereas the bas-relief *Dancing Woman* (fig. 1) derives from the decorative ornamentation of Art Nouveau and the animated figure is inscribed in the oval of a tree trunk, *Desire* displays his typical style of balanced composition, clear form and smooth surface. Inspired by the art of antiquity, Maillol aimed for a harmonious distribution of masses.[8] He frequently exchanged views about classicism with Kessler and was especially enthusiastic about the Olympic Temple of Zeus and its metope frieze with the twelve deeds of Heracles (fig. 2).[9] Possibly inspired by this model, *Desire* was also intended to initiate a twelve-part relief series entitled *Man and Woman*; however, Maillol did not develop this further. Yet his love of classicism caused him to become

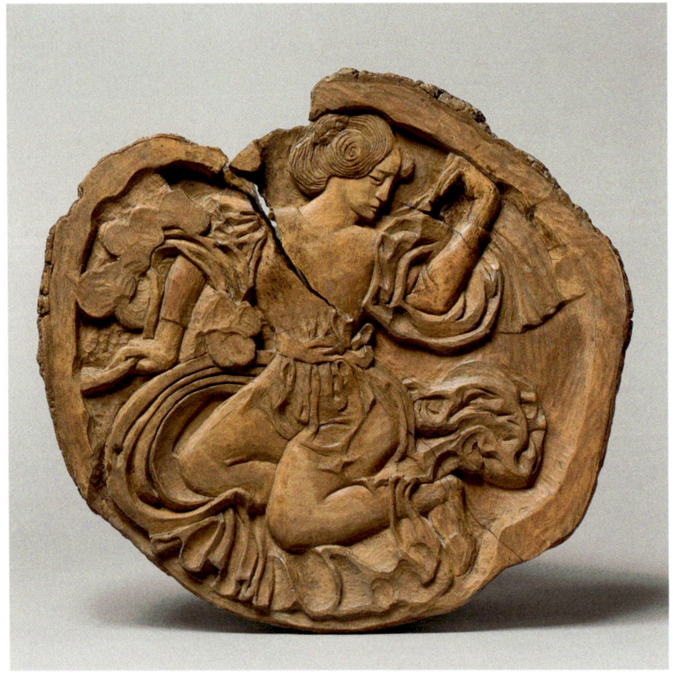

Fig. 1

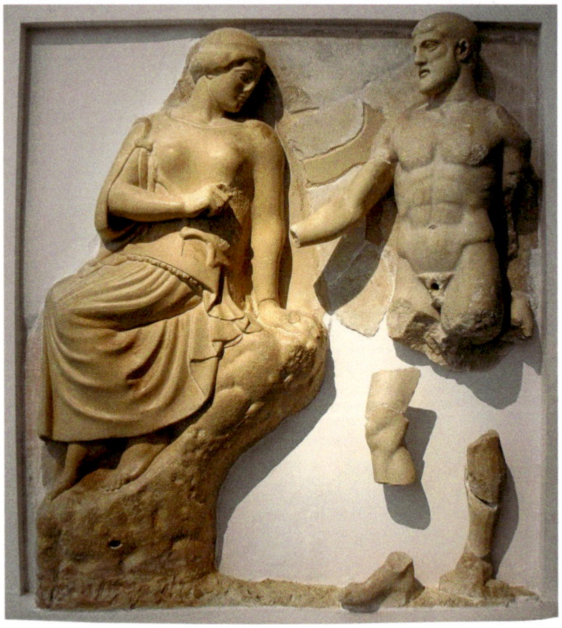

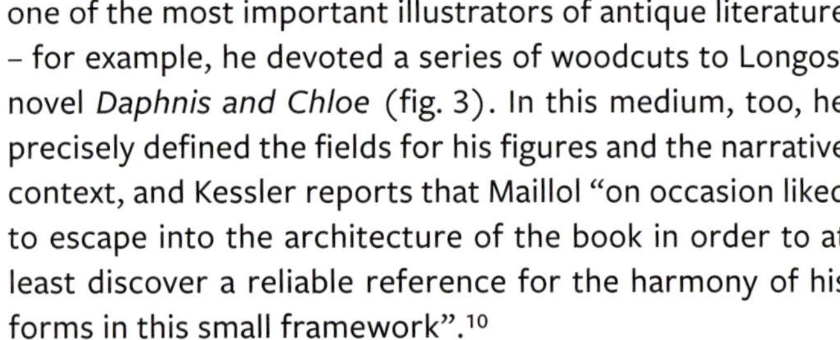

Fig. 2

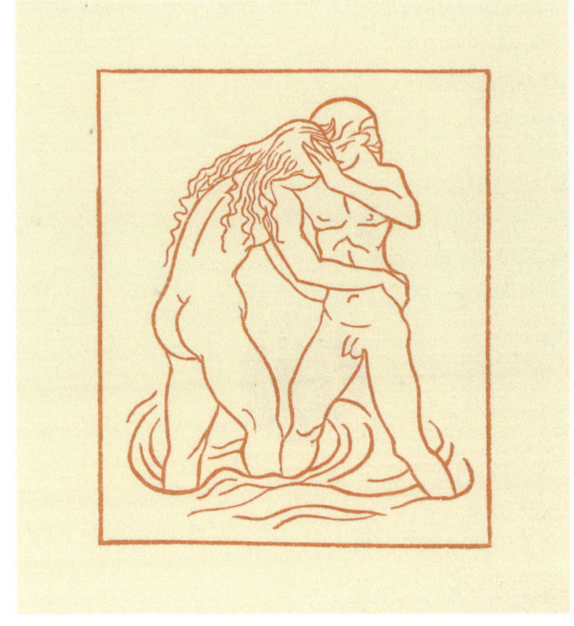

Fig. 3

Fig. 1   Aristide Maillol: *Dancing Woman* (*Danseuse*), 1896, wood,
         Musée d'Orsay, Paris

Fig. 2   *Herakles Brings Athena the Stymphalian Birds*, metope
         of the Temple of Zeus, ca. 460 BCE, marble, Archaeological
         Museum, Olympia

Fig. 3   Aristide Maillol: *Chloe Casting Daphnis into Her Arms*, 1937,
         woodcut in red, Hamburger Kunsthalle, Kupferstichkabinett

one of the most important illustrators of antique literature
– for example, he devoted a series of woodcuts to Longos'
novel *Daphnis and Chloe* (fig. 3). In this medium, too, he
precisely defined the fields for his figures and the narrative
context, and Kessler reports that Maillol "on occasion liked
to escape into the architecture of the book in order to at
least discover a reliable reference for the harmony of his
forms in this small framework".[10]

Maillol's art was an inspiration to many artists, including
the Russian Moissey Kogan, who frequently worked and
lived in Paris. Kogan, too, had initially dealt with medals,

gems and embroidery before turning to sculpture.
Because he lacked both clients and financial means, he
usually carried out reliefs and sculptures in small formats and often in only terracotta or plaster. Like Maillol,
with whom he frequently exchanged ideas between 1921
and 1927,[11] Kogan devoted himself almost exclusively to
the female figure. His idealised nudes hardly changed
over decades. In terms of the symmetry of composition and the dance-like stance of the figures, the bronze
relief *Two Female Nudes in Gothic Framing* (cat. 66),
created in 1927, seems classical. However, the frame

with pendentives bordering the heads is also reminiscent of ecclesiastical niche figures and prompts one to imagine the small-format object being a monumental one. In fact, Kogan was commissioned to produce wall reliefs for the 1914 Cologne *Werkbund Exhibition*, and from then on he dealt with the concept of a human figure as related to the architecture.

Around 1907, as a self-taught sculptor oriented towards the greats of the time, Maillol and Auguste Rodin, the Frenchman Raymond Duchamp-Villon opened himself up to the new movements of Cubism and Futurism. In collaboration with other artists, as a vision of the future he presented the installation *La Maison Cubiste*, for which he created the building façade with a protruding portal in Cubist forms, at the 1912 Paris Salon d'Automne.

Duchamp-Villon's enthusiasm for combining architecture and sculpture continued to come into play when he created the bas-relief *The Lovers* (cat. 67) in 1913 – for which Maillol's work *Desire* served as a model.[12] The sculptor developed his symmetrical composition in a succession of six states. The first two still have distinct architectural character, and the figures are incorporated into a geometrically structured, frieze-like plane (fig. 4). As his work proceeded, Duchamp-Villon visibly removed them from this architectural frame. A preliminary drawing (fig. 5) illustrates how he reduced his composition to simple forms and inter-circulating ovals, and removed the outer geometrical boundaries. In the four states of the relief that followed, the sculptor concentrated entirely on the protruding volumes of the bodies and the surrounding concave forms. Surrounded only by a planar, narrow frame, the erotic motif seemed to dissolve in rhythmic momentum into abstraction, and in doing so completely corresponded with the artist's conviction: "In a harmony of volume, planes and lines, the motif does not play a role at all, or at most a minor one."[13]

While Duchamp-Villon lent his lovers "breathing" space, in her high relief *Nude with Flowing Hair* (cat. 69) Jenny Wiegmann-Mucchi condensed the rendering in the tightest of spaces. She carved an isolated reclining human figure out of the depth of a wooden block. Circumscribed on all sides by a deep, wide frame, the composition nevertheless opens up a wide field of associations: Is the figure confined in a box, is it oppressively constrained? Is it floating in lofty heights with a wafting shock of hair, or is it floating in water with flowing hair? Is its powerful body lifeless or only relaxed prior to its next move?

Nude with Flowing Hair was created in the 1920s during Wiegmann's studies at the Kunstgewerbe- und Handwerkerschule in Berlin-Charlottenburg. With the Austrian sculptor Hans Perathoner, she became familiar not only with the material wood, but also with the formal language of Expressionism and with religious motifs.[14] Only slightly smoothened, her object recalls medieval sculptural or folk art, and since Wiegmann does not clearly define the gender of the muscular nude seen from behind, she may be referring to the uncertain situation of *people* in her time. Beginning in 1923 the artist realised numerous ecclesiastical reliefs in Germany and also Italy – to where she relocated in 1934 – as well as symbolic, free-standing female nudes that lent expression to their own fight against dictatorship. Unlike Maillol, when doing so she never eroticised the female figure.[15]

Erich Buchholz created the works *Black-Red on White* (cat. 70) and *New Panel 3* (*Wood Picture*) (cat. 71) at the same time as Wiegmann produced her relief, and likewise in Berlin. Buchholz had just abandoned painting in favour of architecture, commercial art and stage design; in doing so, he also completed his transition to abstraction and Constructivism. He turned his studio-apartment on Herkulesufer into a playing field for modern design principles and a meeting place for the Berlin avant-garde and kindred spirits from home and abroad (→ Designs of the World). The artist enthusiastically plumbed space in a wide range of media, on paper, in paintings, sculptures and glass objects, as well as in approximately one hundred plaster and wood reliefs. *Black-Red on White* demonstrates his joy in experimentation: mounted on a blockboard, thin pieces of plywood result in a composition consisting of geometric shapes and colour contrasts; however, on the white ground they also form empty and intermediate spaces, segment and whole, boundary and junction. A narrow strip originates at the upper righthand edge of the composition that continues to the lower left corner, where it abruptly ends – using the simplest of means, the frame is thus staged as both an enclosure and an opening. In contrast, *New Panel 3* is clearly circumscribed by a reddish frame. Buchholz carved geometric forms out of the recessed surface of a wooden board that overlap and are grouped around a circle. From 1923 onwards, circle, square, black, red and gold play a pivotal role in his oeuvre. On the one hand, they make reference to the timeless relevance of icons (→ Designs of the World), and on the other, as radical simplifications of form and colour they stand for a modern reality with "new panels". For Buchholz, in contrast to other Constructivists, art was not rational and theoretical, but intuitive, impulsive and spontaneous as well as linked to the human body. The striking signature that his burin left on the ground turns this framed relief into a locus of animated expression.

Swiss artist Sophie Taeuber-Arp occupied a special position within Constructivist art.[16] Ensuing from textile design, she developed her very own colour field compositions in drawing, painting, relief and architecture, whereby she freely combined representational and non-representational art. Whereas in a relief from 1936 (cat. 139) one rather sees geometry and order at work,

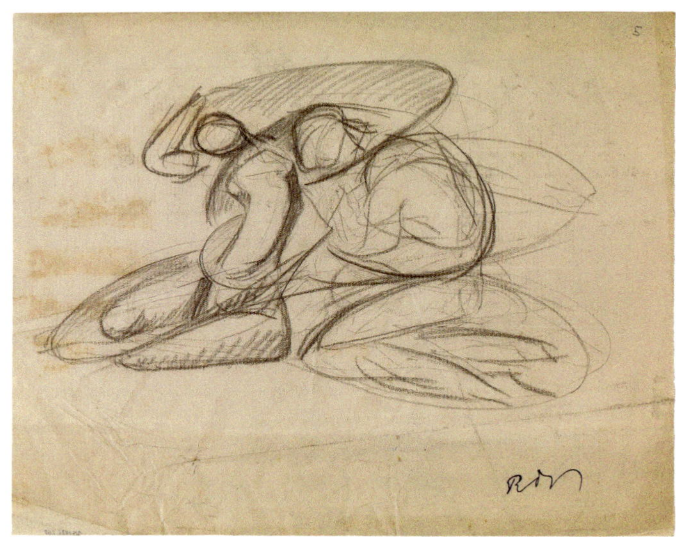

Fig. 5

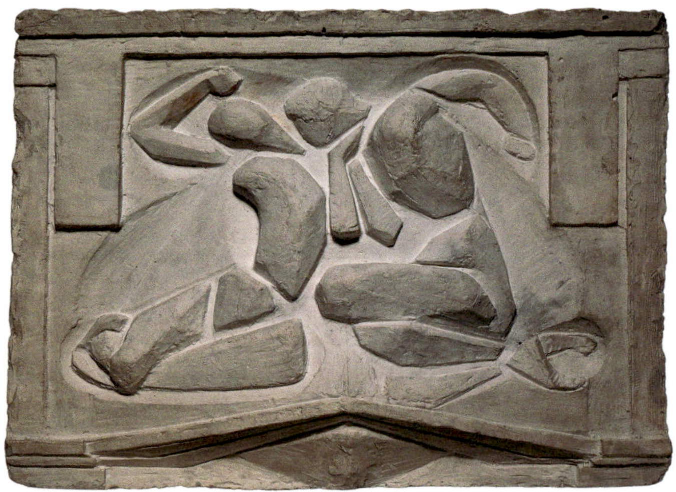

Fig. 4

Fig. 4   Raymond Duchamp-Villon: *The Lovers II (Les Amants II)*, 1913, plaster, Centre Pompidou, Paris

Fig. 5   Raymond Duchamp-Villon: *The Lovers (Les Amants)*, ca. 1913, charcoal on laid paper, Centre Pompidou, Paris

the painting *Composition* (cat. 73) from 1935 is permeated by a graceful dynamism: four curved-straight forms fill the plane of the canvas and seem to move towards the edges of the picture and beyond. They are set in motion not only by tilting in the plane, but also, because of their brightness values, by an optical advancing and receding in the pictorial space. Taeuber-Arp frequently incorporated different forms, such as human, animal, plant (cat. 138), ship, sail or flag shapes, so it is understandable that her partner, Jean Arp, later gave this painting the title *Floating Forms*. The artist finally enclosed her composition in a narrow strip of wood; however, she kept the colouring of the frame so dark that it hardly contrasts with the matt blue-grey of the pictorial ground.[17] For her, a canvas or wooden board, a space or a building were playing fields on which curves and straight lines were allowed to boundlessly vibrate and where coincidences could occur.

Whether figurative or non-representational, modern art took pleasure in exploring its own boundaries, and as an overlap of plane and space, the relief seemed to be particularly suitable for doing so. Around 1920, in his complex object *Ornamental Sculpture on a Divided Frame* (cat. 114)

Oskar Schlemmer intertwined not only the genres of painting and sculpture to bring forth a spectacularly new compound (→ Designs of the World). With four different fields, on which rests a wooden collage as a connecting link, he impressively illustrated the effective power of the frame. By breaking open and at the same time maintaining its wholeness, he pointed out the intermediate realms of perception, meaning, illusion and reality.

Forty years later, artist Niki de Saint Phalle proceeded even more radically: in 1961, the year she became a member of the artists' group Les Nouveaux Réalistes, to which Daniel Spoerri also belonged (cat. 86), she designed small-format, intimate-seeming object pictures such as *Assemblage No. 6* (cat. 72), integrating things of daily life.[18] The objects arranged on a white ground are without exception segments or fragments; they testify to elements of destruction and infirmity in the modern world and at the same time to the beauty of its waste. The fragments became a whole by means of the blue support panel and a frame corner applied to it with glue, which border the composition: yet again, the frame carried out the unity of art and turned the work into the scene of a new reality.

1 See, for example, Werner Ehlich: *Bilderrahmen von der Antike bis zur Romantik*, Dresden 1979.

2 Georg Simmel: "Der Bilderrahmen: Ein ästhetischer Versuch" (1902), in: idem: *Aufsätze und Abhandlungen 1901–1908*, 2 vols., vol. 1, ed. Rüdiger Kramme et al., Frankfurt am Main 1995, pp. 101–108, esp. p. 104.

3 Systems of reference, frameworks or frames are addressed in literary, theatre, film and media studies, as well as in philosophy, linguistics, the social and the neurosciences; see, for example, Claudia Benthien and Gabriele Klein (eds.): *Übersetzen und Rahmen: Praktiken medialer Transformationen*, Paderborn 2017; Uwe Wirth (ed.): *Rahmenbrüche – Rahmenwechsel*, Berlin 2013; Hans Körner and Karl Möseneder (eds.): *Rahmen zwischen Innen und Außen: Beiträge zur Theorie und Geschichte*, Berlin 2010; Ernst Pöppel: *Der Rahmen: Ein Blick des Gehirns auf unser Ich*, Munich 2006.

4 On this, see *In Perfect Harmony: Picture + Frame 1850–1920*, ed. Eva A. Mendgen, exh. cat. Van Gogh Museum, Amsterdam/ Kunstforum Wien, Zwolle 1995.

5 Shortly after the publication of Simmel's essay in November 1901, with reference to the thought that "the frame should *close* the painting", Harry Graf Kessler, a patron of the avant-garde, wrote: "It seems to me that this is based on a profound discrepancy between the view of art. […] an eschewal of designing life itself. Art fundamentally as an escape from life. Romanticism." Quoted in Simmel 1995 (see note 2), p. 359.

6 On the history of its origin, see Antoinette Le Normand-Romain: "L'«idylle enivrante» de l'été 1907: Maillol et Kessler", in: *Aristide Maillol (1861–1944): La quête de l'harmonie*, exh. cat. Musée d'Orsay, Paris et al., Paris 2022, pp. 207f.; Ursel Berger: "Konzeption und Ausführung in Maillols plastischem Werk", in: *Aristide Maillol*, ed. idem and Jörg Zutter, exh. cat. Georg Kolbe Museum, Berlin et al., Munich 1996, pp. 39–62.

7 See exh. cat. Berlin et al. 1996 (see note 6), p. 209.

8 See Berger 1996 (see note 6), pp. 46f.

9 Harry Graf Kessler: "Aristide Maillol", in: idem; *Aufsätze und Reden 1899–1933: Künstler und Nationen*, Frankfurt am Main 1988, pp. 263–271.

10 Ibid., p. 270.

11 See Katharina Henkel: *Moissey Kogan (1879–1943): Sein Leben und sein plastisches Werk*, Düsseldorf 2002, pp. 44f. I thank the author for her advice.

12 See Patrick Jullien (ed.): *Raymond Duchamp-Villon: Catalogue raisonné de l'œuvre sculpté et inventaire de l'œuvre graphique*, Paris 2020, pp. 302–313; Bénédicte Ajac: "Raymond Duchamp-Villon", in: *Collection art modern: La collection du Centre Pompidou, Musée national d'art moderne*, comp. Brigitte Léal, inv. cat. Centre Pompidou, Paris, 2006, pp. 210–214, esp. p. 211.

13 "Dans une harmonie des volumes, des plans et des lignes, le sujet important peu ou pas du tout." Raymond Duchamp-Villon, quoted in Ajac 2006 (see note 12), p. 211.

14 On her life and work, see, for example, *Genni. Jenny Wiegmann-Mucchi (1895–1969): Bildhauerin in Italien und Deutschland*, ed. Andrea Theissen, exh. cat. Zitadelle – Alte Kaserne, Berlin, Berlin 2017.

15 See Catherine McCormack: "Ich schau dir in die Augen, Maillol", in: Kunsthaus Zürich (ed.): *Maillol: Ein anderer Blick*, Zurich 2022, pp. 30–39.

16 See, for example, *Sophie Taeuber-Arp: Gelebte Abstraktion*, ed. Eva Reifert and Anne Umland, exh. cat. Kunstmuseum Basel/The Museum of Modern Art, New York, Munich 2021; *Bewegung und Gleichgewicht: Sophie Taeuber-Arp 1889–1943*, ed. Karin Schick et al., exh. cat. Kirchner Museum Davos/arp museum Bahnhof Rolandseck, Remagen, Bielefeld 2009.

17 The current coat of paint is not original. Arp, who restored numerous of Taeuber-Arp's works after her death, presumably overpainted the original one with a similar colour. I thank Walburga Krupp and Nicoline Zornikau for exchanging their ideas with me on this subject.

18 See *Niki de Saint Phalle*, exh. cat. Zürcher Kunstgesellschaft, Kunsthaus Zürich/Schirn Kunsthalle Frankfurt, Berlin 2022, pp. 27–47.

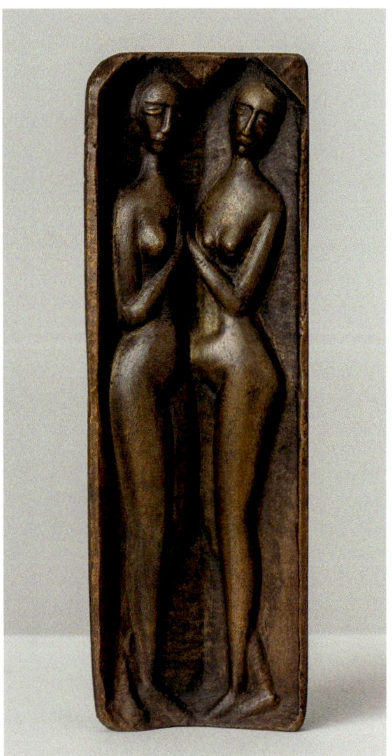

Cat. 66

Cat. 66   Moissey Kogan: *Two Female Nudes in Gothic Framing*,
           ca. 1927, bronze, reddish patina, 17 × 5.7 × 1.8 cm,
           Hamburger Kunsthalle, inv. no. S-1955-52 (Hamburg only)

Cat. 67   Raymond Duchamp-Villon: *The Lovers* (*Les Amants*), 1913,
           plaster, 34.5 × 52 × 6 cm, private collection, London

Cat. 67

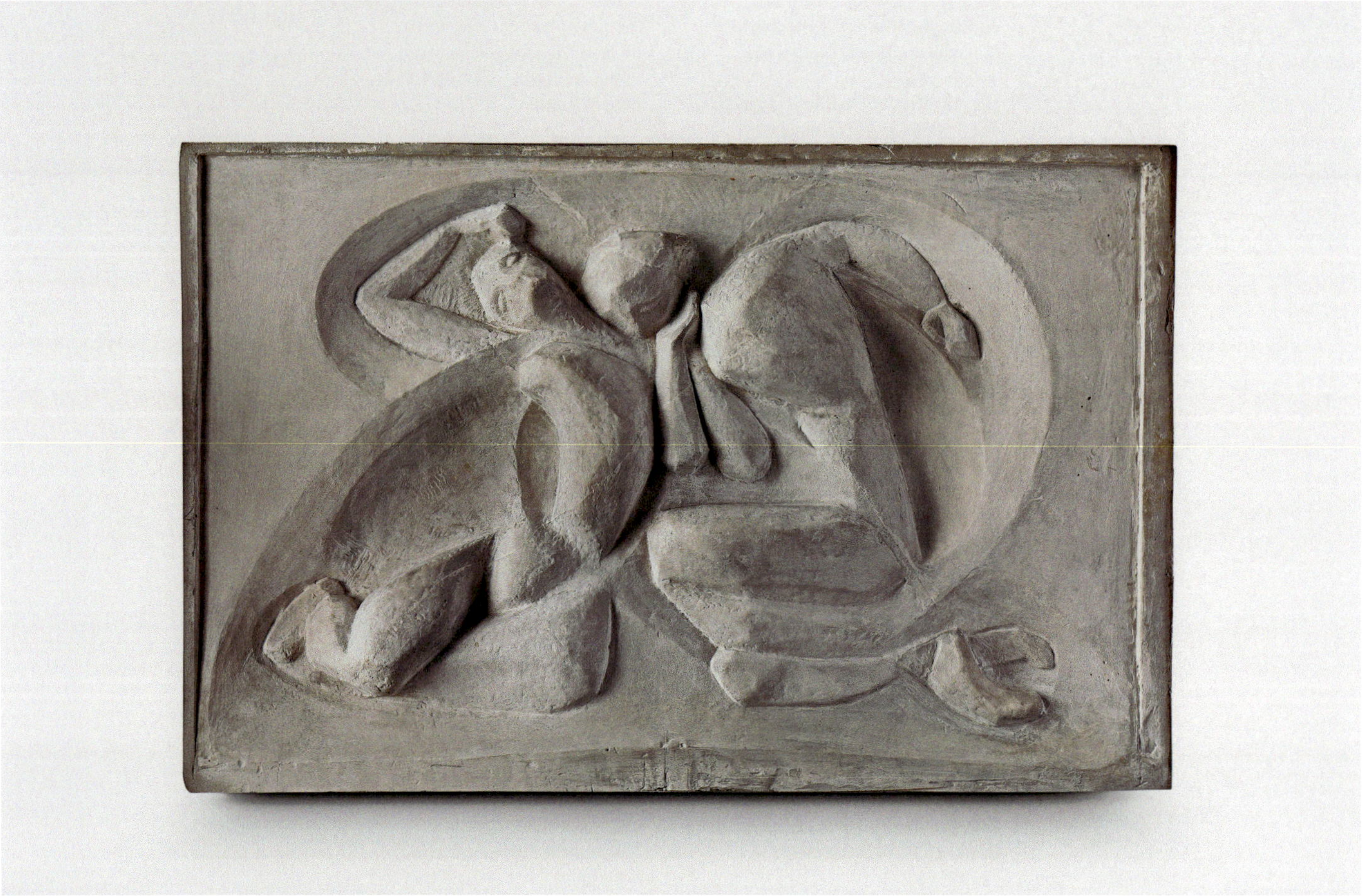

Cat. 68   Aristide Maillol: *Desire* (*Le Désir*), 1907, lead,
119 × 115 × 25 cm, Collection Museum Boijmans
Van Beuningen, Rotterdam, inv. no. BEK 1279 (MK)

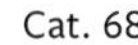

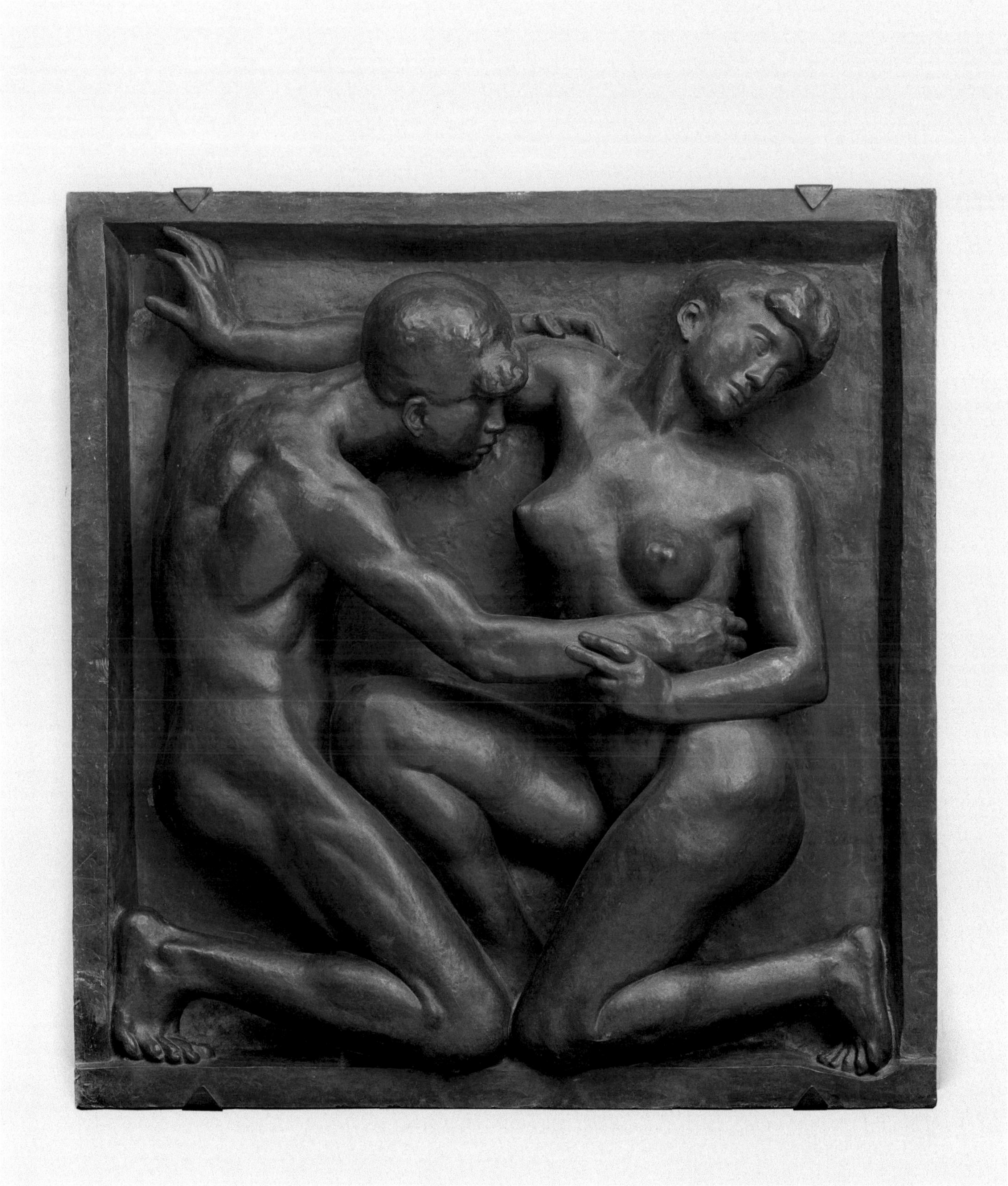

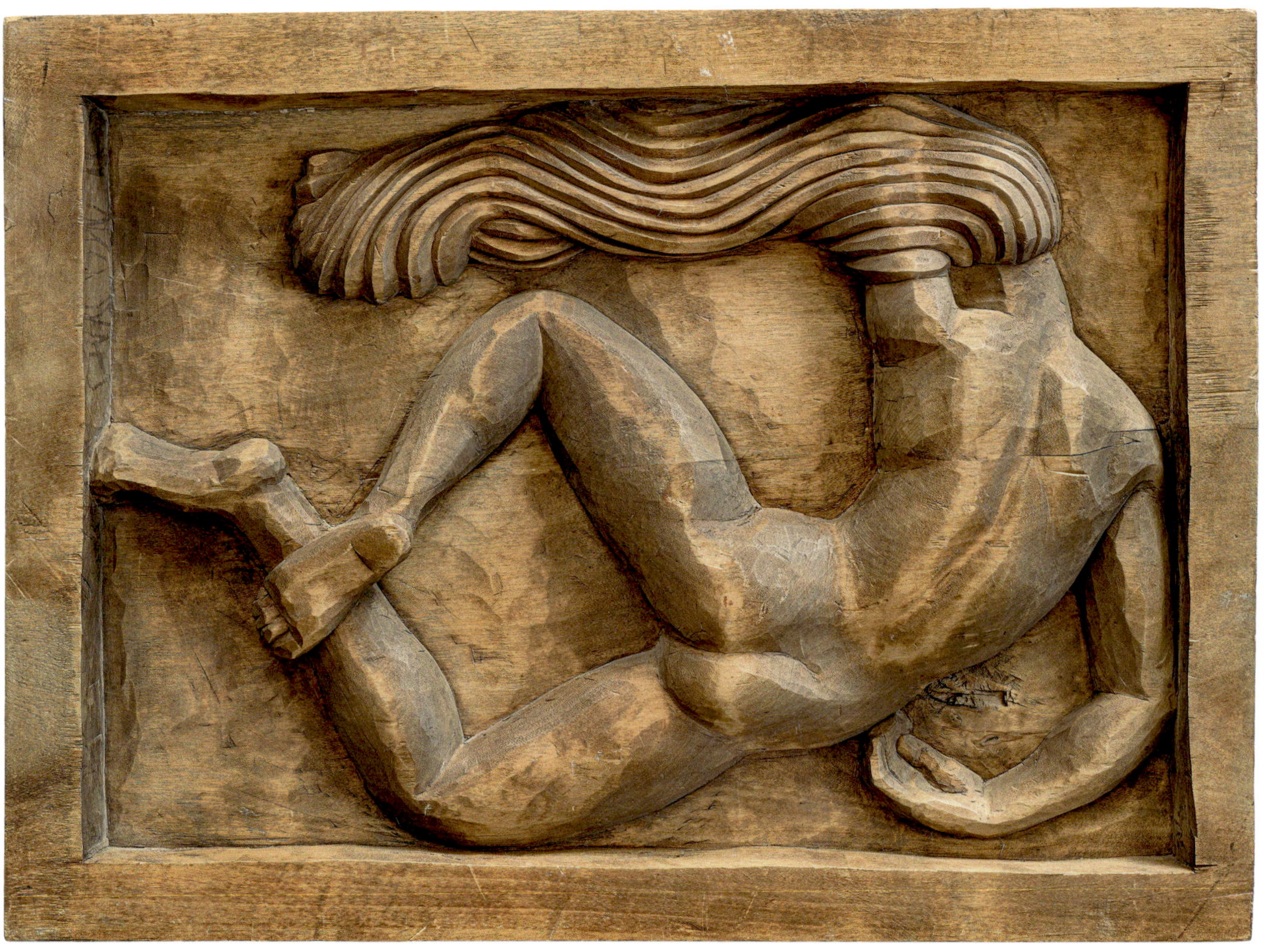

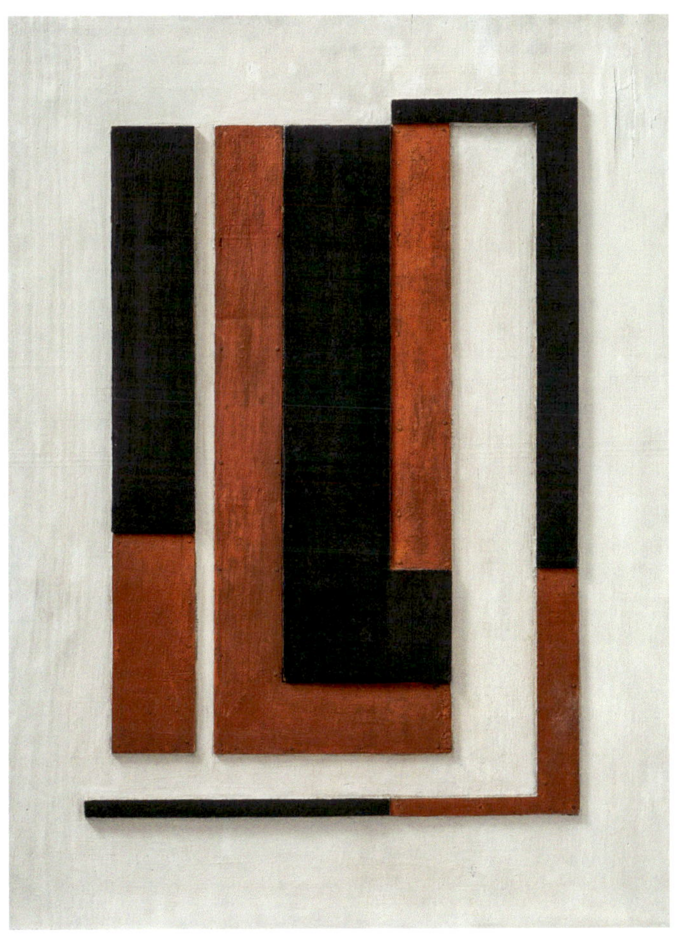

Cat. 70

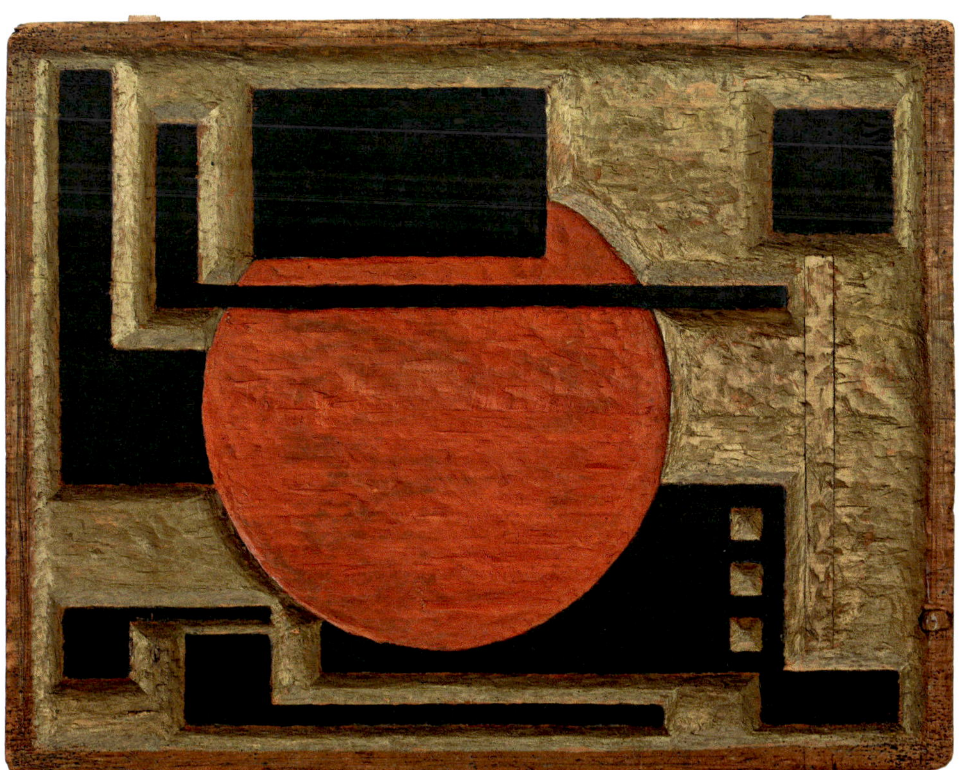

Cat. 71

Cat. 70   Erich Buchholz: *Black-Red on White*, 1922, tempera on plywood, mounted on blockboard, 82.7 × 63.8 cm, Hamburger Kunsthalle, inv. no. HK-5383 (Hamburg only)

Cat. 71   Erich Buchholz: *New Panel 3 (Wood Picture)*, 1923, oil on wood, 55.5 × 71.5 × 3 cm, Staatliche Kunsthalle Karlsruhe, inv. no. 2636

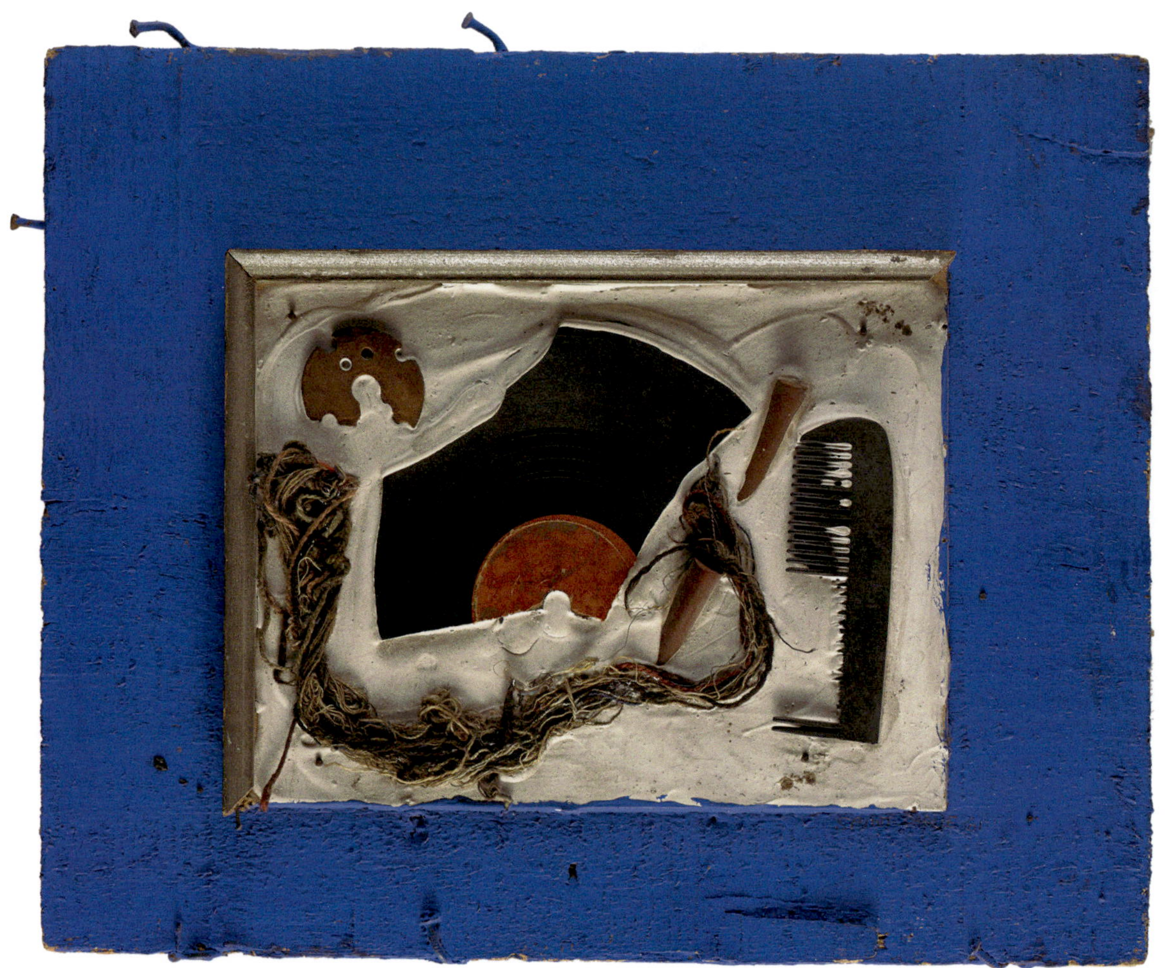

Cat. 72   Niki de Saint Phalle: *Assemblage No. 6*, 1961, assemblage on wooden panel painted blue, 25.5 × 32 × 3.5 cm, ahlers collection, inv. no. 003163 (Hamburg only)

Cat. 73   Sophie Taeuber-Arp: *Composition* (*Floating Forms*),
1935, oil on canvas, 50 × 65 cm, Hamburger Kunsthalle,
inv. no. HK-5229 (Hamburg only)

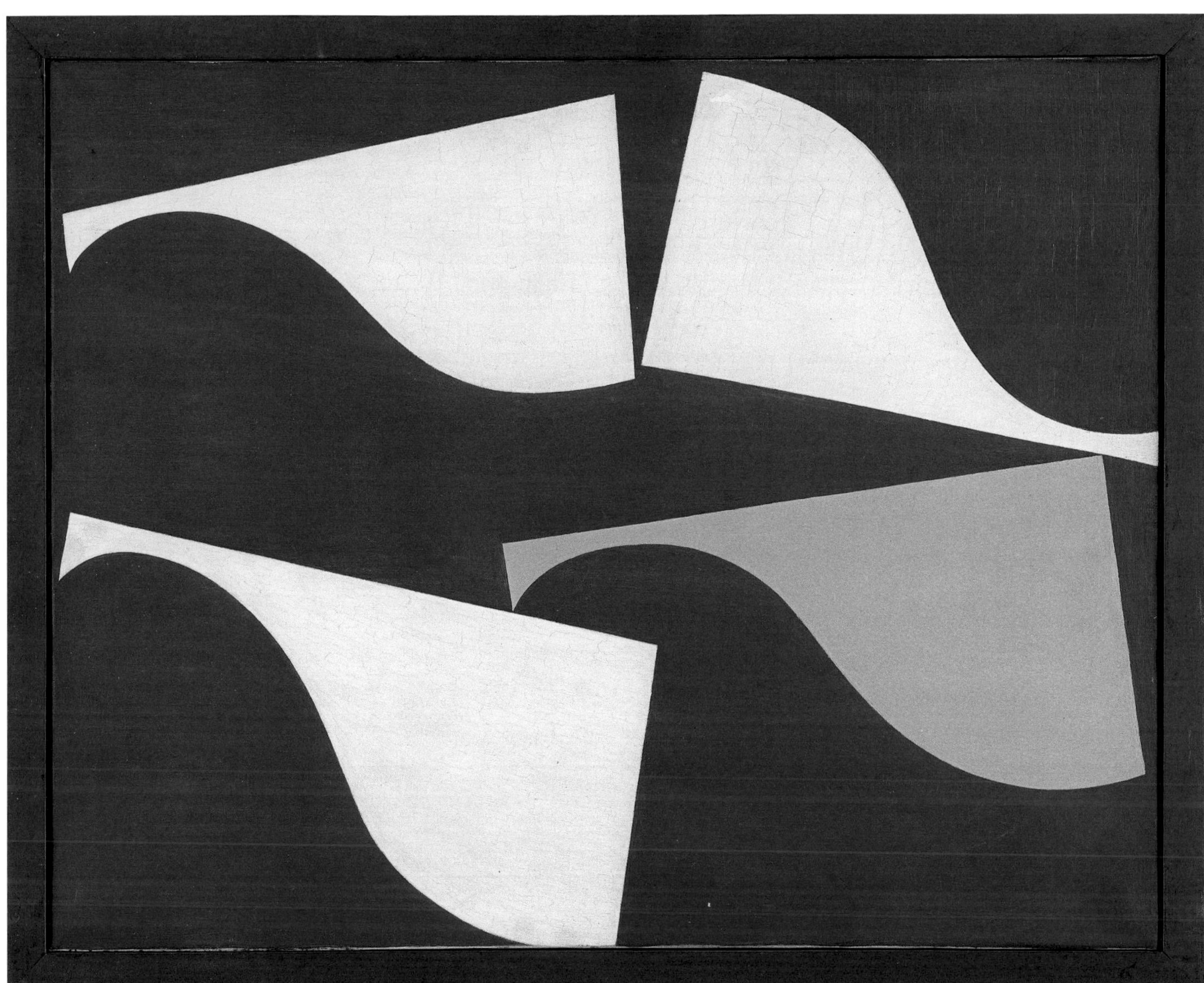

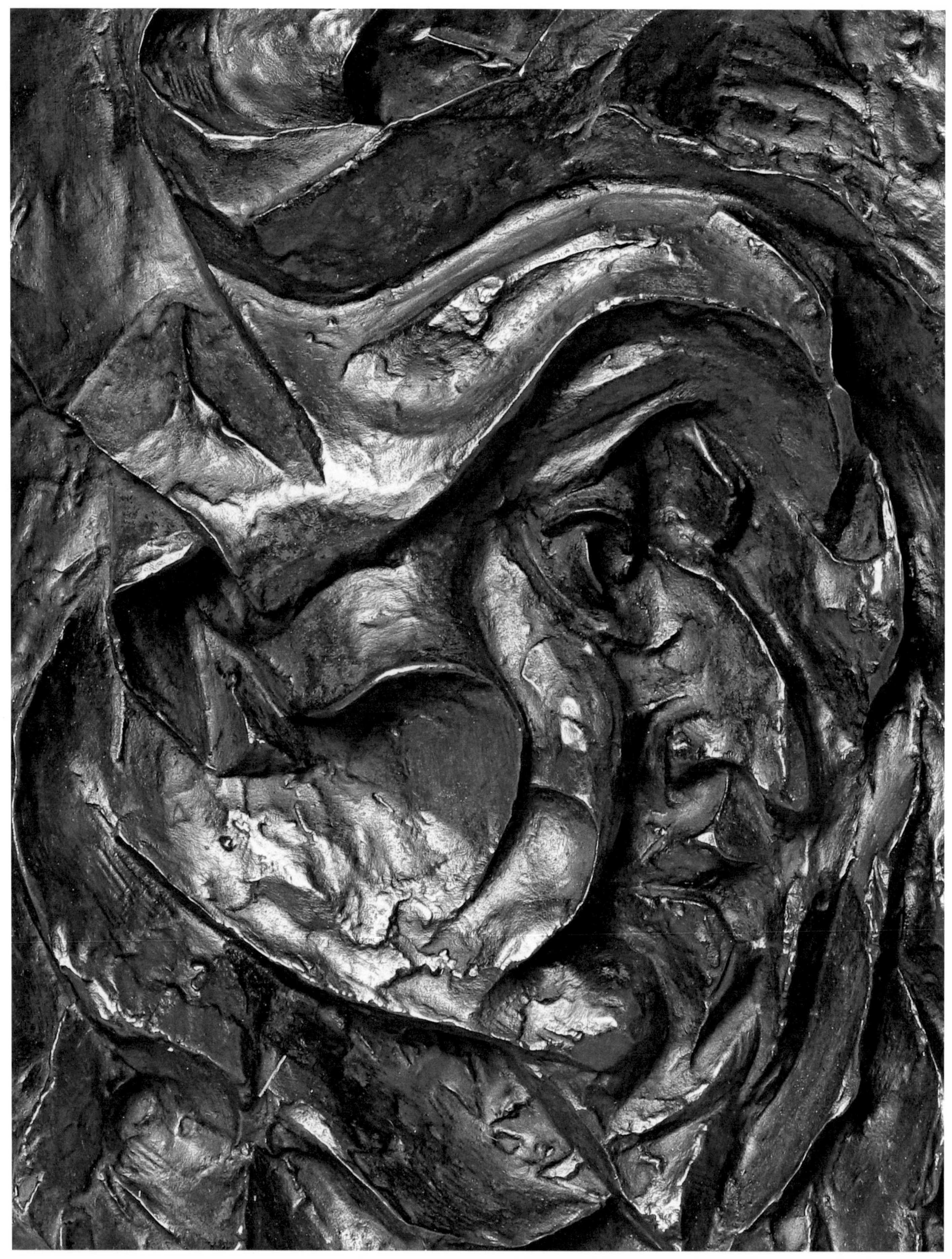

Cats. 74—85

Juliane Au

THE POLY-PERSPECTIVAL GAZE

On Planes in Space and Spatial Planes

With the start of the twentieth century, scientific and technical developments fundamentally changed society, the economy and culture in Europe. It was in particular the theory of relativity published by Albert Einstein in 1905 that cast a new light on correlations in the world. In his theory, Einstein formulated the reciprocal dependency between space and time, which is why from then on one spoke of a fourth possible dimension. Proceeding from the plane, artworks reconquered space, folding, bending and turning themselves into it[1] – as a medium attached to the wall and a spatial medium in equal measure, the relief presented an ideal playing field for this purpose.

Fascinated by this concept, artists developed new manners of representation in which the dimensions of space and the movements that took place within it were to be illustrated by means of the simultaneous rendition of multiple perspectives and vantage points. Especially the metropolis provided an abundance of stimuli and motifs for doing so, as the French writer Eugène Montfort described in a lecture in 1901: "The city dweller sees how his city is transformed. [...] The boulevards are furrowed by rails; street cars run in all shapes and sizes. A huge mechanical coming-and-going; the barbarian cry of the horns ruptures his ears; smoke and fumes from automobiles permeate him. At night, floods of electrical light blaze. Surrounded by moon-coloured light, everything seems strange, artificial, unreal. It is as though passers-by and vehicles are moving on a theatre stage, among props."[2]

In his *Simultaneous Windows* (cat. 74) from 1912, which stems from a series of more than twenty paintings, Robert Delaunay reproduces the Eiffel Tower in bright colours and rhythmical forms. Built on the occasion of the 1889 Exposition Universelle in Paris, it was considered the epitome of modernity, technology and communication, as it was also used by the military as a radio tower. Delaunay broke the motif up into colour fields that he juxtaposed with one another, and in doing so illustrated the dynamics of the modern experience in the inseparable interaction between light, space and movement. He subsumed the resulting kaleidoscope-like effects under the term "simultanéité", as the impressions were not depicted successively but at the same time and were made visible in their interplay.[3] The flickering colour contrasts and detailed colour fields hold the viewer's gaze in constant motion and dynamise the image, which seems to expand out into the surrounding space via the frame, painted in the same manner as the picture (→ Relief and Frame). According to Delaunay, the perceptual process itself became the subject of art: "Without visual sensibility there is no light, no movement. Light in nature creates the movement of colors. Movement is produced by the rapport of odd elements, of the contrasts of colors between themselves which constitutes reality. This reality is endowed with vastness (we see as far as the stars), and it then becomes rhythmic simultaneity."[4] The view of the city becomes a kind of stage area that, still entirely bound to the wall, slides into the viewer's space by means of its rhythmisation. The facets of colour, light and movement condense to become a simultaneous, immediate experience of space and time, which is supported by the physical protrusion of the painting.[5]

At the beginning of the twentieth century, one of the first painters who sought to capture several perspectives simultaneously was Pablo Picasso. Through his examination of the collection of the Musée d'Ethnographie du Trocadéro, among others, beginning in 1906 he produced numerous sketches containing reduced body shapes from various angles of vision, culminating in the large-scale painting *Les Demoiselles d'Avignon* (fig. 4) in the summer of 1907. In this work, Picasso abandoned the central perspective for the first time and combined different views of faces and bodies.[6] Subsequently, he dealt increasingly with space, light and movement, and the possibilities of their portrayal. At the same time he also created sculptural works, about which he told the sculptor Julio González that "it is only necessary to cut them [the paintings] out – the colors are only the indications of different perspectives, of planes inclined from one side to the other – then assemble them according to the indications given by the color, in order to find oneself in the presence of a 'Sculpture'."[7] This is demonstrated by several of Picasso's portraits: for instance, whereas *Clovis Sagot* from the spring of 1909 (fig. 1) plays with polyperspectivity only in the area of the sleeves, the portraits of his companion Fernande Olivier, produced somewhat later, are characterised by a distinct fragmentation of the planes and points of view. The painting *Portrait of Fernande Olivier* (cat. 84) features the head, neck and shoulders as fragmented, geometric forms that open up spatiality in the plane of the canvas. The colours of the individual elements seem independent from one another, even though they were taken from the same earthy palette. A short time later, Picasso produced the bust *Head of a Woman (Fernande)* (fig. 2) by assembling the planar segments of the painting to a sculpted head – thus transferring the simulated space in the painting into real space.[8]

Head of a Woman (Fernande) was bought by the art dealer Ambroise Vollard, regularly put on display, and cast several times in bronze. The Czech art theorist and collector Vincenc Kramář bought one of these casts and, in 1913, presented it in the third exhibition of Skupina výtvarných umělců (Group of Fine Artists).[9] The founding members of this Prague-based group also included the Czech Otto Gutfreund, who went to Paris in 1909/10 to study at the Académie de la Grande Chaumière with the sculptor Émile-Antoine Bourdelle. While there, he came into contact with Cubist works that left a lasting impression on him.[10] In his bronze relief *Head*[11] from 1912 (cat. 75), Gutfreund imbedded a face – possibly his own – reproduced in profile in freely arranged, swirling forms. Supported by dramatic light effects on the animated, reflecting surface, the entire motif seems to get caught in the vortex of its formal composition.[12] Hence, the portrait becomes not only a sensuously tangible vis-à-vis, but expands the frontal arrangement of classic reliefs to produce a psychological image that incorporates both the viewer and space.

Gutfreund's three-dimensional *Cellist* (cat. 76), which was produced at about the same time, is a relief-like form consisting of various planes that unite different perspectives and seem to condense into a single movement: one nearly believes one is seeing the cellist's bow moving expansively over the instrument's strings. The interlocking Cubist volumes translate this fluid movement into a form assembled out of individual views, which allows the musical process to become discernible in its complexity.[13] Beginning in about 1912, Picasso also repeatedly addressed music in his art. He drew on simple materials, as with *Violin* (cat. 80) where he bent, cut and folded four metal sheets, which he painted black, white, brown and blue and provided with smaller iron wire applications. Although the paint is not intended to imitate a real violin, it does make reference to one – the work seems to be an abstracted version of the instrument that was supposedly broken up into its individual parts and then reassembled in order to simultaneously render visible the wide range of views. The f-holes have been replaced by displaced, upright oblong holes cut into the metal, and a horizontal blue object seems to make reference to a bow; both elements are necessary for generating sound in the resonating body.[14] The artist interwove the interior and exterior of the instrument, vibrantly demonstrated by the burst-open surfaces lifted from the wall into space – here, the relief provided Picasso with the opportunity to experiment with sound, surface and their expansion. He produced spatiality in a similar way in his painting *Man with Guitar* (cat. 77), which he created in 1918 on the occasion of the wedding of his friend Guillaume Apollinaire. In this Cubist composition, the individual parts of the design also make reference to the surface as well as its potential to expand, like a relief, into space by means of the effect of colour, form and imagined sound.

In the incipient twentieth century, the subject of music was widespread in art in the context of synaesthetic experiences and considerations with respect to the Gesamtkunstwerk. In 1909, the Ballets Russes began celebrating success on the stages of the French capital. The creative exploration of movement in space by means of light, colour and musical rhythm fascinated many artists, who, like Pablo Picasso and Robert Delaunay, in part designed their own stage sets and costumes and drew inspiration from the stage productions.[15] The idea of a "musicalisation" of visual art can be found in the work of, amongst others, Wassily Kandinsky, Ossip Zadkine and Alexander Archipenko, as well as the Cubist sculptor Jacques Lipchitz[16] who formed his works out of what came across as massive volumes. Lipchitz developed

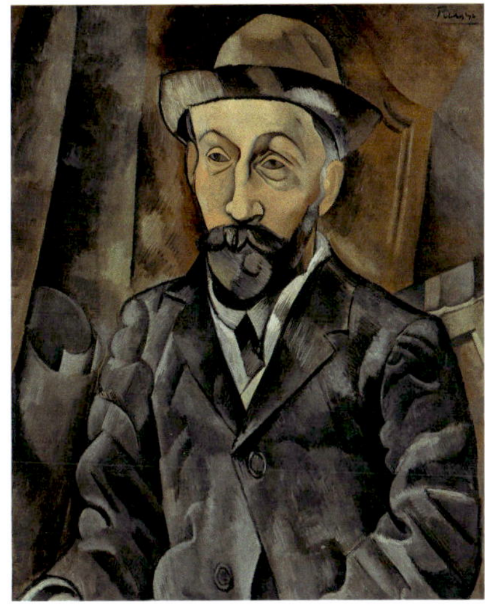

Fig. 1

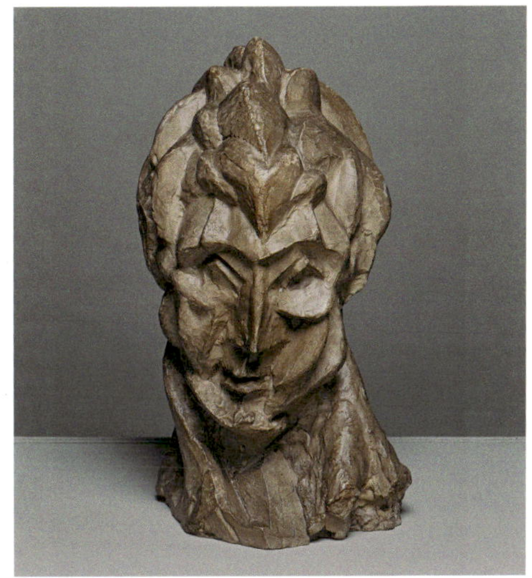

Fig. 2

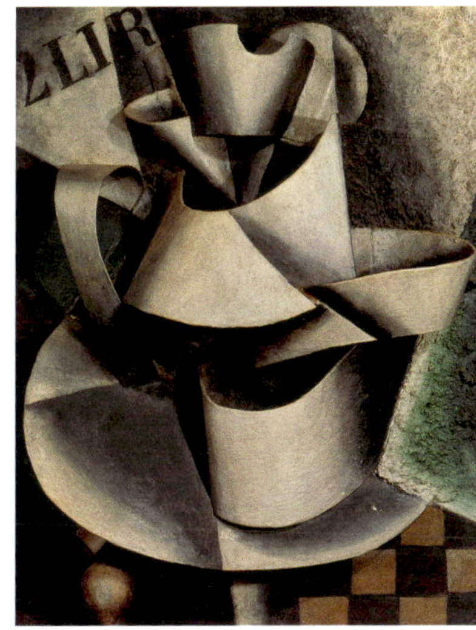

Fig. 3

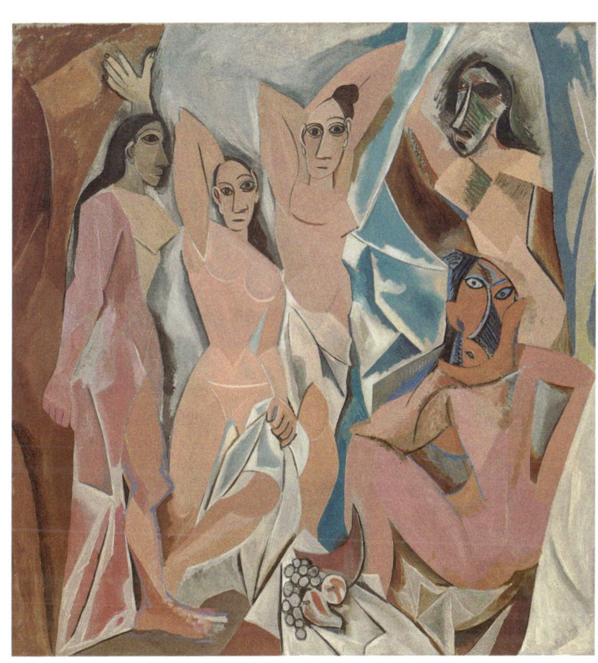

Fig. 4

a formal language based on geometry that, at first glance, seems static yet is full of movement.[17] At the same time, the surface of the material is just as important as the interaction of the different forms and visual axes.[18]

In the case of Lipchitz' sculpture from 1919, *Seated Man with Clarinet II* (cat. 79), the light flows gently over the bronze, whose uneven, animated surface contrasts with the rigour of the Cubist blocks. The shapes of the body being depicted are segmented, and various views of the figure are intertwined, which, among other things, allows one to see the opening of the clarinet's bell. Does Lipchitz want to suggest that the clarinettist is about to raise his instrument in order to play a note or a solo? Are physical movement and sound to be mentally transmitted into space?[19] Despite its polyperspectival nature the work is clearly designed to be oriented towards a wall[20] – here, too, space and effect develop, in the sense of the relief, out of the surface of the rear wall. In Lipchitz' opinion, a sculpture accentuates the space surrounding it in a way that is similar to sounds by means of their resonance. A spatiotemporal experience intended to connect viewers or listeners to the work and space hence first originates in the mind.[21]

In contrast, Alexander Archipenko,[22] who was born in what is today Ukraine and who moved to Paris when he was nineteen, understood sculpture itself as space that is sometimes surrounded and defined by material. *Bather* from 1915 (cat. 83) is an example of his early so-called *sculpto-paintings*, in which

Fig. 1   Pablo Picasso: *The Art Dealer Clovis Sagot*, 1909, oil on canvas, Hamburger Kunsthalle

Fig. 2   Pablo Picasso: *Head of a Woman (Fernande)* (*Tête de femme* [*Fernande*]), 1909, plaster, Tate Modern, London

Fig. 3   Lyubov Popova: *Jug on Table*, 1915, oil on card on panel, State Tretyakov Gallery, Moscow

Fig. 4   Pablo Picasso: *Les Demoiselles d'Avignon*, 1907, oil on canvas, The Museum of Modern Art, New York

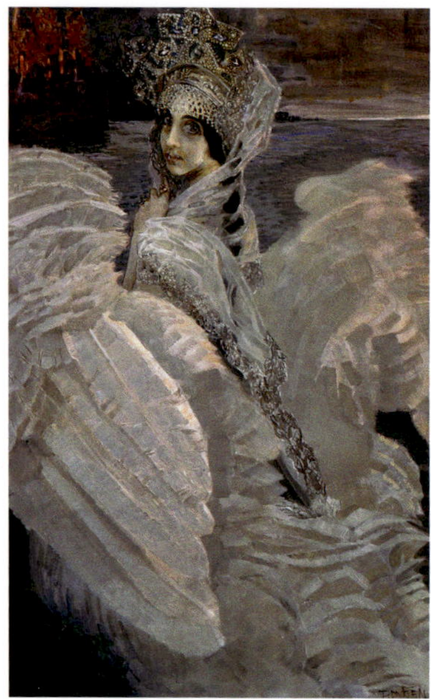

Fig. 5

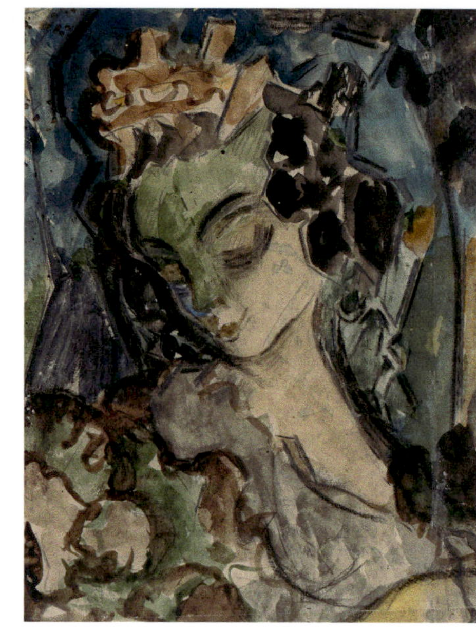

Fig. 6

Fig. 5   Mikhail Vrubel: *The Swan Princess*, 1900, oil on canvas, State Tretyakov Gallery, Moscow

Fig. 6   Naum Gabo: *Young Girl*, 1912, watercolour, chalk and pencil on paper, Berlinische Galerie – Landesmuseum für Moderne Kunst, Fotografie und Architektur

he experimented with a combination of both genres without explicitly creating a classic relief. Archipenko designed polychrome convex and concave forms out of wire, papiermâché and plaster, depicting a standing figure. When viewers move past it, it seems to revolve around itself from out of the plane.[23] Like Henri Laurens' *Woman with Earrings* from 1921 (cat. 81), in its entirety the frontally oriented work appears to be static, whereas the individual elements seem animated.[24] Time and again, Archipenko manages to cause the boundaries of the genres and space to become permeable: when walking round *Female Torso* from 1922 (cat. 82), it also creates the impression of a graceful rotation,[25] and in the relief *Two Glasses on a Table* from 1919/20 (cat. 78), the ordinary motif of a laid table seems to be fragmented into planes and reassembled according to spatial aspects. With his genre-bursting *sculpto-paintings*, which broke away from the wall, Archipenko exerted a great deal of impact on an entire generation of Russian artists, including, for instance, Lyubov Popova (fig. 3), with her "sculptural paintings", and Vladimir Tatlin, who rendered his concepts of space, colour and movement in Constructivist works (→ Designs of the World).[26]

The Russian Naum Gabo[27] likewise experimented with the use of various perspectives and the potential of space, which he wanted to encompass and capture in his sculptures. His *Constructive Head No. 1* from 1915 (cat. 85) – which would be followed by another three of this type – consists of plywood planes fitted together

with the help of indentations. On the one hand, in the faceting of the forms this first head can be traced back to the influential paintings of Mikhail Vrubel (fig. 5), which Gabo had already taken up in a drawing (fig. 6) in 1912, and on the other hand to the compositional schemes of Russian icons in the asymmetry of the shoulders and the inclined posture of the head. Gabo purposely did not work out the volumes of the head, but only alluded to them with the help of the planes and their expansion. Thus he established the surrounding space as a sculptural element (→ Boundary and Space of Possibility) by creating the impression of rhythm and animateness by means of shading, as a result playing with the principles of the relief in a completely new manner.[28]

From an intimate dialogue with portraits by Pablo Picasso, Otto Gutfreund or Naum Gabo to Robert Delaunay's *Simultaneous Windows*, which incorporated all of urban space, the present works testify to various attempts at the outset of the twentieth century to integrate new ideas about space and time into art, and to cause the artwork to extend far beyond itself. Polyperspectival approaches allowed an overcoming of the conventional boundaries of space, time or genre and hence the accommodation of a changing modern reality. In doing so, the relief as something "between" painting and sculpture was not only more current than ever but became the point of departure for a wide variety of planar and spatial concepts that found expression in all genres.

1   See Margit Rowell: "The Planar Dimension 1912–1932: From Surface to Space", in: *The Planar Dimension: Europe, 1912–1932*, ed. idem, exh. cat. The Solomon R. Guggenheim Museum, New York, 1979, pp. 8–31, esp. p. 9.

2   "Le citadin voit sa ville se transformer. […] Les avenues sont sillonnées de rails; des tramways de toutes formes et de toutes dimensions circulent. Un immense va et vient mécanique; le cri barbare des cornes déchire ses oreilles; la fumée, l'odeur automobile l'imprègnent. La nuit, ce sont des flots de lumière électrique. Enveloppés par ces rayons couleur de lune, tout parait étrange, artificiel, irréel. Les passants et les voitures semblent se mouvoir sur une scène de théatre, au milieu de décors." Eugène Montfort: *La Beauté modern: Conférences du Collège d'Esthétique* (*février–juin 1901*), Paris 1902, p. 88.

3   See Simonetta Fraquelli: "Paris als Muse: Die Gemälde von Robert Delaunay, 1909–1938", in: *Robert Delaunay und Paris*, ed. Esther Braun-Kalberer et al., exh. cat. Kunsthaus Zürich 2018, pp. 14–25.

4   He formulated this in the summer of 1912 in his text *La lumière* with an eye towards Michel Eugène Chevreul (*De la loi du contraste simultané des couleurs*, 1839), who made reference to the simultaneity of optical interactions; https://www.artchive.com/ artchive/D/delaunay.html (accessed 13 February 2023).

5   See Pascal Rousseau: "Das Schauspiel der Malerei", in: *Robert Delaunay – Sonia Delaunay: Das Centre Pompidou zu Gast in Hamburg*, ed. Uwe M. Schneede and Karin Schick, exh. cat. Hamburger Kunsthalle, Cologne 1999, pp. 10–22.

6   See Brigitte Léal, Christine Piot and Marie-Laure Bernadac: *The Ultimate Picasso*, New York 2000, pp. 107–118. On the importance of the collections of the Musée du Trocadéro, see *Through the Eyes of Picasso: Face to Face with African and Oceanic Art*, ed. Yves Le Fur, exh. cat. Musée du quai Branly, Paris, Paris 2017.

7   "[…] il suffirait de les découper – les couleurs n'étant somme toute, que des indications de perspectives différentes, des plans inclinés d'un côté ou de l'autre, – puis les assembler selon les indications données par la couleur, pour se trouver en présence d'une 'Sculpture'." Julio González: "Picasso sculpteur: Exposition de sculptures récentes de Picasso", *Cahiers d'Art* 11, nos. 6/7 (1936/37), p. 189. English translation in Museum of Modern Art, *Julio Gonzalez*, trans. Mary S. Coxe, exh. cat. Museum of Modern Art, New York; Minneapolis Institute of Art, Minneapolis 1956, p. 44; www.moma.org/calendar/ exhibitions/3333 (accessed 13 February 2023).

8   See Ann Temkin and Anne Umland: "Picasso Sculpture: An Introduction", in: *Picasso: Sculpture*, ed. idem, exh. cat. The Museum of Modern Art, New York, 2015, pp. 12–17.

9   See ibid.

10   See *Otto Gutfreund*, exh. cat. Museum Kampa, Prague, 2003, n.p.

11   It is uncertain whether Gutfreund provided this work with a title himself. Several titles are mentioned in the literature, in addition to *Head*, *Self-Portrait* and *Portrait of the Artist's Father IV*. Since each of these includes an interpretation of the work, but at the same time cannot be verified, in this text the neutral title of *Head* is used. The National Gallery Prague, which also owns a cast, uses the title *Hlava-reliéf* (*Autoportrét*) (*Head-Relief* [*Self-Portrait*]); see the online collection of the National Gallery Prague, https://sbirky.ngprague.cz/dielo/ CZE:NG.P_5063 (accessed 13 February 2023).

12   See *Czech Modern Art. 1900–1960*, ed. Lenka Bydžovská and Lenka Zapletalová, inv. cat. National Gallery Prague 1995, pp. 100–112.

13   See Tomáš Vlček: "Tschechischer Kubismus in den Jahren 1912–1916: Ouvertüre der Avantgarde in Mitteleuropa", in: *Tschechischer Kubismus 1912–1916*, ed. Agnes Husslein-Arco, exh. cat. Rupertinum, Museum für moderne Kunst Salzburg, 2001, pp. 21–32, esp. p. 28.

14   See exh. cat. New York 2015 (see note 8), p. 81.

15   See Alexandra Keiser: "Encircling Space: An Introduction to Alexander Archipenko", in: *Alexander Archipenko: Space Encircled*, exh. cat. Eykyn Maclean Gallery, New York, 2018, pp. 7–15, esp. p. 10.

16   Born as Chaim Jakob Lipschitz.

17   See Karin Sagner: "Feuerhunde: Der Kamin von Jacques Lipchitz für das legendäre Studio von Jacques Doucet", in: *Jacques Lipchitz: Bildhauer des 20. Jahrhunderts*, ed. Ingrid Mössinger, Karin Sagner and Diana Kopka, exh. cat. Kunstsammlungen Chemnitz, Dresden 2017, pp. 21–41, esp. p. 21.

18   See A. M. Hammacher: "Jacques Lipchitz, 1891–1973: A Concise Survey of His Life and Work", in: Alan G. Wilkinson (ed.): *The Sculpture of Jacques Lipchitz. A Catalogue Raisonné*, vol. 1: *The Paris Years, 1910–1940*, New York et al. 1996, pp. 7–15.

19   See Catherine Pütz: *Jacques Lipchitz: The First Cubist Sculptor*, London 2002, pp. 8–17.

20   See Rowell 1979 (see note 1), p. 11.

21   See Karin Sagner: "Musica humana: Zur Bedeutung der Musik im Werk von Jacques Lipchitz am Beispiel von *Benediction*", in: exh. cat. Chemnitz 2017 (see note 17), pp. 95–119.

22   Born as Олександр Архипенко/ Oleksandr Arkhypenko.

23   See Keiser 2018 (see note 15), pp. 7–15, esp. p. 13.

24   See Thomas Kellein: "Kubismus aus Chartres – Frauen von Gott", in: *Henri Laurens: Frauenbilder, Frauenkörper*, ed. idem, exh. cat. Kunsthalle Bielefeld 2001, pp. 9–22.

25   See Keiser 2018 (see note 15), p. 9.

26   See Christina Lodder: "Archipenko – The Russian Dimension", in: exh. cat. New York 2018 (see note 15), pp. 17–27.

27   Born as Наум Певснер/Naum Pevsner.

28   See Martin Hammer and Christina Lodder: *Constructing Modernity: The Art & Career of Naum Gabo*, New Haven and London 2000, pp. 20–49.

Cat. 74 Robert Delaunay: *Simultaneous Windows (Les Fenêtres simultanées sur la ville. 1re partie, 2e motif, 1re réplique)*, 1912, mixed media on canvas with painted spruce frame, 72.5 × 66 × 7 cm, Hamburger Kunsthalle, permanent loan from the Stiftung Hamburger Kunstsammlungen, inv. no. HK-5055 (Hamburg only)

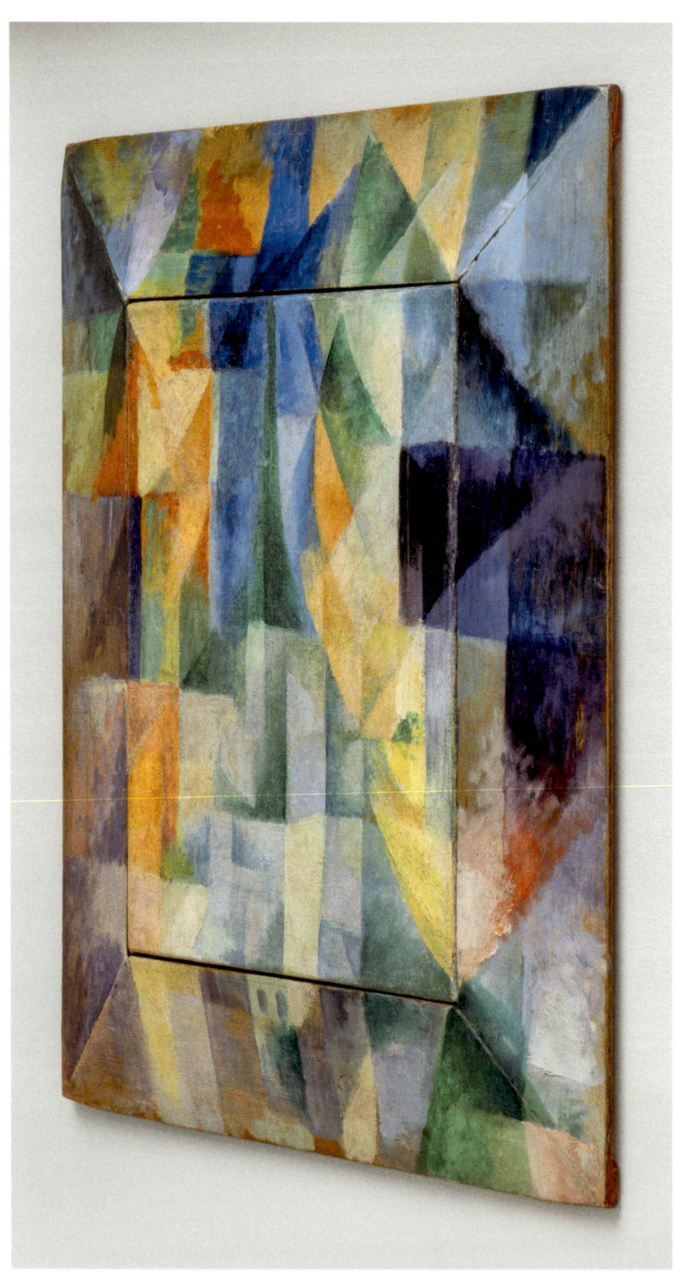

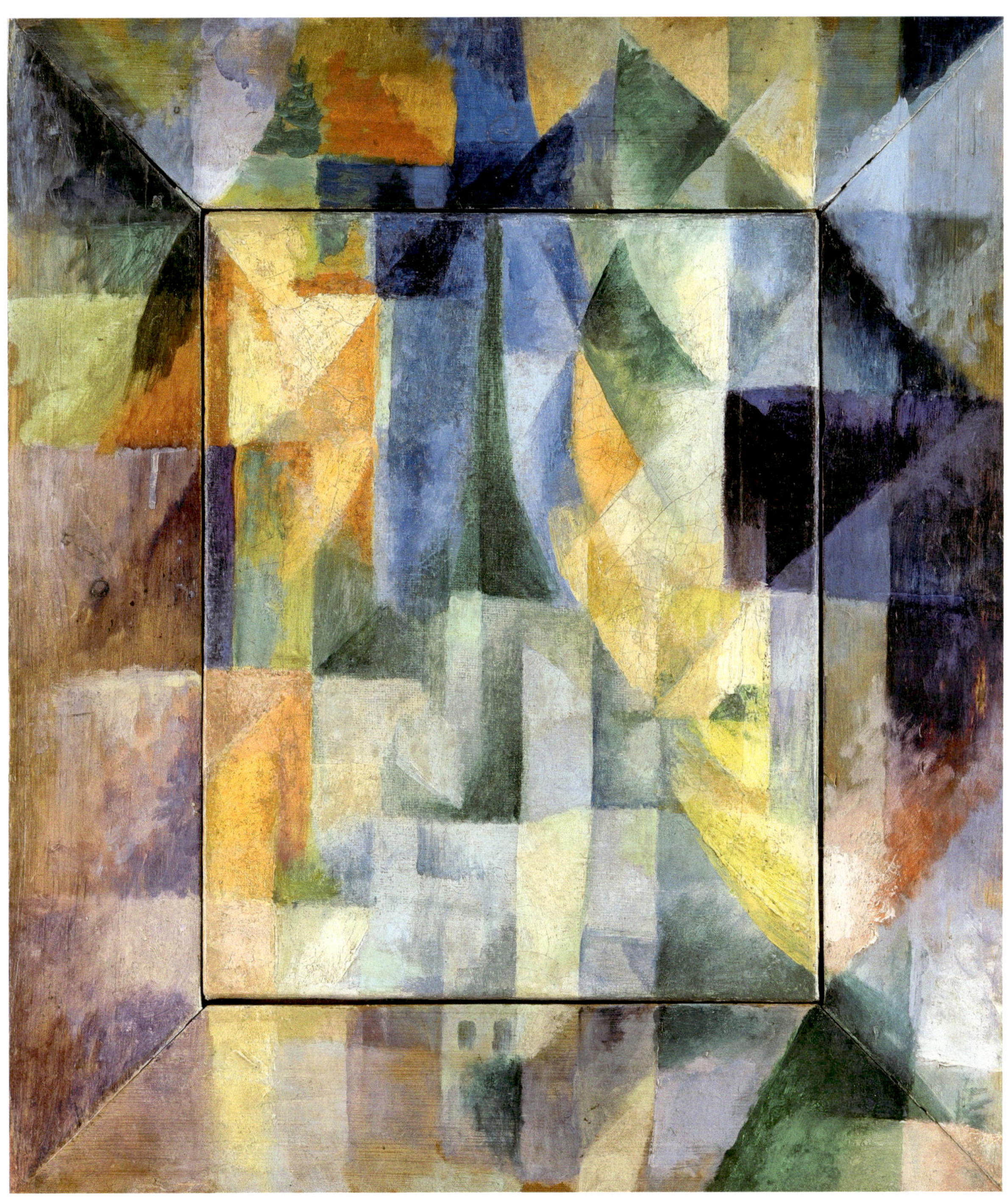

Cat. 75   Otto Gutfreund: *Head*, 1912, bronze, 36 × 27 × 5.5 cm,
private collection, London

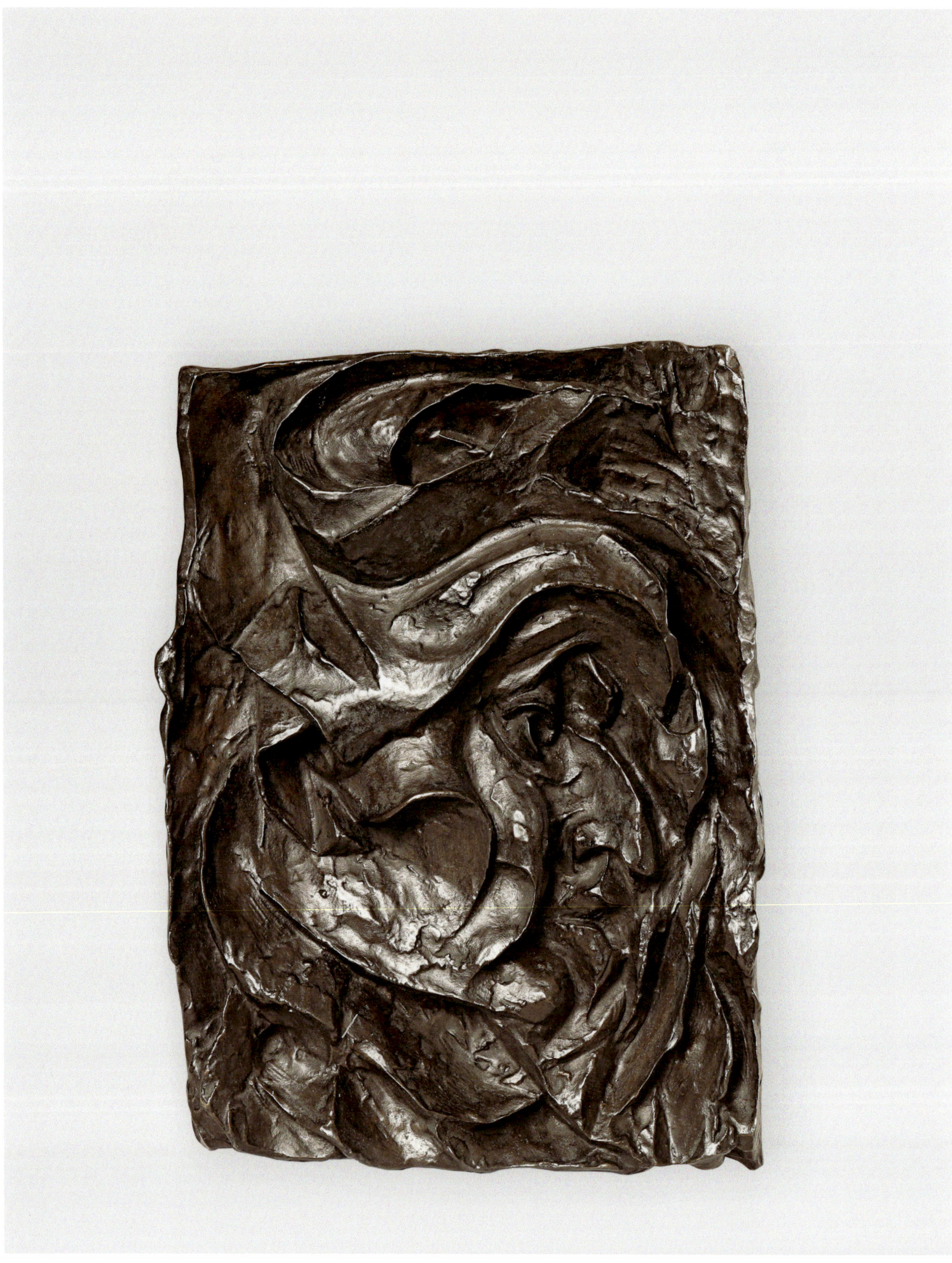

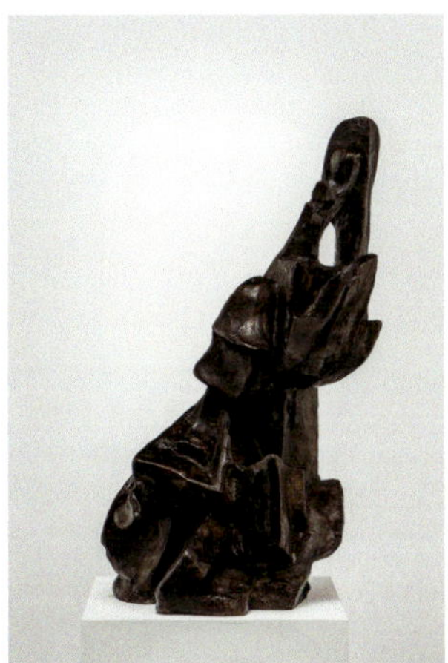

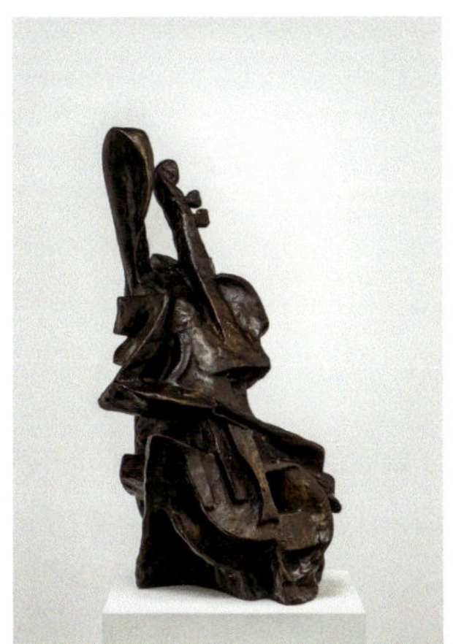

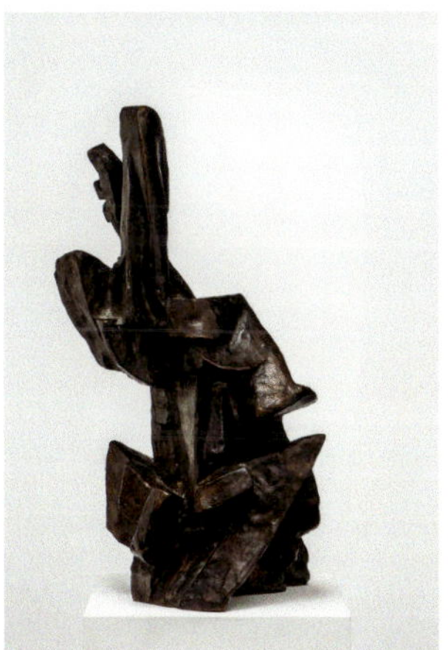

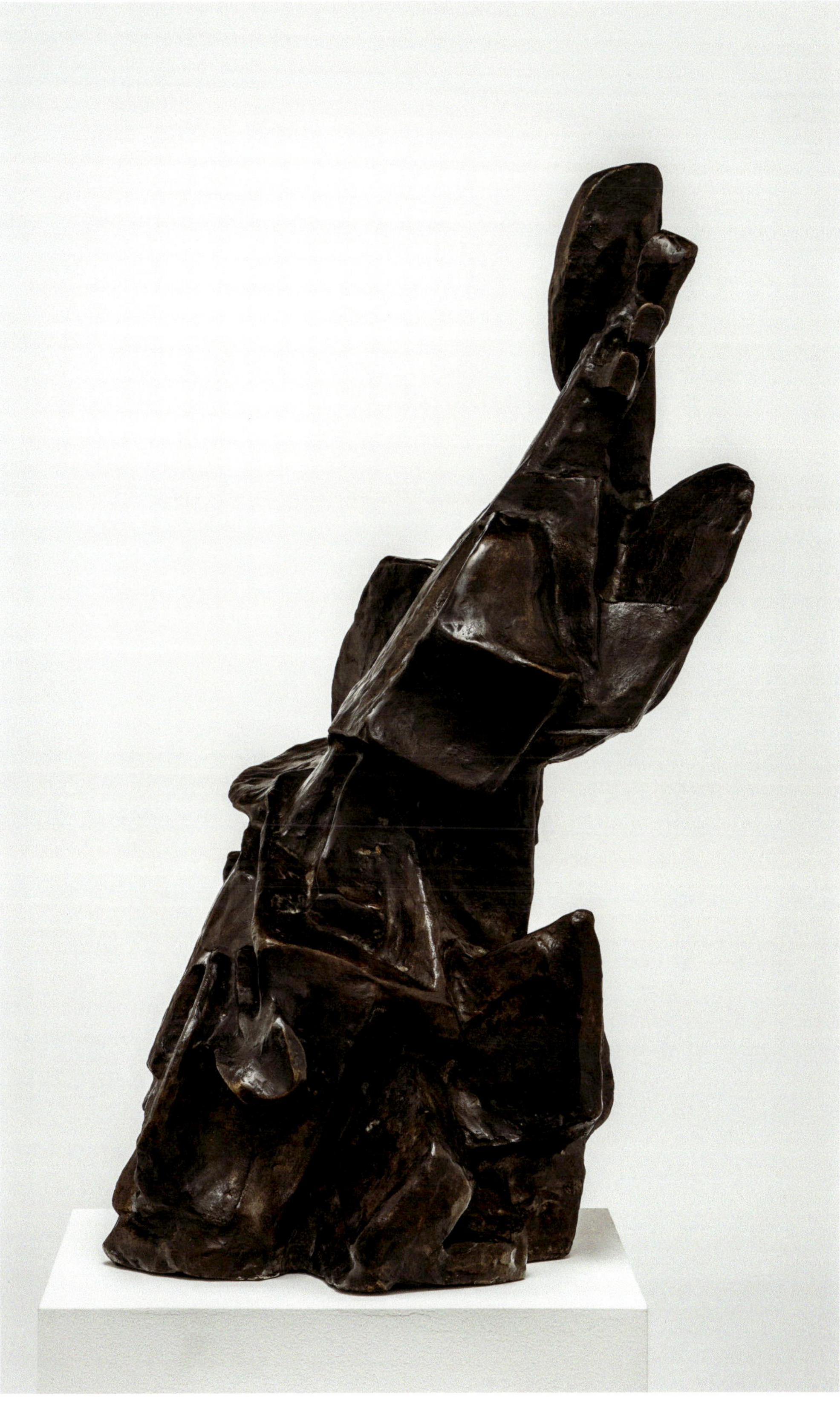

Cat. 77   Pablo Picasso: *Man with Guitar* (*Homme à la guitare*), 1918, oil on canvas, 130 × 89 cm, Hamburger Kunsthalle, inv. no. HK-5151

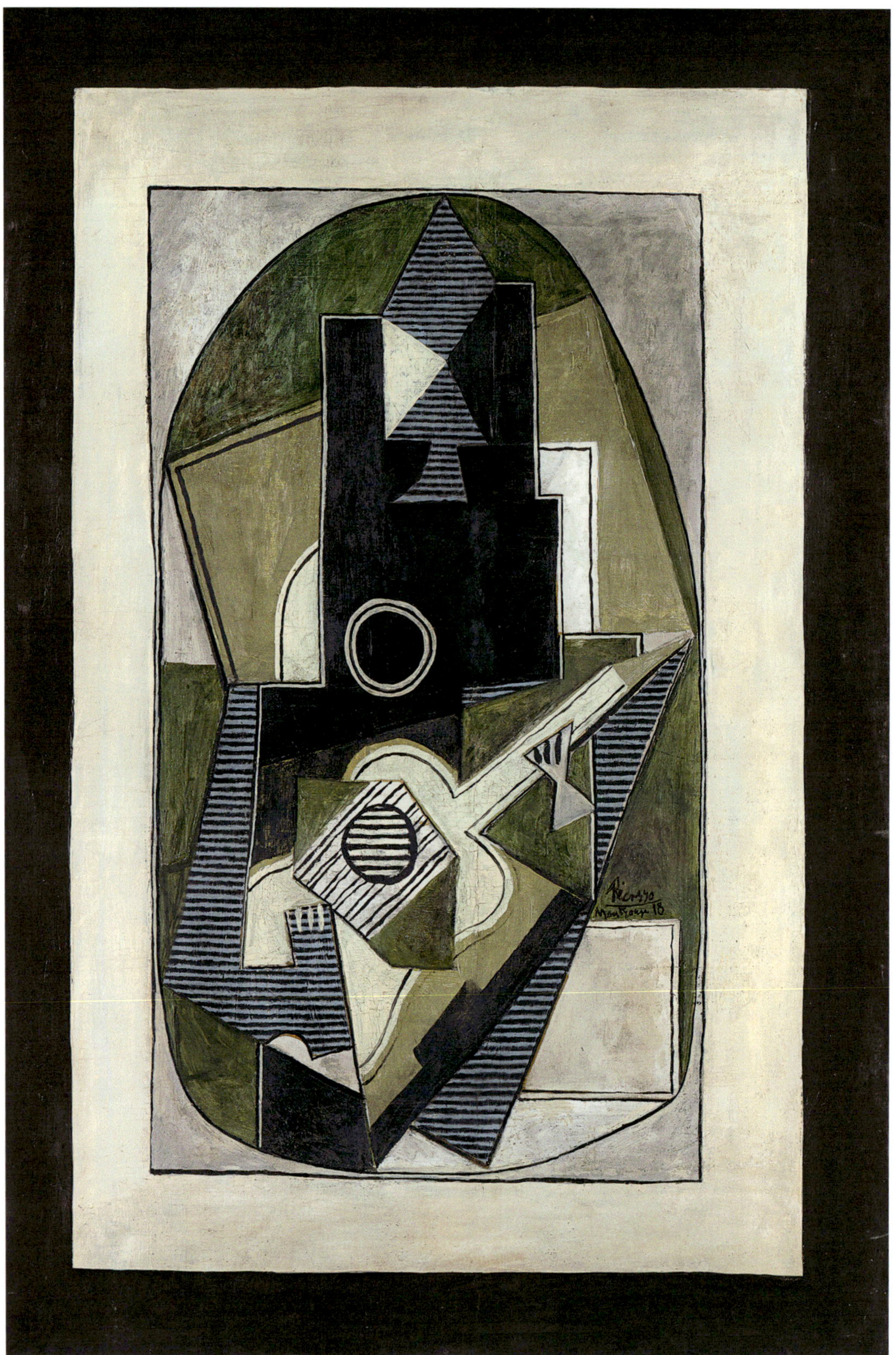

Cat. 78   Alexander Archipenko: *Two Glasses on the Table*
(*Deux verres sur une table*), 1919/20, papier-mâché on wood,
56 × 46 × 4.5 cm, Centre Pompidou, Paris, inv. no. 1428 S

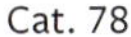

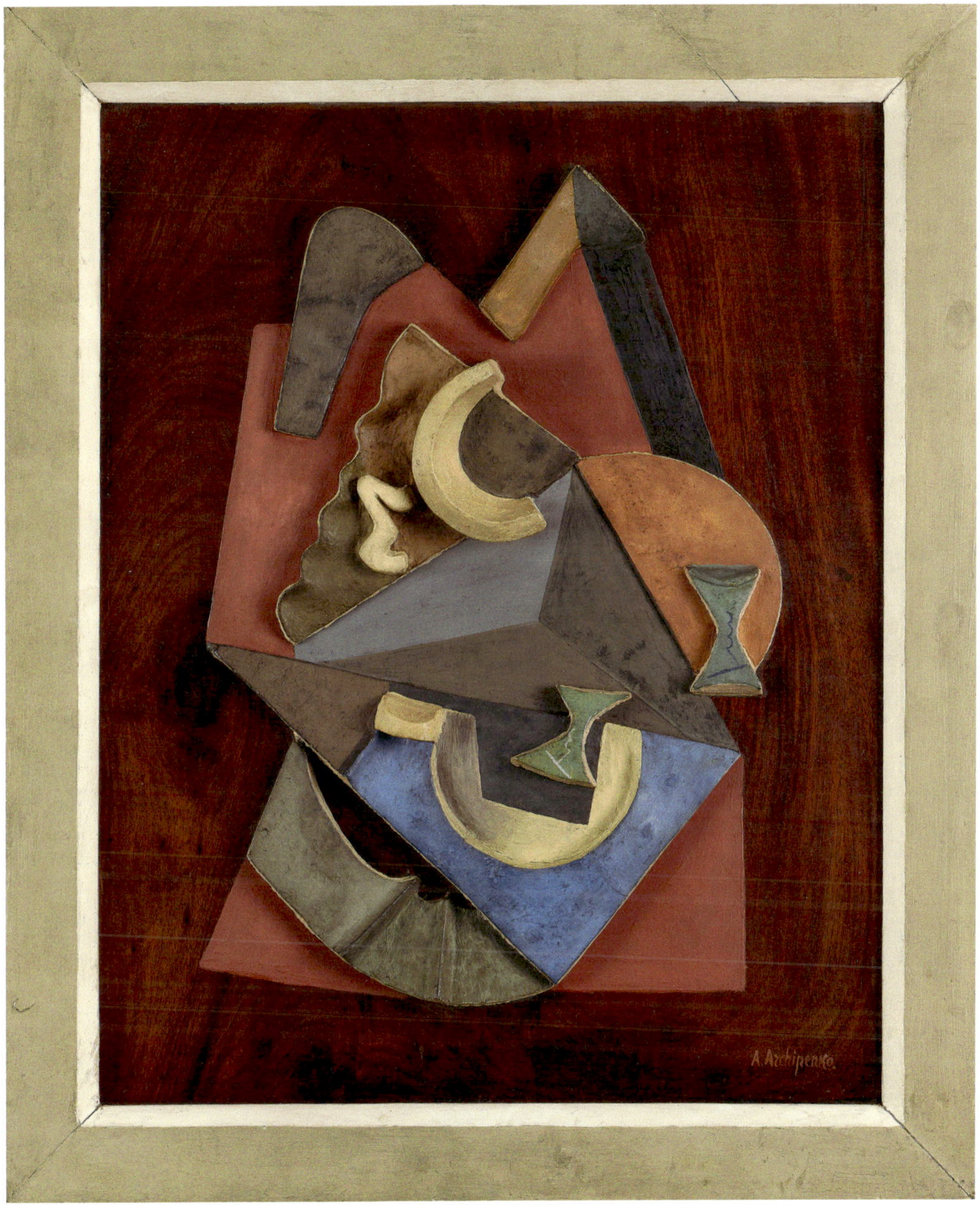

Cat. 79 — Jacques Lipchitz: *Seated Man with Clarinet II*, 1919/20, bronze, 77 × 40 × 30 cm, Hamburger Kunsthalle, permanent loan from the Stiftung Hamburger Kunstsammlungen, inv. no. S-1980-7

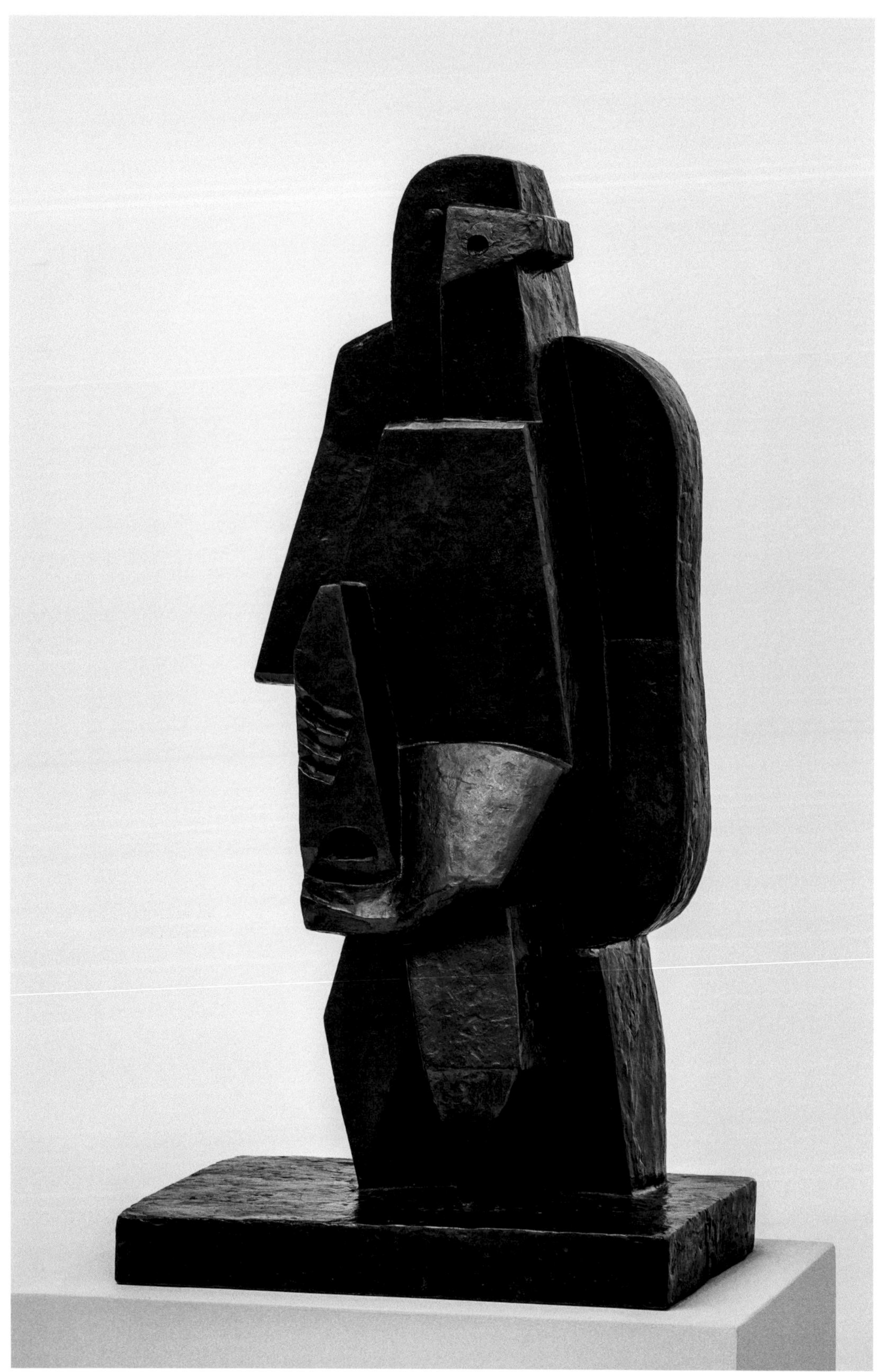

Cat. 80   Pablo Picasso: *Violin* (*Violon*), 1915, sheet metal, painted,
and iron wire, 100 × 63.7 × 18 cm, Musée national Picasso-Paris,
inv. no. MP255

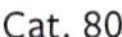

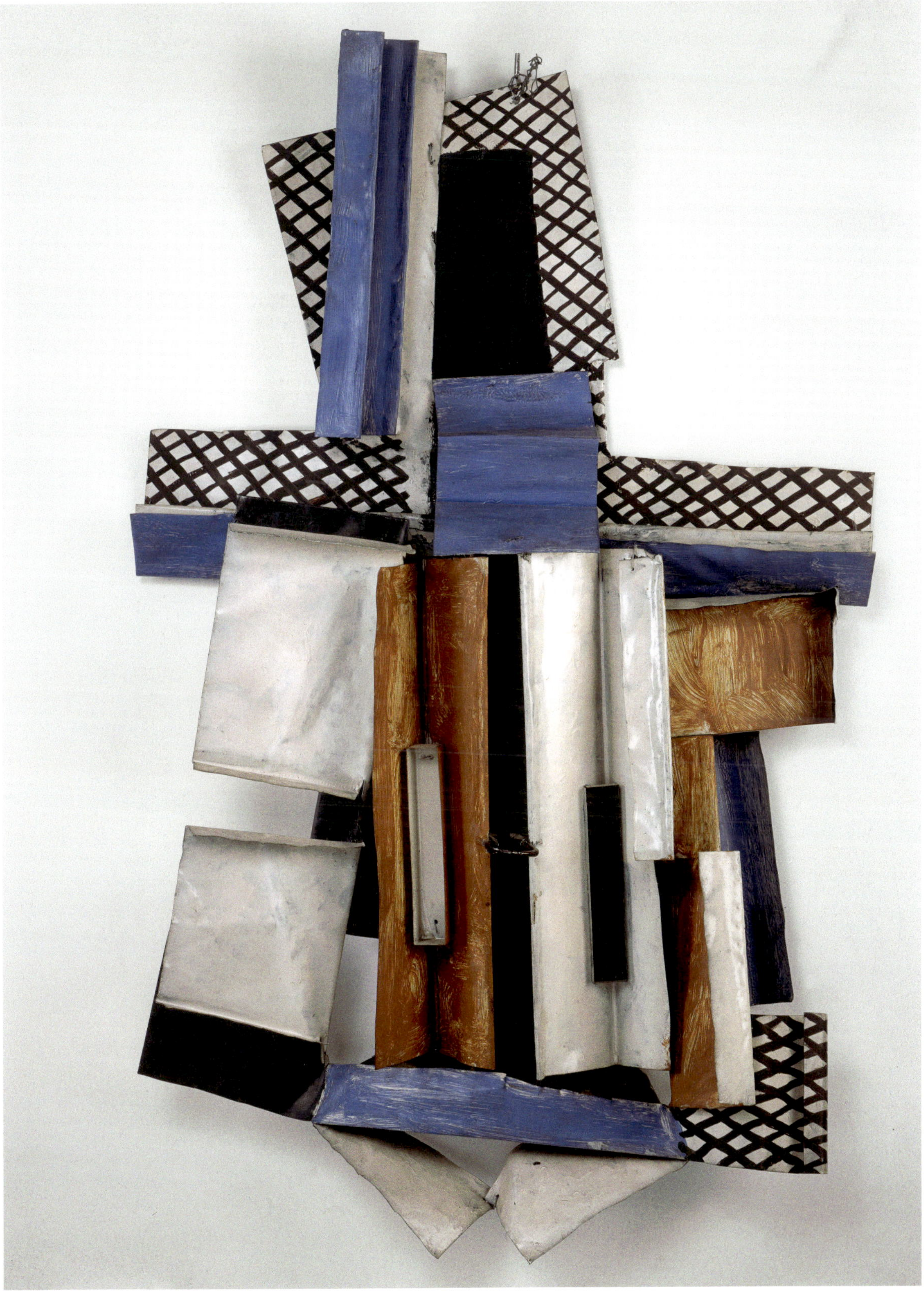

Cat. 81   Henri Laurens: *Woman with Earrings (Femme aux boucles d'oreilles)*, 1921, terracotta, 37 × 12 × 10 cm, Städel Museum, Frankfurt am Main, inv. no. SGP 195 (Frankfurt only)

Cat. 82   Alexander Archipenko: *Female Torso (Torse gris)*, 1922, marble, 47.9 × 24 × 23.4 cm, Städel Museum, Frankfurt am Main, permanent loan from private collection, inv. no. LG 126

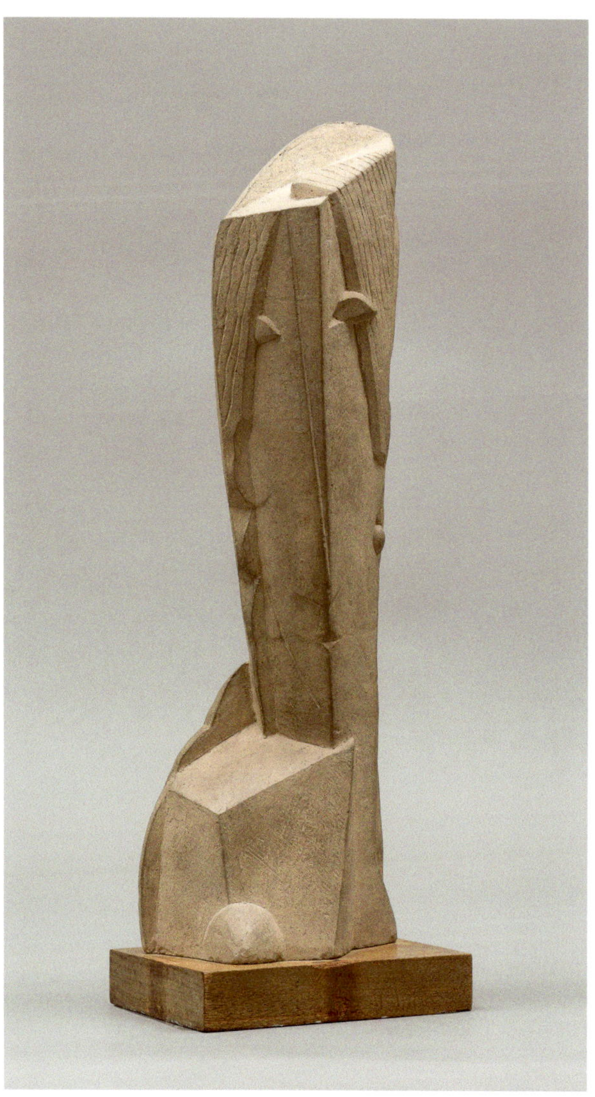

Cat. 81

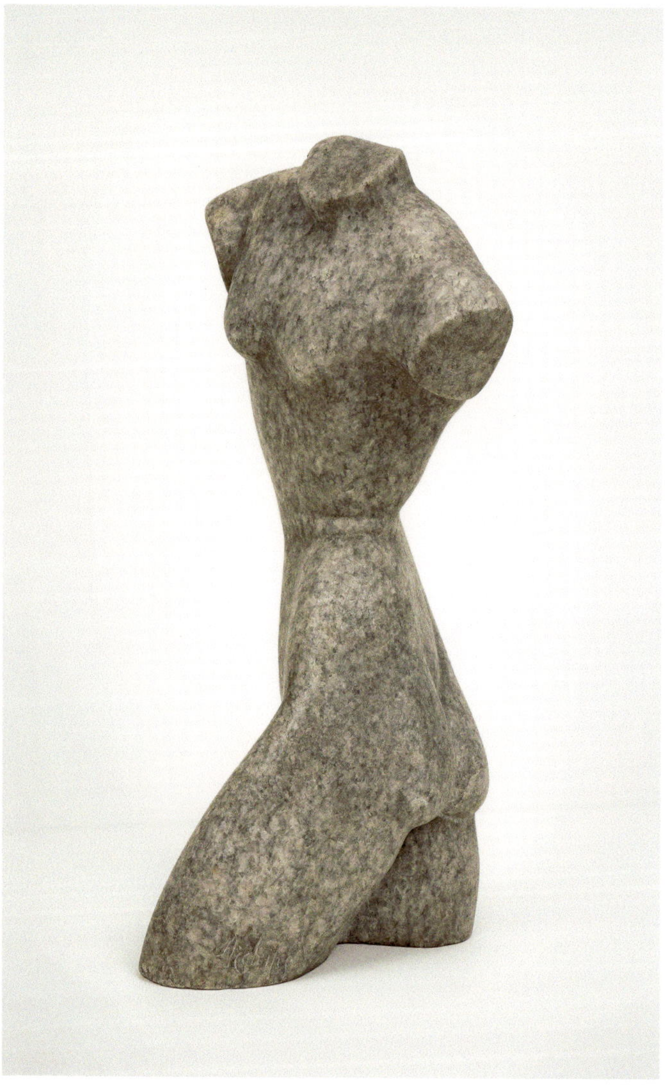

Cat. 82

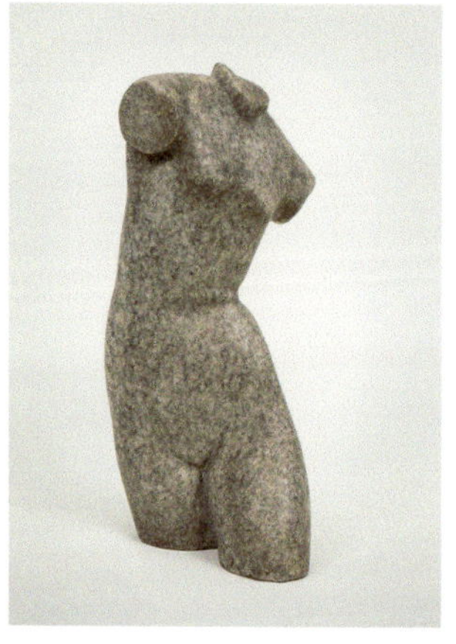
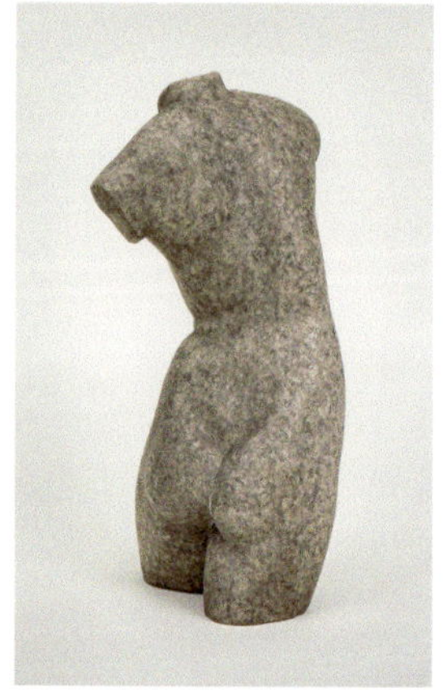

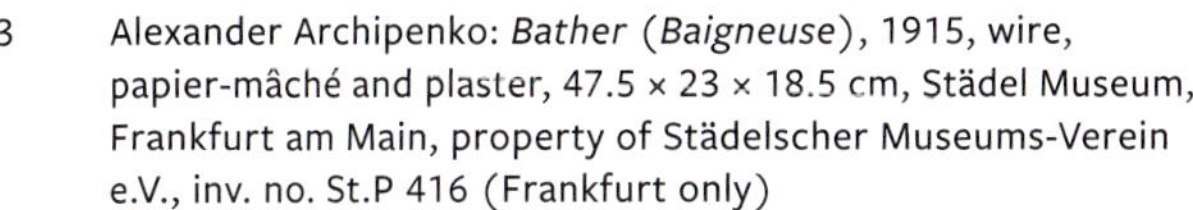
Cat. 83   Alexander Archipenko: *Bather* (*Baigneuse*), 1915, wire, papier-mâché and plaster, 47.5 × 23 × 18.5 cm, Städel Museum, Frankfurt am Main, property of Städelscher Museums-Verein e.V., inv. no. St.P 416 (Frankfurt only)

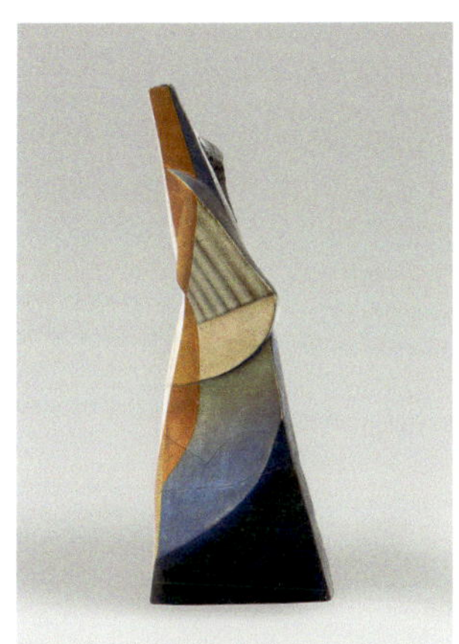

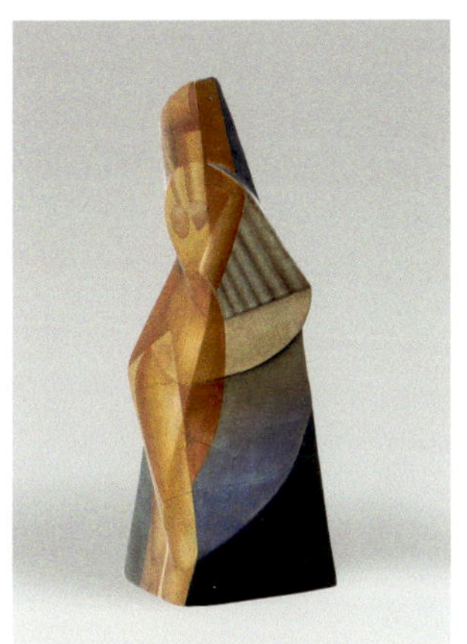

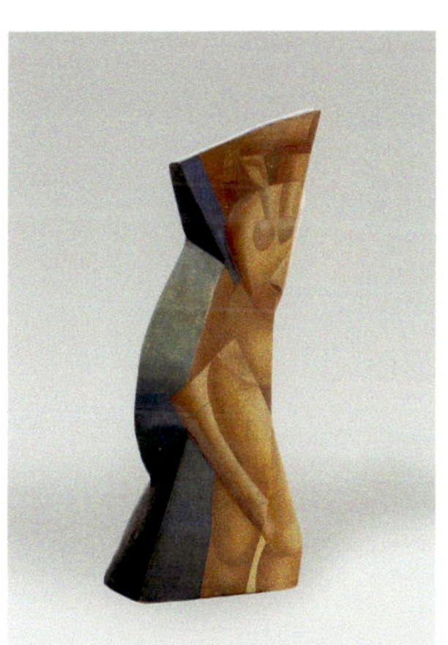

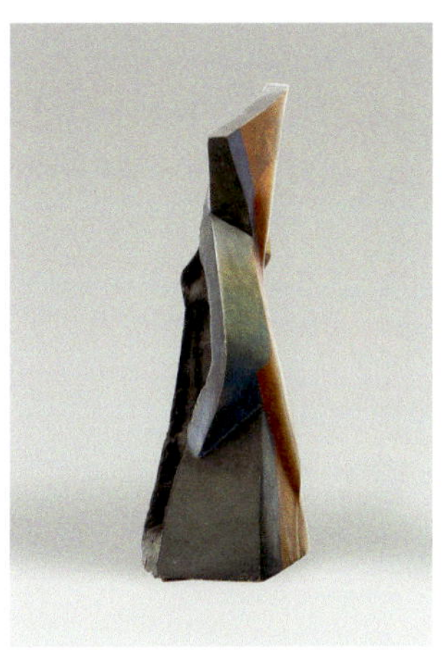

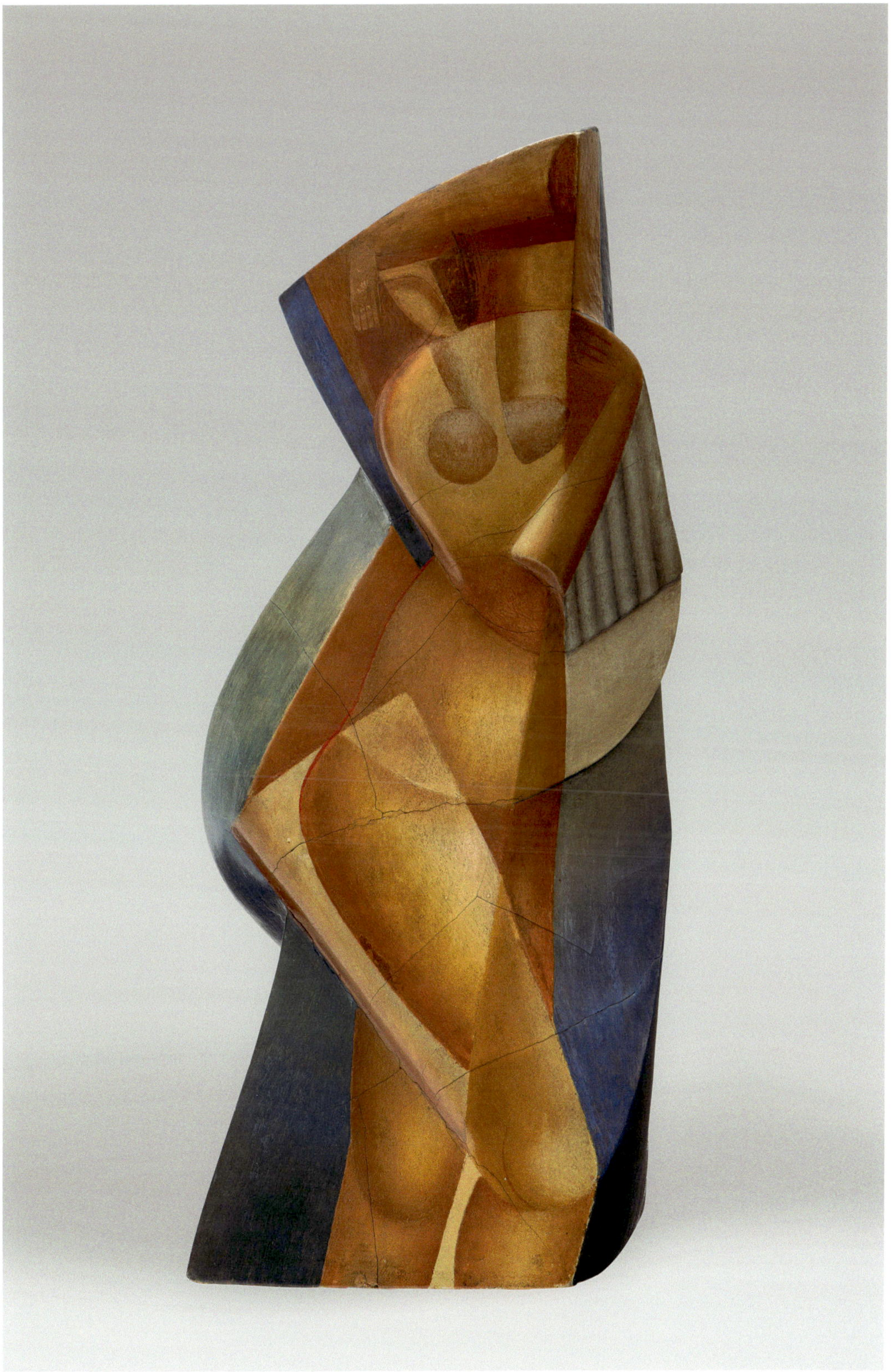

Cat. 84 Pablo Picasso: *Portrait of Fernande Olivier* (*Portrait de Fernande Olivier*), 1909, oil on canvas, 65 × 54.5 cm, Städel Museum, Frankfurt am Main, property of Städelscher Museums-Verein e.V., inv. no. 2110

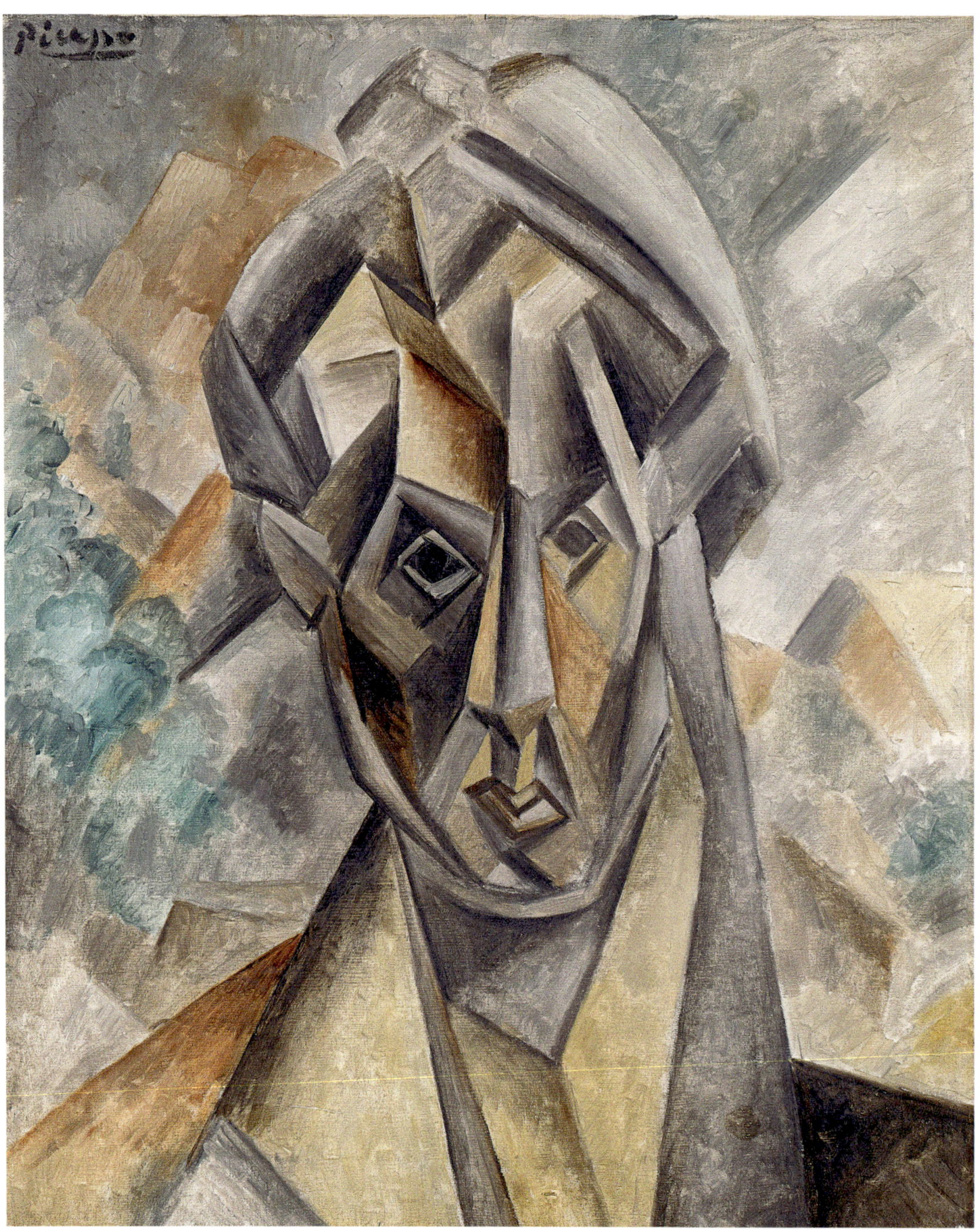

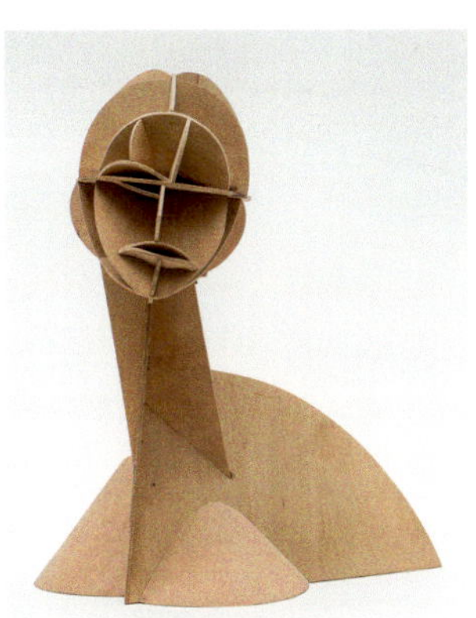

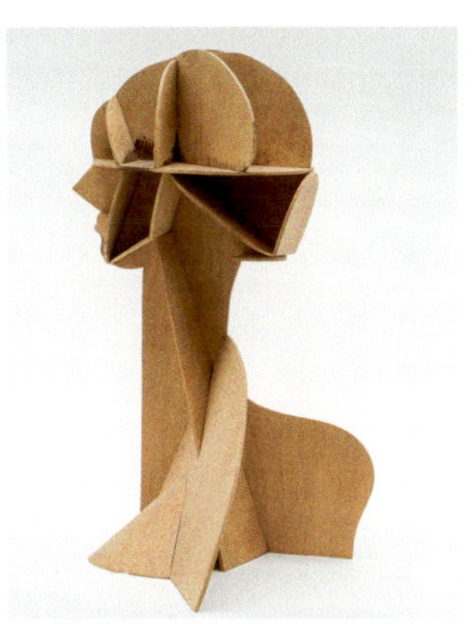

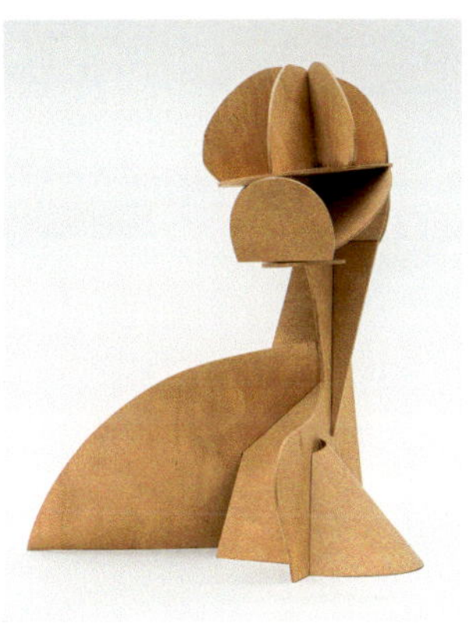

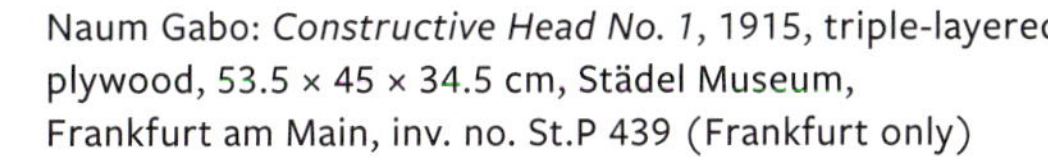

Cat. 85   Naum Gabo: *Constructive Head No. 1*, 1915, triple-layered
plywood, 53.5 × 45 × 34.5 cm, Städel Museum,
Frankfurt am Main, inv. no. St.P 439 (Frankfurt only)

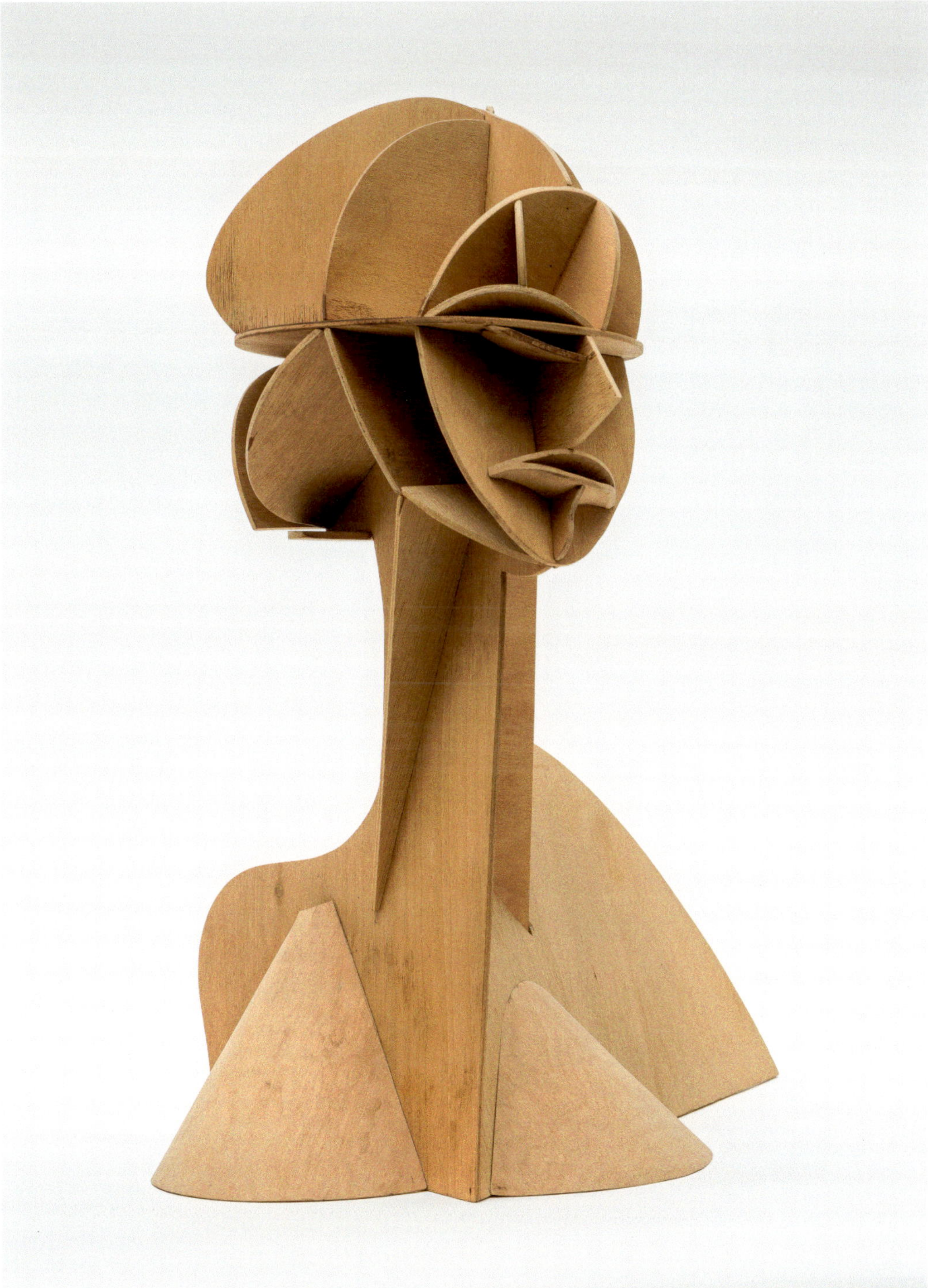

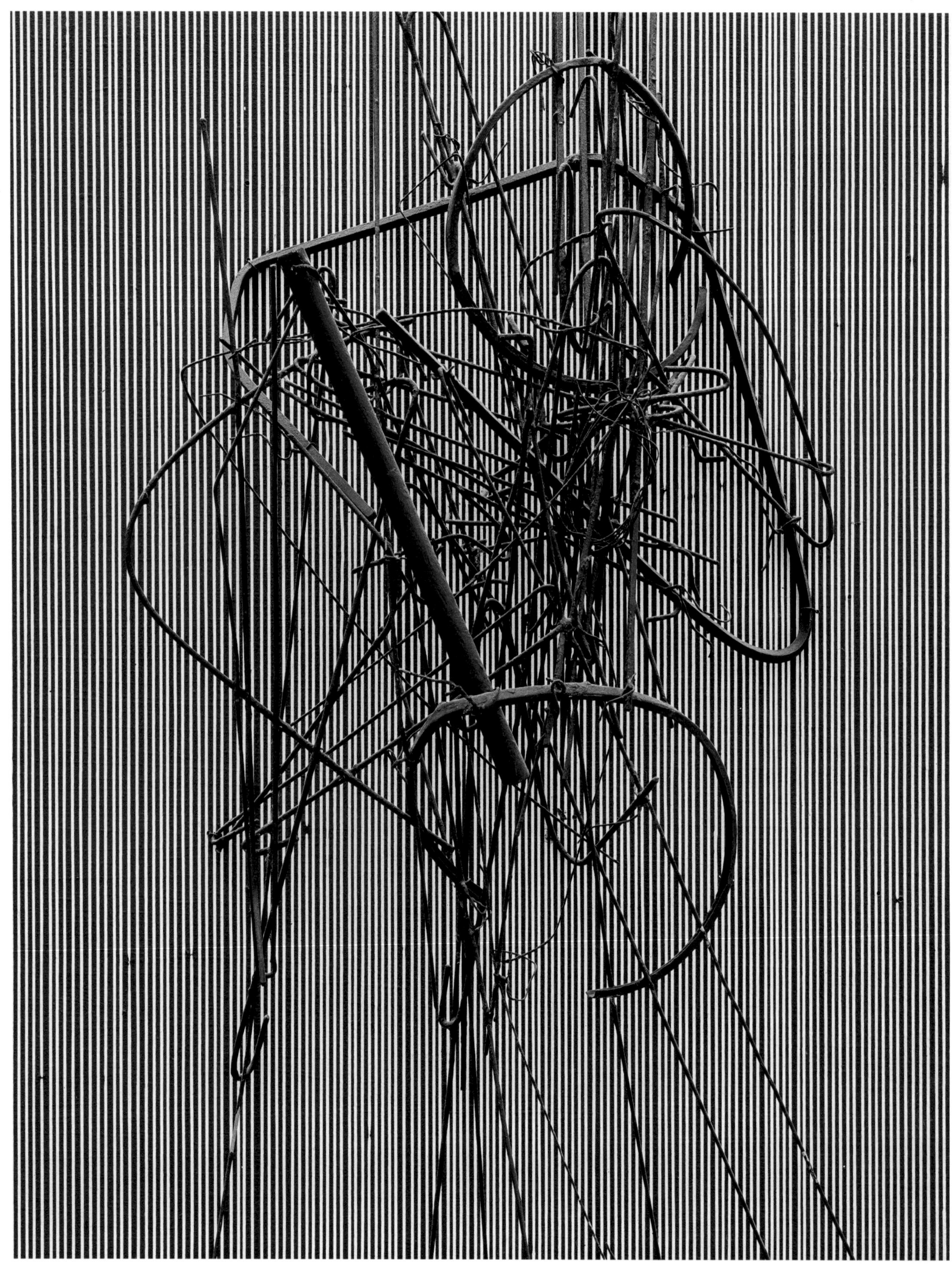

Cats. 86—93

Friederike Schütt

BETWEEN VISION AND TOUCH

Optical Illusion in the Relief

"The people say nothing else except that it is very *deceptive*; [...] that it really looks like a bas-relief! Yes, yes, that's the way the world goes 'round", wrote Philipp Otto Runge in 1802 to his brother Daniel in Hamburg, taking only modest pleasure in the praise he was accorded for the successful trompe-l'oeil in *Triumph of Love* (cat. 87).[1] Evidently, he would have preferred that the aim of the allegorical depiction was appreciated not only by art connoisseurs but by a wider public. The supraporte, which was intended as a wedding gift for the ballroom of the home of his brother Jakob in Wolgast, features a roundelay of putti. The figures of several children arranged in a circular reading direction around Amor, seated on a seashell and playing the lyre, symbolise the various stages of love in the cycle of life. Newly enamoured himself, Runge made (his own) inner emotions the point of departure of his work for the purpose of restaging a well-known motif from antiquity, in the spirit of Romanticism, as an ostensible relief.[2]

In the process of creating reliefs, illusion and dis-illusion lie in close proximity to one another – not just for Philipp Otto Runge. The wide range of artistic potential at the transition from the second to the third dimension positively entices one into putting visual habits to the test with illusions and physicality, space or motion.

Runge's monochrome painting stands in the tradition of sculptural imitations, with which artists of the early modern period sought to stand up to sculptors. In the battle between the disciplines, the *paragone* dealt with in terms of theory and practice until the nineteenth century, painters and sculptors competed not only for a better imitation but also, with respect to physicality and haptics, for the viewer's sense of vision and touch.[3] In this context, the *rilievo* became an important argument (→ Introduction). As countless grisailles since the fifteenth century demonstrate, the nuances of shades of light and shadow are particularly suited for producing *rilievo* in painting.[4] Accordingly, Runge also causes the putti to emerge from the plane by means of subtle light and dark values. In addition, the precise imitation of the stone material contributes to the apparently relief-like haptics.

In the in-between of painting and sculpture, the fiction of the relief tempts one to touch, to the haptic checking of the visual.[5]

It is also tempting to trace with one's finger the outlines of the dishes in Arthur Segal's *Still Life I* (*with Teapot*) (cat. 89) in order to feel the staggering of the surface, which is so difficult to capture in photographs.[6] Segal arranged the teapot and cup as in a painted still life, but without conveying spatiality or depth perspective – a strategy that Giorgio Morandi likewise aspired to in his numerous still lifes in shades of grey when he depicted the everyday objects as if they were floating over the picture plane (cat. 88). The colouration is reminiscent of stone imitations in grisaille. Yet Segal's support and motif are modelled from plaster. Indeed, he calculated in natural light as a sculptural design element. But he intensified the lines of the shadows that the teapot and cup actually cast on the surface of the support by means of painting in order to bond the objects to the ground, while at the same time ensuring their visual raising-out of the second dimension.[7] When considering the possibilities of painting and modelling, Segal did not aim for optical illusion, nor did he take a stance in the sense of the model. What appealed to him was the optical experiment, the "expansion of the painting to become a relief",[8] which in terms of subject and colouration alluded to the art genre of the trompe-l'oeil.

Trompe-l'oeils entered art history in particular as a sub-genre of still life painting. In the Netherlands in the seventeenth century, especially hunting scenes that relied on optical illusion enjoyed enormous popularity.[9] For the best possible illusion, not only was naturalistic imitation perfected in these paintings; the painters also experimented with the spatial expansion outward of the picture planes instead of leading the gaze into the depth (→ Boundary and Space of Possibility).[10] Hence Frans van Cuyck de Myerhop, for example, arranged three life-sized dead birds before a painted frame and simulated the apparent distance of the cadavers from the cracked wall by means of shadows (fig. 1).[11] The activation of the viewer for the exposure of the illusion is an integral part of the effect of the trompe-l'oeil. After all, it is first the "dis-illusionment"[12] that makes for visual pleasure and appreciation of the artistic virtuosity and prompts an inquiry into one's own perception.[13]

Inspiration from trompe-l'oeils such as this one shines through two hundred years later in Otto Scholderer's *Still Life with Two Dead Hazel Grouses* (cat. 90), in which the Frankfurt-based painter frames the staging of the birds, rich in contrast, with a wood imitation that merges with the canvas as the actual support. Scholderer also strove for a proximity to nature in the colours and texture of the plumage. However, without charging the depiction superficially with an intent to deceive or with allusions to vanitas in their simplicity the dead birds completely represent themselves. Like his paragons Jean Siméon Chardin, Gustave Courbet or Édouard Manet (fig. 2), Scholderer was first and foremost interested in the power of the painterly and the intrinsic realism that can be created out of this potential.[14]

The French sculptor Aubert Parent might also have had the mechanisms of trompe-l'oeil painting in mind when, in 1792, he carved, in maple, a dead bird and a mouse stealing its brood from the nest in the impression of a hunting still life (cat. 91). By dispensing with coloured painting, Parent deliberately avoids the intention of optical illusion. Rather, the depiction takes the viewer by surprise by means of the sculptural rendering of a subject allegedly reserved for painting. In addition, Parent designed the animals' feathers and fur with a fragile wealth of detail, which conflicts with the hardness of the wood. By doing so, he visualises a quality of relief design that seeks comparison with painted hunting scenes.[15]

In the *paragone* of the arts, which also comprises the surpassing of the illusion within one and the same medium, the motif of the curtain has become a topos of optical illusion since Plinius' account of the rivalry between the artists Zeuxis and Parrhasios. According to the antique anecdote, Parrhasios outdid Zeuxis' deceptively realistic depiction of grapes, which birds attempted to peck at, with the painting of a curtain, and hence deceived the painter colleague himself.[16] The curtain is per se suitable for the deception manoeuvre, as it lets on that there is something behind it. In painted form, it suggests a surface relief that enters into a relationship of tension with the two-dimensionality of the support and its textile materiality.[17] Gerhard Richter began exploring the

possibilities of the sculptural illusion of the curtain motif in the mid-1960s in a series of paintings of various formats. In the early works, he provided for spatial depth and recognisability of the curtain with a strip at the lower edge of the painting, making it difficult to distinguish between painting and photography by means of blurring (fig. 3).[18] In *Large Curtain* from 1967 (cat. 92), the illusionistic relief of the fall of the folds is taken up in the entire picture plane. The curtain as such, cropped on all sides, can no longer be made out; it loses its concealing purpose. Richter abolished the distinction from the support and intensified the fiction through the all-over in such a way that the painting itself appears to be an undulating surface.[19]

The fluid juxtaposition of the verticals in shades of grey provokes optical fluctuations, in much the same way as they characterise Rafael Soto's *Vibration* (cat. 93). The tangle of wire before the square plane, composed of densely arranged black and white lines, is disorienting. Is it moving or standing still? The construction before a flickering ground seems to change depending on one's position. Yet the kinetics of the artwork develops solely in one's perception; it remains a purely visual effect.[20] When viewing it, it is hardly possible to permeate the layers from the foreground towards the background. The Op artist Soto assembled the components to produce a flickering relief, which becomes the driving force of the illusion and a source of irritation for the viewer.

The impact of Soto's work essentially depends, like that of every trompe-l'oeil, on the viewer's reaction.[21] Trompe-l'oeils push forward into the space of their audience and activate all the senses. In his famous *Snare-Pictures*, Daniel Spoerri carried this approach to extremes with objects that were real instead of ones that deceptively simulated being real. In *Restaurant Spoerri* (cat. 86), the Swiss founder of Eat Art mounted the remains of a dinner party, where guests had sat over alcohol and cigarettes, onto a wooden panel. By tilting the panel vertically, Spoerri made the everyday situation of the abandoned table worthy of being depicted, directing the gaze towards the banality of having become entrapped "in the snare".[22] The artist commented in retrospect: "I actually just put an end to this whole subject of the still life by bulging the trompe-l'oeil, the three-dimensional imitated on two dimensions, out into reality."[23] Beyond optics and haptics, in this case the relief not lastly addresses the sense of smell and taste, and in doing so conquers an additional sphere of extra-pictorial reality.

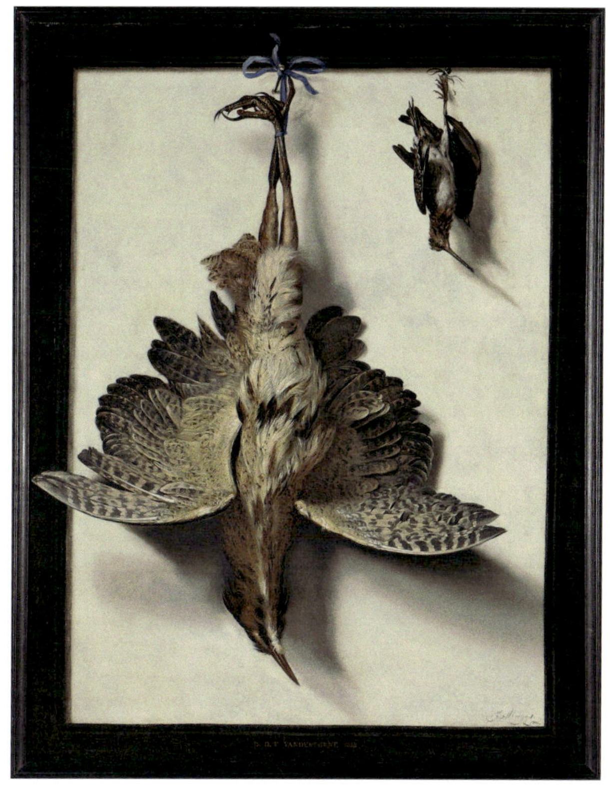

Fig. 1

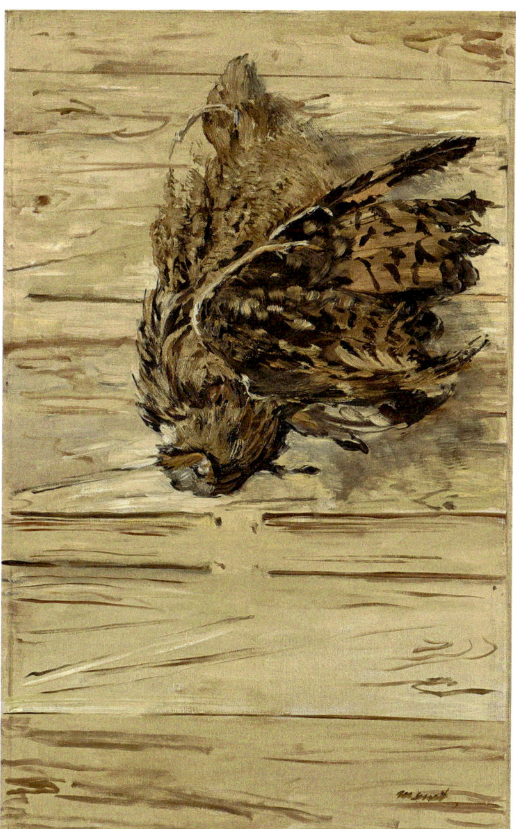

Fig. 2

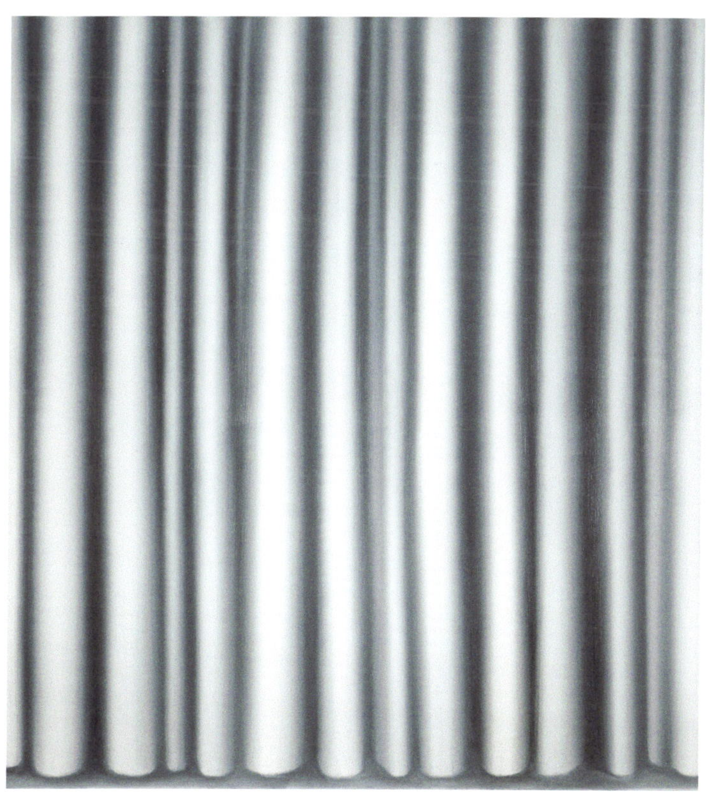

Fig. 3

Fig. 1   Frans van Cuyck de Myerhop: *Still Life with Birds*,
         ca. 1670–80, oil on canvas, Groeningemuseum, Bruges

Fig. 2   Édouard Manet: *Dead Eagle Owl*, 1881, oil on canvas,
         Sammlung Emil Bührle, Kunsthaus Zürich

Fig. 3   Gerhard Richter: *Curtain IV*, 1965, oil on canvas,
         Kunstmuseum Bonn

1   Letter from Philipp Otto Runge to Daniel Runge in Hamburg, Dresden, 30 March 1802, in: Philipp Otto Runge: *Briefe und Schriften*, ed. Peter Betthausen, Berlin 1981, p. 78.

2   See *Kosmos Runge: Der Morgen der Romantik*, ed. Markus Bertsch et al., exh. cat. Hamburger Kunsthalle/Kunsthalle der Hypo-Kulturstiftung, Munich 2010, pp. 88–91.

3   See Ulrich Pfisterer: "Paragone", in: Wolfgang Brassat (ed.): *Handbuch der Rhetorik der Bildenden Künste* (*Handbücher Rhetorik*, vol. 2), Berlin/Boston 2017, pp. 283–312; Claire Barbillon: *Le Relief au croisement des arts du XIXᵉ siècle*, Paris 2014, pp. 143–157; *Wettstreit der Künste: Malerei und Skulptur von Dürer bis Daumier*, ed. Ekkehard Mai and Kurt Wettengl, exh. cat. Haus der Kunst, Munich/Wallraf-Richartz-Museum, Cologne, Wolfratshausen 2002, p. 286 (Stephanie Sonntag); on painted putto reliefs, see ibid., pp. 312–315.

4   See Markus Rath: "Die Haptik der Bilder: *Rilievo* als Verkörperungsstrategie der Malerei", in: idem et al. (eds.): *Das haptische Bild: Körperhafte Bilderfahrung in der Neuzeit*, Berlin 2013, pp. 3–29, esp. pp. 6, 15–23.

5   On haptics in the relief or the fiction thereof in trompe-l'oeil, see Bexte 2022; Bärbel Hedinger, "Trompe-l'œil: Eine moderne Gattung seit der Antike", in: *Täuschend echt. Illusion und Wirklichkeit in der Kunst*, ed. idem, exh. cat. Bucerius Kunst Forum, Hamburg, Munich 2010, pp. 10–15, esp. p. 11.

6   On the "unphotographability" of the relief, see Bexte 2022, pp. 138f.

7   Pavel Liška: "Arthur Segal – Leben und Werk", in: *Arthur Segal 1875–1944*, ed. Wulf Herzogenrath and idem, exh. cat. Kölnischer Kunstverein, Cologne, et al., Berlin 1987, pp. 19–76; on the optical relief, see ibid., pp. 59f.

8   Exh. cat. Münster 1980, p. 170.

9   See Fred G. Meijer: "Virtuosität, Wohlstand und geträumte Trophäen: Niederländische Stillleben mit toten Tieren zwischen 1600 und 1800", in: *Von Schönheit und Tod: Tierstillleben von der Renaissance bis zur Moderne*, ed. Holger Jacob-Friesen, exh. cat. Staatliche Kunsthalle Karlsruhe, Heidelberg 2011, pp. 51–79.

10   See Sybille Ebert-Schifferer: "Der Durchblick und sein Gegenteil", in: exh. cat. Hamburg 2010 (see note 5), pp. 16–23, esp. p. 16.

11   See exh. cat. Karlsruhe 2011 (see note 9), p. 224 (Holger Jacob-Friesen).

12   Gottfried Boehm: "Die Lust am Schein im Trompe-l'œil", in: exh. cat. Hamburg 2010 (see note 5), pp. 24–29, esp. p. 27.

13   See Ebert-Schifferer 2010 (see note 10), p. 18.

14   See Jutta M. Bagdahn: *Otto Franz Scholderer 1834–1902: Monographie und Werkverzeichnis*, Berlin 2020, p. 161; p. 201, no. 199; Boehm 2010 (see note 12), p. 29; Jeanette Falcke: "Otto Scholderer und seine Frankfurter Künstlerkollegen", in: *Otto Scholderer 1834–1902: Die neue Wirklichkeit des Malerischen. Zum 100. Todestag*, exh. cat. Haus Giersch – Museum Regionaler Kunst, Frankfurt am Main, 2002, pp. 11–35, esp. p. 18.

15   See the example of a marble relief with a dead thrush by Jean-Antoine Houdon from 1777 in Pfisterer 2017 (see note 3), p. 305; on the political relevance of iconography, see exh. cat. Karlsruhe 2011 (see note 9), p. 328 (Astrid Reuter).

16   On the curtain motif, see *Hinter dem Vorhang: Verhüllung und Enthüllung seit der Renaissance. Von Tizian bis Christo*, ed. Claudia Blümle and Beat Wismer, exh. cat. Museum Kunstpalast, Düsseldorf, Munich 2016; Philip Ursprung: "Augenwischerei: Trompe-l'œil einst und jetzt", in: *Spiegel geheimer Wünsche: Stillleben aus fünf Jahrhunderten*, ed. Martina Sitt and Hubertus Gaßner, exh. cat. Hamburger Kunsthalle, Munich 2008, pp. 25–37, esp. pp. 25–28.

17   See Christian Spies: "Topologien des Unanschaulichen: Gerhard Richters Vorhangbilder", in: Gottfried Boehm et al. (eds.), *Movens Bild: Zwischen Evidenz und Affekt*, Munich 2008, pp. 118–147, esp. p. 121.

18   See ibid., pp. 121, 127–137.

19   See ibid., pp. 138f.

20   See Rudolf E. Lang: "Wie die Kunst lügt und wir sie darum lieben", in: *Lust der Täuschung: Von antiker Kunst bis zur Virtual Reality*, ed. Andreas Beitin and Roger Diederen, exh. cat. Kunsthalle München/Ludwig Forum für Internationale Kunst, Aachen, Munich 2018, pp. 11–25, esp. pp. 15–22; Paul Wember: "Soto: Kinetische Bilder (1963)", in: *ZERO und Paris: Und heute. Arman, Klein, Soto, Spoerri, Tinguely und andere Künstler in Paris um 1960*, ed. Renate Damsch-Wiehager, exh. cat. Villa Merkel, Galerie der Stadt Esslingen/Musée d'Art Moderne et d'Art Contemporain, Nice, Ostfildern 1997, p. 93.

21   On the role of the recipient in Op art, see Eva Badura-Triska, "Op Art – Manierismus der konkreten Kunst", in: *Vertigo: Op Art und eine Geschichte des Schwindels 1520 bis 1970*, ed. idem and Markus Wörgötter, exh. cat. mumok – Museum moderner Kunst Stiftung Ludwig, Vienna/Kunstmuseum Stuttgart, Cologne 2019, pp. 17–41, esp. p. 18.

22   See Stephan Geiger: "Über alltägliche Realitäten und unsterbliche Anekdoten – Kunsthistorische Betrachtungen zum Werk von Daniel Spoerri", in: *Daniel Spoerri – every, day, life*, exh. cat. Galerie Geiger, Konstanz, 2018, p. 9; Isabelle Schwarz; "Topografien des Zufalls: Zur Verortung des Zufalls im Werk von Dieter Roth und Daniel Spoerri", in: *Purer Zufall: Unvorhersehbares von Marcel Duchamp bis Gerhard Richter*, exh. cat. Sprengel Museum Hannover 2013, pp. 59–76, esp. pp. 65–68; Sybille Ebert-Schifferer: *Die Geschichte des Stillebens*, Munich 1998, pp. 388–392.

23   Daniel Spoerri, quoted in: Konrad Tobler, "Daniel Spoerri: Das Territorium und die Falle der Dinge. Konrad Tobler sprach mit dem Erfinder der Fallenbilder (excerpt 1994)", in: exh. cat. Esslingen/Nice 1997 (see note 20), p. 106.

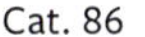

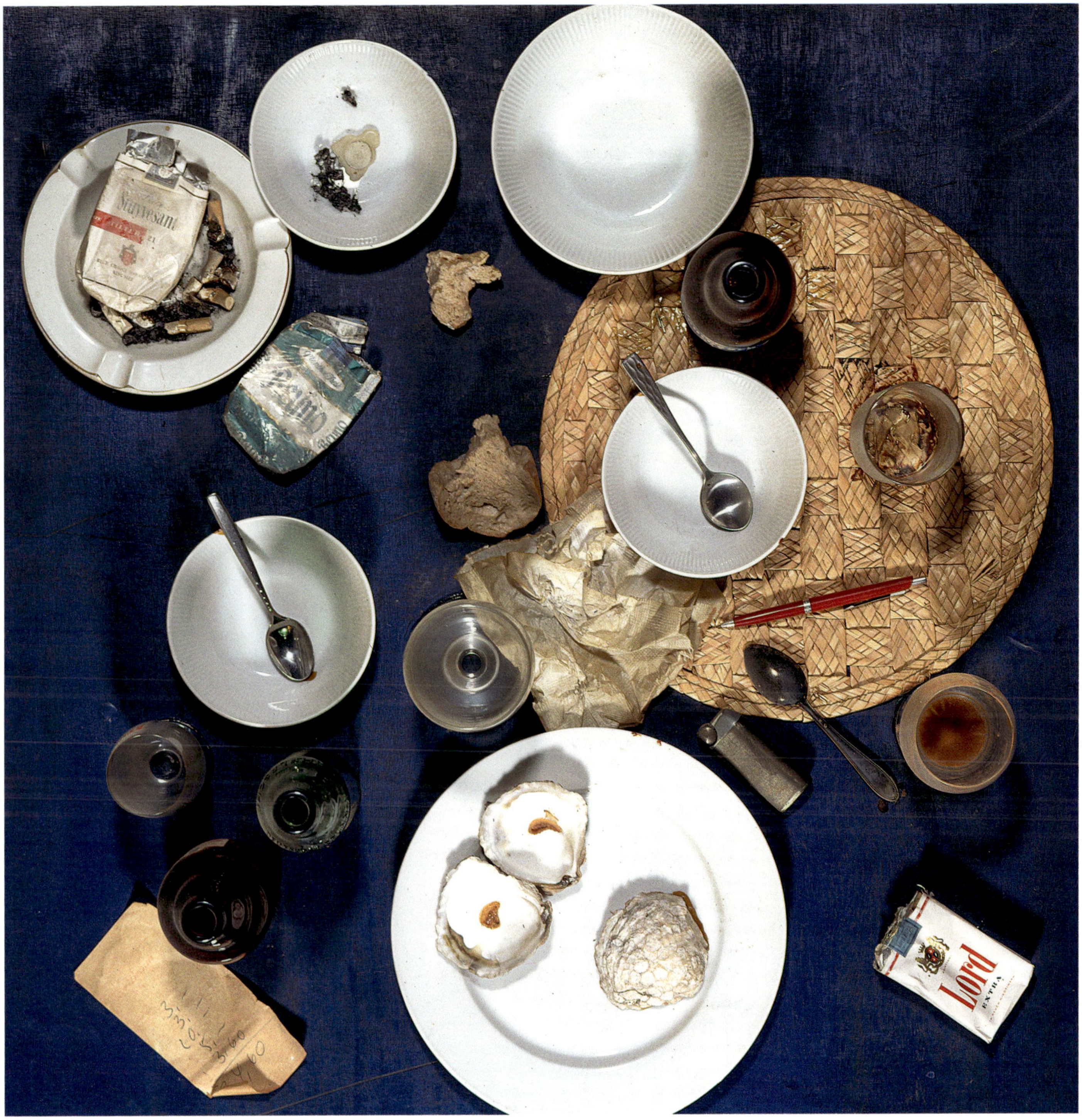

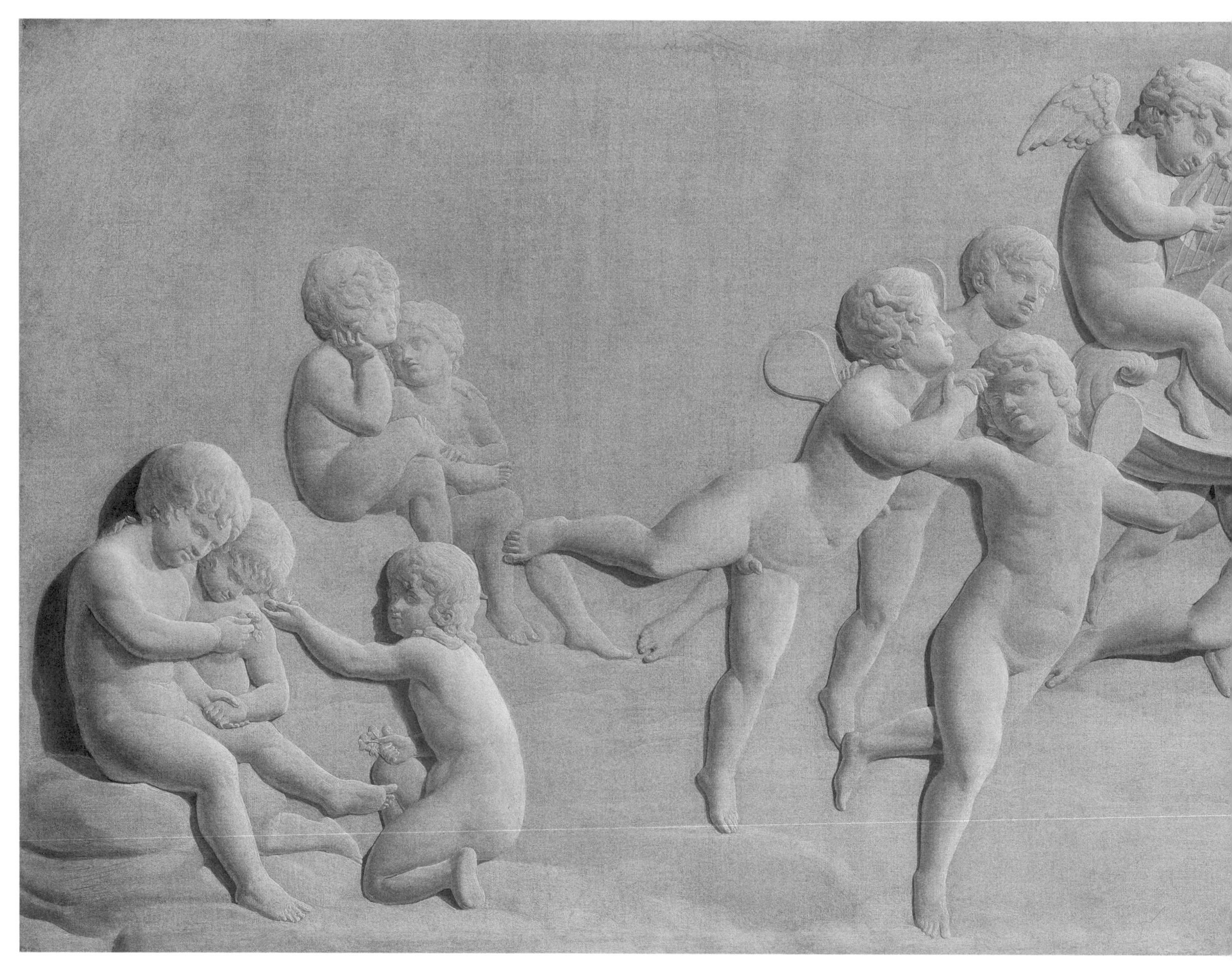

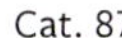

Cat. 87   Philipp Otto Runge: *Triumph of Love*, 1802, oil on canvas,
66.5 × 172 cm, Hamburger Kunsthalle, inv. no. HK-2691

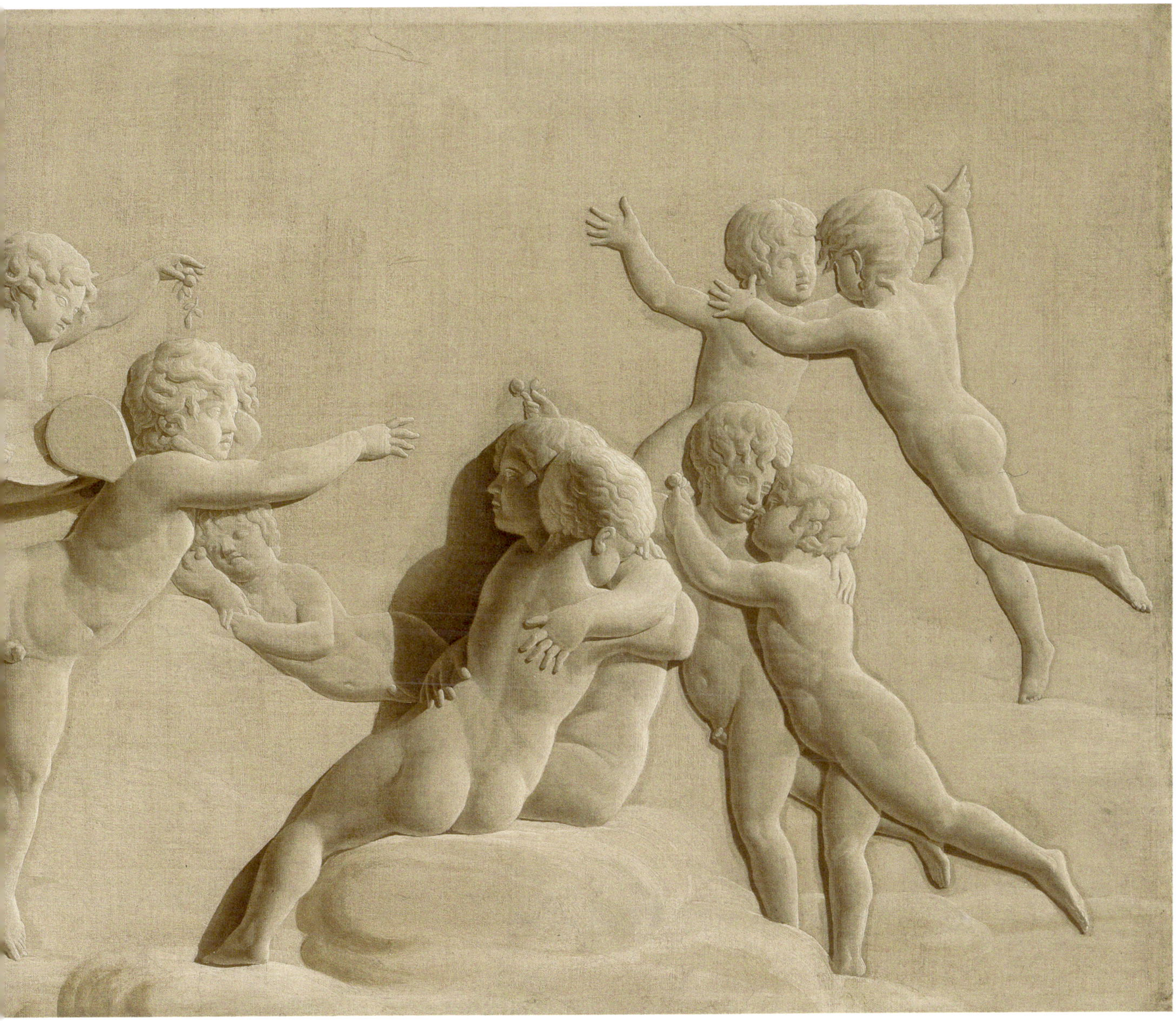

Cat. 88   Giorgio Morandi: *Still Life* (*Natura morta*), 1957, oil on
canvas, 27 × 40 cm, Hamburger Kunsthalle, permanent loan
from the Stiftung Hamburger Kunstsammlungen,
inv. no. HK-5016 (Hamburg only)

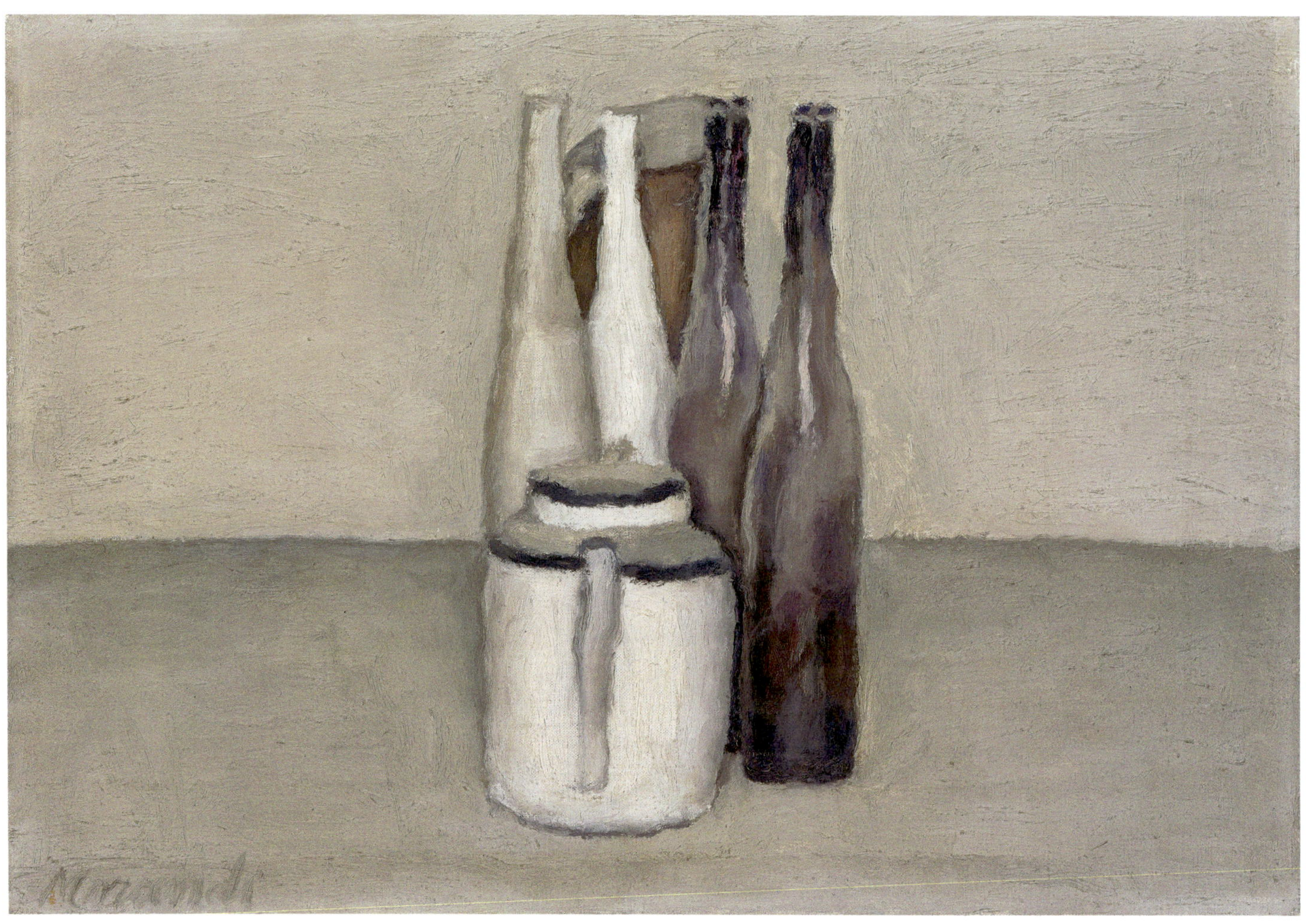

Cat. 89   Arthur Segal: *Still Life I* (*with Teapot*), 1926, plaster, painted, 33 × 38 × 11 cm, Berlinische Galerie – Landesmuseum für Moderne Kunst, Fotografie und Architektur, inv. no. BG-S 0530/77

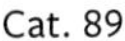

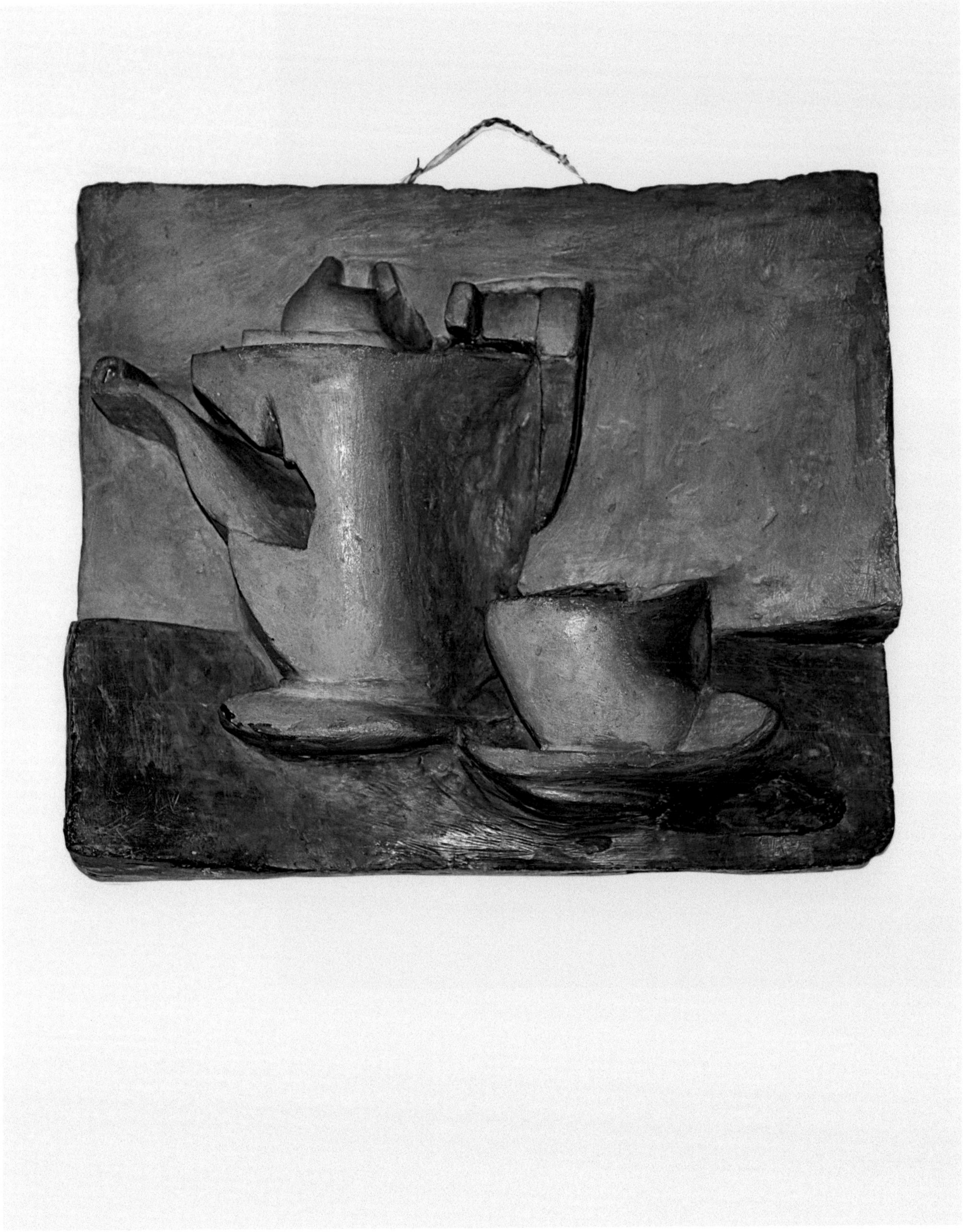

Cat. 90   Otto Scholderer: *Still Life with Two Dead Hazel Grouses*, 1881, oil on canvas, 50.7 × 33.6 cm, Städel Museum, Frankfurt am Main, inv. no. SG 657

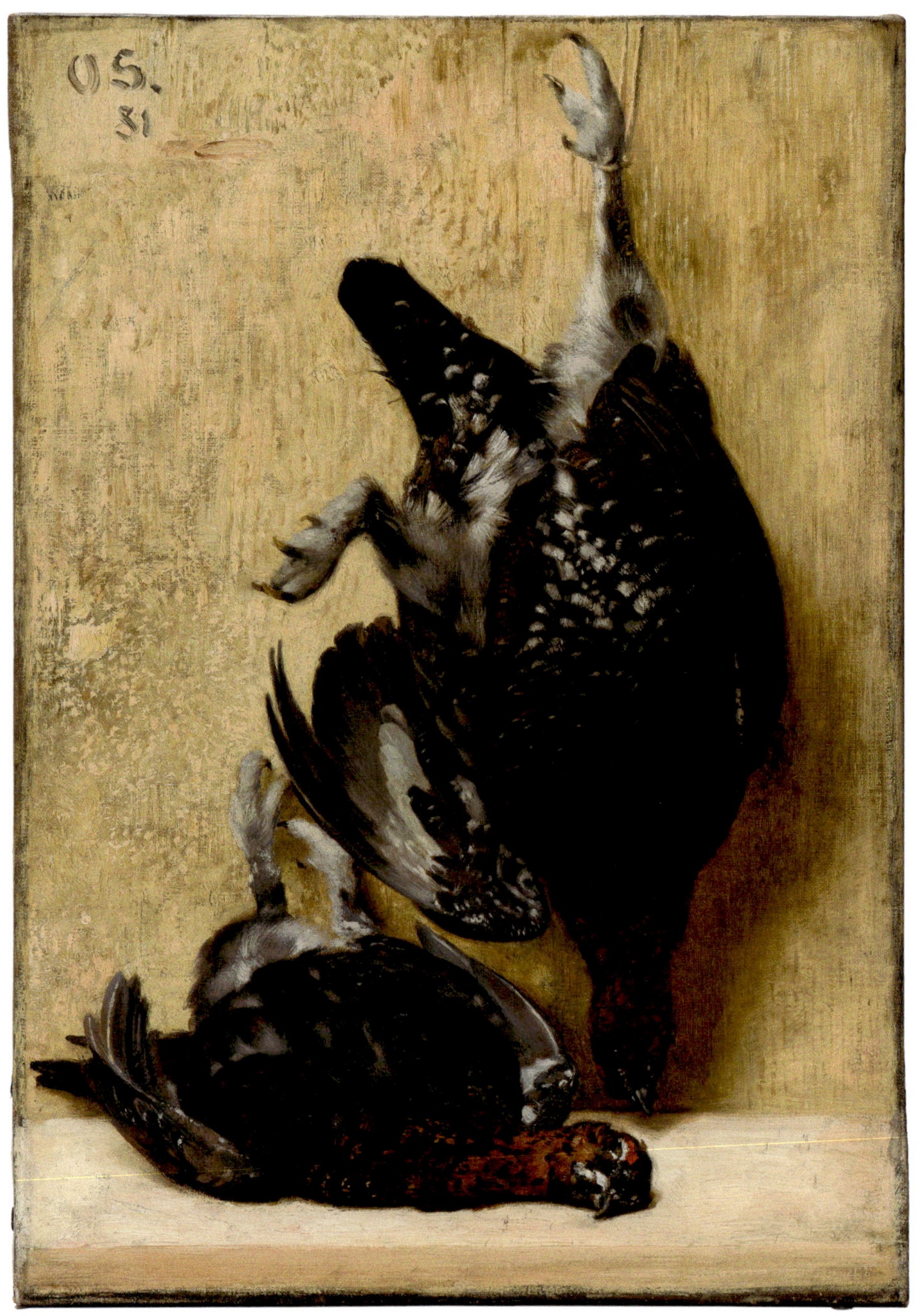

Cat. 91   Aubert Parent: *Bird with a Mouse*, 1792, maple, 28 × 17 cm,
Liebieghaus Skulpturensammlung, Frankfurt am Main,
inv. no. St.P 140

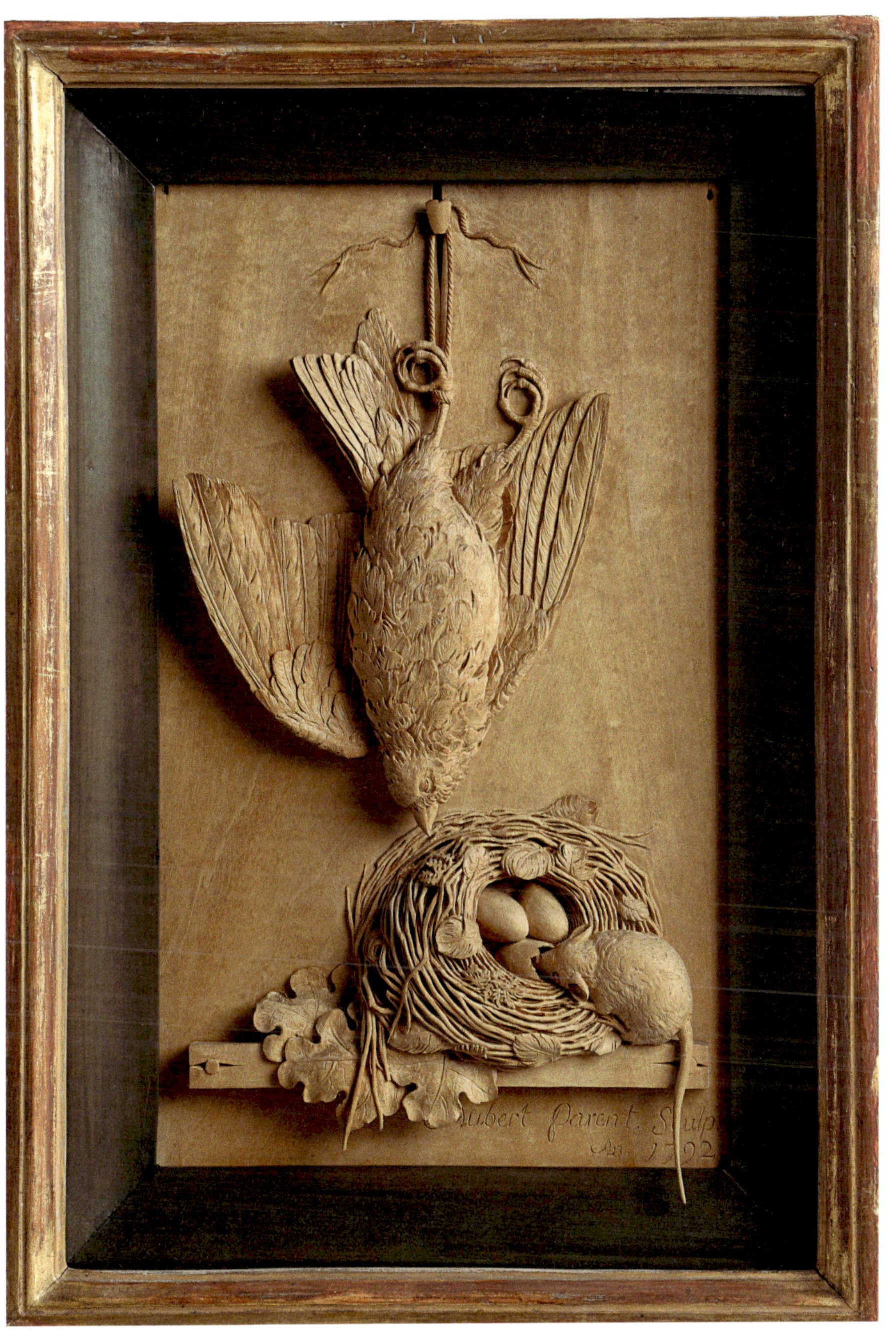

Cat. 92   Gerhard Richter: *Large Curtain*, 1967, oil on canvas, 200 × 275 cm, Städel Museum, Frankfurt am Main, inv. no. SG 1274

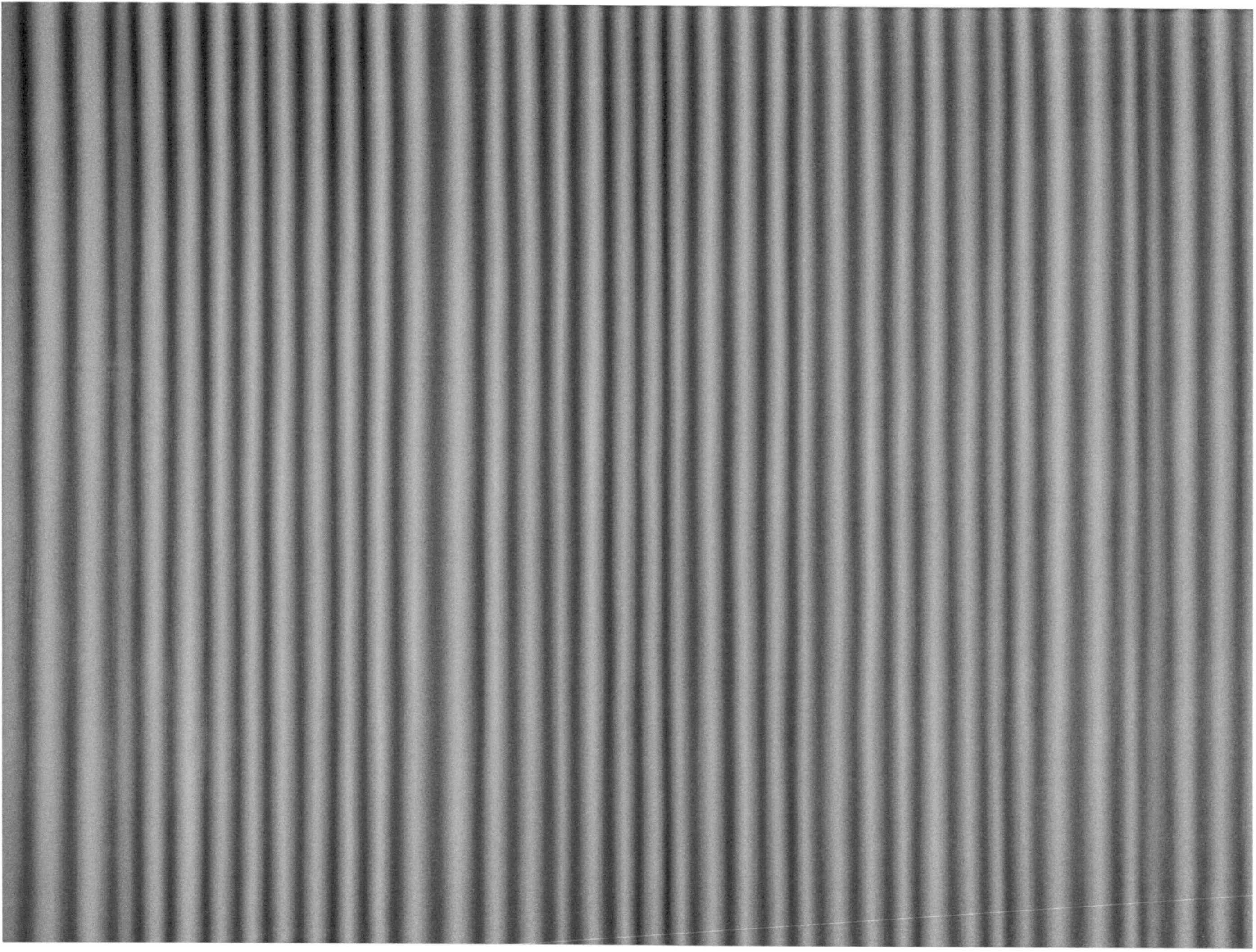

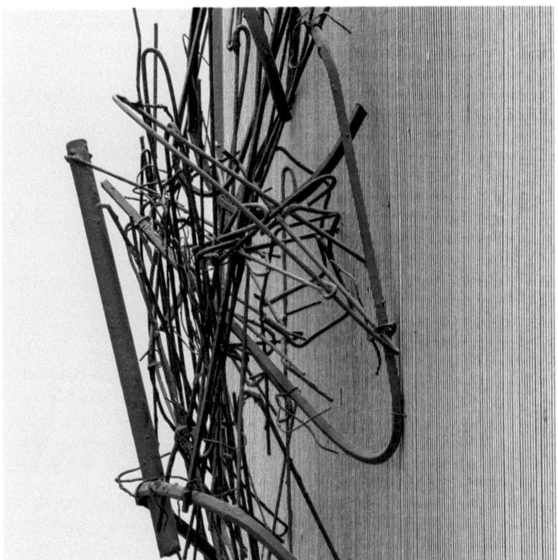

Detail

Cat. 93 Jesús Rafael Soto: *Vibration*, 1961, acrylic on wood and iron wire, 99 × 99.5 × 23 cm, Städel Museum, Frankfurt am Main, inv. no. SG 1243 (Frankfurt only)

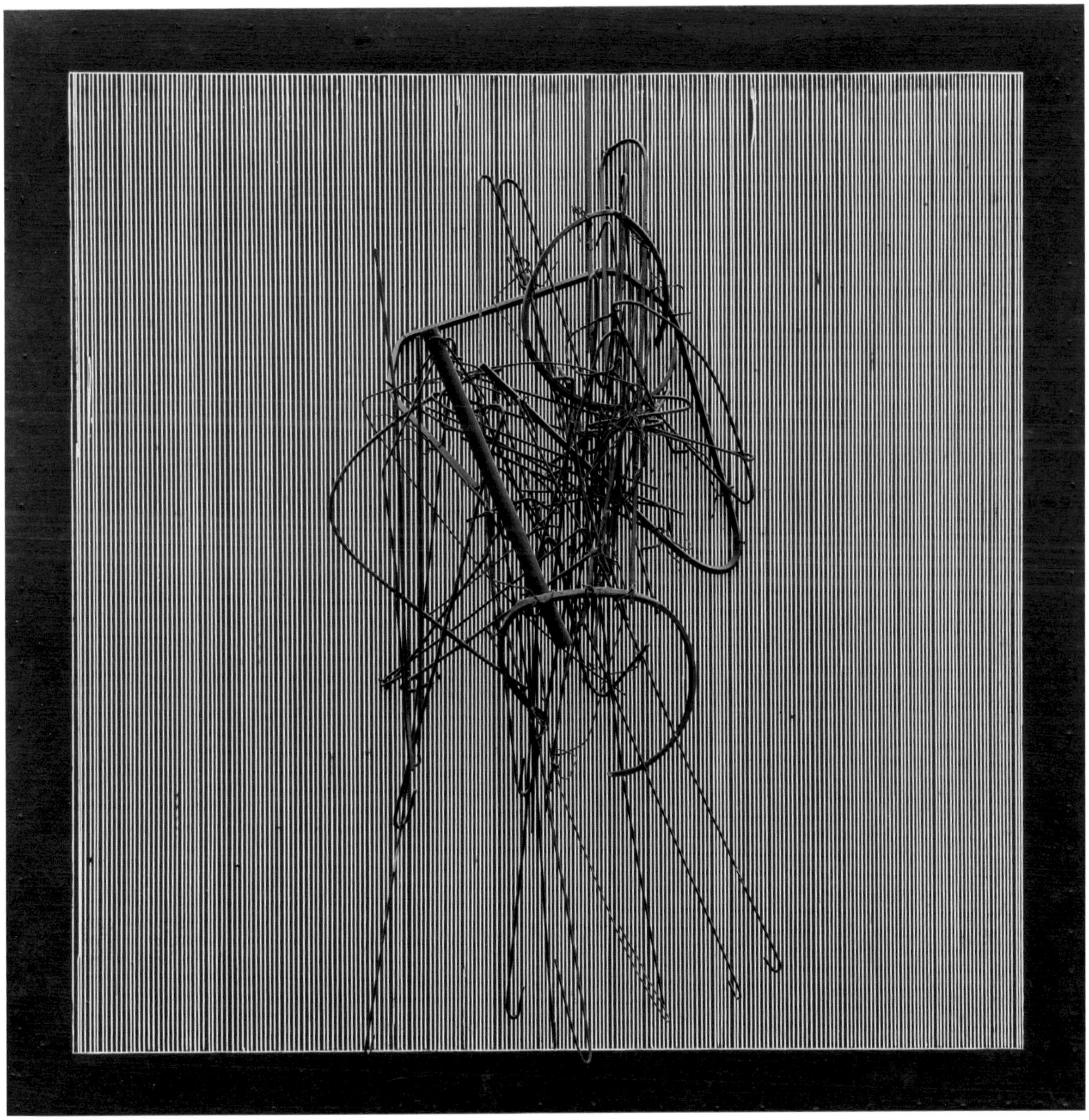

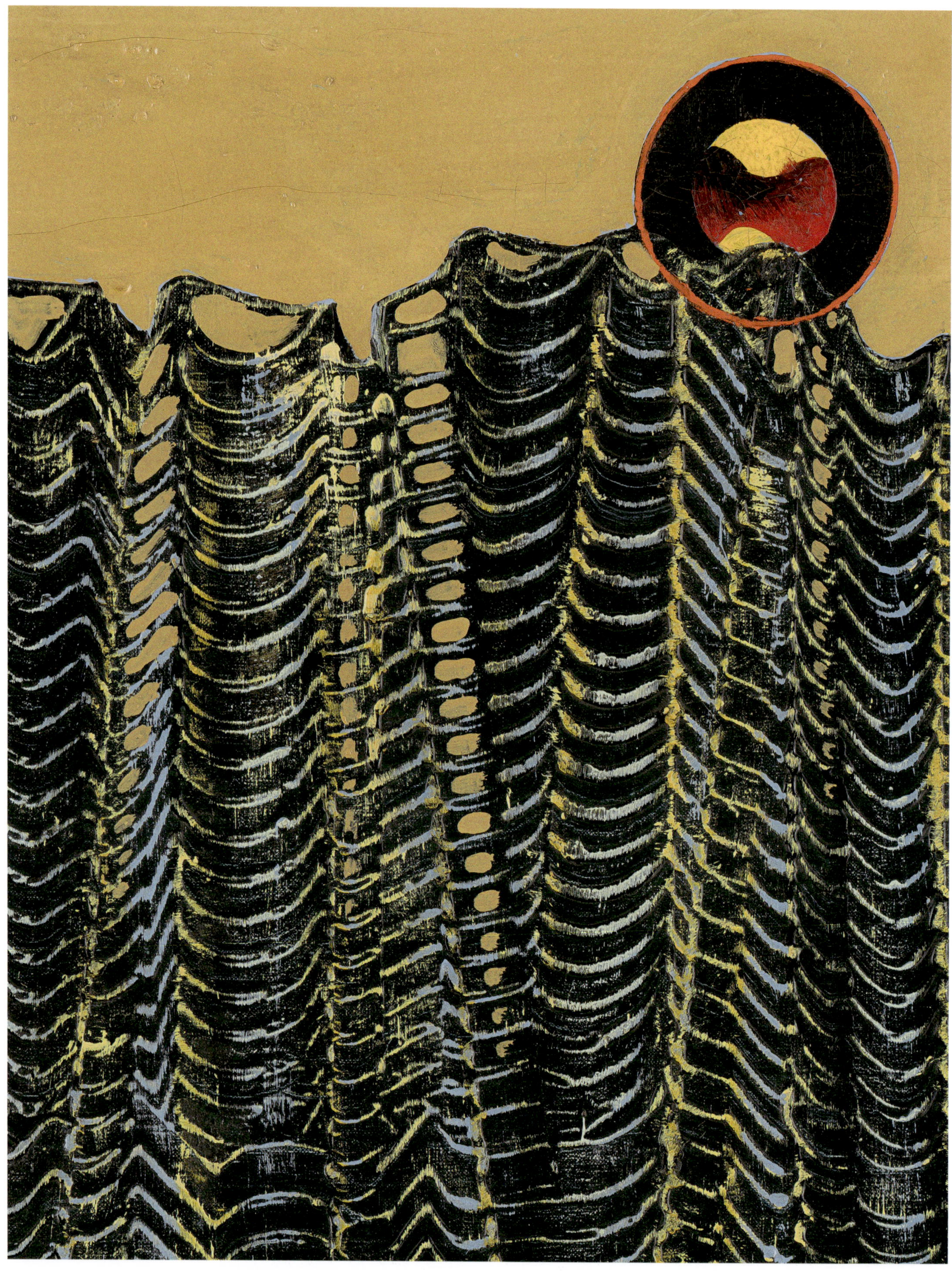

Cats. 94 —104

Alexander Eiling
Eva Mongi-Vollmer
Friederike Schütt

APPROXIMATING NATURE

Untouched nature versus landscape shaped by human intervention: the two had long been considered opposites. By the twentieth century, however, this notion was no longer a central model of thought. Artists had become increasingly less concerned with imitating nature or capturing entire landscape panoramas to serve as backgrounds (fig. 1). They continued the classical study of nature, but in countless works they also addressed the thematic complex of landscape and nature without previous studies in the open air. They no longer drew on familiar examples or specific natural motifs.[1] Emotional immersion in nature and landscape – which were perceived either as threatening or arcadian – was now joined by other aspects. These included creation and formation after the manner of nature, the systematisation of nature modelled on mathematics, the attempt to combine outward and inward images in the encounter with nature, the exploration of nature's haptic qualities, openness of visual observation, and so on.[2] Relief art manifested this fundamental shift in a manner all its own. After all, the artistic relief has a number of properties in common with landscape itself, in that both venture away from the two-dimensional plane. The specific potential of the relief to represent the earth's surface with its highlands and lowlands is used in the geosciences, for example to produce three-dimensional topographical models. In the arts, the properties of the relief – from material to mode of formation to choice of viewing angle – can be used in a wide range of different ways to evoke images of nature or associations with real landscapes.

In contrast to the cartographically precise replication of an existing topography, artists like Yves Klein employed materials taken in part from nature to create reliefs that invite reading as imaginary landscapes. Klein's vivid blue (patented as International Klein Blue, or IKB for short) spreads out evenly across a surface scattered with natural sponges and gravel (cat. 94). The material is reminiscent of the seafloor, while the colour makes us think of the sky: the work seems to radiate into the infinite expanses of the ocean and the cosmos.[3] With the sponge reliefs he had tested on the walls of the Gelsenkirchen Musiktheater between 1957 and 1959, Klein had already proven that he was "a painter of space" (→ Monumental Tasks).[4] For even if the volume of the natural objects sets physical limits to the expansion, the chromatic energy penetrates the third dimension virtually without bounds. On the one hand Klein created a link to reality by drawing on found objects; on the other hand, the monochrome colouration robbed them of their naturalness. The relief was accordingly neither mere illustration nor imitation, but rather the gateway to a new artistic reality.

Jean Dubuffet's *Site of Black Crusts* (cat. 95) resembles works by Klein in that it provides no visual anchor, thus deliberately leaving open the question as to whether the applied structures represent a view from close up or afar. Owing in part to its brown hues, the relief formed unsystematically from papier-mâché, sand and paint conveys the impression of a section of crusted ground. Neither a horizon line nor a figure is present to give us a clue regarding the dimensions or the vantage point. Nor are there any codes such as a palm tree, the sun, or architecture that, in Dubuffet's work *He Has Taken Off His Sandals* (cat. 62), executed immediately after his first stay in the Algerian Sahara, helps at least roughly to localise the landscape.[5] On the contrary, *Site of Black Crusts* from the series *Matériologies* reveals his lifelong fascination with the ground and the composition of sand as a material both grainy and compact.[6] Dubuffet approached his surroundings from the vertical vantage point of the geologist (fig. 2) – not, however, with the aim of achieving topographical precision or reproducing a specific section of ground, but rather to create a surface spectacle with strong tactile appeal, experienceable visually and haptically, from elements of the landscape that had been neglected both artistically and in everyday perception.[7] By refraining from formal and narrative

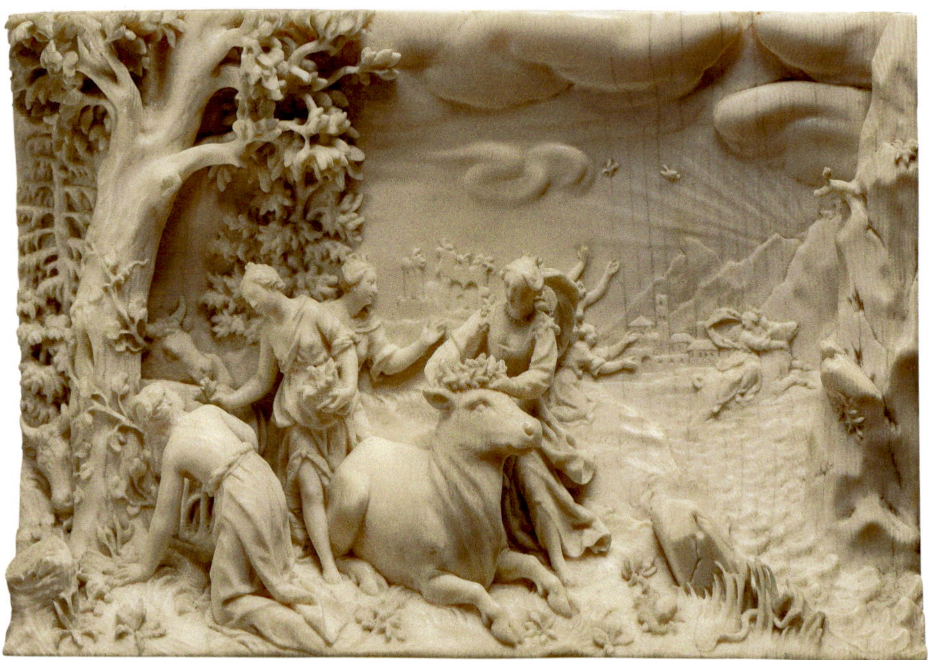

Fig. 1   Johann Michael Schnegg (attributed to): *The Rape of Europe*, ca. 1740–50, ivory,
Liebieghaus Skulpturensammlung, Frankfurt am Main

elements that would have lent structure – and thus in keeping with the *Matériologies* as a whole – he proclaimed the nature-like relief, with its dry, cracked substance and form, the sole object of representation.[8]

Thanks to its scratched surface, Antoni Tàpies' *Collage with the Crosses* (cat. 96) likewise sparks associations with dry, ochre-coloured earth to which the artist added isolated dabs of violet and green paint as well as scraps of paper, virtually transforming it into a poetic reminiscence of blossoms. Our gaze wanders across this seemingly undefined piece of earth at close range; the crosses painted on here and there endow it with symbolic meaning and an atmospheric element. Unlike Dubuffet, who processed the paper into hard crusts, Tàpies employed a collage technique distinguished by a sense of lightness. The distribution of the paper shreds makes them look breeze-blown and introduces rhythm and dynamic to the landscape. Glued on only partially, the paper is as tentatively connected to the painted ground in some places as it is firmly fixed in others. The loose disorder of the surface relief corresponds to the boundlessness of the associative realm created by Tàpies' collage.[9]

Landscape paintings carried out by Paul Klee in the early 1930s form a counterpoint to the undefined and haptic qualities of Dubuffet's and Tàpies' works. In his *Rocky Coast* (cat. 97) and *View into the Fertile Country* (cat. 98), Klee linked the visual experiences of his travels in Egypt with an analytical, systematising gaze. His exploration of the natural

object was also informed by the "knowledge of its inner being", as the artist himself phrased it – an element comprising, among other things, mathematical and musical associations.[10] Klee formed his landscapes without creating the illusion of spatial depth, using instead vertical projections open towards the edges and thus evoking a sense of infinite expansiveness. He constructed the view into the distance with layered geometric forms parallel to the picture plane. It is not perspective that defines what is close or far away, but the contrasts and shades of brightness of the two-dimensionally painted or dot-strewn colour fields.[11]

Klee's views of nature thus adhere entirely to the canvas surface and, with visible brushstrokes, assemble to form landscapes solely with the aid of the colour effects. The Surrealist Max Ernst, on the other hand, devoted himself to a series of paintings similarly reminiscent of landscapes but unambiguously relief-like in character from the mid-1920s onwards. He gave them titles such as *Fishbone Forest* (cat. 99) and *Fishbone Flowers* (cat. 100), and indeed, the trees, plant stems and ground consist of ladder-like structures whose delicate rungs are reminiscent of fishbones. In the Frankfurt example, they are staggered horizontally and vertically to form a hermetically sealed forest that would have reminded the Surrealists of the gloomy and inescapable "thicket" of the soul.[12] A sun-like disc with a red corona shines above the forest's fishbone treetops, its glow so dull as to render it incapable of brightening the fictive

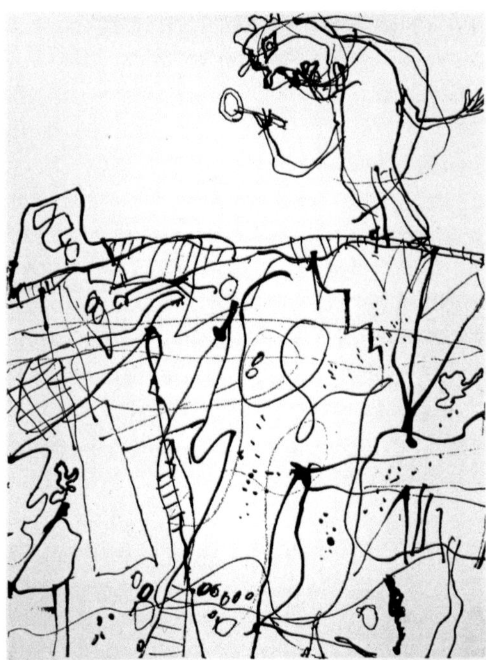

Fig. 2   Jean Dubuffet: *The Geologist with the Magnifying Glass I*
(*Le Géologue à la loupe I*), 1952, ink on paper, private collection

landscape. Ernst described his ambivalent response to the forest in an autobiographical note: "Mixed feelings when he enters the forest for the first time: delight and oppression. [...] Wonderful joy in breathing freely in an open space, but also anxiety at being encircled by hostile trees. Outside and inside at the same time, free and trapped."[13]

Unlike Klein and Tàpies, Ernst did not bring about the landscape's physical expansion into space by way of collage elements, but with the pastose application of black and dark-blue paint, rhythmically modelled with a bristle brush to form a relief.[14] To heighten the impression of plasticity, he then used yellow and light blue to highlight the mounds of paint that had accumulated on either side of every brushstroke. In *Fishbone Flowers*, Ernst employed the conspicuous structures not only for the flower stems but also for the background. An artist who used a wide variety of techniques in his work, he moreover enhanced the painting with marbled zones and shell-shaped forms to create a landscape made up purely of different artistic textures. The viewers are prompted to "feel" the multiform relief structures not by touch but by sight; in doing so, their minds are activated and manifold associations are triggered.[15]

Otto Herbert Hajek's sculpture *Spatial Knots 75* (cat. 104) virtually translates the vertical, scabby repeat pattern of Max Ernst's *Fishbone Forest* into the third dimension. A seemingly infinite continuum of spatial chambers grows out of a multiply linked network of thin, loosely joined rods. Visually, the filigree structure condenses along its longitudinal axis to form a sheer impenetrable wall. At the same time, the artist actively incorporated the empty centre of the three-dimensional body into the work's making and contemplation. He chose the title *Spatial Knots* with the aim of "leading the eyes away from the tangible form of the material [...] in order to enclose the viewer in these chambers, in these streams of space, in their surroundings" (→ Boundary and Space of Possibility).[16] The traces of whitish clay left behind by the casting process – Hajek opted not to remove them – lend the unpolished bronze a dry and brittle quality and, due in part to the copse-like character of the composition, bring natural forms to mind.[17]

Upward-sprouting structures like those in the work by Hajek are levelled by the bird's-eye perspective. The British painter and sculptor William Turnbull, who served as a pilot in the Royal Air Force during the Second World War, created landscapes as unbounded total visions.[18] In 1955 he was commissioned to produce a relief for a building with a curved façade situated in a London street that was only six metres wide. The project was never realised, but the six maquettes (cats. 101–103) have survived (→ Monumental Tasks).[19] Turnbull addressed the challenging conditions by designing the reliefs without a fixed optical reference point. At the same time, they testify to the immense influence of his flight experiences on his artistic work. A pilot could hardly focus on a fixed point. Sight from the cockpit was dominated instead by a lack of clarity about where to look, coupled with uncertainty about what one was seeing. An archaeological site was virtually indistinguishable from a bombed city or an industrial zone. Ultimately, however, both were places that testified to human activity.[20] The long shot of the world landscape – a perspective once associated with divine omnipotence – had given way to the bird's-eye view of a military pilot vainly seeking orientation.[21] Turnbull's reliefs, visually accessible from above in the manner of a camera pan, are a veritable symbol of the viewability of an artwork from many angles and thus bear an analogy to real landscape. It is ultimately the aesthetic of the nature experience that can form the foil for the translation into artificial texture, surface and space and, without claiming to be a direct likeness, can generate an experience of nature and landscape in the beholder – not only in the work of Turnbull. Suggestive of views of the land from the sky, his works are an example of the numerous analogies between the artistically formed relief and the relief of the landscape. Through the use of a wide range of materials, taken in part from nature, and the thorough structuring of the surfaces, the works on display here bear witness to artists' interest in the fanciful recreation of the landscape in the relief medium.

1   See Stefan Gronert: "Die bilderlose Natur: Vom Wandel der Naturerfahrung in der Kunst der neueren Moderne", in: Jörg Zimmermann (ed.): *Ästhetik und Naturerfahrung*, Stuttgart-Bad Cannstatt 1996, pp. 521–536, here p. 521.

2   For an introduction, see Oskar Bätschmann: *Entfernung der Natur: Landschaftsmalerei 1750–1920*, Cologne 1989.

3   On the link between chromatic purity and boundlessness, see Noit Banai: "Vom Mythos der Objekthaftigkeit zur Ordnung des Raums: Yves Kleins Abenteuer in der Leere", in: *Yves Klein*, ed. Olivier Berggruen, Max Hollein and Ingrid Pfeiffer, exh. cat. Schirn Kunsthalle Frankfurt/ Guggenheim Museum Bilbao, Ostfildern 2004, pp. 15–28.

4   Ingrid Pfeiffer: "Yves Klein: Stationen in Deutschland", in: ibid., pp. 55–84.

5   See *Jean Dubuffet: "Er hat die Sandalen ausgezogen"*, ed. Nina Zimmer, exh. cat. Hamburger Kunsthalle/Staatliche Kunsthalle Karlsruhe, Hamburg 2005.

6   On this work as part of the *Matériologies* series, see Max Loreau: *Catalogue des travaux de Jean Dubuffet*, vol. 17, no. 118, Paris 1970.

7   Raphaël Bouvier: "Dubuffets Metamorphosen der Landschaft: Eine Einführung", in: *Jean Dubuffet: Metamorphosen der Landschaft*, ed. idem, exh. cat. Fondation Beyeler, Riehen/Basel, Ostfildern 2016, pp. 11–21, here p. 11; Sophie Berrebi: "Landschaftsdestruktion: Jean Dubuffet und die Prähistorie", in: ibid., pp. 107–113, here p. 110.

8   For a fundamental discussion of the multifariousness of landscape in Dubuffet's oeuvre, see Andreas Franzke: "Erfundene Orte und Situationen: Landschaftswiedergaben im Werk Jean Dubuffets", in: *Dubuffet: Retrospektive*, exh. cat. Akademie der Künste, Berlin et al., Berlin 1980, pp. 167–231, here pp. 168, 172.

9   See *Masterpieces of the Department of Prints and Drawings*, ed. Jutta Schütt and Martin Sonnabend, exh. cat. Städel Museum, Frankfurt am Main, Petersberg 2008, p. 162.

10   Paul Klee: "Wege des Naturstudiums" (1923), in: Bätschmann 1989 (see note 2), pp. 351–353, here p. 352.

11   See *Gärten: Ordnung, Inspiration, Glück*, ed. Sabine Schulze, exh. cat. Städel Museum, Frankfurt am Main/Städtische Galerie im Lenbachhaus und Kunstbau, Munich, Ostfildern 2006, p. 318 (Svenja Kriebel).

12   See Uwe M. Schneede: *Max Ernst*, Stuttgart 1972, p. 110.

13   Max Ernst: "Was ist ein Wald", in: Helmut R. Leppien: *Der Große Wald*, Stuttgart 1967, pp. 22f., here p. 22.

14   In the literature there is reference to pieces of cut sheet metal which the artist used to create the fishbone structure by pressing them into the paint while it was still wet; see Leppien 1967 (see note 13), p. 110. However, this technique can be ruled out for the Frankfurt painting. We thank Stephan Knobloch, the head of the Städel Museum conservation department, for important pointers on how the painting was executed.

15   See the section "Materialbilder – Reliefwirkungen", in: *Max Ernst: Skulpturen Häuser Landschaften*, ed. Werner Spies, exh. cat. Musée National d'Art Moderne, Centre Pompidou, Paris/ Kunstsammlung Nordrhein-Westfalen, Düsseldorf, Cologne 1998, pp. 11–223, here pp. 54–56.

16   Otto Herbert Hajek in a lecture in Stuttgart on 6 March 1979, quoted in Anuschka Plattner: *Otto Herbert Hajek: Konzeptionen der Raumgestaltung – Werkverzeichnis*, diss., Heidelberg 1999, p. 6; trans. JR.

17   Christoph Zuschlag: "Struktur – Rhythmus – Geste: Zur Dynamisierung des Raumes in der Plastik des Informels", in: *Skulptur pur*, ed. Ulrike Lorenz, Stefanie Patruno and Christoph Wagner, exh. cat. Kunsthalle Mannheim, Heidelberg 2014, pp. 76–85, here p. 81; Plattner 1999 (see note 16), pp. 5–7.

18   On total visions in landscape painting, see Bätschmann 1989 (see note 2), pp. 77–83.

19   Amanda A. Davidson: *The Sculpture of William Turnbull*, Aldershot 2005, nos. 43–48.

20   Ben Highmore: "Art, Aftershocks and the Promise of a New World", in: *Postwar Modern: New Art in Britain, 1945–65*, ed. Jane Alison with Hilary Floe and Charlotte Flint, exh. cat. Barbican Art Gallery, London, Munich et al. 2022, pp. 29–33, here p. 32.

21   Davidson 2005 (see note 19), no. 16.

Cat. 94   Yves Klein: *Blue Sponge Relief* (*Little Night Music*), 1960,
sponge, stone and colour pigments on wood and canvas,
145 × 116 cm, Städel Museum, Frankfurt am Main,
inv. no. SG 1254 (Frankfurt only)

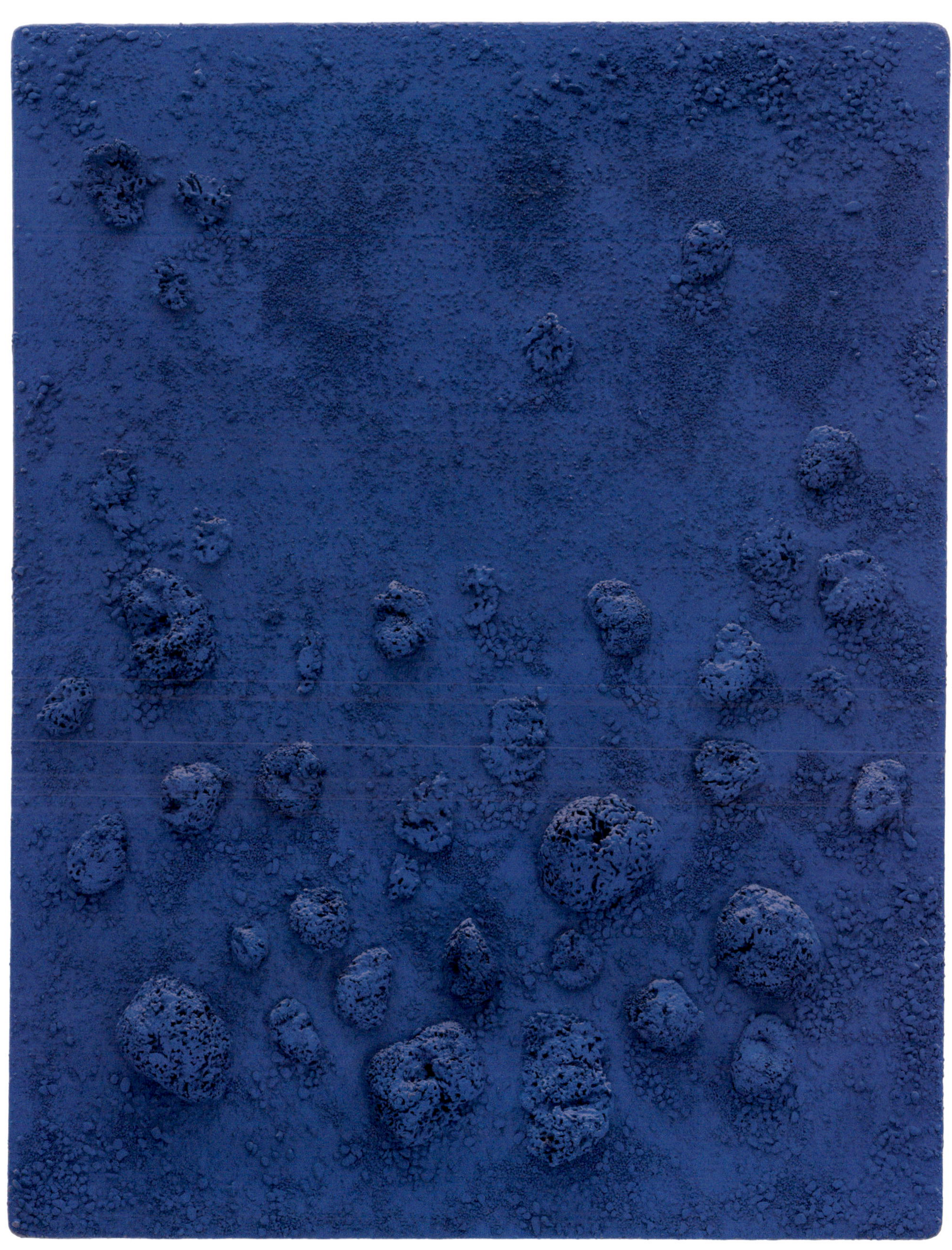

Cat. 95   Jean Dubuffet: *Site of Black Crusts* (*Site aux croûtes noires*),
1960, papier-mâché, sand mixture over plaster and tar (?),
partially coloured, on press board, framed in wood,
55.5 × 66 × 4.5 cm, Städel Museum, Frankfurt am Main,
inv. no. 17887 (Frankfurt only)

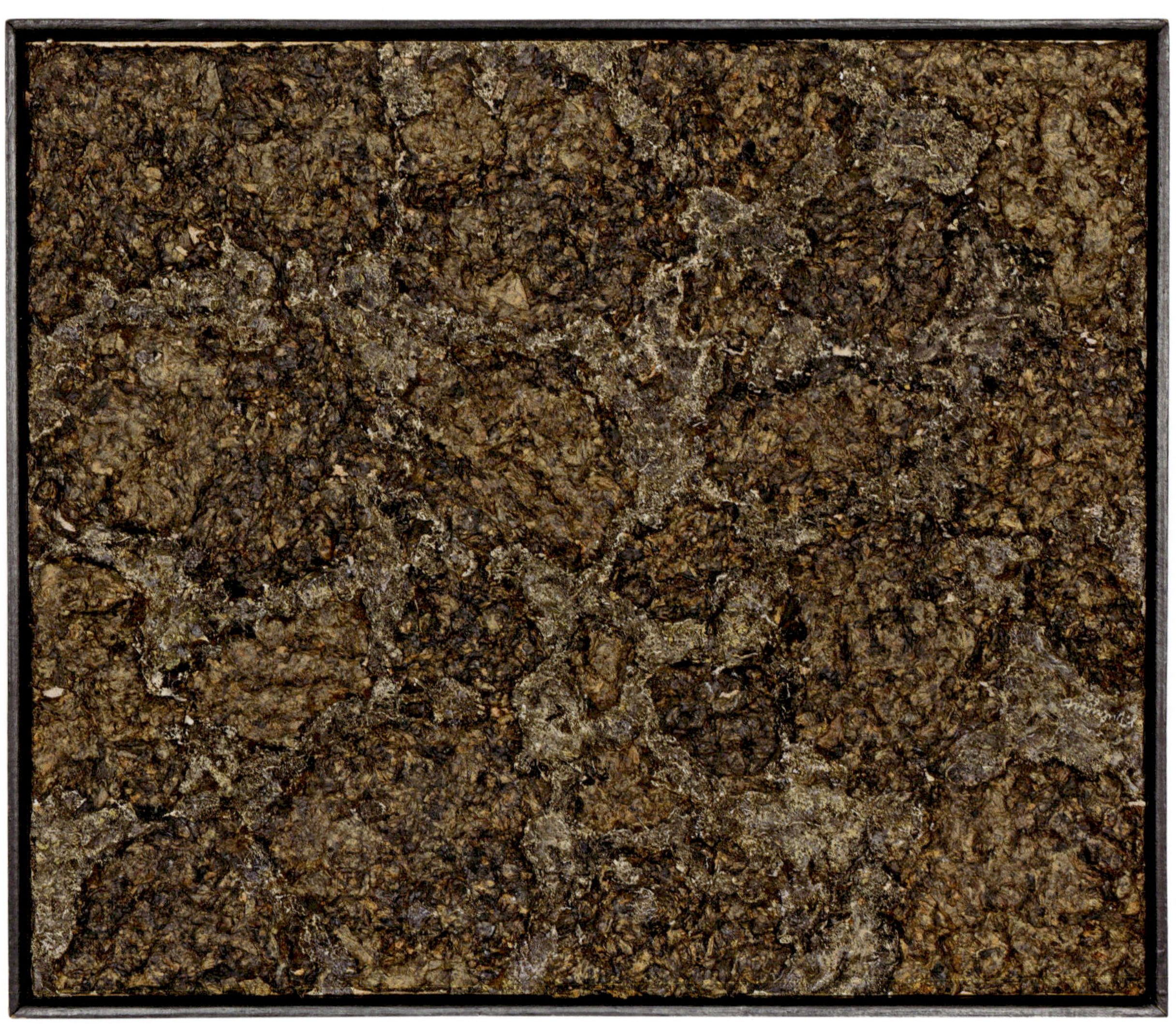

Cat. 96   Antoni Tàpies: *Collage with the Crosses* (*Collage de les creus*),
1947, gouache, chalk, collage and etchings on cardboard,
52.5 × 73.5 cm, Städel Museum, Frankfurt am Main,
inv. no. SG 3386 (Frankfurt only)

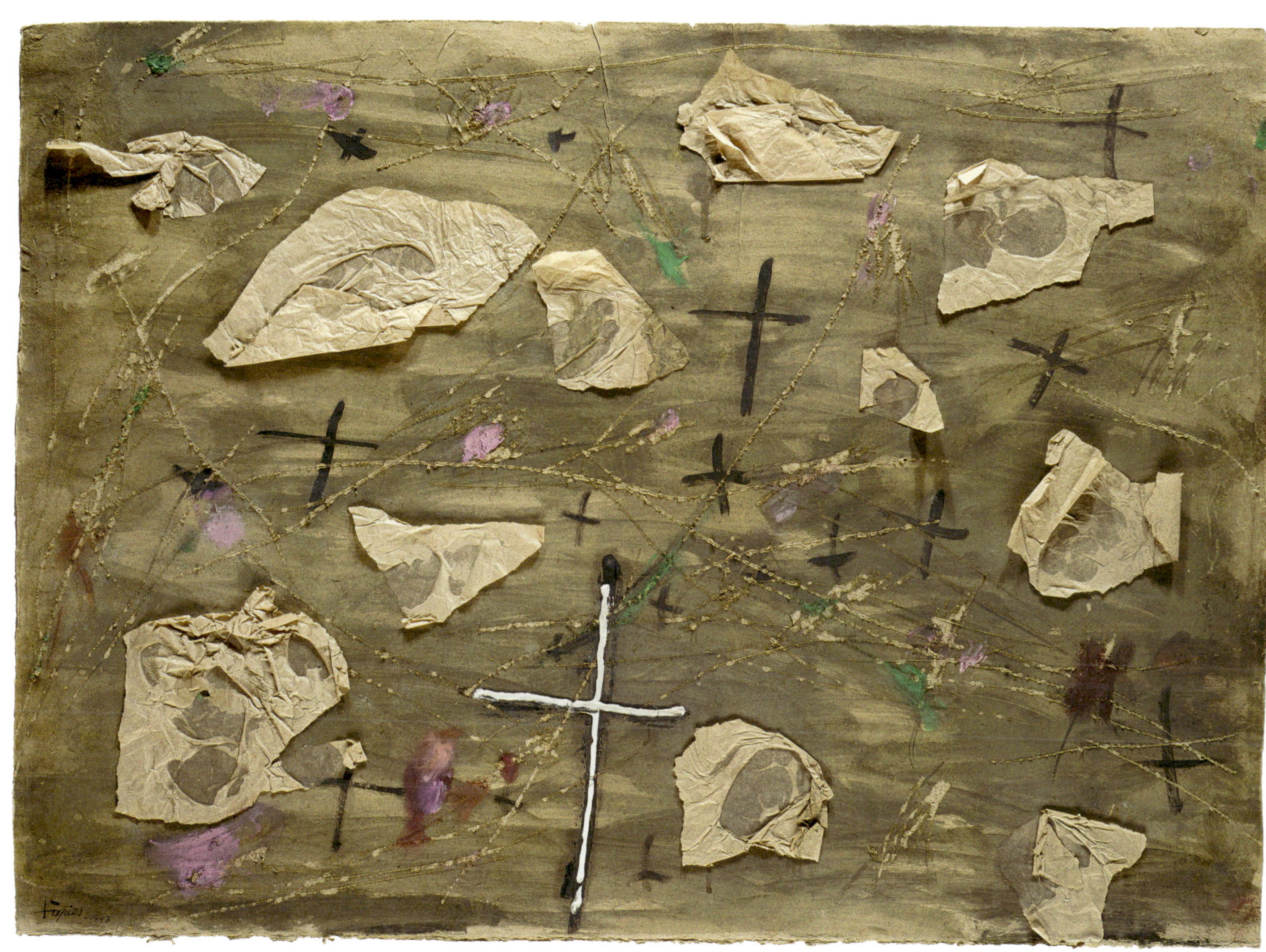

Cat. 97   Paul Klee: *Rocky Coast*, 1931, oil on plywood,
50.6 × 52.7 cm, Hamburger Kunsthalle, inv. no. HK-5053
(Hamburg only)

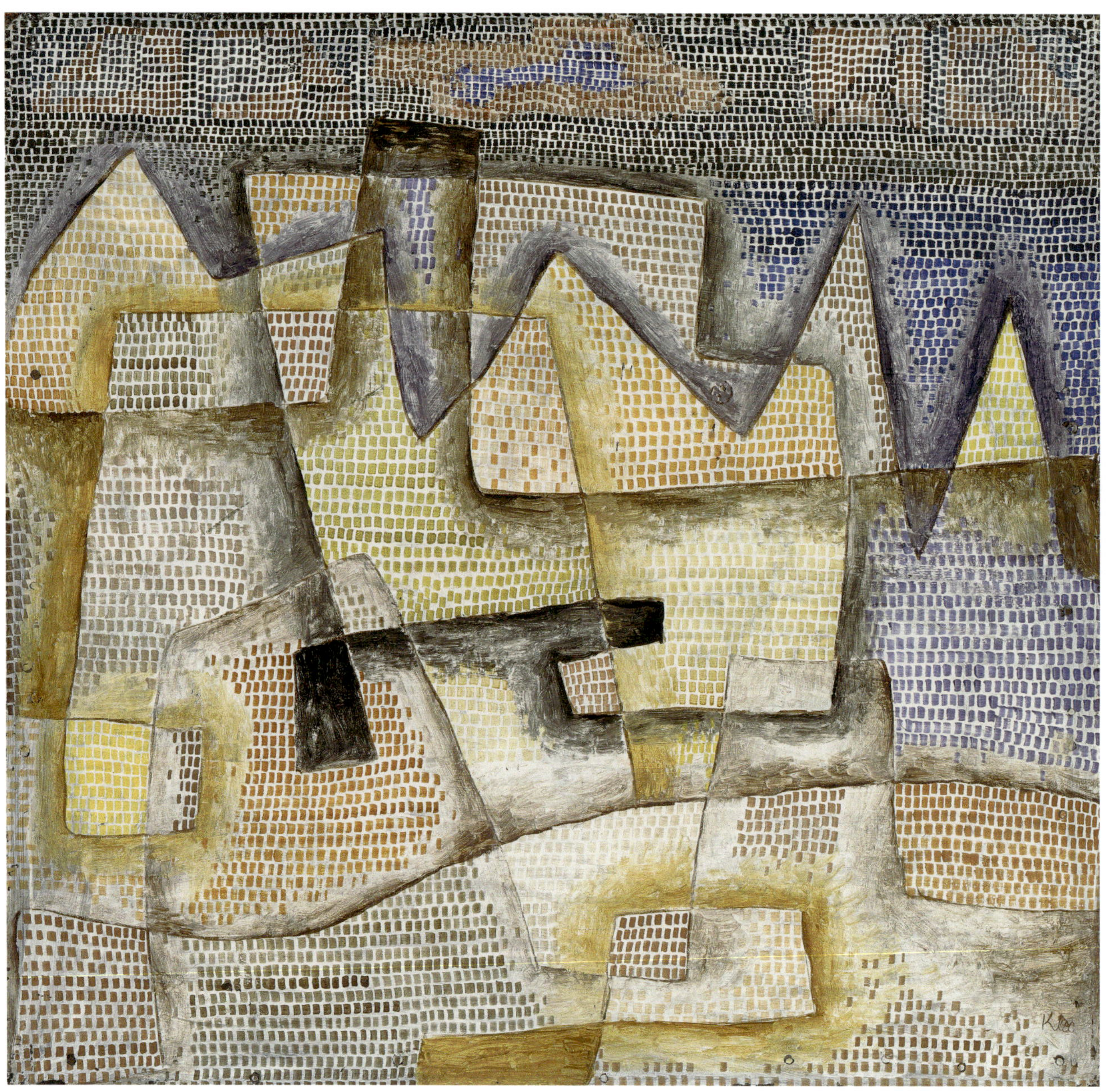

Cat. 98   Paul Klee: *View into the Fertile Country*, 1932,
oil on cardboard, 48.5 × 34.5 cm, Städel Museum,
Frankfurt am Main, inv. no. SG 1221 (Frankfurt only)

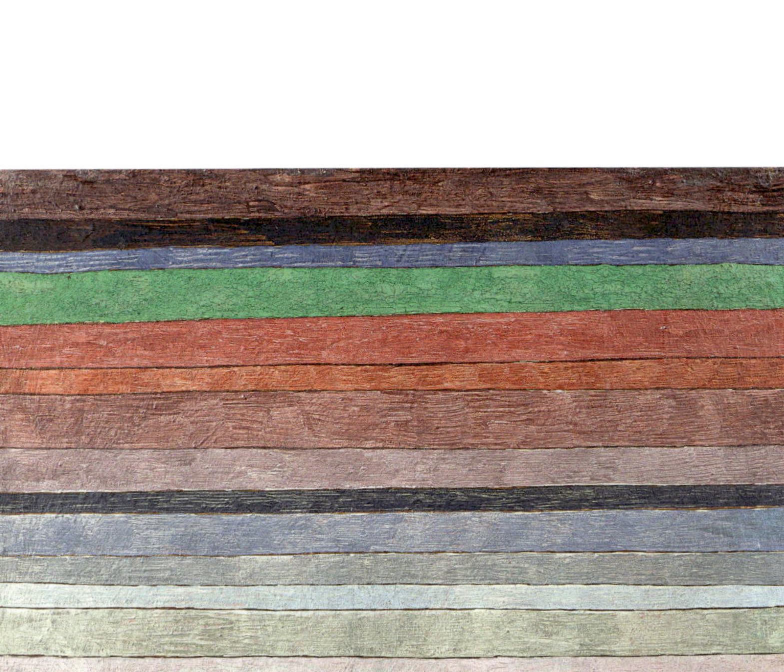

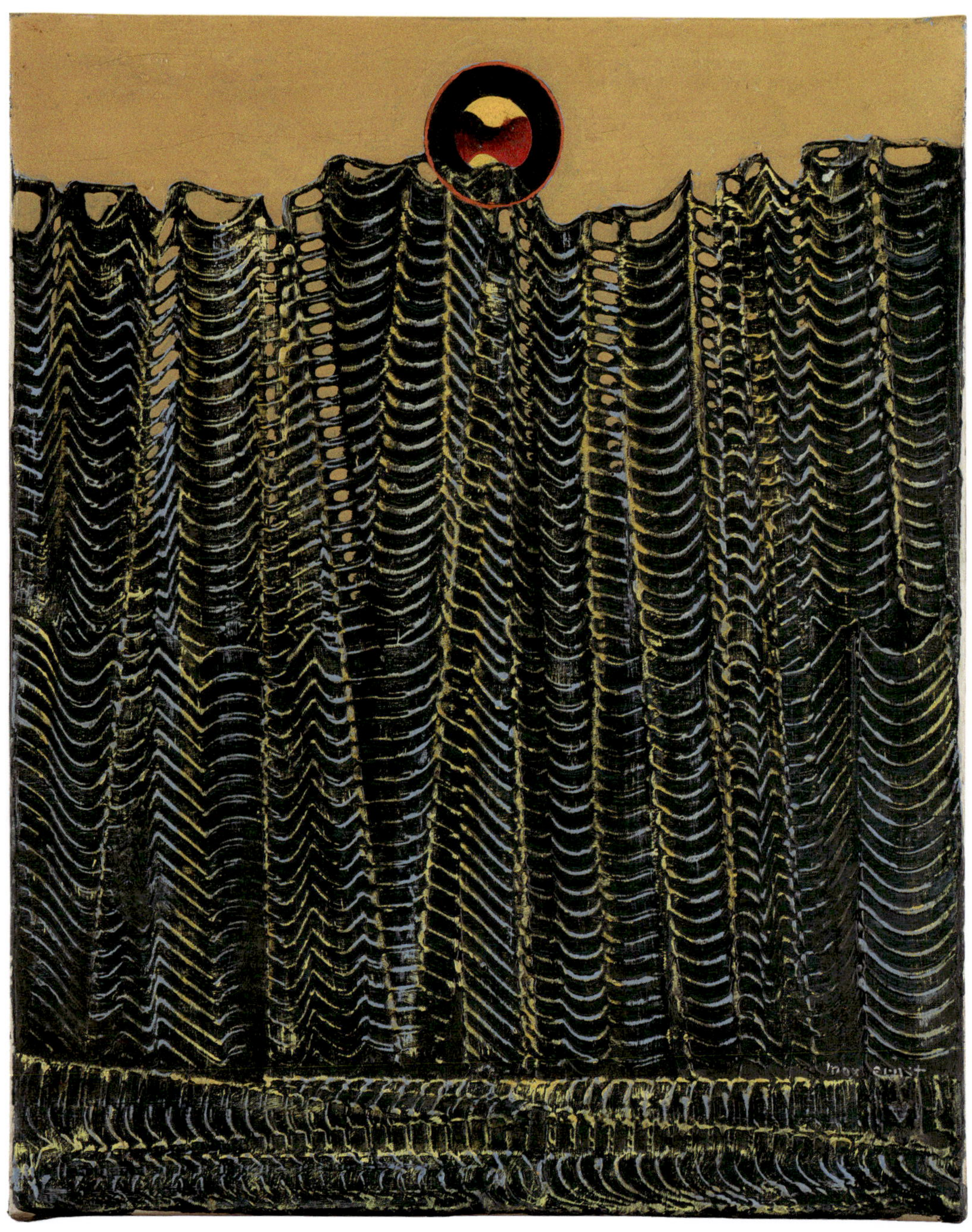

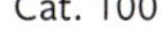

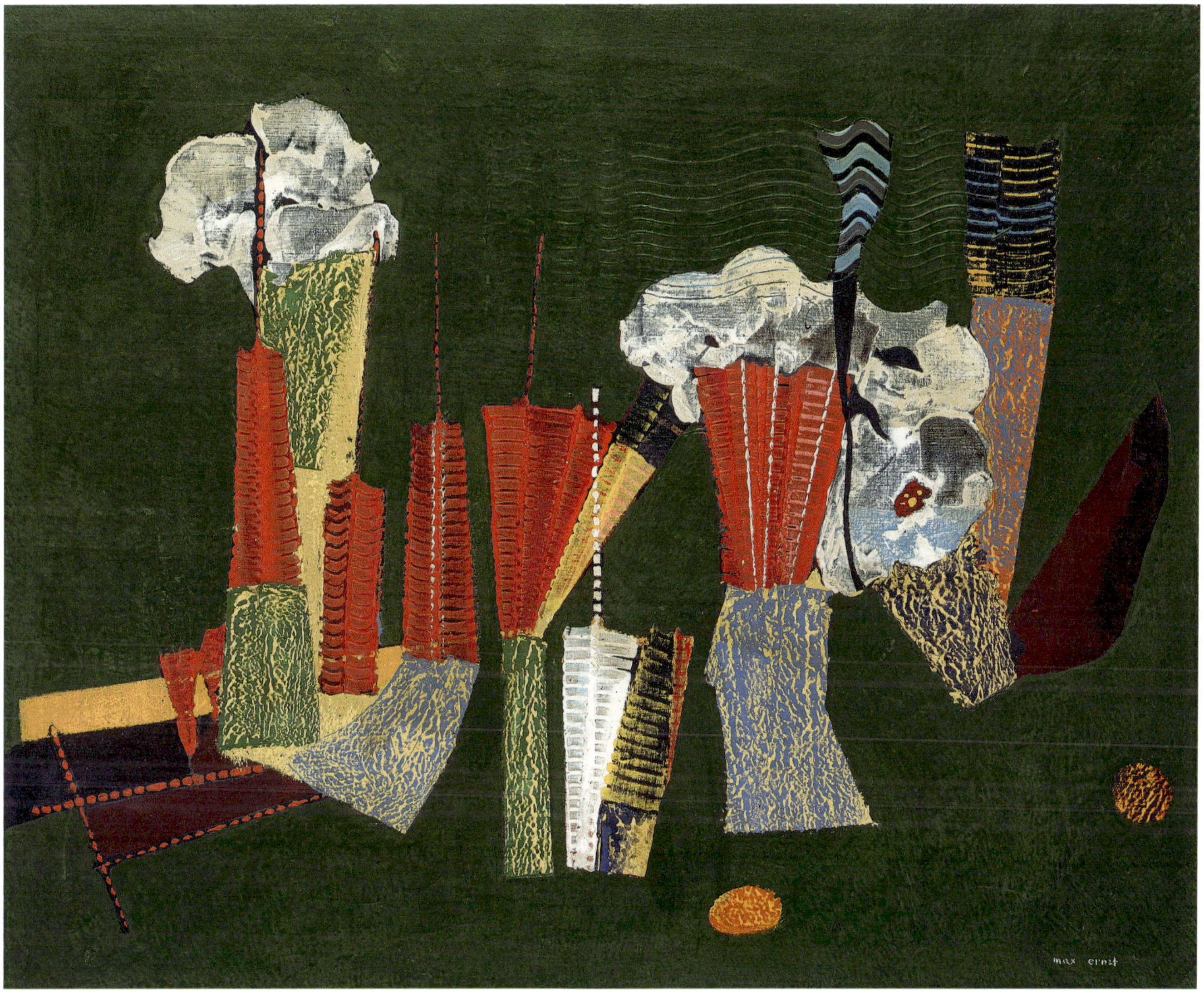

Cat. 101 William Turnbull: *Relief 2*, 1955, bronze, 38.7 × 59 × 2.5 cm,
The William Turnbull Will Trust

Cat. 102 William Turnbull: *Relief 3*, 1955, bronze, 36.8 × 52.1 × 5.7 cm,
The William Turnbull Will Trust

Cat. 103 William Turnbull: *Relief 4*, 1955, bronze, 58.4 × 41.9 × 5.7 cm,
The William Turnbull Will Trust

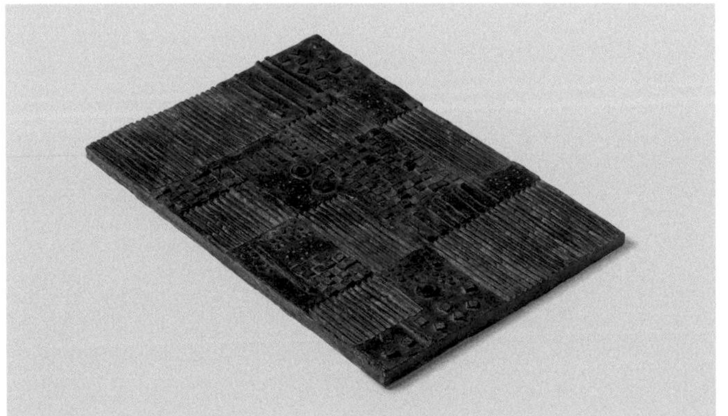

Cat. 101

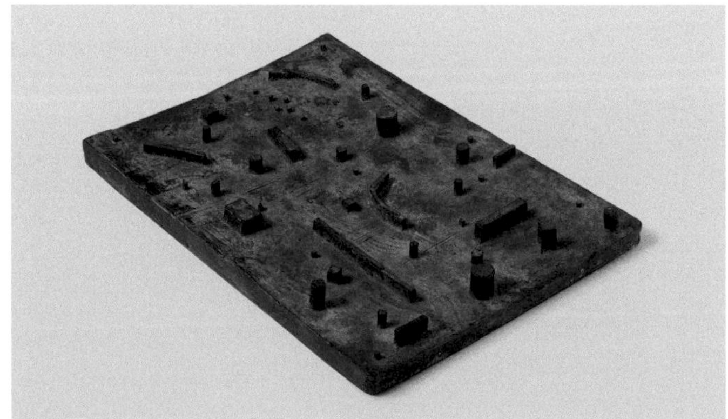

Cat. 102

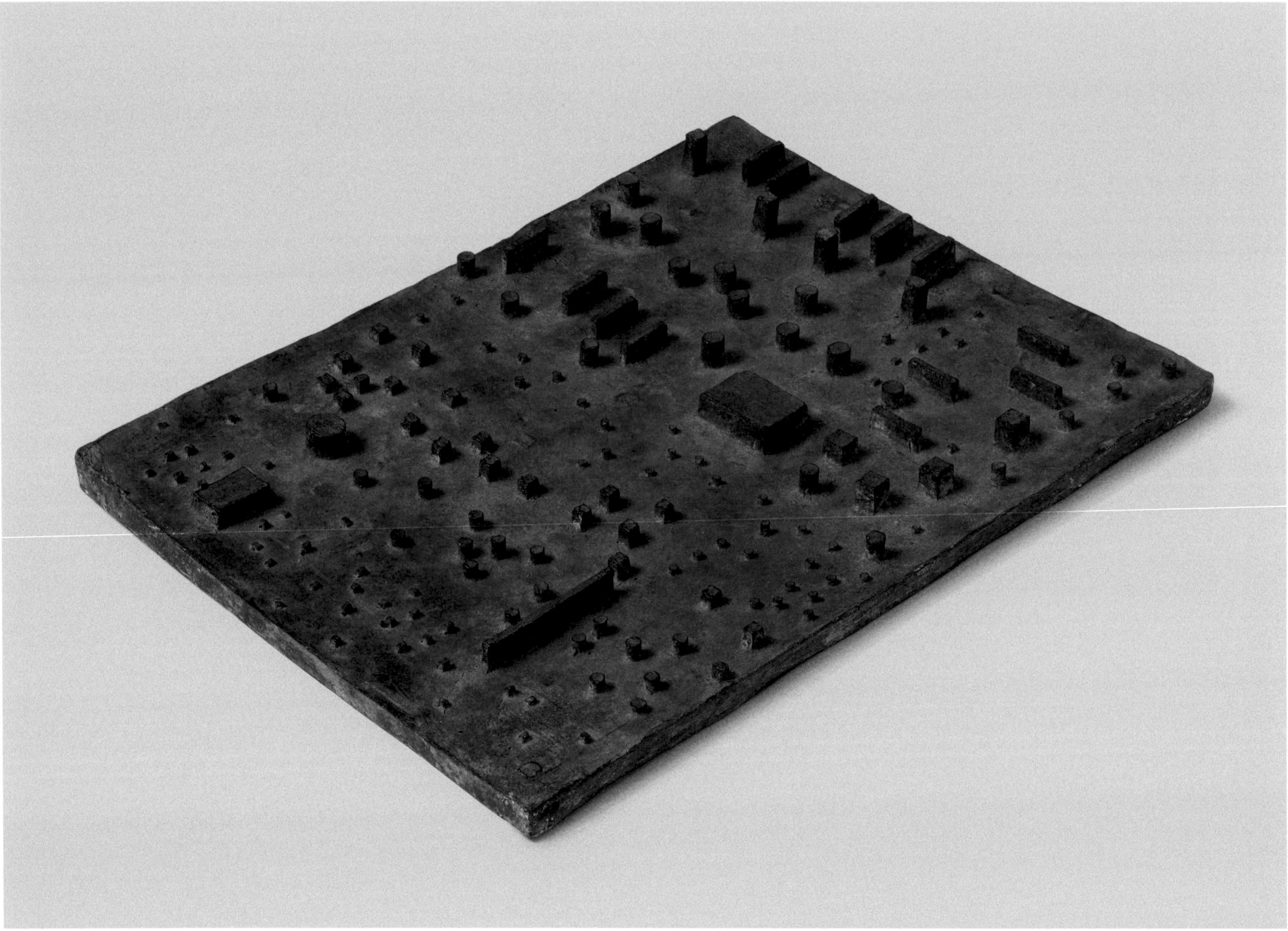

Cat. 103

Cat. 104   Otto Herbert Hajek: *Spatial Knots 75*, 1958, bronze,
40 × 90 × 35 cm, Staatsgalerie Stuttgart, transfer from
the Baden-Württembergisches Kultusministerium 1968,
inv. no. PLNA 138

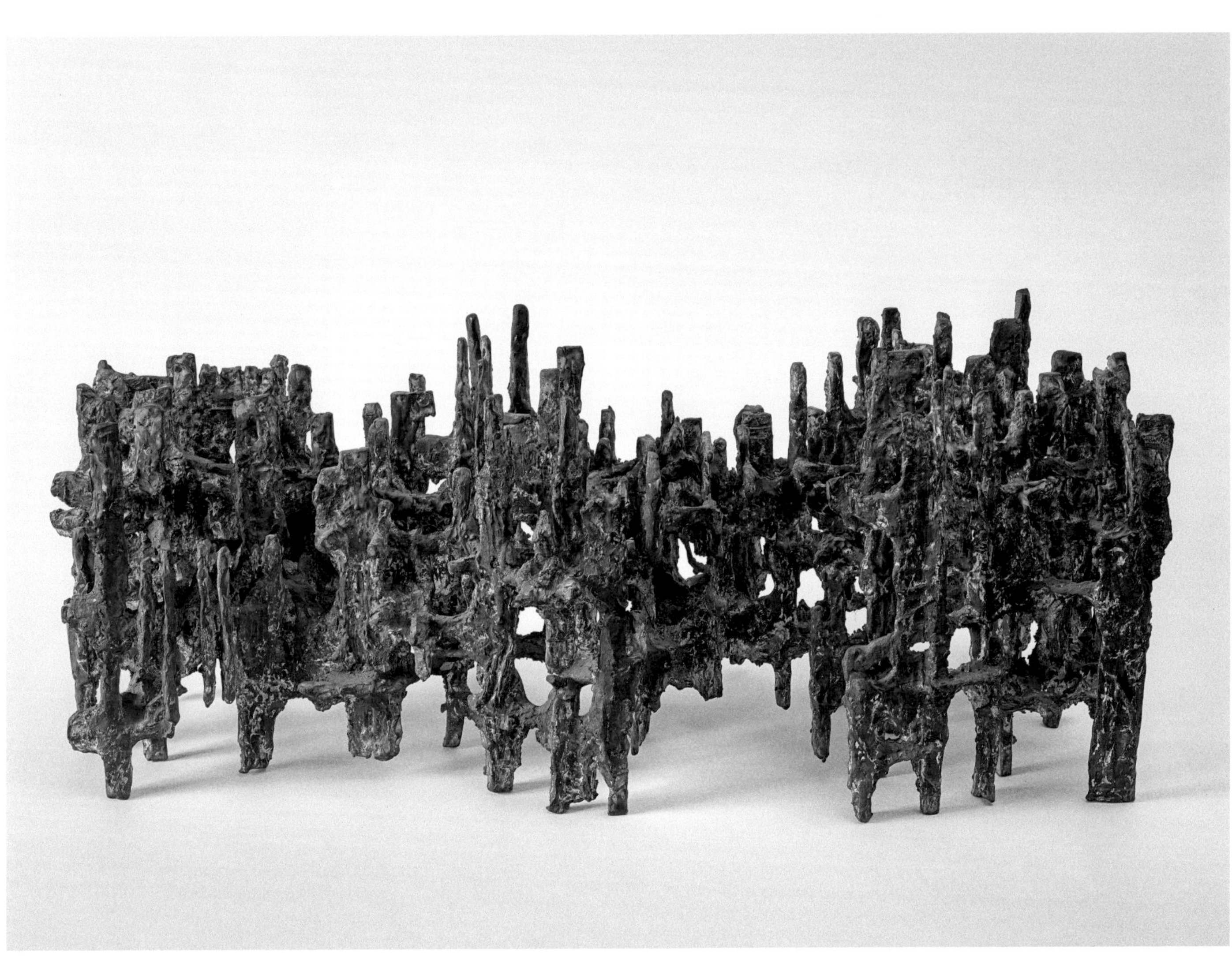

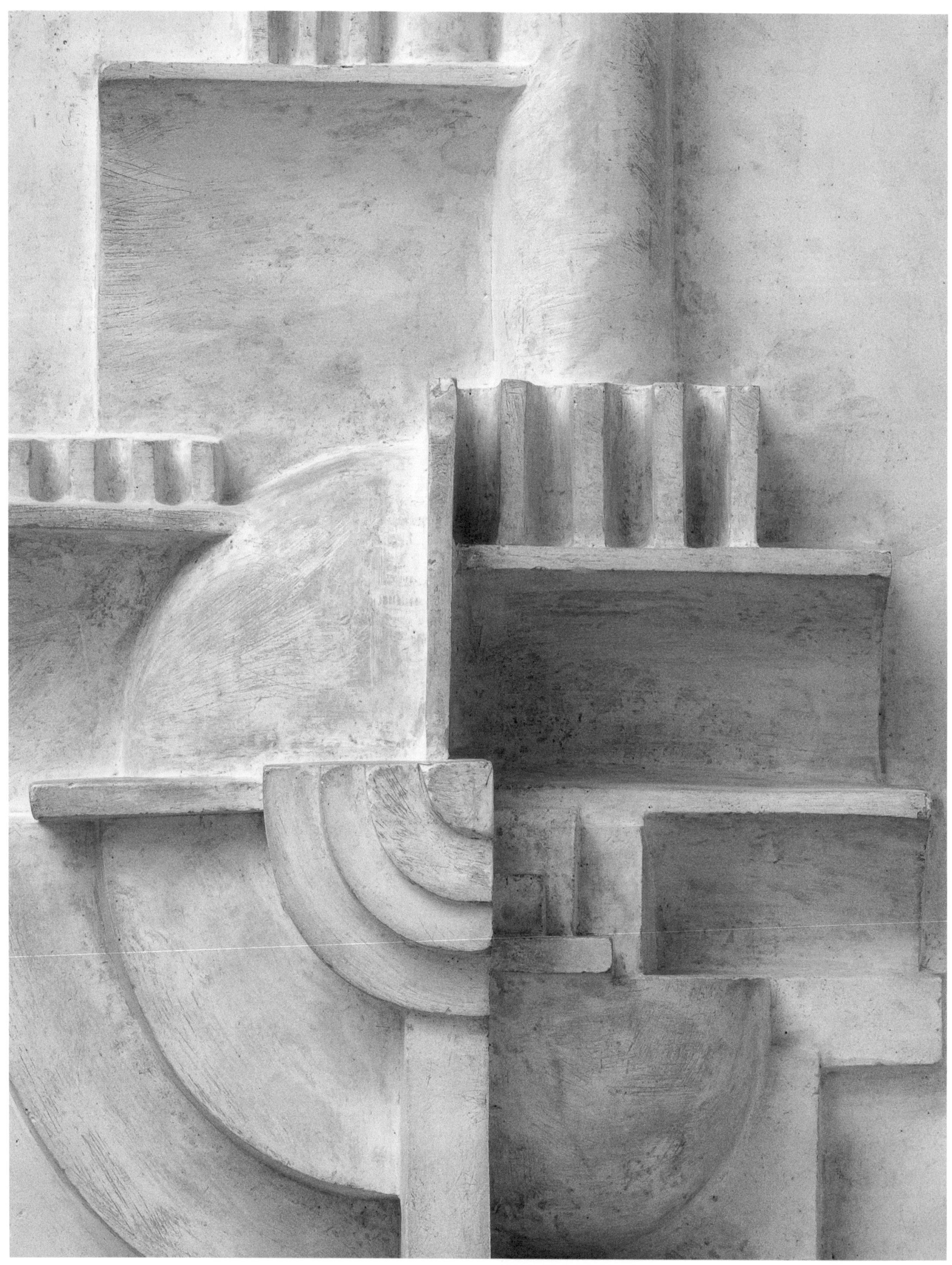

Cats. 105—119

Karin Schick

DESIGNS OF THE WORLD

The Relief as a Construction

A wave of radical changes seized Europe in the nineteenth and early twentieth century: science, technology and industrialisation brought progress, mobility and global communication; politics promised more participation, and imperialism secured economic prosperity. The flip side of these developments was that poverty, exploitation, nationalism, racism, uncertainty and resistance grew among the population. Against the backdrop of the First World War, political revolutions and social upheaval, this led to radical new beginnings in art as well – people wanted to pursue their own visions, to create a new world and a "New Human".[1] Movements with similar aims emerged in numerous countries which established networks beyond national borders and political systems.[2] In the process, as a hybrid art genre that combined painting, sculpture and architecture, the relief played a vital role.

In czarist Russia, uprisings and mass demonstrations had increased since the first Russian Revolution in 1905, which ultimately culminated in the October Revolution in 1917. It was during these explosive times that the avant-garde also began to emerge.[3] Artists demonstrated public presence in 1915 and 1916 in three exhibitions, one of which is regarded as the natal hour of Constructivism: *The Last Futurist Exhibition of Painting 0.10* in Petrograd. The show, which comprised approximately 160 exhibits, was co-organised by Ivan Puni, who was also prominently represented, among other things with the object *The White Sphere* (cat. 107). A drawer module is the showcase for a composition divided diagonally by two areas painted black and green respectively. A three-dimensional element, a white sphere, protrudes from the green area forward into space and backward towards the wall.[4] Despite the radicalness of his means, Puni was not thought of as pioneering; rather, the reliefs he called *Painterly Sculptures* were referred to as Cubist and approximated with a French, form-based aesthetic style of art.[5] As a matter of fact, Puni had sought training

in Paris (returning there in 1924 and establishing himself as Jean Pougny), yet with their interest in multiperspectival spatiality, Cubism and Italian Futurism were an inspiration and model not only for him but for most artists in Russia (→ The Polyperspectival Gaze).

This also applied to the two dominant figures – and fierce competitors – in the exhibition *0.10*: Kazimir Malevich and Vladimir Tatlin. Malevich presented nearly 40 paintings, one of which was today's iconic *Black Square*, and proclaimed Suprematism to be a trendsetting art movement. Non-representational and reduced to geometric forms, it illustrated the "supreme" (Latin: *supremus*) human epistemological principles. However, while Malevich's art remained in the plane of painting – and hence made reference to the spirituality of Russian icons – Tatlin, who was a trained icon painter, now conquered space: he arranged his three-dimensional, often strongly protruding objects on walls covered with white paper at varying heights as well as on angles, and in doing so created the impression of boundlessness and weightlessness (fig. 1).[6] In calling his works *Painterly Reliefs* or *Counter-Reliefs* he expressed his preparedness to fight against rivals, tradition and the bourgeois art business.[7] Like the present composition reconstructed in 1995 (cat. 106), his works were assemblages – that is, spatial collages – primarily consisting of objets trouvés with traces of use.[8] Metal, tin, wood and rope were not only reminiscent of Tatlin's time as a sailor and aroused associations with sails, masts or rigging as well as the vastness of the sea; with the everyday materials, reality also found its way into the sovereign realm of art.

The concentration on media and their purposeful use is characteristic of Tatlin's works. However, in his reliefs he also addressed the vacant space between things and thus the sphere of imagination, indeed, of utopia: later, he augmented his concept of the *Counter-Relief* to develop the model of a 400-metre-high tower – a never-realised *Monument to the Third (Communist) International* –

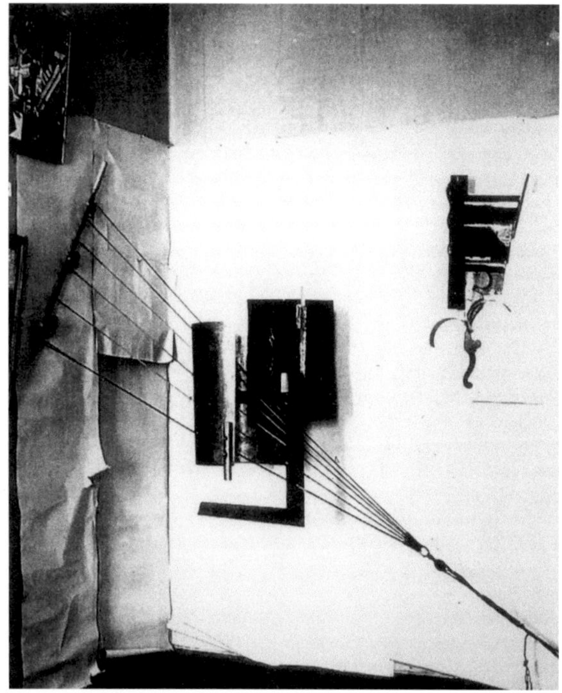

Fig. 1

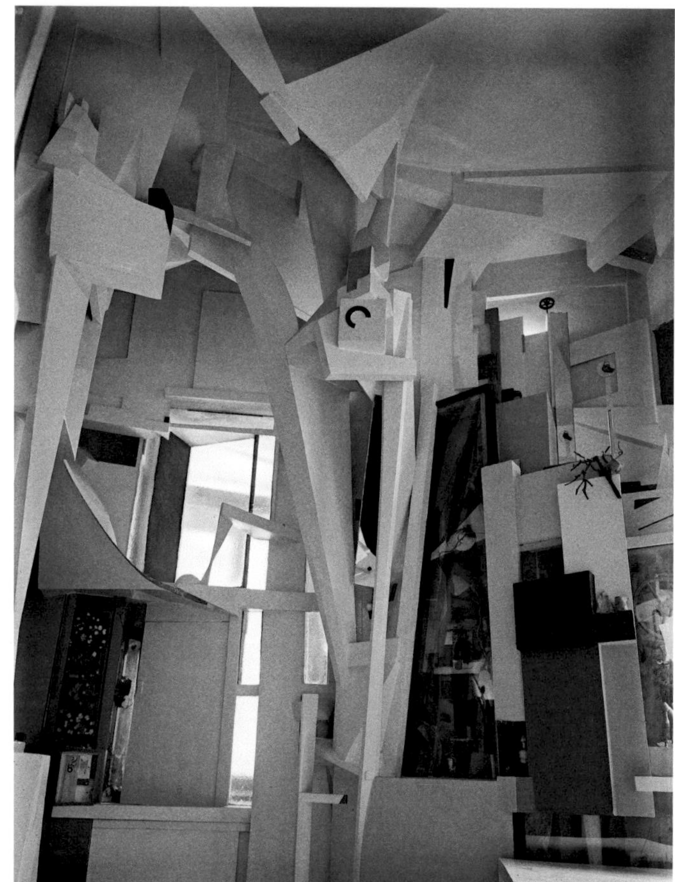

Fig. 2

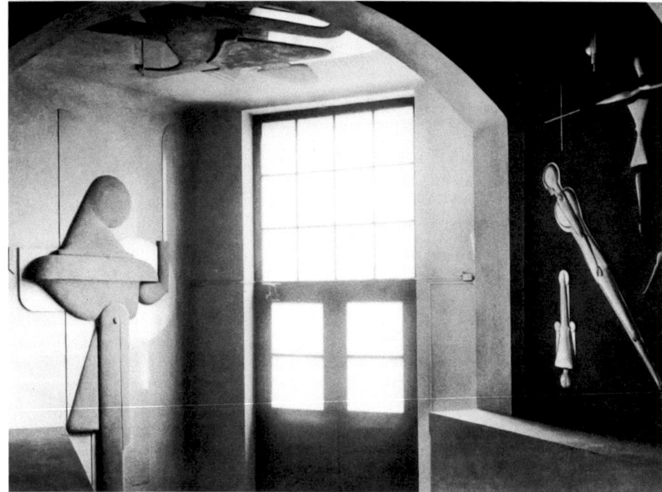

Fig. 3

Fig. 1   Installation view with Vladimir Tatlin's *Corner Counter-Relief*
(1914) and *Counter-Relief with Chair Leg* (1915),
at *The Last Futurist Exhibition of Painting 0.10*, Petrograd,
December 1915/January 1916, photograph

Fig. 2   Kurt Schwitters' *Merzbau*, state: 1933, photograph,
Sprengel Museum Hannover

Fig. 3   Oskar Schlemmer's wall pictures in the workshop building
of the Bauhaus Weimar, view towards the main entrance,
1923, photograph

as well as the suspended sculpture *Letatlin*, both in the spirit of a synthesis of architecture, sculpture and painting, of surface, space and time. Like Malevich's, Tatlin's art was aimed at a liberated society, and he saw himself as an engineer of such a revolution.

The visionary approach of the two artists inspired many of their contemporaries, including Ivan Kliun and Vasily Kamensky, both of whom were also represented in *0.10*. Kliun had found his way to the Suprematism of his friend Malevich by way of a (Cubo-)Futurist work phase (with numerous relief assemblages), and around 1916 he opted for a reduced pictorial language consisting of geometric forms with intensely vibrant colours. In *Suprematist Composition* (cat. 109), he designed a planar picture collage in small format using oil on wood that – thanks to overlapping forms, contrasting colours and varying applications of paint – suggests depth space, indeed, a kind of spherical harmony. An axisymmetric wooden relief (cat. 108) produced around 1915 is attributed to the Futurist poet and painter Kamensky. The starting point of the hieratic sculpture was "a tub like those used to shred cabbage but without side walls and nearly bottomless".[9] By removing superfluous material and adding accents in black, white and blue, Kamensky freed the simple object from its everyday purpose, lending it a timeless presence.

Concurrent with the developments in Russia, an artistic and literary movement formed in Zurich that would spread like wildfire: Dada. While the First World War was raging, politically neutral Switzerland would become a refuge for exiles and a venue for international dialogue. In a protected setting, Dada did away with middle-class as well as artistic conventions, revolted against social norms, and ultimately cast doubt on art itself. In order to break away from traditional forms, one preferred to open the doors to chance, arbitrariness and play, and celebrated a joyous new beginning in anti-art. In February 1916, Cabaret Voltaire was founded in Zurich near the apartment-in-exile of the Russian revolutionary Lenin. There, in the evening, manifestos were read, sound poems recited, dramatic scenes, music or dancing performed, and freedom proclaimed. It was in this setting that the Franco-German Jean Arp, who belonged to the Dada circle along with his Swiss girlfriend and later wife Sophie Taeuber-Arp, created the object *Relief Dada* (cat. 110). Arp had devoted himself to the relief since 1914 and would produce about 800 of them over the course of his career,[10] but he referred to this one as his first Dadaist relief.[11] Based on his own drawings, he had four pieces of wood roughly sawed out, screwed them together in three layers, and finally painted or sprinkled them with slate grey, pink and white. His planar-spatial figure was not meant to depict anything; it was to be unrelated to reality, but, with its oval egg-shape, nevertheless fed on nature. At the time, during trips to nearby Tessin, Arp arrived at the organic forms – which would permanently shape his pictorial language, as shown, for example, by the late sculpture *Threshold with Crenellations* (cat. 142) – as well as at his lifelong themes of growth and metamorphosis.

Dada was infectious and seized many artists, albeit some of them only intermittently, such as Christian Schad. Connected to Expressionism and later to New Objectivity as a painter, Schad experienced an artistic intermezzo in Switzerland, where he had settled in 1915. In Geneva, he developed his experimental *Schadographs*, in which silhouettes of objects were produced by exposing photographic paper to light. As in these planar photograms, in which objects are displayed as white on a dark ground, apparently randomly arranged objets trouvés from reality emerge in the small collage *Composition in N* (cat. 111) – a coin, a piece of lace, a bit of silver foil, a cigarette label – on a piece of wood painted in black.

Another one of Arp's German artist friends advanced to become a master of paper collages and material assemblages: Hannover-based Kurt Schwitters.[12] Schwitters shared the Dadaist approach in many respects; however, he found his way to the word fragment "Merz" (arbitrarily taken from the name Commerzbank). It was under this term that, from 1918 on, he systematically designed his own artistic world out of painting, sculpture, architecture, lectures, magazines, sound poems and music. He wanted to create something positive out of what had been destroyed or discarded, conflating all types of art to produce a large Gesamtkunstwerk, for which his *Merzbau* (fig. 2) became a striking symbol. Starting in 1923, and originating from a single towering sculpture, his multi-part creation comprised of painting, assemblage, sculpture and architecture grew over the next twenty-five years to become an enormous working and living environment.

At the same time, Schwitters developed his *Merz Pictures* and *Merz Reliefs*, which could not be strictly distinguished from another; they connected spatiality with flatness in various ways and could be very different in terms of style. With its rigorously geometric grid and reduced colour palette, *MERZ 1924, 1st Relief with Cross and Sphere.* (cat. 105), for example, exhibits an unmistakable proximity to Constructivism, whereas *Körtingbild* (cat. 112), produced eight years later, manifests as a loose painterly composition. Whereas in *MERZ 1924* one only discovers the metal ladle at second glance, in *Körtingbild* several materials that stem from nature, such as bark and algae, catch one's eye. In *Take (Nimm)* from 1943 (cat. 113), everyday objects and fragments, such as leather, linoleum and a brush, have been nailed to a support and interwoven with oil and brush to form a whole. All of Schwitters' works have relief, since he designed every surface also as space, and it is not surprising that, decades later, his oeuvre, which did away with boundaries and embraced reality, again inspired a new generation of artists, for example the group of Nouveaux Réalistes with Daniel Spoerri and Niki de Saint Phalle (cats. 86, 72).[13]

In the summer of 1920, Schwitters had an exhibition at the Galerie Ernst Arnold in Dresden along with Oskar Schlemmer and Willi Baumeister. The two artist friends, who had studied together at the art academy in Stuttgart, shared a great interest in the figure in space, in the relationship between humans and architecture, and hence in the relief as well. Schlemmer, who was active as a painter, sculptor and stage designer, had already dealt with questions concerning sculpture during the First World War, and now – prior to his appointment to the Staatliches Bauhaus in Weimar in 1921 – he produced dynamic-looking objects comprised of elementary forms. In the multi-faceted work *Ornamental Sculpture on a Divided Frame* (cat. 114), he had combined classic panel painting with a centrally placed wooden sculpture to produce a relief picture – and then instantly dissolved this supposed union by breaking open the frame (→ Relief and Frame). In *Ornamental Sculpture on Oval Backing* (cat. 115), he staged the sculptural centrepiece as an independent object, but then reintegrated it into the wall as a relief by means of the back panel cast along with it in plaster.[14] The complex form of the sculpture was probably derived from the human figure; however, depending on its orientation, it also allows associations with an enormous cabin-ship or a city built on a slope.

That for Schlemmer art was not a formal gimmick but instead always designed for human beings and their lifeworld can be surmised by taking a look at his wall pictures for the workshop building in Weimar (fig. 3). After passing through the main entrance, one was surrounded by figures comprised of basic geometric shapes that were painted on the wall or applied as half reliefs and which related, both visually and haptically, to one's own, real body. As early as November 1919, Schlemmer had programmatically put into words that he was no longer producing images in a familiar sense, but rather "tablets which burst out of their frames and ally themselves with the wall, thus becoming part of a large surface, a larger space than themselves, thus actually becoming part of a thought-of, desired architecture. Compressed in them, reduced to miniature scale, is what should furnish the laws and forms of their surroundings. / In this sense: Tablets of the Law. / The portrayal of man will always remain the great symbol for the artist".[15]

Both premises – the human being as the centre of art and the artwork as part of a space – also applied to Willi Baumeister. Unlike Schlemmer, he never worked as a sculptor, yet he understood the canvas as spatial and always lent relief to his compositions and surfaces. In the 1921 painting *Grey Figure (Upright)* (cat. 117), which belongs to his series *Staggered Figures*, he produced three-dimensionality by overlaying rectangular colour fields, shading the outlines of the figure, providing their heads with lamellae, and causing the arm to seemingly rotate. In the *Wall Pictures* that followed, he included also real relief structures in the geometric figures by adding coloured pieces of card and wood. In *Wall Picture with Semi-Circle* (cat. 116), produced in 1923 on wood, it is only at second glance that one recognises which areas are actually raised and which are painterly illusion. Baumeister was so convinced of the effect of his large-format composition, of which he executed three versions, that he modified it to produce a wall design in an art exhibition in Stuttgart the following year.[16] A reference to the human being is still recognisable in the series *Planar Forces*, in which he avoided any representationalism and created balanced pictures with a variety of colours and forms according to the principles of Constructivism. In *Planar Tension* from 1925 (cat. 118), a vertical rectangle enhanced with sand seems to refer to the popular ingrain wallpaper in modern living environments (→ Spotlight on Structure). Baumeister would even have preferred to embed his paintings into the wall without a limiting frame in order to ideally showcase the protruding relief-like areas.[17]

The art of the period did not pursue an end in itself but pointed to principles of order with a social dimension: because people lived in a new reality of progress, technology and machines, their world should be constituted accordingly. Functionality and a style of design applicable to all areas of life were not only the guidelines for the German Bauhaus, but also for the Dutch De Stijl group, which was founded in 1917 by, among others, Theo van Doesburg, a friend of Schwitters, and Piet Mondrian. In a close dialogue with De Stijl and the Bauhaus, in the seclusion of her domicile Blaricum in the province of Noord-Holland the staunch socialist and pacifist Lou Loeber worked on her art, which was meant to be understandable for people and relevant for a community. Using radiant primary colours, geometric forms and orthogonal grids, she produced Constructivist paintings with representational elements, especially motifs

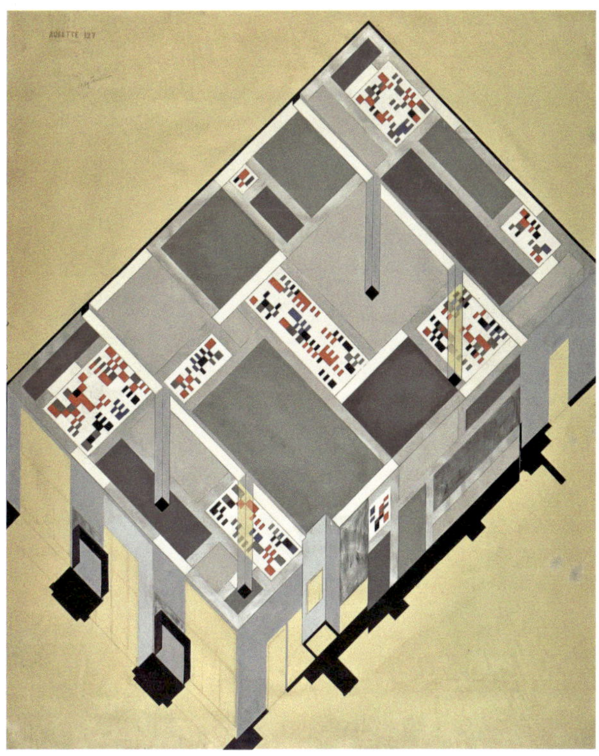

Fig. 4

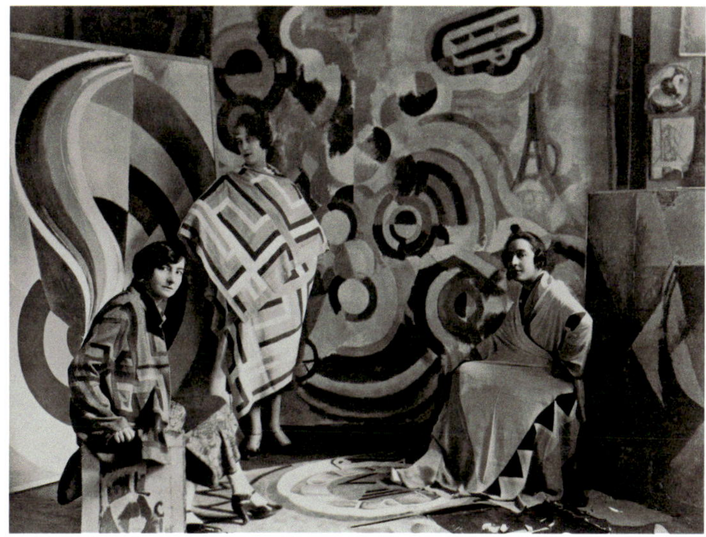

Fig. 5

Fig. 4   Sophie Taeuber-Arp: *Aubette 127* (*Axonometric Drawing of the "Five O'Clock" Tearoom in the Aubette, Strasbourg*), 1927, gouache, metallic paint, ink and pencil on diazotype, Musée d'Art Moderne et Contemporain de Strasbourg

Fig. 5   Sonia Delaunay (right) in the studio with self-designed clothing, 1924, photograph, Département des Estampes et de la photographie, Bibliothèque nationale de France, Paris

from the industrial and working world or everyday life, such as *Sink I* (cat. 119). Whereas Loeber designed visual spaces in the plane in her works, Taeuber-Arp and van Doesburg created a real place for their contemporaries when they transformed the famous "Aubette" building in Strasbourg on the basis of a Constructivist iconographic programme into a cultural and entertainment centre (fig. 4). Situated between painting and architecture, its halls resembled accessible, high-contrast sculptures – and anticipated the depth dimension of Taeuber-Arp's late reliefs (cat. 139), which, when hung on the wall, often come across as models of buildings or urban squares.

    The transnational project of an art that changed the world and shaped society caught on everywhere, and its network grew; for instance, the Russian Suprematist El Lissitzky lived in Germany from time to time and collaborated with Schwitters, Arp, van Doesburg and Baumeister. The new formal language could be experienced not only in the apartment studios of artists like Erich Buchholz in Berlin (→ Relief and Frame) or Piet Mondrian in Paris, but also in public space and through everyday objects: Malevich worked as a product designer, Schwitters as a commercial artist, Taeuber-Arp as an architect, and her friend and fellow painter Sonia Delaunay had become an entrepreneur with her own boutique for "simultaneous clothing" (fig. 5; → The Polyperspectival Gaze).

The new style of art had caught on in society – one could use it, stride through it, or let oneself be enveloped by it.[18] As a hybrid medium, the relief played a crucial role in its success: its reference to the wall and to architecture, as well as its layered, staggered and haptic surfaces, allowed concepts to become palpable and turned them into a reality that individuals and the community could experience sensuously.

181

1 The concept of the "New Human" is examined and discussed critically in: *Der Neue Mensch: Obsessionen des 20. Jahrhunderts*, ed. Nicola Lepp, Martin Roth and Klaus Vogel, exh. cat. Deutsches Hygiene-Museum Dresden, Ostfildern 1999.

2 Artistic modernity as a transnational, worldwide phenomenon is addressed, for example, in: *Die ganze Welt ein Bauhaus*, ed. Institut für Auslandsbeziehungen, exh. cat. ZKM – Zentrum für Kunst und Medien, Karlsruhe, et al., Munich 2019.

3 See Anna Szech: "Chronik 1905–1936", in: *Auf der Suche nach 0,10: Die letzte futuristische Ausstellung der Malerei*, ed. Matthew Drutt, exh. cat. Fondation Beyeler, Riehen/Basel, Ostfildern 2015, pp. 12f.

4 See Irène Mercier: "Jean Pougny", in: *Collection art moderne: La collection du Centre Pompidou, Musée national d'art moderne*, comp. Brigitte Léal, inv. cat. Centre Pompidou, Paris, 2006, pp. 534–536.

5 Anatolij Strigalev: "Auf den Spuren der Ausstellung 0,10", in: exh. cat. Riehen 2015 (see note 3), pp. 46–78, esp. p. 63; Magdalena Nieslony: "Iwan Puni zwischen Paris und Petersburg", in: Ada Raev and Isabel Wünsche (eds.): *Kursschwankungen: Russische Kunst im Wertesystem der europäischen Moderne*, Berlin 2007, pp. 76–82.

6 On the artist, see Museum Tinguely, Basel (ed.): *Tatlin: Neue Kunst für eine neue Welt. Internationales Symposium*, Ostfildern 2013; *Tatlin: Neue Kunst für eine neue Welt*, exh. cat. Museum Tinguely, Basel, Ostfildern 2012.

7 Tatlin had actually visited Pablo Picasso in Paris in 1914 and surely became aware of his principle of the material collage, which in 1915 led to works such as *Violin* (cat. 80).

8 Few original *Counter-Reliefs* have survived – they were probably never intended for eternity – and their reconstruction with new materials can only approximately convey their appearance of that time.

9 Strigalev 2015 (see note 5), p. 52.

10 See Bernd Rau: *Hans Arp: Die Reliefs. Œuvre-Katalog*, Stuttgart 1981.

11 For a detailed description, see *Kunstmuseum Basel: Die Meisterwerke. Gemälde, Skulpturen, Fotografien, Installationen, Videos*, ed. Bernhard Mendes Bürgi and Nina Zimmer, inv. cat. Kunstmuseum Basel, Ostfildern 2011, pp. 196f. (Dorothee Gerkens).

12 On the close dialogue between the two artists, see *schwitters_arp*, ed. Hartwig Fischer, exh. cat. Kunstmuseum Basel, Ostfildern 2004.

13 On Schwitters' continued international impact, see *Aller Anfang ist Merz – von Kurt Schwitters bis heute*, ed. Susanne Meyer-Büser and Karin Orchard, exh. cat. Sprengel Museum Hannover et al., Ostfildern 2000.

14 The plaster relief in Hamburg is the only one of its kind; all of the subsequent casts – five in plaster and eleven in silver – were produced without a circular backing; see Karin von Maur: *Oskar Schlemmer: Monographie und Werkverzeichnis*, 2 vols., Munich 1979, catalogue raisonné nos. P 2–P 3a.

15 Oskar Schlemmer: *The Letters and Diaries of Oskar Schlemmmer*, ed. Tut Schlemmer, trans. Krishna Winston, Middletown 1972, p. 73.

16 See Peter Beye and Felicitas Baumeister (eds.): *Willi Baumeister: Werkkatalog der Gemälde*, 2 vols., Ostfildern 2002, nos. 221 (today Centre Pompidou, Musée national d'art moderne, Paris) and 222 (present version). The site of the third version exhibited in Paris in 1930 is unknown, and the wall design mentioned has not survived. Baumeister had also personally got to know Le Corbusier and Fernand Léger in 1924 in Paris, and this developed into a productive dialogue between the three artists.

17 I would like to thank Felicitas Baumeister for this information.

18 See Karin Schick: "'Auf dem Kleid trägt sie einen Körper': Kunst als Hülle und Raum bei Sonia Delaunay", in: *Robert Delaunay. Sonia Delaunay. Das Centre Pompidou zu Gast in Hamburg*, ed. idem and Uwe M. Schneede, exh. cat. Hamburger Kunsthalle, Cologne 1999, pp. 23–29.

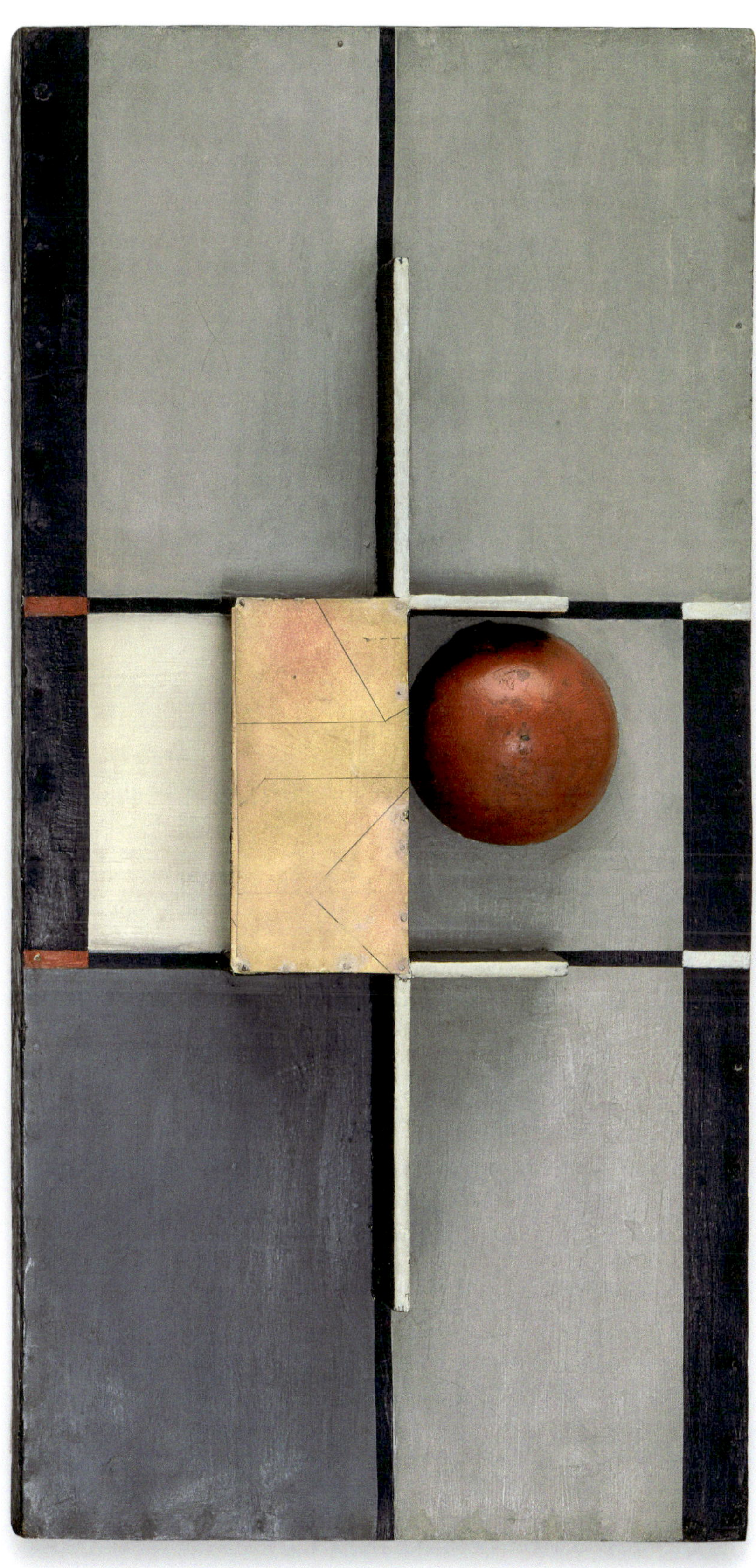

Cat. 105   Kurt Schwitters: *MERZ 1924, 1. Relief with Cross and Sphere.*,
1924, ink (?), oil, card, plastic sheet and metal (ladle)
on wood on cardboard, nailed, 69.1 × 34.4 × 9.3 cm, Sprengel
Museum Hannover, loan Kurt und Ernst Schwitters Stiftung,
Hannover, since 2001, inv. no. 7E+06

Cat. 106 Vladimir Tatlin: *Counter-Relief*, 1916 (reconstruction by
D. N. Dimakow and I. N. Fedotow, Pensa, Russia, 1995),
wood and metal, 124 × 60 × 42 cm, Berlinische Galerie –
Landesmuseum für Moderne Kunst, Fotografie und
Architektur, inv. no. BG-S 8136/96

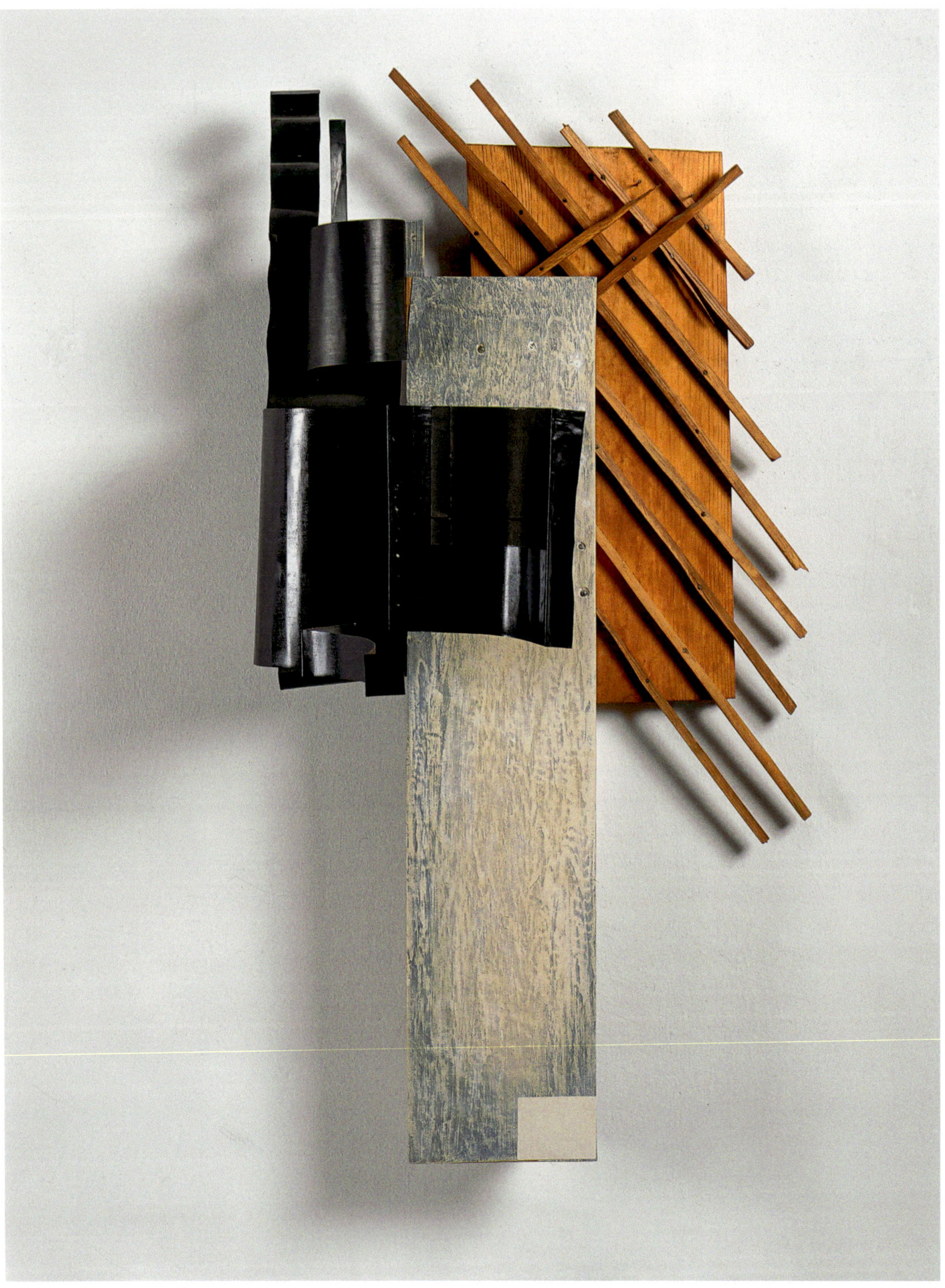

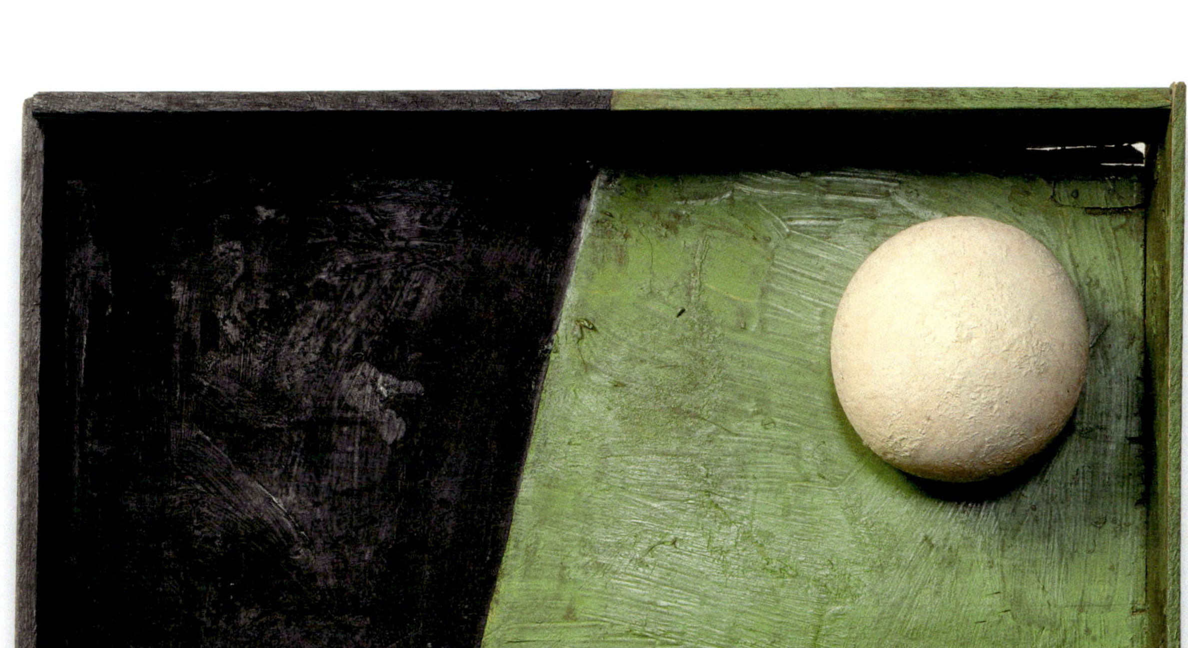

Cat. 107   Ivan Puni: *The White Sphere* (*La Boule blanche*), 1915, wood
            and metal, painted, 34 × 51 × 12 cm, Centre Pompidou, Paris,
            inv. no. AM 1497 S

Cat. 108 Vasily Kamensky (?): *Wooden Relief*, ca. 1915, wood, painted, 60 × 28.5 × 14.3 cm, Hamburger Kunsthalle, inv. no. S-1971-31 (Hamburg only)

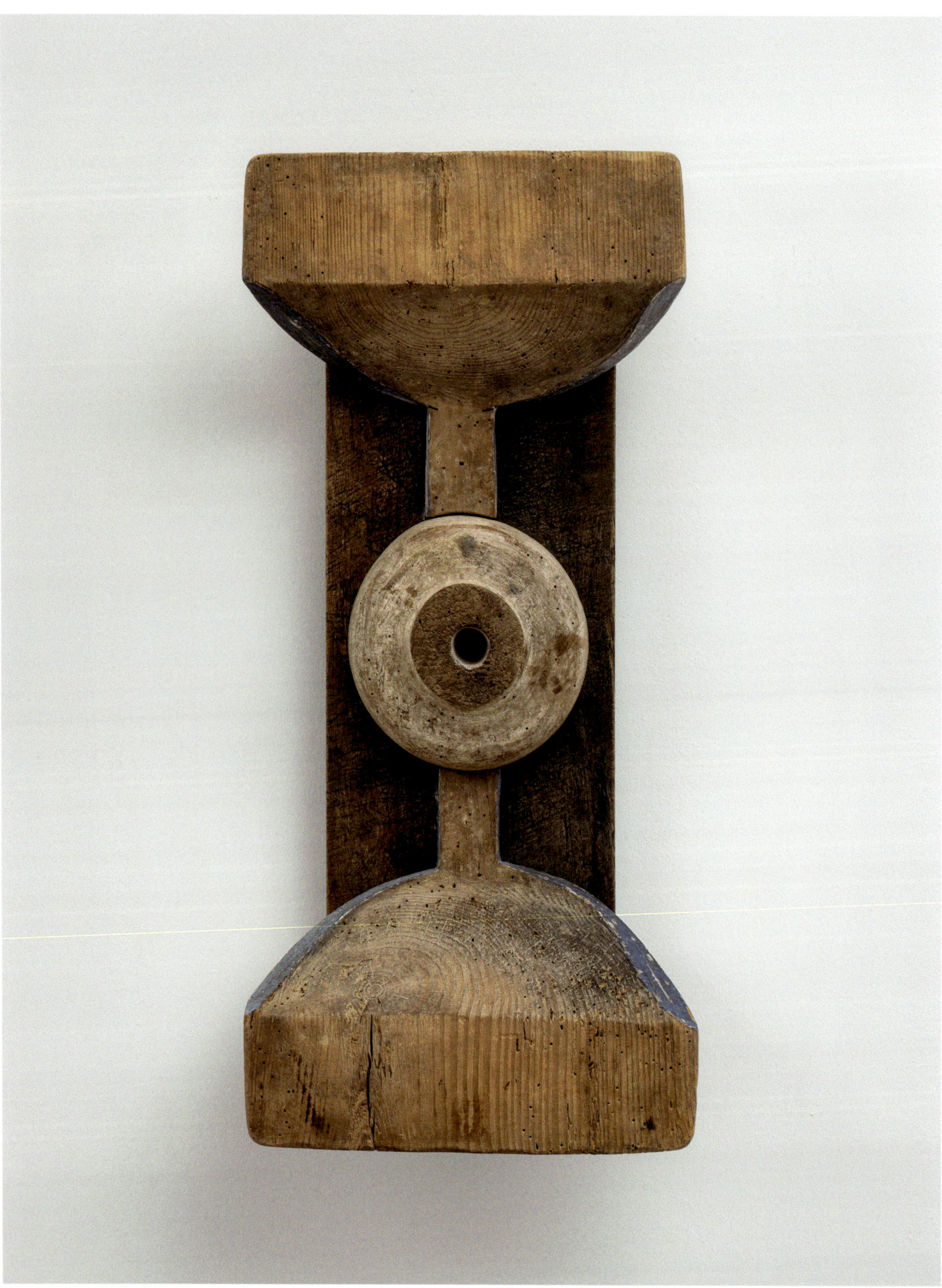

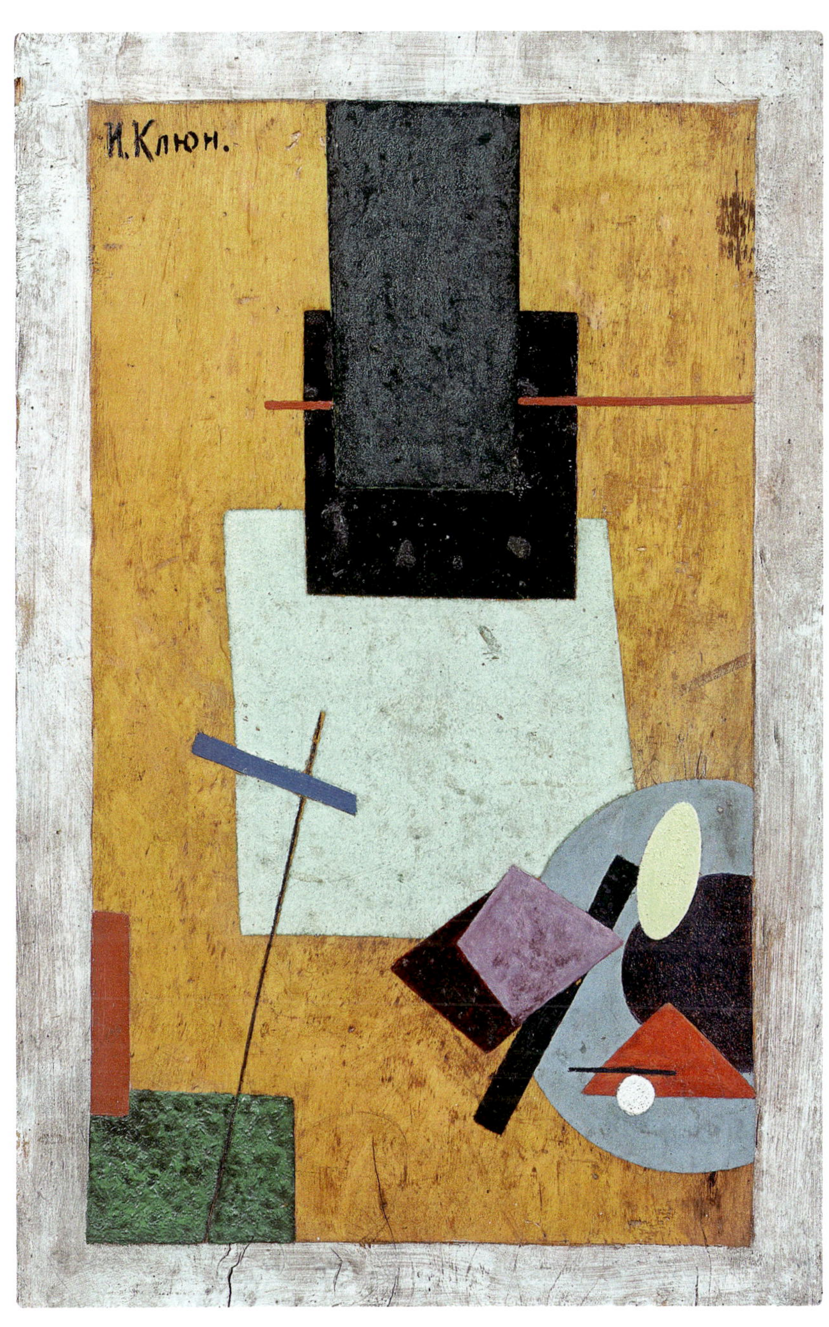

Cat. 109   Ivan Kliun: *Suprematist Composition*, ca. 1916,
oil on wood, 35 × 23 cm, Wilhelm-Hack-Museum,
Ludwigshafen, inv. no. 458/34

Cat. 110   Jean Arp: *Relief Dada*, 1916, wood, painted and screwed, 24 × 17.5 × 8.9 cm, Kunstmuseum Basel, gift from Marguerite Arp-Hagenbach, 1968, inv. no. G 1968.28

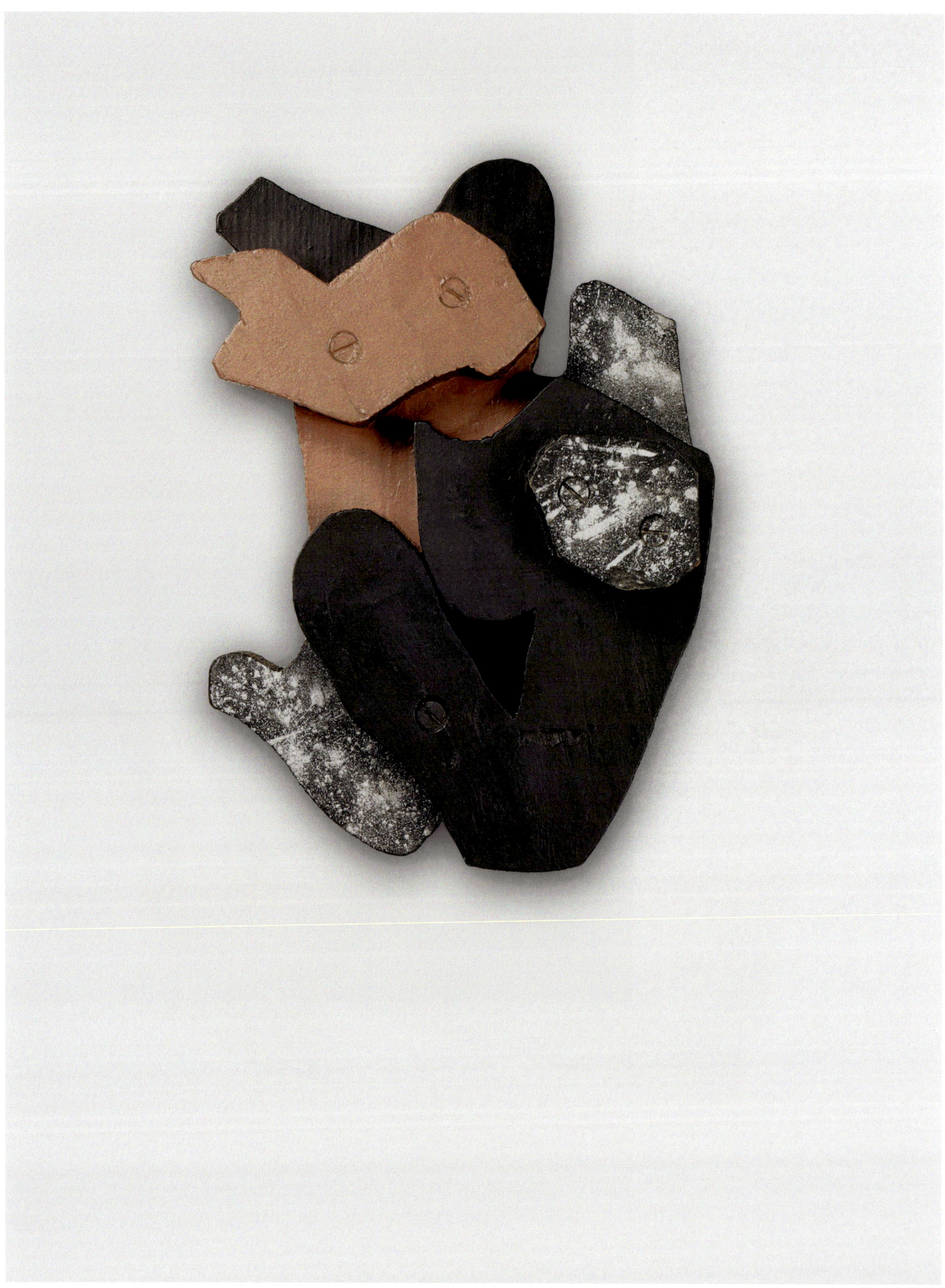

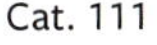

Cat. 111   Christian Schad: *Composition in N*, 1919, collage on painted wood, 18 × 25 × 2.2 cm, Museo Nacional Thyssen-Bornemisza, Madrid, inv. no. 735 (1980.56) (Frankfurt only)

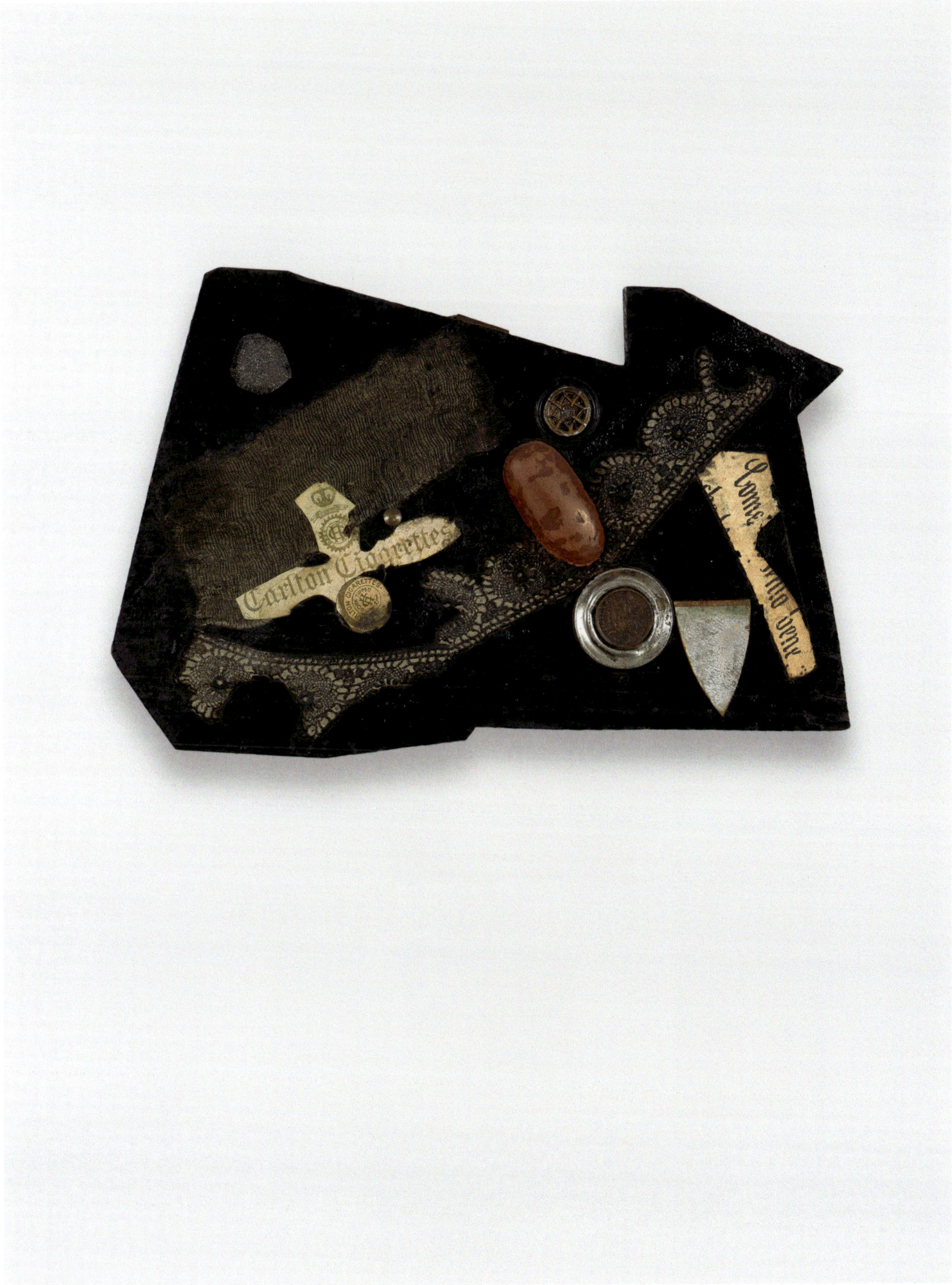

Cat. 112   Kurt Schwitters: *Körtingbild*, 1932, oil, wood, bark,
sheet metal and algae on canvas, nailed, 75.8 × 62.4 cm,
private collection

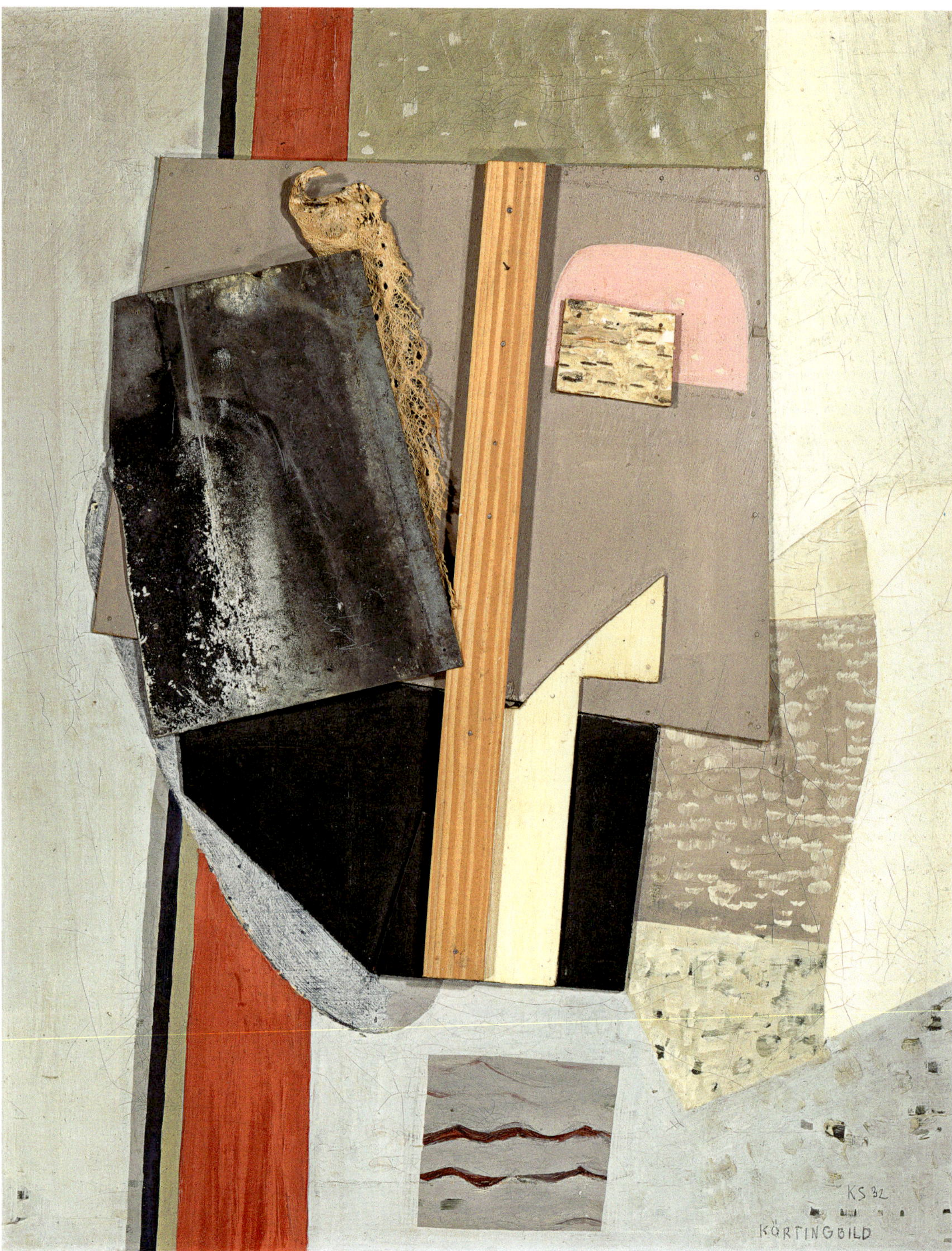

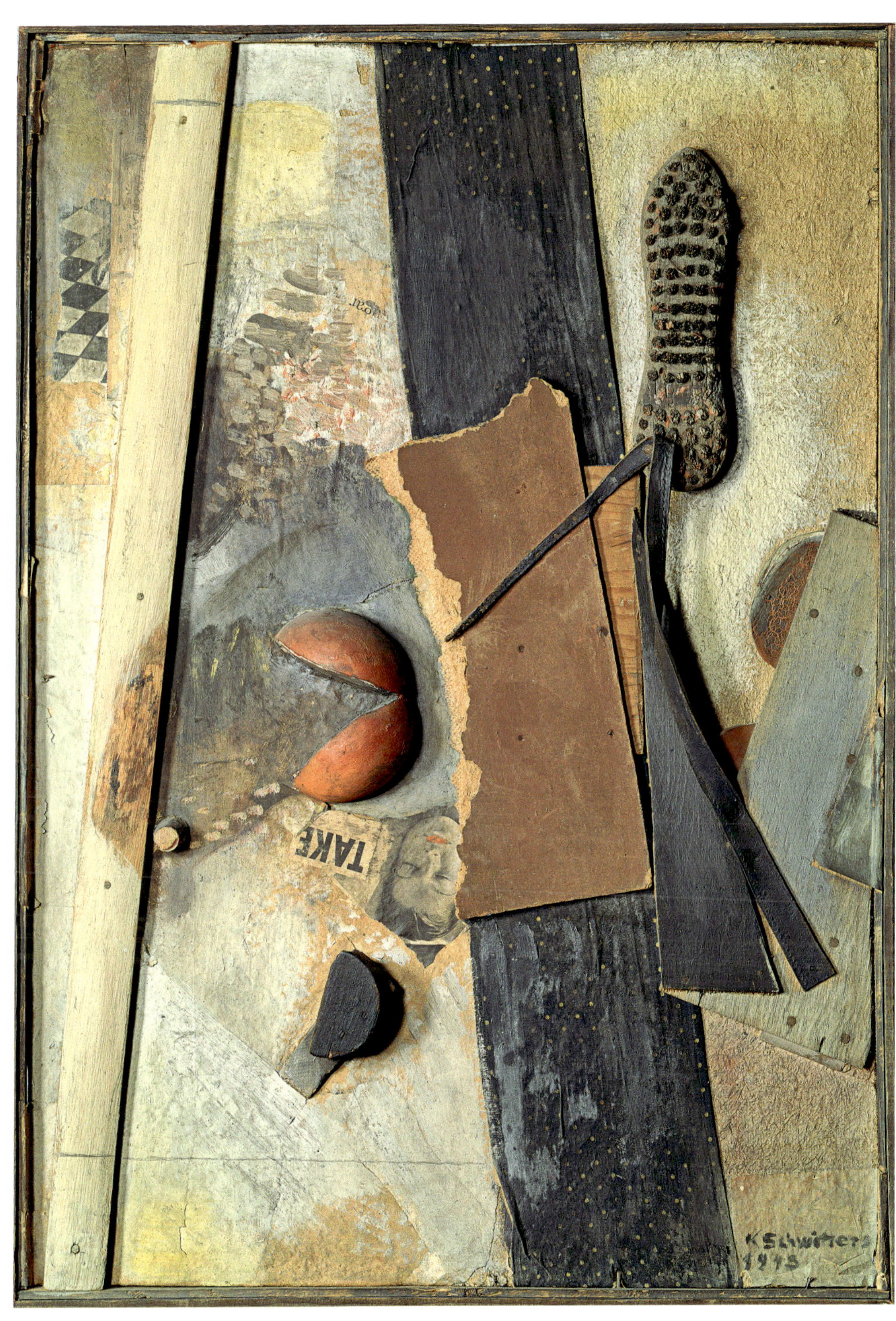

Cat. 113   Kurt Schwitters: *Take* (*Nimm*), 1943, oil, paper, wood,
linoleum, fabric, leather and brush on cardboard, nailed,
79 × 56 cm, private collection

Cat. 114   Oskar Schlemmer: *Ornamental Sculpture on Divided Frame*,
1919/23, wood, painted and brazed, oil on chalk ground,
90 × 68 × 4.2 cm (frame), 47.8 × 20.2 × 11 cm (centrepiece,
linden), Kunstsammlung Nordrhein-Westfalen, Düsseldorf,
inv. no. 200

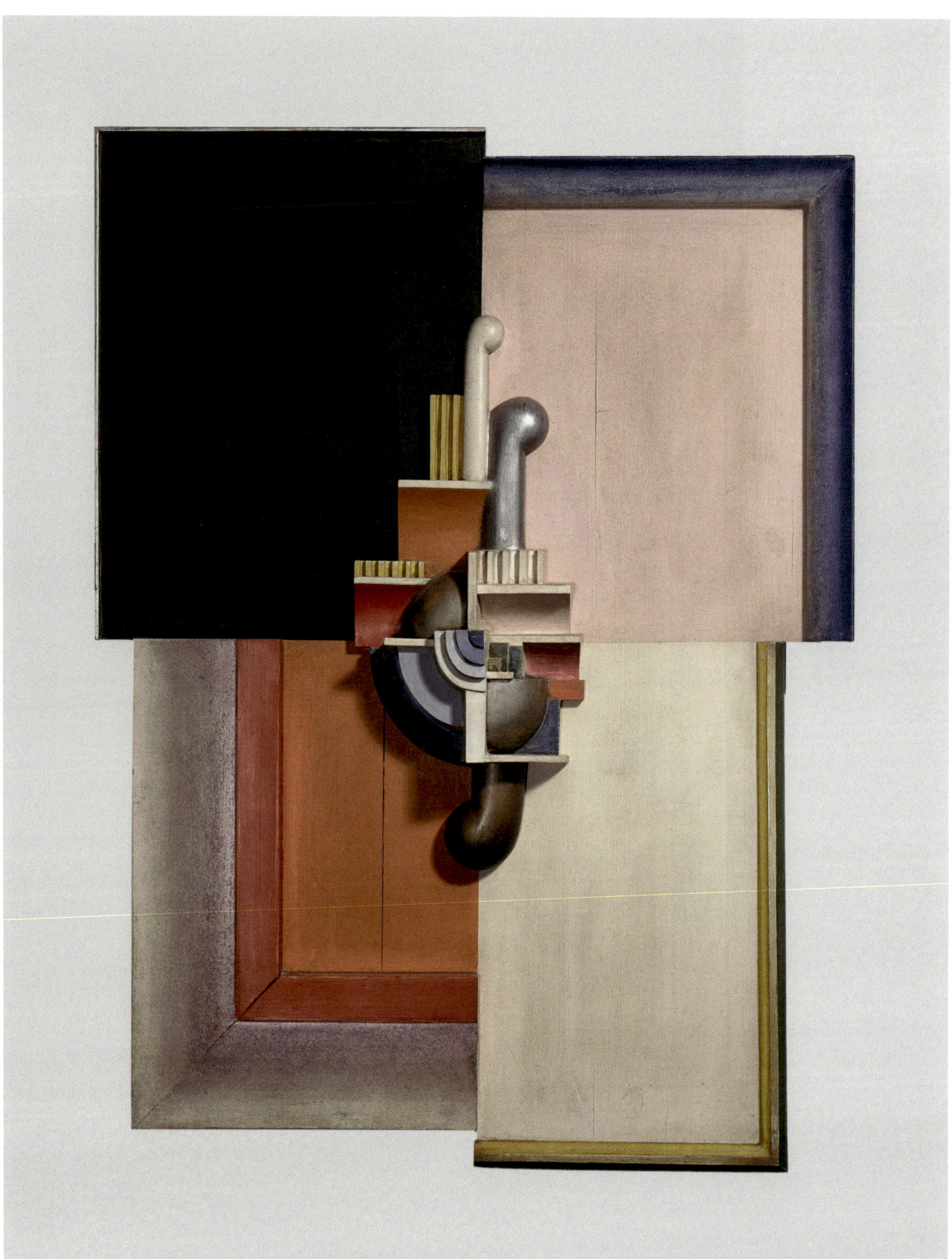

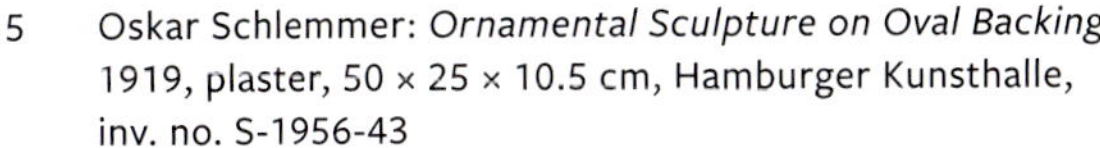

Cat. 115 Oskar Schlemmer: *Ornamental Sculpture on Oval Backing*, 1919, plaster, 50 × 25 × 10.5 cm, Hamburger Kunsthalle, inv. no. S-1956-43

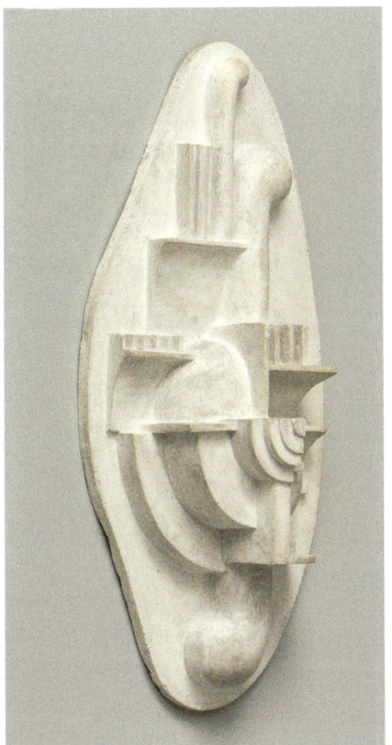

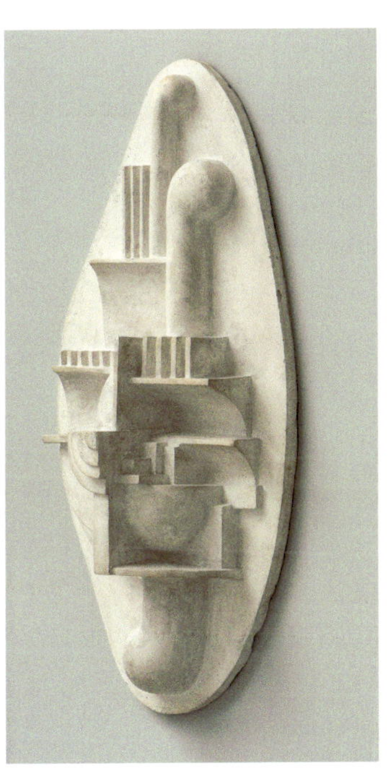

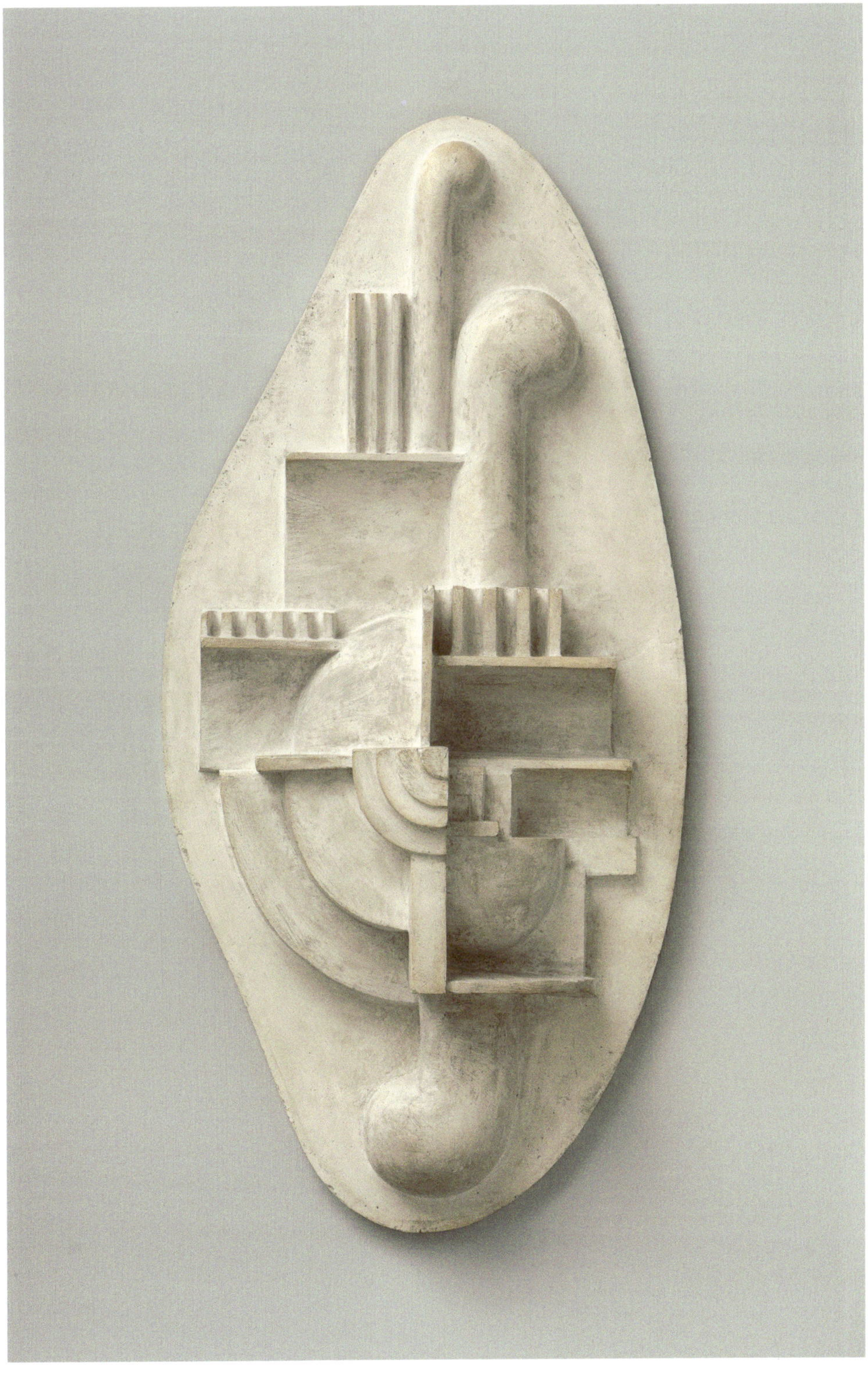

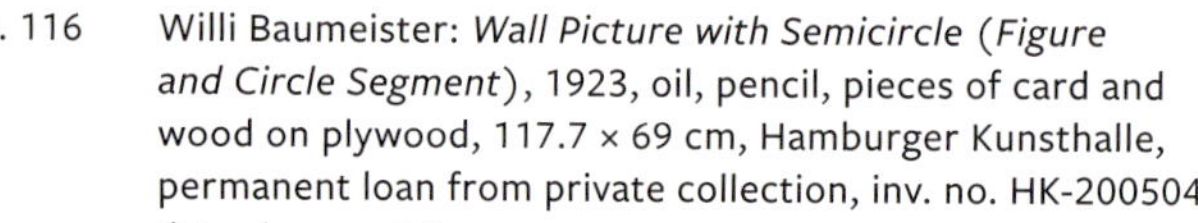

Cat. 116   Willi Baumeister: *Wall Picture with Semicircle* (*Figure and Circle Segment*), 1923, oil, pencil, pieces of card and wood on plywood, 117.7 × 69 cm, Hamburger Kunsthalle, permanent loan from private collection, inv. no. HK-200504 (Hamburg only)

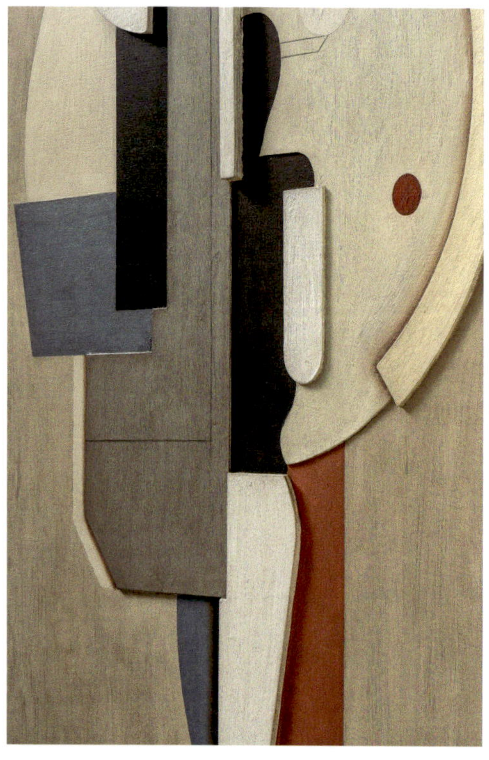

Detail

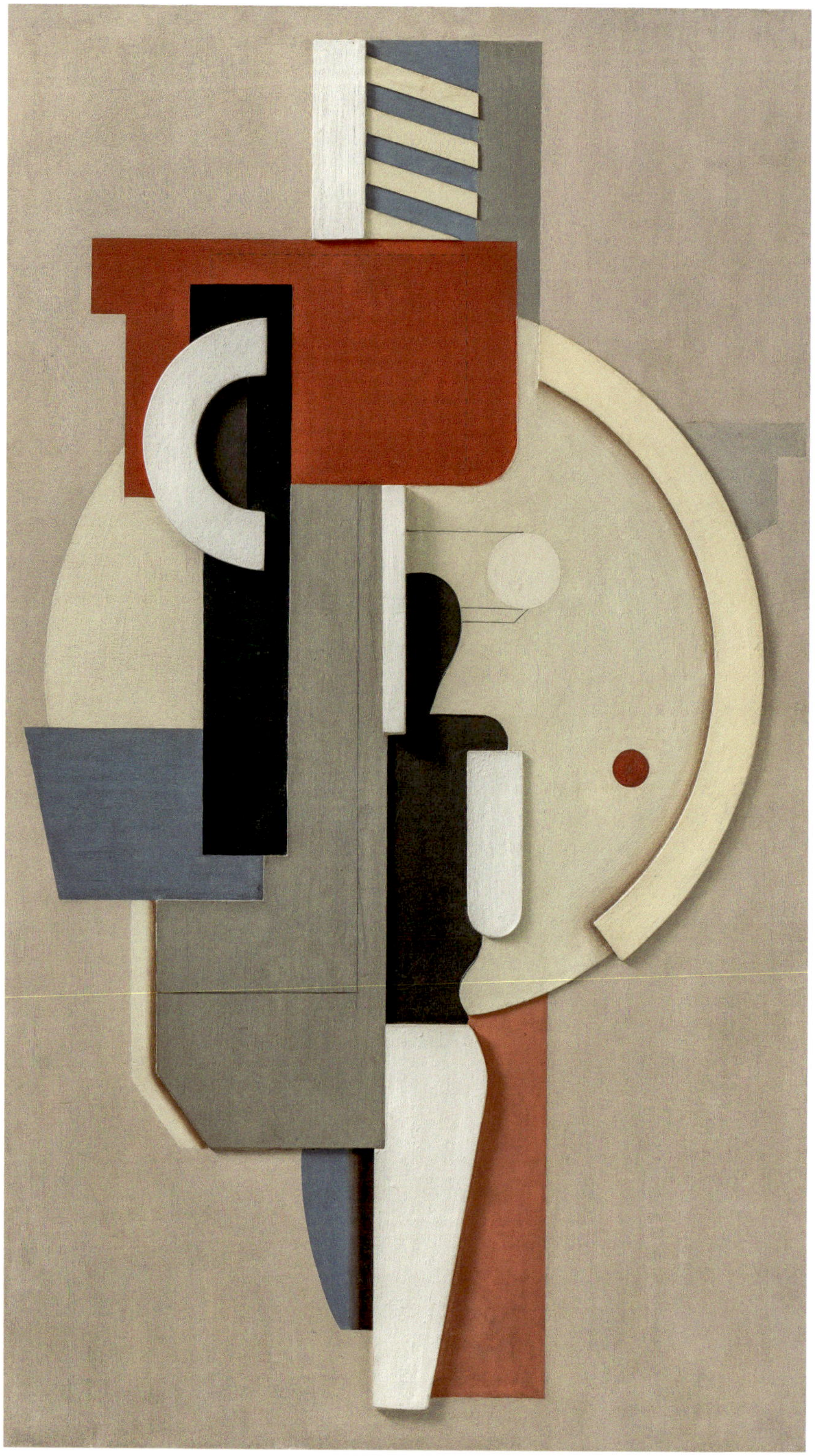

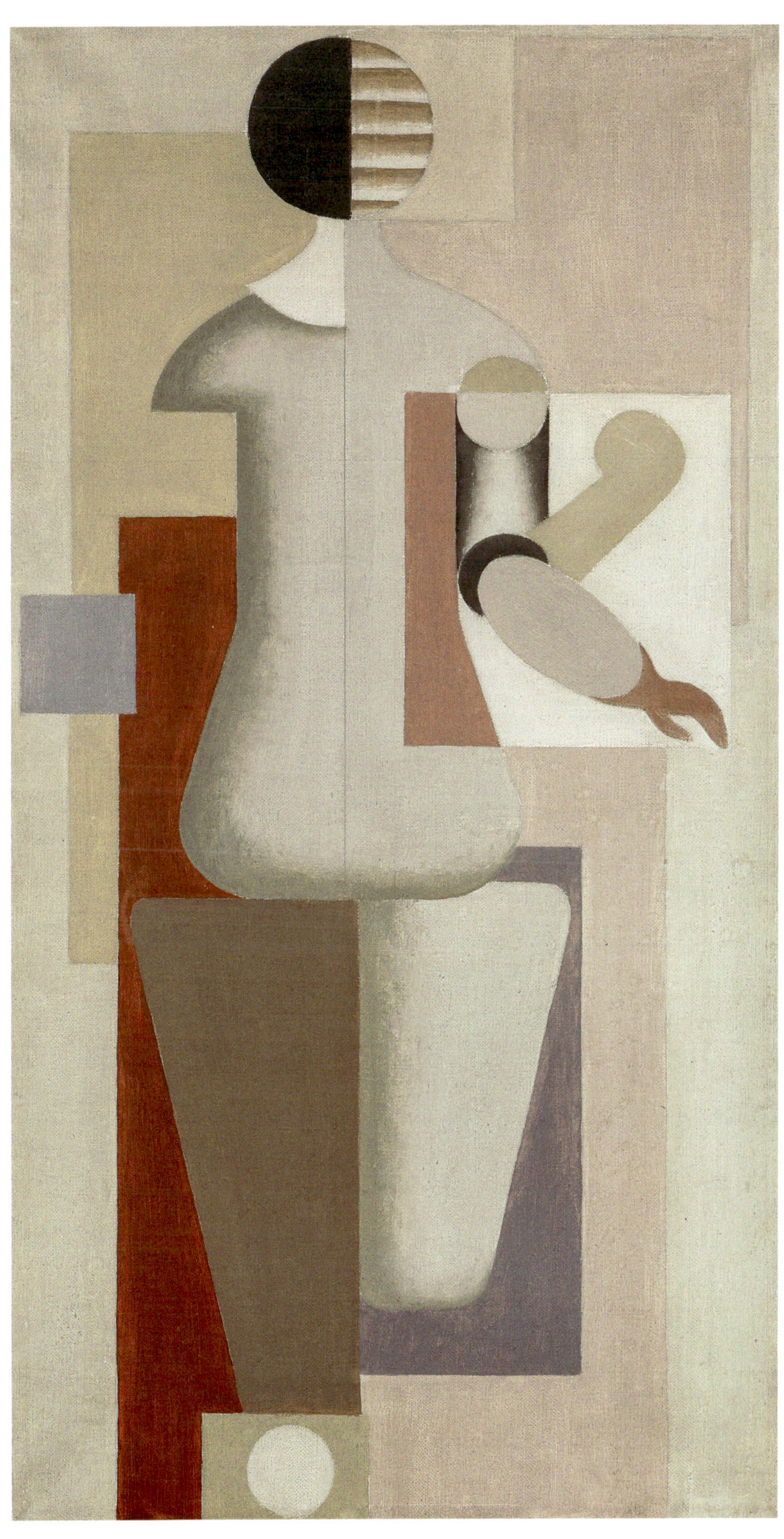

Cat. 117   Willi Baumeister: *Grey Figure (Upright)*, 1921/22, oil
and pencil on canvas, 77 × 41 cm, Hamburger Kunsthalle,
inv. no. HK-2987 (Hamburg only)

Cat. 118   Willi Baumeister: *Planar Tension*, 1925 (reworked in 1936 or later), oil and sand on canvas, 65 × 46 cm, Hamburger Kunsthalle, permanent loan from private collection, inv. no. HK-200503

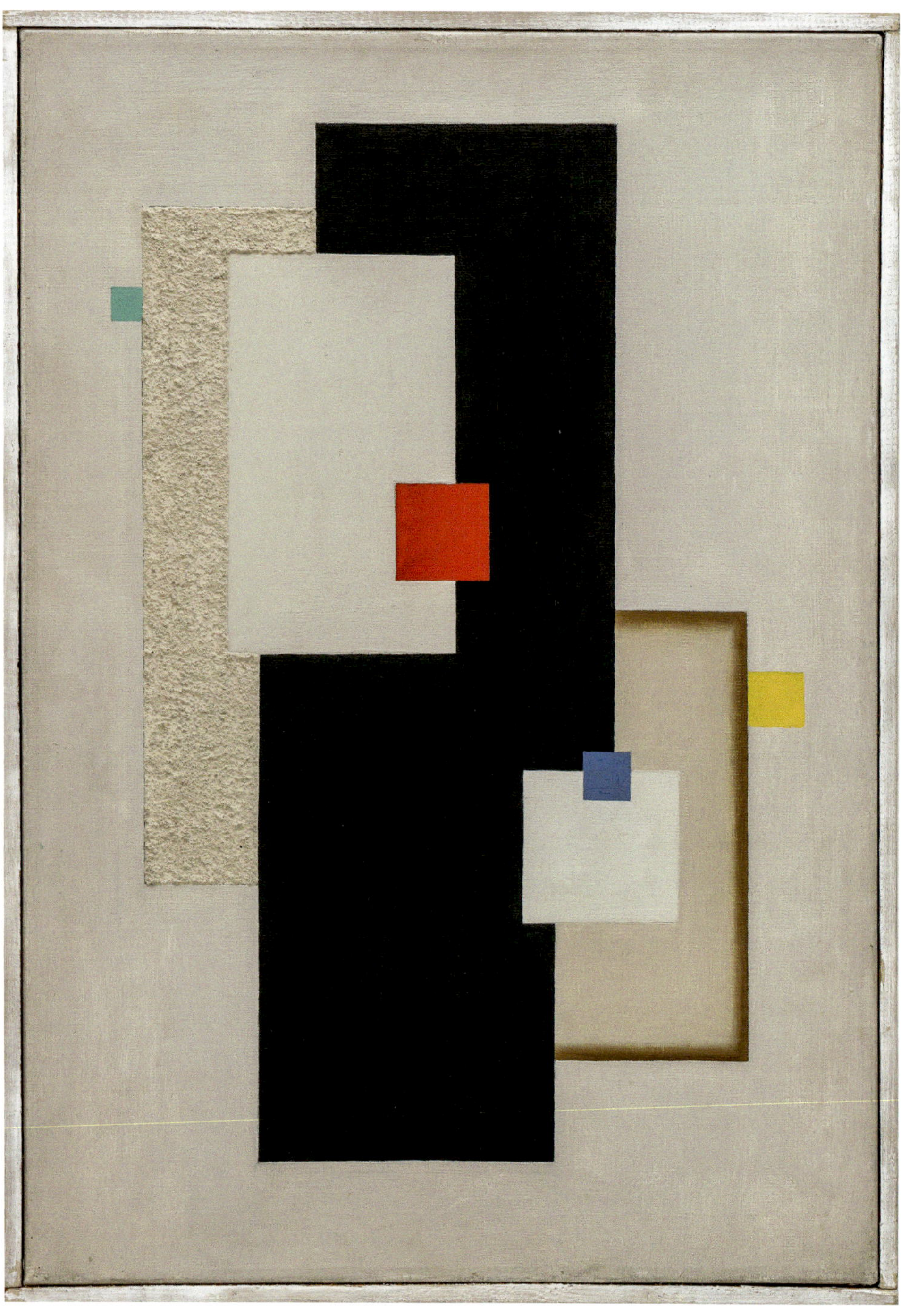

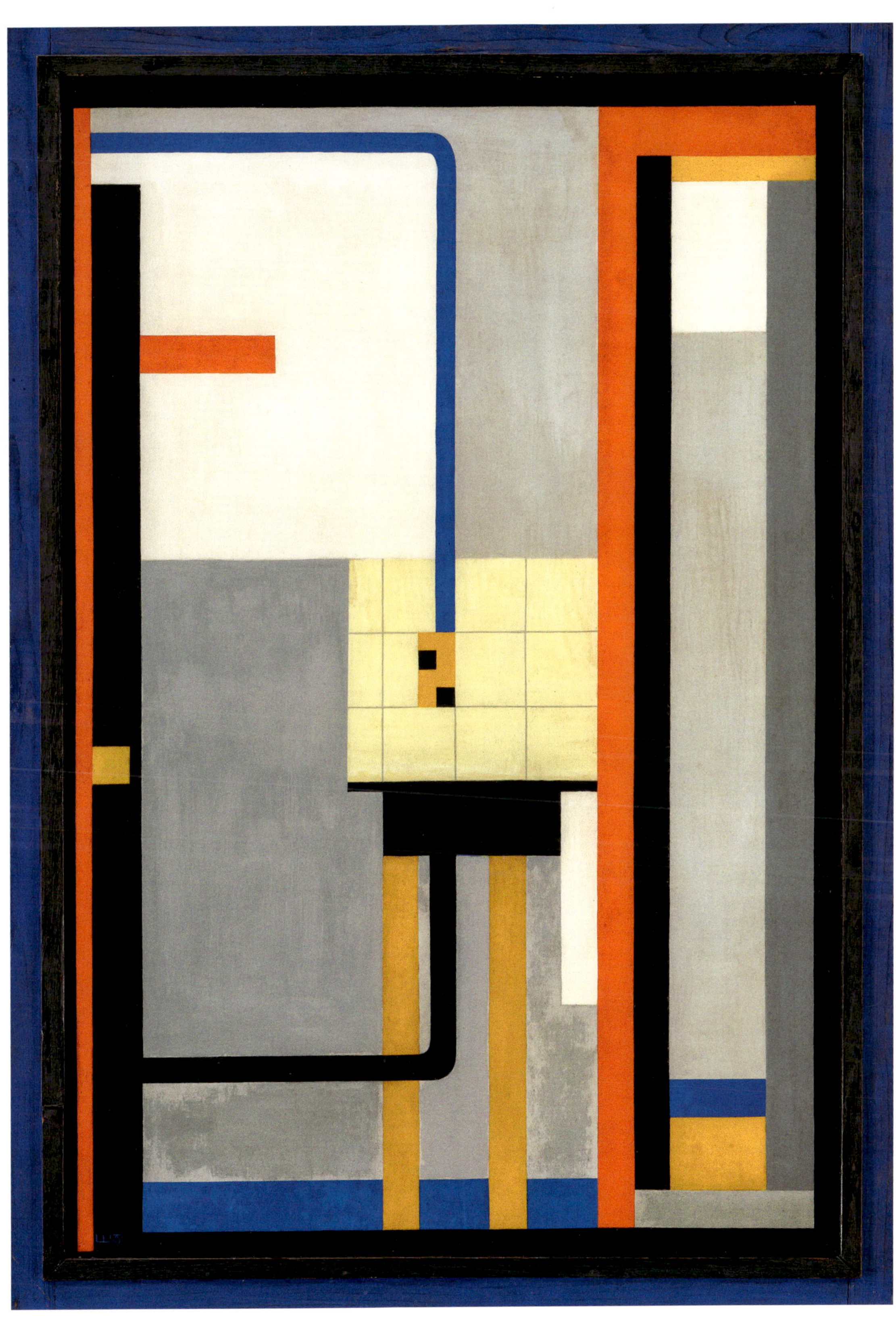

Cat. 119 Lou (Louise Marie) Loeber: *Sink I* (*Gootsteen I*), 1929,
oil on cardboard, 95 × 64.5 cm, Hamburger Kunsthalle,
inv. no. HK-5212

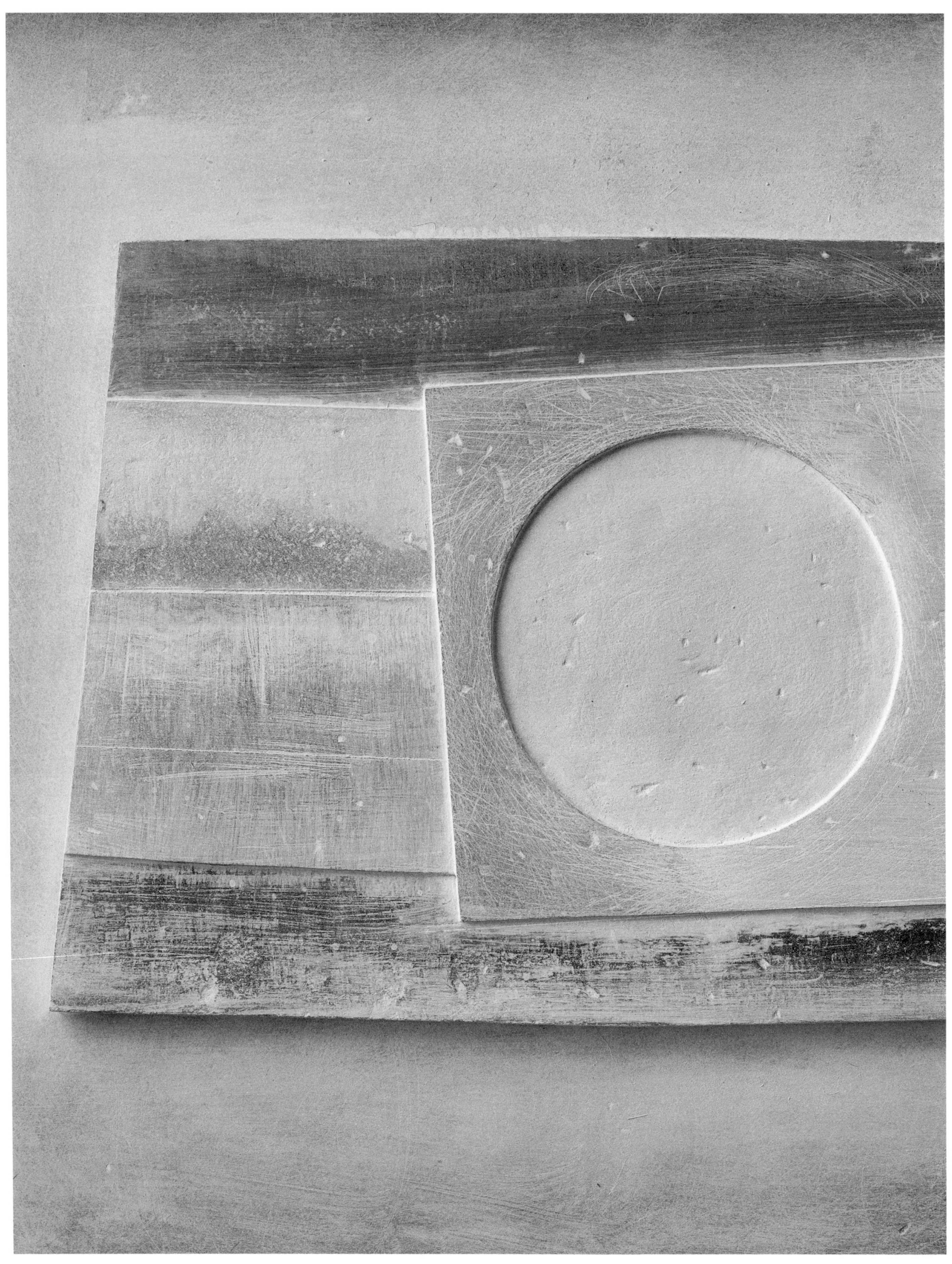

Cats. 120 — 133

Eva Mongi-Vollmer

MONUMENTAL TASKS

Post-War Designs for Wall Reliefs

Monumental wall reliefs demand a high degree of transfer capability, both visual and conceptual, from artists. Not only are there leaps between different dimensions and materials to consider, but also the specific conditions of the installation site. Several designs of the 1950s and 1960s can help us grasp this creative process today.

Following the horrendous destruction caused by the Second World War, the reconstruction and construction of buildings and cities got underway throughout Europe. The efforts usually went hand in hand with government-funded commissions for artworks on and in buildings.[1] This was especially challenging in a Germany still divided among four occupying powers. After all, for the Allies the foremost priority was to exert an influence on the ethically and morally devastated German people, including its artists, by various means such as denazification and re-education. In England, one of the aims of the internationally operating British Council was to forge a link between this policy and culture, in part by way of art exhibitions. Along with the sculptor Henry Moore, Ben Nicholson and Barbara Hepworth were among the artists propagated by that council not least with this purpose in mind.[2] All three of them were accordingly quite visible to the German Federal Republican population. Born in the late nineteenth or early twentieth century, they had all begun to tend towards abstraction (if to varying degrees) as early as the 1920s and were thus representatives of both pre-war modernism and – each in their own way – the post-war present. In the international context, the younger artists' generation was side-lined as a result, a circumstance that sparked critical commentary.[3]

At the first post-war Biennale in Venice in 1948, Henry Moore won the International Prize for Sculpture – a major success. From 1950 onwards, his work was exhibited in Brussels, Paris, Amsterdam, Hamburg (Kunsthalle), Düsseldorf and elsewhere, with a second show touring in 1953, stopping at, among other venues, the Frankfurt Städel (fig. 1). For the accompanying flyer, the influential (art) writer Herbert Read wrote a brief text which, evidently intended to serve didactic purposes, linked the artistic qualities of the works with moral categories. He perceived an "ethical ring" in Moore's striving towards material justice, for example, while branding dynamic surface relief as "deception".[4] The responses to Moore's art in Germany were far-reaching. In 1950, the sculptor Richard Scheibe wrote: "The entire guild moores here."[5] And indeed, the British artist's wide-ranging influence on numerous sculptors[6] is clearly evident, for example in the case of Hans Mettel, who was active in Frankfurt at the time, as well as the Hamburg native Karl Hartung. Yet his oeuvre also met with incomprehension and rejection of the kind that erupted in a letter to the editor in the *Frankfurter Rundschau* in 1953: "If that's not all 'degenerate art', what is 'degenerate art'?"[7] Moore – that much is clear – was an "export hit" and, like Nicholson and Hepworth, ultimately also a perfect fit for the documenta art show that premiered in Kassel in 1955 during the emerging Cold War.[8] It was against this background that the works to be introduced in the following were conceived between 1954 and 1969.

In 1954, Henry Moore received a big commission – in the truest sense of the word – for the Bouwcentrum in Rotterdam (figs. 2, 3), which coordinated the post-war reconstruction of that city's centre following the ravages of war. On the basis of the artist's model, craftsmen executed the relief, a curtain wall measuring 8.61 by 19.2 metres, in front of the brick façade traditional in Central and Northern Europe.[9] The artist, one might add, had a fundamental aversion to architecture-bound commissions of this kind.[10] In the design process, he created ten maquettes, initially in wax or clay, which were subsequently cast in plaster and later in bronze. *Maquette No. 3 and No. 4*[11] (cats. 120, 121) testify to the rich variety of Moore's conception. Now he explored the vertically arranged organic-figural motifs (which he would later develop into three-dimensional figures in a different context),[12] now the linear-geometrical elements by virtue of which the relief approximates an architectural skeleton.[13] The first design was the one ultimately realised. And just as the aspects to be examined in greater depth below merged to form a harmonious whole consisting of curved forms and structures, the relief merged with the architecture of the wall.

Ben Nicholson differed from Moore in that relief was the central theme of his oeuvre. He was initially active as a painter before his interest turned to the three-dimensional cut or carved relief.[14] From the 1950s onwards he developed a penchant for especially hard, resistant material, which he processed with great physical effort, but also, as in the preceding years, with microscopic precision using razor blades. Over time, the colour range of his works transformed from the famous abstract monochrome white reliefs of the 1930s to warm earth tones. Only once – for his third documenta participation in 1964 – did he carry out a relief designed as a wall on a monumental scale in foamed concrete (fig. 4).[15] Nicholson wrote to his friend Jim Ede: "It […] looks to me like a huge chunk of Greece. It is 4 m × 15 m but what fascinates me is that it looks at least twice that size […] it does set up I believe a new poetic kind of architecture which has been lacking since religion ceased to produce this."[16] His other 1960s designs for freestanding relief walls similarly exhibit a finely tuned balance between form, relief depth, composition, rhythm and colour, a case in point being the oil-painted carved board of 1965 (cat. 122). That work goes back to the inspiration the artist took from his travels in Greece in 1959 and 1961. Like Moore's brick relief in Rotterdam, Nicholson's designs for wall reliefs are free of functional architectural limitations; in fact, they are entirely autonomous. In the unity of wall and relief, a "kind of poetic affair", as Nicholson phrased it, materialises self-sufficiently.[17]

Barbara Hepworth was a sculptor somewhat in competition with Moore at both the 1959 Venice Biennale and the first two documenta shows. In 1969 she faced a different task: her relief *Theme and Variations* (fig. 5) for the building of the Cheltenham & Gloucester Building Society in Cheltenham was mounted on the façade at first-floor level. The underlying surface and what would ultimately be a bronze relief measuring 3.5 by 7.6 metres thus did not form a material unity nor was the artist free of restraints posed by the architecture. In other words,

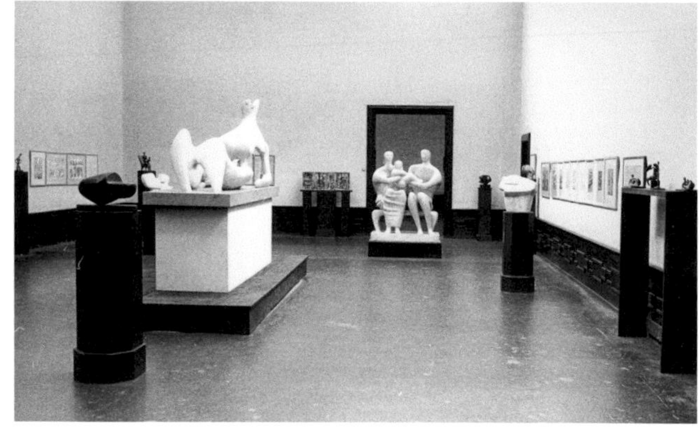

Fig. 1

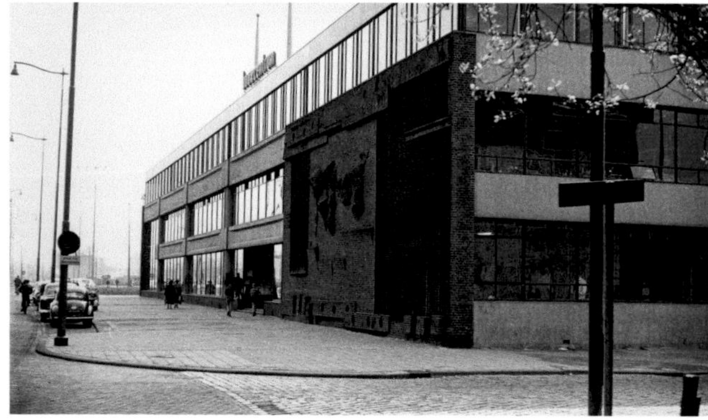

Fig. 2

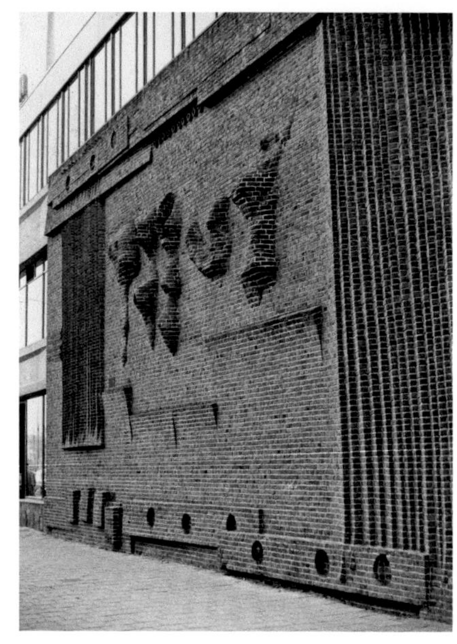

Fig. 3

Fig. 1   View into the Henry Moore exhibition at the Städel, 1953, photograph, Städel-Archiv, Frankfurt am Main

Fig. 2   The Bouwcentrum in Rotterdam, before 1966, photograph, Städel-Archiv, Frankfurt am Main, Nachlass Mettel

Fig. 3   The Bouwcentrum in Rotterdam, before 1966, photograph, Städel-Archiv, Frankfurt am Main, Nachlass Mettel

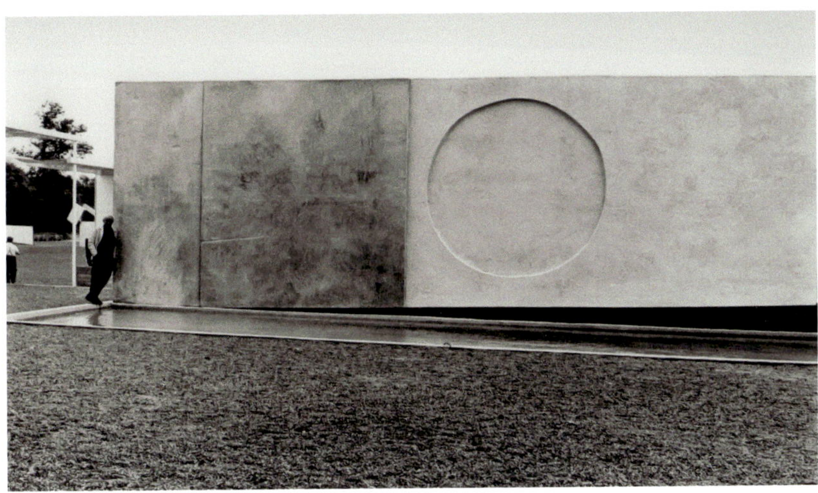

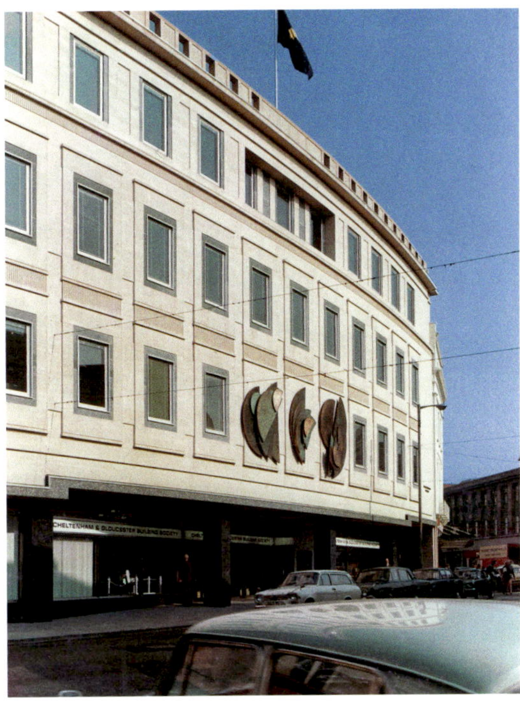

Fig. 4   Felicitas Vogler: *Ben Nicholson at the documenta III, Kassel*, 1964, photograph, Modern and Contemporary Art Archive, National Galleries of Scotland, Edinburgh

Fig. 5   Barbara Hepworth: *Theme and Variations*, 1970, Cheltenham House (formerly Cheltenham & Gloucester Building Society Head Office), Cheltenham, Gloucestershire, photograph, Hepworth Estate

the conditions were of the kind that she, like Moore, tended to reject.[18] When she nevertheless accepted her last public commission, Hepworth wrote that she liked the proportions as well as the customer's wish for an abstract relief.[19] Accordingly, she took a playful approach to filling three fields with overlapping leaf-shaped or semi-circular plates in rhythmic variations, in which context the middle one, with its formal stringency, evidently represented the actual "theme".

Following the wartime devastations, Hepworth regarded the purpose of art, and in particular of sculpture, through a different lens. In 1944 she wrote to Herbert Read: "Sculpture is public – it must have a place, and the people."[20] Numerous large and primarily three-dimensional works in the urban space or the landscape were the consequence, but she produced on a smaller scale and thus for (private) interiors as well. *Theme and Variations* also exists, therefore, in dimensions other than the monumental. A monochrome, white-painted design on hardboard mounted on pine (cat. 123) served as a model for the work's realisation on the building. Taking this design as her point of departure, the artist developed two editions of six, one in silver and one in bronze, on a walnut ground (cat. 124).[21] The

felicitous combination of the reflecting metal and the warm wood testified once again to Hepworth's ongoing search for organic phenomena in abstract forms and how to combine those elements.

The sculptor Karl Hartung sought the same challenge in his late work. Considered politically untarnished, he had been appointed professor of sculpture at the Hochschule für bildende Künste (Academy of Fine Arts) in Berlin six years after the war's end – in biographical analogy to his colleague Hans Mettel of Frankfurt, who was appointed the director of the Städel Schule in 1950. Both artists gained international renown through the first three documenta exhibitions.[22] Starting in 1961, Hartung worked on (among other projects) plaster relief designs that would ultimately come to fruition in 1964 in the almost 100-metre-long, 4-metre-high marble wall on the Westdeutscher Rundfunk (West German Broadcasting Corporation) building in Cologne (fig. 6; cat. 128).[23] In a loosely rhythmic composition of soft, slurred forms, Hartung transformed figural elements into abstract ones and vice versa. Despite the immense scale of many of his reliefs, he never lost sight of the human dimension, an aspect to which not least his drawn notations testify (cat. 127).

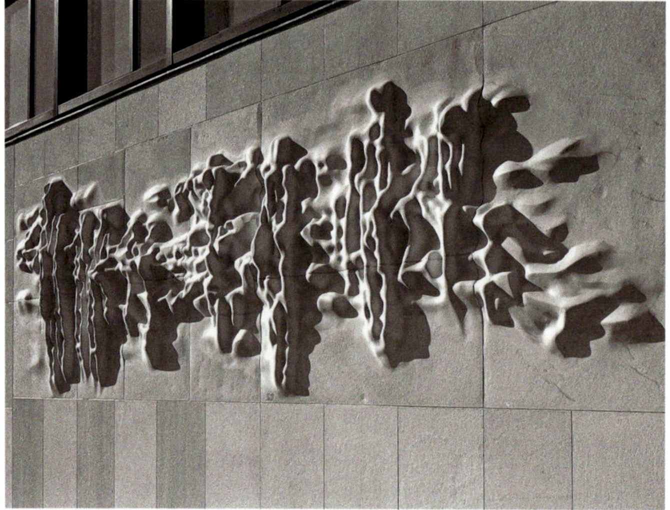

Fig. 6

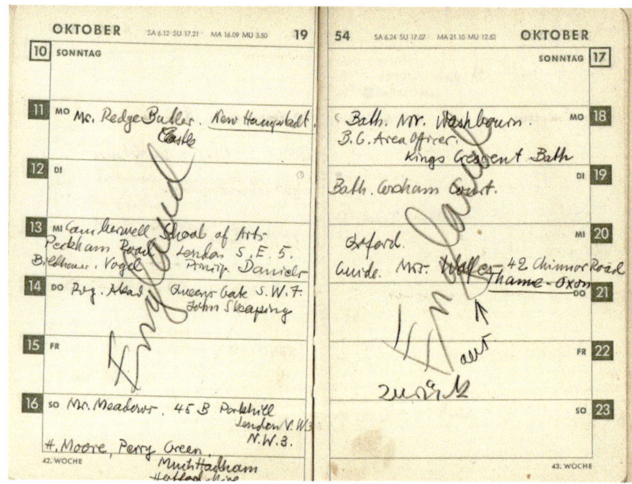

Fig. 7

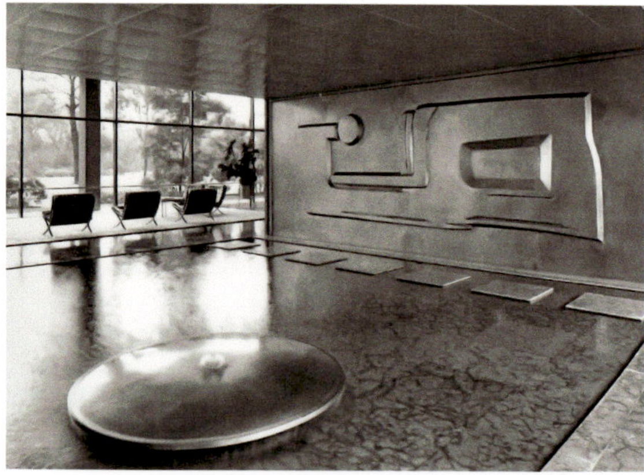

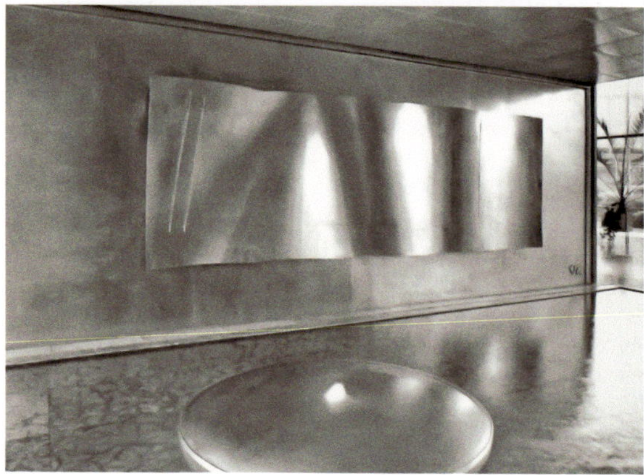

Fig. 8

Over a span of decades, he also created numerous small-scale relief pieces with a wide range of different surfaces as a means of testing various wall structures and their spatial and haptic effects (cats. 125, 126).

Hans Mettel, in contrast, placed the seated and standing human being at the centre of his oeuvre. Inspired by the art of Henry Moore, whose exhibitions in Germany he visited – and to whom he paid a personal visit in England in 1954 (fig. 7) – he moreover adopted the motif of the reclining figure. In the same phase, he turned to abstraction to a degree unusual by his standards, as documented by the 1958 designs for two never-realised wall reliefs for the German conference room in the UNESCO building in Paris (cats. 130–132).[24] Mettel developed his last secular commission (fig. 8) in 1962/63 for the so-called fountain room in the August-Thyssen-Hütte AG administration building in Duisburg-Hamborn, executing the designs in aluminium on wood and in plaster (cats. 129, 133).[25] He conceived two complementary reliefs on the basis of a precisely elaborated principle, which he elucidated in 1963: it took the backlighting that characterises the space for the *Reclining Woman* (executed in 175 by 485 cm) to form and for the *Wave* (executed in 143 by 437 cm) to be set in motion on the surface of the wall. Both reliefs, he added, created an awareness of the light-flooded room's special charm.[26] For this artist, architecture and wall sculpture were thus inseparably linked.

Fig. 6   Karl Hartung: *Wall Relief on the Building of the Westdeutscher Rundfunk Cologne* (detail), 1964, photograph, 2015

Fig. 7   Calendar entries by Hans Mettel, October 1954, Städel-Archiv, Frankfurt am Main, Nachlass Mettel

Fig. 8   Peter Metzger: *Hans Mettel's reliefs in the fountain room of the August-Thyssen-Hütte AG in Duisburg-Hamborn*, 1962/63, photograph, 1960s

1   For a general discussion of the topic, see Eduard Trier: "Reliefs für Architektur", in: *Reliefs: Formprobleme zwischen Malerei und Skulptur im 20. Jahrhundert*, ed. Ernst-Gerhard Güse, exh. cat. Westfälisches Landesmuseum für Kunst und Kulturgeschichte Münster, Bern 1980, pp. 82–91; on the "Kunst am Bau" ("art in architecture") programmes with references to further reading, see Carina Plath: "Die frühen Jahre", in: *Die frühen Jahre: Britische und deutsche Kunst nach 1945*, ed. idem, exh. cat. Sprengel Museum Hannover, Cologne 2014, pp. 69–81, here p. 77.

2   On the work of the British Council (formerly British Council for Relations with Other Countries) and the networks around Herbert Read, see Henry Meyric Hughes: "The Promotion and Reception of British Sculpture Abroad, 1948–1960: Herbert Read, Henry Moore, Barbara Hepworth, and the 'Young British Sculptors'", in: *British Art Studies*, vol. 3, 18 July 2016, https://dx.doi.org/10.17658/issn.2058-5462/issue-03/hmhughes (accessed 13 February 2023); *Henry Moore: Impuls für Europa*, ed. Hermann Arnold, exh. cat. LWL-Museum für Kunst und Kultur Münster, Munich 2016, especially the contribution by Tanja Pirsig-Marshall: "Hier moort die ganze Innung", pp. 67–79; exh. cat. Hannover 2014 (see note 1).

3   For a detailed discussion of this topic, see *Postwar Modern: New Art in Britain, 1945–65*, ed. Jane Alison with Hilary Floe and Charlotte Flint, exh. cat. Barbican Art Gallery London, Munich et al. 2022.

4   "How is such vitality to be achieved? Above all through 'material justice'. This term has an ethical ring." Elsewhere: "To win the beholder with a play on the surface of the stone – with line and relief – is rejected on ethical and not just aesthetic grounds as a kind of deception, because effects of this kind are better suited to painting and drawing." Herbert Read, in: *Henry Moore – Ausstellung von Plastiken und Zeichnungen: 1953–1954. Veranstaltet vom British Council*, flyer, Städel-Archiv, Frankfurt am Main; trans. JR.

5   Letter from Richard Scheibe to Gerhard Marcks, 17 February 1950, quoted in Pirsig-Marshall 2016 (see note 2), p. 67.

6   For authoritative insights, see the extensive research by Christa Lichtenstern et al.: *Henry Moore: Werk – Theorie – Wirkung*, Munich and Berlin 2008.

7   Letter to the editor from Dr. med. Otto Müller, in: *Frankfurter Rundschau*, 17 October 1953, p. 2. Further statements followed in the subsequent days; see Pirsig-Marshall 2016 (see note 2), p. 72.

8   For a fundamental discussion, see *documenta: Politik und Kunst*, ed. Raphael Gross et al., exh. cat. Deutsches Historisches Museum, Berlin, Munich et al. 2021.

9   Herbert Read: *Henry Moore* (1965), Munich and Zurich 1967, pp. 201f. On the history of the relief and the architecture, which has undergone substantial changes since 2012, see "De muur van Moore", https://bouwcentrumrotterdam.nl/?page_id=2957 (accessed 13 February 2023).

10   *Henry Moore and the Challenge of Architecture*, exh. cat. The Henry Moore Foundation, Much Hadham, 2005.

11   Alan Bowness: *Henry Moore: Complete Sculpture*, vol. 3: *Sculpture 1955–64*, London 1986, catalogues raisonnés nos. 367 and 368. The designs, numbering ten in all, were cast in an edition of ten.

12   Scholars are divided on the question of whether the organic forms are found objects pressed into clay; see Alice Correia: "*Upright Motive No. 1: Glenkiln Cross*, 1955–6, Cast 1958–60 by Henry Moore OM, CH", March 2013, https://www.tate.org.uk/art/research-publications/henry-moore/henry-moore-om-ch-upright-motive-no1-glenkiln-cross-r1151461 (accessed 13 February 2023).

13   See Hans-Gerhard Evers: "Gedanken zur Kunst Henry Moores", in: *Henry Moore, 1898–1986: Eine Retrospektive zum 100. Geburtstag*, ed. Wilfried Seipel, exh. cat. Kunsthistorisches Museum Wien, Milan 1998, pp. 59–76, here pp. 63–65.

14   See *Ben Nicholson: From the Studio*, exh. cat. Pallant House Gallery, Chichester, 2021; *Ben Nicholson: Distant Planes 1955–1979*, exh. cat. Piano Nobile Gallery, London, 2020, there esp. Lee Beard: "Unfolding Ideas: Art, Process and Place", pp. 13–24; Sophie Bowness: "The Poetic Painting of Ben Nicholson", in: *Ben Nicholson*, exh. cat. Helly Nahmad Gallery, London, 2001, pp. 5–12.

15   The so-called *Nicholson Wall* in Sutton Place, 1980–1982, is a late echo, but is based on a relief of 1937/38 not conceived as a wall; see Louise Campbell: "'Architecture and the Painter': The Studios of Ben Nicholson", in: exh. cat. Chichester 2021 (see note 14), pp. 107–119.

16   Letter from Ben Nicholson to John Ede, presumably 12 July 1964, quoted in Beard 2020 (see note 14), p. 24.

17   Ibid.

18   Penelope Curtis: "From Bridgewater to Otterlo: Hepworth, CIAM and 'The Synthesis of the Arts'", in: *Barbara Hepworth: Sculpture for a Modern World*, ed. idem and Chris Stevens, exh. cat. Tate Britain, London, et al. 2015, pp. 98–104, here pp. 101f.

19   Letter from Barbara Hepworth, 1 December 1969, quoted in *Barbara Hepworth: A Retrospective*, ed. Penelope Curtis and Alan G. Wilkinson, exh. cat. Tate Gallery Liverpool et al., London 1994, p. 156. For a more detailed discussion of the commission and the work's genesis, see Sophie Bowness: "Barbara Hepworth's Studio Practice: Plaster for Bronze", in: idem (ed.): *Barbara Hepworth – The Plasters: The Gift to Wakefield*, Farnham et al. 2011, pp. 31–95, here pp. 86–89.

20   "Sculpture is public – it must have a place, and the people." Letter from Barbara Hepworth to Herbert Read, 14 May 1944, quoted in Penelope Curtis: "The Artist in Post-War Britain", in: exh. cat. Liverpool et al. 1994 (see note 19), pp. 125–149, here p. 127.

21   Bowness 2011 (see note 19), pp. 164–167; there both the plaster maquette for the execution on the building, inv. no. BH503, and the hardboard model for the realisations in wood and metal, inv. no. BH512A.

22   Kerstin Schlüter: "Hans Mettel – der Nachlass im Städel", in: *Von Köpfen und Körpern: Frankfurter Bildhauerei aus dem Städel*, exh. cat. Museum Giersch, Frankfurt am Main, 2006, pp. 71–83; idem: *Der Bildhauer Hans Mettel: Mit einem kritischen Werkkatalog der plastischen Arbeiten*, diss., Marburg 1998, Frankfurt am Main et al. 2001; *Karl Hartung 1908–1967: Metamorphosen von Mensch und Natur. Monographie und Werkverzeichnis*, ed. Markus Krause, exh. cat. Germanisches Nationalmuseum, Nuremberg, et al., Munich 1998; Irmtraud von Andrian-Werburg (ed.): *Karl Hartung: Werke und Dokumente*, Nuremberg 1998. I thank Michael Mohr for pointing me to Mettel's 1954 calendar (see fig. 7) in the Mettel estate, Städel-Archiv, Frankfurt am Main.

23   Exh. cat. Nuremberg et al. 1998 (see note 22), catalogue raisonné no. 740a.

24   Schlüter 2001 (see note 22), catalogue raisonné no. E 92.

25   Ibid., catalogue raisonné no. 106.

26   The complete quotation is found in: ibid., pp. 132f.; see exh. cat. Frankfurt am Main 2006 (see note 22), p. 231 (Manfred Großkinsky).

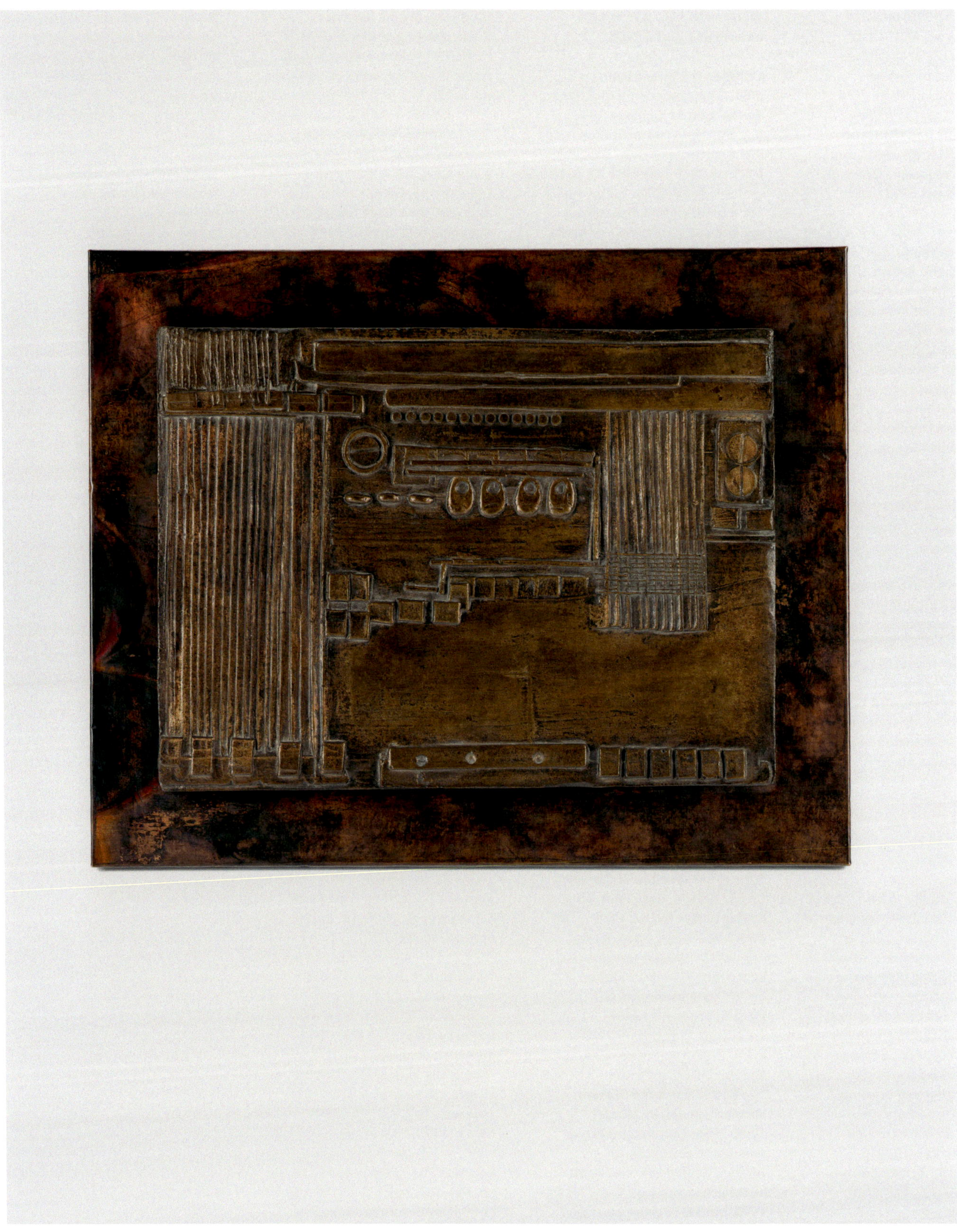

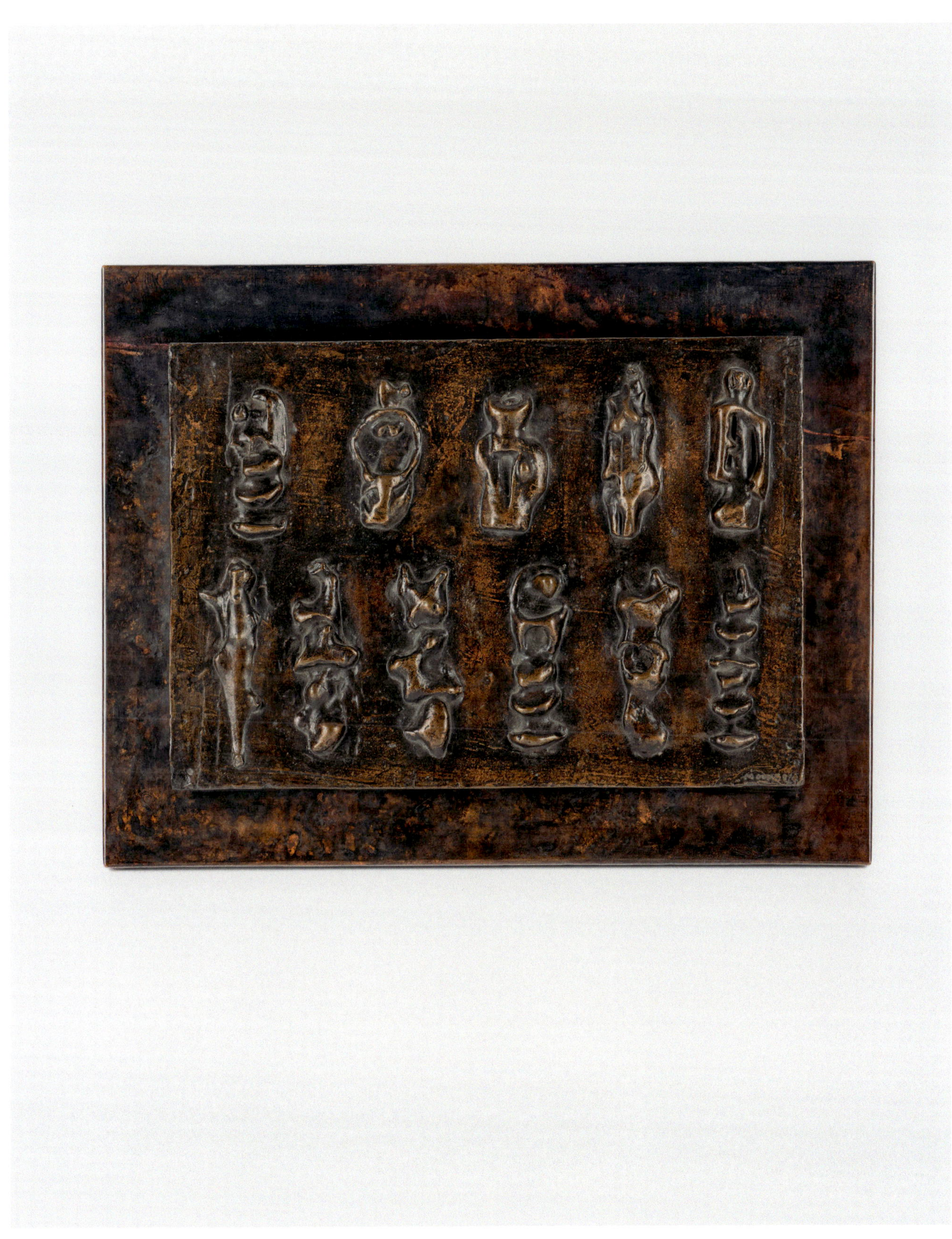

Cats. 120, 121   Henry Moore: *Maquettes No. 3 and No. 4 for the Brick Wall of the Rotterdam Bouwcentrum*, 1954/55, bronze, 56.5 × 44.5 × 5.3 cm / 60 × 45 × 5.5 cm, Museum für Kunst und Gewerbe Hamburg, property of the Stiftung Hamburger Kunstsammlungen, inv. no. 1967.273.ab / St. 258a-b

Cat. 122   Ben Nicholson: *1965 (Kos – Concept for a Free-Standing Wall)*, 1965, oil on carved board, 34.2 × 49 × 4.2 cm, Pallant House Gallery, Chichester, permanent loan from private collection (2018)

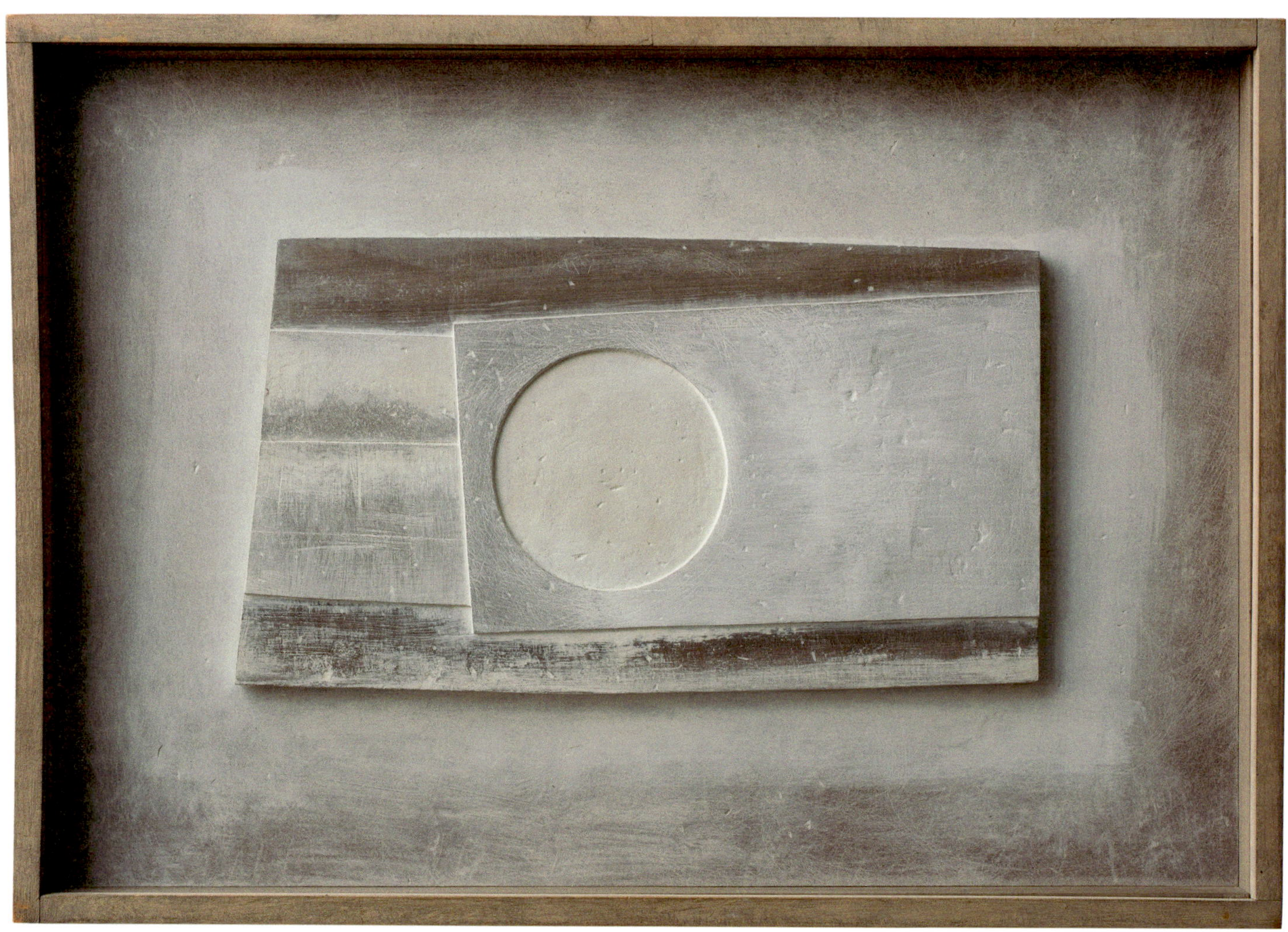

Cat. 123   Barbara Hepworth: *Maquette: Theme and Variations*, 1970,
fibreboard, painted, on pinewood, 39.5 × 72.5 × 5 cm,
The Hepworth Wakefield, presented by the artist's daughters,
Rachel Kidd and Sarah Bowness, through the Trustees of
the Barbara Hepworth Estate and the Art Fund

Cat. 124   Barbara Hepworth: *Maquette: Theme and Variations*, 1970,
silver on walnut, 31 × 66 × 16 cm, private collection,
courtesy of Simon Studer Art, Geneva

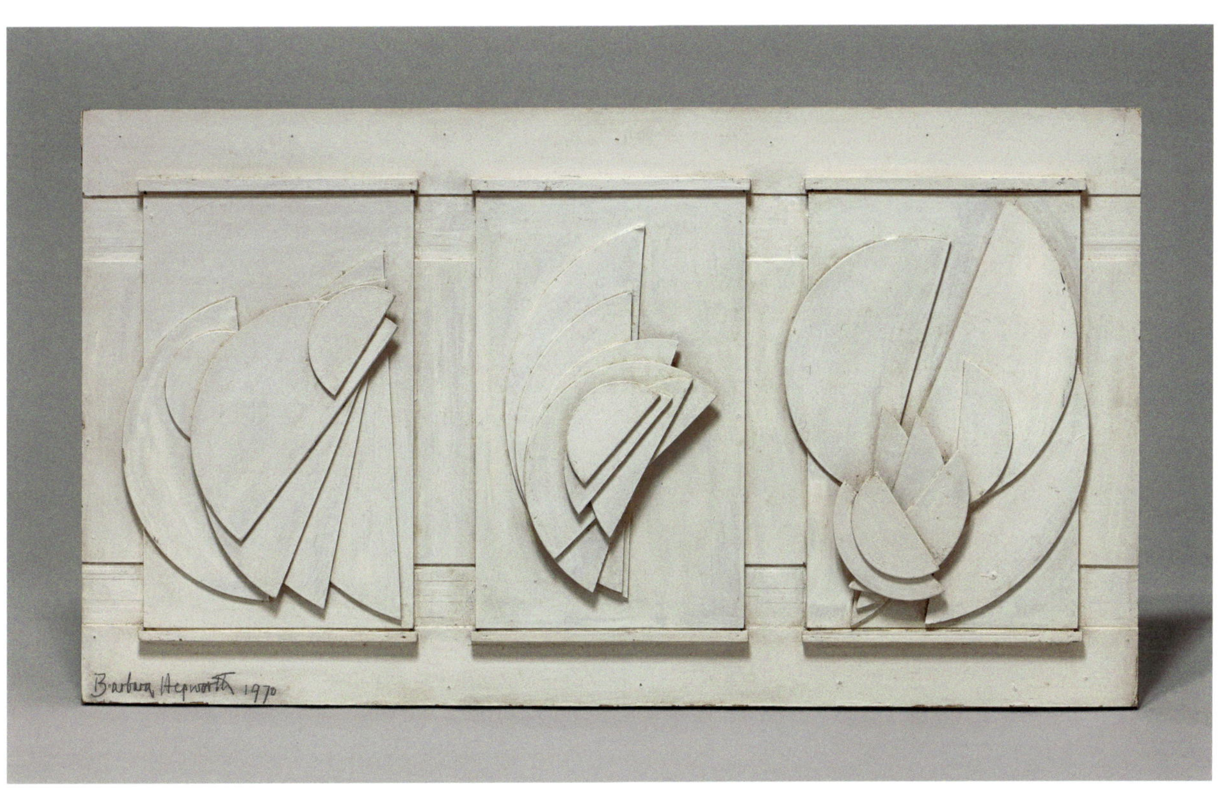

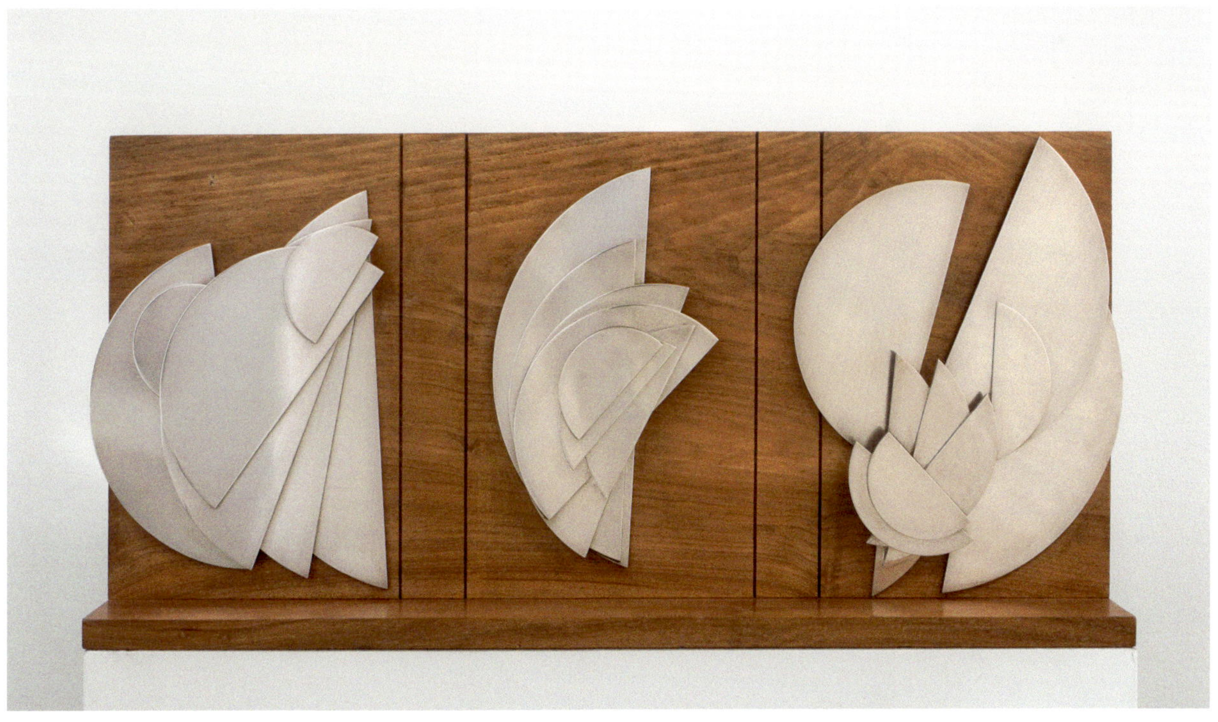

Cat. 125   Karl Hartung: *Relief*, 1958, travertine, 12 × 28.2 × 3.3 cm,
             Nachlass Karl Hartung (Hamburg only)

Cat. 126   Karl Hartung: *Relief*, 1958, sandstone, 19 × 36.5 × 6 cm,
             Nachlass Karl Hartung (Hamburg only)

Cat. 127   Karl Hartung: *Figure in Front of a Relief Wall* (*Lanzarote*),
             undated, felt pen on paper, 29.7 × 21 cm, Nachlass Karl
             Hartung (Hamburg only)

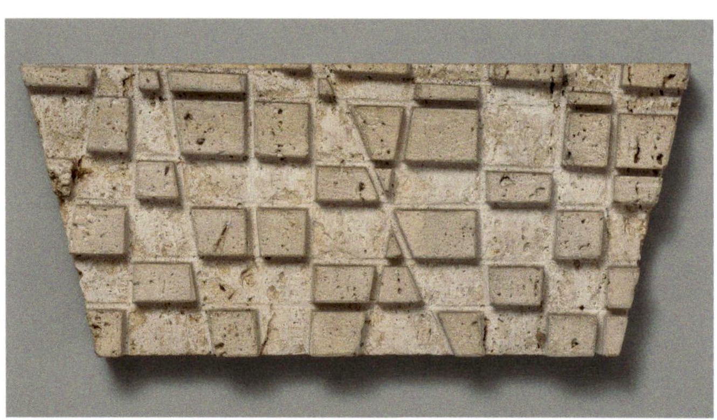

Cat. 125

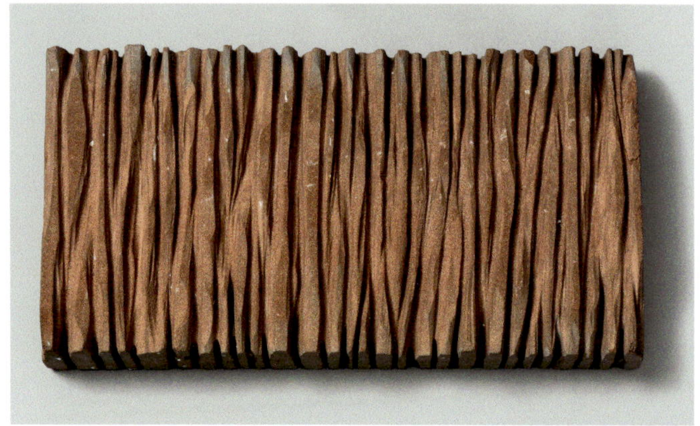

Cat. 126

Cat. 127

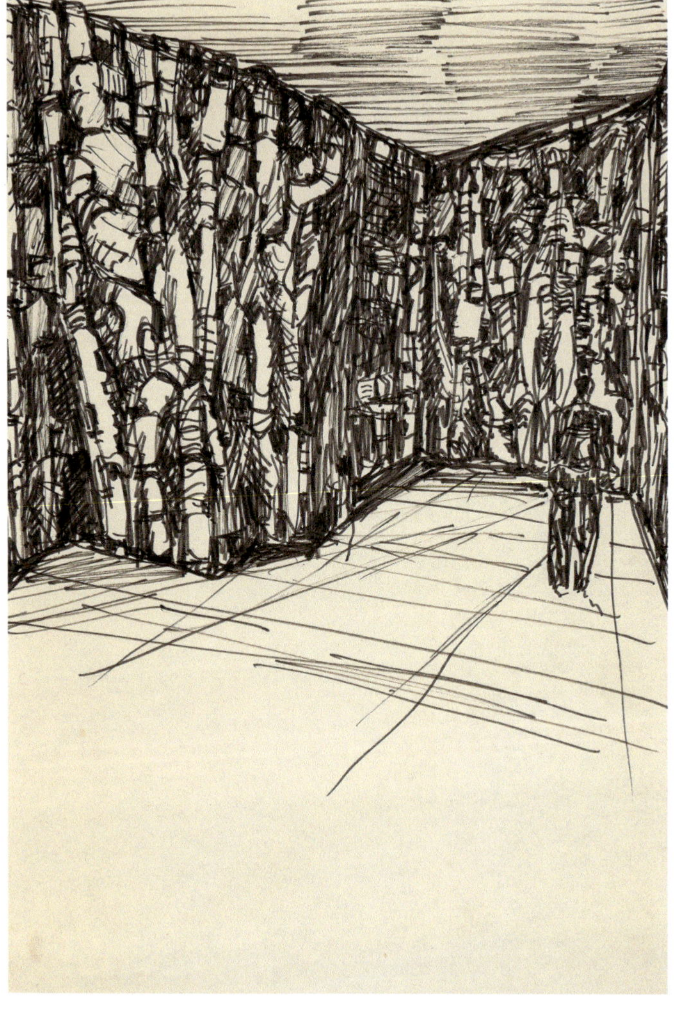

Cat. 128   Karl Hartung: *Detail of the Wall Relief, Westdeutscher Rundfunk, Cologne*, ca. 1961/62, plaster, 90.7 × 107 × 6 cm, Nachlass Karl Hartung (Hamburg only)

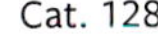

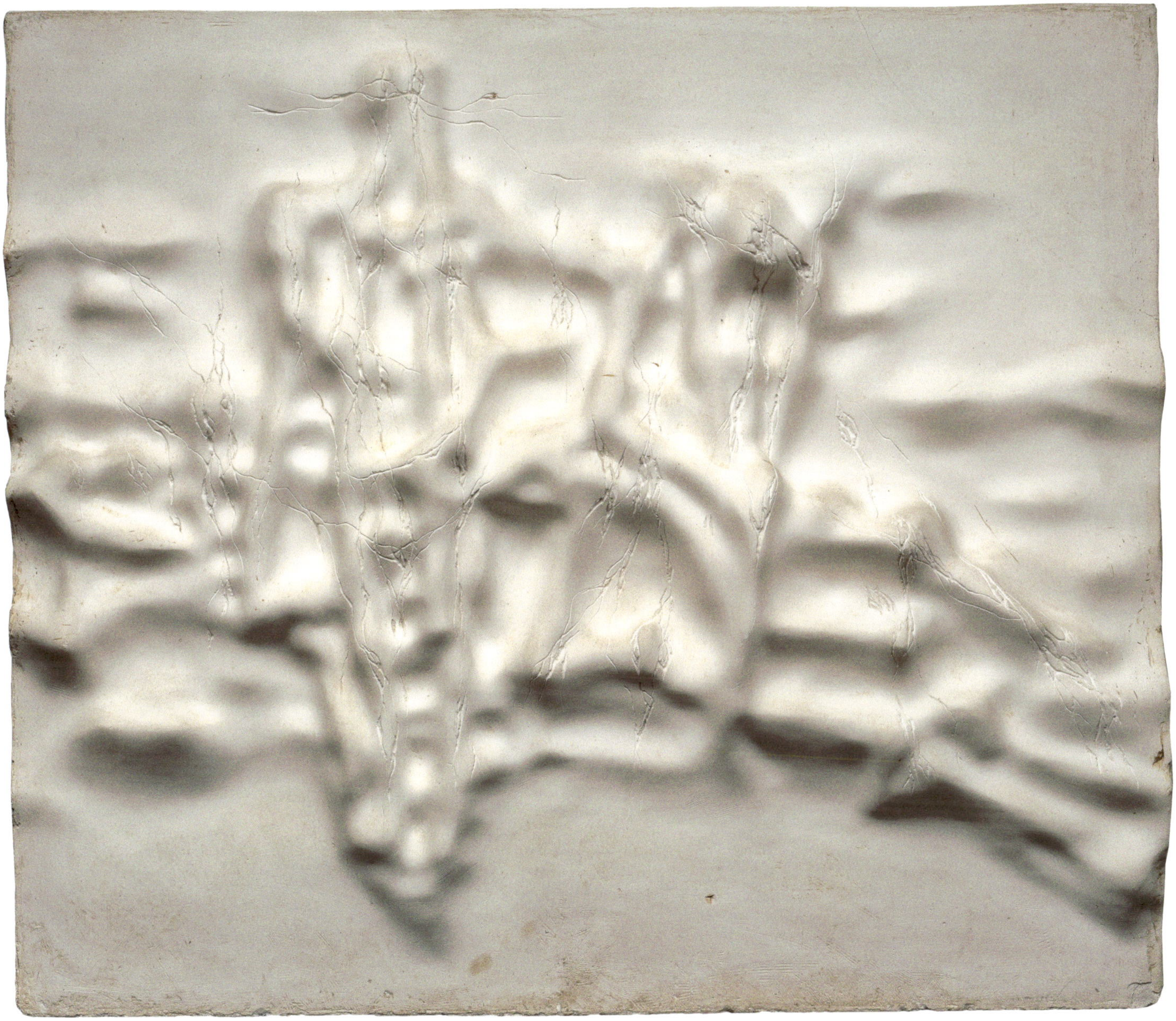

Cat. 129 Hans Mettel: *Wave, Model for the Fountain Room in the Administrative Building of the August-Thyssen-Hütte AG, Duisburg-Hamborn*, 1962/63, aluminium on wood, 49 × 126.3 × 6.5 cm, Städel Museum, Frankfurt am Main, inv. no. St.P 551 (Frankfurt only)

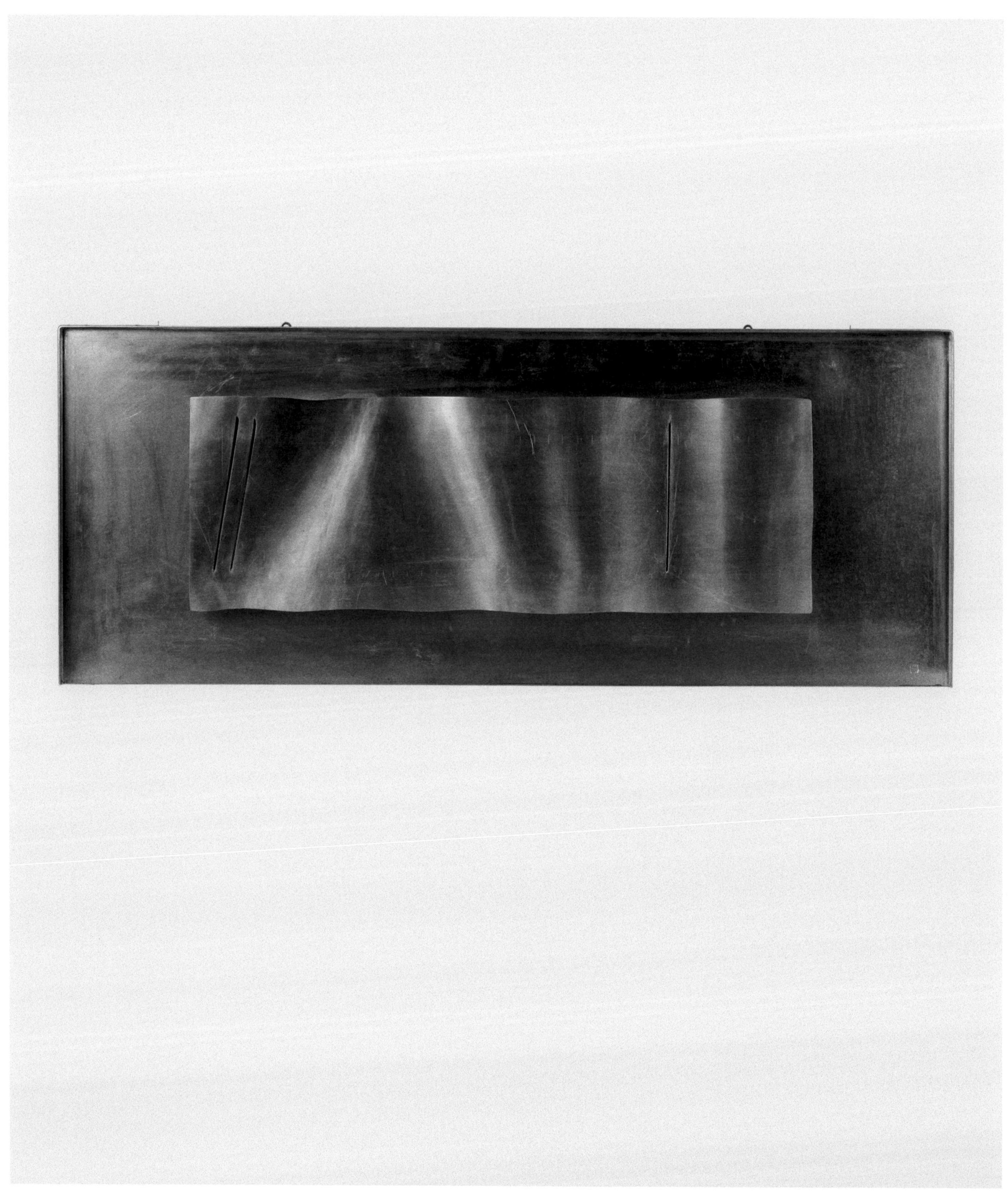

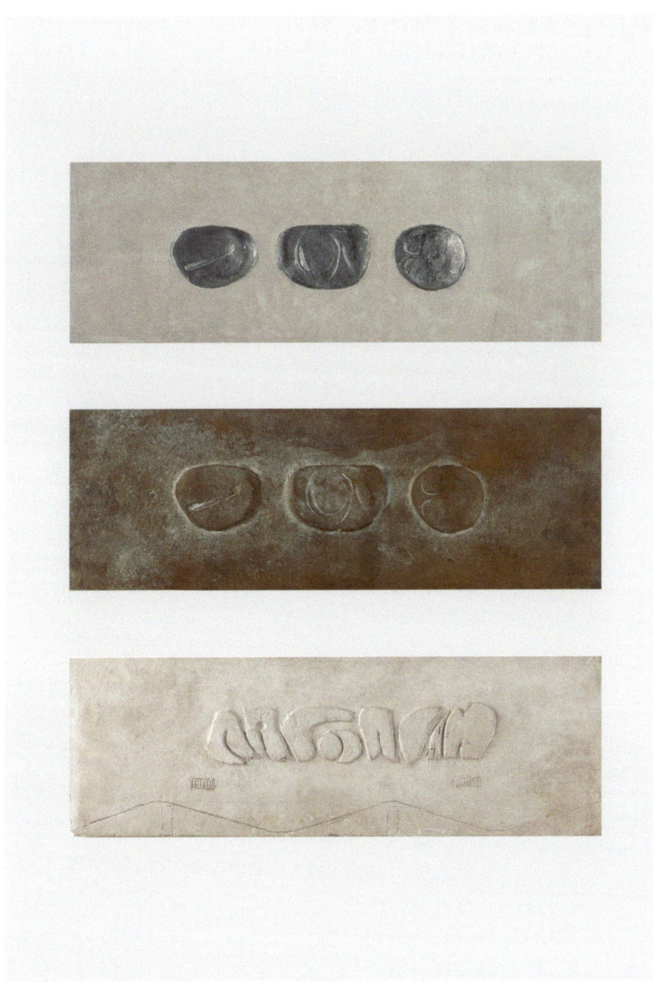

Cat. 130   Hans Mettel: *Model for a Wall Relief for the German Conference Room in the UNESCO Building, Paris*, 1958, plaster with metal-leaf plating, painted, 20.8 × 60.5 × 2.5 cm, Städel Museum, Frankfurt am Main, inv. no. St.P 533 a (Frankfurt only)

Cat. 131   Hans Mettel: *Model for a Wall Relief for the German Conference Room in the UNESCO Building, Paris*, 1958, bronze, cast after the plaster, 19 × 56.5 × 0.3 cm, Städel Museum, Frankfurt am Main, inv. no. St.P 533 (Frankfurt only)

Cat. 132   Hans Mettel: *Model for a Wall Relief for the German Conference Room in the UNESCO Building, Paris*, 1958, plaster with pencil drawing, 20.4 × 60.5 × 2.3 cm, Städel Museum, Frankfurt am Main, inv. no. St.P 533 b (Frankfurt only)

Cat. 133   Hans Mettel: *Reclining Woman, Model for the Fountain Room in the Administrative Building of the August-Thyssen-Hütte AG, Duisburg-Hamborn*, 1962/63, plaster, brazed, 12.3 × 31.5 × 3 cm, Städel Museum, Frankfurt am Main, inv. no. St.P 537 (Frankfurt only)

Cats. 130–132

Cat. 133

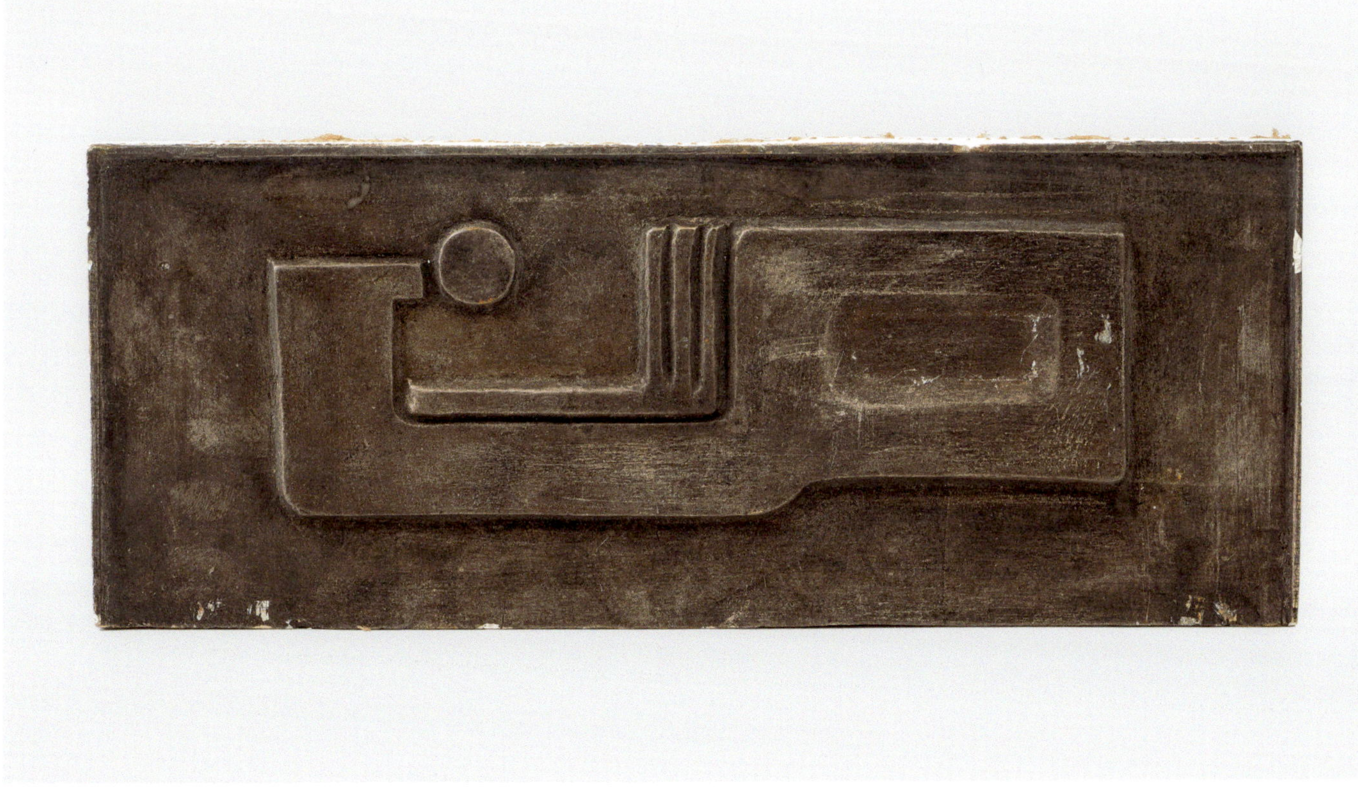

Cats. 134 — 149

Svenja Grosser

BACK AND FORTH

The Image Support as Boundary and Space of Possibility

Across the centuries, artists have repeatedly redefined the canvas as a support. It was the starting point for the most pioneering discussions in painting. While in the Renaissance it was understood as a window to the world, hence negating its planarity, modern artists highlight precisely this. The canvas became the locus of new negotiations in art, at the latest in the avant-garde and neo-avant-garde: it could either become a sculptural artwork or be done away with outright. Works were created that questioned and expanded the supposed boundaries of painting, or even transgressed them.[1]

> This ultimately resulted in three possibilities for artists to deal with what was once the sacrosanct support in the advancing twentieth century: from the execution at the point of origin itself, i.e., the plane of the pictorial ground, regardless of whether it was out of wood or out of linen, through the expansion into space, to the disclosure of what was behind it. Thus three levels of (pictorial) space emerged to be dealt with and viewed: that of the work, that of the viewer, and that of the exhibition space.

The Italian avant-garde artist Lucio Fontana is exemplary for the radicalness of the manifestations such negotiations can assume: in the 1960s, he perforated or cut through the painted canvas, and in doing so broke open the support at the boundary between the viewer and pictorial space. In traditional painting, depth and space were produced through the use of perspective, light and shadow. In contrast, Fontana structured his canvas with the simplest of means: with puncture-like holes (*Buchi*; cat. 135) or with carefully placed gashes (*Tagli*; cat. 136). Three clean, slightly vertical-running incisions were made in the intense shade of blue of *Concetto spaziale – Attese* (cat. 136). They cut through the canvas and yet deny us a view of the underlying wall, as Fontana covered the gashes on the reverse side of the canvas with black gauze. The artist elevated the canvas itself to become the pictorial object and – paradoxically – destroyed it at the same time. The obscurity behind the canvas opens up an imaginary space: neither pictorial nor exhibition space, this includes a further component that evades the viewer's and the curator's control.

> Whereas Lucio Fontana took advantage of perspective, light and shadow in the style of painting, instead of producing space in a painterly way he created it by means of real incisions.[2] Or as Otto Piene wrote about the beginnings of the *Tagli*: "The incisions transform the planes of the canvas into a relief whose dialectic suggests a space."[3]

As early as the 1920s, the wood relief by Dadaist Jean Arp actually enabled seeing the wall and hence integrated the (exhibition) space in the work. At the same time, it is helpful to know that Arp had found his way to the relief via painting, drawing and collage.[4] The painterly influence is demonstrated exemplarily in his early wood relief *Tower Clock* (*Horloge*) from 1924 (cat. 137). Arp already burst the classic rectangle format of the support by trimming the wood to produce an irregular circle. He painted the wood in a dark colour palette consisting of extensively applied shades of blue, green and red. Arp created plasticity by means of a cut-out and the attachment of five elements. By doing so, he not only turned the exhibition surface into part of the work, but allowed it to open up into the space. The organic, coloured sections lend the objects a visual dynamic and are reminiscent of their purpose specified in the title: the display of time. The longer sawn-out shape can be interpreted as a clock hand, and according to Arp the pieces of wood attached represent a naval, a torso and a bottle.[5] The Surrealist-Dadaist relationship of reality and absurdity finds expression in this curious, seemingly arbitrary combination of objects and the alienation of the purpose of the hand, which manifests here as a static element. In the case of this work, even though the support is broken through, a balanced interaction develops between positive and negative.[6]

Jean Arp's wife Sophie Taeuber-Arp also explored the joining of positive and negative forms; however in *Shells and Flowers* (*Coquilles et fleurs*) from 1938 (cat. 138), one of her few round reliefs, she did not allow them to cut through to the wall.[7] Like Jean Arp, she too chose the circular form as a basic structure. The circle, one of the elements she preferred during this period (cat. 139), now became the carrier and the pictorial form.[8] *Shells and Flowers* is one of a three-part series of tondi with identical diameters. Each of them consists of four wooden boards, placed one on top of the other, that have been aligned in such a way that they direct one's gaze from the uppermost board to the bottom. They differ in two details only: all are arranged differently, and whereas the two other works are kept entirely in white, in the present version from the Aargauer Kunsthaus collection the interior forms are accented with edges painted yellow. Hence, the yellow radiates to the surfaces and affects their shade of white.[9]

In retrospect, it cannot be reconstructed why Sophie Taeuber-Arp painted this tondo only, yet the colour has a defining influence on the object and its distinction from the underlying surface. All three reliefs are the result of dealing with the creation of depth and space by means of plasticity. Taeuber-Arp did not paint the shadows necessary to achieve this, but realised them physically by means of layering the three levels. She reinforced their sculptural perception through the additional application of colour. Nevertheless, she did not carry out the more radical step towards a complete breach – perhaps because she did not want to let chance, in the form of the surrounding space and including the non-influenceable colour of the wall and structuring, intervene in her clear formal language. Hence, a coloured wall would distract too much from the concentrated examination of light and shadow.

The painterly title of *Shells and Flowers* could suggest that Taeuber-Arp wanted to add a lyrical component to her work, yet this was assigned to it posthumously.[10] Taeuber-Arp rarely gave titles to her works, and when she did, she oriented herself towards their formal characteristics.[11] This approach illustrates that she placed her focus on formal investigations, which may likewise be reflected in the serial arrangement of her reliefs.[12]

The American sculptor Louise Nevelson also focussed her attention on composition when she painted her relief-like assemblages in monochromatic colours and arranged them in wooden boxes. In the spirit of the readymade, space and work converged in *Royal Fire* from 1960 (cat. 134) and, by means of the uniform gilding, now merged to produce a precious art object.

Jean Arp deliberately employed the happenstance that the exhibition space cannot always be influenced by the artist as a stylistic means (cats. 137, 140, 141).[13] Especially in the case of *Eyes–Nose–Moustache* (*Yeux–nez–moustache*), a framed work on card from 1928 (cat. 140), the wall serves not only as a mounting background but as part of the concept. By means of the frame, the omitted areas are consciously included in the relief. Hence the positive forms are not the sole determinants of the basic form of the work. By doing so, Arp purposely transgressed the boundary of the support into real space. The relief first takes shape as a second level owing to the layer of the underlying wall.[14] The opposite applies, for example, in the case of the reliefs *Leaving the Echelon* (*Quittant l'échelonnement*) by Arp (cat. 143) and *Relief, Constr.* by Rudolf Jahns (cat. 144), both of which build on a pictorial ground, albeit a retracted one. However, works such as Arp's *Free Form with Two Holes* (*Forme libre à deux trous*) from 1935 (cat. 141) stand out from the wall and act – independently from the rectangle – as separate pictorial forms. Here, the interior structures produced by the negative forms literally enclose the space instead of revealing what lies behind it. It is the viewer who must decide whether they want to engage with the resulting positive or negative forms. Thus the relief acts as a kind of boundary – a boundary of the pictorial level, which the viewer's eye can transgress in one or the other direction. Arp explicitly addresses the phenomenon of the boundary towards the end of the 1950s with his *Threshold Sculptures* (cat. 142), a group of works in which planar, regular bodies stand freely in space and can consequently be viewed from all sides, with the primary focus on the front and back side. He commented on them as follows: "The quality of the space between the door frame is not the same as the space immediately before or after crossing the threshold."[15] This makes it more than clear that the surrounding space has to be seen as an essential part of the artwork that is actively filled by the viewer – it is the counterplay between positive/negative, inside/outside, mass/void.

Naum Gabo's *Linear Construction No. 1* (*Variation*) from 1963/64 (cat. 146) demonstrates how the enclosing space can become the essence of the work of art. Entirely in the spirit of the "Realist Manifesto" from 1920, which he

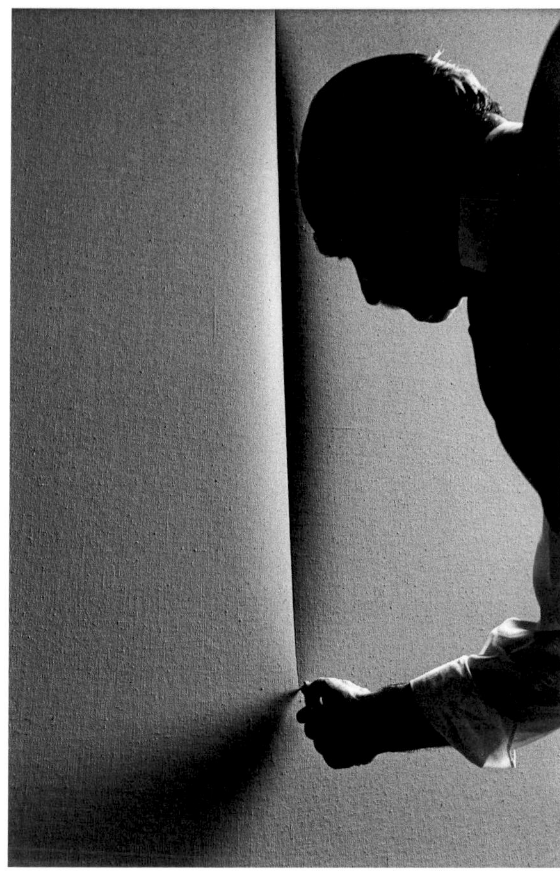

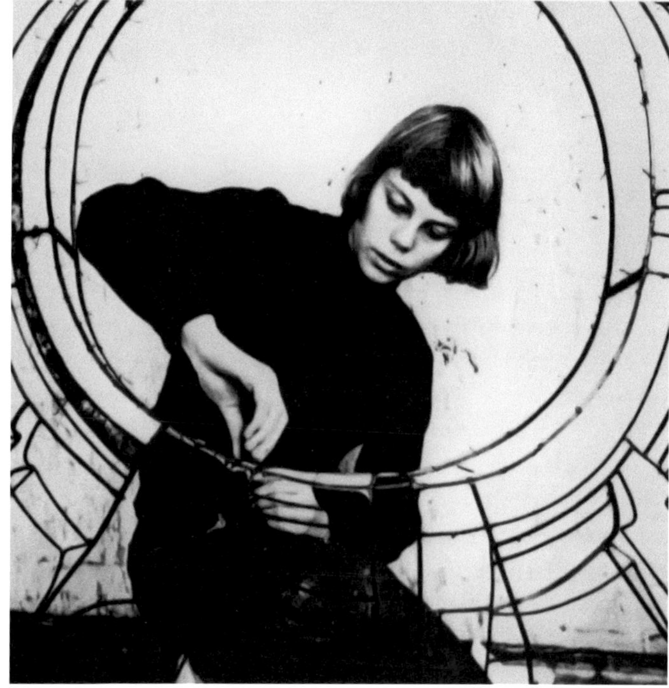

Fig. 2

Fig. 1   Ugo Mulas: *Lucio Fontana, "Taglio"*, Milan, 1965, photograph,
courtesy of Galleria Civica d'Arte Moderna e Contemporanea, Turin

Fig. 1

Fig. 2   Giulia Niccolai: *Lee Bontecou*, photograph, ca. 1960/61

wrote in collaboration with his brother, Antoine Pevsner (cat. 148), the sculpture's mass does not determine its perception, but rather the space it creates and the depth associated with it. In order to transfer this space into the sculpture as an independent part, Gabo used closely strung nylon threads, spanning them around an acrylic glass construct that he had developed. The density of the transparent threads creates an illusionistic surface that encloses an ellipsis-shaped void. As the crucial element, it changes from a negative into a positive form when one walks around the sculpture, while the viewer's eye, uncertain about what it should focus on, perceives the void as a distinct volume.

The American artist Lee Bontecou ventured the ultimate step towards the viewer in the 1960s in the form of her relief constructions (cats. 147, 149). In her work from 1960, she sewed patches of raw linen over a steel frame-work to form a crater-shaped surface (cat. 147). The polygonal surfaces stagger in various shades of beige and brown. Like irregular steps, they rise and fall, penetrate the viewer's space and simultaneously retreat back into the pictorial surface.[16] By doing this, Bontecou reinterpreted the purpose of the linen, which traditionally served as a painting ground. Instead of creating the illusion of spatiality with painterly means, she used her patchwork technique to work into space. Characteristic of these early reliefs by the artist is the black hole which, in different versions, is always located near the centre. It seems to look back at the viewer like an eye. However, it also directs their gaze into the work – a reciprocal relationship. Here, as with Lucio Fontana's works, appearances are deceptive. Bontecou attempted to evoke endlessness, and to do so she lined the hole with black velvet, so that the human eye can barely perceive the pictorial ground. In most cases, what is located in the centre of the image is also the thematically most important element. In Lee Bontecou's work, it is the "void" hiding behind the black hole. Or as Donald Judd aptly noted: "The black hole does not allude to a black hole; it is one."[17] It was not by chance that all of Bontecou's works were untitled and hence open up scope for associations of every kind.[18]

Bontecou's relief not only extends into the exhibition space, but expands physical space to become an impalpable sphere. You would think that she and Fontana aimed for the demystification of art when they allegedly enabled looking at the underlying wall. But the opposite is the case: they opened up the pictorial space, which was now neither the window to the world nor to the exhibition space, and developed it into a new, unknown dimension – a fourth level. However, transgressing boundaries does not always have to involve the actual expansion of the support, as Hermann Glöckner proved in his cardboard panels coated with black lacquer (cat. 145). He did not produce spatiality – in this respect comparable to Fontana and Bontecou – with the use of painterly-illusionist techniques. Indeed, instead of abolishing the two-dimensionality of the picture plane by means of plasticity or perforating it, he took a step back, virtually reversing the method into its opposite: he folded Japanese tissue paper, subsequently placing it on the damp paint of the small-format panels – transforming space into plane.[19]

Artists such as Lucio Fontana, Jean Arp, Sophie Taeuber-Arp, Louise Nevelson, Lee Bontecou and Hermann Glöckner transgressed the boundaries of the planar pictorial support, explored new possibilities, and in doing so also sharpened our view of painting itself. Yet what all of them share is the fact that the support continued to constitute the starting point of their considerations and that painting seems to consistently resonate as a counterpart or companion to the relief.

1 On the coherence between the declared "death of painting" and its material transgression of boundaries as well as the expansion into space, see Martin Engler: "Diesseits wie jenseits des Bildes: Die Erweiterung des Malerischen", in: idem and Max Hollein (eds.): *Gegenwartskunst: 1945–heute im Städel Museum*, Ostfildern 2016, pp. 215–219.

2 See Hannelore Kersting: *Lucio Fontana: Concetto spaziale Attese 1962/63 (Kleine Werkmonographie*, vol. 15), Frankfurt am Main 1979, n.p.

3 Otto Piene, quoted in Jole de Sanna: *Lucio Fontana: Materie, Raum, Konzept*, Klagenfurt 1995, p. 197.

4 See Gabriele Mahn: "Die Reliefs von Hans Arp", in: *Hans Arp*, ed. Christine Hopfengart, exh. cat. Kunsthalle Nürnberg, Ostfildern 1994, pp. 44–55, esp. p. 44.

5 See Stefanie Poley: *Hans Arp: Die Formensprache im plastischen Werk*, Stuttgart 1978, p. 94.

6 See ibid.

7 A total of five round reliefs are listed in the catalogue raisonné from 1948: according to the Sophie Taeuber-Arp Research Project, eight are known to have been produced; see Anna Schrader: "Relief en Bois", in: Sophie Taeuber-Arp Research Project, 8 August 2022, https:// sophietaeuberarp.org/coquilles-et-fleurs-relief-rond-en-quatre-hauteurs-2/ (accessed 13 February 2023).

8 See Rudolf Koella: "Coquilles et fleurs", in: Stephan Kunz (ed.): *Sophie Taeuber-Arp 1889–1943*, Aarau 2010, pp. 53–61, esp. p. 53.

9 See ibid., p. 56.

10 See Walburga Krupp: "Floral-linear: Figuration und Abstraktion im Werk von Sophie Taeuber-Arp", in: *Sophie Taeuber-Arp: Heute ist Morgen*, ed. Thomas Schmutz and Friedrich Meschede, exh. cat. Aargauer Kunsthaus, Aarau/Kunsthalle Bielefeld, Zurich 2014, pp. 217–225, esp. p. 225.

Jean Arp probably supplied the title; see ibid. Elsewhere, the work is also associated with the title *Relief en Bois*, for the first time in 1940, in: "Allianz" Vereinigung moderner Schweizer Künstler (ed.): *Almanach neuer Kunst in der Schweiz*, Zurich 1940. This early date in the artist's lifetime would by all means also attribute its title to Taeuber-Arp herself; hence, the Sophie Taeuber-Arp Research Project assigns it as the most probable title; see Schrader 2022 (see note 7).

11 See Krupp 2014 (see note 10), p. 225.

12 It has not been definitively clarified whether all three of the works were created during her lifetime; see Schrader 2022 (see note 7).

13 On the component of chance in the reliefs around 1924 in terms of pictorial composition, see Poley 1978 (see note 5), pp. 93f.

14 See ibid.

15 Jean Arp, in: Denys Chevalier: "Ein Gespräch mit Hans Arp", in: *Hans Arp*, exh. cat. Kunstmuseum Winterthur 2016, pp. 53–61, esp. p. 59.

16 See Jeremy Melius: "Living with the Void", in: *Lee Bontecou*, ed. Joan Banach and Laura Stamps, exh. cat. Gemeentemuseum Den Haag, London 2017, pp. 22–31, esp. p. 28.

17 Donald Judd: "Lee Bontecou, 1965", in: idem; *Writings*, ed. Flavin Judd and Murray Caitlin, New York 2016, pp. 162–167, esp. p. 165.

18 Besides the eye, further body openings such as the mouth or the vagina are invoked. In addition, there are technical associations: the lens of the camera or the screen of a tube television, to mention only the most well-known interpretations.

19 On Hermann Glöckner's role in the expansion of the panel picture, see Engler 2016 (see note 1), pp. 215f.

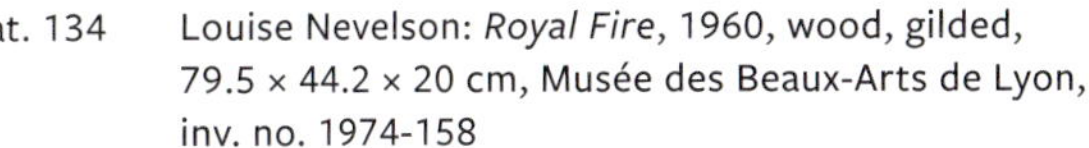

Cat. 134   Louise Nevelson: *Royal Fire*, 1960, wood, gilded,
79.5 × 44.2 × 20 cm, Musée des Beaux-Arts de Lyon,
inv. no. 1974-158

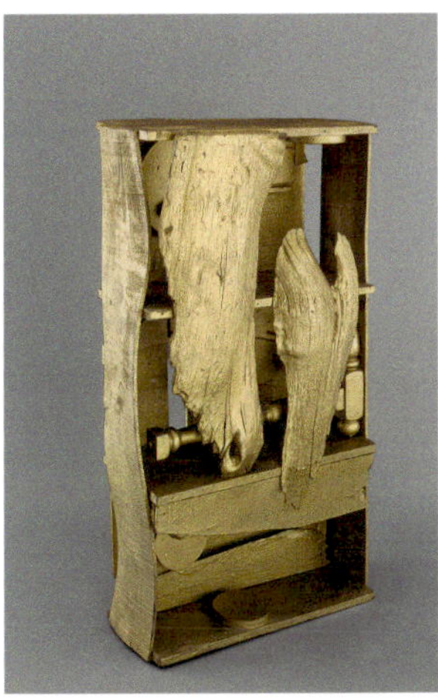

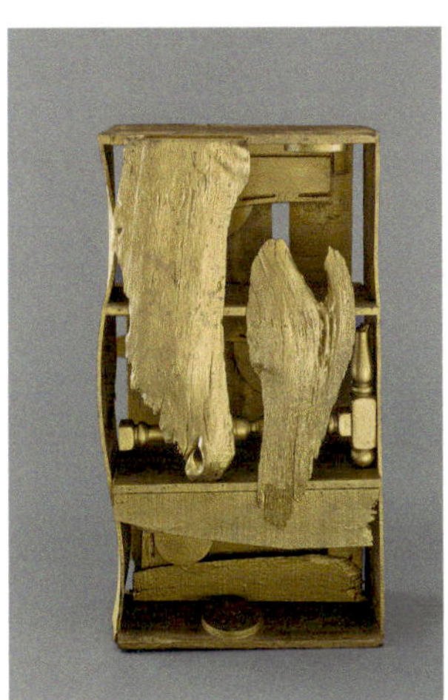

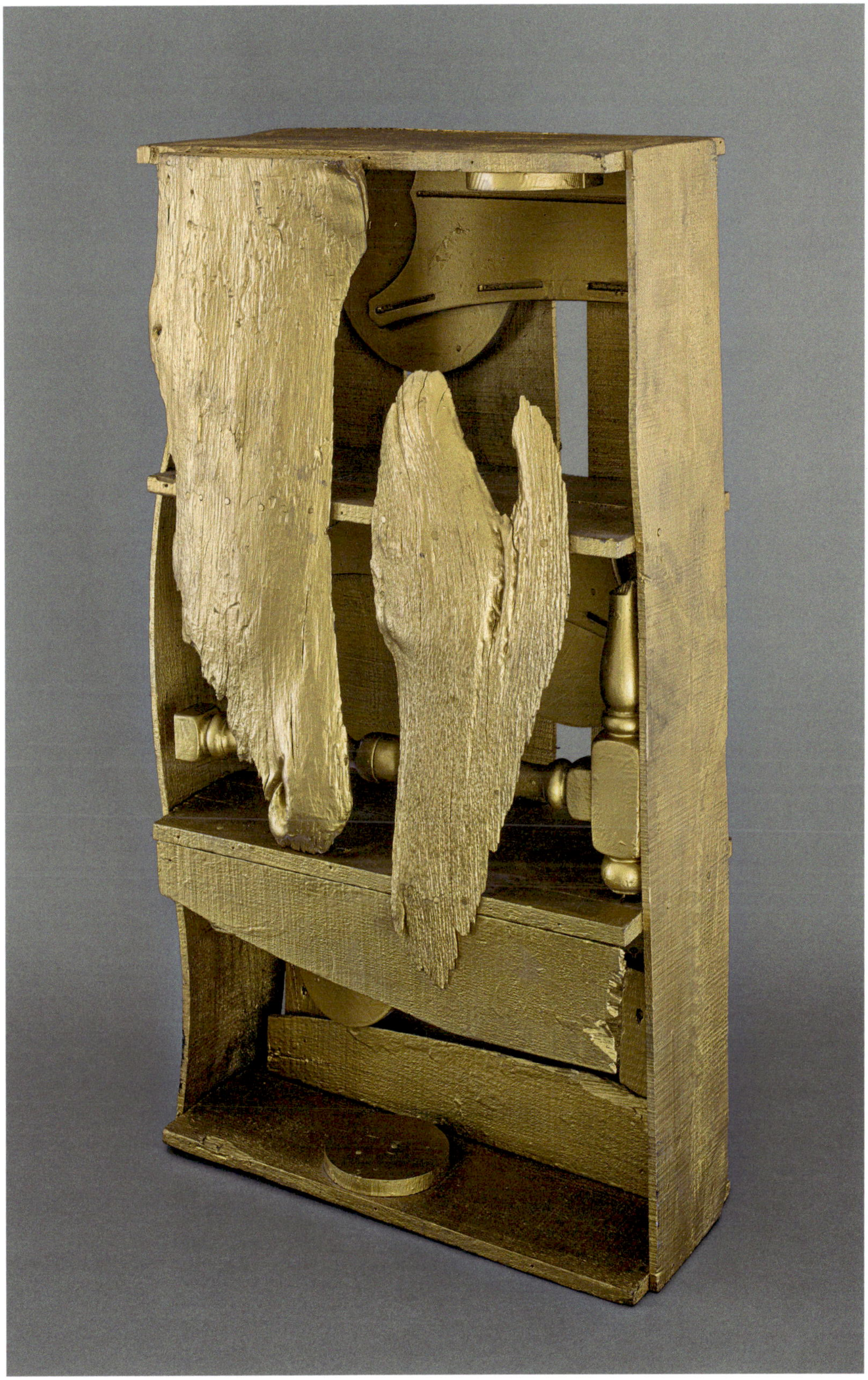

Cat. 135   Lucio Fontana: *Spatial Concept* (*Concetto spaziale*), 1960, oil on canvas, 99.5 × 81.4 cm, Hamburger Kunsthalle, inv. no. HK-5385 (Hamburg only)

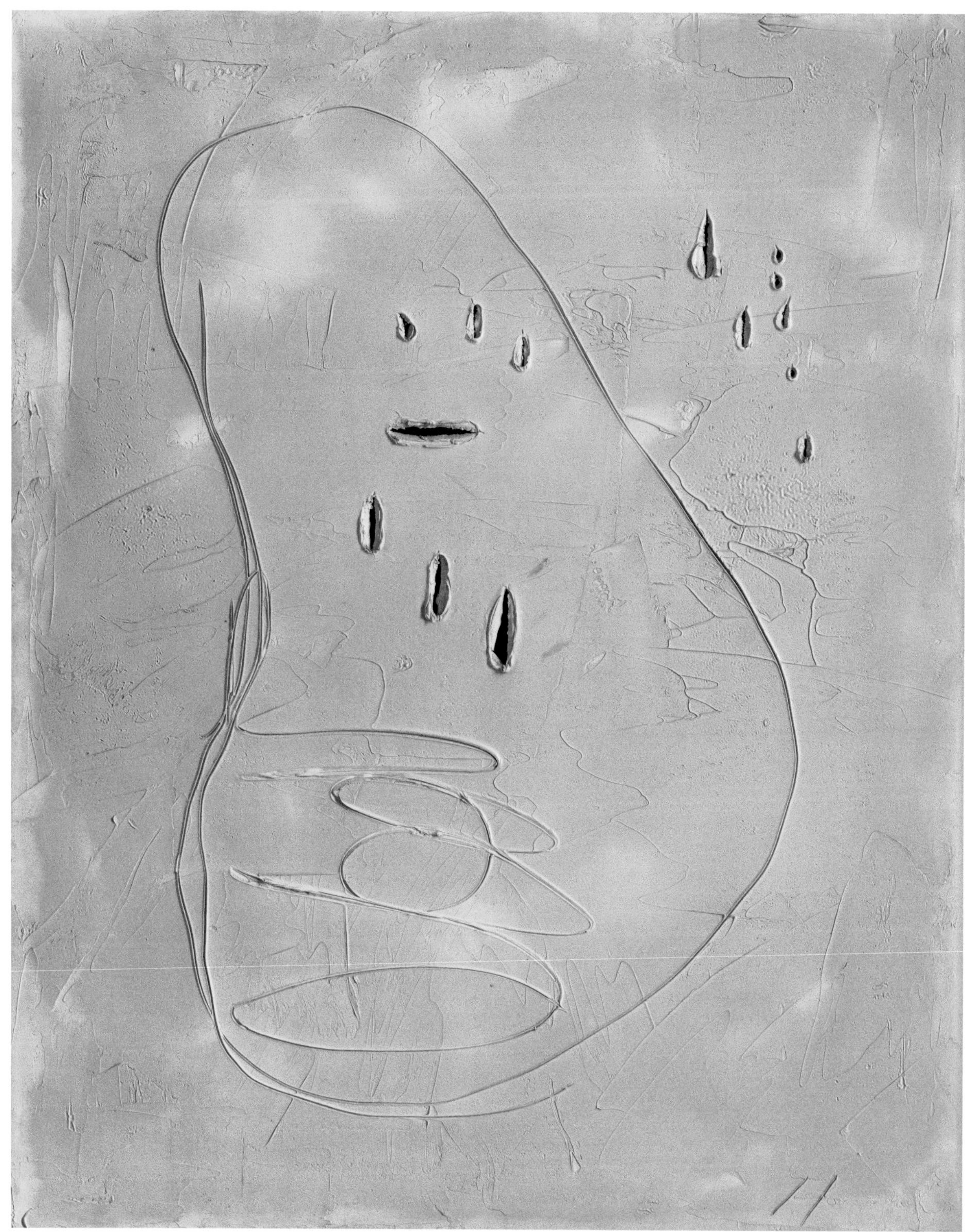

Cat. 136   Lucio Fontana: *Spatial Concept – Expectations* (*Concetto spaziale – Attese*), 1962/63, oil on canvas, 92 × 73 cm, Städel Museum, Frankfurt am Main, inv. no. SG 1240 (Frankfurt only)

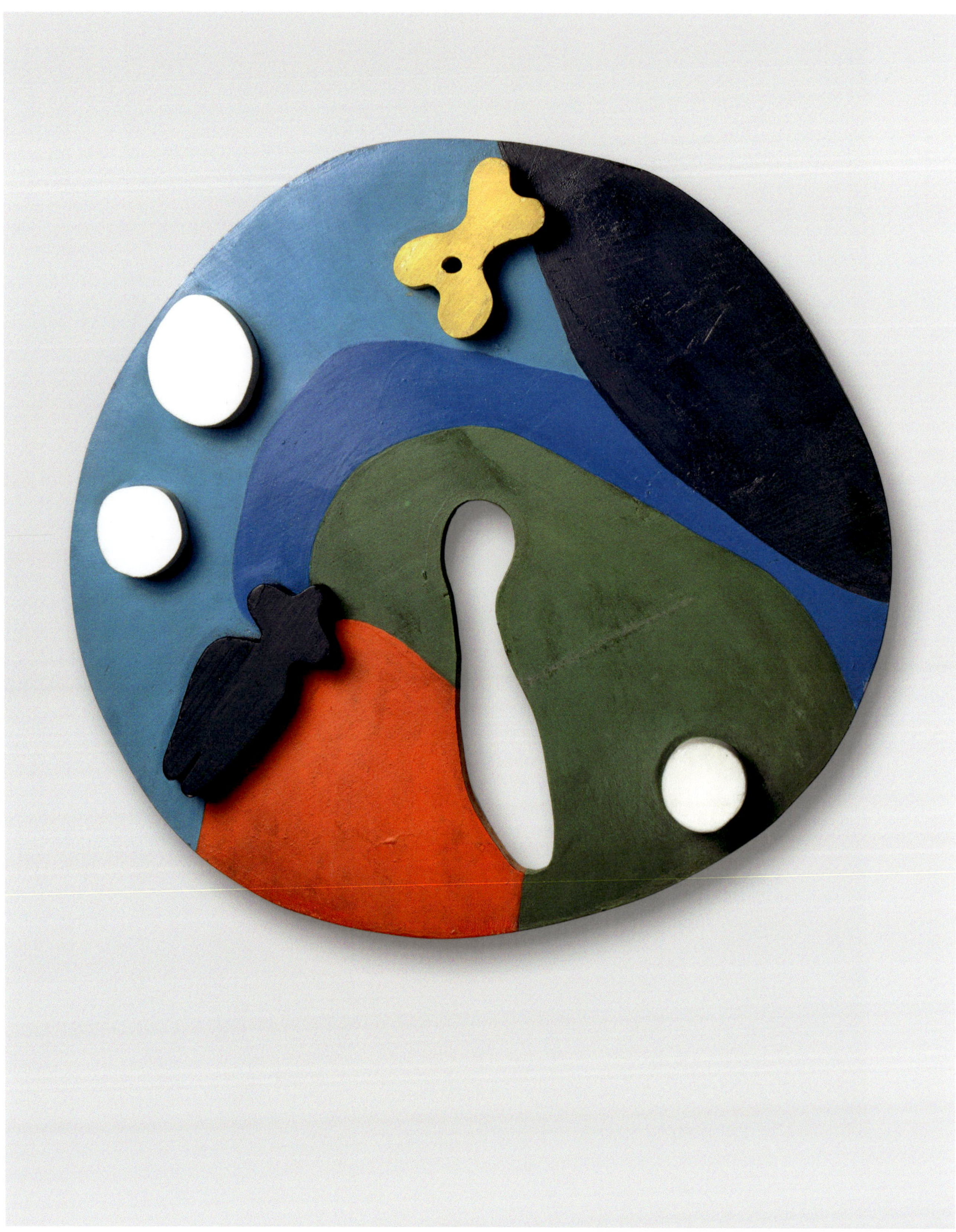

Cat. 137   Jean Arp: *Tower Clock* (*Horloge*), 1924, wood, painted, 53.5 × 53 × 6 cm, Kunstmuseum Basel, gift from Marguerite Arp-Hagenbach, 1968, inv. no. G 1968.31

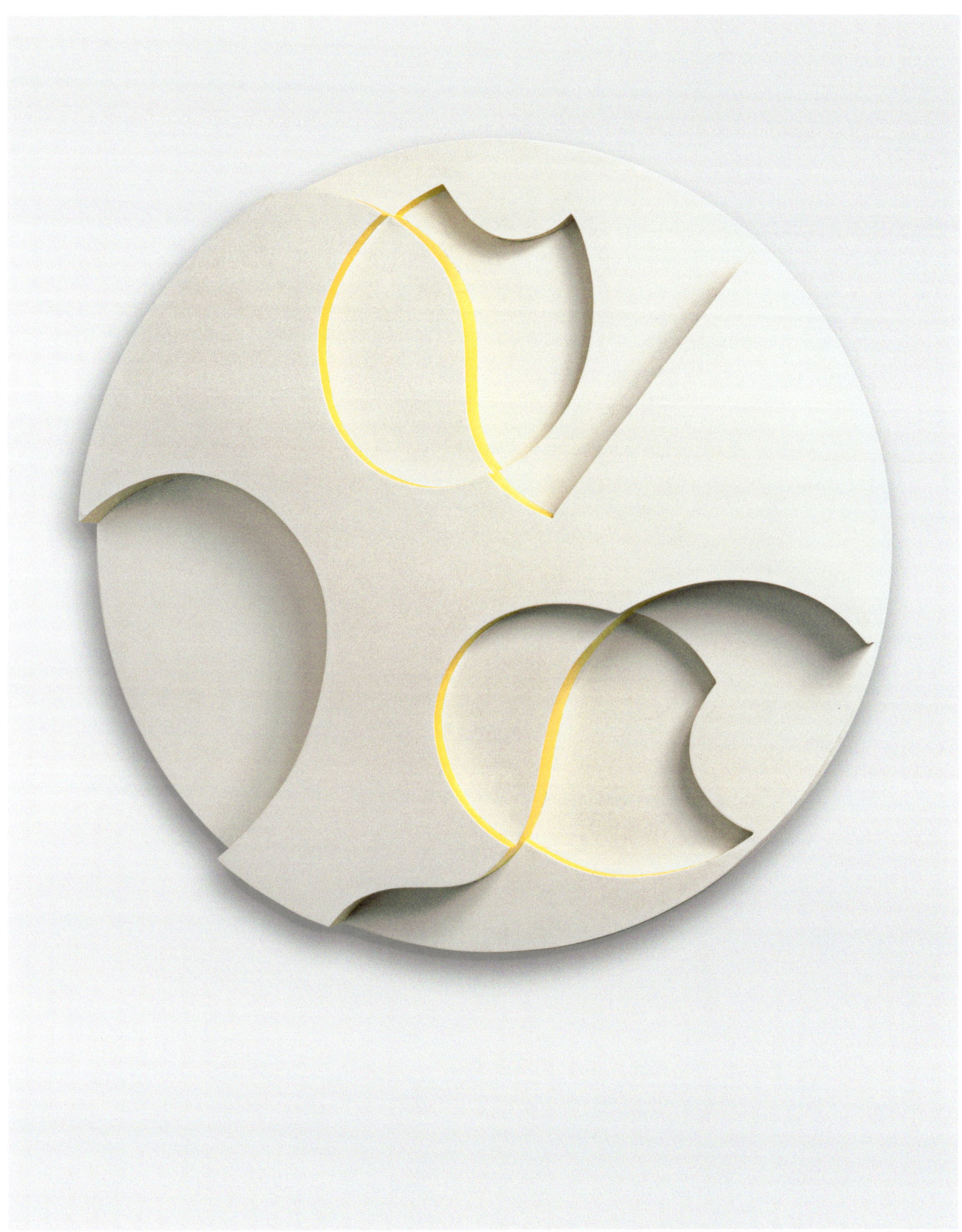

Cat. 139   Sophie-Taeuber-Arp: *Relief*, 1936, wood, painted, 50 × 68.5 cm,
Kunstmuseum Basel, gift from Marguerite Arp-Hagenbach,
1968, inv. no. G 1968.107

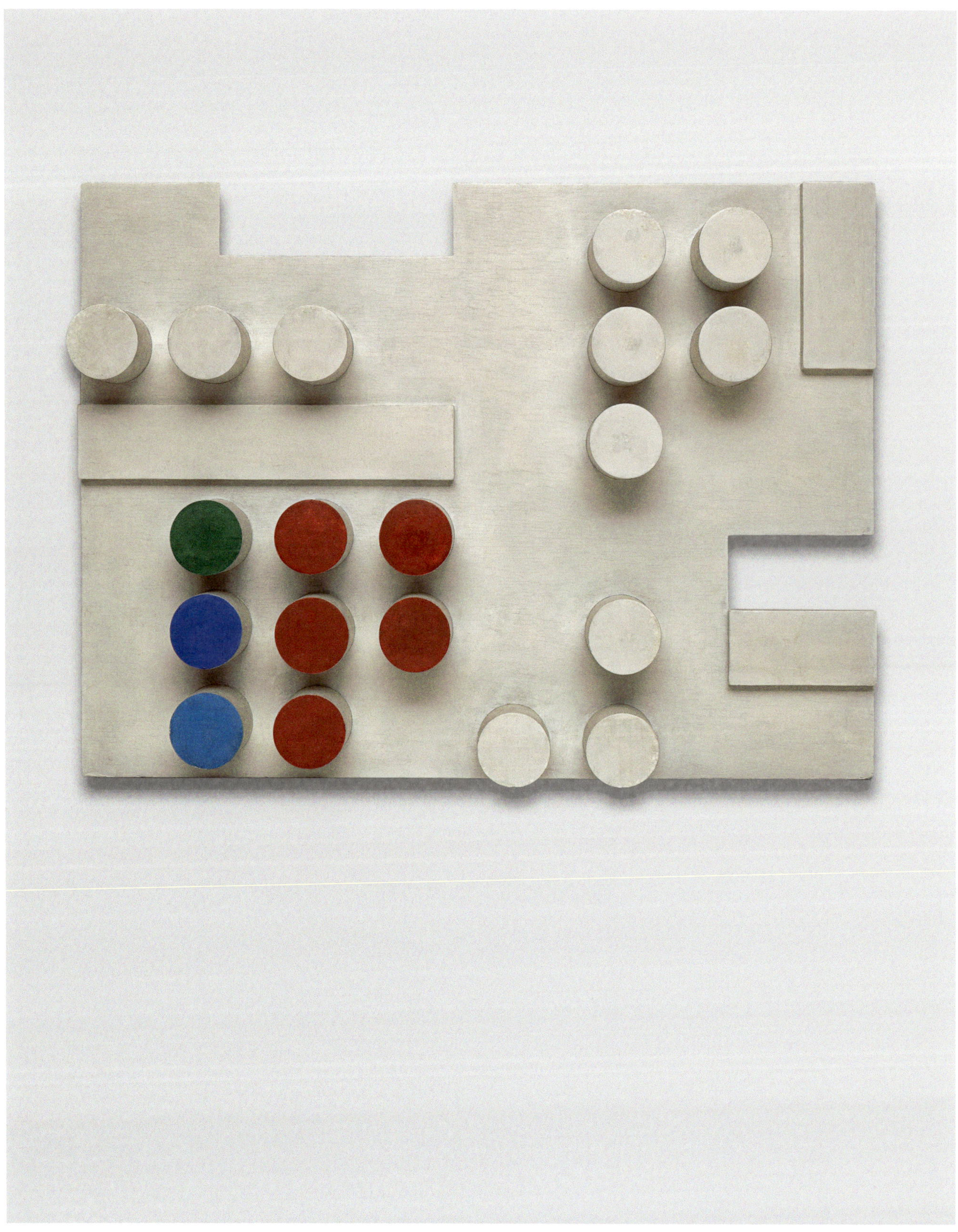

Cat. 140   Jean Arp: *Eyes-Nose-Moustache* (*Yeux–nez–moustache*),
1928, oil on cardboard, 51 × 38.7 cm, Hamburger Kunsthalle,
inv. no. HK-5184

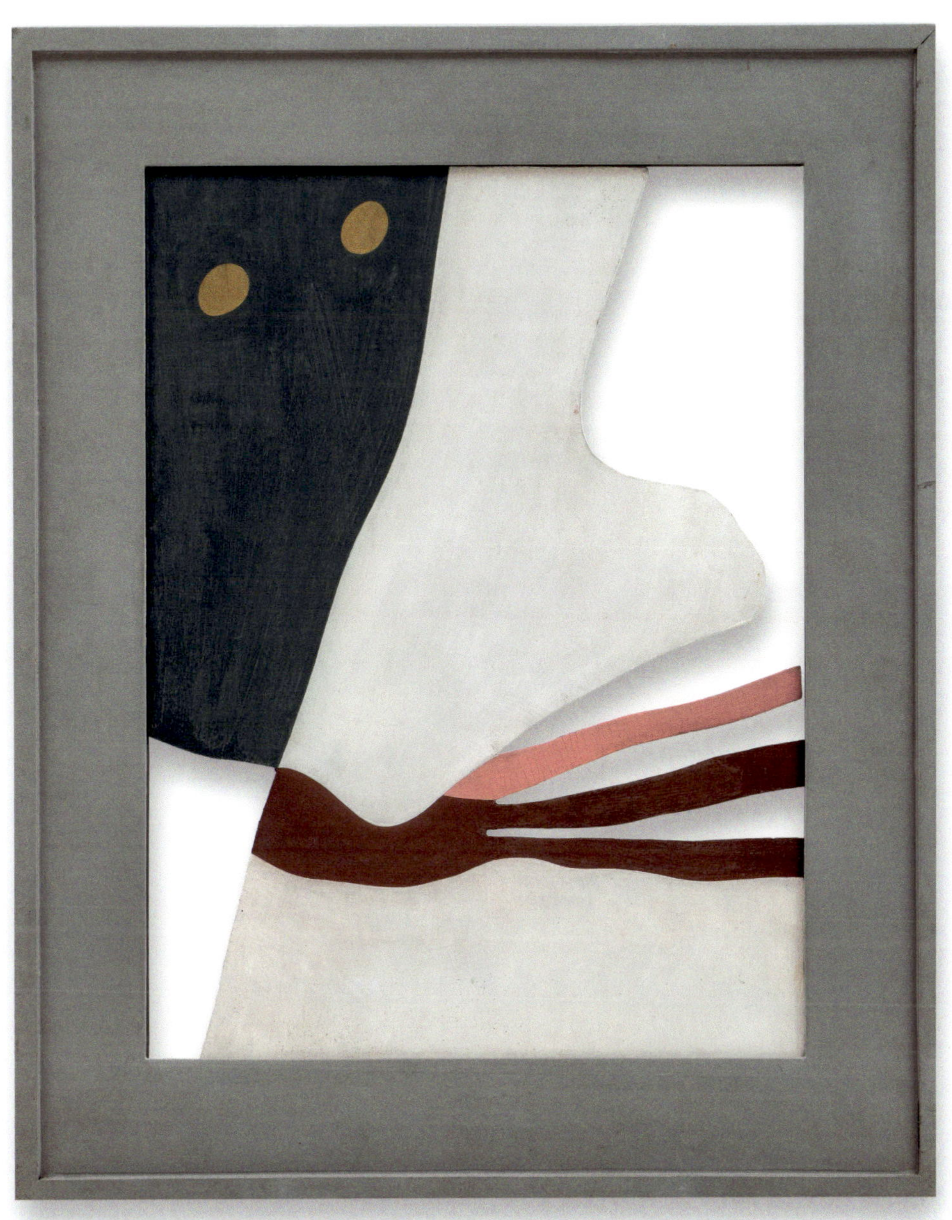

Cat. 141 Jean Arp: *Free Form with Two Holes* (*Forme libre à deux trous*), 1935, wood, 32 × 41 × 3 cm, Emanuel Hoffmann-Stiftung, gift from the Sammlung Maja und Emanuel Hoffmann 1998, on permanent loan to the Öffentliche Kunstsammlung Basel, inv. no. H 1998.12

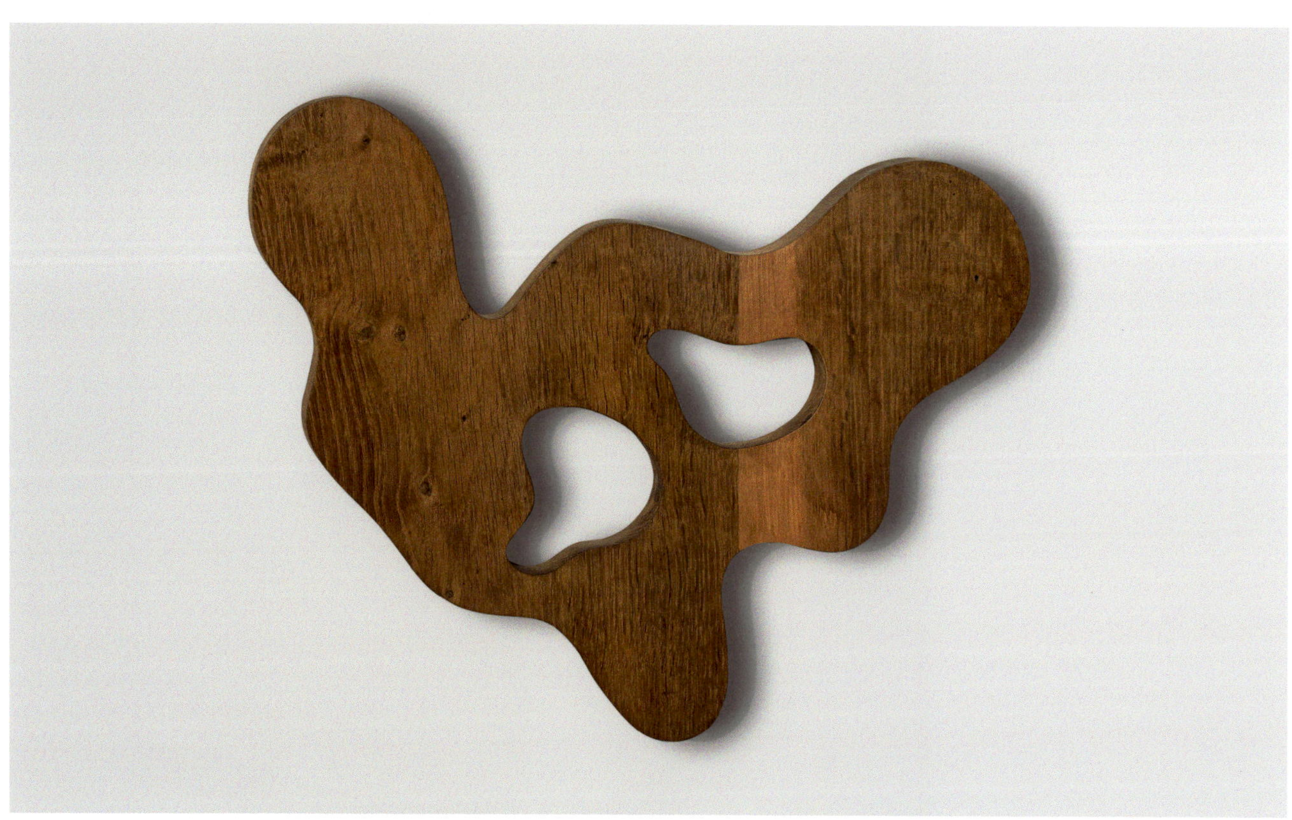

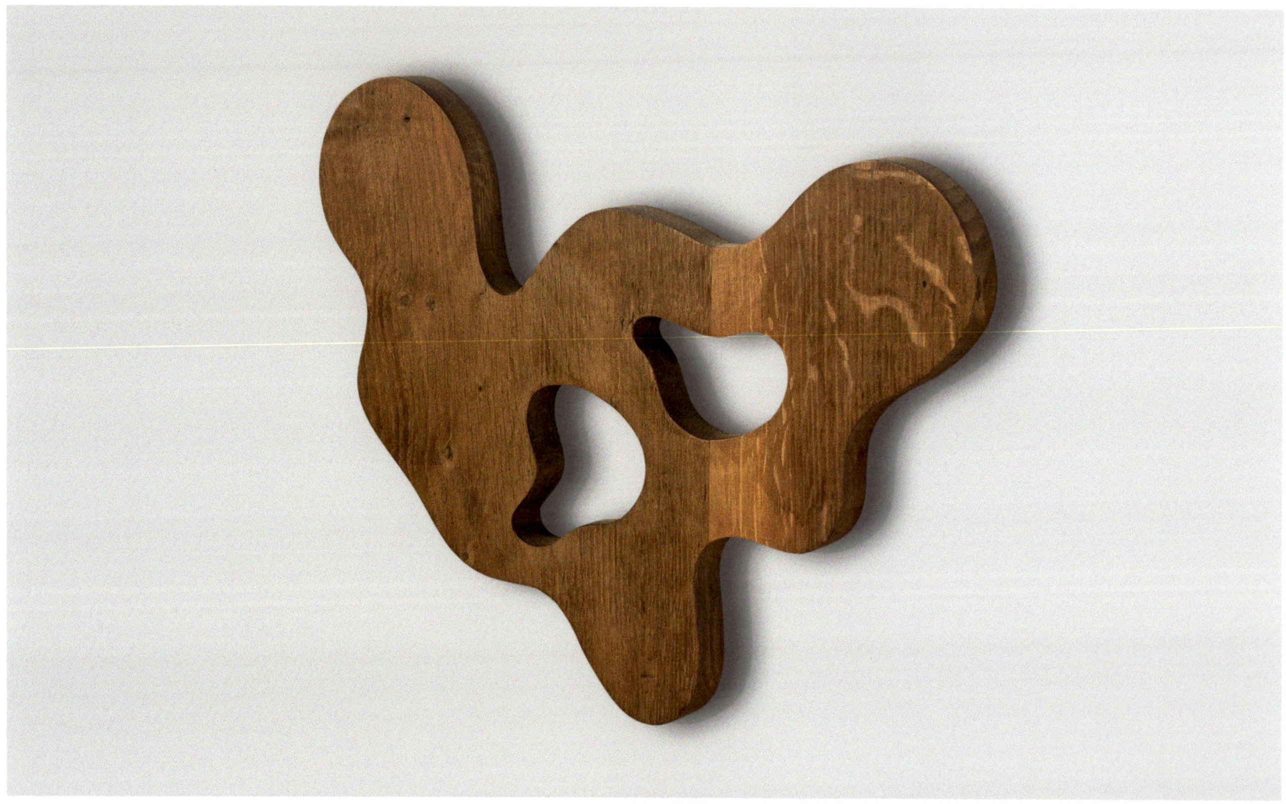

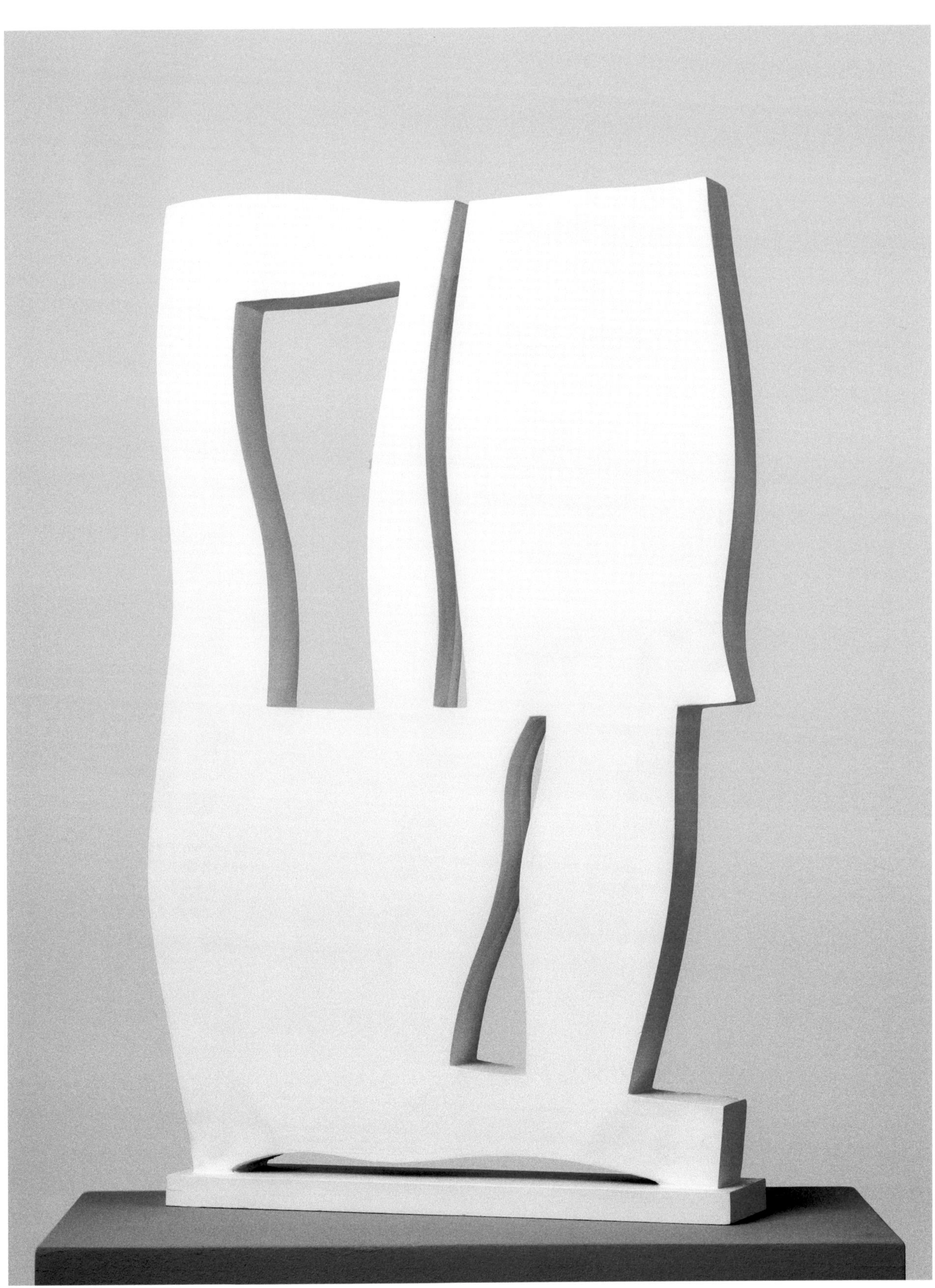
Cat. 142   Jean Arp: *Threshold with Crenellations*, 1959, plaster,
75 × 45 × 10 cm, Hamburger Kunsthalle, inv. no. S-1976-11

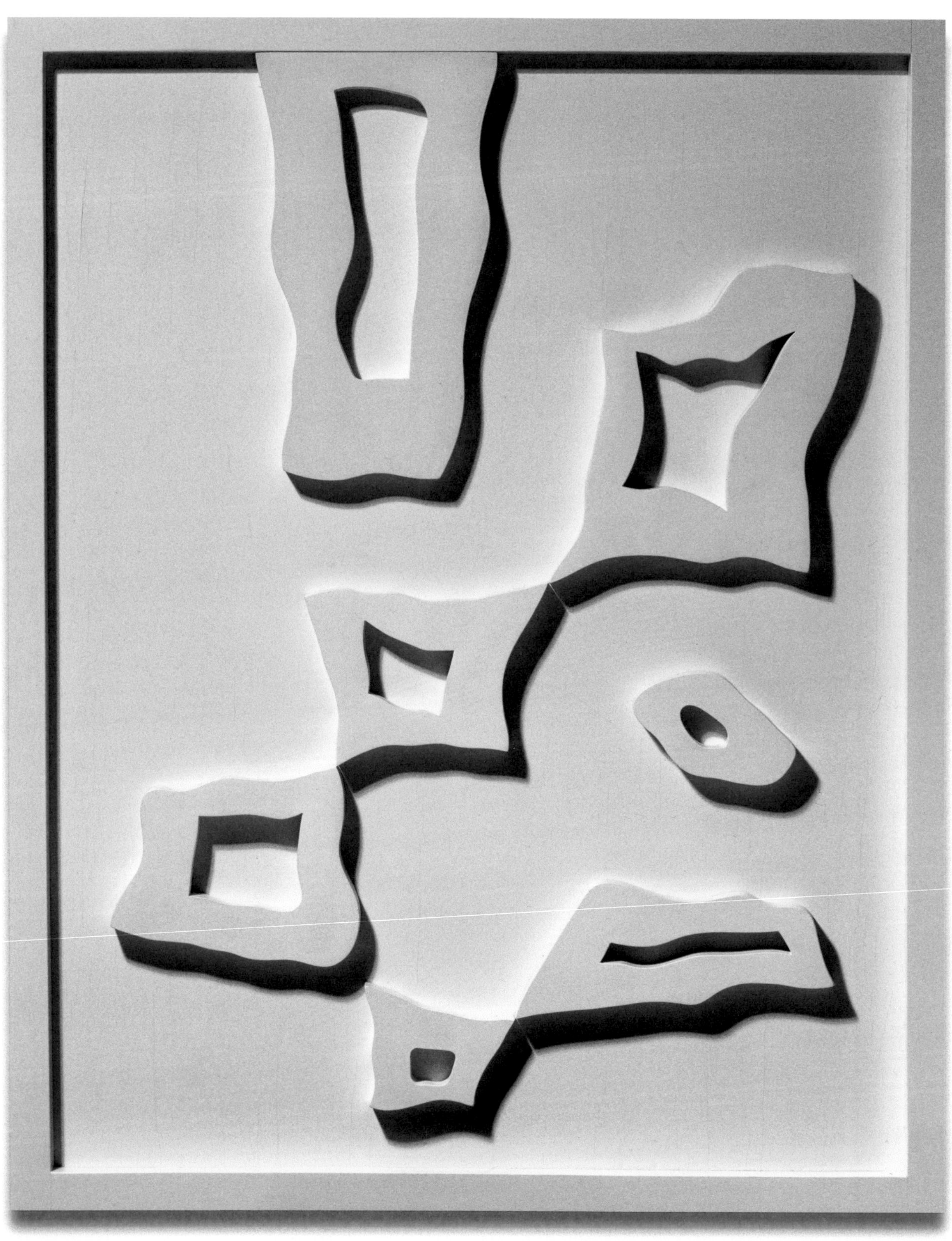

Cat. 143   Jean Arp: *Leaving the Echelon* (*Quittant l'échelonnement*), 1959, wood, painted, 105 × 85 cm, private collection

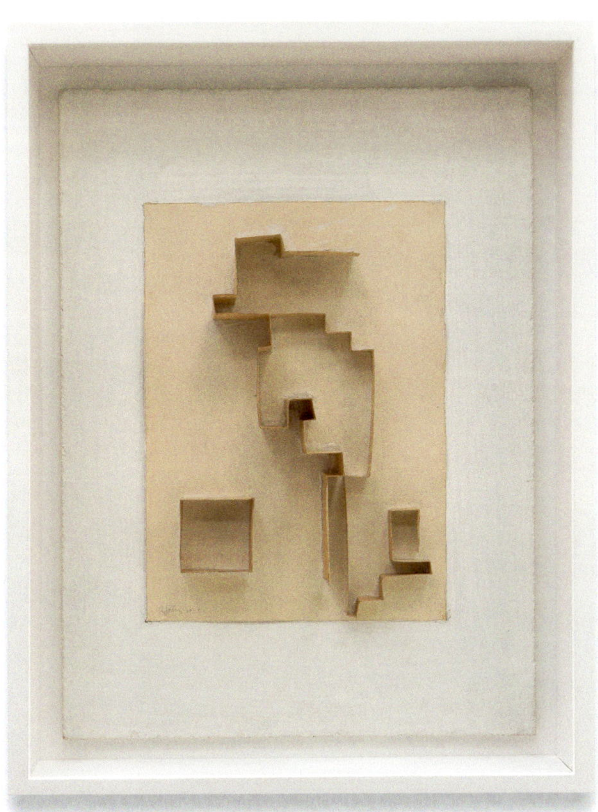

Cat. 144

Cat. 145

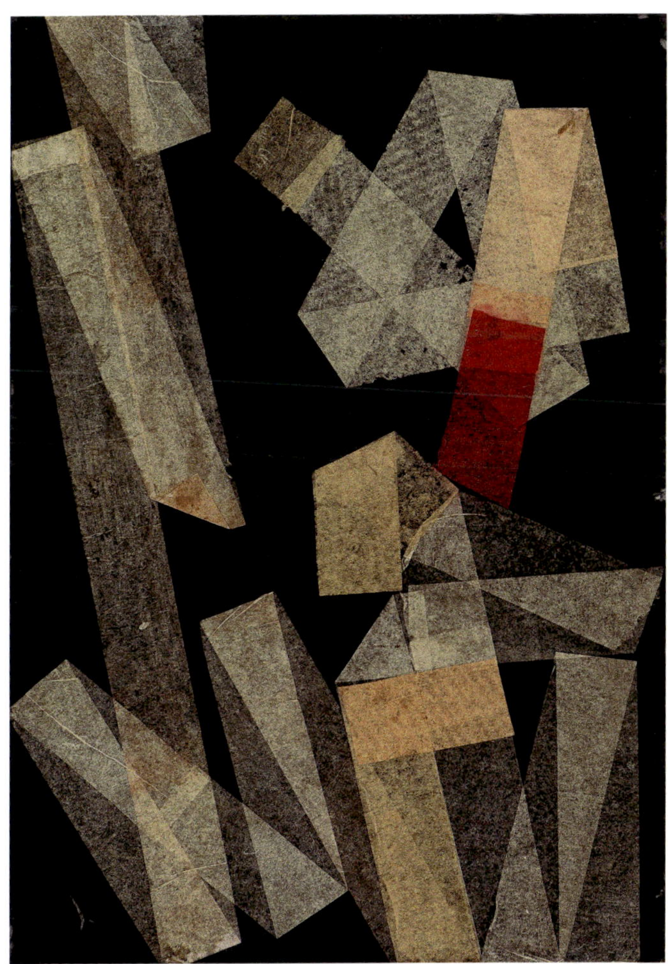

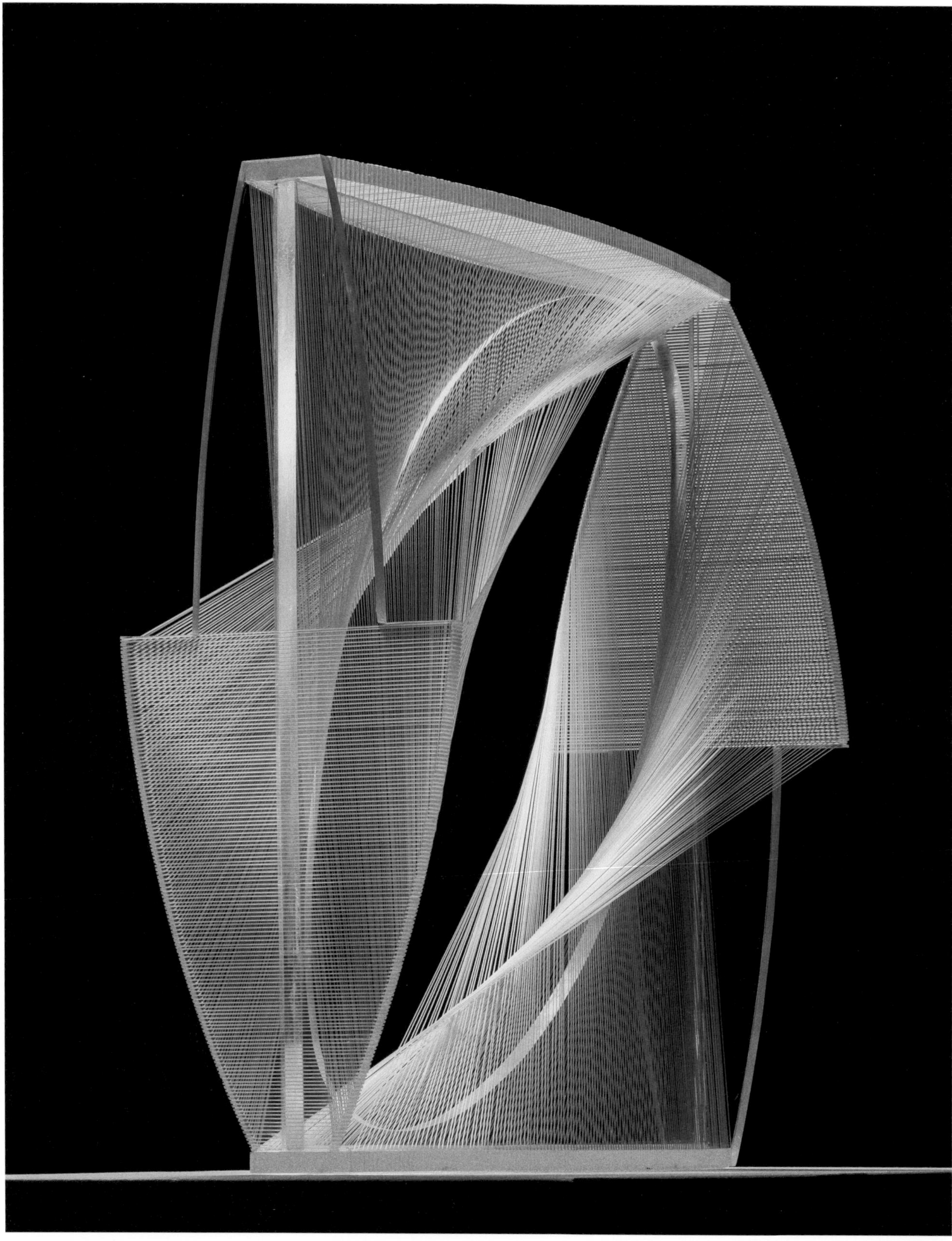

Cat. 146   Naum Gabo: *Linear Construction No. 1* (*Variation*), 1963/64
(draft 1942/43), acrylic glass and nylon, 46 × 46 × 18 cm,
Hamburger Kunsthalle, inv. no. S-1981-3

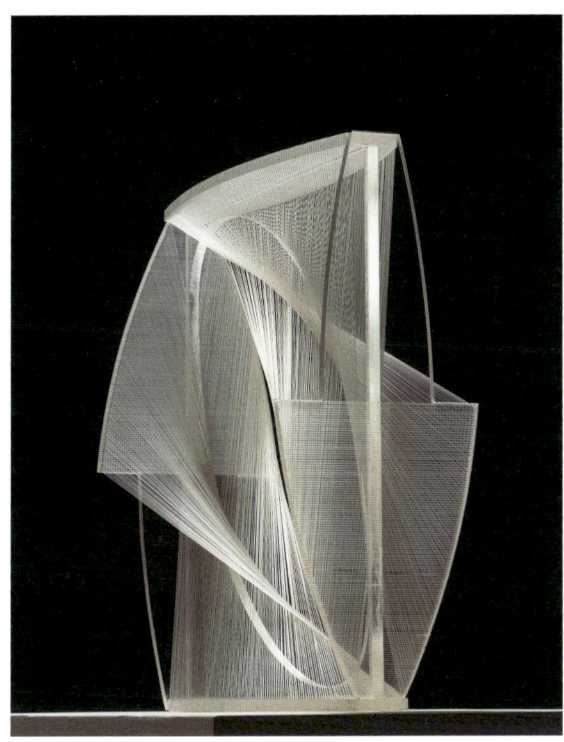

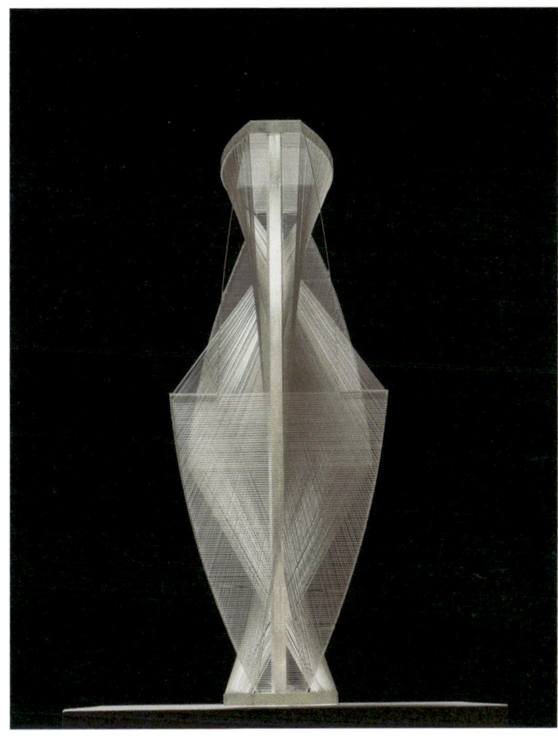

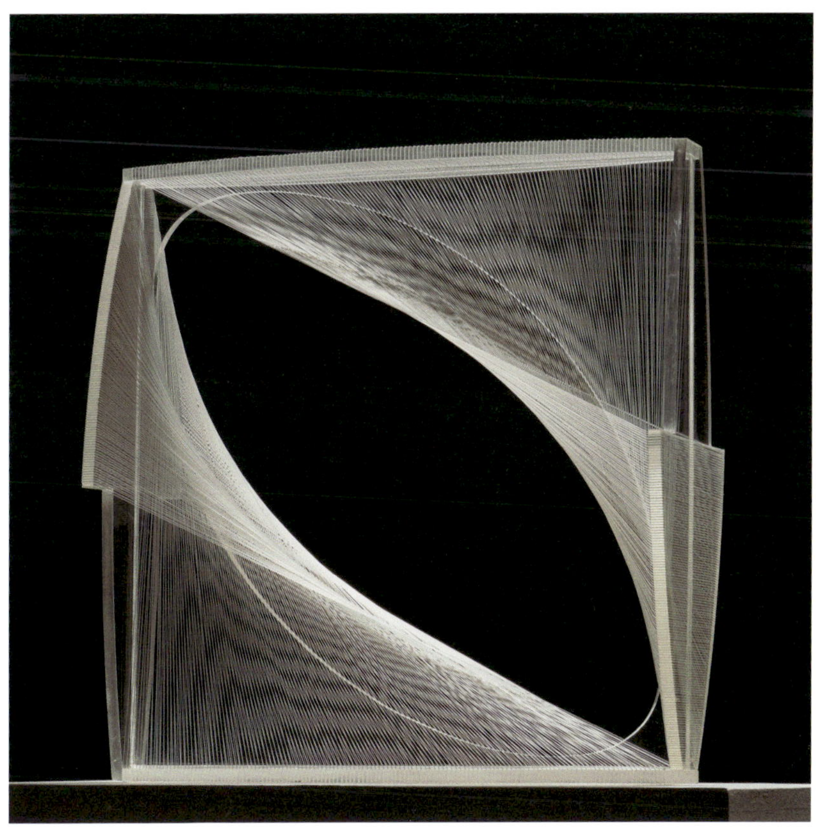

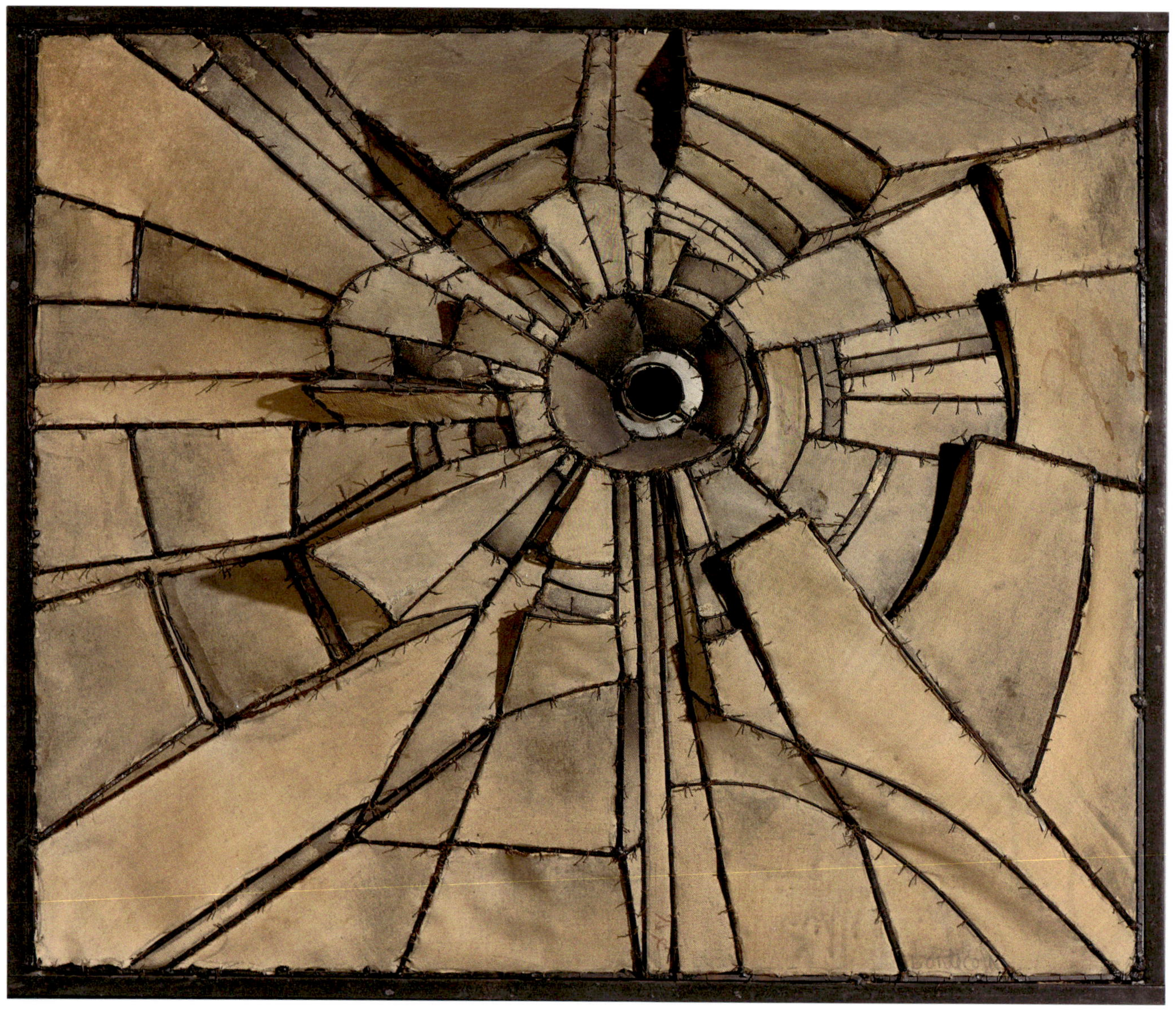

Cat. 147   Lee Bontecou: *Untitled*, 1960, linen, welded steel
and copper thread, 61 × 73.3 × 17.8 cm, Kunstmuseum
Den Haag, inv. no. 1E+06

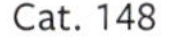

Cat. 148   Antoine Pevsner: *Dynamic Construction* (*Construction dynamique*), 1947, brass on fibreboard, painted, 95 × 87 × 38 cm, Centre Pompidou, Paris, inv. no. AM 1348 S

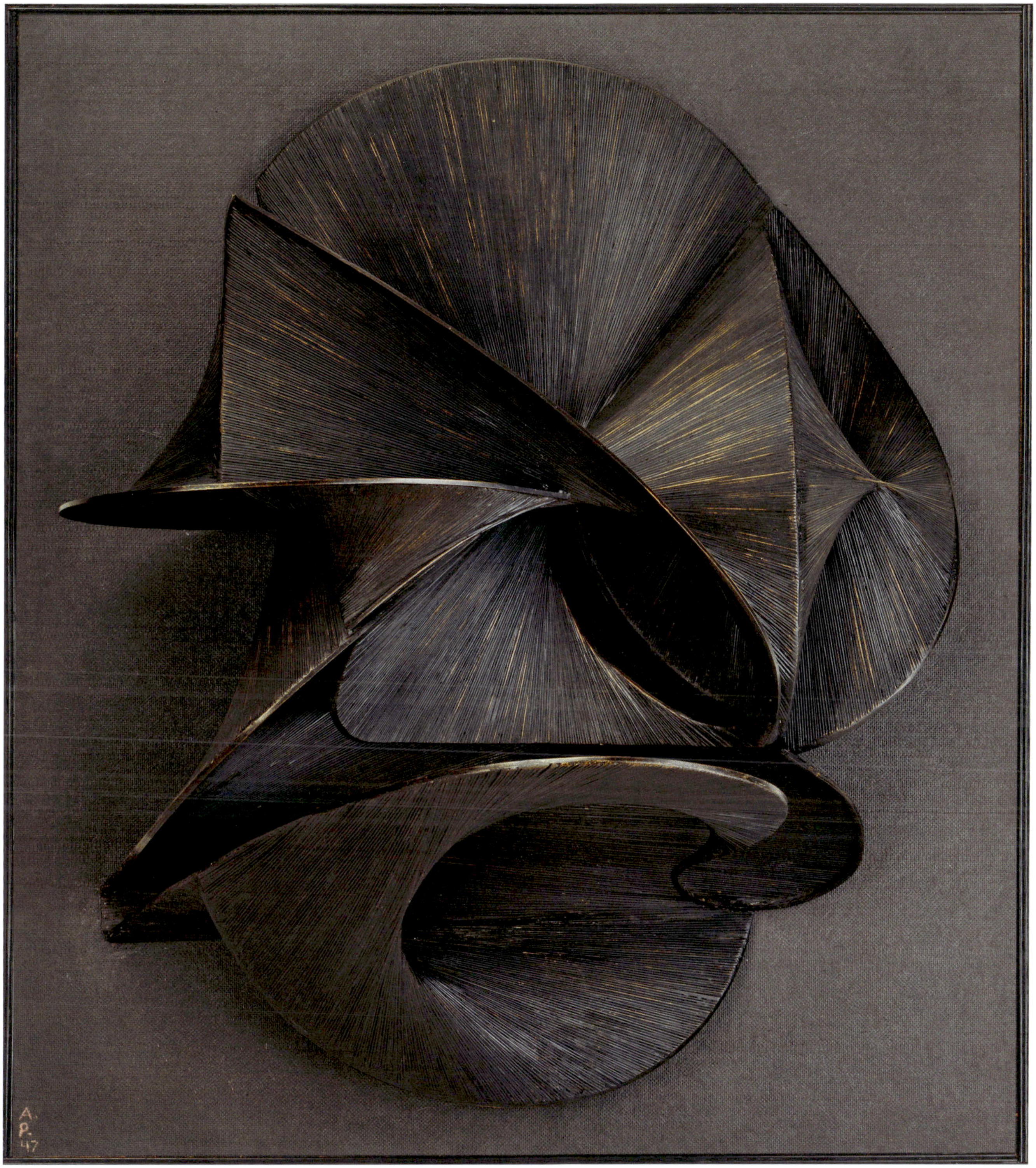

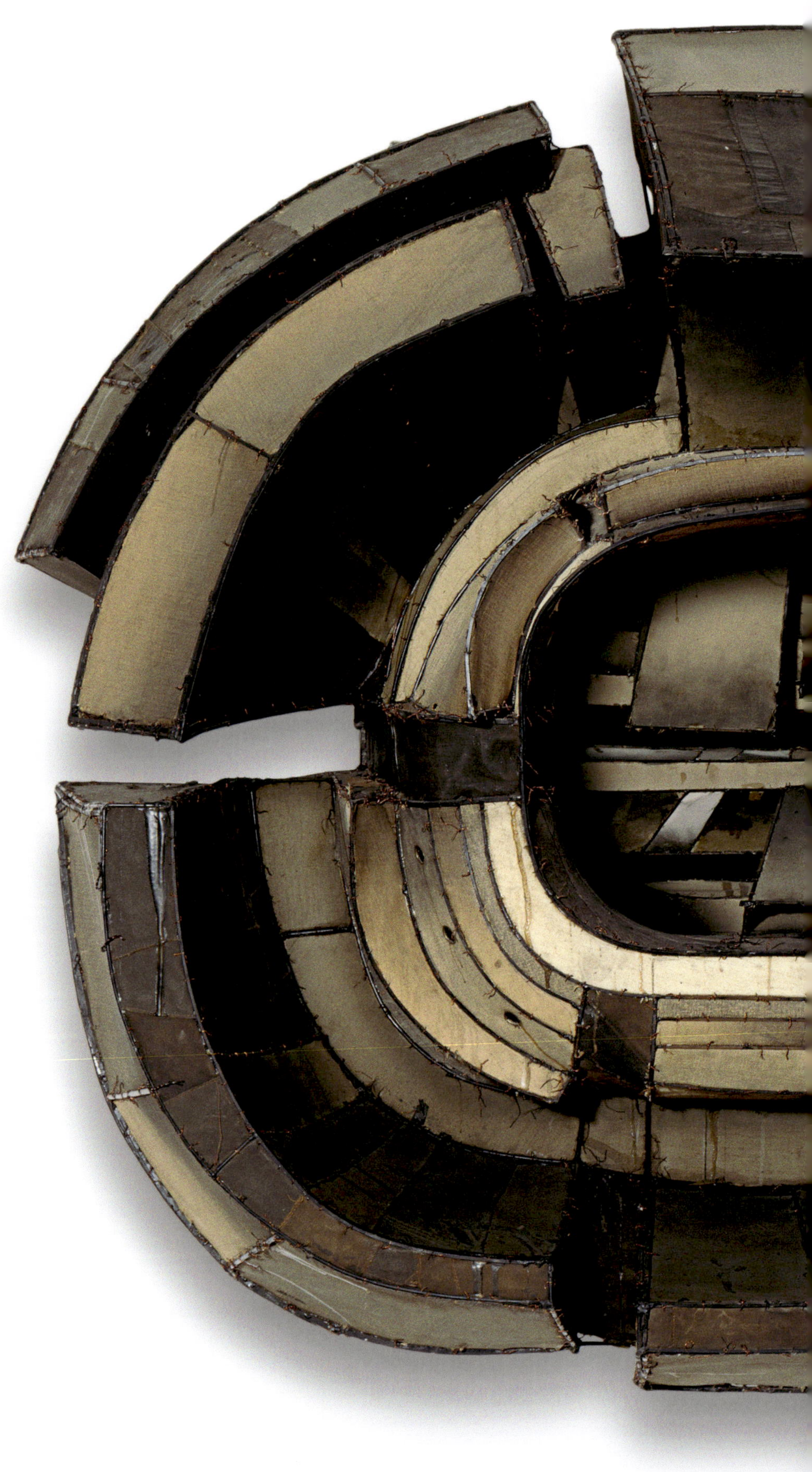

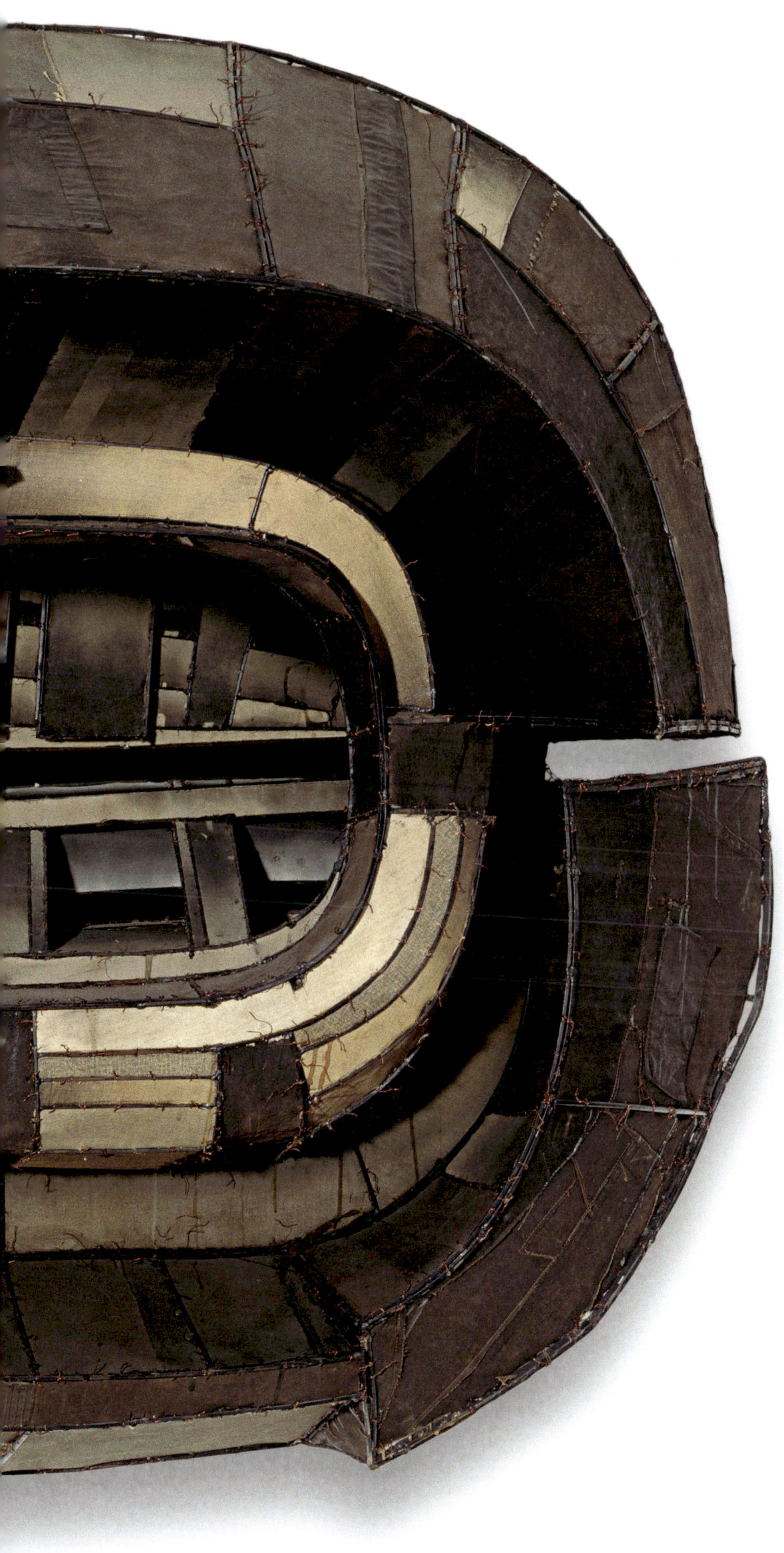

Cat. 149 Lee Bontecou: *Untitled*, 1962, welded steel, canvas, wire and soot, 184 × 218.5 × 81 cm, Emanuel Hoffmann-Stiftung, on permanent loan to the Öffentliche Kunstsammlung Basel, inv. no. H 1966.2

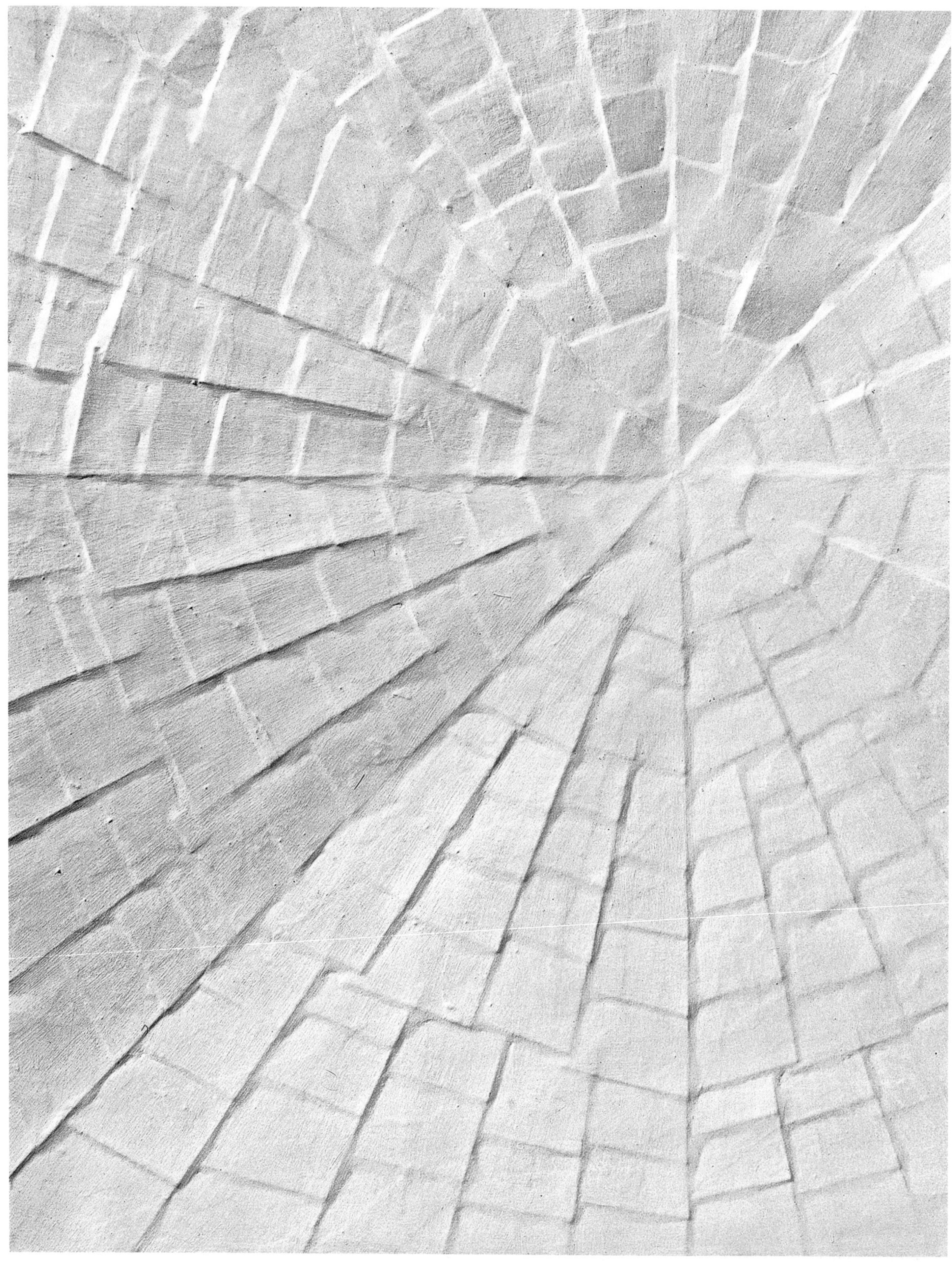

Cats. 150—164

Juliane Au

"THE PAINTING HAS NO LOCUS – IT OCCURS EVERYWHERE"[1]

A Spotlight on Structure

Structured surfaces, serially arranged everyday objects, and colors reduced all the way to monochromy – at first glance, some of the objects assembled here may come across as monotonous and rather lacklustre. However: rays of light fall on the works, brightening some sections, immersing others in deep shadows, and in this way giving rise to rhythm. The interplay of structure, material and light lend the works a vibrant dynamic. Many artists, especially in the 1950s and 1960s, examined materials and recurring structures. While in the United States, with the advent of Minimalism a style of reduced painting developed through the use of geometric, massive forms and nearly monochromatic coloration,[2] in Europe a wide range of different artists addressed grids and their influence on perception. When, in 1961, the exhibition *nove tendencije* took place in Zagreb, artists came together who experimented with optical phenomena related to planes, structures and objects. In part unbeknownst to one another, they all dealt with similar content, as art was intended to directly affect people whose perception became essential. Consequently, the so-called Nouvelles Tendances became a collective movement of individual actors and artistic groups throughout Europe and South America.[3] But structure and material had already become important factors as early as the beginning of the twentieth century.

"It is our mission to give our new world a new shape with the means of today."[4] This call by Hannes Meyer, the later director of the Bauhaus, to rethink design became a manifesto. The trained stonemason and bricklayer expanded the architecture department of the Bauhaus and intensified its contact to industry. Affordability and functionality became important parameters for furnishings;[5] Meyer saw standardised (industrial) products as features of community and of both mental as well as financial relief.[6] In collaboration with the wallpaper factory run by the Rasch brothers, a competition was announced among students that, in September 1929, resulted in a sample book (cat. 150). Criticised at first, the wallpapers quickly became the Bauhaus' greatest commercial success (cats. 151–153), and with their various patterns, hatchings and colours (fig. 1) soon became an essential part of modern interior design. They turned the wall itself into a space-shaping element.[7] In order to distinguish itself from middle-class, luxurious representation, a new, social home décor developed that was defined by functionality, clear lines and light-filled spaces. For the purpose of community, notions of design and style pervaded people's entire life and everyday world.[8]

In the 1920s, other visual artists also thought along similar lines. Jean Arp, for example, experimented with relief-like découpages. They are not shaped but layered one over the other, painted, and seem almost playful (cat. 111; → Designs of the World).[9] *The Eggboard* (cat. 155), produced in 1922, consists of a board to which have been applied differently coloured, slightly laterally inclined forms reminiscent of paddles, to which oval shapes have been fixed. The work and its title refer to an imaginary parlour game Arp made up, one rule of which is to throw raw eggs at each other. This was intended to expose the blind obedience and social submission of the middle classes. With its reference to everyday objects, a tension between order and chaos, a set of rules and the deliberate breaking of them, *The Eggboard*, which stems from Arp's time as a Dada artist in Zurich, was intended to encroach on society as a social corrective (→ Designs of the World).[10] In contrast, Auguste Herbin integrated thoughts on architecture and space in his colour concept. His *Polychrome Relief* from 1920 (cat. 162) as well as his *Four-Sided Relief* from 1921 (cat. 163) play with the effects of different colours, multi-perspectivity and ornamentality. The sometimes coloured geometric forms combine to become a comprehensive structure that dissolves the boundaries of the works into space. The "paintings in space", as Herbin called them, continuously alternate between planarity and depth, painting and sculpture, and explore their similarities and dependencies.[11] In doing so, Herbin also understood his art as a means of shaping society according to an ideal of the collective.[12]

Even stronger emphasis was placed on society and those who viewed art in the 1950s and 1960s. What numerous works from that period share is a seriality that potentially extends ad infinitum. In his 1967 essay "Art and Objecthood", the American Michael Fried stressed that what is central for Minimalism is "[e]ndlessness, being able to go on and on, even having to go on."[13] This observation also applied to artists in Europe: the painter and object artist Peter Roehr created montages that were completely devoted to serial sequences. In *O. T. (OB–138/5)* from 1967 (cat. 160), he attached industrially manufactured, plastic slide mounts to hardboard to produce a grid structure.[14] The repetition of everyday objects in large panels helped him put the world in order, but also to reflect: objects found by chance or pre-produced objects are recontextualised in the work.[15] Patterns seem to develop in the continuous repetition. The focus is on the arrangement and structure of the individual parts; one can envisage the work extending into the plane, as well as into space.[16] Cast shadows deepen reliefing that is only slightly pronounced but crucial, since the protruding of the work is understood conceptually. It extends into one's lifeworld and world of experience as well as into the social environment of those viewing it, integrates objects from their surroundings, and causes them to appear in a new light (cat. 158). As Roehr himself aptly noted: "The painting has no locus – it occurs everywhere."[17] The meaning and potential of these objects, the availability of resources, and consumption are called into question and redefined, as are the customary practices of art reception.[18] Peter Roehr and numerous other Nouvelle Tendances artists were very interested in Zen Buddhism.[19] In this context, one can detect parallels especially with respect to concentration on the present moment and the creative process as a meditative act.[20] The notion of conscious non-consciousness, a concentrated state of mind free of thought, had been adopted by various artists for quite some time, in particular in abstract and concrete art – from Kazimir Malevich (fig. 2) and Yves Klein (fig. 3; cat. 94) to Günther Uecker (cats. 20, 164).[21] The sought-after de-individualisation was translated into monochrome works, frequently done in the non-colours of white and black, that play with dematerialisation.

The Conceptual artist Piero Manzoni similarly operated with the possibilities (and impossibilities) of material. In his work, it is the supports themselves that are elevated to become the content.[22] The *Achrome* works (cats. 156, 157) he began developing in 1957 are radically reduced to their materiality by staging the canvas through folding or gathering.[23] Texture and dynamic develop mainly through the light that dances on the surfaces.[24] Concentrating on the material allows a questioning of painting and sculpture, and because the objects were not suitable as a projection surface for viewers, they were also directed against a middle-class understanding of art.[25] In the 1950s and 1960s, monochrome, primarily white works became a popular artistic principle, based on Lucio Fontana's "Manifiesto Blanco" of 1946. He therein demanded a new formal language that shifted the focus to light, space and movement and was meant to involve the public visually in the formation process of the works.[26] Such works were free of references to the figurative world or the psychological effects of colour, and hence open to interpretation. The aim was integrating life into art in order to fundamentally expand its possibilities in terms of space and time.[27] This could take on monumental form, as was the case in works by the sculptor and painter Louise Nevelson, who collected objects from urban space and remnants from her environment to fashion monochrome sculpture walls as well as smaller-format collages and paper reliefs, some of which, such as *Dawn's Clouds* (cat. 154), were shaped as wet paper pulp with the aid of a model. Thus, would-be remains from everyday life themselves became auratic works of art that reached into space and our lifeworld.[28] In his reliefs, Dutch artist Jan Schoonhoven, founding member of the Nul-groep, also worked with light impressions on sculpturally shaped material, primarily corrugated cardboard and papier-mâché (cat. 161).[29] Beginning in 1960, he painted his objects uniformly white for the purpose of calling attention to the act of perception – depending on the viewer's standpoint, the structures of his objects change, with the result that they seem to be in constant, vibrant motion.[30]

The phenomenon of individual perception is also addressed in the form of various kinetic grids, as created, for example, by Gerhard von Graevenitz (fig. 4), Dadamaino (fig. 5), and Klaus Staudt with his object *White-Grey* (cat. 159). Serially arranged elements appear to float in the pictorial spaces they create.[31] The statics inscribed in the works is rescinded

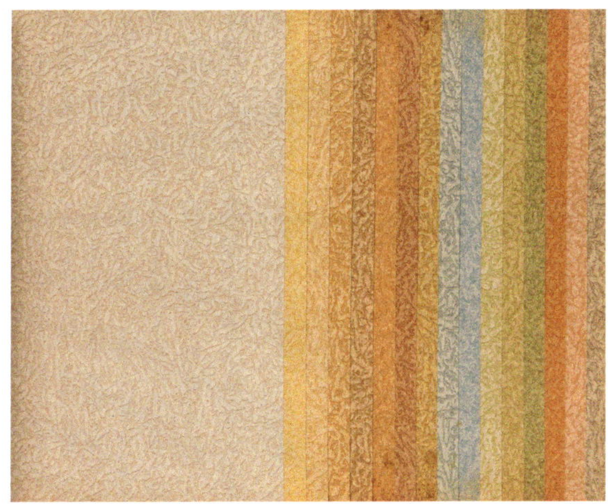

Fig. 1

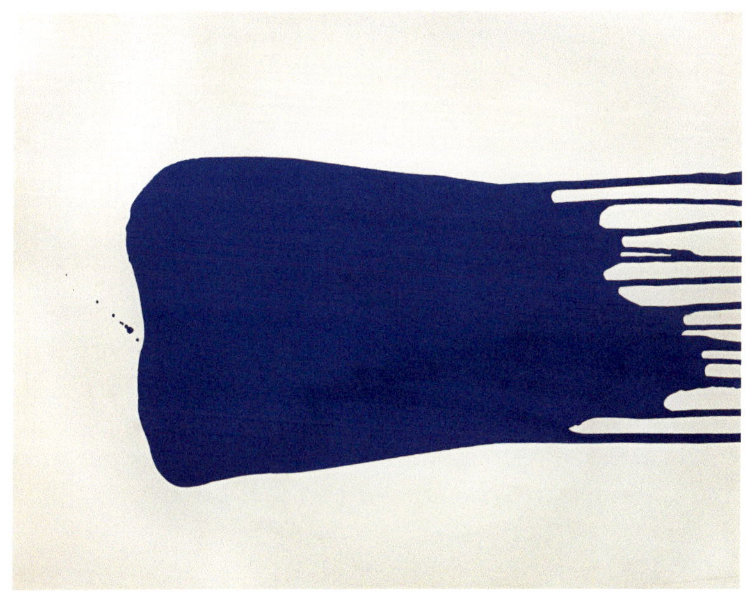

Fig. 3

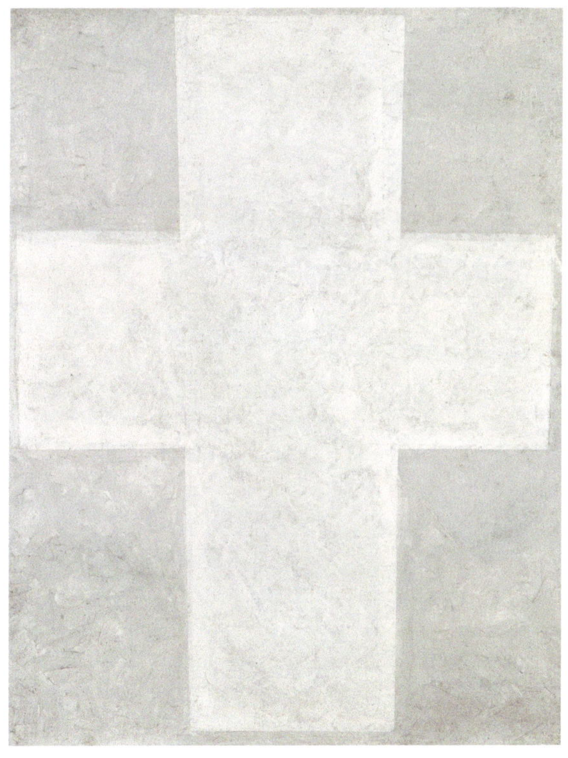

Fig. 2

Fig. 1   Wallpaper factory Gebr. Rasch & Co., G.m.b.H., Bramsche: *Sample Card bauhaus 1934, Wallpaper Series B 58 A–Q*, 1934, glue print wallpaper, Rasch-Archiv, Bramsche

Fig. 2   Kasimir Malevich: *White Suprematist Cross*, 1920/21, oil on canvas, Collection Stedelijk Museum Amsterdam

Fig. 3   Yves Klein: *Monochrome bleu sans titre* (*IKB 27*), ca. 1957, pigment and synthetic resin on paper, Succession Yves Klein, Paris

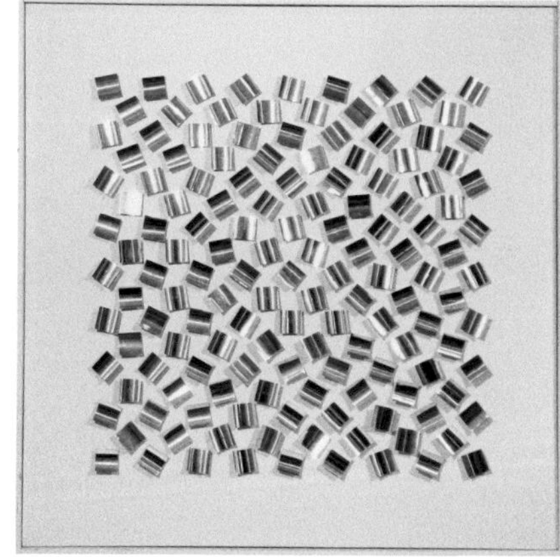

by the incident light and set in motion by countless reflections.[32] This process is supported by the colour white, which in this context acts as the equivalent of light.[33] In contrast to the reserved, clear aesthetic of those objects, Günther Uecker's *Poetry of Destruction* from 1983 (cat. 164) exhibits brutal traces of an axe on a canvas, which was first painted black and then covered with a dense network of steel nails. In his nail work, Uecker combines painting with space and animates viewers to approach it from different perspectives in order to appreciate its formation process. A similar play with haptic experience and the stimulating of and dealing with vision itself can also be detected in works by François Morellet (fig. 6). Thus, the object's physical extension into space is accompanied by the time-related aspect of how the object is dealt with. In Uecker's work, the supposed "destruction" becomes a creative act that shapes and claims space, dynamised by means of light and shadow.[34]

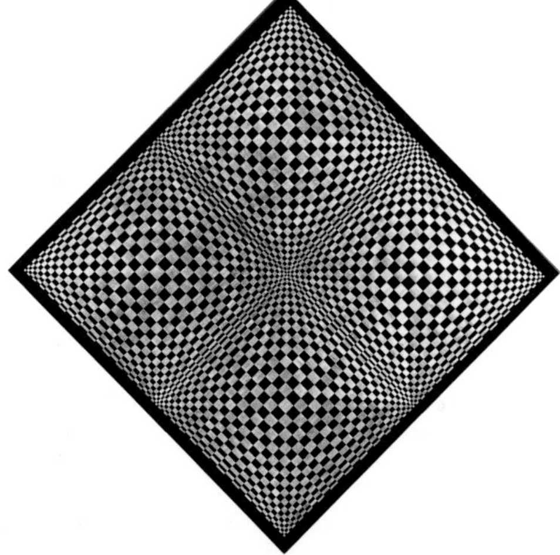

In these clearly structured works, the physical relief seems to recede into the background in favour of intellectual considerations by placing emphasis on light and perception and their individuality, dynamic, and susceptibility to deception. Viewers become an integral part of the work, determining its genesis as a fully formed work. Beyond rigid systems of order, these works also enter the viewers' worlds of thought and perception and inquire into the undiscovered potentials latent in material and human beings beyond structure and seriality – the relief breaks loose from its three-dimensional boundaries.

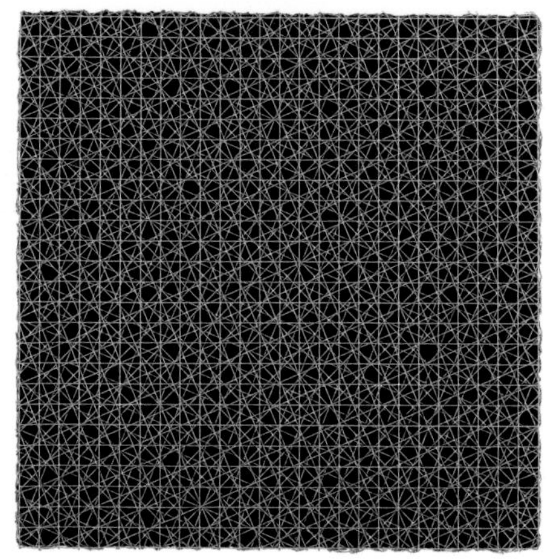

Fig. 4   Gerhard von Graevenitz: *Kinetic Object I*, 1963, wood, metal, rubber, motor, private collection

Fig. 5   Dadamaino (Eduarda Emilia Maino): *Oggetto ottico dinamico*, 1962, aluminium on painted wooden panel, Museo di arte moderna e contemporanea di Trento e Rovereto, Sammlung VAF-Stiftung

Fig. 6   François Morellet: *4 Superimposed Wire Grids (0°, 22°5, 45°, 67°5; 38 mm)* (*4 grillages superposés [0°, 22°5, 45°, 67°5; 38 mm]*), 1970, wire grids on wood painted black, Sammlung Heinz und Anette Teufel im Kunstmuseum Stuttgart

1 Peter Roehr, 1965, quoted in Gerd de Vries (ed.): *Über Kunst: Künstlertexte zum veränderten Kunstverständnis nach 1965*, Cologne 1974, p. 245.

2 See *Black & White: Von Dürer bis Eliasson*, ed. Lelia Packer and Jennifer Sliwka, exh. cat. Kunstpalast Düsseldorf/National Gallery, London, Munich 2017, pp. 196–200.

3 *A Little-Known Story about a Movement, a Magazine, and the Computer's Arrival in Art: New Tendencies and Bit International, 1961–1973*, ed. Margit Rosen, exh. cat. Neue Galerie Graz am Landesmuseum Joanneum/ZKM – Zentrum für Kunst und Medien, Karlsruhe, Karlsruhe et al. 2008, pp. 10–12.

4 Hannes Meyer: "The New World" (1926), in: idem: *Buildings, Projects, and Writings*, ed. C. Schnaidt, trans. D. Q. Stephanson, Teufen 1965.

5 See Sabine Thümmler: *Die Geschichte der Tapete: Raumkunst aus Papier*, Kassel 1998, p. 188.

6 Hannes Meyer: "Die neue Welt", 1926, quoted in Meyer 1980 (see note 4), p. 29.

7 Burckhard Kieselbach: "90 Jahre – Die Geschichte der Bauhaustapete im Überblick", in: *bauhaustapete – neu aufgerollt*, ed. Maren Waike-Koormann, exh. cat. Museumsquartier Osnabrück, Bramsche 2019, pp. 15–31, esp. pp. 15f.

8 Thümmler 1998 (see note 5), pp. 188–190.

9 Bernd Rau: *Hans Arp: Die Reliefs. Œuvre-Katalog*, Stuttgart 1981, pp. XXXVIIIf.

10 In a poem written in 1927, also titled "Das Eierbrett", he once more explains the rules of the game; see Jane H. Hancock: "Jean Arp's *The Eggboard* Interpreted: The Artist as a Poet in the 1920's", *The Art Bulletin* 6, no. 65, 1 March 1983, pp. 122–137.

11 Serge Lemoine: "La Peinture et les mots", in: *Auguste Herbin: Une rétrospective 1900–1960*, exh. cat. Galerie Lahumière, Paris, 2010, pp. 9–18, esp. p. 11.

12 In his case, it was a communist ideal committed to the collective. Herbin had been a founding member of the Communist Party of France since 1920.

13 Michael Fried: "Art and Objecthood" (1967), in: idem: *Art and Objecthood: Essays and Reviews*, Chicago and London 1998, pp. 148–172, esp. p. 166.

14 Sarah Hayden and Paul Hegarty: *Peter Roehr: Field Pulsations. Avant-Garde Artist of the 1960s*, ed. Renate Wiehager, Cologne 2018, pp. 75f.

15 There was an extensively annotated copy of Walter Benjamin's essay *The Work of Art in the Age of Mechanical Reproduction* in Roehr's library; see Werner Lippert and Paul Maenz: *Peter Roehr*, Frankfurt am Main 1991, pp. 10f.

16 Ibid., pp. 18f. Roehr was familiar with Minimal Art through his friend Paul Maenz.

17 Peter Roehr, 1965, quoted in De Vries 1974 (see note 1), p. 245.

18 *Peter Roehr 1944–1968: Die Sammlung Paul Maenz*, vol. 2, ed. Gerda Wendermann, exh. cat. Neues Museum Weimar, Ostfildern 2000, pp. 55–59. The materials are an expression of capitalism and economic growth, but they also address a new culture of political debate and a fascination with the approach to new media.

19 Lippert/Maenz 1991 (see note 15), pp. 10f. For example, there was also a German edition of Daisetz Teitaro Suzuki's publication *Zen and Japanese Culture* (Hamburg 1958) in Roehr's library at the time of his death.

20 In this school of Mahâyâna Buddhism, established in the sixth century CE, it is essential to open up the nature of things through contemplation or meditation in order to achieve an understanding of oneself and the world; for more on this, see Helmut Brinker: "Vom Wesen des Zen", in: *Zen und die westliche Kunst*, ed. Hans Günther Golinski and Sepp Hiekisch-Picard, exh. cat. Museum Bochum, Cologne 2000, pp. 11–25.

21 Helen Westgeest: "Zen und Nicht-Zen: Zen und die westliche Kunst", in: ibid., pp. 61–111.

22 See exh. cat. Weimar 2000 (see note 18), p. 13.

23 Barbara Spahn: *Piero Manzoni (1933–1963): Seine Herausforderung der Grenze von Kunst und Leben*, Ph.D. diss, Munich 1999, pp. 21–23, 26f.

24 Exh. cat. Weimar 2000 (see note 18), p. 13.

25 Spahn 1999 (see note 23), pp. 26f.

26 See *neue tendenzen 1955–1965: Lucio Fontana, Gerhard von Graevenitz, Gotthard Graubner, François Morellet, Uli Pohl*, exh. cat. Kunsthandel Wolfgang Werner, Berlin, Berlin and Bremen 2015, p. 1.

27 Spahn 1999 (see note 23), pp. 23, 137f. This idea acquired a completely new level of meaning due to the concurrent onset of spaceflight, in particular with the launch of the Soviet *Sputnik 1* on 4 October 1957.

28 *Louise Nevelson. Skyggernes Skulptør*, ed. Majbritt Løland and Stinna Toft, exh. cat. Kunsten Museum of Modern Art, Aalborg, 2020, pp. 181f.; see Yuval Etgar: "Out of Order: The Collages of Louise Nevelson", *Mousse Magazine Online*, 10 May 2022, https://www.moussemagazine.it/publishing/from-out-of-order-the-collages-of-louise-nevelsonby-out-of-order-the-collages-of-louise-nevelson/ (accessed 13 February 2023).

29 Max Imdahl: "Schoonhovens weiße Reliefs und Zeichnungen", in: *Jan J. Schoonhoven – retrospektiv*, exh. cat. Museum Folkwang Essen et al., Düsseldorf 1995, pp. 43–49.

30 Karin Schick: "Jan J. Schoonhoven", in: *Kunstmuseum Stuttgart*, ed. Marion Ackermann, coll. cat. Kunstmuseum Stuttgart, Ostfildern 2005, p. 158.

31 Simone Schimpf: "Das Raster als Hardware", in: *Klaus Staudt: Horizonte*, ed. Renate Goldmann, exh. cat. Leopold-Hoesch-Museum, Düren et al., Cologne 2017, pp. 36–47.

32 Hans-Peter Riese: "Von der sinnlichen Anmutung des Konkreten", in: *Klaus Staudt. Retrospektive 1960–1997*, ed. Peter Reindl, exh. cat. Museum für Konkrete Kunst, Ingolstadt, et al., Dortmund 1997, pp. 10–28.

33 Peter Reindl: "Klaus Staudt – Zwischen Statik und Kinetik: Wieviel Bewegung verträgt die Kunst nach dem futuristischen Manifest?", in: ibid., pp. 130–145.

34 Edouard P. Derom and Eric R. Kandel: "Günther Uecker und die Suche nach einer neuen Brücke zwischen Malerei und Skulptur", in: *Uecker*, ed. Gabriele Lauser and Marion Ackermann, exh. cat. Kunstsammlung Nordrhein-Westfalen, Düsseldorf, Berlin 2015, n.p.

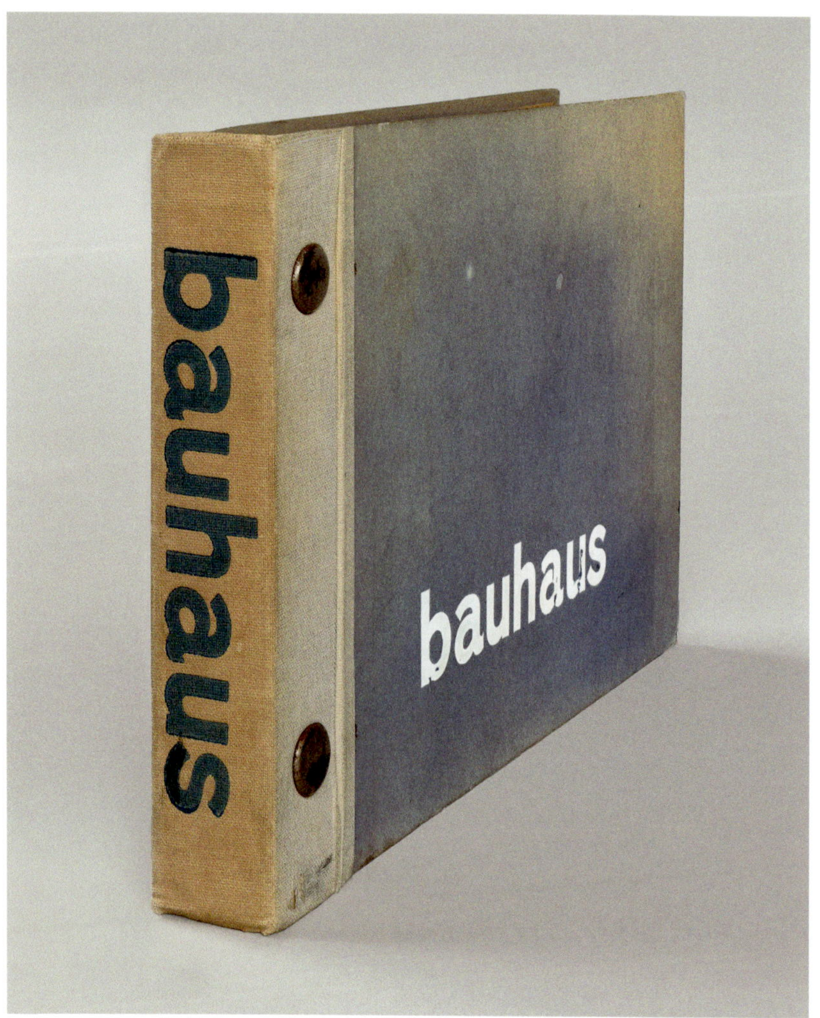

Cat. 150

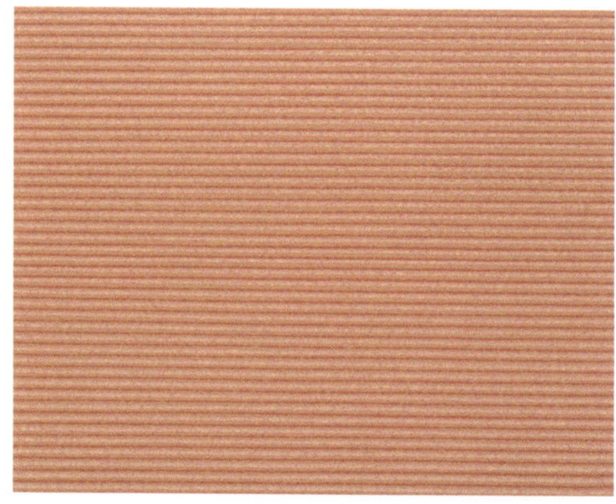

Cat. 150　Wallpaper factory Gebr. Rasch & Co., G.m.b.H., Bramsche: *Sample Card bauhaus 1930*, 1930/31, pasteboard with linen-covered back, book nails, glue print wallpaper samples, 15.9 × 23.9 cm, Sammlung Freese

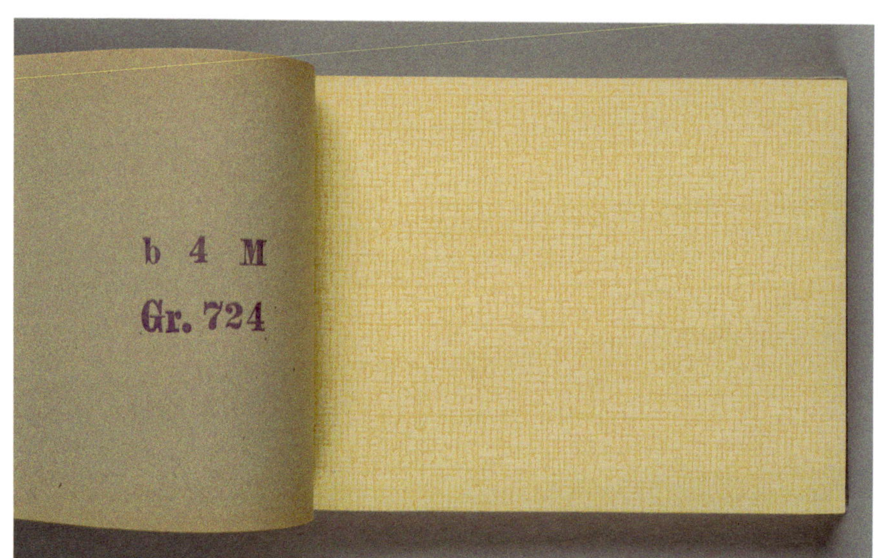

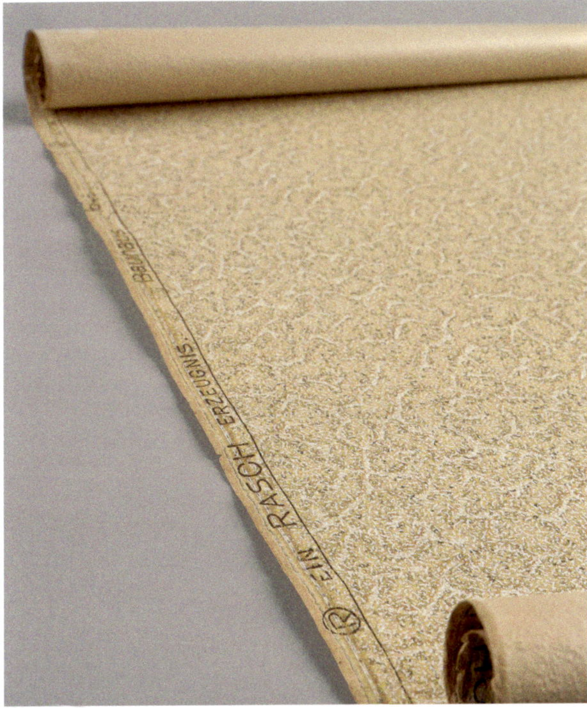

Cat. 151

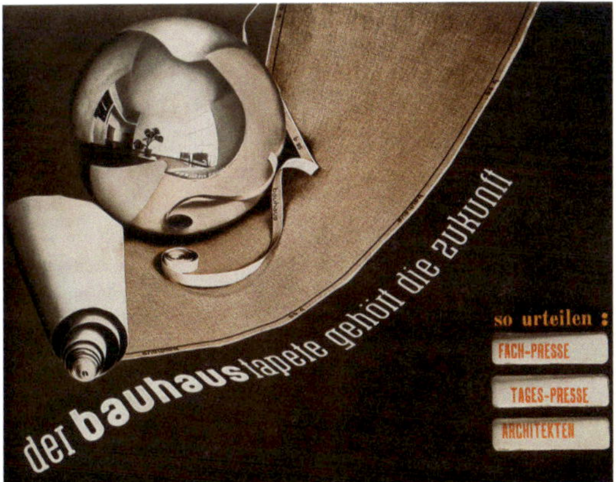

Cat. 152

Cat. 153

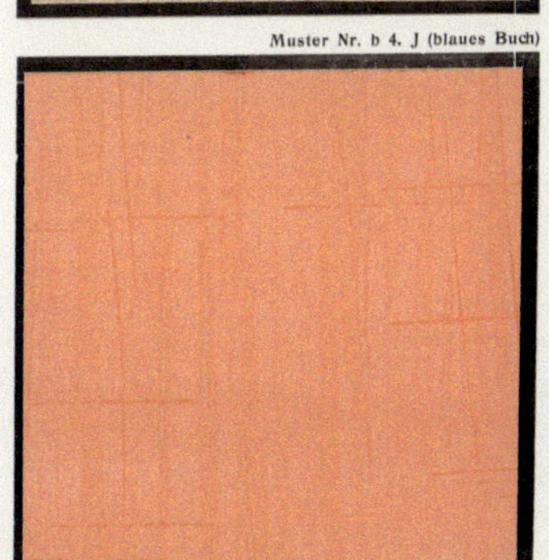

Cat. 151 Wallpaper *Bauhaus b48. Ein RASCH Erzeugnis*, ca. 1933, paper, 50.5 × 142 cm, Sammlung Freese

Cat. 152 Wallpaper factory Gebr. Rasch & Co., G.m.b.H., Bramsche: *Advertisement for Bauhaus Wallpaper*, ca. 1930, paper with glued-on wallpaper samples, 26 × 23 cm, Sammlung Freese

Cat. 153 Cover and wallpaper samples from the advertising *der bauhaustapete gehört die zukunft*, design: Joost Schmidt, 1931, paper, 14.5 × 21 cm, Sammlung Freese

BAUHAUS-TAPETEN

MUSTER:
Bauhaustapeten sind unaufdringlich und zurückhaltend gemustert. Entwurf und Farbgebung besorgte das Bauhaus Dessau. Die durchweg hellen Farbtöne beruhen auf gemeinsamer Farbenskala. Die Auswahl umfaßt 150 Blatt Leimdruckmuster, die in der blauen Bauhauskarte und 100 Blatt Öldrucktapeten, die in der gelben Karte enthalten sind. Beide Karten sind in Dinformat a 5.

FARBEN:
Die Farben für die Tapeten des blauen Buches sind aus den lichtechtesten Rohstoffen der I. G. Farbenindustrie A. G. in eigener Farbenfabrik der Tapetenfabrik Rasch & Co., Bramsche, hergestellt. Dagegen ist es bisher nicht möglich, die wasserfesten Öldruckfarben der gelben Bauhauskarte in derselben Lichtechtheit der Farben herzustellen. Wer mehr Wert auf Lichtechtheit als auf Wasserfestigkeit legt, wählt deshalb aus der blauen Karte.

PAPIER:
Das Papier sämtlicher Bauhaustapeten ist 90 gr. pro qm schwer und von bester Qualität.

PREISE:
Der Preis beträgt RM. 1,— bis 1,75.

WO ERHÄLTLICH?
In den besseren Spezialtapetengeschäften. Daselbst Musterbücher.

Muster Nr. b 21. H. (gelbes Buch)

Muster Nr. b 17. K. (blaues Buch)

Muster Nr. b 4. J (blaues Buch)

Hersteller: Tapetenfabrik Gebr. Rasch & Co., G.m.b.H., Bramsche bei Osnabrück.

Cat. 154   Louise Nevelson: *Dawn's Clouds*, 1977, cast paper,
70.3 × 99.7 cm, Städel Museum, Frankfurt am Main,
inv. no. 67964 (Frankfurt only)

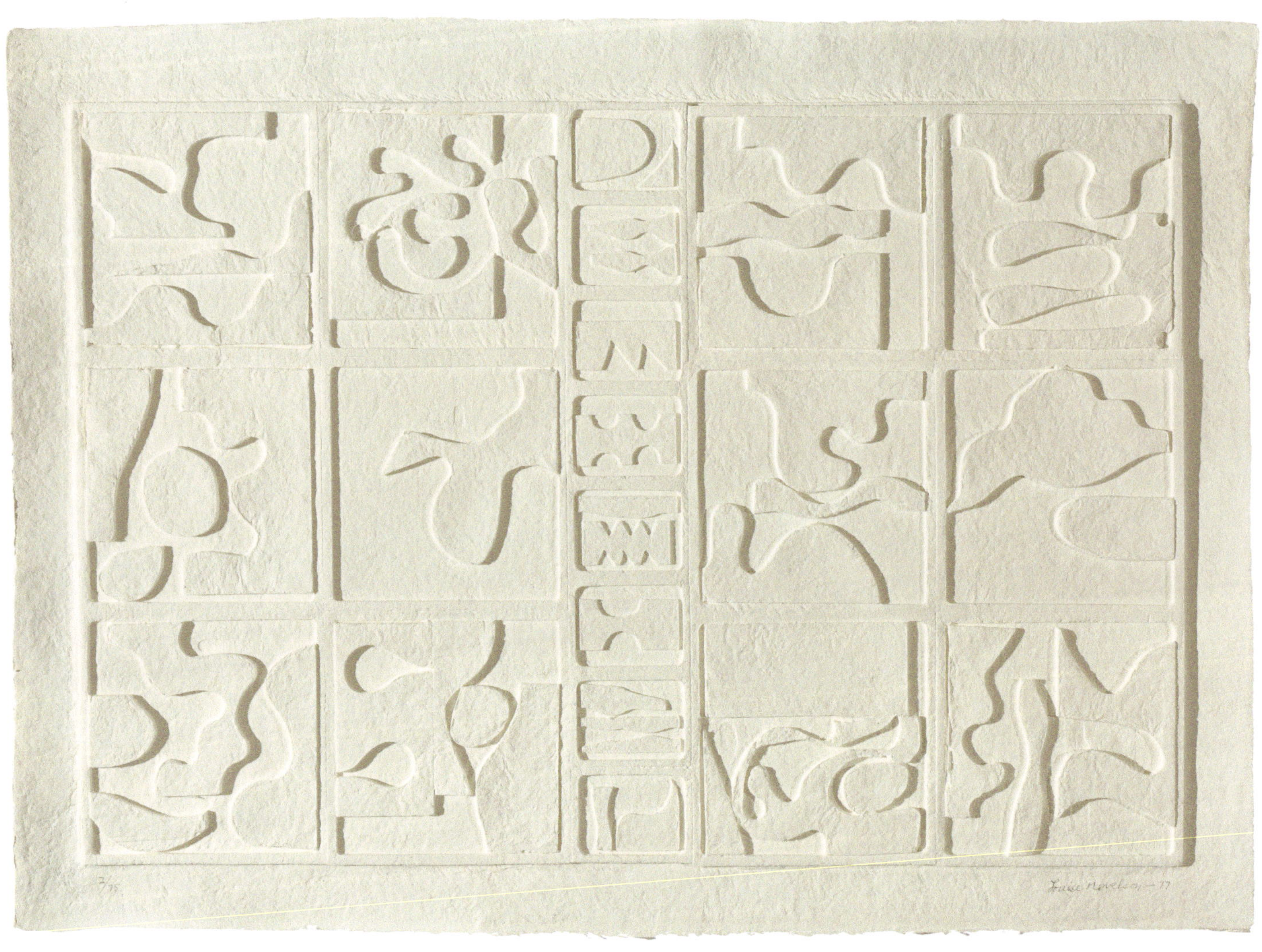

Cat. 155   Jean Arp: *The Eggboard* (*La planche à œufs*), 1922, wood, painted, 76.2 × 96.5 cm, private collection

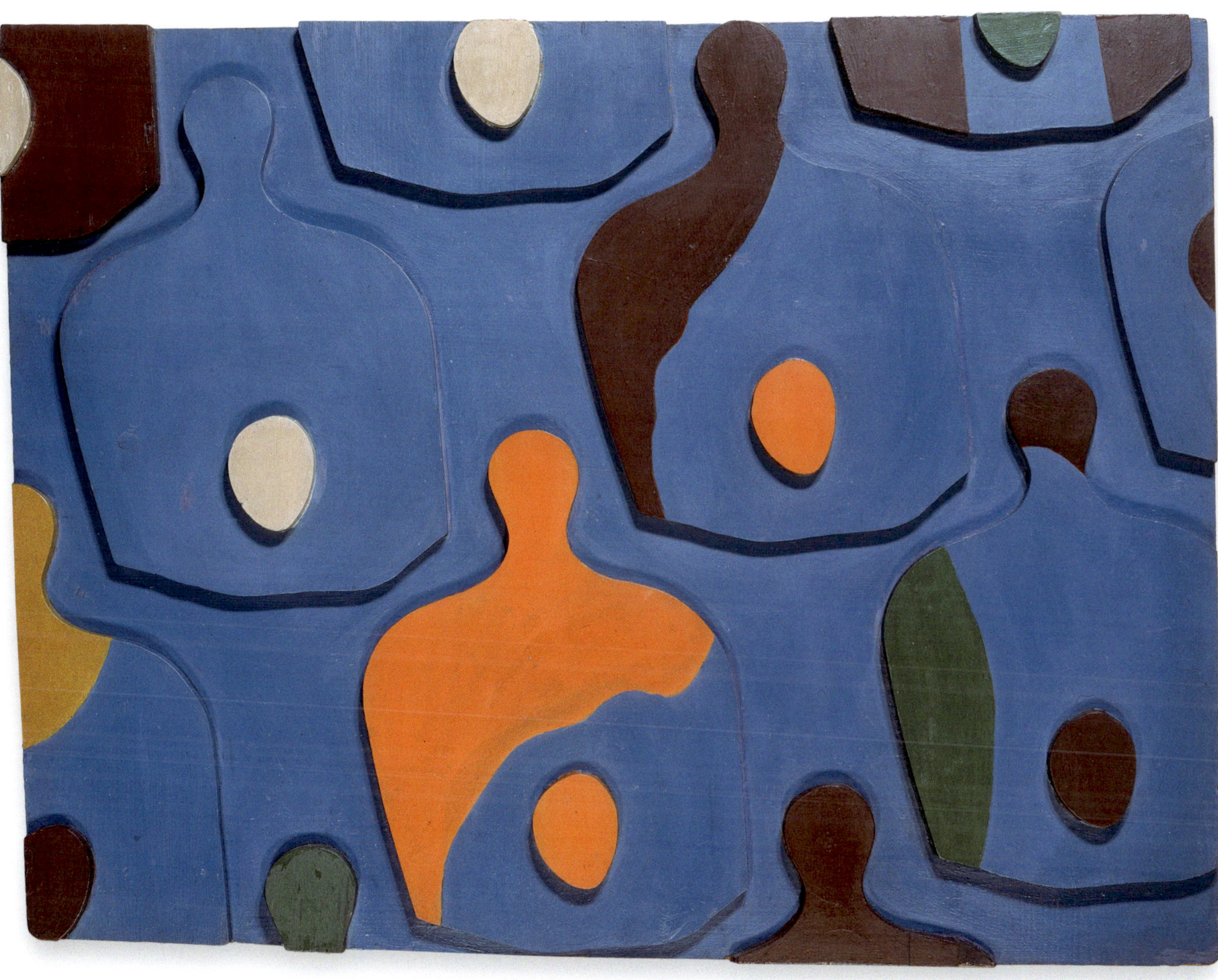

Cat. 156   Piero Manzoni: *Achrome*, 1959/60, kaolin on canvas, 80 × 100 cm, Städel Museum, Frankfurt am Main, inv. no. SG 1242 (Frankfurt only)

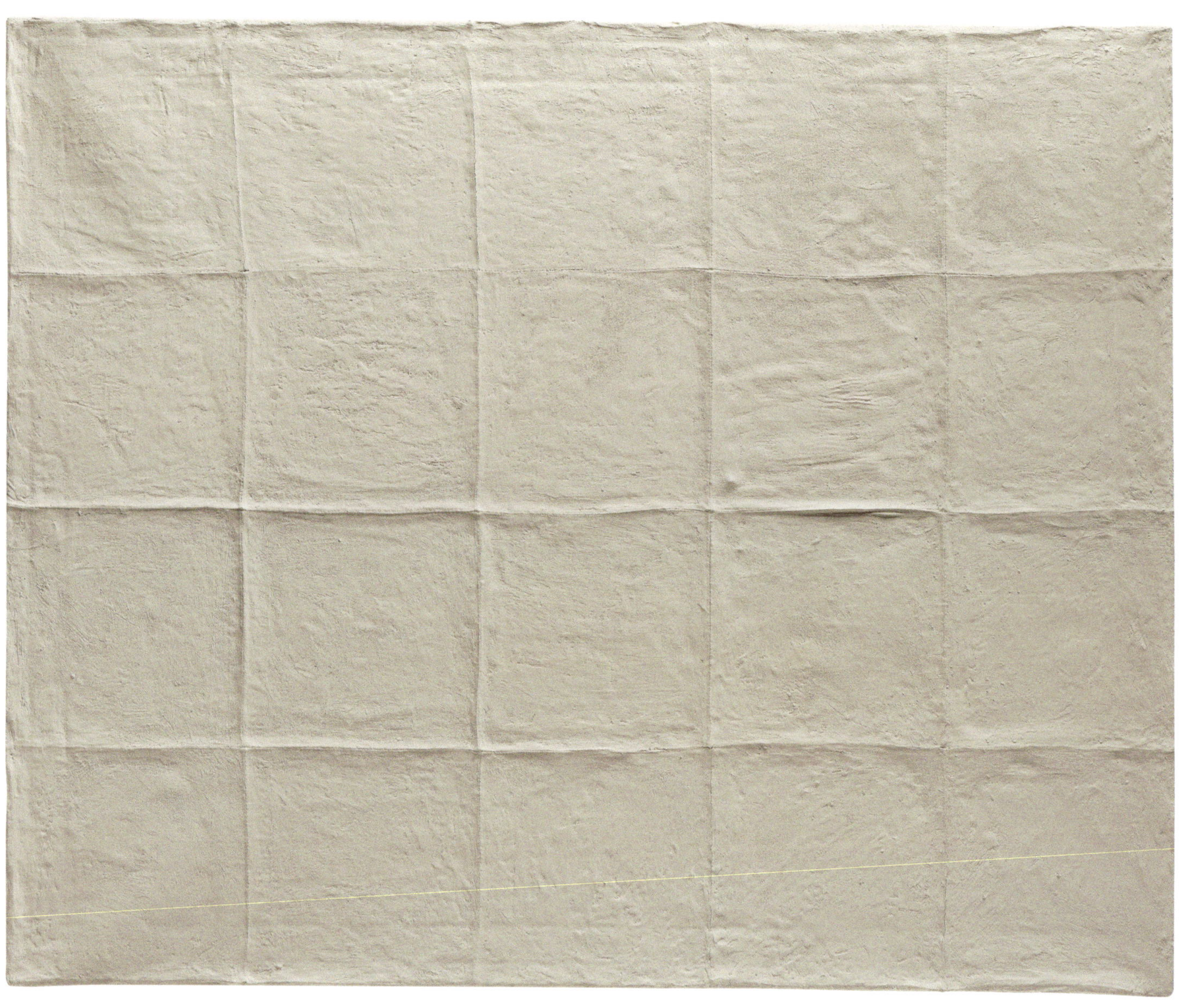

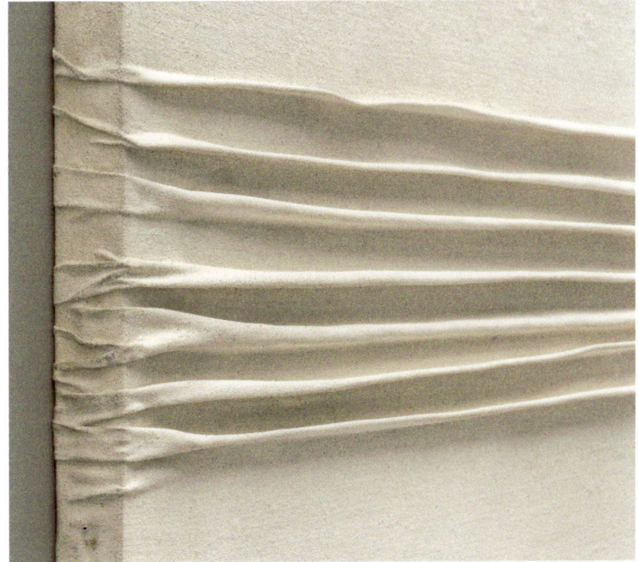

Detail

Cat. 157   Piero Manzoni: *Achrome*, 1959, kaolin and glue on canvas,
61 × 61 cm, Hamburger Kunsthalle, inv. no. HK-5198
(Hamburg only)

Cat. 158   Adolf Luther: *Texture for Light* (*Relief with Eggs*),
1967, eggshells, plaster, paint, wood, acrylic glass plate,
68 × 68 × 10.5 cm, Städel Museum, Frankfurt am Main,
permanent loan from the Adolf-Luther-Stiftung,
inv. no. LG 123 (Frankfurt only)

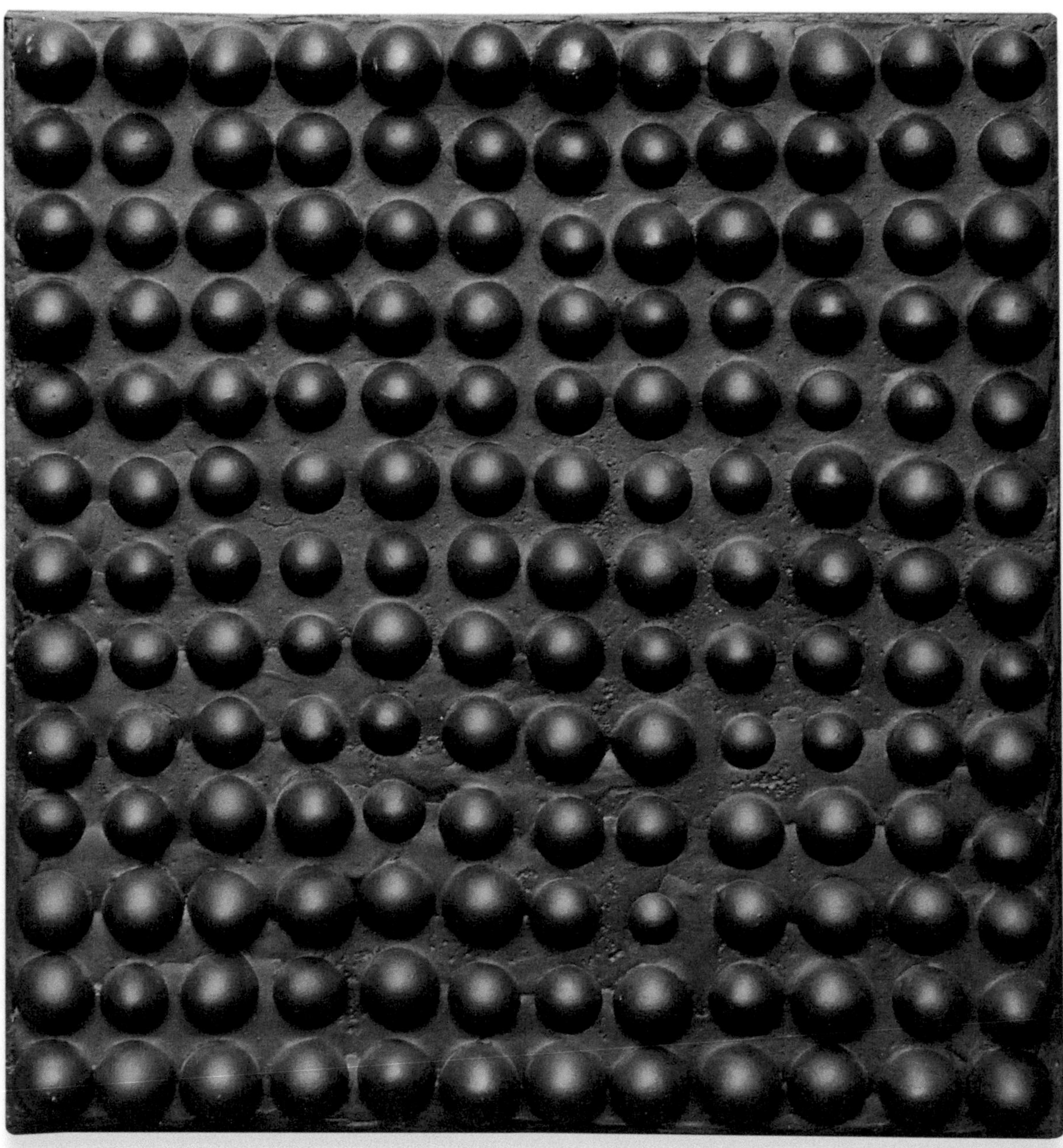

Cat. 159   Klaus Staudt: *White-Grey*, 1964/65, wood, dispersion
paint and acrylic glass, 96 × 96 × 10 cm, Städel Museum,
Frankfurt am Main, inv. no. 2561

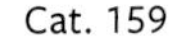

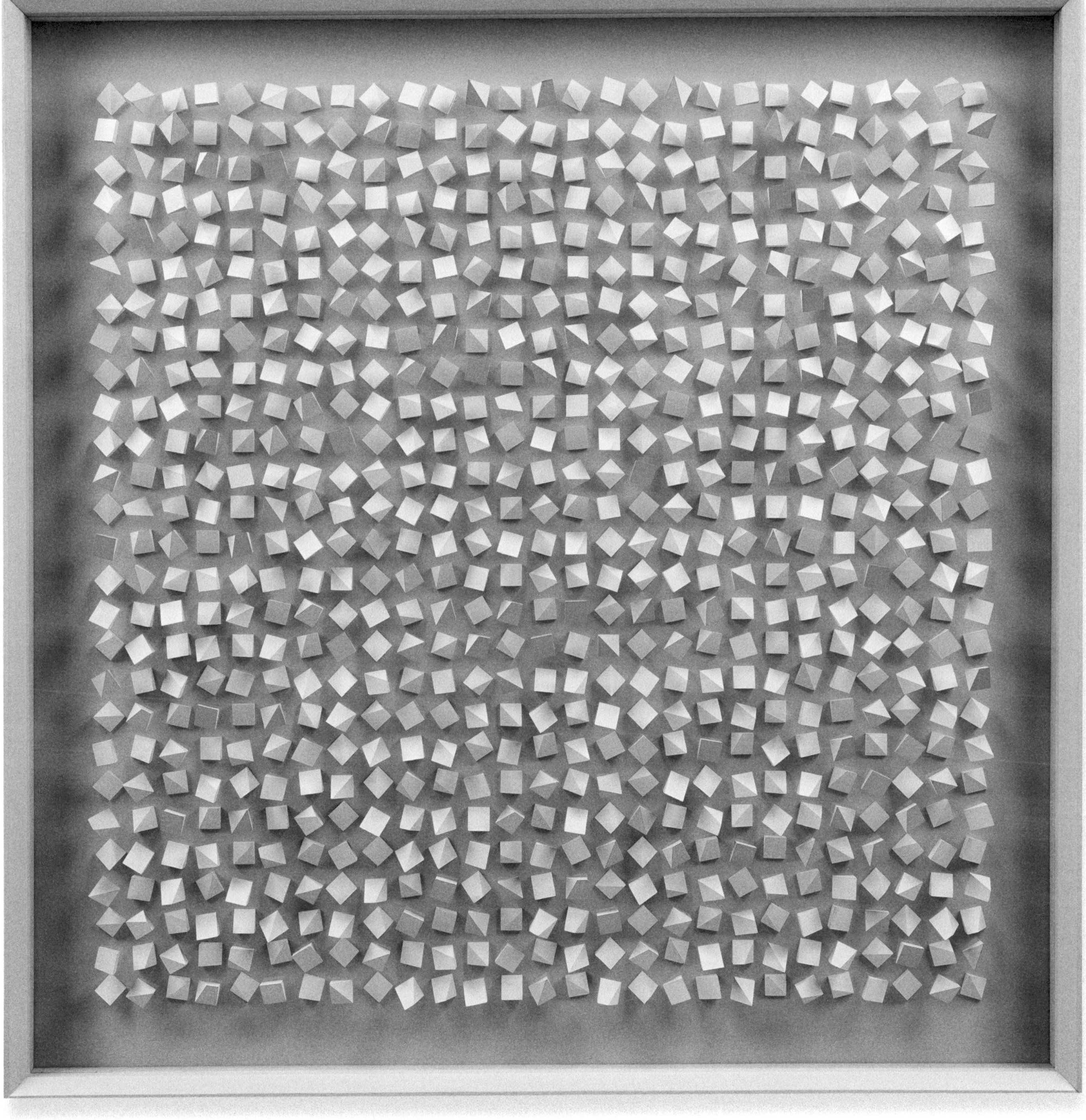

Cat. 160   Peter Roehr: *Untitled (OB–138/5)*, 1967, plastic mounted on laminated hardboard, 35 × 35 cm, Städel Museum, Frankfurt am Main, inv. no. 2160

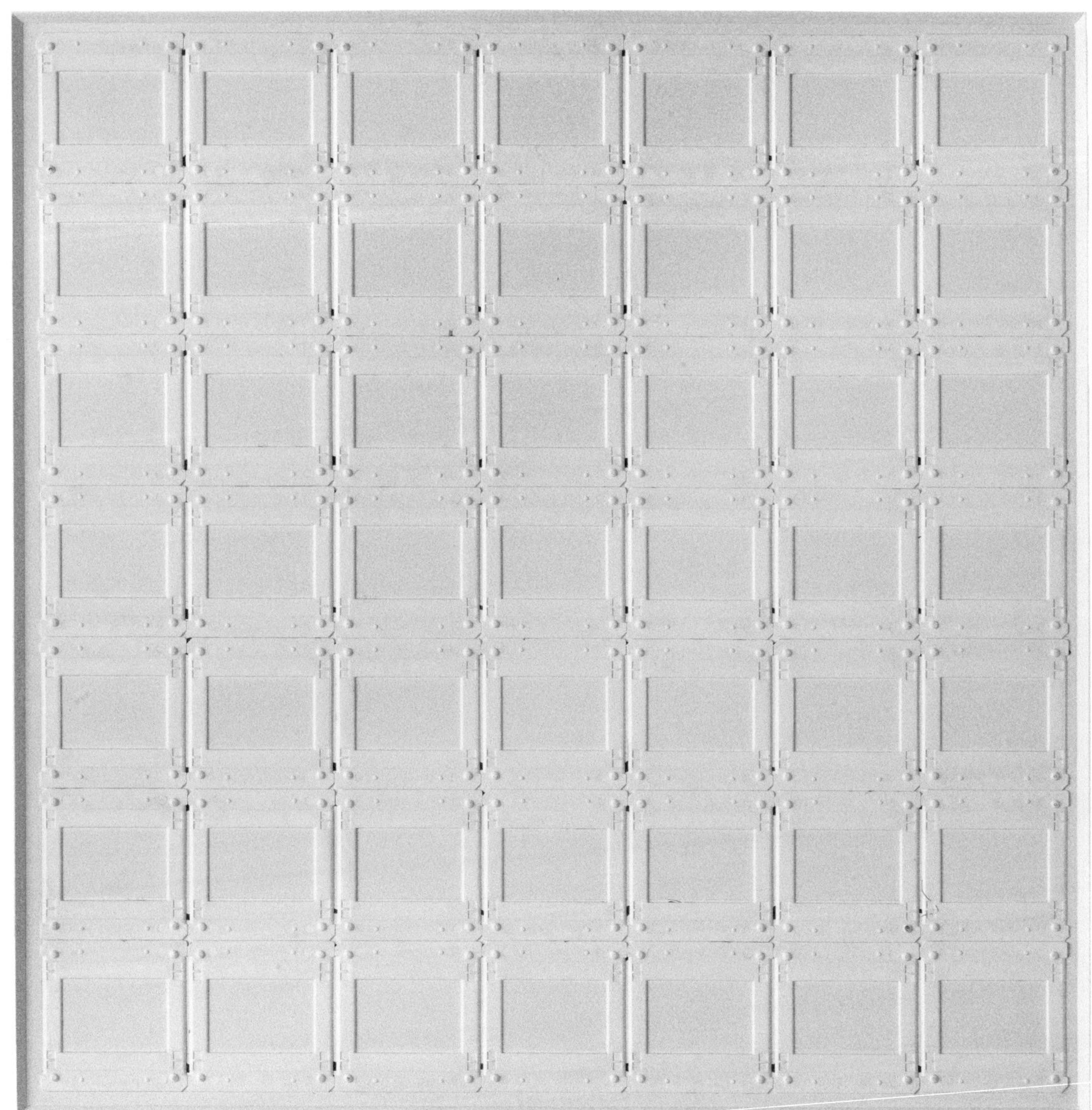

Cat. 161   Jan Schoonhoven: *Square Dish Relief*, 1966, latex paint,
paper and cardboard on wood and hardboard,
100 × 100 × 11 cm, Sammlung Heinz und Anette Teufel
im Kunstmuseum Stuttgart, inv. no. 2009-114

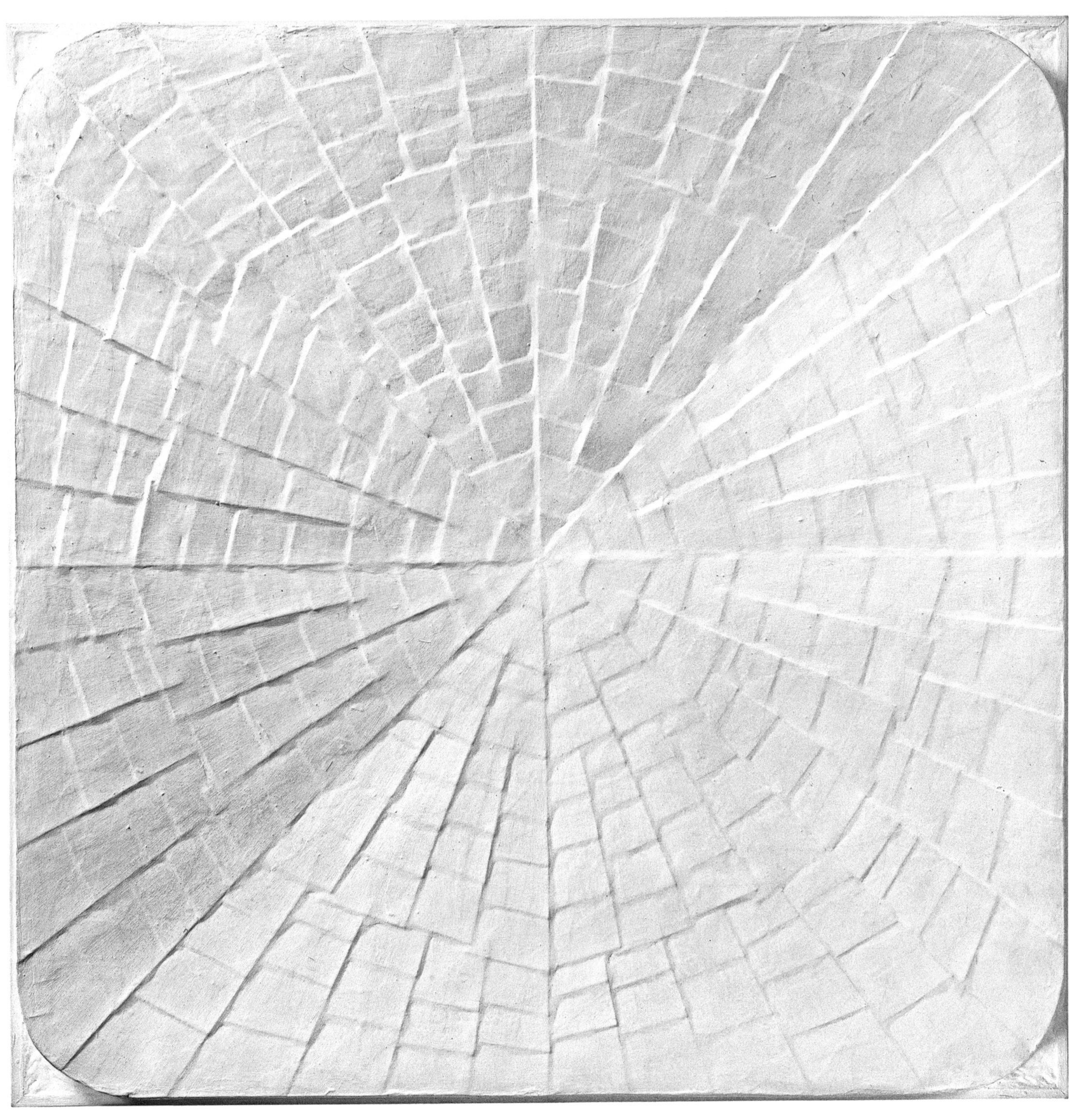

Cat. 162   Auguste Herbin: *Polychrome Relief* (*Relief polychrome*), 1920, assemblage made from painted wood, 88.5 × 69 × 15 cm, Musée d'Art Moderne de Paris, inv. no. AMS 593

Cat. 163   Auguste Herbin: *Four-Sided Relief* (*Colonne relief quatre faces*), 1921, cement, painted, 53 × 13.5 × 13.5 cm, Hamburger Kunsthalle, inv. no. S-1981-1 (Hamburg only)

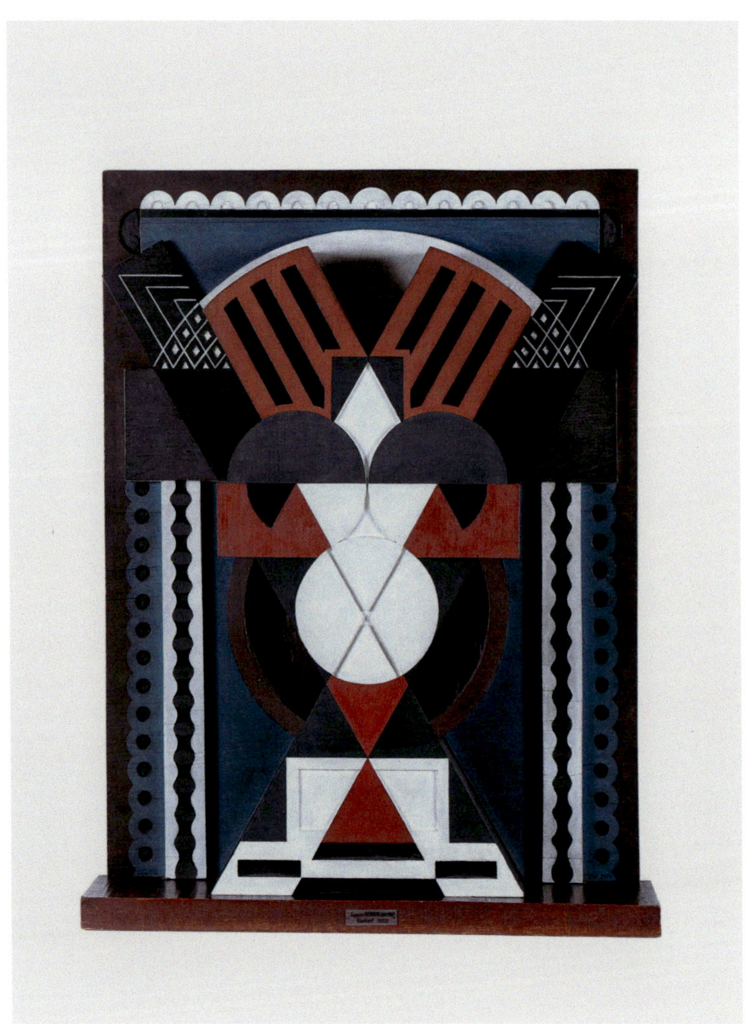

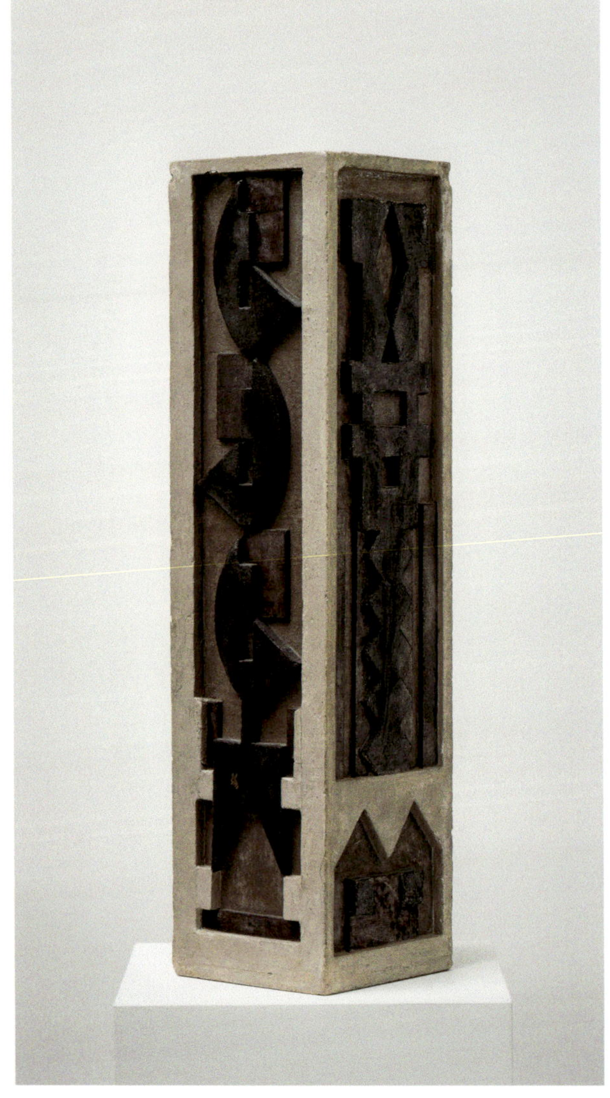

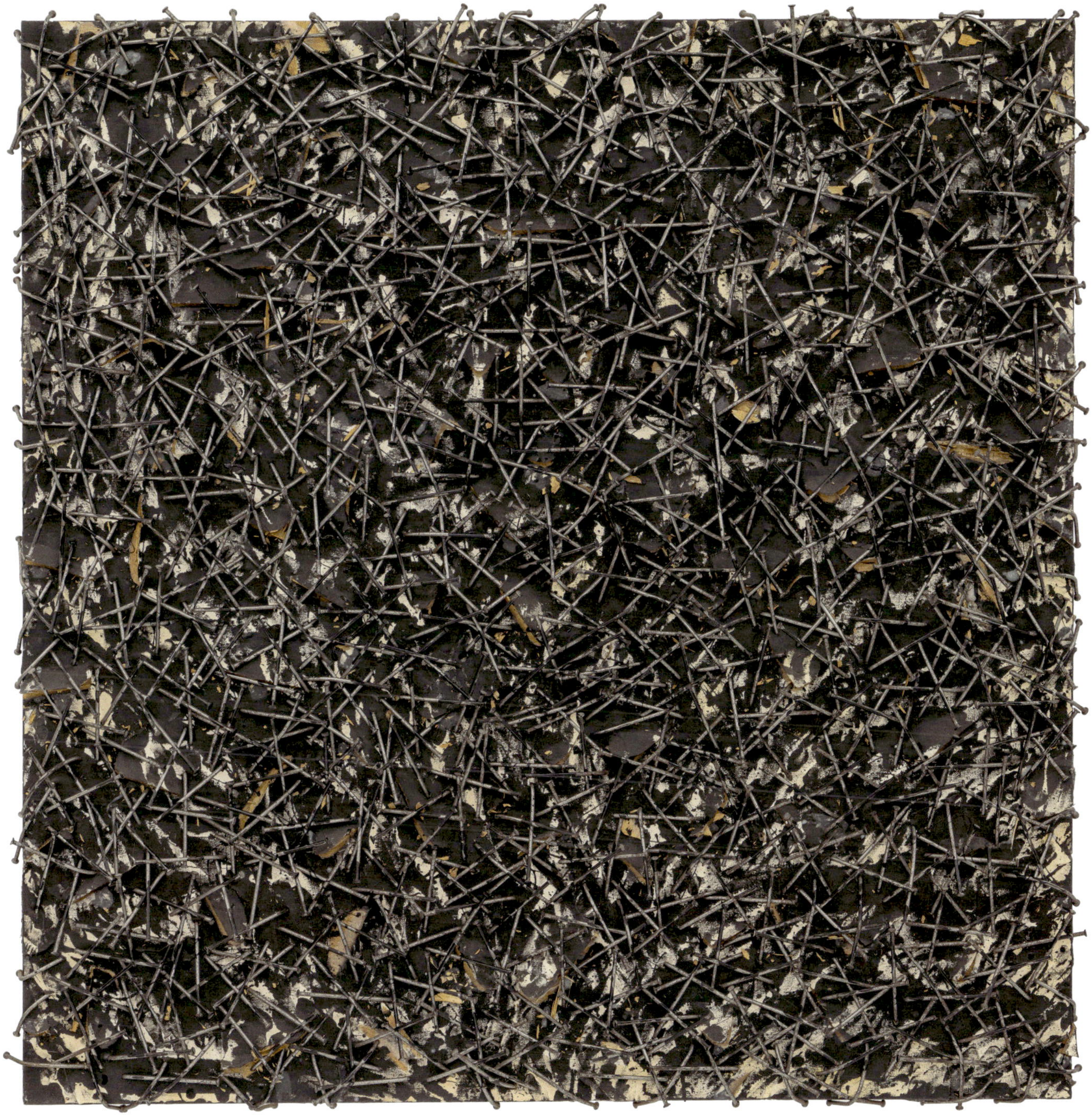

Cat. 164   Günther Uecker: *Poetry of Destruction*, 1983, black paint
and nails on canvas on wood, 124 × 125 × 16 cm,
Hamburger Kunsthalle, inv. no. G-1985-15 (Hamburg only)

THE ARTISTS

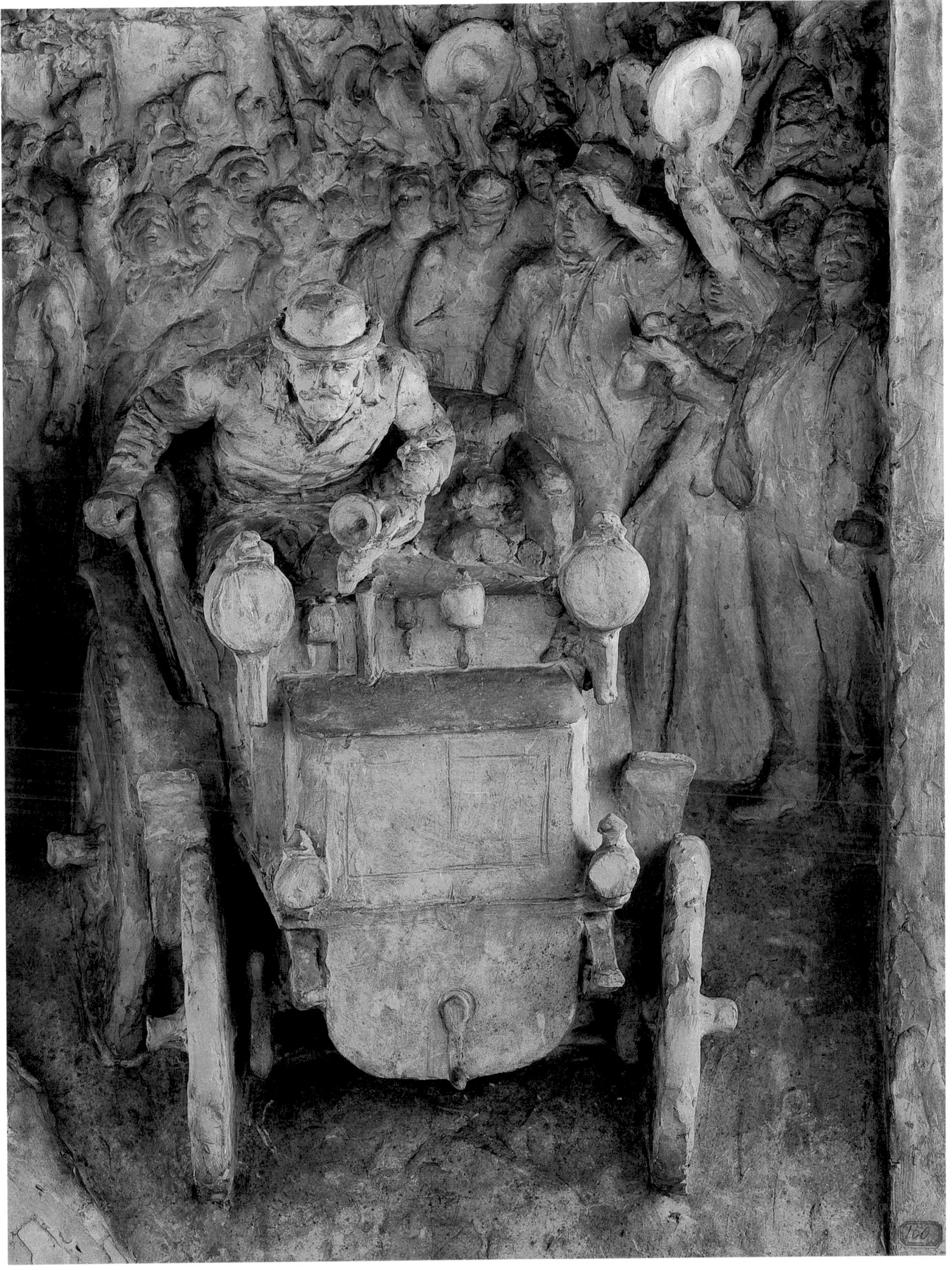

HUBERT PONSCARME 1827–1903
→ Cats. 48, 49

IVAN PUNI 1892–1956
→ Cat. 107

R CHRISTIAN DANIEL RAUCH 1777–1857
→ Cat. 18

GERHARD RICHTER *1932
→ Cat. 92

AUGUSTE RODIN 1840–1917
→ Cat. 34

PETER ROEHR 1944–1968
→ Cat. 160

MEDARDO ROSSO 1858–1928
→ Cats. 37, 38

PHILIPP OTTO RUNGE 1777–1810
→ Cat. 87

S NIKI DE SAINT PHALLE 1930–2002
→ Cat. 72

CHRISTIAN SCHAD 1894–1982
→ Cat. 111

JOHANN GOTTFRIED SCHADOW 1764–1850
→ Cats. 2, 3

OSKAR SCHLEMMER 1888–1943
→ Cats. 114, 115

OTTO SCHOLDERER 1834–1902
→ Cat. 90

JAN SCHOONHOVEN 1914–1994
→ Cat. 161

LUDWIG SCHWANTHALER 1802–1848
→ Cat. 19

KURT SCHWITTERS 1887–1948
→ Cats. 105, 112, 113

ARTHUR SEGAL 1875–1944
→ Cat. 89

JESÚS RAFAEL SOTO 1923–2005
→ Cat. 93

DANIEL SPOERRI *1930
→ Cat. 86

KLAUS STAUDT *1932
→ Cat. 159

T SOPHIE TAEUBER-ARP 1889–1943
→ Cats. 73, 138, 139

ANTONI TÀPIES 1923–2012
→ Cat. 96

VLADIMIR TATLIN 1885–1953
→ Cat. 106

BERTEL THORVALDSEN 1770–1844
→ Cat. 21

WILLIAM TURNBULL 1922–2012
→ Cats. 101–103

U GÜNTHER UECKER *1930
→ Cats. 20, 164

V AUGUSTO VARNESI 1866–1941
→ Cat. 54

ARTUR VOLKMANN 1851–1941
→ Cat. 11

W JENNY WIEGMANN-MUCCHI 1895–1969
→ Cat. 69

Y OVIDE YENCESSE 1869–1947
→ Cats. 47, 50, 51

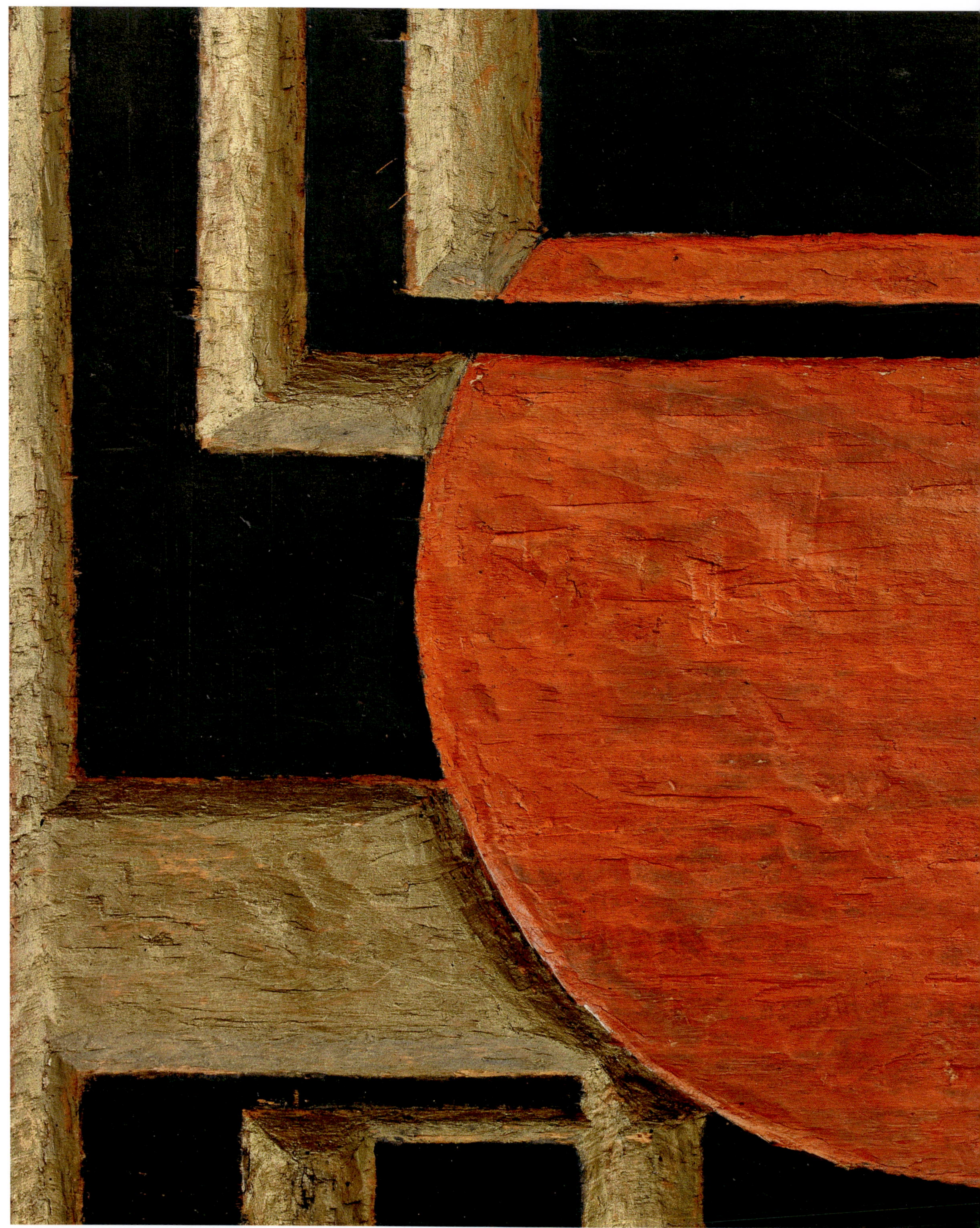

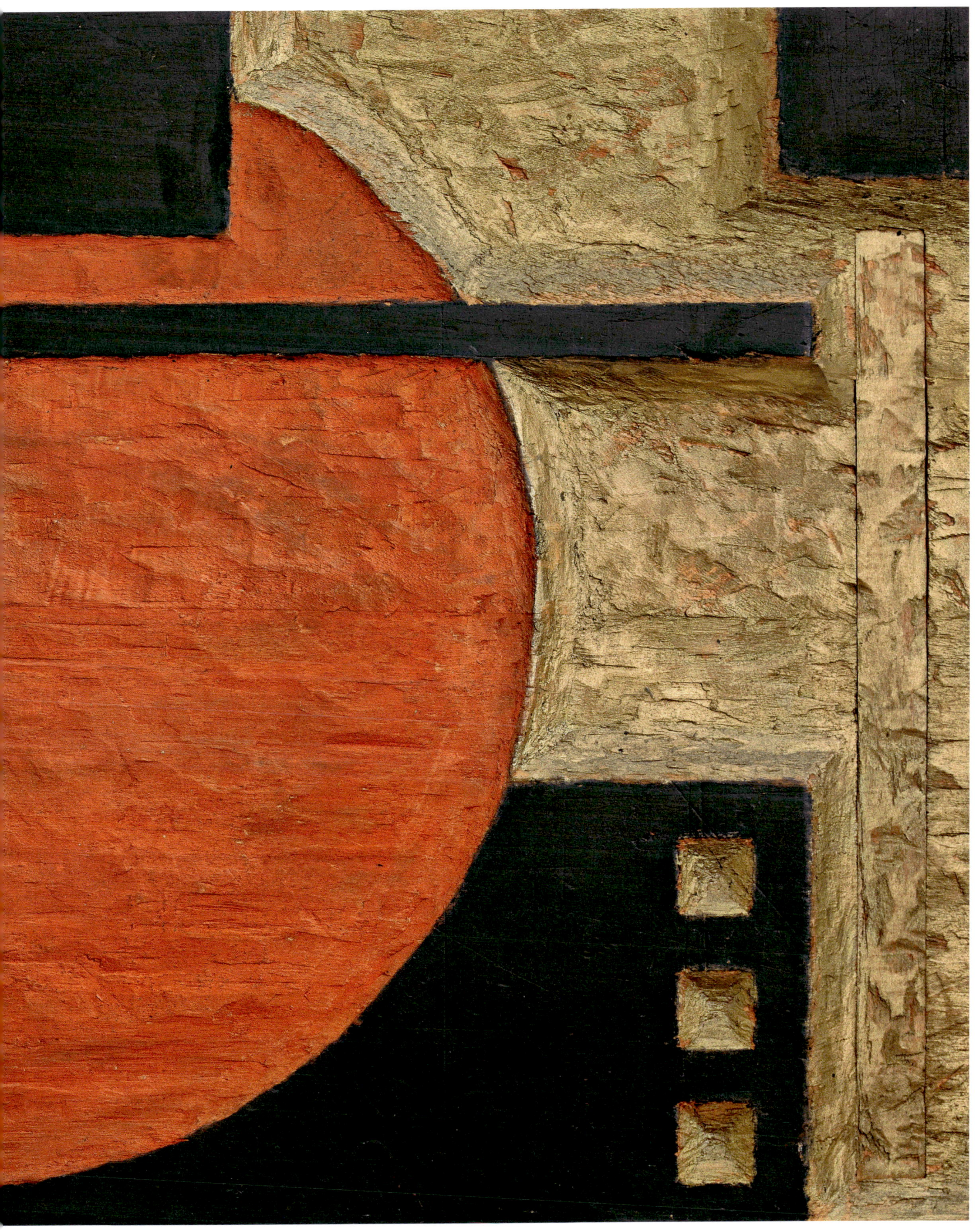

COLOPHON

This catalogue has been published in conjunction with

Outstanding! The Relief from Rodin to Picasso
Städel Museum, Frankfurt am Main, 24 May – 17 September 2023

Outstanding! The Relief from Rodin to Taeuber-Arp
Hamburger Kunsthalle, 13 October 2023 – 25 February 2024

An exhibition of the Städel Museum, Frankfurt am Main,
and the Hamburger Kunsthalle

Editors
Alexander Eiling, Eva Mongi-
Vollmer, Karin Schick

Editing
Friederike Schütt

Catalogue Management Frankfurt
Eva Mongi-Vollmer

Catalogue Management Hamburg
Juliane Au

Graphics/Corporate Design
Sandra Adler-Krause

Design and Layout
tonique, Frankfurt am Main
Alexander Horn, Lukas Schmidt,
Tim Schötensack

Copyediting and Proofreading
Sarah Quigley

Translation
Judith Rosenthal (Introduction,
Echo of the Parthenon, Poly-
chrome Reliefs, Painterly-
Sculptural Reliefs, Approximating
Nature, Monumental Tasks);
Rebecca van Dyck (Greetings,
Forewords, Sculptural Narration,
Faces in Relief, Relief and
Frame, The Polyperspectival Gaze,
Optical Illusion in the Relief,
Designs of the World, Boundary
and Space of Possibility,
A Spotlight on Structure)

Editorial Direction Prestel
Markus Eisen

Production
Cilly Klotz

Separations
Helio Repro GmbH, Munich

Printing and Binding
Grafisches Centrum Cuno
GmbH & Co. KG, Calbe

Typeface
Freight Sans

Paper
Arctic Volume White 150 g/sqm

Penguin Random House
Verlagsgruppe FSC® N001967

A CIP catalogue record for
this book is available from the
British Library.

Library of Congress Control
Number: 2023935931

In respect to links in the book,
Penguin Random House Verlagsgruppe expressly notes that no
illegal content was discernible on
the linked sites at the time the
links were created. The Publisher
has no influence at all over the
current and future design, content or authorship of the linked
sites. For this reason Penguin
Random House Verlagsgruppe
expressly disassociates itself from
all content on linked sites that
has been altered since the link was
created and assumes no liability
for such content.

© 2023 Städel Museum, Frankfurt
am Main, Hamburger Kunsthalle,
the authors, and Prestel Verlag,
Munich · London · New York 2023,
A member of Penguin Random
House Verlagsgruppe GmbH, Neu-
markter Strasse 28 · 81673 Munich

Museum Edition
ISBN 978-3-947879-20-5 (German)
ISBN 978-3-947879-21-2 (English)

Trade Edition
978-3-7913-7985-2 (German)
978-3-7913-7986-9 (English)

Printed in Germany
www.prestel.com

Städel Museum

Director
Philipp Demandt

Assistants to the Director
Susanne Lorenz, Johanna Schick

Curators
Alexander Eiling, Eva Mongi-
Vollmer in collaboration with
Friederike Schütt

Project Management
Friederike Schütt

Modern Art
Alexander Eiling, Juliane Betz;
Eva-Maria Höllerer, Jule Mylin,
Catharina Rother, Aude-Line
Schamschula, Neela Struck

Exhibition Organisation
Katja Hilbig-Bergmann, Sven
Lubinus; Dominik Auvermann,
Beatrice Drengwitz, Hannah
Vietoris, Albrecht Wild

Conservation
Works on paper: Jutta Keddies,
Brigitte Halder-Kaplan (freelance)
Paintings and sculptures:
Stephan Knobloch; Eva-Maria
Bader, Lilly Becker, Linda Schmidt
Liebieghaus Skulpturensammlung:
Harald Theiss; Miguel González
de Quevedo

**Technical Department/
Installation Crew**
Thomas Pietrzak, Nils Jahnke;
Michael Götz, Thorsten Knapp,
Thomas König, Ralf Lappe

**External Partners/
International Relations**
Johanna Schick

Education Department
Chantal Eschenfelder,
Anna Huber, Anne Sulzbach;
Janine Burnicki, Anne Dribbisch,
Antje Lindner, Natalie Wasiljew

Marketing
Bernadette Mildenberger,
Annabell Hurle; Sarah Merabet,
Rebekka Zajonc

Graphics/Corporate Design
Sandra Adler-Krause,
Martin Kaufmann

Press/Public Relations
Pamela Rohde, Franziska von
Plocki; Carolin Fuhr, Susanne
Hafner, Romy Kahler, Elisabeth
Pallentin, Vanessa Tron

Engagement (Sponsorship)
Julia Lange; Hannah Krämer

Engagement (Fundraising)
Stefanie Jerger; Andrea Canthal,
Claudia Kaschube, Hannah Ruiz

Administration
Heinz-Jürgen Bokler, Iris Sauer;
Vilizara Antalavicheva, Victoria
Diefenbach, Adelheid Felsing,
Elisabeth Graczyk, Diana Hillesheim,
Jutta Okos, Anja Pontoriero,
Vanessa Schäfer, Susann Schürer,
Weronika Szarafin, Sophie Voß

IT Department
Sebastian Heine; Tihomir Kukic,
Benjamin Schiller

Events
Kerstin Schultheis; Franziska
Boguslaw, Jakob Domes,
Anila Kamberaj

Museum Shop
Anke Gordon; Marcus Lackmann,
Anette Riede

Museum Café
Hammam Alshami, Sarah Seefelder

**Supervisory Service/
Cashier Desk**
Edwin Cifuentes Montenegro,
Jolanta Radtke, Catrin Röttinger-
Zengel, Ruzica Skrijelj

Library
Elena Ganzlin; Michael Mohr

Provenance Research/Archives
Iris Schmeisser

Städel Museum
Städelsches Kunstinstitut
und Städtische Galerie
Schaumainkai 63
60596 Frankfurt am Main
Tel. +49 69 60 50 98-0
Fax +49 69 60 50 98-111
www.staedelmuseum.de

Colophon

Hamburger Kunsthalle

Management Board
Director
Alexander Klar
Managing Director
Norbert Kölle

Curator of the Exhibition
Karin Schick

Research Assistant
Juliane Au

Assistance Director
Katharina Hoins, Catharina Joithe,
Ifee Tack
Assistance Managing Director
Oliver Scheid
Management Board Assistance
Anja Breuer-Achouri

Human Resources
Head Marion Blicke; Katja Weiß

Press & Public Relations
Head Mira Forte; Julia Schmid,
Mareike Wacha

Support & Partnerships
Head Gesa-Thorid Huget,
Anna Punke-Dresen; Lilian Adlung
Schönheit, Sonia Mahnkopf,
Miriam Runte, Lisa Warnke

Project Data Space
Christian Auffahrt, Petra Bassen,
Clara Blomeyer

Collections & Exhibitions
Old Masters
Sandra Pisot
19th Century
Markus Bertsch
Modern Art
Karin Schick
Contemporary Art
Brigitte Kölle, Petra Roettig
Department of Prints
and Drawings
Head Andreas Stolzenburg;
Jan Steinke; Digitalization Project:
David Klemm, Christoph Irrgang
Coins & Medals
Annabelle Görgen-Lammers
Provenance Research &
Collection History
Ute Haug
Research Assistants
Juliane Au, Selvi Göktepe,
Johanna Hornauer
Projects
Leona Marie Ahrens, Nadine
Bauer, Ann-Kathrin Hubrich,
Sylvia Karges, Ruth Stamm,
Ifee Tack
Curatorial Assistance for Project
and Exhibition Implementation
Elisabeth Lutz-Bachmann
Office Collections
Elisabeth Lutz-Bachmann,
Ursula Trieloff

Library, Archive &
Documentation
Head Katharina Gietkowski;
Frederik Hänlein, Frieda Weber,
Monika Wildner, User Service:
Michaela Pens, Archive: Jenny
Beringmeier

Conservation & Art Technology
Head & Old Masters
Silvia Castro
19th Century
Eva Keochakian
Modern Art
Nicoline Zornikau
Contemporary Art
Julia Langenbacher,
Barbara Sommermeyer
Paper and Photograph
Conservation
Sabine Zorn, Martina Ingold,
Ella Solomon, Hannah Zettner

Education
Head Andrea Weniger;
Aida Bakhtiari, Melanie Fahden,
Anja Gebauer, Ute Klapschuweit,
Jenny Saitzek, Sophie Winckel
and team

Registrars' Department &
Exhibition Coordination
Head Meike Wenck;
Kazusa Haii, Konstanze Jäger,
Shannon Ort
Media Technology
Tobias Boner
Art Handling
Head Jochen Möhle; Ulugbek
Ahmedov, Sebastian Conrad,
Oliver Meier, Joshua Sassmanns-
hausen, Fenna Winkler
Archivists
Sören Schubert, Ursula Sdunnus
Bookbinding
Anja Zuschke

Event Management &
Program Coordination
Sina Fuhrmann, Marejke Fries

Museum Attendants
Head Małgorzata Tonak-Renka;
Hassan Daneschwar, Gerhard
Kruse, Pauletta Piniane and team

Communication & Marketing
Head Jan Metzler;
Anastasia Panagiotopulu

Digital Media
Head Martina Gschwilm;
Social Media: Lea Ziegler

Visitor Services
Head Joanna von Graefe;
Sylvia Komstke, Anna-Lena
Schumacher

Controlling & Finance
Accounting
Head Kathrin von Gönner;
Oxana Königstuhl
Coordination Cash Registers
Jörg Reinholz

Building & Technology
Head Ralf Suerbaum
IT & System Administration
Matthias Heine
Building Technology
Andreas Horn, Florian Krause
Caretaking
Volker Ruge, Carlos Leandro
and team
Assistance Caretaking
Thomas Schmid

Hamburger Kunsthalle
Glockengießerwall 5
20095 Hamburg
Tel. +49 (0)40 428131 200
Fax +49 (0)40 428131 884
www.hamburger-kunsthalle.de

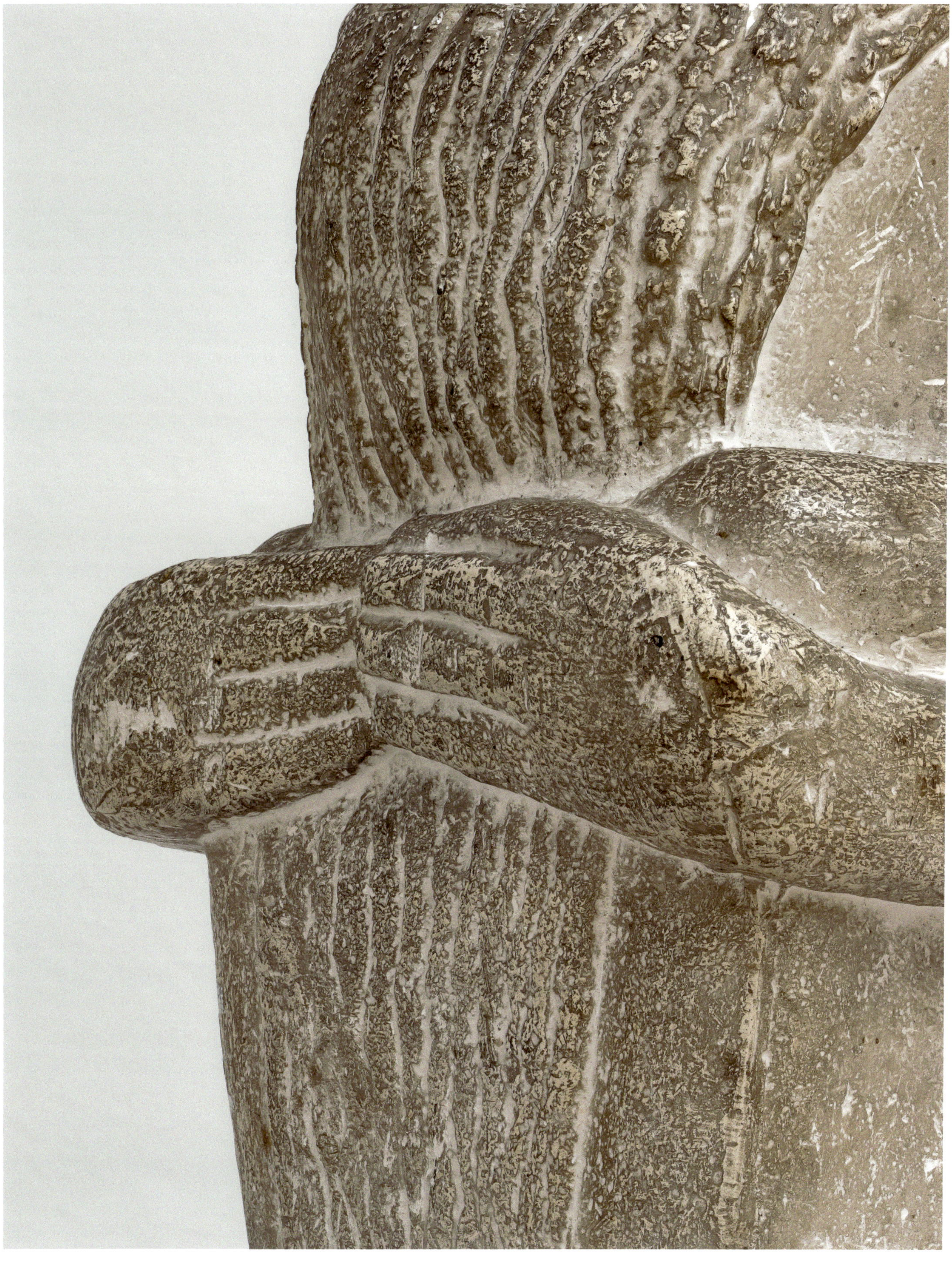

Photo Credits and Artists' Copyrights

Aargauer Kunsthaus Aarau und Gottfried Keller-Stiftung, Bundesamt für Kultur, Bern/Jörg Müller: cat. 138

Agence photographique du Musée Rodin, Paris/ Jerome Manoukian: p. 22, fig. 12

ahlers collection/Thomas Ganzenmüller, Hanover: cat. 72

Albertinum – Skulpturensammlung, Staatliche Kunstsammlungen Dresden/Hans-Peter Klut, Elke Estel: cats. 47–51

Antikensammlung und Skulpturensaal der Goethe-Universität Frankfurt am Main/Horst Ziegenfusz: cat. 1

Archiv Baumeister im Kunstmuseum Stuttgart: cat. 8

Bibliothèque nationale de France, Paris: p. 181, fig. 5

Bildarchiv Foto Marburg/Thomas Scheidt: cat. 12

Birmingham Museums Trust (CC0): p. 37, fig. 1

Bowness/Image courtesy of PIANO NOBILE, London: cat. 124

bpk/Berlinische Galerie – Landesmuseum für Moderne Kunst, Fotografie und Architektur, Berlin: cats. 89, 106

bpk/Berlinische Galerie – Landesmuseum für Moderne Kunst, Fotografie und Architektur, Berlin/Anja Elisabeth Witte: p. 134, fig. 6

bpk/Centre Pompidou, Paris/CNAC-MNAM/ Jacqueline Hyde: cat. 78

bpk/Centre Pompidou, Paris/CNAC-MNAM/ Georges Meguerditchian: p. 122, fig. 5

bpk/Centre Pompidou, Paris/CNAC-MNAM/ Adam Rzepka: cats. 107, 148; p. 122, fig. 4

bpk/Germanisches Nationalmuseum, Nuremberg/Monika Runge: p. 49, fig. 2

bpk/Hamburger Kunsthalle/Christoph Irrgang: cats. 2, 3, 5, 36, 41, 58, 60, 66, 70, 73, 76, 108, 115, 119, 135, 140, 142, 146, 157, 163, 164; p. 19, fig. 6; p. 28, fig. 19

bpk/Hamburger Kunsthalle/Elke Walford: cats. 14, 38, 63, 77, 87, 97, 100, 117; p. 120, fig. 3

bpk/Kunstmuseum Stuttgart, Sammlung Heinz und Annette Teufel/Uwe Seyl: cat. 161; p. 238, fig. 6

bpk/Kunstsammlung Nordrhein-Westfalen, Düsseldorf/Walter Klein: cat. 114

bpk/Meßbildarchiv: p. 67, fig. 2

bpk/Musée national Picasso-Paris/RMN – Grand Palais/Béatrice Hatala: cat. 80

bpk/Nationalgalerie, SMB/Klaus Göken: p. 22, fig. 11

bpk/Paris Musée, Dist. RMN – Grand Palais/ image ville de Paris: cat. 162

bpk/RMN – Grand Palais, Paris/Hervé Lewandowski: p. 23, fig. 13; p. 120, fig. 1

bpk/RMN – Grand Palais, Paris/Tony Querrec: cat. 16; p. 23, fig. 14

bpk/RMN – Grand Palais, Paris/Michel Urtado: p. 69, fig. 4

bpk/Saint-Germain-en-Laye, Musée Maurice Denis – Le Prieuré/RMN – Grand Palais, Paris/ Benoît Touchard: cat. 15

bpk/Scala: p. 133, fig. 3; p. 134, fig. 5

bpk/Scala – courtesy of the Ministero Beni e Att. Culturali: p. 49, fig. 1

bpk/Skulpturensammlung und Museum für Byzantinische Kunst, Staatliche Museen zu Berlin/Antje Voigt: p. 51, fig. 4

bpk/Sprengel Museum Hannover/Michael Herling, Uwe Vogt: cat. 105

bpk/Sprengel Museum Hannover/Wilhelm Redemann: p. 178, fig. 2

bpk/Staatliche Antikensammlungen und Glyptothek, Munich/Jochen Remmer: p. 49, fig. 3

bpk/Staatliche Kunsthalle Karlsruhe/Wolfgang Pankoke: cat. 71

bpk/Staatsgalerie Stuttgart: p. 85, fig. 4

bpk/Staatsgalerie Stuttgart, Überstellung des Baden-Württembergischen Kultusministeriums: cat. 104

Collection Museum Boijmans Van Beuningen, Rotterdam/Tom Haartsen: cat. 68

Collection Stedelijk Museum Amsterdam: p. 237, fig. 2

Georg Kolbe Museum, Berlin, Dauerleihgabe (Nachlass Familie Blumenthal)/Markus Hilbich: cats. 24–28

Emanuel Hoffmann-Stiftung, Depositum in der Öffentlichen Kunstsammlung Basel/ Bisig & Bayer, Basel: cat. 141

Emanuel Hoffmann-Stiftung, Depositum in der Öffentlichen Kunstsammlung Basel/ Martin P. Bühler: cat. 149

Barbara Hepworth © Bowness: cat. 123; p. 201, fig. 5

Historisches Museum Frankfurt/Horst Ziegenfusz: cats. 53–57

Institut Mathildenhöhe, Städtische Kunstsammlung Darmstadt/Gregor Schuster: cat. 4

Kirchner Museum Davos: cat. 17

Kunsthalle Mannheim/Margita Wickenhäuser: cat. 86

Kunstmuseum Basel/Martin P. Bühler: cats. 110, 137, 139

Kunstmuseum Basel/Max Ehrengruber: cat. 10

Kunstmuseum Basel/Jonas Haenggi: cat. 139

Kunstmuseum Den Haag: cat. 147

Kunstsammlungen der Veste Coburg: cat. 9

Liebieghaus Skulpturensammlung, Frankfurt am Main: cats. 19, 21, 52, 91; p. 26, fig. 17; p. 164, fig. 1

Lyon MBA/Martial Couderette: cat. 134

MART – Archivio fotografico e Mediateca: p. 238, fig. 5

Musea Brugge/Hugo Martens: p. 151, fig. 1

Musée Rodin, Paris/Christian Baraja: cat. 34

Museo Nacional Thyssen-Bornemisza, Madrid: cat. 111

Museum Folkwang, Essen – ARTOTHEK: cat. 43

Museum für Kunst und Gewerbe Hamburg, Eigentum der Stiftung Hamburger Kunstsammlungen/Joachim Hiltmann: cats. 120, 121

Nachlass Jenny Wiegmann-Mucchi, courtesy of Galerie Poll, Berlin/Friedhelm Hoffman: cat. 69

Nachlass Karl Hartung/Christoph Irrgang: cats. 35, 125–128

Nationalgalerie, SMB/Christian Daniel Rauch-Museum, Bad Arolsen/Frank Hellwig: cat. 18

Ny Carlsberg Glyptotek, Copenhagen/Anders Sune Berg: cat. 40

Pallant House Gallery, Chichester, UK (on loan from a private collection, 2018): cat. 122

Paris Musées/Petit Palais, Musée des Beaux-Arts de la Ville de Paris (CC0): cat. 31; p. 85, fig. 3

Private collection/Horst Ziegenfusz: cat. 32

Private collection, London/Erik and Petra Hesmerg: cat. 67

Private collection, London/Heinrich Schneebeli: cats. 29, 33, 42, 75

Private collection in the Hamburger Kunsthalle/ bpk/Christoph Irrgang: cats. 116, 118

Gerhard Richter/David Ertl – ARTOTHEK: p. 151, fig. 3

Sammlung Freese/Horst Ziegenfusz: cats. 150–153

Sammlung Oskar Reinhart "Am Römerholz", Winterthur: p. 84, fig. 1

SHK/Hamburger Kunsthalle/bpk/Christoph Irrgang: cats. 44, 74, 79

SHK/Hamburger Kunsthalle/bpk/Elke Walford: cats. 62, 88; p. 133, fig. 1

SMÄK, Munich/Marianne Franke: p. 17, fig. 4

Städel Museum, Frankfurt am Main: cats. 6, 7, 11, 20, 22, 37, 39, 45, 46, 59, 61, 65, 81–85, 90, 92–96, 98, 99, 129–133, 136, 144, 145, 154, 156, 158–160; p. 16, fig. 1; p. 19, fig. 7; p. 67, fig. 1; p. 101, figs. 2, 3

Städel-Archiv, Frankfurt am Main: p. 37, fig. 2; p. 200, figs. 1–3; p. 202, fig. 7

Courtesy of Stuart Lochhead Sculpture: cats. 13, 30

Succession Alberto Giacometti/Adagp, Paris, 2023/Adagp images: p. 101, fig. 1

Succession Picasso/DACS 2018, courtesy of private collection/Tate: p. 133, fig. 2

Succession Yves Klein/Adagp, Paris, 2023/Adagp Images: p. 237, fig. 3

The Miriam and Ira D. Wallach Division of Art, Prints and Photographs: Print Collection, The New York Public Library: p. 69, fig. 5

The Museum of Modern Art/Scala, Florence: p. 25, fig. 15; p. 133, fig. 4

The William Turnbull Will Trust/Mark Dalton: cats. 101–103

Altay Tuz, Christoph Irrgang: p. 237, fig. 1; p. 238, fig. 4

Wilhelm-Hack-Museum, Ludwigshafen: cat. 109

IMAGE DETAILS

Cover: cat. 148; p. 2: cat. 107, p. 4: cat. 13; pp. 12/13: cat. 69; p. 15: cat. 155; p. 33: cat. 147; p. 34: cat. 1; p. 46: cat. 9; p. 64: cat. 20; p. 82: cat. 37; p. 98: cat. 58; p. 118: cat. 70; p. 130: cat. 75; p. 148: cat. 93; p. 162: cat. 94; p. 176: cat. 115; p. 198: cat. 122; p. 212: cat. 136; p. 234: cat. 161; p. 253: cat. 31; p. 257: cat. 157; pp. 258/259: cat. 71; p. 263: cat. 60

COPYRIGHTS

© Lee Bontecou 2023, all rights reserved, for Lee Bontecou

© Bowness, for Barbara Hepworth

© Christian Schad Stiftung Aschaffenburg/VG Bild-Kunst, Bonn 2023, for Christian Schad

© Comissió Tàpies/VG Bild-Kunst, Bonn 2023, for Antoni Tàpies

© The Estate of Yves Klein/VG Bild-Kunst, Bonn 2023, for Yves Klein

© Estate of Jacques Lipchitz, for Jacques Lipchitz

© Lucio Fontana by SIAE/VG Bild-Kunst, Bonn 2023, for Lucio Fontana

© Karel Appel Foundation/VG Bild-Kunst, Bonn 2023, for Karel Appel

© Barbara Klemm, for Barbara Klemm

© Niki Charitable Art Foundation/VG Bild-Kunst, Bonn 2023, for Niki de Saint Phalle

© Gerhard Richter 2023 (0061), for Gerhard Richter

© Succession Brancusi, all rights reserved/ VG Bild-Kunst, Bonn 2023, for Constantin Brancusi

© Succession Alberto Giacometti/VG Bild-Kunst, Bonn 2023, for Alberto Giacometti

© Succession H. Matisse/VG Bild-Kunst, Bonn 2023, for Henri Matisse

© Succession Picasso/VG Bild-Kunst, Bonn 2023, for Pablo Picasso

© Ugo Mulas Estate/Courtesy of GAM Galleria Civica d'Arte Moderna e Contemporanea, Turin/Fondazione per l'Arte Moderna e Contemporanea CRT-owned, for Ugo Mulas

© Angela Verren Taunt, all rights reserved/VG Bild-Kunst, Bonn 2023, for Ben Nicholson

© VG Bild-Kunst, Bonn 2023, for Alexander Archipenko, Jean Arp, Willi Baumeister, Jean Dubuffet, Max Ernst, Lucio Fontana, Hermann Glöckner, Otto Herbert Hajek, Karl Hartung, Auguste Herbin, Rudolf Jahns, Eugène Leroy, Lou (Louise Marie) Loeber, Adolf Luther, Piero Manzoni, Giorgio Morandi, François Morellet, Rolf Nesch, Louise Nevelson, Antoine Pevsner, Ivan Puni, Peter Roehr, Jan Schoonhoven, Jesús Rafael Soto, Daniel Spoerri, Klaus Staudt, William Turnbull, Günther Uecker, Jenny Wiegmann-Mucchi

© Nina & Graham Williams/Tate, for Naum Gabo

The remainder of the illustrations stem from the archives and authors of the Städel Museum and the Hamburger Kunsthalle. It was not possible to identify the copyright holders of the illustrations in all cases. Warranted claims will naturally be settled within the scope of the customary agreements.